W9-AXQ-355

PE PLE
in Time and Place

WORLD GEOGRAPHY

UTHORS

Dr. Linda L. Greenow
Associate Professor of Geography
SUNY — The College at New Paltz
New Paltz, NY

Dr. W. Frank Ainsley, Jr.
Professor of Geography
University of North Carolina
Wilmington, NC

Dr. Gary S. Elbow
Professor of Geography
Texas Tech University
Lubbock, TX

SERIES CONSULTANTS

Dr. James F. Baumann
Professor of Reading Education
Associate Director, National Reading Research Center
The University of Georgia
Athens, GA

Dr. Theodore Kaltsounis
Professor of Social Studies Education
University of Washington
Seattle, WA

LITERATURE CONSULTANTS

Dr. Ben A. Smith
Assistant Professor of Social Studies Education
Kansas State University
Manhattan, KS

Dr. John C. Davis
Professor of Elementary Education
University of Southern Mississippi
Hattiesburg, MS

Dr. Jesse Palmer
Assistant Professor, Department of Curriculum and Instruction
University of Southern Mississippi
Hattiesburg, MS

COVER PHOTOGRAPH
Replica of an Italian globe, 1578

SILVER BURDETT GINN

MORRISTOWN, NJ • NEEDHAM, MA
Atlanta, GA • Deerfield, IL • Irving, TX • San Jose, CA

SERIES AUTHORS

Dr. W. Frank Ainsley, Professor of Geography, University of North Carolina, Wilmington, NC

Dr. Herbert J. Bass, Professor of History, Temple University, Philadelphia, PA

Dr. Kenneth S. Cooper, Professor of History, Emeritus, George Peabody College for Teachers, Venderbilt University, Nashville, TN

Dr. Claudia Crump, Professor of Elementary Social Studies Education, Indiana University Southeast, New Albany, IN

Dr. Gary S. Elbow, Professor of Geography Texas Tech University, Lubbock, TX

Roy Erickson, Program Specialist, K12 Social Studies and Multicultural Education, San Juan Unified School District, Carmichael, CA

Dr. Daniel B. Fleming, Professor of Social Studies Education, Virginia Polytechnic Institute and State University, Blacksburg, VA

Dr. Gerald Michael Greenfield, Professor and Director, Center for International Studies, University of Wisconsin — Parkside, Kenosha, WI

Dr. Linda Greenow, Associate Professor of Geography, SUNY — The College at New Paltz, New Paltz, NY

Dr. William W. Joyce, Professor of Education, Michigan State University, East Lansing, MI

Dr. Gail S. Ludwig, Former Geographer-in-Residence, National Geographic Society, Geography Education Program, Washington, D.C.

Dr. Michael B. Petrovich, Professor Emeritus of History, University of Wisconsin, Madison, WI

Dr. Norman J.G. Pounds, Former University Professor of History and Geography, Indiana University, Bloomington, IN

Dr. Arthur Roberts, Professor of Education, University of Connecticut, Storrs, CT

Dr. Christine L. Roberts, Professor of Education, University of Connecticut, Storrs, CT

Parke Rouse, Jr., Virginia Historian and Retired Executive Director of the Jamestown-Yorktown Foundation, Williamsburg, VA

Dr. Paul C. Slayton, Jr., Distinguished Professor of Education, Mary Washington College, Fredericksburg, VA

Dr. Edgar A. Toppin, Professor of History and Dean of the Graduate School, Virginia State University Petersburg, VA

GRADE LEVEL WRITERS/ CONSULTANTS

Claudette Butler Hatfield, Social Studies Department Chairperson, Williams Middle School, Florence, South Carolina

Pat Kelly-Coupar, Teacher, Thomas Jefferson Middle School, Edison, New Jersey

Cay Hoh, Teacher, Hayes Junior High School, St. Albans, West Virginia

Alvin Lindsey, Teacher, Donnan Junior High School, Indianapolis, Indiana

ACKNOWLEDGMENTS

Page 29: *The Sea Around Us* by Rachel Carson. Copyright © 1950, 1951, 1961 by Rachel L. Carson; Renewed 1979 by Roger Christie. Oxford University Press.

Page 41: By M. Scott Carpenter et al. Used by permission of Simon & Schuster Inc.

Page 47: © Copyright 1971 Cherry Lane Music Publishing Company, Inc. All rights reserved. Used by permission.

Page 64: Copyright © 1992 by The New York Times Company. Reprinted by permission.

Page 102: Reprinted by permission of Macmillan Publishing Company from RICHARD HALLIBURTON'S COMPLETE BOOK OF MARVELS. © 1960, renewed 1988 by Macmillan Publishing Company.

Pages 134, 136: From THE BERNAL DIAZ CHRONICLES as translated by Albert Idell. Used by permission of Doubleday & Company.

Page 140: From *Anthology of Mexican Poets* translated by Edna W. Underwood.

Page 145: Reprinted with permission from book #60660 The Log of Christopher Columbus, by Robert Fuson. Copyright © 1987 by Robert Fuson. Published by International Marine Publishing Company, a division of TAB BOOKS, Blue Ridge Summit, PA 17294 (1-800-233-1128 or 717-794-2191).

Page 170: Copyright © 1987 by The New York Times Company. Reprinted by permission.

Page 200: Reprinted with permission of Four Winds Press, an imprint of Macmillan Publishing Company from COATA INDIAN FAMILY: Children of the Incas by David Mangurian. Copyright © 1979 by David Mangurian.

Continued on page 753

CONTENTS

UNIT 1 LEARNING ABOUT THE EARTH

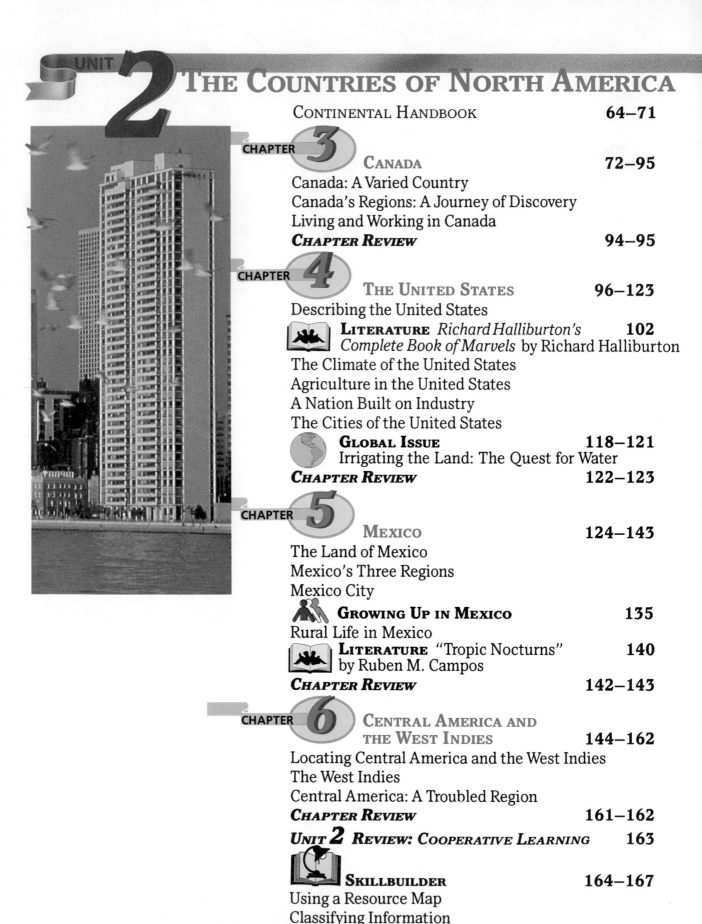

UNIT 2 THE COUNTRIES OF NORTH AMERICA

UNIT 3 THE COUNTRIES OF SOUTH AMERICA

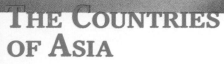

UNIT 5 THE COUNTRIES OF ASIA

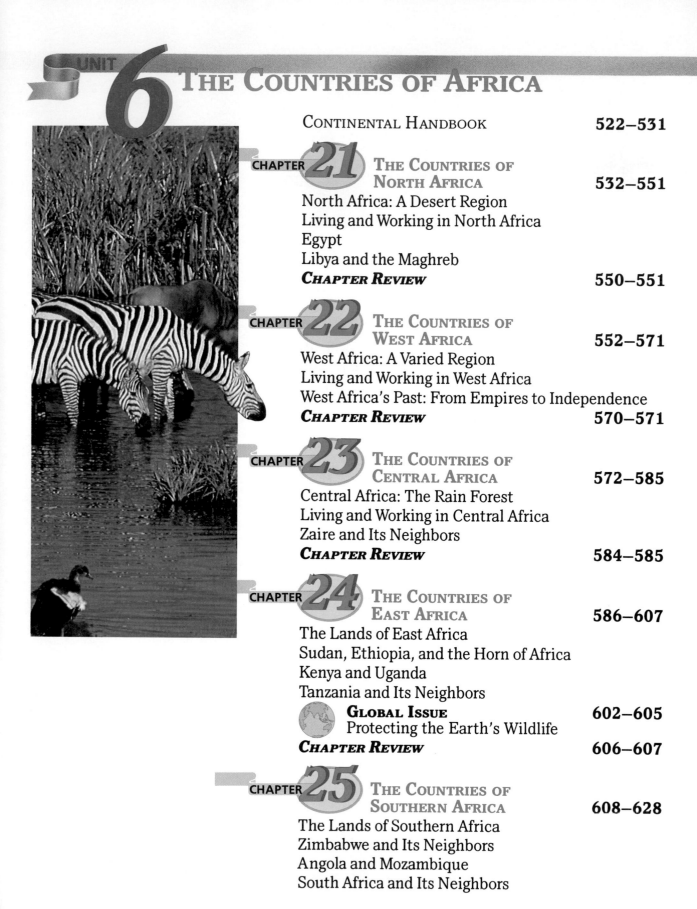

UNIT 6 THE COUNTRIES OF AFRICA

UNIT 7 AUSTRALIA, NEW ZEALAND, AND THE PACIFIC ISLANDS

ATLAS

TIME LINES

GRAPHS

TABLE OF COUNTRIES

TABLES

CHARTS

DIAGRAMS

SPECIAL FEATURES

USING SOURCE MATERIAL

LITERATURE

GROWING UP IN

GLOBAL ISSUES

SKILLBUILDERS

SOCIAL STUDIES

LANGUAGE ARTS

GRAPH APPENDIX

MAP SKILLS HANDBOOK

Knowing how to work with maps is a skill that everyone should have. You cannot thoroughly learn about geography without being able to read maps. Maps also have uses that go beyond what you learn in school.

Watch the nightly news on television. How many times are maps used during the broadcast? The next time you are in a library, look at a newspaper or weekly news magazine. How many times are maps used to help explain the subject of articles? Are maps used in any advertisements on television or in magazines?

If you kept track of how many times you saw maps on television and in newspapers and magazines during one week, you would see that maps are an important source of information. You would also see how important it is to be able to understand maps.

As you study geography, you will use map skills that you have already learned. You will also learn some new map skills. This Map Skills Handbook presents many of the map skills you will need to get the most out of your textbook — and many of the map skills that you can use to understand the world around you.

LESSON 1

Map Essentials

SPAIN: POLITICAL

Bay of Biscay
1 **2** FRANCE **3**
•Bilbao
A
PYRENEES ← ANDORRA
Ebro River
Valladolid Saragossa•
Douro River
Barcelona
PORTUGAL
Madrid⊙
Tagus
40°N
S P A I N
River
Guadiana River Valencia•
BALEARIC
ISLANDS
B
Córdoba•
Mediterranean
•Seville
W — E
Sea
ATLANTIC
OCEAN Málaga•
S
Strait of
Gibraltar
4°W 0° 36°N

⊙ National capital   0   150   300 miles
• Other cities   0 150 300 kilometers

8°W 4°E

2

Showing the Earth on a Map

NEW YORK CITY: CENTRAL PARK

Manhattan

Hudson River

Henry Hudson Pkwy.

Broadway

Central Park

Park Ave.

FDR Dr.

East River

0   1/2   1

Scale: 1 inch stands for 1 mile

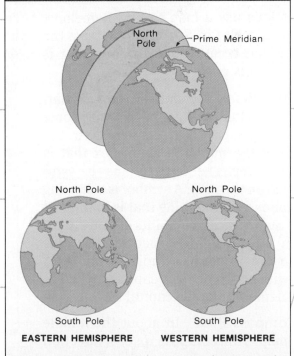

From Round Earth to Flat Paper

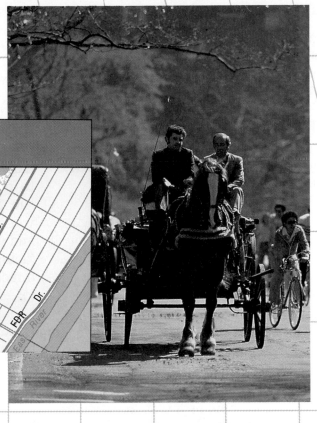

EASTERN AND WESTERN HEMISPHERES

North Pole

Prime Meridian

North Pole

North Pole

South Pole

South Pole

EASTERN HEMISPHERE

WESTERN HEMISPHERE

3

Map Essentials

CONNECTIONS

To read a map you must know the elements, or parts, of a map. Look at the map on this page. Name the parts of the map that you recognize. Now point out the parts you don't recognize.

TERMS

key, compass rose, grid system, latitude, longitude, scale, kilometer

FOCUS

What are the elements and symbols that are found on a map?

A. The Parts of A Map

Finding a City Almost 11,000 athletes represented 172 countries at the 1992 Summer Olympics in Barcelona (bahr suh LOH nuh), Spain. "Barcelona, Spain?" you ask yourself. Where is that?

No doubt, some of you do know where Barcelona is. But how would you describe its location to someone who doesn't? You probably already know the answer: By using a map.

So let's use a map to find Barcelona. Since it is a city in Spain, we will use the map of that country like the one that is shown on this page.

The Key Before we start looking for Barcelona, let's take a moment to review some of the map's essential elements. At the bottom of the map is a small box that is the map's **key**. The key explains the symbols used on the map. A symbol is a drawing that stands for something that is in the real world. Symbols can be points or dots, lines, shaded areas, or little pictures. On this map, a dot is used to indicate a city. A circle with a star means a capital city. What is the name of Spain's capital city?

The Compass Rose In about the middle of the map is the **compass rose**, or direction

marker. This shows where the cardinal directions are on the map. As you know, the cardinal directions are north, south, east, and west. The compass rose also shows the intermediate directions: northeast, northwest, southeast, and southwest.

Cartographers, the people who draw maps, have used these directions for centuries. The cardinal directions were originally determined by where the sun appears to rise, which is the east, and where the sun appears to set, which is the west. If you stand with your right arm to the east and your left arm to the west, then you are facing north, and south is the direction directly behind you.

SPAIN: POLITICAL

Bay of Biscay • Bilbao FRANCE • ANDORRA PYRENEES Ebro River Valladolid Saragossa • Barcelona Douro River PORTUGAL Madrid ✪ Tagus River S P A I N 40° N Guadiana River Valencia BALEARIC ISLANDS Córdoba • Mediterranean Sea Seville • Málaga • ATLANTIC OCEAN Strait of Gibraltar 4° W 0° 36° N 8° W 4° E

✪ National capital
• Other cities

0   150   300 miles
0   150   300 kilometers

Cities 250,000 to 499,000	
Bilbao	A-2
Córdoba	B-1
Valladolid	A-1

Cities 500,000 to 999,999	
Málaga	B-1
Saragossa	A-2

Seville	B-1
Valencia	B-2

Cities 1,000,000 or more	
Barcelona	A-3
Madrid	A-2

The population of Spain is almost 40,000,000.
▶ What are Spain's two most populated cities?

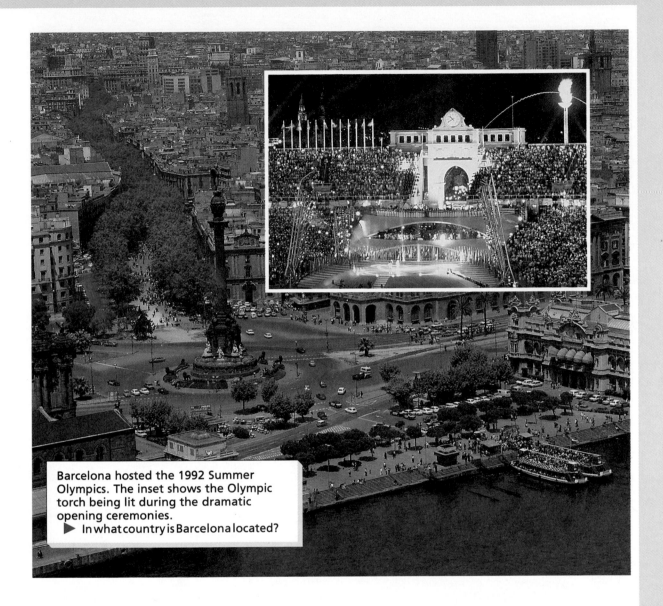

Barcelona hosted the 1992 Summer Olympics. The inset shows the Olympic torch being lit during the dramatic opening ceremonies.
▶ In what country is Barcelona located?

B. The Grid System

The Gazetteer On a small map like this one, it is easy enough to pick out Barcelona. And you can use the key and the compass rose for help in describing exactly where Barcelona is—to the northeast of Madrid, the capital city of Spain. In this book the important places mentioned in a chapter are listed in a section called the Gazetteer. Turn to the Gazetteer, on pages 707–720. You can see that each city has an important fact reported about it. After that fact are the **latitude** and **longitude** of the city.

What are latitude and longitude? They are part of the **grid system** that cartographers have created to help us find places on maps. The horizontal lines on this grid system are lines of latitude, and the vertical lines are lines of longitude.

Latitude Lines of latitude are called parallels. They circle the earth in an east-west direction and are parallel to the Equator. Parallels measure distance north and south of the Equator. You can see from the map on page 6 that each line of latitude has a measurement in degrees. The Equator is at

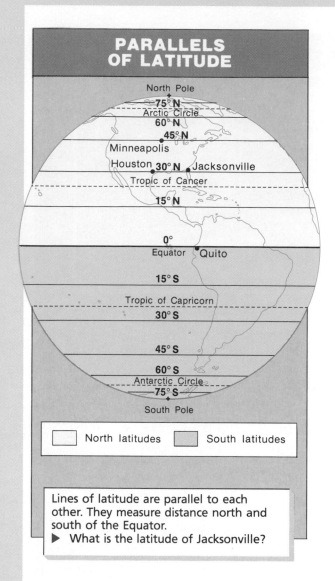

PARALLELS OF LATITUDE

North Pole
75° N
Arctic Circle
60° N
45° N
Minneapolis
Houston 30° N Jacksonville
Tropic of Cancer
15° N
0°
Equator Quito
15° S
Tropic of Capricorn
30° S
45° S
60° S
Antarctic Circle
75° S
South Pole

☐ North latitudes   ☐ South latitudes

Lines of latitude are parallel to each other. They measure distance north and south of the Equator.
▶ What is the latitude of Jacksonville?

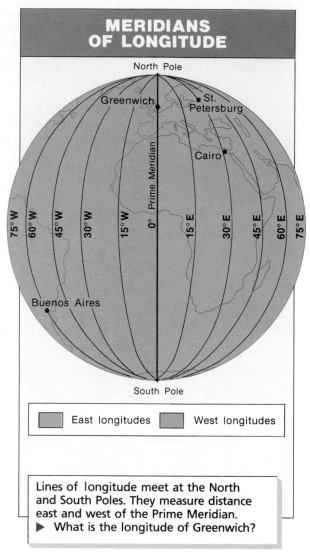

MERIDIANS OF LONGITUDE

North Pole
Greenwich • St. Petersburg
Cairo
Prime Meridian
75° W 60° W 45° W 30° W 15° W 0° 15° E 30° E 45° E 60° E 75° E
Buenos Aires
South Pole

☐ East longitudes   ☐ West longitudes

Lines of longitude meet at the North and South Poles. They measure distance east and west of the Prime Meridian.
▶ What is the longitude of Greenwich?

0° latitude. Lines of latitude north of the Equator are called lines of north latitude. On a map, they are shown as 20°N, 30°N, and so on. The latitude for the North Pole is 90°N.

Lines of latitude south of the Equator are called lines of south latitude. On a map they are shown as 20°S, 30°S, and so on. The South Pole is 90°S.

Longitude The lines of longitude in the grid system are called meridians. Meridians run from the North Pole to the South Pole. They are used to measure distance east and

west of the starting point, called the Prime Meridian. The Prime Meridian passes through Greenwich, England. Greenwich is a town located near London. Sometimes the Prime Meridian is called the Greenwich Meridian because of its location. Find the Prime Meridian on the map above.

Longitude is also measured in degrees. The Prime Meridian is the starting point, so it is numbered 0°. Lines of longitude to the west of the Prime Meridian are called west longitude. Lines of longitude to the east are called east longitude.

The lines of longitude are numbered east

and west to 180° from the Prime Meridian. The meridian of 180° lies on the opposite side of the earth from the Prime Meridian.

Coordinates If you look up Barcelona in the Gazetteer, you will find that its latitude and longitude are listed there as 41°N/2°E. This set of numbers, or *coordinates*, locate the city precisely.

Suppose you had to find Barcelona on a world map, such as the one below. Unless you already knew where Spain was, you would have a hard time looking through all the countries on the map to first find Spain and then Barcelona. You can see how useful the coordinates are.

Another Grid System If you look again at the map of Spain on page 4, you will see at the top the numbers 1, 2, and 3. Along the left-hand side of the map you will see the letters *A* and *B*. These letters and numbers identify the boxes that the lines of latitude and longitude form.

Look at the listing of cities under the map. This *city index* lists all the cities shown on the map. The name of each city is followed by the letter and the number of the box in which the city is located. For example, the city index for this map tells us that Barcelona is in box A-3, which is where row *A* and column 3 meet. Once you find the box, you can scan it and locate Barcelona. The city index and the grid system allow us to easily find places on this or any other map.

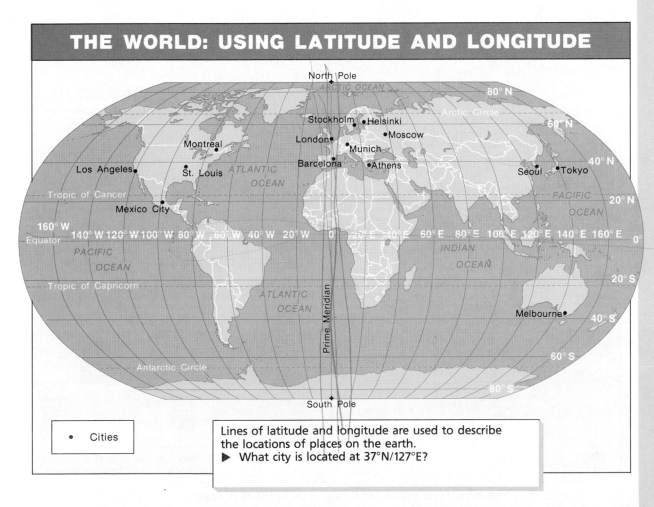

THE WORLD: USING LATITUDE AND LONGITUDE

Cities

Lines of latitude and longitude are used to describe the locations of places on the earth.
▶ What city is located at 37°N/127°E?

FROM PHOTOGRAPH TO MAP

	Fairways		Sand traps		Ponds		Highway
	Putting greens		Paths		Rivers		Other land

Compare the photograph above with the map below it. You can see that the map uses colors to represent real things shown in the photograph. Blue is used to represent the ponds, and yellow represents the golf course's sand traps.
▶ What color is used on the map to show the highway?

The Metric System of Measurement

If you turn to the scale bar shown on the map of Spain on page 4, you will see that measurement is given in both miles and **kilometers**. A kilometer is a measure of distance in the metric system.

This system is used for measuring distance. It is also used for measuring weight, capacity, and temperature. The metric system is in use or is being introduced in all the major countries of the world except the United States. Thus, it is important that we become familiar with this system.

To help you become familiar with the metric system, we have used both customary measurements, which are in general use in the United States, and metric measurements in this book. When a customary measurement appears, it is followed in parentheses ( ) by the metric measurement that is about equal to it.

As you read this book, you will see that inches are followed by centimeters (cm), feet and yards by meters (m), miles by kilometers (km), and acres by hectares (ha). Pounds are followed by kilograms (kg), and quarts by liters (l). Degrees Fahrenheit (°F) are followed by degrees Celsius (°C).

C. Drawing a Map to Scale

From Photo to Map All maps are drawings of parts of the earth. But maps do not show everything that exists on the part of the earth being mapped. The photograph and the map on page 8 illustrate how maps show only some details of the earth. The photograph shows details not shown on the map, such as the grass and the trees of the golf course. The map uses colors to show the parts of the golf course that the cartographer wanted on the map.

Scale All maps are drawn to a certain **scale**. Scale means that a certain number of inches on the map represents or stands for a certain number of feet or miles on the earth's surface. The scale bars found on maps give you this relationship.

Scale can be shown in three different ways. On some maps, the scale is shown as "One inch equals 200 feet." Scale is also shown a second way, by a fraction or ratio. For example, the ratio scale, or fraction on a map might read "1:2,400." This means that one unit of measurement on the map equals 2,400 units of the same length in the real world.

The third way to show scale is by a bar scale. If you turn back to the map of Spain on page 4, you can see that the bar scale is the straight line in the key with the distances marked off on it. All three of these scales show the relationship between the actual distance on the earth's surface and the distance shown on the map.

LESSON 1

Review

REVIEWING MAIN IDEAS
A. How is the key on a map used?
B. Why is the grid system useful for locating places?
C. What are the three ways of showing scale on a map?

SKILLS CHECK

MAP SKILL
Turn to the Gazetteer on pages 707–720. Find the coordinates of the following cities.

Athens   Mexico City
Los Angeles   London

Showing the Earth on a Map

CONNECTIONS

Suppose you were going on a trip across the United States. What kinds of maps would you need for your trip?

TERMS

landform, physical map, contour line, distribution map

FOCUS

What are some of the different kinds of maps that can be used to describe an area?

A. Different Maps for Different Purposes

One of the projects you might be assigned this year is to write a report on one of the world's countries. An important part of any country report is a map of the country you are writing about. But what kind of map should you draw? One map of a country can show only a limited amount of information about the country. For example, an outline map of the country would show only the country's shape and its boundaries with other countries.

One way to avoid this problem is to include several different kinds of maps of the country. You could show a map of the continent the country is located on. You could also draw a map showing the country's major **landforms**. Landforms are features of the earth's surface that are made by nature. They include mountains, hills, rivers, lakes, and oceans.

B. Maps Have Different Scales

You might run into a problem when you begin to draw the maps. How can you fit a map of a continent and a map of a country on pages that are the same size? For example, a map of Asia would have to be larger than the size of the notebook

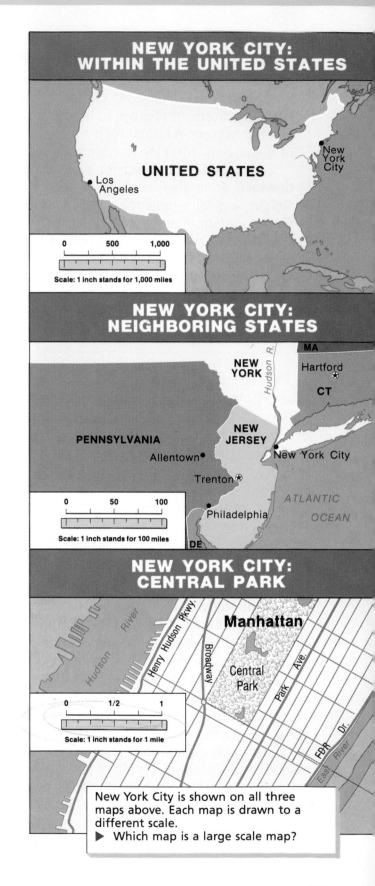

NEW YORK CITY: WITHIN THE UNITED STATES

UNITED STATES

New York City

Los Angeles

0   500   1,000

Scale: 1 inch stands for 1,000 miles

NEW YORK CITY: NEIGHBORING STATES

MA

NEW YORK

Hartford

Hudson R.

CT

PENNSYLVANIA

NEW JERSEY

Allentown

New York City

Trenton

0   50   100

ATLANTIC OCEAN

Scale: 1 inch stands for 100 miles

Philadelphia

DE

NEW YORK CITY: CENTRAL PARK

Manhattan

Hudson River

Henry Hudson Pkwy.

Broadway

Central Park

Park Ave.

FDR Dr.

East River

0   1/2   1

Scale: 1 inch stands for 1 mile

New York City is shown on all three maps above. Each map is drawn to a different scale.
▶ Which map is a large scale map?

10

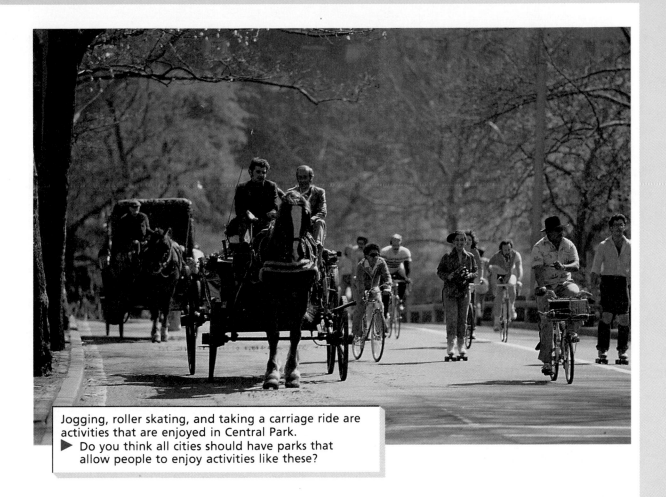

Jogging, roller skating, and taking a carriage ride are activities that are enjoyed in Central Park.
▶ Do you think all cities should have parks that allow people to enjoy activities like these?

paper if a map of China, which is located in Asia, is drawn to fill the entire page.

To fit all the maps on pages of the same size, you would have to use different scales for the different-size areas. As you learned in Lesson 1, maps are scale drawings of the real world. The maps you include in your country report would have to be drawn at different scales in order to fit on same-sized pages.

For example, on page 10 the maps showing New York City are drawn to three different scales. The bottom map shows part of New York City. With this map, we are able to find some of New York's landmarks, such as Central Park and Broadway. This is called a large-scale map. To show more detail of an area, a cartographer uses a large-scale map.

The middle and top maps show New York City's neighboring states and its location in the United States. These maps show much less detail about New York City, but they do show more of the area that surrounds New York. These maps are called small-scale maps. Small-scale maps show large parts of the earth's surface; large-scale maps show small parts of the earth.

Here's another example of how scale works. If you drew a map of your classroom, you would have a large-scale map. Then, if you mapped the neighborhood around the school, you would show more area in less detail. This map of the neighborhood would be a small-scale map. If you went on to map the whole town, you would be using a still smaller scale. And a map of even smaller scale would be needed for the state.

Contour lines are a good way to show elevation of the land and how steep the land is. An elevation map tells about the height of the land.
▶ What is the highest elevation point on map A?

C. Showing the Earth's Relief on Maps

Physical Maps One map that should be in your report is a **physical map** of the country. A physical map shows the earth's features, such as mountains and plains. It also shows what the elevation, or height, of the land is.

The best way to get an accurate picture of the earth's surface on a map is to use **contour lines**. A contour line is a line drawn on a map that connects all points of land that are the same height above sea level.

Sea level is considered to be 0 feet (0 m). Map A on this page shows how the contour lines connect elevations at 1,000 feet (305 m), 2,000 feet (610 m), and 5,000 feet (1,524 m).

You can learn many things about the land from contour maps. If the contour lines are close together, the slope of the hill or mountain is steep. The slope is more gentle the farther apart the lines are. If a contour map has very few contour lines, it means the land is almost level. Look at the contour map of Sri Lanka on the opposite page. Which part of the island has the steepest slope? What is the elevation of Colombo and Jaffna? What is the elevation of Kandy? What is the average height of the island's highest point?

Showing Elevation On the physical maps you will use this year, the areas between the contour lines are colored. These colored areas show the different elevations. Compare the contour map of Sri Lanka on the opposite page with the elevation map of the same area. The key on map B indicates that green is used to show elevations between sea level and 1,000 feet (300 m). Then different shades of orange and purple are used to show higher elevations.

Physical maps have a variety of uses. People who build roads and railroads need to know where the most level land is, so they use physical maps. They are also useful for determining where to build houses.

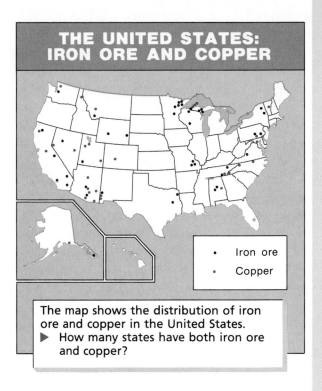

THE UNITED STATES: IRON ORE AND COPPER

- • Iron ore
- • Copper

The map shows the distribution of iron ore and copper in the United States.
▶ How many states have both iron ore and copper?

D. Other Kinds of Maps

There are several other kinds of maps that you could use in your country report. A daily weather map would show the weather patterns across the country. Another interesting kind of map to include is a **distribution map** of the country's resources. A distribution map shows the range of people, crops, or resources in a country or region.

The map at the top of this page shows the distribution of iron ore and copper deposits in the United States. Distribution maps help us understand why some industries develop in certain parts of the country. For example, in which part of the country do you think copper mining is the major industry? In which part of the country is iron-ore mining important?

Look at the distribution map of oil and natural gas fields. Which part of the country has the largest oil fields? Is it the same part of the country that has a large number of natural gas fields?

UNITED STATES: OIL & NATURAL GAS FIELDS

Oil fields
• Natural gas fields

The map shows the distribution of oil and natural gas in the United States.
▶ Does your state have deposits of either oil or natural gas?

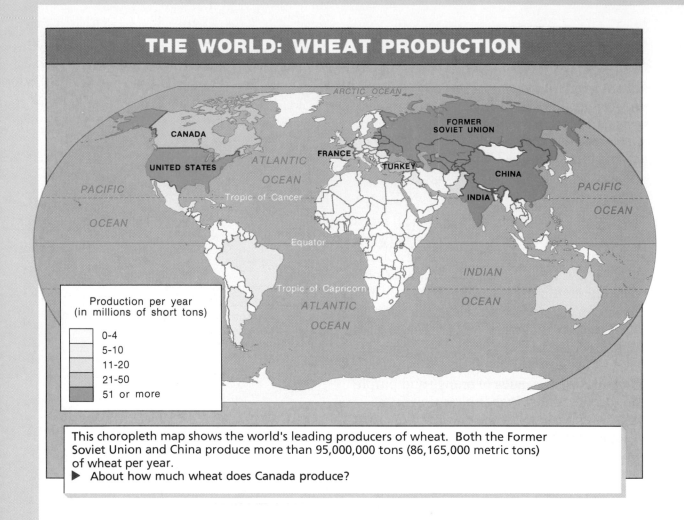

THE WORLD: WHEAT PRODUCTION

Production per year (in millions of short tons)

- 0-4
- 5-10
- 11-20
- 21-50
- 51 or more

This choropleth map shows the world's leading producers of wheat. Both the Former Soviet Union and China produce more than 95,000,000 tons (86,165,000 metric tons) of wheat per year.

▶ About how much wheat does Canada produce?

Another map that shows distribution is a *choropleth* (KOR uh pleth) map. A choropleth map uses different colors to show the distribution of a product in a region or in the world. The colors also show how much of the product is produced by the countries.

The map on this page is a choropleth map of wheat production. The map key explains what each color means on the map. For example, on this map, you can see that the darkest green means that a country produces 51 million tons or more of wheat. Yellow means that a country produces between 0 and 4 million tons of wheat. You can use the choropleth map to find the world's largest and smallest producers of wheat.

LESSON 2

Review

REVIEWING MAIN IDEAS

A. What is a landform?
B. What is the difference between small-scale maps and large-scale maps?
C. How do physical maps show elevation?
D. Name three kinds of special-purpose maps.

SKILLS CHECK

MAP SKILL

Turn to the Atlas, on pages 688-706, and name the kinds of maps you find there for each continent. Choose one of the continents and explain how you would use the maps to describe that continent.

14

From Round Earth to Flat Paper

CONNECTIONS

If someone said to you that the earth was flat, how would you prove to him or her that it is round?

TERMS

cartography, distortion, projection, great circle, hemisphere

FOCUS

What are map projections and how are different projections used?

The cartographer in the above photograph is tracing the outline of a country for a map.
▶ How is she tracing the outline?

A. Measuring the Round Earth

Long ago in Egypt, there lived a wise man named Eratosthenes (er uh TAHS thuh-neez). Eratosthenes had a revolutionary idea—he believed that the earth was round. Most people in Eratosthenes' time thought the earth was flat and that if they went too far in any direction, they would fall off the edge into everlasting darkness.

Eratosthenes set out to prove that these people were wrong. Some scientists before Eratosthenes had also believed that the earth was round. Eratosthenes used these scientists' arguments and took them one step further—he showed how large the round earth really was.

Eratosthenes knew that at the beginning of summer, the sun would shine directly down into a deep well at a place called Syene (now Aswan) on the Nile River. This told him that the sun was directly overhead at that point. Eratosthenes also had observed that the sun was never directly overhead at Alexandria, which was about 500 miles (800 km) north of Syene.

These observations about the sun's rays led Eratosthenes to calculate that the distance around the earth must be 25,000 miles (40,225 km). He was very close to being absolutely correct. With modern instruments, scientists have found that the distance around the earth is actually 24,860 miles (40,000 km). Amazingly, Eratosthenes was not that far off!

Even after Eratosthenes' discovery, some people continued to believe that the earth was flat. Gradually, however, most people came to believe that the earth really was round. Of course, today almost everyone has seen photographs showing the earth from space. From these photographs, we know that the earth is a sphere revolving in space around the sun.

B. Making a Map of a Globe

Mapping the Earth The perfect model of the earth is a globe. Like the earth, a globe is round in shape, and it shows the earth's continents and oceans. But what are maps? Maps, too, are representations of the earth. The difference is that a map is drawn on a flat piece of paper, not on a round ball. Why do we need maps? One answer is simple. Maps are easy to fold or roll up and carry along with us everywhere we go. Imagine trying to carry a large globe along as you travel.

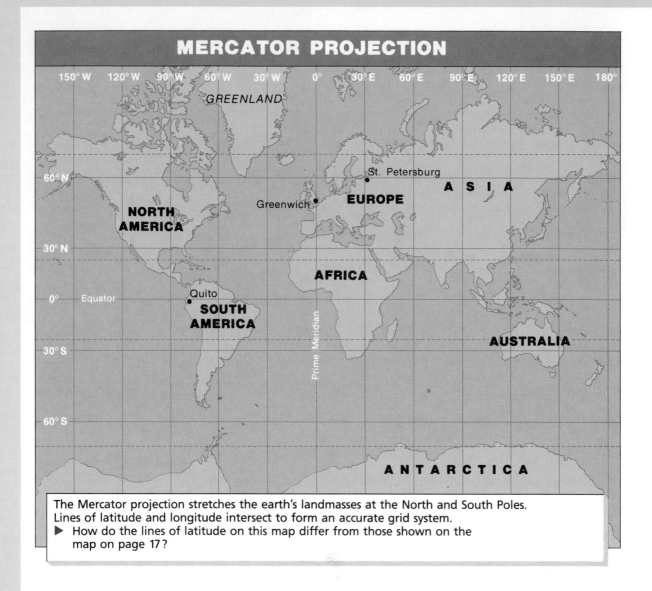

MERCATOR PROJECTION

| | | | | | | | | | | | |
|150°W|120°W|90°W|60°W|30°W|0°|30°E|60°E|90°E|120°E|150°E|180°|

GREENLAND

60° N

St. Petersburg

ASIA

NORTH
AMERICA

Greenwich

EUROPE

30° N

AFRICA

0° Equator

Quito

SOUTH
AMERICA

Prime Meridian

30° S

AUSTRALIA

60° S

ANTARCTICA

The Mercator projection stretches the earth's landmasses at the North and South Poles. Lines of latitude and longitude intersect to form an accurate grid system.
▶ How do the lines of latitude on this map differ from those shown on the map on page 17?

The early explorers knew that maps were more practical to use than globes. One of the main fields of geography during the Age of Exploration was **cartography**, or map making. Cartographers drew maps of all the new places being discovered.

The Distorted Earth But the cartographers found that showing the round earth on a flat map was not so easy. Why? Because when cartographers transfer the round globe to a flat surface, some changes occur in the earth's directions, shapes, sizes, and distances. These changes are **distortions**, or errors in the way the earth actually looks.

Through the years cartographers have developed many ways to draw the round earth on flat surfaces. Each of these different ways is called a **projection**. All projections, however, distort the way the earth looks on a globe. Some projections distort the sizes of continents; some distort the shapes; and others distort distances and directions.

C. The Mercator Projection and Navigation

A Navigator's Map One of the most famous map projections is called the Mer-

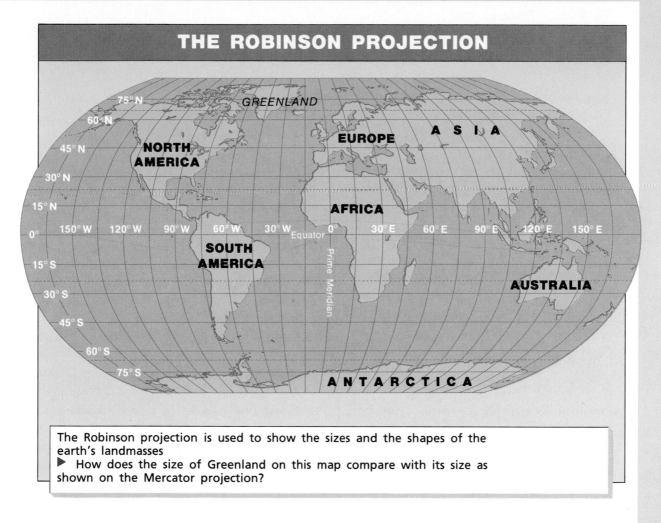

THE ROBINSON PROJECTION

75° N

GREENLAND

60° N

EUROPE   A S I A

45° N

NORTH
AMERICA

30° N

15° N

AFRICA

0°   150° W   120° W   90° W   60° W   30° W   0°   30° E   60° E   90° E   120° E   150° E
Equator

SOUTH
AMERICA

15° S

Prime Meridian

30° S

AUSTRALIA

45° S

60° S

75° S

A N T A R C T I C A

The Robinson projection is used to show the sizes and the shapes of the
earth's landmasses
▶ How does the size of Greenland on this map compare with its size as
shown on the Mercator projection?

cator (mur KAYT ur) projection. In the 1500s, explorers and sailors needed a map that would allow them to find their way around the oceans of the world. A cartographer named Gerardus (juh RAHR dus) Mercator developed a new projection, which was named for him. Mercator's projection showed the positions of places on the map exactly as they appear on a globe. Ships could easily find their destinations with a compass and Mercator's map.

The Mercator projection was great for the sea captains and sailors navigating the world's oceans. But Mercator's map was not good at all for showing the correct shapes and sizes of lands near the poles.

You can see this is true if you compare a Mercator map with a globe. Look at the

Mercator map on page 16 and compare the size of Greenland with that of South America. Now look at the same two areas on the globe in your classroom. You will see from the globe that Greenland is only about one-eighth the size of South America. On the Mercator map, however, Greenland is much larger than South America. The Mercator projection stretches lands near the North and South Poles to much bigger sizes than they actually are.

Robinson Projection If you want to show the correct sizes and shapes of the continents, you must use another projection. In this book, we have chosen the Robinson projection. You can see what this kind of map looks like above. The Robinson pro-

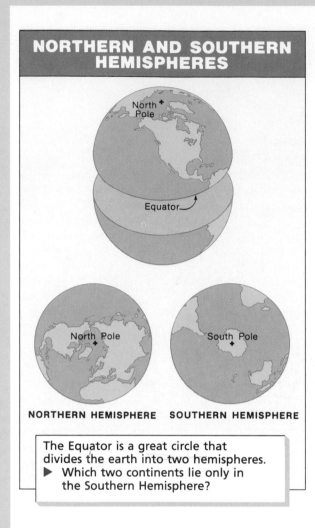

NORTHERN AND SOUTHERN HEMISPHERES

North Pole

Equator

NORTHERN HEMISPHERE   SOUTHERN HEMISPHERE

North Pole   South Pole

The Equator is a great circle that divides the earth into two hemispheres.
▶ Which two continents lie only in the Southern Hemisphere?

EASTERN AND WESTERN HEMISPHERES

North Pole — Prime Meridian

North Pole   North Pole

South Pole   South Pole

EASTERN HEMISPHERE   WESTERN HEMISPHERE

The Prime Meridian divides the earth into eastern and western hemispheres.
▶ In which hemisphere is the United States?

jection shows the size and shape of the continents with little distortion. Compare the size of Greenland and South America on this map. You can see that Greenland is much smaller. This is closer to the actual size and shape of Greenland on a globe.

D. Great Circles and Straight Lines

The Hemispheres The Mercator projection shows that ships and planes can travel in a straight line from, say, London, England, to New York. But on the globe, a straight line is not the shortest or the quickest way to travel. Instead, a **great circle** is the shortest possible distance between any two places on the surface of the earth.

A great circle is any circle you can draw on a globe that divides it into equal parts. If you were to cut a globe along a great circle, the knife would pass through the center of the globe and divide it into **hemispheres**, or two equal parts.

The Equator is a great circle because it divides the earth into northern and southern hemispheres. The Prime Meridian is also a great circle. As you can see from the map above, it divides the earth into eastern and western hemispheres.

Great Circle Routes Ships and airplanes often follow the curve of a great circle. By following great circle routes, ships and airplanes use less fuel, and passengers and cargo reach their destinations sooner.

GREAT CIRCLE ROUTES

Singapore (24-1/2 hrs)
Bangkok (24-1/2 hrs)
Hong Kong (16-1/2 hrs)
Beijing (21 hrs)
Tokyo (16 hrs)
New Delhi (17 hrs)
Moscow (11 hrs)
Berlin (8-1/2 hrs)
Cairo (11-1/2 hrs)
London (7 hrs)
Madrid (7 hrs)
Honolulu (11 hrs)
Chicago (2 hrs)
San Francisco (5-1/2 hrs)
New York (1 hr)
Washington, D.C.
Melbourne (21-1/2 hrs)
Mexico City (5 hrs)
Caracas (5-1/2 hrs)
Equator
0°
Cape Town (18 hrs)
Rio de Janeiro (10-1/2 hrs)

Numbers in parentheses show flying time, in hours, from Washington, D.C.

Great circle routes are the shortest possible distance between any two locations on the globe.
▶ How many hours would it take to fly from Washington, D.C. to Moscow?

Great circle routes are best shown on maps that we sometimes call polar projections. A polar projection puts the North Pole or South Pole at the center of the map. Two of the maps on page 18 are polar projections. Can you tell which ones they are? The map on page 675 is another example. Polar projections allow great circle routes to be drawn in straight lines across the map.

Look at the map above. It is similar to a polar projection. The red lines shown on this map are parts of great circle routes.

LESSON 3

Review

REVIEWING MAIN IDEAS
A. What is the size of the earth?
B. How do maps distort the earth?
C. Why was the Mercator projection useful to navigators?
D. What is a polar projection?

SKILLS CHECK

MAP SKILL

What projection is used to show Antarctica on page 675?

MAP SKILLS HANDBOOK REVIEW

REVIEWING TERMS

On a separate sheet of paper, write the letter of the term that best matches each numbered statement.

a. key
b. compass rose
c. latitude
d. longitude
e. physical map
f. contour line
g. cartography
h. distortion
i. projection
j. hemisphere

1. An error in the way the earth actually looks
2. A marker that shows where the cardinal directions are on a map
3. A way to draw the earth on a flat surface
4. Distance, measured in degrees, east and west of the Prime Meridian
5. A line drawn on a map that connects all points of land which are the same height above sea level
6. Distance, measured in degrees, north and south of the Equator
7. The work of making maps
8. The part of a map that explains the symbols used on the map
9. A map that shows the earth's relief, or physical features, and land elevations
10. Half the earth or the globe

REVIEWING THE FACTS

On a separate sheet of paper, answer the following questions in complete sentences.

1. What are the four cardinal directions?
2. What is the starting point of longitude called?
3. What relationship does scale show?
4. What kind of map would a cartographer use to show more detail of an area?
5. How can you tell which land forms are represented by contour lines?
6. How are physical maps used?
7. Why do different map projections have distortions?
8. What distortion is found in a Mercator projection?
9. Why is the Robinson projection used in this book?
10. How are great circle routes best shown on a map?

WRITING ABOUT GEOGRAPHY

Imagine that you are designing a new ski area for the town of Innsbruck, Austria. Explain what maps you would find useful to help you select the best location.

THINKING CRITICALLY

On a separate sheet of paper, answer the following questions in complete sentences.

1. How does the grid system help to locate places on a map?
2. Why do maps have different scales?
3. What map would you use to compare the resources of the United States with those of Canada?
4. Why, do you think, might Eratosthenes' discovery have encouraged explorers to seek new lands?
5. Why is it important to develop accurate maps?

On a separate sheet of paper, draw a graphic organizer that is like the one shown here. Copy the information from this graphic organizer to the one you have drawn. Under the main idea for each lesson, write three statements that you think best support the main idea.

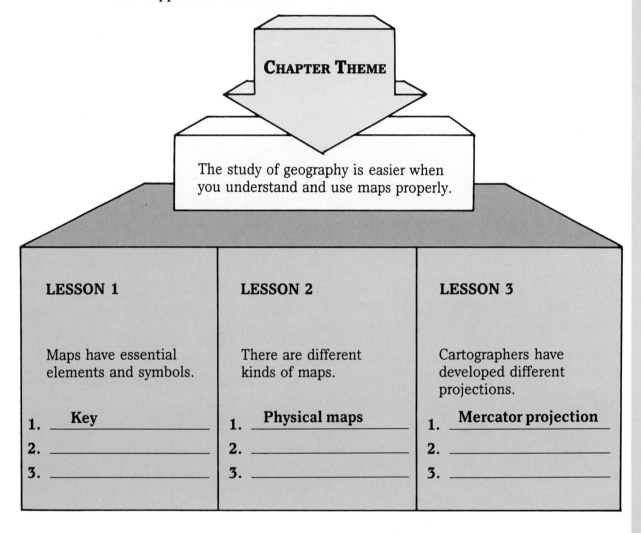

CHAPTER THEME

The study of geography is easier when you understand and use maps properly.

LESSON 1

Maps have essential elements and symbols.

1.   Key
2.
3.

LESSON 2

There are different kinds of maps.

1.   Physical maps
2.
3.

LESSON 3

Cartographers have developed different projections.

1.   Mercator projection
2.
3.

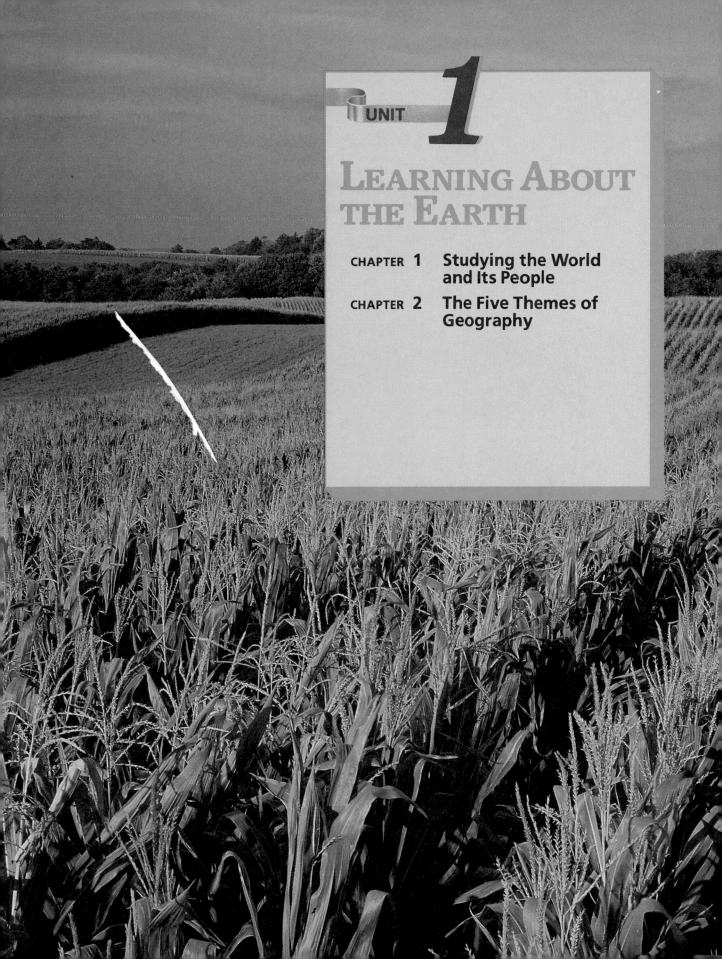

UNIT 1

LEARNING ABOUT THE EARTH

STUDYING THE WORLD AND ITS PEOPLE

1. **Robinson Crusoe's Life on a Deserted Island**

2. **People Have Many Different Ways of Life**

3. **Making a Living in the World**

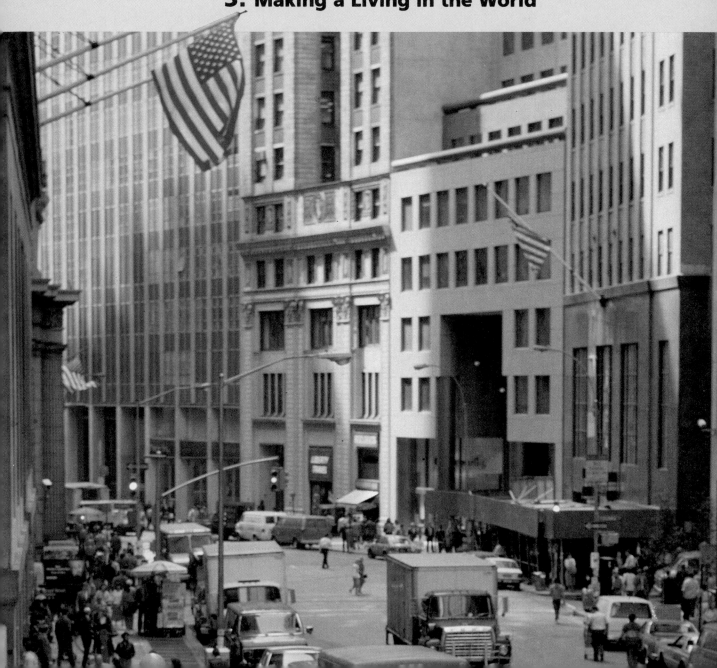

Robinson Crusoe's Life on a Deserted Island

CONNECTIONS

Imagine you are on a deserted tropical island and have only a hammer and an axe. With a partner, list the ways you would use these tools to gather food and build a shelter on the island.

TERMS

plantation, geography, natural resource, atmosphere, weather, climate, domesticate

FOCUS

In what ways do we use our physical environment to live?

A. Robinson Crusoe and His Island Home

September 30, 1659—I, poor miserable Robinson Crusoe, being shipwrecked during a dreadful storm, came on shore this dismal unfortunate island, . . . all the rest of the ship's company being drowned, and myself almost dead. . . .

I had neither food, house, clothes, weapon nor place to fly [flee] to; and in despair of any relief saw nothing but death before me; either that I should be devoured by wild beasts, murdered by savages, or starved to death for want of food. At the approach of night I slept in a tree for fear of wild creatures. . . .

This is the first entry from a journal kept by Robinson Crusoe. Crusoe was the hero of a fictional adventure story called *Robinson Crusoe*, which was written in 1719 by a British writer named Daniel Defoe. *Robinson Crusoe* tells the story of young Crusoe's adventures after he decided to become a sailor and leave England. Crusoe eventually sailed to Brazil, the largest country in South America, and became the owner of a **plantation**, which is a large, commercial farm that grows only one crop.

Some fellow plantation owners asked Crusoe to join them in a trip to the west coast of Africa. There the owners would buy slaves and bring them back to Brazil to work on their sugar and tobacco plantations.

Crusoe agreed to take the long and dangerous trip across the Atlantic Ocean. Unfortunately, this was to be a journey filled with incredible misfortune and adventure for both Crusoe and the ship's crew. A few days after the start of the journey, Crusoe's ship ran straight into the path of a powerful hurricane. This huge ocean wave capsized the ship, drowning the ship's crew and sweeping Crusoe onto the beach of a deserted island.

B. Crusoe and the Geography of His Deserted Island

To survive, Crusoe had to learn the **geography** of his new island home. Geography is the study of the earth and how people use the earth. Geography may not seem as exciting as the adventure story about Crusoe. You probably think geography is only the memorization of the names of important mountain ranges and rivers, and learning the products of countries. It is true that you will be expected to learn many facts about the world. Knowing the names and locations of countries, cities, mountains, and rivers is the foundation of geography. After all, you can't talk about skiing in the Rocky Mountains unless you know what and where they are.

But geography is much more than memorizing facts. Geography explains the world around us. It answers questions such as why is it cold at the North Pole, why is Florida just right for swimming in January, and why do palm trees grow in California but not in Kansas? Most important, geography shows us how people use the earth and change it to produce the food we eat, to make the clothes we wear, and to build the homes in which we live.

▶ Workers hurry to their jobs on Wall Street in New York City.

Crusoe built a raft to carry the many supplies he retrieved from the wrecked ship. With the supplies, he was able to build a shelter, hunt, and farm.
▶ What kinds of supplies did Crusoe find on the ship?

C. Crusoe's Exploration of the Island

Crusoe decided that the beach, which was swampy and wet, was not a good spot to stay and build a shelter. He thought over what a good location should offer him.

I consulted several things in my situation, which I found would be proper for [my new home]. Firstly, health and fresh water. . . . Secondly, shelter from the heat of the sun. Thirdly, security from ravenous [starving] creatures, whether men or beasts. Fourthly, a view to the sea, that if God sent any ship in sight I might not lose any advantage for my deliverance, of which I was not willing to banish all my expectation yet.

Crusoe studied the landscape of the island, hoping to find a proper site for a new home. Near a small stream he found a flat, grassy plain beside a rising hill. Crusoe decided that this should be the site of his new home.

Crusoe now set to work building a permanent shelter. Fortunately, Crusoe had retrieved some tools, guns, and other supplies from the ship, which lay wrecked near the island. With these he dug a small cave in the side of the hill. In the front of the cave mouth, he pitched his tent, which was made from the sails of the wrecked ship. Crusoe felt he needed protection, so with great effort he cut down several trees and built a log wall around his tent and cave.

D. From Hunting to Farming

Hunting "I went out [once a day]," Crusoe wrote in his journal, "with my gun . . . to see if I could kill anything fit for food." At first, Crusoe hunted the wild goats he found on the island. He also fished in the surrounding ocean waters and dug for turtle eggs hidden in the beach sands.

As time passed, Crusoe continued to explore his island and found other foods to eat. Looking through a tangle of vines one day, he found bunches of grapes. Near the grapes he discovered a grove of lemon trees and other fruit trees.

Crusoe also discovered a few barley plants and rice plants on the island. Instead of immediately cooking and eating the plants, Crusoe allowed them to bear seeds. He then planted these seeds after heavy rains occurred. Crusoe's first crop of barley failed to grow.

> *Finding my first seed did not grow, which I easily imagined was by the drought, I sought for a moister piece of ground. . . . I dug up a piece of ground near my new bower [home], and sowed the rest of my seed in February, a little before the vernal equinox. And this having the rainy months of March and April to water it, sprung up very pleasantly, and yielded a good crop. . . .*

Even though he planted after the rains, a drought, or dry period without rain, killed the plants. It was only after Crusoe understood when the rainy season occurred that his crops of barley and rice grew.

By Crusoe's second year on the island, he had a steady supply of food from his garden. Later, he caught some young goats and **domesticated** them. *Domesticate* means to "tame wild animals to live with humans." The goat herd provided Crusoe with meat, which freed him from having to worry about hunting every day.

Natural Resources Crusoe could build a home and grow food because he learned to

The island's abundant rainfall allowed Crusoe to grow a large wheat crop.
► How did Crusoe harvest his crop of wheat?

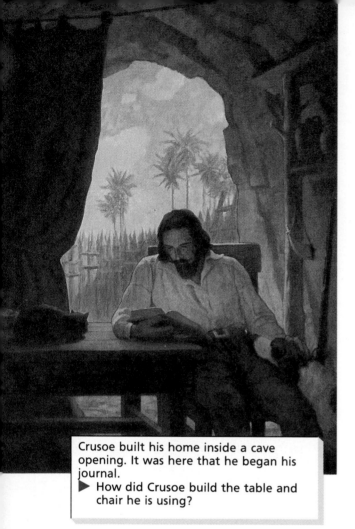

Wilmington Institute Library, photo courtesy of Brandywine River Museum.

Crusoe built his home inside a cave opening. It was here that he began his journal.
▶ How did Crusoe build the table and chair he is using?

use the island's **natural resources**. Natural resources are materials made by nature that people can use. What were the natural resources Crusoe used? He used the soil to grow crops and trees to build the fort. The animals living on the island provided him with what he needed for food and to make clothing.

The natural resources we find on the earth are the source of our food, clothing, and shelter. But these natural resources require the labor, or work, of people to make them useful products. These products are usually processed, or changed into different forms. This is exactly what Crusoe had to do. He used the barley he grew to make bread. He took the skin from his goats and cut and sewed them into a vest and pants.

Crusoe also had to learn about the island's seasons and the changes in the island's temperature in order to grow his crops. The temperature, the amount of sunshine, and the amount of rainfall are all conditions of the **atmosphere**. The atmosphere is the blanket of air that covers the earth. If the earth had no atmosphere, there could be no life.

We use two words to describe the atmosphere. One word that we use all the time is **weather**. Weather is how the atmosphere is at a certain time and place. A weather report on television or a weather forecast in the newspaper describes what the weather is today or predicts what it will be tomorrow. Another word we use to describe the atmosphere is **climate**. Climate is the pattern of weather that a place has over a period of time. Crusoe's island had a climate that was warm all year, and it had rainy seasons and dry seasons.

E. Crusoe's Story and Our Life Today

Learning from Crusoe Crusoe survived on his island for almost 30 years, until he was finally rescued by the crew of a passing ship. During those 30 years, the resources of the earth and Crusoe's hard labor provided Crusoe with abundant food and adequate clothing and shelter.

You will probably never be lost on an island without food, shelter, and clothing. And if you ever are, you will have learned a few lessons from Crusoe about how to survive. But there is a more important lesson to learn from Robinson Crusoe that we can apply to our everyday lives. Today it seems that humans can do almost anything with their tools and imagination. We have flown to the moon and are exploring the frontiers of the universe. Television gives us instant information about almost any part of the world. We can microwave our dinners in a few minutes and we can

FROM: # The Sea Around Us

Rachel Carson

Crusoe came upon an island that was well stocked with natural resources. But at one time, the island—like all islands—was nothing more than a barren, rocky, empty piece of land surrounded by the ocean. How did it come to be covered with trees, grasses, birds, and animals? In her book, *The Sea Around Us*, Rachel Carson wrote about how newly born islands come to be alive with so many different forms of life.

We can only guess how long after its emergence from the sea an oceanic island may lie uninhabited. Certainly in its original state it is a land bare, harsh, and repelling [disgusting] beyond human experience. No living thing moves over the slopes of its volcanic hills; no plants cover its naked lava fields. But little by little, riding on the winds, drifting on the currents, or rafting in on logs, floating brush, or trees, the plants and animals that are to colonize it arrive from the distant continents.

So deliberate, so unhurried . . . are the ways of nature that the stocking of an island may require thousands or millions of years. It may be that no more than half a dozen times in all these eons [years] does a particular form, such as a tortoise, make a successful landing on its shores. To wonder impatiently why man is not a constant witness of such arrivals is to fail to understand the majestic pace of the process. . . .

The wide-ranging birds that visit islands of the ocean in migration may . . . have a good deal to do with the distribution of plants, and perhaps even some of the insects and minute [small] land shells. . . .

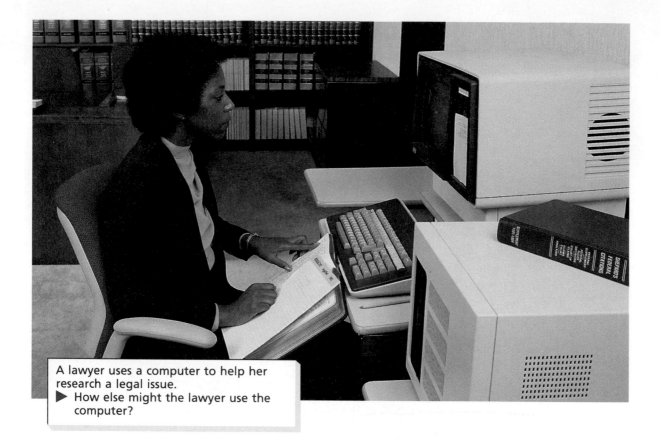

A lawyer uses a computer to help her research a legal issue.
▶ How else might the lawyer use the computer?

program computers to solve math problems that would take a person several years to figure out.

Using the Earth   Crusoe's struggle for food, shelter, and clothing seems very distant and removed from these modern-day accomplishments. Yet, like Crusoe, we still use the earth's resources—even to make tools like computers and microwaves. Knowing what these resources are and how we use them will give us a fuller understanding of the world we live in.

Robinson Crusoe was an explorer, an observer, and a learner. He investigated his island, he examined the island's landscape, and he learned how to live on the island. You, too, can follow in his footsteps this year as you explore the world, observe its people and places, and learn how these people and places affect you.

LESSON 1

Review

REVIEWING MAIN IDEAS

A. Why did Crusoe decide to sail to Africa?
B. Why is the study of geography important?
C. Name the four things Crusoe wanted his home to have.
D. How did Crusoe obtain food on his deserted island?
E. What message does the story of Robinson Crusoe have for people today?

SKILLS CHECK

WRITING SKILL

Reread Crusoe's first journal entry, on page 25. Imagine that you have landed on a deserted island. Write a journal entry that describes how you would feel and what your plans would be to find food, clothing, and shelter.

People Have Many Different Ways of Life

CONNECTIONS
Have you ever eaten any foods that tasted different from what you normally eat? Describe what you liked or disliked about the food.

TERMS
culture, language family, mosque

FOCUS
How does culture shape the way we live?

A. Culture and Crusoe's Island Life

Robinson Crusoe survived on a deserted island by using the island's natural resources. The way Crusoe used these resources was based on his **culture**. Culture is the way a person or people live. The language we speak, our religion, and our beliefs about what is good and bad are all parts of our culture. Culture also includes the clothes we wear, the music we listen to, and almost everything else that makes up our way of life.

Crusoe's way of life on the island was based on the English culture in which he was raised. Crusoe could have lived perfectly well by hunting goats and other wild animals on his island and by picking wild fruits and berries. But he immediately set to work trying to tame the wild goats and trying to grow grain to make bread. If someone from a different culture had landed on the island, he or she would have found different ways of surviving, because that person would have used the island's resources differently.

B. Language and Our Thoughts

Learning Language Robinson Crusoe lived alone on his island for 25 years before he rescued a man from some cannibals who had landed on the island. The rescued man, whom Crusoe named Friday, was a South American Indian who had been brought to the island for sacrifice by the cannibals. Crusoe described his first encounter with Friday after the rescue.

He spoke some words to me, and though I could not understand them, yet I thought they were pleasant to hear, for they were the first sound of a man's voice that I had heard, my own excepted, for about twenty-five years. . . . I was greatly delighted with him, and made it my business to teach him everything . . . but especially to make him speak and understand me. . . .

Until Friday and Crusoe could speak the same language, they could only communicate by pointing at objects and by making signs with their hands. Once Friday learned English, the men could talk to each other and Friday could begin to learn about Crusoe's culture.

Language is one of the most important parts of culture. Thousands of languages are spoken today by the more than 5 billion people who live on the earth. Most people in the United States speak English, which comes to us from England, the European country that once controlled our country.

At one time, England had the largest empire in the world, and the English language spread with England's empire. Today the lands England once controlled are independent countries, but English is still spoken by many people in these countries. In fact, English is one of the most widely spoken languages in the world.

Language Family English is a Germanic language, which means that it is related to languages spoken in northern Europe. Germanic is a **language family**. A language family is a group of languages that all come from one common ancestor language. The other important European language families are the Romance languages of southern Europe and the Slavic languages that are used in Eastern Europe.

31

Many important languages are not related to the European language families. Arabic is spoken by millions of people in northern Africa and the Middle East. In Asia, Chinese and Japanese are the most important languages. Swahili is an important language in Africa, and Quechua (KECH wah) is still spoken by Indians in some parts of the Andes mountains of South America. These are only a few of the thousands of languages used by the different peoples on the earth.

C. Religion: An Important Part of Culture

Different Religions Robinson Crusoe was English. His religion was Protestant, one of the Christian religions that was the religion of most people in England during the time the story was written. Do you remember that Crusoe lived in Brazil for a time? Brazil was controlled by people from Portugal, who were Roman Catholics, another Christian religion. In an earlier adventure in the book, Crusoe was captured by pirates off the coast of Africa. The pirates were Muslims, which is the name for the followers of the Islamic religion.

These are only a few of the many religions practiced by people around the world. Not all religions share the same beliefs. For example, most Christians believe that Sunday is a day of worship. This belief shapes the work schedule of most Christians, who work from Monday through Friday or Saturday. For Muslims, Friday is a day of rest, and for Jews, Saturday is the day of worship.

Religion affects more than just work schedules. People who belong to the Hindu religion in India do not eat meat. Muslims do not eat pork, and Jewish dietary laws place restrictions on the preparation and kinds of foods Jews can eat.

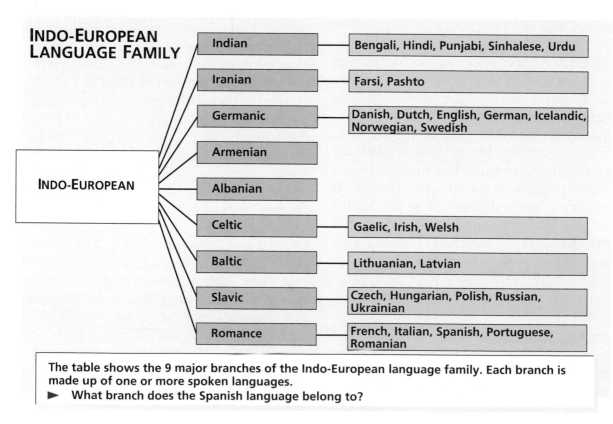

The table shows the 9 major branches of the Indo-European language family. Each branch is made up of one or more spoken languages.
► What branch does the Spanish language belong to?

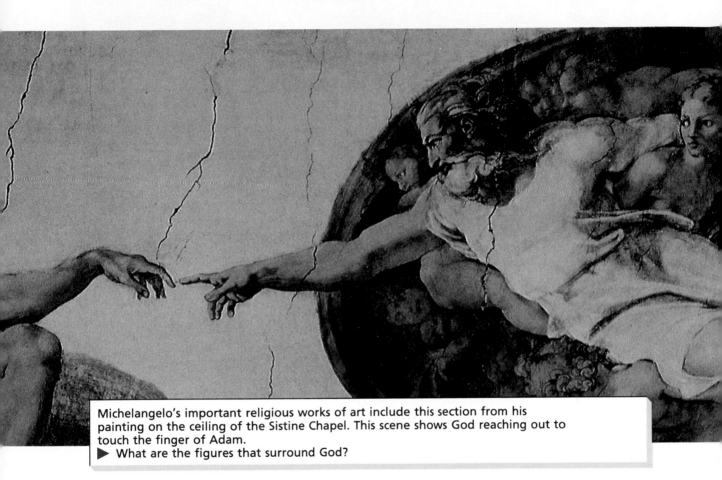

Michelangelo's important religious works of art include this section from his painting on the ceiling of the Sistine Chapel. This scene shows God reaching out to touch the finger of Adam.
▶ What are the figures that surround God?

Religious Art Much of the greatest art in the world is religious art. Michelangelo was a great artist who lived in Italy in the sixteenth century. His best-known paintings and sculptures are of scenes from famous Bible stories. In fact, much of the great European art in the centuries before and after Michelangelo has religion as its subject matter.

Art works from other parts of the world also have religious roots. Statues of Buddha, the founder of the Buddhist religion, are important artworks from China, India, and Southeast Asia. Sculptures of Hindu gods from India are found in art museums around the world. Art museums also have collections of African masks and wood carvings. Most of these were originally made for religious ceremonies or for other religious purposes.

Each religion also has its own special kind of church or temple architecture. Because of this, we can easily identify a Christian cathedral in France; an Islamic **mosque**, or Islamic place of worship, in Turkey; or a Buddhist shrine in Burma. Other religions around the world also have their own special style of art and their own way of building places of worship.

D. Culture and the Way We Eat

If you were invited to eat dinner in the home of an Arab Bedouin, what would you eat? Bedouins are wandering herders who live in the deserts of the Middle East and North Africa. You begin by washing your hands. Then the men are invited into the tent where your host lives. Because men and women eat separately, the women will eat after the men have finished.

A group of Arab men sit cross-legged around their meal. The pieces of bread are eaten with the dinner.
▶ Which hand is used to eat with?

All the men sit on rugs around a huge platter. On the platter is a large, flat wheat bread that looks like a giant pancake. Rice is mounded on top of the bread. Then pieces of boiled lamb are put on top of the rice, and a seasoned butter sauce is poured over the rice and lamb.

You won't be given any silverware. Instead, you will be expected to pick the rice and lamb from the platter with your right hand. After the men have eaten, they relax and enjoy cups of strong Arab coffee.

This is only one example of the many different foods and the customs for preparing and eating food that you can find in the countries of the world. We can also find different foods in our own country. Perhaps you have eaten in a Chinese restaurant. Unless you learned to use chopsticks as a child, you would find that eating with chopsticks is very different from using silverware.

Certainly the foods we eat are partly influenced by the places where we live. An Arab living in the interior of a desert is not likely to eat seafood, which would not be easy to get so far from the ocean. However, the ways in which foods are prepared are largely determined by the unique culture or customs practiced by the people who live in a region.

LESSON 2

Review

REVIEWING MAIN IDEAS

A. What do we mean when we use the term *culture*?
B. Why is English so widely spoken throughout the world?
C. Name two ways in which culture is influenced by religion.
D. Give an example of how the way people eat is influenced by their culture.

SKILLS CHECK

THINKING SKILL

Describe how music, clothing, or food is an important part of our culture today.

Making a Living in the World

Describe a career you might want to pursue when you finish your education. Explain why that career appeals to you.

TERMS

subsistence, ore, pastoralism, alloy, nomad

FOCUS

How have people used the earth's resources to make a living?

A. People as Resources

Subsistence Economy You have learned how Robinson Crusoe had to use the natural resources of his environment to survive. There are other resources that are as important as natural resources. You may be surprised to learn that people, too, are a resource. In fact, it is human resources, that is, people, who do the work to make natural resources useful.

Like Crusoe, our ancestors had to learn about natural resources and use their human resources to make them into useful products. Like Crusoe, early humans survived by hunting animals and gathering any edible plants they could find. Edible plants are the fruit, leaves, roots, or other plant parts that are good to eat. Unlike Crusoe, these early people did not have guns. Instead, they hunted with weapons such as traps, slingshots, and spears.

People who live from hunting and gathering have a **subsistence** economy. A subsistence economy is one in which the people collect only enough food to feed themselves.

When Crusoe first arrived on his island, he had a subsistence economy. He hunted when he needed meat, and he gathered grapes and other plants. As you may remember from Lesson 1, Crusoe domesticated some wild goats, which gave him a more secure food supply.

Pastoralism Early humans also tamed animals to make them pets or to use their meat, milk, and hides. Larger animals could be used for pulling carts or for riding. Eventually, people who lived in the great grasslands of Asia and the semidesert regions of Africa learned to herd animals for a living. Herding animals for a living is called **pastoralism.**

The pastoralists had to move their herds of animals to find enough good grasses for the animals to graze on. They became **nomads**, people who have no permanent home. Nomads move from place to place, living in tents or other movable shelters.

An African boy herds his family's cattle and sheep. Pastoralism is still practiced in many parts of the world.
▶ Why is the boy carrying sticks?

35

EARLY WESTERN CIVILIZATIONS

Mesopotamia

Egypt

Present-day
national boundaries

• Ancient cities

0   300 miles

0   300 kilometers

Black
Sea

Mediterranean
Sea

Ebla

Euphrates

Tigris River

River

Babylon

Akkad

Jordan
River

Jericho

Lagash

Memphis

Nile River

Persian Gulf

Some of the earliest civilizations
began in Mesopotamia and Egypt.
▶ What ancient cities were located
   between the Tigris and Euphrates
   Rivers?

B. Farming and the Rise of Cities

Growth of Farming When Robinson Crusoe began planting grain, he changed his economy, or way of making a living, from hunting and gathering to farming. Early humans also went through a similar change. They realized that certain plants could be grown in one area where they could be protected and where they might be more easily harvested than in the wild. This new way of growing crops was the beginning of agriculture, or farming.

The change from hunting and gathering to farming is one of the most important events in human history. Farming made it possible for people to produce a surplus of food. When they had a surplus, they could store it for times when crops failed. But

surplus food also meant that not everyone had to spend time hunting and gathering or farming. Some people could spend their time doing other kinds of work. These people became specialists, or people who do only one kind of job. Some people made weapons and tools, and others made baskets or pottery.

The number of people living in one place also started to grow. Camps became villages and villages became towns. Eventually, the first cities began to develop. These cities required a government to keep everything running smoothly. Since many goods were gathered in the cities, armies were created to provide protection.

Growth of Trade Trade began to develop between cities when people realized that goods produced in one city could be traded for different goods produced in another city. Trade routes sprang up between cities as merchant caravans carried loads of goods for trading.

The people living in the cities developed a way of life known as civilization. Civilizations have productive farms, governments, armies, a system of writing, large ornate buildings, and great works of art. Civilizations began to grow in many parts of the world.

One early center of civilization was Mesopotamia, the area between the Tigris and Euphrates rivers in what is today the country of Iraq. Great cities were built here between 5,000 and 6,000 years ago. About the same time, another important Western civilization began along the banks of the Nile River in Egypt.

C. The Rise of Manufacturing

Using Resources The people living in cities learned new ways to use natural resources. They melted **ores**, or rocks that contain minerals, to make metals such as copper and iron. Later they improved these

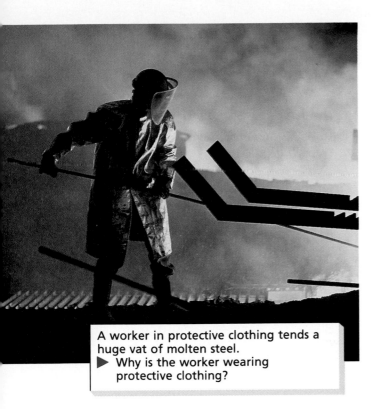

A worker in protective clothing tends a huge vat of molten steel.
▶ Why is the worker wearing protective clothing?

metals by mixing them in **alloys** such as bronze and steel. Alloys are mixtures of metals that are harder or stronger than the individual metals from which they are made. Both of these processes allowed people to make stronger weapons and tools.

About 200 years ago a revolutionary advance was made in our ability to use energy. In England, James Watt made the first steam engine. Steam engines could be used to run machines in factories. They could also be mounted on carts that ran on rails; these became the first railroads. About the same time, steam engines were put on ships. Now ships could sail under their own power rather than depend on wind to move them.

These inventions and others made it possible to build large factories. The first factories made cloth for clothing and other uses. Soon, more factories were built to manufacture tools, guns, transportation equipment, and thousands of other goods for people to use.

D. Work Today and in the Future

Manufacturing is still an important part of the economy of most countries. But as in the past, the way people make a living is again changing. Today some major countries are moving from manufacturing to information and service industries as their most important economic activities. Information industries gather, process, and store information in computers. Service industries provide services for other people. Service industry jobs include work in education, health, restaurants, and tourism.

Some experts believe that in the future most people will work in these kinds of jobs. These experts also believe that by using computers and other new electronic tools, people may be able to work from their homes. Even today, some companies have given workers computers to use at home. The home computers are linked to other computers at the company's office. The workers send the work they have done on their home computers to the main company computer.

LESSON 3

Review

REVIEWING MAIN IDEAS
A. What early human activity is part of a subsistence economy?
B. What effects did surplus food have on people's lives?
C. How did the invention of the steam engine change the way in which people produced goods?
D. How might the industries of the future affect the way people work?

SKILLS CHECK

MAP SKILL
Turn to the map of South America in the Atlas. Crusoe's ship is to have wrecked near 7°N/50°W. Name the countries that are near this coordinate.

REVIEWING TERMS

Match each term with the correct definition. Write your answers in sentence form.

atmosphere	geography
nomad	natural resource
culture	pastoralism
weather	service industry
climate	language family

1. A material made by nature that people can use
2. The way a person or people live
3. A person with no permanent home
4. The blanket of air that covers the earth
5. A group of languages from one common ancestor language
6. An economy based on the herding of animals
7. Work that provides services rather than goods
8. The condition of the atmosphere at a certain time or place
9. The pattern of weather a place has over a period of time
10. The study of the earth and how people use the earth

REVIEWING THE FACTS

On a separate sheet of paper, answer the questions in complete sentences.

1. What were the natural resources that Crusoe used to survive on his island?
2. What do weather and climate describe?
3. How did English become one of the most widely spoken languages in the world?
4. Name three religions that help shape the culture of people around the world.

5. Why can we say that Crusoe had a subsistence economy?
6. Why did pastoralists become nomads?
7. Why did trade develop between ancient cities?
8. What was the result of creating alloys such as bronze and steel?
9. What were wind and water used to power?
10. What are service industries?

WRITING ABOUT GEOGRAPHY

When Crusoe met Friday, they could not understand each other's language. Write a paragraph explaining how you would teach someone from another country how to speak a few sentences in English.

THINKING CRITICALLY

On a separate sheet of paper, answer the following in complete sentences.

1. How can the study of geography help you plan a vacation to a foreign country?
2. How could the lessons of Crusoe's survival have been applied to man's first landing on the moon?
3. In what ways does culture influence the way people live?
4. How did the beginning of agriculture allow the development of civilization?
5. Why was the steam engine a revolutionary advance in technology?

On a separate sheet of paper, draw a graphic organizer like the one shown here. Copy the information from this graphic organizer to the one you have drawn. Next to each main idea, write three statements that you think best support it. The first statement has been done for you.

CHAPTER THEME

Geography is the study of the earth and the way people live on the earth.

Lesson 1   People use the physical environment in many different ways.

1. To grow food
2. _____
3. _____

Lesson 2   Culture shapes the way we live.

1. The language we speak
2. _____
3. _____

Lesson 3   There are many ways of using the earth's resources to make a living.

1. Hunting and gathering
2. _____
3. _____

CHAPTER **2**

THE FIVE THEMES
OF GEOGRAPHY

The Earth and Its Regions

CONNECTIONS

Imagine that you are an astronaut standing on the moon. Describe what the earth would look like to you.

TERMS

region, relief, glacier

FOCUS

Why do we divide the earth into regions?

A. Viewing the Earth from Space

This was it. We were 100 miles up and going at a velocity of 25,730 feet per second. Now for the first time, I could look out the window and see back along the flight path. I could not help exclaiming over the radio about what I saw. "Oh," I said, "that view is tremendous!" It really was. I could see for hundreds of miles in every direction—the sun on white clouds, patches of blue water beneath, and great chunks of Florida and the southeastern U.S.

I saw the Canary Islands through the periscope and then saw them through the window. They were partially hidden by clouds. While I was reporting in by radio to the Canary Islands tracking station, I had my first glimpse of the coast of Africa. The Atlas Mountains were clearly visible through the window. Inland, I could see huge dust storms blowing across the desert, as well as clouds of smoke from brush fires raging along the edge of the desert. One of the things that surprised me most about the flight was the percentage of the earth that was covered by clouds. They were nearly solid over central Africa and extended out over most of the Indian Ocean and clear across the Pacific.

These words were written by John Glenn, the first American to orbit the earth. Glenn made his historic trip on Tuesday, February 20, 1962, in the spacecraft named *Friendship* 7. The fascinating scenes that unfolded beneath *Friendship* 7 as it moved through space gave John Glenn a new and different view of the earth. You, too, will see the earth in a special way when you study geography. But unlike Glenn, one of the ways you will view the earth is by looking at its different **regions**. A region is a part of the earth that has one or more common characteristics.

The Five Themes Region is one of the five themes, or main ideas, of geography. The other four themes are absolute and relative location, place, relationships within places, and movement.

The themes are like telescopes, since each theme gives us a special way of looking at the earth. In this chapter you will learn how the themes work, and how you can use them to understand the world around you.

This view of the earth from space shows how Africa looked to Glenn.
▶ What other continent is visible in the photograph?

41

▶ A Landsat photograph taken from a satellite shows part of San Francisco Bay.

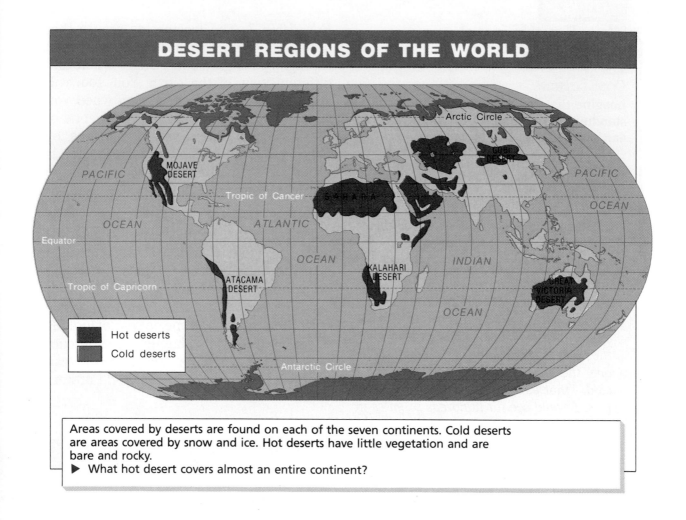

DESERT REGIONS OF THE WORLD

Arctic Circle

MOJAVE DESERT

PACIFIC OCEAN

GOBI DESERT

PACIFIC OCEAN

Tropic of Cancer

SAHARA

ATLANTIC OCEAN

Equator

INDIAN OCEAN

ATACAMA DESERT

KALAHARI DESERT

Tropic of Capricorn

GREAT VICTORIA DESERT

OCEAN

Hot deserts
Cold deserts

Antarctic Circle

Areas covered by deserts are found on each of the seven continents. Cold deserts are areas covered by snow and ice. Hot deserts have little vegetation and are bare and rocky.
▶ What hot desert covers almost an entire continent?

B. Defining Different Regions

Regions vary according to the characteristics, or qualities, that we use to identify them. One example of this is the climate regions of the world. These are areas that have similar climates that often cover a large part of a continent. The map on this page shows the regions of the world that are covered by desert climates. What other characteristics might these regions have in common?

Regions can also be defined according to economic activities, such as farming and manufacturing. Cultural traits, such as language, religion, and food, can also be used to identify a region. Political divisions, such as the boundaries between countries or states, also identify regions. During a news

program on radio or television, you may have heard the announcer say, "Today in Southeast Asia . . ." or "Yesterday in Western Europe. . . ." You may have read a newspaper story about Southern Africa, Eastern Europe, the Middle East, or Central America. These names refer to geographical regions of the earth that are made up of many countries.

An area can also be part of more than one region. The city of Philadelphia, Pennsylvania, for example, is in the mid-Atlantic region of the United States. It is also part of a region known as Megalopolis, an area of large cities and many people in the eastern part of the country. This Megalopolis stretches from Boston, Massachusetts, to Washington, D.C.

C. The Many Forms of the Land

O beautiful for spacious skies,
For amber waves of grain,
For purple mountain majesties
Above the fruited plain.

Do you recognize these lines? They are from the first verse of the song "America the Beautiful," which was written in 1893 by Katharine Lee Bates. In the summer of that year, Bates made a trip from Massachusetts to Colorado. From the top of Pikes Peak, she could see the Rocky Mountains stretching off to the west. Turning to the east, she could see the Great Plains fading off into the distance. This view so impressed Bates that she later composed her song. The purple mountains are the Rocky Mountains, and the fruited plain is covered by the Great Plains.

Landforms The Great Plains and the Rocky Mountains are landform regions of the United States. Landforms are the forms or shapes of the earth. Plains, plateaus, hills, and mountains are the four main kinds of landforms. Each of these landforms is different from the others because of its **relief**.

Relief is the difference in the elevation or height of the land.

A plain is an almost flat area, with little difference in elevation between the high parts and the low parts. This is why we say plains have low relief. There are many different kinds of plains. Coastal plains are areas near the ocean coast that were once underwater. Lake plains were once the bottoms of lakes that were exposed when the lakes dried up.

A plateau is a plain that has been raised up by pressures inside the earth so that it stands high above the areas around it. Plateaus often have canyons that cross them. The canyons were formed by many rivers that cut into the surface of the plateau. The Grand Canyon is an example of such a canyon. Sometimes the surface of the plateau may be broken by hills or mountains, too.

Hills are areas of moderate relief. This means that the difference in elevation between the tops of hills and the bottoms of the valleys is between 300 feet (91 m) and 1,000 feet (305 m). Hills may have either steep or gentle slopes.

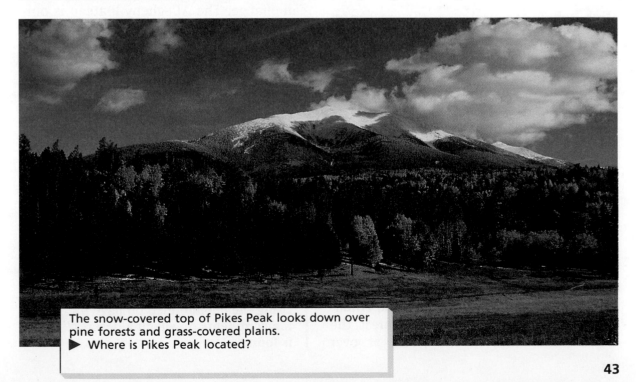

The snow-covered top of Pikes Peak looks down over pine forests and grass-covered plains.
▶ Where is Pikes Peak located?

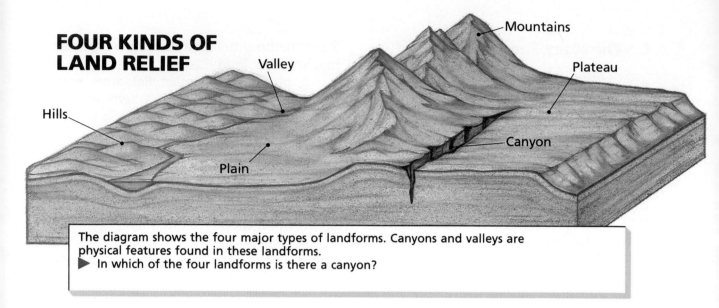

FOUR KINDS OF LAND RELIEF

Mountains

Plateau

Valley

Canyon

Hills

Plain

The diagram shows the four major types of landforms. Canyons and valleys are physical features found in these landforms.
► In which of the four landforms is there a canyon?

Hills often form in an area where there was once a plateau. The hills occur when rivers that flowed across the plateau cut so many canyons and valleys in the plateau that there is little or none of the original flat plateau surface left. The Allegheny Plateau in the eastern United States is an example of a plateau that has worn down so much that it is really a region of hills. However, geographers continue to call it a plateau.

High Relief Mountains are the most spectacular landforms. Mountains have high relief, which means that a mountain's peak is at least 1,000 feet (305 m) above the land around them. Many mountains are so tall that they have snow on them all year round. The snow can harden into ice and form **glaciers**, large wide rivers of ice that slowly flow down the sides of a mountain, carving the mountain into a sharp, pointed peak. Many of the peaks in the Rocky Mountains and the Sierra Nevada Mountains of the United States were once covered by glaciers.

Mountains often form in long rows that are called mountain ranges. The tallest mountain range in the world is the Himalaya Mountains in Asia. Mount Everest, the highest mountain in the world at over 29,000 feet (8,840 m), is found in the Himalayas.

The longest mountain range in the world is the Andes in South America. The Andes extend all the way down the western side of South America. They are over 4,000 miles (6,436 km) long, which is greater than the distance between New York and Los Angeles.

An important thing to remember about all these landforms is the fact that each can change. The Allegheny Plateau is only one example of how weather and rivers can wear down and slowly change a landform.

LESSON 1

Review

REVIEWING MAIN IDEAS
A. What is meant by a region?
B. Name three different ways in which a region can be defined?
C. What are the four major landform regions?

SKILLS CHECK

MAP SKILL
Using the climate map on page 42, name the continents on which a desert climate is found.

Location and Place

CONNECTIONS

Name the landmarks you would use if you wanted to direct a friend from your school to your home.

TERMS

navigator, meteorologist, absolute location, relative location

FOCUS

How do we use location and place?

A. John Glenn's Return to Earth

Navigation You read about what John Glenn saw from space. Now let's see what happened when he came back to the earth. Glenn's spacecraft was pulled to the earth by gravity. Gravity is the force that attracts objects toward the earth. Friction with the atmosphere slowed the spacecraft down a little, but giant parachutes were used before the craft landed. These kept the ship from hitting the earth so hard that Glenn would be injured. The impact of landing was also reduced by aiming the spacecraft at the Atlantic Ocean.

Unlike the pilots of today's space shuttles, Glenn could not steer his spacecraft. As a result, no one was sure exactly where he would land in the Atlantic. How could the United States Navy's ships find Glenn? There were no landmarks on the ocean to guide people who had the job of finding Glenn and his spacecraft.

Fortunately, we have invented a way of telling where anything is on the earth, even if there aren't any landmarks to go by. **Navigators** are people who are responsible for locating ships and planes. These same people were also responsible for finding Glenn's spacecraft after it splashed down. Navigators have created a system of imaginary lines that divide up the earth. This system is called the grid system, which you learned about in the Map Handbook.

The longitude and latitude numbers that make up the grid system allow us to locate a country or object anywhere on earth. If we know the latitude and longitude of a place, we can find its location, no matter where it is.

Absolute Location The latitude and longitude of a place is called **absolute location**. Using sophisticated computers and maps, the navigators on the ships that were to pick up John Glenn were able to determine the absolute location where Glenn had landed. They had no trouble finding the spacecraft when it landed.

Knowing how to find the absolute location of a place is a basic skill in geography, since it is the quickest way to find a place on a map. Throughout this year, you will often be asked to find the absolute location of the earth's cities, towns, lakes, and rivers.

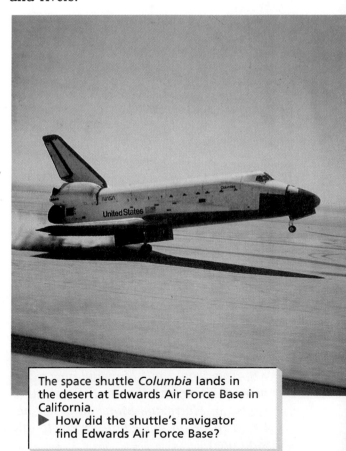

The space shuttle *Columbia* lands in the desert at Edwards Air Force Base in California.
▶ How did the shuttle's navigator find Edwards Air Force Base?

45

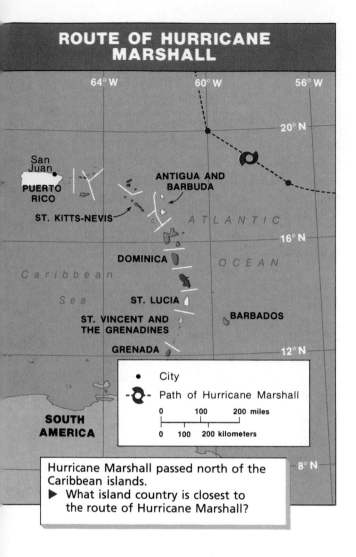

ROUTE OF HURRICANE MARSHALL

Hurricane Marshall passed north of the Caribbean islands.
▶ What island country is closest to the route of Hurricane Marshall?

How is the location of the hurricane given in this newspaper report? Perhaps you noticed that the article gives the absolute location of the hurricane. The storm was 18°N and 57°W at 6 P.M., and it was expected to move to 20°N and 60°W by the next morning. These locations are very useful for **meteorologists**, the scientists who study the weather, because the locations allow them to follow the storm's exact progress. But absolute location is not very useful to people who don't have maps showing latitude and longitude lines.

Relative Location The newspaper also tells you that the hurricane is located 600 miles (965 km) east of San Juan, Puerto Rico. If you know where the city of San Juan is, or if you have a map that shows it, you can estimate how far 600 miles (965 km) is and know just about where the hurricane is. When we find the location of a place by telling how far and in what direction it is from somewhere else, we are using **relative location**. Relative location gives the location of a place relative to some known landmark.

Imagine that you had to tell someone how to find your school. You might say, "My school is one block north of the Greengate Shopping Center, which is on Elm Street." When you give these kinds of directions, you are using relative location. You have told the person the distance and direction of the school from the shopping center, and you have told him or her what street the school is on. If you were telling a person where your town is located, you would probably begin by noting its relative location to the nearest large city, or some significant landform.

Most of us use relative location every day to find the places where we need to go. Absolute location is used by navigators, meteorologists, and others who need to find exact locations without having to depend on landmarks.

B. Finding Our Way by Relative Location

At 6 P.M. Central Daylight Time, Hurricane Marshall was centered near the latitude 18°N and longitude 57°W, or about 600 miles (965 km) east of San Juan, Puerto Rico. The storm is traveling northwest at about 12 miles per hour (19 km per hour), and is expected to be centered at about 20°N latitude and 60°W longitude by 6 A.M. This would put Marshall about 200 miles (322 km) northeast of the island of Barbuda. Hurricane Marshall is not believed to be an immediate threat to any land area.

C. Natural and Human Features of Places

Almost heaven, West Virginia,
Blue Ridge Mountains, Shenandoah River.
Life is old there,
Older than the trees,
Younger than the mountains
Blowin' like a breeze.

Country Roads, take me home
To the place I belong:
West Virginia,
Mountain Momma
Take me home,
Country Roads.

All my mem'ries gather round her,
Miner's lady, stranger to blue water.
Dark and dusty, painted on the sky,
Misty taste of moonshine,
Teardrop in my eye.

Describing the Land These words are from a popular song, "Take Me Home, Country Roads," which was written and recorded by John Denver. What impressions do you get from this song? You may think of West Virginia as a state with mountains and rivers. Maybe the lines "Miner's lady, stranger to blue water. / Dark and dusty, painted on the sky" made you think that mining is an important part of West Virginia's economy. Of course, the "miner's lady" is West Virginia, and "stranger to blue water" and "dark and dusty" are references to how coal mining has changed the land and water of the state.

Many popular songs, poems, novels, and paintings have a theme similar to the one in "Take Me Home, Country Roads." They show in words or pictures what some part of the earth is like. Most of these works of art also show how both nature and human beings have shaped the character of a place. Nearly every place on the earth is the way it is because of the way people have used and changed the natural environment.

Think about the place where you live. The natural environment of your area includes the kind of climate it has. For example, in the southeastern United States summers are long, hot, and humid, and winters are short and mild. Vegetation such

Deep inside a mine, a coal miner uses a machine to cut away coal from a tunnel wall. The coal is then gathered and sent to the surface.
▶ What do you think it is like to work in a coal mine?

as forests, grasslands, and deserts is part of the natural environment. Landforms such as mountains, plateaus, plains, and hills are also considered to be parts of the natural environment.

Human Characteristics of a Place You can see how people shape the character of a place by looking at the diagram below. Each section of the diagram shows the changes that have occurred in a particular area. In the first section, the land is untouched by humans. But this does not mean changes do not occur. Even in nature, the land constantly changes. Trees die, rivers change course, and new weather patterns can create deserts where there was once forest.

In the second section, people have moved onto the land and have begun to farm it. A few houses built from the area's natural resources are scattered about. Some of the forest has been cleared to grow crops for the individual families.

In the third section, the individual farms have started to disappear as a village begins to grow. A road has been built to connect the farms to the village. The fields are no longer just small patches in the forests. Notice also that the village is located on the stream that flows through the section. Can you guess what uses the village might make of the stream?

The fourth and the fifth sections show how the farming village slowly changes into a community that is no longer based on farming. These two sections show the effects of a new way of making a living. This is especially clear from the fifth section. Factories have been built, the stream has been covered over, and the paths have become paved roads.

In the sixth section, a modern city has grown from the factory town. Freeways have replaced the one-lane roads. Office buildings stretch into the sky, allowing thousands of people to work together in a small area. Most of the land is covered by buildings and highways; now only a few of the forest's trees are left.

The human and natural characteristics of a place change over time. As you can see from this diagram, the modern city, such as this one in Europe, began as a few scattered houses. These became farming villages that slowly grew into trading towns. Beginning in the eighteenth century, towns developed factories and business

As you can see from section six, some of the past changes to the land continue to exist in the modern city. But few of the earlier buildings and roads remain in the modern city. And it is hard to see what the natural environment of the land used to be. Both the human characteristics and the natural features of this place have changed.

Changing the Land Now think about the different ways in which people have changed the natural environment in the community where you live. You would want to note whether there is farming where you live, what kind of transportation moves people and goods into and out of the community, and where the transportation routes go.

You would also want to think about the cities and towns that have been built in your area. How many people live in them, and what are their major economic activities? For example, are there factories, farms, mines, ports, rail yards, or other evidence of how people earn a living? You might also want to look at the kinds of houses and other buildings people have built. These are only a few of the many ways that human activities can change the characteristics of the places in which people live.

LESSON 2

Review

REVIEWING MAIN IDEAS
A. How was Glenn's spacecraft located when it landed?
B. How is relative location different from absolute location?
C. What shapes the character of a place?

SKILLS CHECK
WRITING SKILL
Write a paragraph in which you describe the natural and human features of your community. Include landforms, other towns or cities, and states.

sections. By the twentieth century, the city had become a massive, widespread urban region that covered the natural landscape.
▶ What are some of the human characteristics of this place that have changed over the centuries?

Human Changes to the Earth

CONNECTIONS

Imagine that you are a geographer who is studying the area where you live. How would you describe the landscape of this area?

TERMS

technology, irrigation, reservoir, ground water

FOCUS

How do people change the land?

A. The Great Plains 200 Years Ago

Imagine that you had a time machine and could go back to the Great Plains as it was 200 years ago. The land that now covers the middle part of North America from Texas to Canada and from the Rocky Mountains to the centers of Kansas, Nebraska, and South Dakota, was once covered by this vast grassy plain.

Herds of buffalo sent huge columns of dust up into the sky as they thundered across the Great Plains. The only human inhabitants were Indians, or Native Americans. These nomadic people lived in temporary camps in which they set up teepees, or cone-shaped tents made of buffalo hides. The Indians didn't farm, living instead from hunting buffalo and gathering the few useful plants that grew on the plains. If the Indians had disappeared, they would have left little evidence that they had ever lived on the Great Plains.

B. The Great Plains Today

What is the Great Plains like today? The Indians now live on reservations, public lands that have been set aside by the government for Native Americans. The vast herds of buffalo that roamed the Great Plains are now gone. The buffalo survive only in parks or on a few ranches.

The grasslands that stretched from horizon to horizon have been plowed up and the land is now used for growing wheat and other grains or as pasture for cattle. Many rivers that cross the plains have been dammed to control floods, to provide water for crops, to generate electricity, and to make lakes for recreation. The Indian trails that led across the grassy plains are now railroads, roads, and freeways for trains, trucks, and cars. In the towns and cities of the Great Plains, there are stores, schools, churches, and a thousand other things that the Indians never knew. And, unlike the Indian camps, the settlements are permanent, not temporary.

The Indians lived much the same way for hundreds of years. What has caused the rapid change on the Great Plains? The answer is that different people with a different culture and a more advanced **technology** came to the Great Plains. Technology is the knowledge and skill people use to make things. With their new technology, the people who took over the Indians' lands were able to make great changes.

C. The Interaction of Humans with the Environment

Interaction The way the earth is today is the result of the ways in which people have interacted with the environment. The Indians of the Great Plains had a very simple technology. They adapted to the environment by learning to make tools from stone, bone, and other natural materials. If they couldn't find buffalo to hunt, they would go hungry. In the winter they kept warm by building fires from dry buffalo dung, or excrement, called buffalo chips, because there were no trees to use for wood.

Many of the Indians who lived in North America farmed for at least part of their food. Why didn't the Indians of the Great Plains do the same? Agriculture would have given them an extra food supply and made

50

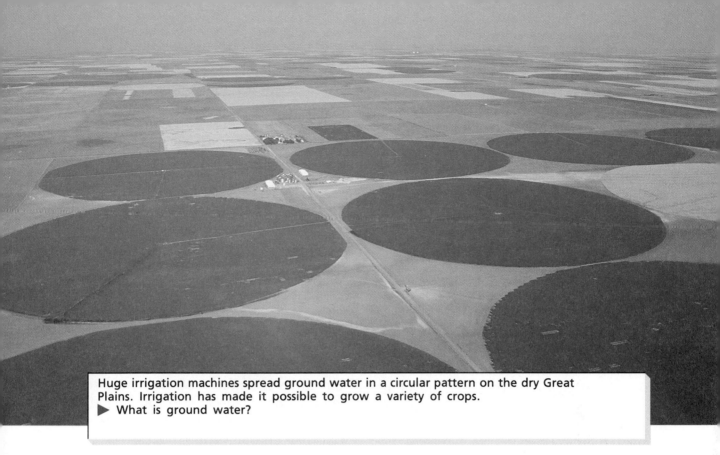

Huge irrigation machines spread ground water in a circular pattern on the dry Great Plains. Irrigation has made it possible to grow a variety of crops.
▶ What is ground water?

their lives more secure. The Plains Indians were unable to farm because the plains are too dry for dependable farming. For the Plains Indians, hunting was the most dependable way to get food.

Why are there farms in the Great Plains today? Part of the answer is in the kinds of plants that are grown. Wheat and other grains that are grown in the Great Plains can grow with small amounts of water. The Indians did not have these crops.

Irrigation Another answer is **irrigation**. Irrigation is the watering of crops or other plants by pipes, canals, or ditches. To irrigate their crops, modern farmers in the Great Plains use **reservoirs**, or lakes and other areas where water is stored for use. Another source of irrigation is **ground water**, which is rainwater that collects in underground rocks. Farmers can drill wells to bring the ground water to the surface.

These are but two examples of the hundreds of different ways that people have learned to adapt to and change the world's environments in order to survive. This year, you will learn about the many different ways that the world's people have learned to make the environment yield the things they need to survive and improve their lives.

LESSON 3

Review

REVIEWING MAIN IDEAS
A. Why did the Indians of the Great Plains live in temporary camps?
B. How did technology change life on the Great Plains?
C. Why is farming possible on the Great Plains today?

SKILLS CHECK
THINKING SKILL
Irrigation and other forms of technology changed the Great Plains. How, do you think, might the same technology be used to change a desert region?

The Importance of Movement

CONNECTIONS

List the different ways you could send a message to a friend who lives in another neighborhood.

TERMS

import, consumer

FOCUS

How are transportation and communication important to our lives?

A. Transportation and Trade

Commuting How far do members of your family travel to work each day? If you live in or near a large city, they may travel as few as 5 miles (8 km) or as many as 30 miles (48 km) or more to get from your home to their workplace. The people of the United States and other industrialized countries are highly mobile. Our society is dependent on transportation. Many of us travel long distances each day to go to work, to go shopping, or for entertainment. We may travel hundreds or even thousands of miles for vacations or to visit relatives. Each year, millions of people move from one city to another, to another part of the United States, or even to a foreign country. These people move to attend school, to get a new job, or to find a place that they think is better to live in.

But this isn't the only way in which we might think of our society as being mobile. Even if you never moved from the home where you live now, never took a vacation, and worked in your home, you would still be dependent on transportation for most of the things you need to live.

For example, look at the labels on the clothes you are wearing. Most likely, at least one piece of your clothing was made outside the United States. If you have a television, a videocassette recorder, or a stereo, it was probably **imported**, or brought into the country from another country.

Even when goods are not imported, movement is essential to getting them to the **consumers** who will buy and use them. Consumers are people who buy and use many types of goods. The food you ate this morning was probably bought in a nearby store. Have you ever thought how that food got to the store?

Moving Goods Let's take the example of breakfast cereal. Cereal is made of grain that may have been grown on a farm in Kansas or Nebraska. The farmer took the harvested grain to a grain elevator, where it was stored until it was shipped by railroad to a mill perhaps in Kansas City, Missouri. From there the processed grain was sent to another city, such as Minneapolis, Minnesota, where the cereal company made it into cereal and put it into boxes.

The boxes were sent to a warehouse, where they were stored before they were shipped to grocery stores throughout the country. Even if you live in one of the states where the grain in your breakfast cereal was grown, it probably traveled hundreds or even thousands of miles before it finally got to the store where you bought it.

A similar story could be told for nearly everything you buy. Unlike the Plains Indians, we grow and make very little of what we need to survive. Instead, we depend on a complex system that moves the things we need from the places where they are produced to stores near where we live.

B. The Movement of Information

Electronic Information Communication is another kind of movement—the movement of information. The way information is moved is quite different from the way goods are moved. Why? Information can be moved through wires as electronic impulses. It can also be moved through the air as radio waves.

THE UNITED STATES: MAJOR HIGHWAYS

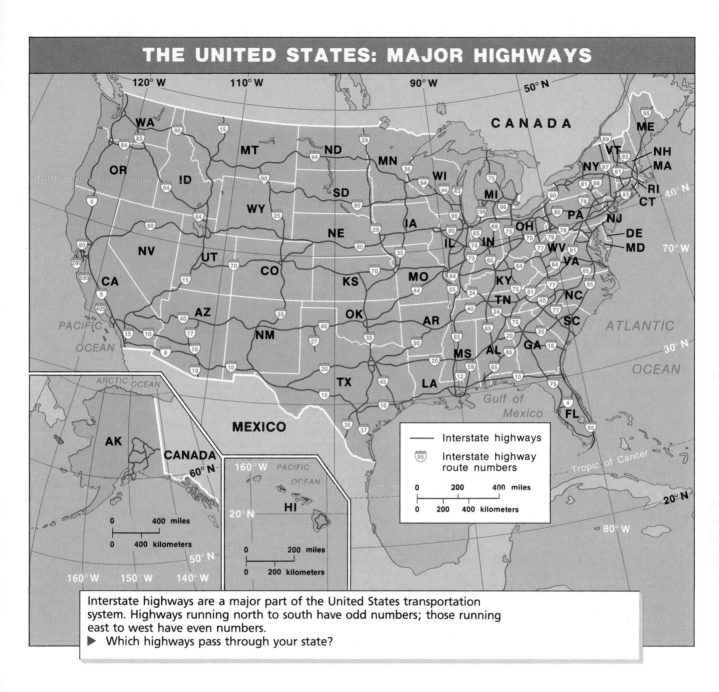

Interstate highways are a major part of the United States transportation system. Highways running north to south have odd numbers; those running east to west have even numbers.

▶ Which highways pass through your state?

Think about how communication has changed our lives. Do you have relatives or friends who live in another town? If you want to talk with them, all you have to do is pick up the telephone and dial their number. We can call nearly any city in the world by telephone. We take this convenience for granted, but before that, there was no way to send voice messages farther than the loudest shout.

Communicating Today Now we can use radio, television, computers, and satellites to send information almost instantly to any part of the world and to space. You can watch live sporting events on television from anyplace in the world, and you can learn about important events almost at the same time that they occur.

Rapid communications have changed business even more than our private lives.

Important papers can be delivered overnight by air express services. If overnight isn't fast enough, computers can send large amounts of information to each other by telephone. Drawings and other documents can be sent by fax, or facsimile, machines. These machines transform the drawings or words into electronic signals. The signals are sent by telephone in a few minutes to other fax machines, where they are printed out immediately on paper. In fact, you could send a copy of this book to any place in the world where there is a telephone and a fax machine.

Transportation and communication provide important links between places. They make it possible for you to buy goods from all parts of the world. And they make it possible for businesses to have offices or factories in different cities or countries.

C. Putting the Five Themes of Geography Together

This chapter has introduced you to the five important themes of geography. In the first lesson you learned about the theme of regions. In the second lesson you read about the theme of absolute location and relative location. You also learned a third theme — that every place has distinct characteristics or features. In the third lesson, you read about the way humans interact with and change their environment. Environment is the fourth theme. In this lesson you learned about the importance of movement in connecting different places on the earth. This is the fifth theme.

These five themes all fit together. Every place has a location on the earth. The combination of natural environment and human activities gives each place a special quality. The way people live in a place shows us how they have adapted to the environment. Technology allows people to make great changes in the natural environment of a place and to develop productive economies. Movement connects places and allows products, people, and ideas to travel from place to place. Similar kinds of places can be grouped into regions. Each region has a location and a special character that comes from the environment and the way of life of the people who live there. As you read the chapters that follow, you will see how the five themes of geography help to explain why there are so many different and unique lands, peoples, and ways of life on the earth.

In 1873, a French writer named Jules Verne wrote a novel titled *Around the World in Eighty Days*. The hero of this book made a bet that he could travel all the way around the world in 80 days. In those days no one had ever traveled around the world so quickly. This book will take you on a trip around the world, too. It will take you longer than 80 days to make your tour, but by the time you return you will have learned many useful and interesting things about the fascinating world in which we live.

LESSON 4

Review

REVIEWING MAIN IDEAS
A. Why is transportation so important in our society?
B. How has the movement of information changed in recent years?
C. What are the five themes of geography?

SKILLS CHECK

MAP SKILL
A box of cereal can travel a long way before it gets to the grocery shelf. Use the scale on the map of the United States on page 692 to find the distance in miles between the following cities. Add the distances between the cities to find the total distance the cereal traveled.
1. Kansas City, MO
2. Minneapolis, MN
3. Sacramento, CA

REVIEWING TERMS

region technology
relief irrigation
glacier reservoir
absolute reservoir
  location import
relative consumer
  location

On a separate sheet of paper, write the word or words from the list above that best complete the sentences.

1. Southeast Asia is a political _____ of the earth that is made up of countries.

2. "The supermarket is two blocks from my home." This statement gives the supermarket's _____.

3. For more variety, a jeweler may want to _____ gems from another country.

4. The _____ of Detroit, Michigan is 42°N/83°W.

5. The movement of a _____ can create pointed mountain peaks.

6. An advanced _____ can change a landscape.

7. Desert farming is possible because of _____.

8. Melting winter snow and heavy spring rains help to keep up water levels in a _____.

9. Some people will argue that a good _____ carefully checks prices.

10. Across North America one finds a varied _____ of mountains, hills, valleys, and canyons.

REVIEWING THE FACTS

On a separate sheet of paper, answer the questions in complete sentences.

1. What are the five themes of geography?

2. What are some of the characteristics of a region?

3. What is the major difference between plains, hills, and mountains?

4. What are the tallest and longest mountain ranges?

5. What is the job of a navigator?

6. How are locations useful for meteorologists?

7. How does life on the Great Plains today compare with life on the Great Plains two hundred years ago?

8. What changed life on the Great Plains?

9. Why do we say that the people of the United States live in a mobile society?

10. What forms of movement provide the links between places?

WRITING ABOUT GEOGRAPHY

Absolute location and relative location are two ways of describing where a place is located. Absolute location is used less frequently in our daily lives. Most people use relative location, especially when giving directions. Write a paragraph that gives the relative location of your school. Write another paragraph that gives the relative location of your state capital.

THINKING CRITICALLY

Answer the following questions in complete sentences.

1. What are the characteristics of your natural environment?
2. Look at the diagram on pages 48–49. At what stage of change would you place the community in which you live? Give examples to defend your choice.
3. How have rapid means of communication changed our lives?
4. "The Five Themes of Geography" is the title of this chapter. Which of the five themes would apply to viewing another planet?
5. The two songs in this chapter relate to the natural environment and to humans changing the environment. Write a song, poem, or paragraph that shows how you feel about the natural environment you described in answer to question 1.

SUMMARIZING THE CHAPTER

On a separate sheet of paper, draw a graphic organizer like the one shown here. Copy the information from this graphic organizer to the one you have drawn. Below each main idea, write two statements that you think best support it. The first statement for each main idea has been done for you.

CHAPTER THEME

We can use the five themes of geography to study the earth and the way people live on the earth.

LESSON 1 Regions are defined by the characteristics we use to identify them.

1. By climate _____
2. _____
3. _____

LESSON 2 Finding location is important to many people.

1. Navigators need to locate planes and ships.
2. _____
3. _____
   _____

LESSON 3 People change the land.

1. Forests are cleared to grow crops.
2. _____
3. _____

LESSON 4 Movement is important in connecting different places on the earth.

1. Goods can be imported into a country.
2. _____
   _____
3. _____

COOPERATIVE LEARNING

In Unit 1 you learned how people survive in the world by using the natural resources around them. It is important for us to understand how to use these resources.

Robinson Crusoe needed to learn the geography of his new island home to survive. He learned to hunt and farm and use the natural resources wisely. He investigated his island, he examined the island's landscape, and he learned how to live on the island.

PROJECT

Your group will work together to create a board game about Robinson Crusoe's life on a deserted island. You may decide that your game will contain facts about the geography of his island home. Or perhaps it may contain facts about Crusoe's way of life. Or the group may decide to design a game that includes a variety of ideas about geography and living conditions on the island.

Work together to design a game board. Think about other games you have played and about how the boards are designed. Also decide how the pieces in your game will advance. Many games use spinners, cards, or dice to determine how the player will move. Sometimes, bonus cards give players extra turns and chances to move ahead. Penalty cards make players lose a turn or move backward. The cards could in-clude topics such as geography, hunting, farming, natural resources, and other details about Crusoe's way of life.

Once your group has discussed and chosen a design, each group member should work to construct part of the game. One person should sketch the board on butcher paper. The others should make the game pieces, dice, cards, or spinner. Each group member could write three bonus cards and three penalty cards.

Finally, your group should meet to put the game together. Don't forget to give it a name.

PRESENTATION AND REVIEW

Your group should test your game by playing it together. By testing the game, you will be able to find and fix any problems. When the group is pleased with the way the game works, present it to the rest of the class.

Then trade games with other groups in your class. Ask them to tell you how they liked your game. Ask if they have any suggestions that would improve the game.

Your group should meet again to discuss how well you worked together. Did everyone have a chance to speak? Did everyone take part in making the game? List the advantages of working with a group. How could you improve the group activity?

REMEMBER TO:
- Give your ideas.
- Listen to others' ideas.
- Plan your work with the group.
- Present your project.
- Discuss how your group worked.

SKILLBUILDER

UNDERSTANDING CLIMOGRAPHS

WHY DO I NEED THIS SKILL?

Your geography textbook is a study of the many different regions of the world. An important part of this study is the influence of climate on the people and land of these regions. As you have learned, climate is the pattern of weather in a particular place over a period of time. Climate can vary from region to region and can help explain many of the differences in how people around the world live.

The two major elements of climate are temperature and precipitation. By looking at temperature and precipitation data for a particular place, you can determine what type of climate that place has. A **climograph** combines a line graph with a bar graph to provide temperature data and precipitation data.

LEARNING THE SKILL

As you know, temperature is the amount of heat in the atmosphere, or air, and precipitation is the amount of moisture that falls to the earth as rain, snow, sleet, hail, or mist. The climographs in this textbook show the average monthly temperature and the average monthly precipitation for certain cities over the course of a year.

For example, the climograph on this page shows the annual temperature and precipitation data for New York City, New York. On the bottom of the climograph are abbreviations for the 12 months of the year. The scales on the left side of the climograph show average monthly temperature in two ways: in degrees Fahrenheit (°F) and in degrees Celsius (°C). The scales on the right show average monthly precipitation both in inches (in.) and in centimeters (cm).

The average temperature for each month is shown by a dot on the graph, and all 12 dots are connected by a line. By looking at this line graph, you can see how the city's temperature may vary from month to month. You can also determine the annual temperature range by finding the difference between the highest and lowest temperatures that occur during the year. For example, the annual temperature range for New York City is about 43°F (24°C).

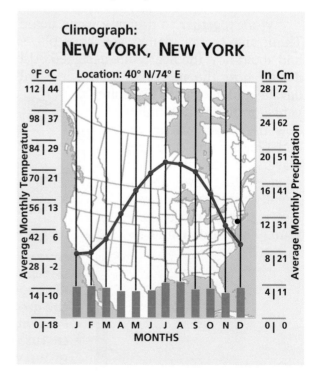

The average precipitation for each month is shown by a bar rising from the bottom of the graph. By looking at the bar graph, you can see how the city's precipitation varies during the year. For example, the climograph for New York shows that the amount of precipitation the city receives from month to month is fairly constant. What is the difference between the lowest and highest amounts of precipitation that New York receives?

You can see from the climograph that on the average, New York receives the most precipitation in July and August. You can also see that these are the warmest months, with temperatures over 70°F (21°C). What are the two coldest months of the year in New York City?

Climograph:
CAIRO, EGYPT

Location: 29°N/31°E

Average Monthly Temperature

°F °C
112|44
98|37
84|29
70|21
56|13
42|6
28|-2
14|-10
0|-18

In Cm
28|72
24|62
20|51
16|41
12|31
8|21
4|11
0|0

Average Monthly Precipitation

MONTHS: J F M A M J J A S O N D

PRACTICING THE SKILL

Use the climograph for New York and the climograph for Cairo, Egypt, shown on this page, to answer the following questions.

1. During which month does Cairo have its highest average temperature?
2. What is the coldest month in Cairo, and what is the average temperature during that month?
3. In which city is the average temperature lower during May—New York or Cairo?
4. What is the average precipitation in New York during October?
5. What is the average precipitation in Cairo during October?
6. Which city receives more precipitation in a year?
7. Which of these two cities do you think might be located on or near a desert?
8. What problems would the climate of each city create for someone who wanted to grow and maintain a flower garden in the city?

APPLYING THE SKILL

As you study the different regions of the world, you can use the climographs in your geography textbook to understand the climate of particular cities in these regions. The climate data will help you understand the relationship between climate and how people in different regions live. In addition, by comparing climograph data with climate data presented in other ways for other places in the world, you will be able to predict or infer what type of climate these other places may have.

SKILLBUILDER

USING SQR

WHY DO I NEED THIS SKILL?

Your social studies book contains abundant amounts of information about people, places, and events. Therefore, you must try to learn and remember many facts and ideas. In this Skillbuilder you will learn to use a strategy, or plan of action, for reading a social studies lesson. The strategy is called **SQR.** These letters stand for *Survey, Question,* and *Read.* Using **SQR** will help you learn and remember the important ideas found in this book and in the other textbooks that you use.

LEARNING THE SKILL

There are three steps in the **SQR** strategy. They are as follows:

Step 1: Survey the lesson. *Survey* means "look over what you will read to get a general idea of what the lesson is about." Begin your survey by reading the lesson title. Ask yourself if you already know some things about the topic of the lesson. Then read the list of terms and the headings in the lesson. The headings are the boldface statements that have the letters *A, B, C,* and so on in front of them. As you read the headings, try to make some guesses or predictions about what will be in the lesson.

Be sure to look at any pictures, photographs, maps, charts, or other visuals in the lesson. This will also help you get a general idea of what the lesson is about. After surveying the lesson, you will be prepared to read and understand it.

Step 2: Ask questions. Think of any questions you may have about the lesson from the survey you just did. Use the words *who, where, when, why, what,* and *how* to help you think of questions. Then read the questions asked by the author of your book. Read the focus question, which is found at the beginning of the lesson and which asks about the main idea of the lesson. Also read the questions that ask about the photographs and other visuals. Finally, read the questions in the lesson review box.

Now fold a sheet of paper lengthwise. On the left-hand side, write down the questions that you plan to answer as you read the lesson. Select five to seven questions that you think deal with important ideas.

Step 3: Read the lesson. As you read the lesson, look for the answers to your questions. Write the answers on the right-hand side of your paper. Add to your list any other questions that come to mind as you read.

PRACTICING THE SKILL

Practice using **SQR** for the first part of Lesson 3 in Chapter 2, on page 50. Refer to the "Using SQR" table if you need help in remembering the steps in the strategy. After you finish, answer these questions.

1. How are the Great Plains today different from what they were like 200 years ago?
2. How has technology played a role in the changes that have occurred in the Great Plains?

The **SQR** strategy helps you learn and remember important ideas. It is also helpful when you study for a test. Save your **SQR** questions and answers, and use them to review the materials before a test.

Use **SQR** as you read the next chapter, which is about Canada. See if using **SQR** helps you to learn, understand, and remember the ideas in the lessons in that chapter. Try using **SQR** when you read the textbooks for all of your classes.

USING SQR			
Survey	• Look at headings, questions, vocabulary words, and visuals.	• Think about what you already know about the topic.	• Make predictions about the lesson topic.
Question	• Think about the questions already in the lesson.	• Use vocabulary words, headings, and other lesson features to prepare your own questions.	• Make predictions about the lesson content.
Read	• Read to answer your questions.	• Write down the answers or say them to yourself.	• Ask and answer any other questions that come to mind as you read.

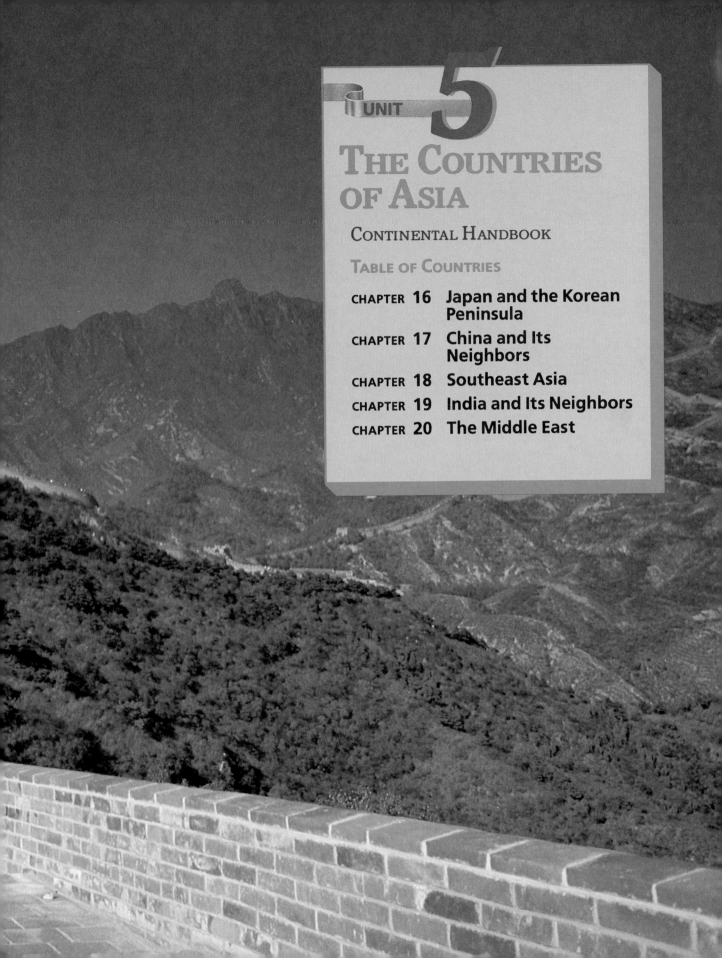

UNIT 5

THE COUNTRIES OF ASIA

CONTINENTAL HANDBOOK

TABLE OF COUNTRIES

CONNECTIONS
What are some of the products you use daily that come from Asia?

TERMS
Pacific Rim

FOCUS
What makes Asia a region?

Japan Is Said To Be Richest

TOKYO, Aug. 1—Japan became the world's richest nation on paper in 1987, supassing the United States in national assets for the first time with $43.7 trillion worth of land, factories, stock and other wealth, a leading Japanese newspaper said today.

A. Growing Ties Between the United States and Asia

This newspaper article probably startled some Americans who are used to thinking of the United States as the richest country in the world. In recent years, however, the economies of Japan and many other Asian countries have grown dramatically. These countries have become important customers of American-made goods. Asian countries also produce many of the goods we buy in the United States, such as televisions, videocassette recorders, and other electronic goods.

In addition to being important trade partners with the United States, Japan and other Asian countries are taking on new responsibilities. For example, Japan is giving some of its new wealth to poor countries around the world, just as the United States does. In the future, Japan is also expected to help maintain international peace by contributing money and troops to peace-keeping forces. Americans must learn about Asia to cooperate with our economic and diplomatic partners.

B. Large and Small in Asia

No other continent on earth has as many great contrasts between large and small countries, cities, and physical features as Asia does. For example, Asia includes six of the world's ten most populated countries. China has more peo-

Asia is the largest continent on the globe. It includes the deserts of the Middle East and the snow-covered peaks of the world's highest mountains.
▶ What mountain range is Mt. Everest located in?

Mountain peak

Elevations

Feet   Meters

10,000 3,000
5,000   1,500
2,000   600
1,000   300
0   0

Land below sea level

0   400   800 miles

0   400   800 kilometers

The Himalaya Mountains

PACIFIC OCEAN

AUSTRALIA

EUROPE

ARCTIC OCEAN

Bering Sea

Sunday / Monday
International Date Line

KAMTCHATKA PENINSULA

HOKKAIDO

HONSHŪ

Sea of Japan

Korea Strait

40°N

30°N

Beijing

Yellow River

He

NORTH CHINA PLAIN

East China Sea

Tropic of Cancer

Philippine Sea

HONG KONG (U.K.)

LUZON

MINDANAO

South China Sea

130° E

120° E

CELEBES

KALIMANTAN (BORNEO)

TIMOR

Coral Sea

Arafura Sea

10° S

GOBI

WEST SIBERIAN PLAIN

Lake Baikal

Lake Balkhash

TIEN SHAN

Mt. Everest
29,028 ft.
(8,848 m)

THE PAMIRS

HINDU KUSH

HIMALAYAS

Katmandu

Ganges River

Dacca

Bay of Bengal

Sunda

SRI LANKA

EASTERN GHATS

DECCAN PLATEAU

WESTERN GHATS

INDOCHINA PENINSULA

Gulf of Siam

River

MALAY PEN.

Strait of Malacca

Singapore

SUNDA ISLES

SUMATRA

BALI

110° E

100° E

90° E

80° E

INDIAN OCEAN

Aral Sea

Caspian Sea

ELBURZ MTS.

ZAGROS MOUNTAINS

Tigris River

Baghdad

Euphrates River

Persian Gulf

Gulf of Oman

ARABIAN PENINSULA

Gulf of Aden

Arabian Sea

20° N

10° N

Ankara

Beirut

Red Sea

Equator

0°

50° E

60° E

70° E

AFRICA

Arctic Circle

ple than any other country on earth, over a billion people. India is the second largest, with nearly 900 million people.

Yet Asia also includes countries with small populations. For example, the nation of Qatar (ke TAHR) has fewer than half a million people.

In area, too, Asia has both large and small countries. China is one of the largest countries of the world, with 3,691,502 square miles (9,560,990 sq km) of territory. This means that China is slightly larger than the United States. On the other hand, the tiny state of Singapore is really just a large city. Singapore covers an area of 225 square miles (583 sq km). The smallest state of the United States, Rhode Island, is more than five times as large as the nation of Singapore.

C. What Makes Asia a Region?

Why are such different countries called the region of Asia? One reason that they are grouped together is they share the same landmass. Bodies of water meet most of the edges of this landmass. The Pacific Ocean marks the eastern edge of Asia, and the Indian Ocean defines the southern edge. Along the western edge of Asia is the Red Sea, which separates Asia from Africa. The Mediterranean Sea divides Asia from Europe.

The northern border of Asia runs along Russia's northern border. As you read in Chapter 15, most of Russia's territory is in Asia. But it is not considered an Asian country, because its largest cities and most of its people are in the European part of the country.

Within Asia itself there are several regions. These are East Asia, which in-

cludes China and Japan; South Asia, which includes India and its neighbors; the countries of Southeast Asia; and the Middle East, which stretches from Afghanistan to Lebanon.

Within Asia's gigantic landmass are some of the world's most dramatic landscapes. The mighty Himalayas form a huge, rugged knot near the center of this region. These mountains stretch across the border of China into the nations of India and Nepal.

Mount Everest, the world's highest mountain, is located in the Himalayas. Mount Everest is 29,028 feet (8,848 m) high. This means that if you climbed to the peak of Mount Everest, you would be almost 6 miles (9 km) above the earth's surface. Many teams of mountain climbers have tried to do just that, and some of them have actually reached the top.

In addition to having the highest mountain, Asia also has the lowest point on the earth's surface. This is the Dead Sea, 1,302 feet (397 m) below sea level.

Along with high peaks and low lands, the huge landmass of Asia also has great contrasts in climate. One of the driest regions on earth, the Arabian Desert, is found on the Arabian Peninsula. Some areas of the Arabian Peninsula receive almost no rainfall for many years and have almost no vegetation or people.

But not all of Asia is this dry. The islands of Indonesia, the Philippines, and the coasts of countries such as Vietnam, Malaysia, and Thailand are covered with thick, dense rain forests that receive over 80 inches (203 cm) of rainfall each year. People in these regions grow crops such as rice, which requires large amounts of water and a warm climate.

The countries of Asia include some of the richest and poorest nations in the world.
▶ How many nations share the island of Borneo?

ASIA: POSITICAL

National capitals ⊛
Other cities •

| 0 | 400 | 800 miles |
| 0 | 400 | 800 kilometers |

PACIFIC OCEAN

ARCTIC OCEAN

INDIAN OCEAN

EUROPE

AFRICA

AUSTRALIA

RUSSIA

CHINA

INDIA

MONGOLIA

KAZAKHSTAN

Yekaterinburg
Chelyabinsk
Omsk Novosibirsk
Barnaul
Kemerovo Krasnoyarsk
Novokuznetsk
Irkutsk
Khabarovsk
Vladivostok

Karaganda

UZBEKISTAN
Tashkent
TURKMENISTAN
Ashkhabad
TAJIKISTAN
Dushanbe
KYRGYZSTAN
Bishkek
Alma-Ata

Meshed
IRAN
Tehran
Isfahan
Baghdad
IRAQ
Damascus
SYRIA
LEBANON
Beirut
JORDAN
Amman Jerusalem
ISRAEL
Jidda
Riyadh
SAUDI ARABIA
San'a
YEMEN

Al-Kuwait
KUWAIT
Manama
BAHRAIN
Doha
QATAR
Abu Dhabi
UNITED ARAB EMIRATES
Masqat
OMAN

AFGHANISTAN
Kabul
PAKISTAN
Faisalabad
Lahore
Islamabad
Karachi
Hyderabad
Ahmadabad
Bombay
Pune
Bangalore
Nagpur
Madras
Colombo
SRI LANKA
Male
MALDIVES

Delhi
New Delhi
Kanpur
NEPAL
Katmandu
BHUTAN
Thimbu
Calcutta
BANGLADESH
Dacca
Chittagong

MYANMAR
Rangoon

THAILAND
Bangkok

LAOS
Vientiane

VIETNAM
Hanoi
Ho Chi Minh City

CAMBODIA
Phnom Penh

MALAYSIA
Kuala Lumpur
SINGAPORE
Singapore

BRUNEI
Bandar Seri Begawan

INDONESIA
Medan
Jakarta
Bandung
Semarang
Surabaja

PHILIPPINES
Quezon City
Manila

Ulan-Bator

Beijing
Tianjin
Taiyuan
Lanzhou
Xi'an
Chengdu
Chongqing
Wuhan
Nanjing
Shanghai
Qingdao
Jinan
Luda
Shenyang
Anshan
Fushun
Changchun
Harbin
Guangzhou
HONG KONG (U.K.)
MACAO (PORT.)

NORTH KOREA
Pyongyang
SOUTH KOREA
Seoul
Inch'on
Taegu
Pusan

JAPAN
Sapporo
Tokyo
Yokohama
Kawasaki
Nagoya
Kyōto
Kōbe
Osaka
Hiroshima
Kitakyūshū
Fukuoka

TAIWAN
Taipei
Kao-hsiung

TURKEY
Ankara
Istanbul
Izmir

MONGOLIA

PAPUA NEW GUINEA
Port Moresby

Aral Sea
Caspian Sea
Persian Gulf
Gulf of Oman
Arabian Sea
Red Sea
Gulf of Aden

Bay of Bengal

Sea of Japan
Yellow Sea
East China Sea
South China Sea
Philippine Sea
Coral Sea
Arafura Sea

URAL MOUNTAINS

PORT. = PORTUGAL
U.K. = UNITED KINGDOM

LACCADIVE ISLANDS (INDIA)
ANDAMAN ISLANDS (INDIA)
NICOBAR ISLANDS (INDIA)
KURIL ISLANDS (U.S.S.R.)
RYUKYU ISLANDS (JAPAN)
SULAWESI (CELEBES)
KALIMANTAN (BORNEO)
SUMATRA
JAVA
BALI
TIMOR
NEW GUINEA

Huang He
Chang Jiang
Xi Jiang
Mekong River
Irrawaddy River
Salween
Brahmaputra River
Ganges River
Indus River
Tigris River
Euphrates River

Tropic of Cancer
Equator

D. Old and New in Asia

Some of the world's oldest civilizations began in Asia. Three thousand years ago the area along the Huang He, a river of northern China, became the heartland of Chinese civilization. The area between the Tigris and Euphrates rivers in Iraq also held important ancient civilizations.

Asia has a long history, but the region is not trapped in the past. In many ways, Asia is as modern as the countries of Europe and the United States. The people of Japan, South Korea, and Taiwan have earned a reputation as brilliant engineers who have developed new electronic goods, scientific equipment, and automobiles.

Nearly 40 percent of Asia's people live in small villages and on farms. Only Africa has a greater proportion of people who live in rural areas. But Asia also has some of the world's largest cities. Tokyo, the capital city of Japan, has grown so large that it has spilled over into the nearby city of Yokohama. Together these two cities have over 20 million residents and form one of the world's largest urban centers.

The people in Asia's cities communicate with people all over the world through radio, telephone, television, and newspapers. Asia's cities also have many of the same problems that are found in large American and European cities, such as housing shortages, pollution, and traffic jams.

E. The Future of Asia

Asia has valuable resources, although some countries lack certain minerals. Nations in the southwestern part of Asia, such as Saudi Arabia, Kuwait, and Iran, have gigantic reserves of petroleum. Countries all over the world depend on this oil to run factories and vehicles, and to make plastic products.

Some Asian countries, such as Taiwan, South Korea, and Japan, have built industries that produce goods bought by millions of people throughout the world, but especially by those in North America and South America. The Taiwanese, South Koreans, and Japanese also buy many products produced in the United States, Canada, Mexico, and the other countries of Latin America.

For this reason, we say that most of the countries around both sides of the Pacific Ocean belong to the region known as the **Pacific Rim.** Trade, cultural exchange, and diplomatic relations are growing stronger each year among nations of the Pacific Rim. Many people believe that the Pacific Rim countries will become the world's largest and strongest economic area.

Review

REVIEWING MAIN IDEAS

A. In what ways is Japan an important economic partner of the United States?
B. Which Asian country has the largest territory and the largest population?
C. What are the highest and lowest points in Asia?
D. In what ways are Asian cities like cities in the United States or Europe?
E. Why is the Pacific Rim an important region?

SKILLS CHECK

MAP SKILL

Turn to the world map on pages 688–689 of the Atlas. Name the countries that form the Pacific Rim of North and South America.

ASIA

	FLAG AND PRINCIPAL LANGUAGE(S)	POPULATION AND LANDMASS	PRINCIPAL PRODUCTS EXPORT	IMPORT

▶ AFGHANISTAN

Kabul ★

Pashto, Dari

POPULATION
14,800,000
59 per sq mi/23 per sq km

LANDMASS
250,775 sq mi/649,507 sq km

Natural Gas

Vehicles

▶ BAHRAIN

Manama

Arabic, English,
Persian

POPULATION
500,000
1,961 per sq mi/757 per sq km

LANDMASS
255 sq mi/660 sq km

Crude Oil

Crude Oil

▶ BANGLADESH

★Dacca

Bengali, English

POPULATION
114,700,000
2,081 per sq mi/803 per sq km

LANDMASS
55,126 sq mi/142,776 sq km

Jute Products

Crude Oil

▶ BHUTAN

★Thimbu

Dzongkha, Nepali

POPULATION
1,500,000
94 per sq mi/36 per sq km

LANDMASS
16,000 sq mi/41,440 sq km

Cement

Food

▶ BRUNEI

Bandar Seri
Begawan

Malay, English,
Chinese

POPULATION
300,000
135 per sq mi/52 per sq km

LANDMASS
2,226 sq mi/5,765 sq km

Crude Oil

Machinery

▶ CAMBODIA

Phnom Penh
★

Khmer

POPULATION
6,800,000
99 per sq mi/38 per sq km

LANDMASS
68,898 sq mi/178,446 sq km

Rubber

Machinery

▶ CHINA

★
Beijing

Chinese

POPULATION
1,103,900,000
299 per sq mi/115 per sq km

LANDMASS
3,691,502 sq mi/9,560,990 sq km

Crude Oil

Machinery

▶ INDIA

★
New Delhi

Hindi, English,
Assamese, Bengali

POPULATION
835,000,000
679 per sq mi/262 per sq km

LANDMASS
1,229,424 sq mi/3,184,208 sq km

Tea

Crude Oil

ASIA

	FLAG AND PRINCIPAL LANGUAGE(S)	POPULATION AND LANDMASS	PRINCIPAL PRODUCTS EXPORT	IMPORT
INDONESIA ★Jakarta	Indonesian, Dutch English	**POPULATION** 177,000,000 227 per sq mi/88 per sq km **LANDMASS** 779,675 sq mi/2,019,358 sq km	Crude Oil	Machinery
IRAN ★Tehran	Farsi, Turkish, Kurdish, Arabic	**POPULATION** 53,900,000 85 per sq mi/33 per sq km **LANDMASS** 635,932 sq mi/1,647,064 sq km	Crude Oil	Machinery
IRAQ ★Baghdad	Arabic, Kurdish, Persian, Turkish	**POPULATION** 18,100,000 107 per sq mi/41 per sq km **LANDMASS** 168,927 sq mi/437,521 sq km	Crude Oil	Machinery
ISRAEL ★Jerusalem	Hebrew, Arabic, English	**POPULATION** 4,500,000 563 per sq mi/217 per sq km **LANDMASS** 7,992 sq mi/20,699 sq km	Diamonds	Machinery
JAPAN Tokyo ★	Japanese, English	**POPULATION** 123,200,000 858 per sq mi/331 per sq km **LANDMASS** 143,619 sq mi/371,973 sq km	Electrical Machinery	Crude Oil
JORDAN ★Amman	Arabic, English	**POPULATION** 4,000,000 106 per sq mi/41 per sq km **LANDMASS** 37,737 sq mi/97,739 sq km	Phosphates	Crude Oil
KUWAIT ★Kuwait	Arabic, English	**POPULATION** 2,100,000 339 per sq mi/131 per sq km **LANDMASS** 6,200 sq mi/16,058 sq km	Crude Oil	Vehicles
LAOS ★Vientiane	Lao, French, English	**POPULATION** 3,900,000 43 per sq mi/16 per sq km **LANDMASS** 91,428 sq mi/236,799 sq km	Timber	Rice

	FLAG AND PRINCIPAL LANGUAGE(S)	POPULATION AND LANDMASS	PRINCIPAL PRODUCTS EXPORT	IMPORT
LEBANON Beirut ★	Arabic, French, English	**POPULATION** 3,300,000 836 per sq mi/323 per sq km **LANDMASS** 3,949 sq mi/10,228 sq km	Services	Food
MALAYSIA Kuala Lumpur ★	English, Malay, Chinese, Tamil	**POPULATION** 17,400,000 135 per sq mi/52 per sq km **LANDMASS** 128,727 sq mi/333,403 sq km	Crude Oil	Machinery
MALDIVES ★ Malé	Divehi, English	**POPULATION** 200,000 1,739 per sq mi/671 per sq km **LANDMASS** 115 sq mi/298 sq km	Fish	Petroleum
MONGOLIA Ulan Bator ★	Mongolian	**POPULATION** 1,900,000 4 per sq mi/3 per sq km **LANDMASS** 604,247 sq mi/1,565,000 sq km	Livestock	Machinery
MYANMAR Rangoon ★	Burmese, English	**POPULATION** 40,800,000 156 per sq mi/60 per sq km **LANDMASS** 261,789 sq mi/678,034 sq km	Teak	Machinery
NEPAL Katmandu ★	Nepali	**POPULATION** 18,700,000 344 per sq mi/133 per sq km **LANDMASS** 54,362 sq mi/140,798 sq km	Textiles	Food
NORTH KOREA Pyongyang ★	Korean	**POPULATION** 22,500,000 483 per sq mi/186 per sq km **LANDMASS** 46,609 sq mi/120,717 sq km	Metals	Machinery
OMAN ★ Masqat	Arabic	**POPULATION** 1,400,000 17 per sq mi/7 per sq km **LANDMASS** 82,000 sq mi/212,380 sq km	Crude Oil	Machinery

ASIA

	FLAG AND PRINCIPAL LANGUAGE(S)	POPULATION AND LANDMASS	PRINCIPAL PRODUCTS EXPORT	IMPORT

PAKISTAN

Islamabad ★

Urdu, Baluchi, Punjabi, Pushtu

POPULATION
110,400,000
356 per sq mi/137 per sq km

LANDMASS
310,403 sq mi/803,944 sq km

Cotton

Machinery

PHILIPPINES

★Manila

Filipino, English, Spanish

POPULATION
64,900,000
561 per sq mi/217 per sq km

LANDMASS
115,651 sq mi/299,536 sq km

Electronics

Crude Oil

QATAR

★Doha

Arabic, English

POPULATION
400,000
91 per sq mi/35 per sq km

LANDMASS
4,400 sq mi/11,396 sq km

Crude Oil

Machinery

SAUDI ARABIA

★
Riyadh

Arabic

POPULATION
14,700,000
17 per sq mi/6 per sq km

LANDMASS
873,972 sq mi/2,263,587 sq km

Crude Oil

Machinery

SINGAPORE

Singapore
★

Chinese, English, Malay, Tamil

POPULATION
2,700,000
12,000 per sq mi/4,633 per sq km

LANDMASS
225 sq mi/583 sq km

Petroleum

Crude Oil

SOUTH KOREA

★Seoul

Korean

POPULATION
43,100,000
1,134 per sq mi/438 per sq km

LANDMASS
38,022 sq mi/98,477 sq km

Ships

Crude Oil

SRI LANKA

Colombo
★

Sinhali, Tamil, English

POPULATION
16,900,000
667 per sq mi/258 per sq km

LANDMASS
25,332 sq mi/65,610 sq km

Tea

Crude Oil

SYRIA

Damascus
★

Arabic, Kurdish, Armenian, Turkish

POPULATION
11,800,000
165 per sq mi/63 per sq km

LANDMASS
71,498 sq mi/185,180 sq km

Crude Oil

Crude Oil

	FLAG AND PRINCIPAL LANGUAGE(S)	POPULATION AND LANDMASS	PRINCIPAL PRODUCTS EXPORT	IMPORT

TAIWAN

★Taipei

Chinese

POPULATION
20,000,000
1,440 per sq mi/556 per sq km

LANDMASS
13,887 sq mi/35,967 sq km

Electrical Machinery

Crude Oil

THAILAND

★Bangkok

Thai (Siamese), Chinese, English

POPULATION
55,600,000
280 per sq mi/108 per sq km

LANDMASS
198,445 sq mi/513,998 sq km

Rice

Crude Oil

TURKEY

★
Ankara

Turkish

POPULATION
55,400,000
184 per sq mi/71 per sq km

LANDMASS
301,380 sq mi/780,574 sq km

Clothing

Crude Oil

UNITED ARAB EMIRATES

Abu Dhabi★

Arabic

POPULATION
1,700,000
53 per sq mi/20 per sq km

LANDMASS
32,278 sq mi/83,600 sq km

Crude Oil

Machinery

VIETNAM

★Hanoi

Vietnamese, English French, Chinese

POPULATION
66,800,000
512 per sq mi/198 per sq km

LANDMASS
130,486 sq mi/337,912 sq km

Clothing

Crude Oil

YEMEN

★
San'a

Arabic

POPULATION
9,400,000
50 per sq mi/19 per sq km

LANDMASS
187,365 sq mi/485,275 sq km

Petroleum

Crude Oil

CHAPTER **16**

JAPAN AND THE KOREAN PENINSULA

Land and Sea in Japan and the Two Koreas

CONNECTIONS

Thinking back on the units you have already studied, name as many island nations and peninsula nations as you can.

TERMS

Ring of Fire

FOCUS

What are the principal landforms of Japan, North Korea, and South Korea?

A. Making a Geographical Comparison

Two Island Nations You might think that the nation of Great Britain could not possibly be similar in any way to the nation of Japan. After all, they are almost on opposite sides of the earth. But surprisingly, these two nations have quite a few things in common.

For example, if you compare the map on page 398 with the map on page 264, you can see that Japan's location off the east coast of Asia is somewhat similar to Great Britain's location off the west coast of Europe. Both Japan and Great Britain are island nations. Japan is separated from the mainland of Asia by the Korea Strait, which is only about 120 miles (193 km) wide, and by the Sea of Japan. The English Channel and the North Sea separate Great Britain from the European continent.

Another feature shared by both nations is their dependence on the seas and channels around them. Like the people of Great Britain, the Japanese use the ocean and the nearby seas as transportation routes. In the 1800s and 1900s, Great Britain established a vast overseas empire. The Japanese also built an empire but it was much smaller than Great Britain's. Like the British, they are trading experts. Today, Japanese products are famous around the world, and Japanese companies have offices in many countries.

Both Japan and Great Britain have economies that depend on trade and manufacturing. Both countries import food and raw materials for their industries and export manufactured goods to pay for these imports. Foreign trade is the lifeblood of Japan and Great Britain.

B. Japan, a Nation of Islands

Four Islands One of the great gifts of the Japanese people to the world is a style of poetry called *haiku* (HY koo). A haiku is a verse form in which there are only 17 syllables. The syllables are usually divided into three lines, with 5 syllables in the first line, 7 in the second line, and 5 in the third line, as in this example.

Wet snow is sweeping
Over the red-berry bush. . .
Two sparrows chirping.

A haiku often paints for the reader a scene from nature and usually gives an impression of peace and tranquility. Through their haiku, the Japanese describe their land with great affection.

What is their land like? Japanese poets never run out of scenes to describe, because the Japanese landscape is full of fascinating and varied views. Japan is an archipelago, or a group of islands quite close to each other. The Japanese archipelago consists of 4 main islands. The largest island is Honshu (HAHN shoo). To its north is the island of Hokkaido (hah KYD oh). The southernmost of the islands are Shikoku (shi-KOH koo) and Kyushu (kee OO shoo). Nearly 4,000 small islands are found in the ocean that surrounds these 4 large islands.

Ring of Fire Most of Japan's islands are the peaks of a large mountain chain that rises from the floor of the North Pacific Ocean. A number of the mountains are

▶ Hirosaki Castle on the main island of Honshu

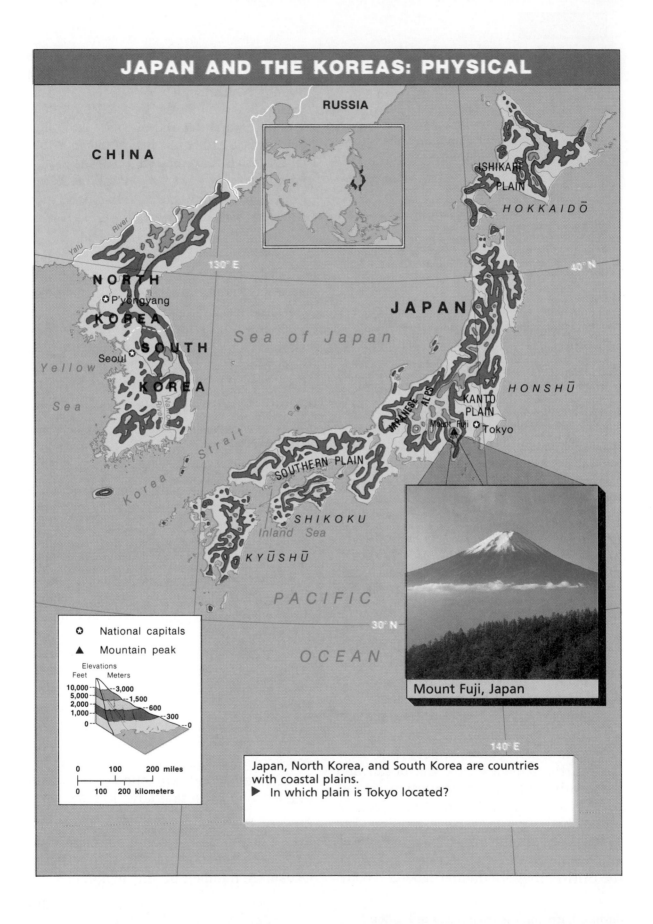

JAPAN AND THE KOREAS: PHYSICAL

RUSSIA

CHINA

NORTH

KOREA

⊙ P'yongyang

SOUTH

KOREA

Seoul ⊙

Yalu River

Yellow

Sea

Han River

Korea Strait

SOUTHERN PLAIN

SHIKOKU

Inland Sea

KYŪSHŪ

ISHIKARI PLAIN

HOKKAIDŌ

40° N

JAPAN

Sea of Japan

JAPANESE ALPS

KANTO PLAIN

HONSHŪ

Mount Fuji ▲ ⊙ Tokyo

130° E

30° N

PACIFIC

OCEAN

140° E

Mount Fuji, Japan

⊙ National capitals

▲ Mountain peak

Elevations

Feet   Meters

10,000 ─ ─3,000
5,000 ─
2,000 ─ ─1,500
1,000 ─ ─600
0 ─ ─300
─0

0   100   200 miles

0   100   200 kilometers

Japan, North Korea, and South Korea are countries with coastal plains.
▶ In which plain is Tokyo located?

volcanos, and many are still active. As you read earlier, volcanic eruptions are caused when heat and pressure build up deep inside the earth. This process is similar to the way that bubbles in a pot of soup rise to the surface and burst, releasing heat and steam. When the volcanos erupt, they vent smoke, fumes, and sometimes lava. Because of the many fiery eruptions, the mountain ranges on the coasts around the Pacific Ocean, including that of Japan, make up what is called the **Ring of Fire.**

The earthquakes in Japan that often accompany volcanic activity are usually mild. But an earthquake that struck Japan in 1923 destroyed the entire city of Yokohama and much of the city of Tokyo. Approximately 100,000 people died in that earthquake. Since more than 1,000 earthquakes occur in Japan each year, it is no wonder that the Japanese appreciate the peaceful settings that they describe in their haiku poetry.

The highest, most scenic mountains of Japan are the Japanese Alps, which are located near the center of Honshu. Mount Fuji, the highest peak in the Japanese Alps, rises more than 12,300 feet (3,700 m) above sea level. Of all the mountain peaks in the world, the beautiful snowy peak of Mount Fuji is perhaps the most photographed. The Japanese regard Mount Fuji as a sacred mountain. Many poems have been written about it, including this one.

> Struck with awe by high
> and sacred Fuji's summit
> towering in the sky,
> Even the clouds dare not go
> over it, but trail below!

C. From Snowy Peaks to Sunny Plains

Climates The islands of Japan stretch out about 1,400 miles (2,253 km) from northeast to southwest. By looking at the map on page 398, you can see that the most northern point of Japan is located at a latitude of about 45°N and that the most southern point is at about 31°N.

Imagine that we could move the islands of Japan into the Atlantic Ocean and spread them along the East Coast of the United States. Japan would reach as far north as the northern borders of Vermont and New Hampshire. It would then stretch south along the coast all the way to the northern edge of Florida.

Japan has a range of climates similar

ロッカールーム➡ ル受付➡
ファミリーレストラン➡ テリア➡
チケット売場 レンタルスキー➡
テンバー第1リフト プロショップ➡

The cold, snowy winters in northern Japan are perfect for winter sports.
▶ Which East Coast states in our country have similar winter weather?

to that of our East Coast. In northern Hokkaido, winters are long and icy, as are winters in northern Vermont and New Hampshire. Winter temperatures rarely go above 32°F (0°C). Heavy blankets of snow cover the ground and fill the roads, blocking the routes of travelers. Winters in Hokkaido are so difficult that people look forward with great joy to the coming of spring.

On Kyushu, the southernmost island of Japan, winters are mild. During the daytime the temperature usually reaches 45°F (7°C). The air is clear and crisp, and little snow falls.

Japan Current Kyushu, Shikoku, and Honshu are warmed by the Japan Current, an ocean current that brings warm water to Japan from the southern part of the Pacific Ocean. The waters of this current warm the air above the water's surface and keep temperatures mild. The Japan Current flows north along Kyushu, Shikoku, and Honshu, but just at the northern tip of Honshu, the Japan Current veers toward the east. Its warmth doesn't reach as far north as Hokkaido. That is why Hokkaido's winters are colder and harsher than winters in other parts of Japan.

On Honshu, Shikoku, and Kyushu, summers are long, hot, and humid. In Tokyo, the temperature often reaches as high as 85°F (29°C) during the day. Farther south on Kyushu, summer temperatures frequently climb to 90°F (32°C). This is a time of the year when vacationers appreciate Hokkaido's cooler temperatures and travel to the northern island for rest and relaxation.

D. The Four Islands of Japan

Japan has a population of over 121 million people, which is about one-half the population of the United States. But Japan's land area is only 143,619 square miles (371,830 sq km), whereas the land area of the United States is 3,615,123 square miles (9,359,553 sq km), which makes the United States approximately 25 times larger than Japan. As a result, Japan has an average of 858 people per square mile (331 people per sq km), compared with 69 people per square mile (27 people per sq km) in the United States.

Japan's population is not evenly spread out over all its islands. Honshu, the largest island, has the largest population, and most people are concentrated in two important

JAPAN: POPULATION DENSITY

⊛ National capital
• Other cities

Persons per	
square mile	square kilometer
0	0
250	100
750	300
1,250	500
2,500	1,000

THE 25 LARGEST CITIES OF JAPAN

Tokyo	8,355,000	Sendai	700,000
Yokohama	2,993,000	Okayama	572,000
Ōsaka	2,636,000	Kumamoto	556,000
Nagoya	2,116,000	Kagoshima	531,000
Sapporo	1,543,000	Higashiōsaka	523,000
Kyōto	1,479,000	Hamamatsu	514,000
Kōbe	1,410,000	Amagasaki	509,000
Fukuoka	1,160,000	Funabashi	507,000
Kawasaki	1,089,000	Niigata	476,000
Kitakyūshū	1,056,000	Shizuoka	468,000
Hiroshima	1,044,000	Himeji	453,000
Sakai	818,000	Hachiōji	427,000
Chiba	789,000		

Almost one half of the 25 largest cities of Japan have a population of more than 1 million.
▶ What is Tokyo's population density?

400

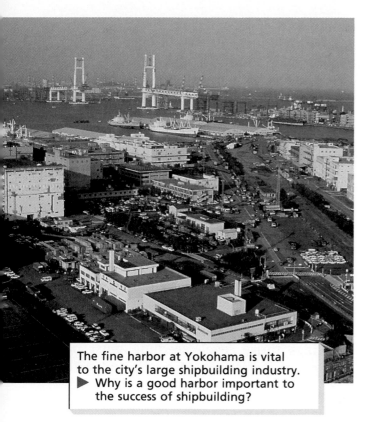

The fine harbor at Yokohama is vital to the city's large shipbuilding industry.
▶ Why is a good harbor important to the success of shipbuilding?

few small valleys and narrow plains provide a limited amount of level land. Until recently this peninsula consisted of one country, Korea. Japan ruled Korea before World War II. When Japan was defeated in 1945, Soviet troops occupied northern Korea, and the United States Army moved into southern Korea to help South Koreans build a new government. In 1945 a border was drawn across the peninsula near the 38th parallel (38°N), separating the two regions.

In 1948 the people north of this line formed their own country, called the Democratic People's Republic of Korea, or North Korea. Their capital city is P'yongyang (pee ONG yahng). North Korea has a Communist form of government and a strong friendship with communist China. The people south of the dividing line formed their own country, called the Republic of Korea, or South Korea. Its capital city is Seoul (sohl). South Korea has a democratic form of government and strong friendships with the United States and Japan.

urban areas, Tokyo and Yokohama. Tokyo is the capital city and industrial center of Japan. Nearby is the city of Yokohama. Together these cities have over 22 million residents. These urban areas have more people, industries, shipyards, and businesses than any other areas of Japan.

The remaining three large islands of Japan are quite different from Honshu and from one another. Forests, farms, and fishing villages are typical of Hokkaido. Shikoku and Kyushu look across the beautiful Inland Sea to the large island of Honshu. Shikoku is the smallest of the four main islands. Mountains cross the island from east to west. Kyushu also has steep mountains, which are covered by forests. But Kyushu does have a small level area in the north, with cities and industries.

E. Comparing North Korea and South Korea

Like Japan, most of the land of North Korea and South Korea is mountainous. A

LESSON 1

Review

REVIEWING MAIN IDEAS

A. What similarities are there between Great Britain and Japan?
B. Why do earthquakes occur in Japan?
C. How is the climate of Japan similar to the climate of the East Coast of the United States?
D. How is Honshu different from the other three regions of Japan?
E. How did Korea become separate nations?

SKILLS CHECK

MAP SKILL

Use the Gazetteer on pages 707–720 to find the latitude and longitude of these cities: Tokyo, Seoul, P'yongyang. Write your answers on a separate sheet of paper.

Japan's Economic Miracle

CONNECTIONS

Japan is famous for producing automobiles, cameras, and electronic equipment. Name a Japanese product in each of these categories that is available in the United States.

TERMS

seedbed, paddy, synthetic material

FOCUS

How do the Japanese produce so many goods with so few natural resources?

A. Living on a Farm in Honshu

Raising Rice Most of Japan is made up of hills and mountains. There is little level land for farming. On Honshu, only the Kanto Plain near Tokyo has level land.

Tadashi Matsumoto, a Japanese schoolboy, knows how much effort it takes to farm in Japan. Tadashi lives with his family in a small village near the city of Kobe (KOH bee), in the foothills of the Japanese Alps. Tadashi's family raises rice, tea, bamboo, mushrooms, melons, and onions in its fields. Tadashi attends school, and after school he does homework or plays baseball. Often he must help his family with the farm work.

One such task is the care of rice seedlings, or young rice plants. Rice seeds are planted in a special area called a **seedbed** at the edge of an irrigated rice field, called a **paddy**. The rice seeds are sprouted in the seedbed, and then planted in the paddy.

When the paddy has been prepared and the seedlings shoot up in the seedbed, the family transplants the tender seedlings into the paddy. To make sure that the seedlings thrive, each seedling must be planted at just the right depth and with the right amount of space around it. Although a person working carefully can perform this delicate task much better than a machine, today some people use a motorized planter to set the seedlings in place.

The photograph on the left shows people harvesting a crop of rice.
▶ What stage in rice farming is shown in the photograph on the top right?

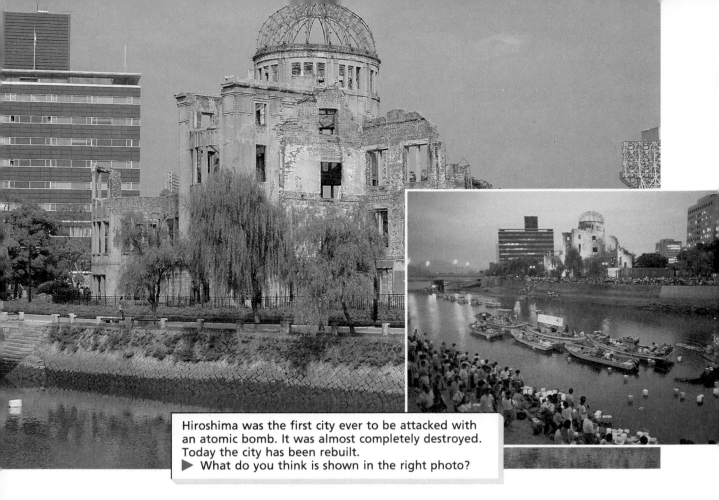

Hiroshima was the first city ever to be attacked with an atomic bomb. It was almost completely destroyed. Today the city has been rebuilt.
▶ What do you think is shown in the right photo?

Terrace Farming Tadashi's family also uses hilly areas on its land by making terraces. On the terraces, paddies can be irrigated. If Tadashi's father planted rice on a hillside slope without terraces, the water would just run off the hill and the seedlings would not survive. As in the Andes, terraces turn useless land into productive farmland.

On slopes where terraces are too difficult to construct, Tadashi's family and neighbors raise peach, apple, or mandarin orange trees, or they grow potatoes, vegetables, or tea bushes.

Very little land in Japan is used for grazing cattle or other animals. This is true even on the Kanto Plain and in the lower hills of Honshu. In countries where land is scarce, farmers use their small plots of land for growing food crops rather than for grazing livestock. They can produce more food by cultivating each acre of land than by leaving it as pastureland.

B. Japan's Economic Growth

A New Economy Today, names of Japanese corporations such as Honda, Toyota, Sony, and Panasonic are known all over the world. But a few decades ago, it seemed as though Japan's economy was crushed and would never recover. When Japan was defeated in World War II and forced to surrender, its economy was greatly weakened. Many large cities, such as Hiroshima (hihr uh SHEE muh) and Nagasaki (nahg uh SAHK ee), had been destroyed. Many factories throughout Japan had been leveled, and thousands of people had been killed.

How did Japan succeed in becoming a world economic giant when its factories had lain in ashes such a short time before?

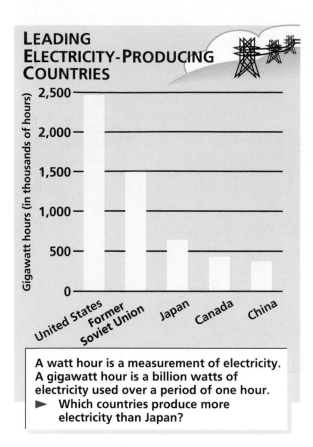

LEADING ELECTRICITY-PRODUCING COUNTRIES

Gigawatt hours (in thousands of hours)

2,500
2,000
1,500
1,000
500
0

United States
Former Soviet Union
Japan
Canada
China

A watt hour is a measurement of electricity. A gigawatt hour is a billion watts of electricity used over a period of one hour.

► Which countries produce more electricity than Japan?

In the years after World War II, Japan received many loans and much aid from the United States and other countries. But money alone could not work the economic recovery that Japan experienced, because Japan lacks almost all the raw materials needed for industry.

Resources A list of Japan's natural resources is short. It includes a small amount of coal on Hokkaido and Kyushu, and mountain forests that produce lumber and wood pulp for making paper. Iron ore and minerals such as silver, lead, and copper are found only in limited amounts. Japan has a severe shortage of petroleum. Almost every drop of oil that Japan uses must be imported. To reduce the expense of im-

porting oil, factories in Japan use electricity as much as possible.

In the Japanese Alps near the industrial zones of Honshu, there are short, swift rivers that have been dammed to generate massive amounts of hydroelectric power. Except for the United States and the former Soviet Union, Japan produces more electricity than any other country. Yet Japan still cannot produce enough power for all its factories and industries. So Japan imports large amounts of oil and natural gas. Indonesia and the Middle East, especially Saudi Arabia, are Japan's main suppliers of oil.

With few raw materials or fuels, how does Japan continue to be an industrial giant? Its secret is to buy raw materials from other countries and import them through excellent harbors at Yokohama, Nagasaki, and Osaka. Factories then use the most modern equipment and techniques to produce goods efficiently. With large amounts of high-quality goods to export, Japanese industries earn a great deal of money. They spend this money on even more efficient machinery, better methods of manufacturing, and high wages for their workers.

Japan began this policy of exporting goods soon after World War II. The country's leaders believed that this would be the best way for Japan to develop its economy. One of the first export industries developed in the country was the textile industry. The profits earned from the export of textiles were then used to build new factories. These factories produced more sophisticated goods, such as cameras and televisions, for export.

C. Honshu's Industrial Zones

Three Industrial Centers Honshu has more than farms like the one belonging to Tadashi's family. It also has most of Japan's industries and large cities. In the industrial city of Tokyo and its neighboring city Yokohama, huge factories produce steel, children's toys, optical equipment, and parts for oceangoing ships. Yokohama has an especially fine harbor and a large shipbuilding industry. Japan is a major world producer of steel, cement, electronic equipment, automobiles, and chemicals. It is also a major world producer of microchips. Microchips are the "brains" of computers.

Most of these industries are located in the Tokyo–Yokohama industrial zone.

Japan's engineers are working hard to make Japan a leader in the production of computer products such as microchips. In fact, the country hopes to be able to build the world's fastest computer soon. It has also invested huge sums of money to create artificial intelligence programs for computers.

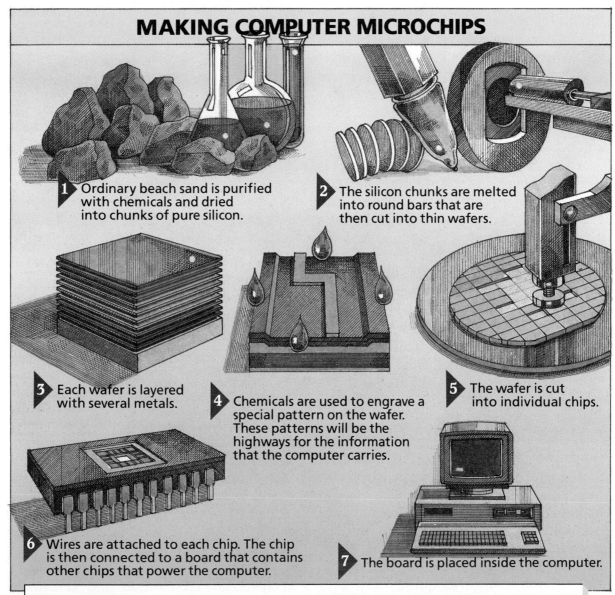

MAKING COMPUTER MICROCHIPS

1 Ordinary beach sand is purified with chemicals and dried into chunks of pure silicon.

2 The silicon chunks are melted into round bars that are then cut into thin wafers.

3 Each wafer is layered with several metals.

4 Chemicals are used to engrave a special pattern on the wafer. These patterns will be the highways for the information that the computer carries.

5 The wafer is cut into individual chips.

6 Wires are attached to each chip. The chip is then connected to a board that contains other chips that power the computer.

7 The board is placed inside the computer.

Microchips are the source of the computer's power and speed. The chips must be manufactured in an extremely clean environment.
▶ What skills, do you think, are required to create a microchip?

Honshu's second industrial zone is shared by the cities of Kobe and Osaka. Together, Kobe and Osaka have approximately 4 million people. Until World War II, Osaka was Japan's leading trade and manufacturing city. Osaka's economy was built on trade with China, carried out by ships that crossed the Inland Sea and the Sea of Japan. Find these bodies of water on the map on page 398. Osaka was especially famous for its many textile factories, which used cotton brought in by ship up the Inland Sea to Osaka's harbor. Most of Osaka's textile factories were built in the 1940s and 1950s. They can no longer make textiles as cheaply as newer factories in Taiwan and South Korea. Today, other factories in Osaka and Kobe produce parts for ships, engineering equipment, clothes, and other manufactured goods.

The third industrial zone of Honshu is the city of Nagoya (nuh GOI uh), which is located between the Tokyo-Yokohama and Osaka-Kobe industrial zones. Nagoya's population of nearly 2.5 million is much smaller than that of the other two industrial zones. Yet Nagoya is now the first-ranking Japanese city for producing cotton, wool, and textiles made from **synthetic materials**. A synthetic material is made from materials produced by people, not by nature, and is often made from chemicals. Polyester, nylon, and rayon are synthetic materials.

D. Hokkaido, Shikoku, and Kyushu

Hokkaido Plain Hokkaido, the most northern of Japan's four main islands, is less populated than Honshu. The Ishikari Plain in the southern part of Hokkaido has enough level land for agriculture, but the growing season is short and cool. Many farmers on the Ishikari Plain raise a special type of rice that grows quickly and does not need a warm climate. They also produce crops that are typical of Eastern Europe's

Many of Japan's major products are in turn used in the manufacture of another of its major products, automobiles.
▶ How does this help Japan's economy?

farms, such as oats, hay, and potatoes. Some farmers on Hokkaido also grow pasture grasses and graze dairy cattle and beef cattle. This is a young and growing form of agriculture in Japan. As a result, the Japanese are eating much more meat than ever before.

Hokkaido also has an important tourist industry. The long, snowy winters create ideal conditions for skiing and other winter sports. Tunnels and bridges connect Honshu with Japan's three other main islands. One tunnel allows high-speed trains to travel between Hokkaido and the large cities of Honshu, allowing city people to get to Hokkaido quickly to enjoy a winter weekend.

There are no large plains on Shikoku as there are on Honshu and Hokkaido. Instead, Shikoku has rugged mountains covered by forests, and a narrow strip of coastal land along the Inland Sea, where small cities and rice paddies cover the landscape. Many people live in fishing villages and around the edge of the island.

Commercial Fishing   Japan has one of the largest and most productive fishing industries in the world. In contrast to the small-scale fishing of Shikoku, commercial fishing is done by companies that own huge modern ships. These ships travel through the Pacific Ocean and fish off the coasts of Alaska and South America, catching salmon, tuna, and other ocean fish. The ships are large enough to carry the supplies needed for the crew to live at sea for weeks. Often a "factory ship" accompanies the fishing vessel. Workers on the factory ship clean and refrigerate or freeze each day's catch so that the fish do not spoil before the ship anchors in a harbor. Some of the catch is exported to North and South America. The bulk of the fish is used in Japan, because fish is an important part of the Japanese people's diet.

Coal Mining   Kyushu, the most southern of Japan's large islands, has Japan's largest coalfield. Coal mines are located along the northern coast of Kyushu. You can see from the map on page 398 that coal can be loaded onto ships in northern Kyushu and sent eastward through the Inland Sea toward the three industrial zones of Honshu. Unfortunately for Japan, most of Kyushu's coal is of a poor quality and unsuitable for industrial use. And Kyushu's coal supplies have decreased, because the mines have been operating for many years. Most of Japan's coal mines will be depleted by the year 2000. Much of the country's coal is now imported from Australia, China, and Canada and the United States.

WORLD FISH CATCH

Japan 13%

Former U.S.S.R. 12%

Other 54%

China 10%

U.S. 6%

Chile 5%

Japan leads the world in the amount of fish caught. Most of the fish is used domestically.
► What percentage of the world total is caught by Japan and China?

LESSON 2

Review

REVIEWING MAIN IDEAS
A. Why is farming so difficult in Japan?
B. Why is it so remarkable that Japan has become an economic giant?
C. Where are the three industrial zones of Honshu located?
D. What are the main economic activities of Hokkaido, Shikoku and Kyushu?

SKILLS CHECK

THINKING SKILL

Imagine that you are asked to visit a small country that has few mineral resources and only small areas of level land. Make a list of the materials the country might import, and the products that could be manufactured and exported with those materials.

Old and New Lifestyles in Japan

CONNECTIONS

What topics would you consider if you wanted to compare ways people in Japan live with the ways in which people in the United States live?

TERMS

futon, tatami

FOCUS

In what ways, do you think, is Japan's culture a blend of old and new life styles?

A. Japan, a Nation Without Minority Groups

Few Immigrants One of the unique features of Japan's people is that hardly anyone belongs to a minority group. Almost everyone in Japan today is simply Japanese, whereas in the United States there are many minority groups. Ancestors of today's Americans came to the United States from all over the world and blended their cultures to create an American culture. In Japan, almost everyone has kept the same culture for many centuries.

Why does Japan have hardly any minority groups? One reason is that in the sixteenth century, Japan almost completely closed its doors to outsiders, especially Europeans. The Japanese feared that Europeans would take over their land. So they forced foreign missionaries, traders, and visitors to leave Japan.

Allowing Visitors Japan kept its doors closed to foreigners until 1853. In that year, Commodore Matthew Perry arrived at Tokyo Bay with three United States Navy warships. He persuaded Japan's leaders to sign a treaty giving the United States trading

Like haiku, traditional Japanese watercolors usually have nature as their theme.
▶ What is shown in the watercolor?

rights and other privileges. Slowly, Japan began accepting outside people, but only a very few. Even recently, Japan has been reluctant to allow foreigners to immigrate permanently. In the 1970s, when hundreds of thousands of Vietnamese fled from the war in their homeland, many countries around the world allowed the Vietnamese to come to their nations. Altogether, nearly 1 million of these people left Vietnam, but the Japanese allowed fewer than 200 of them to enter Japan.

B. What Is Japan's Culture Like?

Early Settlers Before Japan closed its doors to outsiders in the sixteenth century, its islands were settled by people from all over Asia. Many of the early settlers arrived in Japan by traveling through China and the Korean peninsula and then crossing the Korea Strait.

The early Japanese adopted many ideas and techniques from the Chinese and from the Koreans. In past centuries, Japanese students went to China to study its *philosophy*, or basic ideas about the nature and meaning of life, its laws, and its government. The Japanese used some of China's ideas in organizing their own governments.

The Japanese adopted some Chinese ways and rejected others. For example, the Japanese borrowed and simplified the Chinese form of writing. They then created a new written language, Japanese, which has different characters from Chinese.

Religion Many Japanese believe in Shintoism, a collection of ideas about gods who lived in mountains, in the sea, and everywhere in nature. Some Shinto ceremonies and festivals are designed to ask the gods in nature for help in growing a good crop or in avoiding floods in the rainy season. Other ceremonies thank the gods for a rich harvest or for good weather. Shintoism is not quite the same as other religions, because it does not call people together for

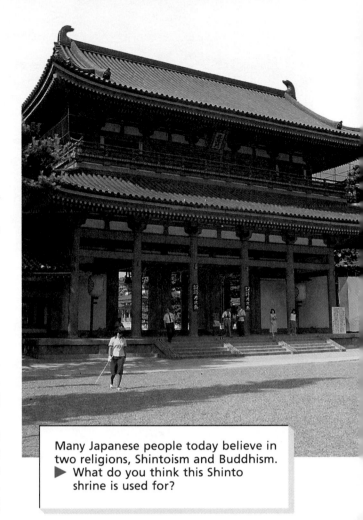

Many Japanese people today believe in two religions, Shintoism and Buddhism. ▶ What do you think this Shinto shrine is used for?

worship. In the beginning there were not even any Shinto priests.

Beginning in the sixth century, many Buddhists began arriving in Japan from China and Korea. Buddhists believe in the teachings of Buddha, the founder of the Buddhist religion. He taught that happiness comes from being kind to others. He also taught that material things are not important for happiness.

The early Japanese added the teachings of Buddhism to their beliefs of Shintoism. Many people in Japan today follow both religions, celebrating some events with a Shinto ceremony and others with a Buddhist ceremony. The combination of Shinto and Buddhist beliefs is unique in Japan and not found extensively in other parts of Asia.

This photograph shows the Ginza district, one of the busiest sections of Tokyo. The Ginza is famous for its shops, restaurants, and nightclubs.
▶ What cities in the United States have sections famous for shops, restaurants, or entertainment?

C. Busy Tokyo

Daily Life City life in Japan is much like city life everywhere in the world. For example, the morning rush hour in Tokyo is similar to rush hours in most large cities. As you read the following paragraph, think of other cities that fit the same description.

It is morning in a Tokyo train station, and you are being pushed along by a great crowd of people hurrying toward the train that will take them to work. The crowd is so dense that you could not turn back even if you wanted to. If you dropped a package or a shoe, you would not dare stoop down to pick it up for fear of being trampled. When you reach the train, there are no seats left, so you crowd against the other people standing in the aisle. On schedule the doors close, and the train begins to move.

Yoshiko Uchimura is a young Japanese girl who lives with her family in Tokyo. Life in Tokyo is busy and hectic for Yoshiko, her family, and her friends. Tokyo is one of the most crowded cities in the world. Yet many Japanese customs make it possible for people to live together in crowded conditions and still maintain peace.

Like most people in Tokyo, the Uchimura family lives in a huge building containing many apartments, each with only one or two rooms. Yoshiko's entire family shares one large room that is used as a bedroom at night, as a dining room for meals, and as a living room for relaxing and studying. Many Japanese homes do not have solid wood walls, but have sliding walls of heavy paper. The walls can be opened or shut to make smaller rooms out of one large room. Heavy padded quilts called **futons** are rolled out at night for sleeping. They are stored away in chests during the day, so they don't take up much valuable space.

When Yoshiko goes out shopping or visiting friends, she usually wears blue jeans and a blouse or sweater. But at home she often wears a comfortable kimono, a soft, warm robe with a large sash around the waist. Like most Japanese, Yoshiko removes her shoes when entering her home. The most common type of floor covering in Japanese homes is the **tatami**, a soft woven floor mat. Wearing street shoes in the home would dirty the tatami, so by custom, people remove their shoes on entering a room and use soft slippers instead.

Japanese Culture Popular western culture and ways are becoming more common every day in Japan. Western culture comes from the United States and Europe, and includes things that are familiar to American teenagers, such as rock music, comic books, and movies. Tokyo even has its own Disneyland, built in 1983 on the edge of the city.

But the Japanese also follow many old traditions. Yoshiko and her family sometimes spend January 1, New Year's Day, visiting the Imperial Palace, near downtown Tokyo. This huge complex of buildings contains the modern palace where the emperor of Japan lives with his family. This section of the Imperial Palace is open to the public only on special holidays. Parts of the old palace where former emperors lived are also located here.

Gardens and nature are important to the Japanese, perhaps because their cities

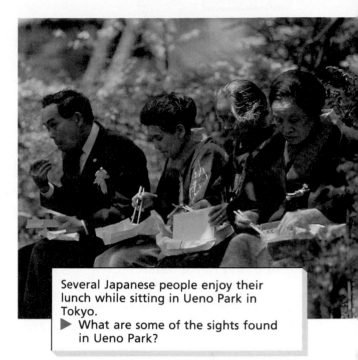

Several Japanese people enjoy their lunch while sitting in Ueno Park in Tokyo.
▶ What are some of the sights found in Ueno Park?

are so congested. Tokyo's beautiful Ueno (WAY noh) Park has several large museums, an art gallery, and a zoo. It is a favorite place for people to stroll and enjoy nature right in the middle of the city.

LESSON 3

Review

REVIEWING MAIN IDEAS
A. Why does Japan have so few minority groups?
B. How has Japan's culture been influenced by the cultures of China and Korea?
C. In what ways is daily life in Japan different from daily life in the United States?

SKILLS CHECK
WRITING SKILL
Imagine that you are visiting Tokyo. Write a short letter home describing what you have seen on your visit.

North Korea and South Korea

Using what you have already learned about the Korean peninsula, name what you think are important economic activities of North Korea and South Korea.

TERMS
demilitarized zone

FOCUS
How do the economies of North Korea and South Korea differ?

A. Korea as a Colony of Japan

Korea's Modernization Like the Japanese, the Koreans tried to avoid contact with outsiders for several centuries. Their culture, which had adopted many features of Chinese culture, did not change much while Korea's doors were closed to people from other countries.

In 1895, Japan took Korea as a colony and imposed rapid changes on the people of the peninsula. The people of Korea had always farmed, but the Japanese forced them to modernize, or change to meet the needs of the times. The Japanese built more irrigation canals in order to build new rice paddies. They also introduced basic farm machinery to the Koreans and showed them how to grow crops such as tobacco and cotton. The Japanese also modernized Korean fishing boats and taught the Koreans how to fish more efficiently and catch greater numbers of fish. Although the Japanese helped to improve the Korean economy, the Koreans were not happy to be a colony of Japan.

Independence By the time Japan was defeated in World War II and had to give up its colony of Korea, life was quite different for the Koreans. They had begun to cut large amounts of wood from their forests for fuel. People worked in coal mines and iron ore mines that the Japanese had opened up in the northern part of Korea. The Japanese had built roads and railroads to connect important cities and ports on the peninsula. With good transportation the Japanese could ship coal, iron ore, and other minerals to their own factories in Japan. After Korea became independent, the Korean people built and added on to what the Japanese had introduced to them.

In 1950, Communist North Korea invaded South Korea. This action grew into the Korean War. The United States and some other members of the United Nations fought to protect South Korea. The Chinese Communists fought for North Korea, which also received help from the Soviet Union. North Korea was unable to take over South Korea. In 1953, North Korea and South Korea agreed to a division of the Korean peninsula at the 38th parallel. A narrow strip of land called a **demilitarized zone** lies on either side of the boundary. That zone is an area where there are no troops or weapons. It helps to keep the two countries separate.

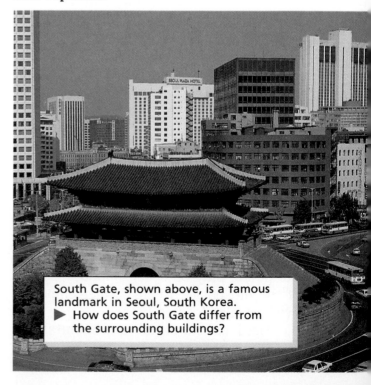

South Gate, shown above, is a famous landmark in Seoul, South Korea.
▶ How does South Gate differ from the surrounding buildings?

B. Northern and Southern Agriculture

Rugged North Korea The northern end of the Korean peninsula has rugged mountains along the border between North Korea and China. These mountains are not especially high, and most of the peaks do not even reach 9,000 feet (2,743 m). But between the peaks, rivers have cut through the mountains like knives, leaving deep, narrow gorges that are almost impossible to travel through.

The land of North Korea is difficult for people to live in, and the climate of the northern mountains is hostile. Summers are warm, with temperatures often reaching 85°F (29°C). In contrast, winters are long and bitterly cold. Cold winds from Siberia bring frigid temperatures. Daytime temperatures usually reach only about 27°F (-3°C). Rivers in North Korea are frozen for three or four months every winter. Ice forms along the coasts and blocks the harbors.

Under these conditions, farmers have a difficult time growing crops. Cool-weather crops, such as corn, potatoes, and wheat, are commonly grown in North Korea. Most of North Korea's level land is located around the capital city of P'yongyang. In rural areas, there is little land for growing food for North Korea's population of about 22 million people.

South Korea's Agriculture The climate of South Korea is milder than that of North Korea. High temperatures in wintertime often pass 32°F (0°C). With less frigid winters, farmers in South Korea are able to grow vegetables such as cabbage, potatoes, and sweet potatoes in the cooler months. In warmer summer months, farmers grow rice, soybeans, and onions. By planting crops during their longer growing season, South Korean farmers produce more food than North Korean farmers.

South Korea also has another advantage for agriculture. A large, level plain is

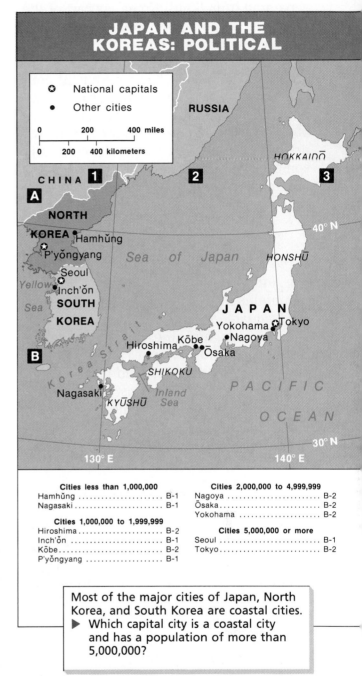

JAPAN AND THE KOREAS: POLITICAL

⊕ National capitals
• Other cities

Cities less than 1,000,000	
Hamhŭng	B-1
Nagasaki	B-1

Cities 1,000,000 to 1,999,999	
Hiroshima	B-2
Inch'ŏn	B-1
Kōbe	B-2
P'yŏngyang	B-1

Cities 2,000,000 to 4,999,999	
Nagoya	B-2
Ōsaka	B-2
Yokohama	B-2

Cities 5,000,000 or more	
Seoul	B-1
Tokyo	B-2

Most of the major cities of Japan, North Korea, and South Korea are coastal cities.
▶ Which capital city is a coastal city and has a population of more than 5,000,000?

located between the Naktong River and the capital city of Seoul. The plain provides farmers with much more level land than the North Korean farmers have.

Before 1945 the lack of agriculture in North Korea was not a serious problem, because North Korea had not yet been

413

separated from South Korea. As part of the nation of Korea before 1945, South Korea supplied food to all the people of Korea.

Today, North Korea is working hard to modernize its farms. The government controls most of the farmland and organizes farm households into collective farms, with about 300 families on each farm. Families are usually paid with part of the crops and some cash, too. North Korea's farmers now produce almost all the food needed to feed their country's population.

C. Two Different Paths of Industrialization

An Industrial Nation North Korea's mountains make farming difficult, but they hold valuable resources, such as coal, iron ore, tungsten, and zinc. Steel and machinery are two of North Korea's main industrial products, but chemicals and fertilizers are valuable products, too. Most of North Korea's industries are located near the capital city of P'yongyang.

North Korea has most of the Korean peninsula's important minerals. But the standard of living in North Korea is low. Why? One reason is the Communist economic system. All economic decisions are made by the government. Individual factory owners must follow government plans about what to produce and how much to produce. As you read in Chapter 15, this is how the Soviet Union's economic system used to work. Perhaps North Korea's government will also make changes in its economic system now that communist rule in the Soviet Union has ended.

An Economic Power South Korea's economy offers an interesting contrast to North Korea's. South Korea has few mineral or energy resources. The country used to pay for electricity sent by transmission lines from North Korea. When Korea was divided in 1945, the transmission lines were cut and South Korea was left without a reliable source of cheap power. But South Korea has one of the world's fastest growing

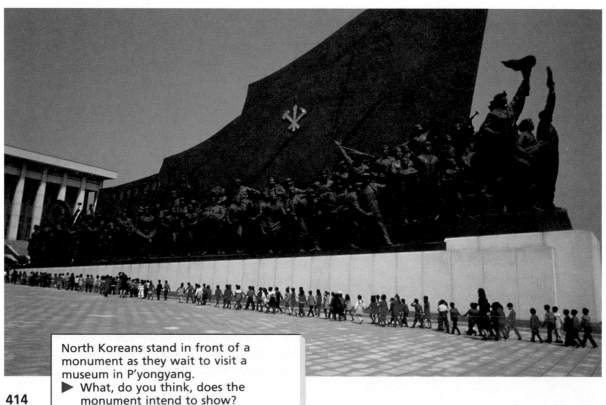

North Koreans stand in front of a monument as they wait to visit a museum in P'yongyang.
► What, do you think, does the monument intend to show?

South Korea is a leading producer of steel, and in turn, shipbuilding has become a major industry there.

▶ What part of a ship is shown here?

economies; in fact, South Korea is said to have experienced an economic miracle much like Japan has.

South Korea's economic success is the result of several factors. One is that South Korea's people are better educated than North Korea's. Another reason is that the government borrowed money from other countries to create new industries.

Another factor has been South Korea's development of its few mineral resources. Recently, small deposits of iron ore were found in the southeast, and coalfields were discovered in the east. With these resources and imported petroleum, South Korea is growing as an industrial nation. It is one of the world's leading producers of steel. Shipbuilding, which depends on steel production, is a major industry in South Korea. At the same time, its business leaders have worked hard to build industries that produce clothing, shoes, computer equipment, televisions, and other electronic goods. South Korea's own people and many millions more in other countries purchase these products in great numbers. As a result, South Korea's economy has grown rapidly in the past 20 years.

Unfortunately, not all of South Korea's people have benefited from the economic miracle. People in the cities have a higher standard of living than people who live in rural areas.

LESSON 4

Review

REVIEWING MAIN IDEAS

A. How did Japan influence the economy of the country of Korea before World War II?

B. Why do farmers in North Korea have more difficulty producing food than South Korean farmers do?

C. What kinds of industries are most important in North Korea and South Korea?

SKILLS CHECK

THINKING SKILL

Why do you think South Korea's economy has become more developed than North Korea's economy?

REVIEWING TERMS

On a separate sheet of paper, write the term that best completes each sentence.

> paddy
> synthetic material
> futon
> tatami
> demilitarized zone

1. Many Japanese homes have a type of floor covering called a _____.
2. A _____ is made from materials produced by people, not by nature.
3. A _____ helps to keep two countries separate and does not allow troops or weapons within its boundaries.
4. Rice seedlings are transplanted into an irrigated rice field, which is called a _____.
5. In Japan, a heavy padded quilt called a _____ is often used for sleeping.

REVIEWING THE FACTS

On a separate sheet of paper, answer the following questions in complete sentences.

1. Why are the mountain ranges on the coasts around the Pacific Ocean called the Ring of Fire?
2. How does the Japan Current affect the climate of Japan?
3. On what island is Tokyo, the capital of Japan, located?
4. How do the governments of North Korea and South Korea differ?
5. What are some of the ways Japanese industries continue to improve their products?

6. What are some goods produced in Honshu's industrial zones?
7. What are the two main religions practiced in Japan?
8. Why did Japan give up its colony of Korea?
9. How does the geography of North Korea differ from the geography that is found in South Korea?
10. Why are the mountains of North Korea important?

WRITING ABOUT CULTURE

In addition to rock music, comic books, and movies, what other parts of western culture, do you think, may eventually become common in Japan? Write a paragraph or two explaining your views.

THINKING CRITICALLY

On a separate sheet of paper, answer the following questions in complete sentences.

1. Why can potatoes and fruit trees, but not rice, be grown on slopes that do not have terraces?
2. Why is the ship that usually accompanies a fishing vessel called a factory ship?
3. What reasons might Japan have for wanting to limit the number of immigrants it allows?
4. What minority groups does the United States have?
5. Why would Japan want to have Korea as a colony?

SUMMARIZING THE CHAPTER

On a separate sheet of paper, draw a graphic organizer like the one shown here. Copy the information from this graphic organizer on the one you have drawn. Under the main idea of each lesson, write three statements that you think best support that main idea.

CHAPTER THEME

Japan's historical development was mostly separate and isolated. Today, Japan is a modern, industrialized nation. Its neighbors, the Koreas, offer many contrasts.

Lesson 1 Japan, North Korea, and South Korea have a variety of landforms.
1. _____
2. _____
3. _____

Lesson 2 The Japanese produce many goods even though their land has few natural resources.
1. _____
2. _____
3. _____

Lesson 3 Japan's culture is a blend of old and new lifestyles.
1. _____
2. _____
3. _____

Lesson 4 North Korea and South Korea have different economies.
1. _____
2. _____
3. _____

CHINA AND ITS NEIGHBORS

China, the Giant of East Asia

CONNECTIONS
Name the ways in which you think China is different from Japan.

TERMS
alpine, tableland

FOCUS
What are the differences between eastern and western China?

A. Planning a Trip to China

Climbing Mount Everest One day in 1984, Peter Jenkins, a writer and mountain climber from Tennessee, received an important telephone call from his friend Skip. After the phone call, Peter was so excited that he was hopping around like a dancing stork. Skip had just invited him to join a mountain-climbing expedition. The team would climb to the top of Mount Everest, the highest mountain in the world. Mount Everest rises to a height of 29,028 feet (8,848 m). This incredibly high mountain belongs to a long mountain range called the Himalayas. The Himalayas stretch across China's southwestern border. The Himalayas cover a part of China that is now called Xizang (SHEE ZANG), but it was once known as Tibet.

Peter and Skip tried to imagine where Tibet and Mount Everest are. In his journal, which was later published in his book, *Across China,* Peter wrote down the following conversation.

> *"Where is Tibet?" I asked. Skip paused, trying to figure it out himself.*
> *I could not picture that part of the world.*
> *"Tibet's in the far southwestern corner of China. . . . I think Tibet borders with India, Nepal, and Bhutan."*
> *Every country he mentioned sounded more intriguing.*

China's Neighbors Skip correctly named India, Nepal, and Bhutan as China's neighbors. China has eleven other neighbors as well. China shares its northern border with Russia and Mongolia. Mongolia is landlocked between Russia and China.

North Korea touches China along China's northeastern border. China shares its southern border with India, Bhutan, Nepal, Vietnam, Laos, and Myanmar, which used to be named Burma. China's western border includes Pakistan, Afghanistan, and three former republics of the Soviet Union that are now independent—Tajikistan, Kyrgyzstan, and Kazakhstan.

B. Crowded East, Empty West

A Vast Country China, which is officially called the People's Republic of China, occupies most of eastern Asia. China's total area of 3,691,502 square miles (9,560,990 sq km) makes China slightly larger than the United States.

When Peter's mountain-climbing team left for China in August 1984, they flew from Seattle, Washington, to Beijing, formerly Peking, the capital city of China. This almost 17-hour trip took them about 5,500 miles (8,850 km) across the Pacific Ocean. Once the team arrived in China, they had to fly another 1,600 miles (2,574 km) to reach the city of Lhasa, which is near Mount Everest. But this was only the beginning of the trip. It would be two more months before they reached the peak of Mount Everest.

The team left Lhasa and traveled in old trucks to the foot of Mount Everest, a distance of about 300 miles (480 km). On a modern highway in the United States, a car could travel that distance in about six hours. For Peter's team, the trip took several days. They had to travel slowly because the **alpine**, or mountainous, roads were narrow, twisted, and dangerous. Getting to the bottom of Mount Everest was almost as difficult as climbing to its peak!

419

▶ One of the six temples in the Forbidden City in Beijing, China

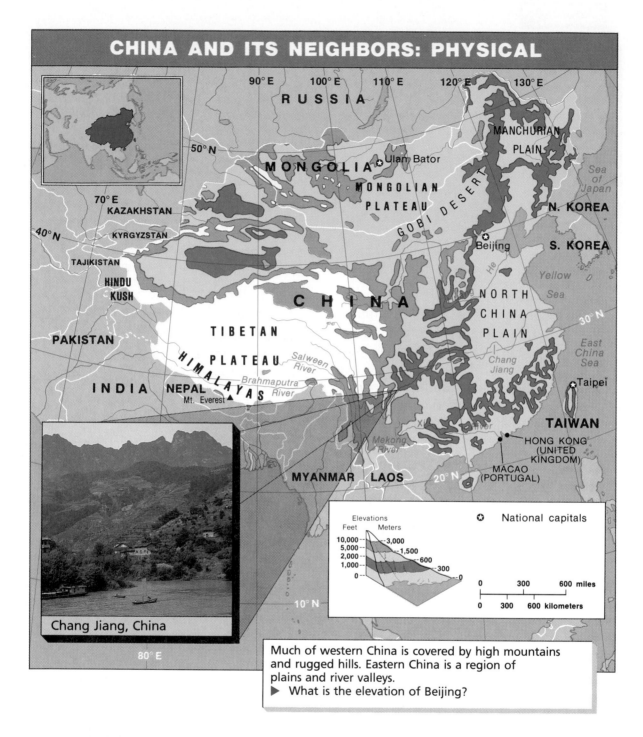

CHINA AND ITS NEIGHBORS: PHYSICAL

90° E   100° E   110° E   120° E   130° E

RUSSIA

MANCHURIAN PLAIN

50° N

MONGOLIA   ☉ Ulan Bator

Sea of Japan

MONGOLIAN PLATEAU

GOBI DESERT

N. KOREA

70° E

KAZAKHSTAN

☉ Beijing

S. KOREA

40° N

KYRGYZSTAN

He

Yellow Sea

TAJIKISTAN

CHINA

NORTH

HINDU KUSH

CHINA

30° N

PAKISTAN

TIBETAN

PLAIN

East China Sea

PLATEAU

Salween River

Chang Jiang

☉ Taipei

HIMALAYAS

Brahmaputra River

INDIA   NEPAL

Mt. Everest ▲

TAIWAN

Xi

River

HONG KONG (UNITED KINGDOM)

Mekong River

MACAO (PORTUGAL)

MYANMAR   LAOS

20° N

Elevations

☉   National capitals

Feet   Meters

10,000 -- --3,000
5,000 -- --1,500
2,000 --
1,000 -- --600
0 -- --300
-- 0

0   300   600 miles

0   300   600 kilometers

10° N

Chang Jiang, China

80° E

Much of western China is covered by high mountains and rugged hills. Eastern China is a region of plains and river valleys.
▶ What is the elevation of Beijing?

The Populated East As Peter and his team made their way to Mount Everest, they saw only a few houses, farms, or other travelers. Why was this western part of China so empty when China has the largest population of any country on earth—over 1 *billion* people? The answer is that most of China's people live in eastern China. Western China is mainly barren, a land of mountains, plateaus, and deserts.

Much of eastern China is covered by broad river valleys. If you look at the map above, you can see that the northernmost river is the Huang He (hwang hih), or Yellow

How would you translate the Chinese characters for the word *Beijing*? Translating Chinese characters into the alphabet used in English and many other languages has always been a difficult task. In the early 1900s, two Englishmen developed the Wade-Giles (jiles) system of translating Chinese. The Wade-Giles system was used for most of this century, and many people still recognize placenames based on that system.

In the 1950s the Chinese government introduced the Pinyin system for writing Chinese words in the Roman alphabet. The Chinese believe that the Pinyin spelling comes closer to the correct pronunciation of Chinese.

In this book, we are using the Pinyin system. Whenever we have used the Pinyin term, we have also mentioned its older, Wade-Giles spelling. That is why we tell you that Xizang was once called Tibet and that Beijing was once known as Peking.

River. This 2,903-mile-long (4,671-km-long) river begins in central China and makes two large loops as it crosses the country. Before it empties into the Yellow Sea, the Huang He crosses the wide North China Plain, which is China's most important agricultural region.

South of the Huang He is China's longest river, the Chang Jiang (chahng jee-AHNG), or Yangtze River. The Chang Jiang also begins in central China, but it winds eastward for 3,434 miles (5,525 km) before it empties into the East China Sea.

The Western Region Western China, where Peter's group traveled to Mount Everest, is a rugged, sparsely populated region. Only a few towns and villages are found in its narrow valleys. To the north of the Himalayas is a high, dry region called the Tibetan plateau. The plateau is level and flat, so it is called **tableland**, but the cold, dry climate makes farming difficult.

C. The People of China

About 95 percent of China's citizens belong to one ethnic group—the Chinese. Although the Chinese speak the same language, they use many different dialects. Some of the dialects are so different from each other that they sound almost like other languages. More than 50 other ethnic groups with different languages and customs also live in China. The Tibetans are among the most important of these groups. They speak Tibetan and live mainly in southern and western China.

The Mongols are an important ethnic group in northern China. Their language, Mongolian, is completely different from Chinese and is similar to the languages of the Muslim people who live in the Central Asian nations of the former Soviet Union.

LESSON 1

Review

REVIEWING MAIN IDEAS
A. Which countries are neighbors of China?
B. Why is eastern China more densely populated than western China?
C. What are three important ethnic groups in China?

SKILLS CHECK
MAP SKILL
Using the map on page 423, name the river that is nearest to each of these Chinese cities: Guangzhou, Shanghai, Tianjin.

China's Varied Regions

CONNECTIONS

If you were going on a trip to China, what kinds of clothes would you pack for your stay there?

TERMS

triple cropping, loess, alluvial soil

FOCUS

How are China's three regions different from one another?

A. The Three Regions of China

Studying China Peter Jenkins had studied China's geography before he began his trip, so he was not surprised to see large areas of uninhabited land in the west. He had learned that China has three regions—the western interior, northeastern China, and southeastern China. Peter's trip to China took him to all three regions. These regions can be seen on the map on page 420.

Peter began his trip in the western interior. This region includes Mount Everest and the rest of the Himalayas. The second region Peter traveled through is southeastern China, which is located between the Chang Jiang and the southern border of China. Finally he traveled through the third region, northeastern China. The Chang Jiang forms this region's southern border, and the coast of the Yellow Sea makes up its eastern border.

Two Different Climates Before Peter packed his suitcase for his trip, he made two lists of clothing to take. One list included wool socks, wool pants, a wool sweater, gloves, and a heavy parka. These were the clothes he would need while traveling in the western interior.

At the top of the second list, Peter wrote "For travel in China—hot and humid weather." This list was completely different from the first one. It included sandals, cotton socks, a lightweight sweater, jeans, T-shirts, and sunglasses. These were the clothes Peter needed for traveling in northeastern and southeastern China. Peter knew he would need a variety of clothing because the lands and climates in China's three regions are very different.

B. The Western Interior

I'd never experienced so many mountains. There seemed to be a million of them. . . . Over every pass, around every cliff, and through every narrow valley arose more and more mountains.

This was Peter's journal entry as the mountain-climbing team traveled through the Himalayas toward Mount Everest.

The Himalayas are one of the four major landforms of the western interior. The three other landforms are the Tibetan plateau and two deserts, the Xinjiang and the Gobi.

In the Himalayas, Peter's team took tanks of oxygen to help them breathe at elevations above 20,000 feet (6,096 m). They also had to wear heavy parkas and gloves to keep warm. It was a tough climb to the top. As the leader of Peter's team said later, everyone finally reached the summit of Mount Everest "despite a cracked rib, frozen eyeballs, bad avalanches and winds faster than a race car."

The climate in most areas of the Himalayas is cold. Peter noted that his team

passed several clusters of . . . homes with smoke fluffing out from the tops of their flat roofs. It was the dead of summer [August] and a chilly high forties this morning.

The Rooftop of the World Located north of the Himalayas is the Tibetan plateau. This plateau is often called the "Rooftop of the World," because it is the world's largest high-elevation plateau. The Tibetan plateau is crisscrossed by mountain ranges,

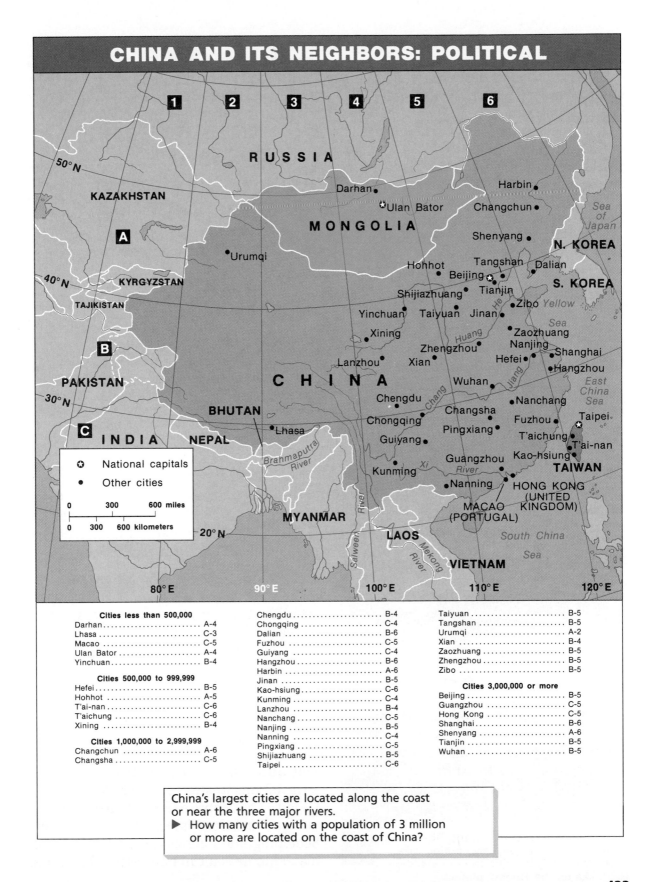

CHINA AND ITS NEIGHBORS: POLITICAL

Legend:
- ✪ National capitals
- • Other cities

0 300 600 miles
0 300 600 kilometers

Cities less than 500,000

Darhan	A-4
Lhasa	C-3
Macao	C-5
Ulan Bator	A-4
Yinchuan	B-4

Cities 500,000 to 999,999

Hefei	B-5
Hohhot	A-5
T'ai-nan	C-6
T'aichung	C-6
Xining	B-4

Cities 1,000,000 to 2,999,999

Changchun	A-6
Changsha	C-5

Chengdu	B-4
Chongqing	C-4
Dalian	B-6
Fuzhou	C-5
Guiyang	C-4
Hangzhou	B-6
Harbin	A-6
Jinan	B-5
Kao-hsiung	C-6
Kunming	C-4
Lanzhou	B-4
Nanchang	C-5
Nanjing	B-5
Nanning	C-4
Pingxiang	C-5
Shijiazhuang	B-5
Taipei	C-6

Taiyuan	B-5
Tangshan	B-5
Urumqi	A-2
Xian	B-4
Zaozhuang	B-5
Zhengzhou	B-5
Zibo	B-5

Cities 3,000,000 or more

Beijing	B-5
Guangzhou	C-5
Hong Kong	C-5
Shanghai	B-6
Shenyang	A-6
Tianjin	B-5
Wuhan	B-5

China's largest cities are located along the coast or near the three major rivers.
▶ How many cities with a population of 3 million or more are located on the coast of China?

423

but they are not as high or spectacular as the Himalayas.

In the valleys of these mountains, farmers grow barley, wheat, and vegetables in small plots. Most people on the Tibetan plateau make their living by herding yaks, animals that are similar to oxen.

Peter's group hired yak herders to help carry their climbing gear to their base camp at Mount Everest. There were no roads in that area, but each yak could carry about 100 pounds (45 kg) of food and equipment on the rocky trails.

The yak herders told Peter and his friends that yaks have several uses. The herders use their yaks to carry food and clothing or to pull a plow in a farmer's field. Yak hair is woven into clothing, and yak milk is made into butter. When yaks

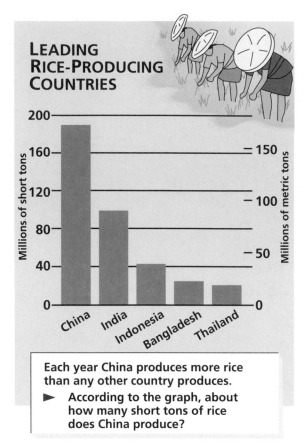

LEADING RICE-PRODUCING COUNTRIES

Each year China produces more rice than any other country produces.

► According to the graph, about how many short tons of rice does China produce?

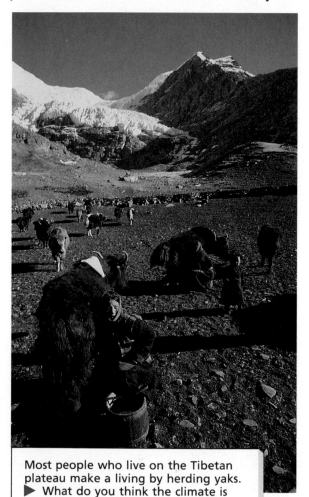

Most people who live on the Tibetan plateau make a living by herding yaks.
► What do you think the climate is like on the Tibetan plateau?

become very old or must be killed, their meat is eaten and their hides are used to make sandals and other products that are usually made from leather.

The Xinjiang Desert The Xinjiang Desert is the third major landform of the western interior. It is found north of the Tibetan plateau. This dry region includes several broad basins and a few small rivers. All of the western interior is far from the Pacific and Indian oceans, and it rarely receives any precipitation. Total annual precipitation in the western interior is less than 10 inches (254 mm).

The Gobi Desert The fourth major landform of the western interior is the Gobi Desert. The Gobi, like other parts of the western interior, is sparsely populated. Scorching hot summers and frigid winters make life difficult in both the Gobi Desert and the Xinjiang Desert. Fierce winds there carry blinding dust but little moisture.

C. Southeastern China

A Humid, Rainy Climate After leaving the Himalayas, Peter traveled by plane to Chengdu, a city in southeastern China. As soon as Peter's plane landed in Chengdu, he noticed that the weather there was much warmer and more humid than that of the Himalayas and the Tibetan plateau. In his journal, Peter wrote, "My clothes stuck to my skin and palm trees sagged under the hammer of summer in tropical China. . . . It was about 95° [35°C]."

The Chang Jiang, which runs along the northern edge of southeastern China, is this region's most important river. Many smaller rivers flow out of the western mountains and across southeastern China to the South Sea. Between the rivers are rolling hills and broad, flat valleys.

Triple Cropping Southeastern China's level land and warm, rainy climate provide excellent conditions for agriculture. Most farmers here can plant crops throughout the year. As soon as they harvest one crop, they begin planting another. This is called **triple cropping**. Triple cropping allows farmers to get three times as much food from their land as farmers in cold climates, who plant only one crop a year.

Rice is the main crop grown in southeastern China. The tremendous amount of rice grown here helps to make China the world's largest rice producer.

Peter learned about the other crops grown in southeastern China by studying the menus of Chengdu's restaurants. In the western interior, he had mainly eaten goat meat, butter made from yak's milk, and bread made of uncooked dough. In Chengdu the foods were quite different. Chengdu is located in the province of Sichuan (SEE-chwahn), and Sichuan cooking is famous everywhere, including the United States.

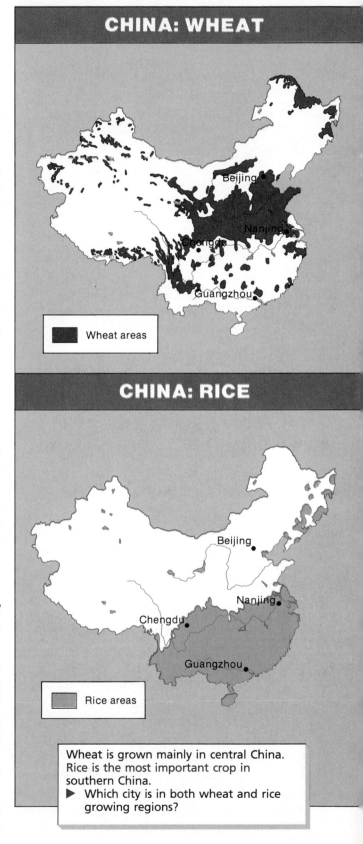

CHINA: WHEAT

Wheat areas

CHINA: RICE

Rice areas

Wheat is grown mainly in central China. Rice is the most important crop in southern China.
▶ Which city is in both wheat and rice growing regions?

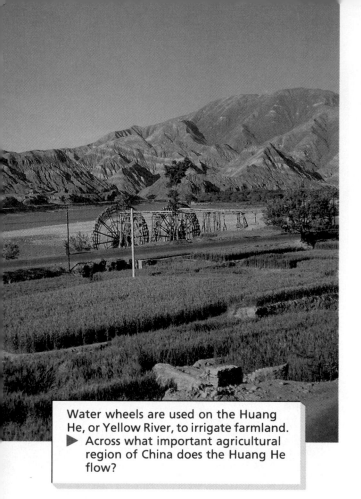

Water wheels are used on the Huang He, or Yellow River, to irrigate farmland.
▶ Across what important agricultural region of China does the Huang He flow?

Shanghai also receives agricultural products and manufactured goods from northern China. Coastal shipping lines carry the products to Shanghai. They are then sent up the Chang Jiang and sold to the millions of people in small towns and villages of southeastern China.

Shanghai is also an important industrial center. Tungsten, which is found in great quantities in southern China, is processed here. Other industries include shipbuilding, rice milling, processing of fruits and vegetables, and new industries that produce metals and chemicals.

Guangzhou (GUAHNG joh), or as it was once called, Canton, is the second largest city in southeastern China. It is much smaller than Shanghai, with about 3 million people. Guangzhou is located near the mouth of the Xi (shee) Jiang, or West River, making the city a major port. In turn, shipbuilding has become a major industry in Guangzhou.

Farmers from all over southern China send their products to Guangzhou. The raw materials needed for the city's textile industry are among these products. Guangzhou has several cotton mills and silk mills for manufacturing cloth.

Guangzhou's main industry is the processing of tea, sugarcane, and rice. Hydroelectricity generated from the Xi Jiang powers other factories, which produce textiles, fertilizers, and farm machinery.

Guangzhou is a center of international trade. In fact, twice each year the city plays host to China's largest trade fair, the Export Commodities Fair, which attracts thousands of foreign merchants.

D. Northeastern China

China's Heartland Northeastern China is the cultural and industrial heartland of China. It is also the oldest inhabited region in China. Archaeologists have discovered human fossils showing that people lived

Peter ate many tasty dishes made of pork, chicken, and fish. In a restaurant he watched a chef cook onions, green peppers, garlic, and vegetables with these meats. He also drank a lot of tea, which is another major product of southeastern China, and he ate many bowls of rice and special Sichuan noodles.

Shanghai and Guangzhou Huge cities are found throughout southeastern China. The largest is Shanghai, which is located near the mouth of the Chang Jiang. Shanghai has a population of over 6 million people. For centuries, Shanghai has been one of China's most important trade centers. Many of the goods and crops produced in southeastern China are shipped down the Chang Jiang to Shanghai. There they are loaded onto large boats and ships. The products are sold to buyers in other parts of China or are exported.

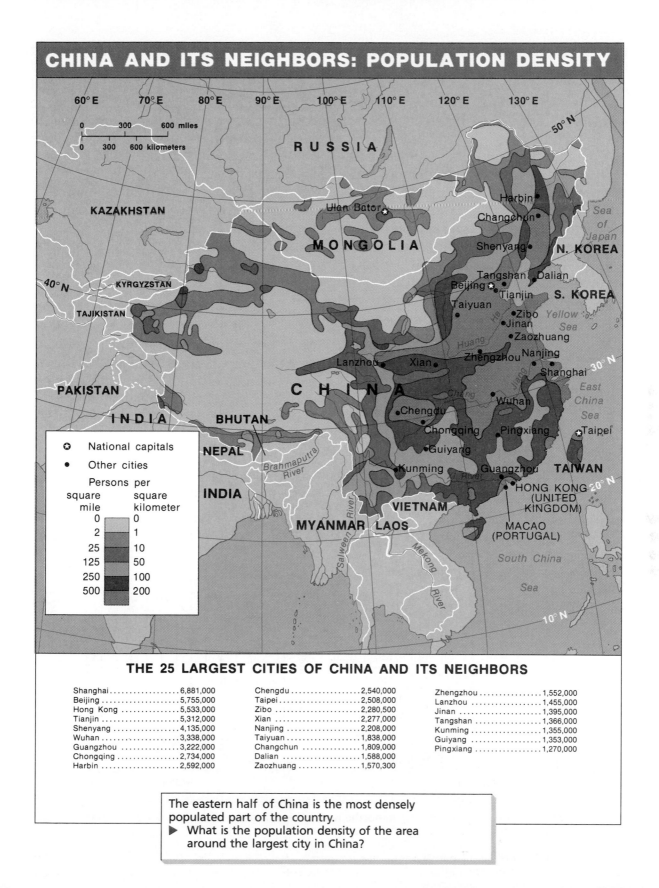

CHINA AND ITS NEIGHBORS: POPULATION DENSITY

National capitals
Other cities

Persons per

square mile	square kilometer
0	0
2	1
25	10
125	50
250	100
500	200

THE 25 LARGEST CITIES OF CHINA AND ITS NEIGHBORS

Shanghai 6,881,000	Chengdu 2,540,000	Zhengzhou 1,552,000
Beijing 5,755,000	Taipei 2,508,000	Lanzhou 1,455,000
Hong Kong 5,533,000	Zibo 2,280,500	Jinan 1,395,000
Tianjin 5,312,000	Xian 2,277,000	Tangshan 1,366,000
Shenyang 4,135,000	Nanjing 2,208,000	Kunming 1,355,000
Wuhan 3,338,000	Taiyuan 1,838,000	Guiyang 1,353,000
Guangzhou 3,222,000	Changchun 1,809,000	Pingxiang 1,270,000
Chongqing 2,734,000	Dalian 1,588,000	
Harbin 2,592,000	Zaozhuang 1,570,300	

The eastern half of China is the most densely populated part of the country.
▶ What is the population density of the area around the largest city in China?

near Beijing in 600,000 B.C. Farmers began to practice agriculture along the Huang He about 5000 B.C.

The name *Huang He* means "yellow river" in Chinese. The river's color comes from the yellowish soils that have been washed into the river from the Loess (LOH-es) Plateau. A powdery, fertile soil, **loess** is excellent for agriculture since it holds moisture so well.

Rich **alluvial soils** are found along other stretches of the Huang He. Alluvial soils are rock fragments and silt deposited on the land when a river floods during the rainy season. For thousands of years the Huang He has flooded every spring, spreading a blanket of rich soil across the Huang He valley and the North China Plain.

The North China Plain is a large, flat area of alluvial soils near the mouth of the Huang He. The North China Plain and Huang He valley make up China's most important agricultural region. More than one fourth of all of China's agricultural products comes from this area. It is the country's largest wheat-growing region. In fact, as you can see from the map on page 14, China is one of the world's largest producers of wheat.

This region also produces enormous amounts of corn, tobacco, cotton, and soybeans. Soybeans are used for animal feed, food products, and in industrial products, such as paint.

Climate and Resources The crops grown in northeastern China are different from those grown in southeastern China. Why? Using the climographs on this page, compare the temperatures of Beijing and Shanghai. The area around Beijing has a colder and drier winter than Shanghai does. This makes it impossible to grow in Beijing the

Winter in the area around Beijing, in northeastern China, is generally colder and drier than winter in the area around Shanghai, in southeastern China.

▶ During which month is the difference between the temperature in Beijing and the temperature in Shanghai the greatest?

tea, rice, sugarcane, and other crops grown in southeastern China.

Northeastern China has many of China's mineral and fuel resources. Most of China's enormous deposits of coal—which are the largest in the world—are found in the northeast. Important coal and iron ore deposits are found near the city of Shenyang.

Near the border with North Korea, China has large deposits of minerals such as lead, zinc, tin, and copper. Factories and steel mills in Shenyang process these raw materials into heavy machinery, tools, bicycles, and other metal goods.

Beijing and Tianjin are the two largest cities in northeastern China. Since it is China's capital city, Beijing has many important government offices. It also has ancient palaces, shrines, and beautiful gardens. Tianjin, to the east of Beijing, is northeastern China's industrial center. The government has enlarged and modernized Tianjin's port and has encouraged the growth of industries such as chemicals, textiles, and iron and steel mills.

Transportation Northeastern and southeastern China have most of the country's people, farms, and industries. However, it is difficult to transport goods across the enormous distances that separate the cities in each region. Because of the mountains and rivers that cross these regions from east to west, only a few roads, highways, or railroads have been built to connect the cities of northeastern and southeastern China. However, over the centuries the Chinese have built many canals that crisscross the rivers that flow through these two regions. The longest is the Grand Canal, which extends for over 1,000 miles (1,600 km) and connects Beijing and the city of Hangzhou near Shanghai. This and other canals have made it possible to ship foods, minerals, and manufactured goods cheaply from the north to the south.

The Grand Canal is the longest of the canals that connect China's rivers and allow trade between the southeastern and northeastern regions.
▶ How long is the Grand Canal?

LESSON 2

Review

REVIEWING MAIN IDEAS
A. What are China's three regions?
B. What are the four major landforms of the western interior region of China?
C. Why is Shanghai an important trading center for southeastern China?
D. What makes northeastern China a fertile farming region?

SKILLS CHECK
THINKING SKILL
Why is triple cropping practiced only in southeastern China, and not in the western interior or northeastern China?

429

Ways of Life in China

CONNECTIONS

What are some of the ways in which life in a mountainous region might be different from life on a plain?

TERMS

dynasty, commune

FOCUS

Why do people living in the desert and mountain areas of China have different languages and religions from other Chinese?

A. Beijing, the "Northern Capital"

Beijing One of the first things tourists notice when they visit Beijing is the bicycles. Hundreds of bicycles wheel through the streets, carrying business people, workers, and students to their work or homes. Bicycles are found throughout China's cities, but Beijing has the most—over 3 million, more than any other city in the world. Beijing is special for another reason—it is China's capital city and home to an incredible number of fascinating palaces.

Bicyclists on a street in Beijing.
▶ What do you think is one of the benefits of using bicycles instead of cars in a city?

Beijing, whose name means "northern capital" in Chinese, has been the capital of China since 1421. For thousands of years before then, it had been only a small town. It became an important political center beginning in the 1200s, when the great Mongol emperor Kubla (KOO bluh) Khan took over China. Kubla Khan decided to rebuild Beijing and create two sections for the city, the Inner City and the Outer City. The Outer City, in southern Beijing, was where ordinary people lived and worked. The Inner City was the section where the rulers lived. This section of Beijing was surrounded by high walls.

Inside the Inner City was another enclosed area, called Imperial City. This zone held the offices of the ruler's closest advisors. The Imperial City enclosed yet another city—the Forbidden City.

The Forbidden City The Forbidden City was a protected area where the emperors of China lived and worked. China's emperors usually belonged to a **dynasty**, or a family that ruled China for many generations. No one was allowed to pass through the gates into the Forbidden City without permission. Most ordinary people never saw the inside of the Forbidden City. When the Communist party took control of China in 1949, the government opened up the Forbidden City as a museum for the public, making it possible for all to marvel at its great treasures and architecture.

The Forbidden City is huge, covering 250 acres (101 ha). Inside are many palaces, temples, bridges, roadways, and courtyards. The most important part is an area of six palaces. Here the emperors of China presided over ceremonies, watched military parades, met with their advisors, and held huge banquets.

These six palaces stretch out along a straight walkway. Like the emperor and his visitors in the past, tourists today can walk down this walkway, passing through many gates and archways with names such as the Gate of Supreme Harmony and the Gate of Heavenly Purity.

Outside the Forbidden City is a huge plaza called Tiananmen (TEE en ahn mun) Square. This has been the traditional meeting place for the Chinese people to voice criticism of the government. It was here in 1989 that thousands of students and workers demonstrated for democracy in China. The Communist government would not accept their demands and decided to end the demonstration by sending in soldiers. Over 1,000 of the demonstrators were killed by the soldiers in the areas around the square.

B. The Mongols and China

The Great Wall   In the third century B.C., the Chinese became worried about invaders and built a massive fortified wall to protect themselves from Asians who might attack from the north. This wall, which is called the Great Wall, is about 4,000 miles (6,400 km) long and wide enough to allow five

horses to travel together along the road built on top of it. The Great Wall winds across northern China from its border with North Korea to the edge of the Xinjiang Desert. This remarkable structure is the only object made by humans that is visible from the moon.

The Mongols   The Great Wall was not an effective barrier to invaders. In fact, China was invaded many times both before and after the Great Wall was built. One of the most important invaders was Kubla Khan, the emperor who rebuilt Beijing. Kubla Khan was a Mongol from the Gobi Desert of the western interior. Although the Mongols ruled China between the thirteenth and the fourteenth centuries, their culture did not influence Chinese culture. Even today, Mongols are quite different in their culture.

Peter Jenkins desperately wanted to visit a Mongolian village while he was in China. He had read about the ancient Mongolian horsemen and wanted to see

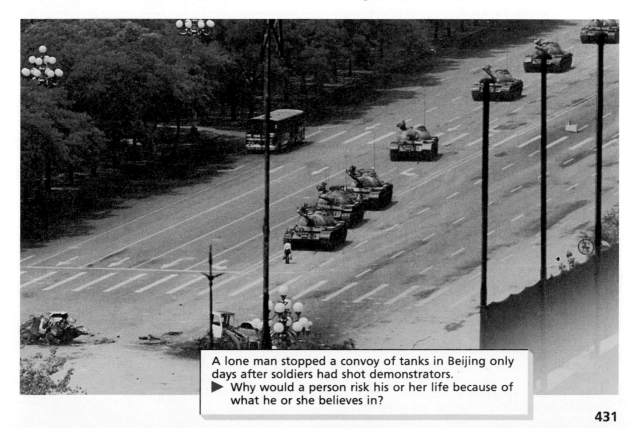

A lone man stopped a convoy of tanks in Beijing only days after soldiers had shot demonstrators.
▶ Why would a person risk his or her life because of what he or she believes in?

431

how their descendants live today. He received permission from the government to visit a village near the city of Hohhot, on the southern edge of the Gobi Desert.

The Mongol family that Peter visited herded cattle and sheep, and raised horses to help with the livestock. Many Mongol families live in mud-brick houses in small villages that have only a few families. The people and their language, Mongolian, are related to Turkish. Their way of life is similar to that of people in the nearby nation of Mongolia.

The language of the Mongols is completely different from Chinese. As you read earlier, even the Chinese language has many different dialects. Chinese dialects spoken in northern China are distinct from the Chinese spoken in Shanghai, Guangzhou, or other parts of China. Often two people speaking different dialects of Chinese cannot speak each other's language at all.

C. Religions of China

Lamaism in Tibet Religions in China also vary. For example, Tibetans living in the valleys of the Himalayas and in the Tibetan plateau practice Lamaism, which is a form of the religion called Buddhism. For centuries the Tibetan people considered their religious leaders to be their political leaders as well. Many young Tibetan men studied to be *lamas*, or holy men, in Tibet's thousands of monasteries and temples.

Tibet was part of the Chinese empire for centuries. In 1911, China granted Tibet independence. Independence did not last long, however, because China took over Tibet again in 1951. Then Chinese troops destroyed monasteries and shrines through-

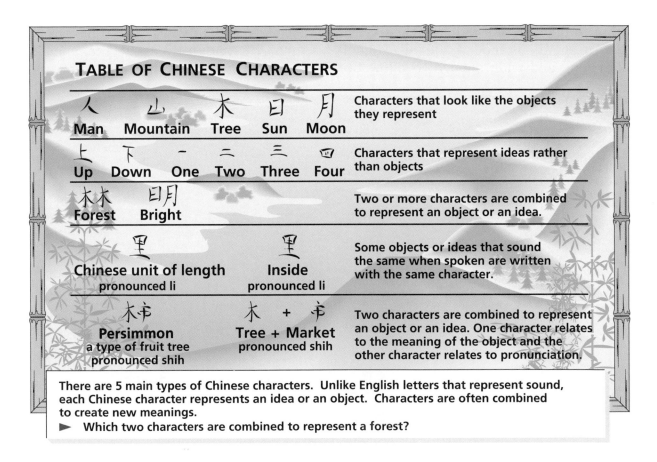

TABLE OF CHINESE CHARACTERS

Characters					Description
人 **Man**	山 **Mountain**	木 **Tree**	日 **Sun**	月 **Moon**	Characters that look like the objects they represent
上 **Up**	下 **Down**	一 **One**	二 **Two**	三 **Three**	四 **Four**	Characters that represent ideas rather than objects
林 **Forest**	明 **Bright**				Two or more characters are combined to represent an object or an idea.
里 **Chinese unit of length** pronounced li		里 **Inside** pronounced li			Some objects or ideas that sound the same when spoken are written with the same character.
柿 **Persimmon** a type of fruit tree pronounced shih		木 + 市 **Tree + Market** pronounced shih			Two characters are combined to represent an object or an idea. One character relates to the meaning of the object and the other character relates to pronunciation.

There are 5 main types of Chinese characters. Unlike English letters that represent sound, each Chinese character represents an idea or an object. Characters are often combined to create new meanings.

► Which two characters are combined to represent a forest?

out Tibet and the other regions of China. The Chinese believed that to be good Communists, people must not believe in any religions. Many Tibetan monks and religious leaders escaped to the neighboring nations of Nepal and India. Recently the Chinese government has allowed the Tibetans to rebuild some of their shrines and temples.

Buddhism The Chinese government has tried to crush religion, but religious teachings and writings still influence people's everyday behavior. Most Chinese practice Buddhism, a religion that first appeared in northern India in the sixth century B.C. Buddhists learn self-discipline and the correct way to do even small daily tasks. Buddhist *monks* study meditation and learn to ignore hunger and pain. In China, most Buddhists also follow the teachings of Confucius (kun FYOO shus), a Chinese philosopher who lived during the fifth century B.C. Confucius taught people that they should do good deeds and treat others the way they would like to be treated themselves. His teachings are collected in a book called the *Analects.* Here are some of his ideas.

> *The Master said, Even when walking in a party of no more than three, I can always be certain of learning from those I am with. There will be good qualities that I can select for imitation and bad ones that will teach me what requires correction in myself.*
>
> *A follower asked, Is there any single saying that one can act upon all day and everyday? The Master said, Perhaps the saying about consideration: Never do to others what you would not like them to do to you.*

D. Rural Life in China

An Agricultural Nation China is unusual in that over half of its people live in villages and small towns; only about a fourth of the people in the United States live in small

The Chinese philosopher Confucius lived from about 551 B.C. to 479 B.C.
▶ About how old was Confucius when he died?

communities. Most Chinese are farmers, although some may have second jobs in small factories or businesses. Despite this fact, Chinese farmers have difficulty producing enough food to feed a steadily growing population.

Chinese farmers and consumers are careful not to waste farmland or food. Farmers grow grain and vegetables instead of using their scarce land to raise pasture grasses to feed cattle and large animals. For much of China's history, however, Chinese farmers have tried to grow crops without the equipment or technology to fight floods, droughts, and insects. The

433

FROM: # The Good Earth

by Pearl S. Buck

Pearl S. Buck, an American who grew up in China where her parents were missionaries, is famous for her books about life and people in China. Her best-known novel, *The Good Earth*, tells about a farmer named Wang Lung who loves the land and struggles for many years to keep his crops growing. Wang Lung endures droughts, floods, and locusts, insects that eat farmers' crops.

. . . **I**n these parts, where Wang Lung had lived all his life and his father and his father's father had lived upon the land, there were famines once in five years or so, or if the gods were lenient, once in seven or eight or even ten years. This was because the heavens rained too much or not at all, or because the river to the north, because of rains and winter snows in distant mountains, came swelling into the fields over the dykes which had been builded by men for centuries to confine it.

Time after time men fled from the land and came back to it, but Wang Lung set himself now to build his fortunes so securely that through the bad years to come he need never leave his land again but live on the fruits of the good years, and so subsist until another year came forth. He set himself and the gods helped him and for seven years there were harvests, and every year Wang Lung and his men threshed far more than could be eaten. He hired more laborers each year for his fields until he had six men and he builded a new house behind his old one, a large room behind a court and two small rooms on each side of the court beside the large room. The house he covered with tiles, but the walls were still made of the hard tamped earth from the fields, only he had them brushed with lime and they were white and clean. Into these rooms he and his family moved, and the laborers, . . . lived in the old house in front.

Huge billboards that tie family planning to patriotism are a common sight in China.

▶ What is the English translation of the slogan on this billboard?

government has tried many agricultural experiments to encourage farmers to produce as much food as possible.

Communes In the 1950s, China's Communist government took control of all farmland and divided it into huge state farms called **communes**. About 20,000 people worked on each commune. The government made all the decisions about what the commune should grow and how it should operate.

The communes did not produce much more food than the old system. So gradually the government broke down the huge communes into smaller units called collectives. Many people were allowed to rent small plots of land and keep any profits they could make with their crops.

Family Planning Food production increased, but the population was increasing even more quickly. By the early 1980s, Chinese officials had adopted a plan to encourage *family planning*. Under the plan,

people would be rewarded for having only one child. The government hoped to slow down population growth and avoid huge famines in the future. Their population control plan has had some success. But China's greatest problem for the future is going to be feeding its growing population.

LESSON 3

Review

REVIEWING MAIN IDEAS

A. How did China's emperors close the Forbidden City to outsiders?
B. Why was the Great Wall built?
C. What are two of the religions of China?
D. How has the Chinese government tried to increase food supplies?

SKILLS CHECK

WRITING SKILL

Write an advertisement for tourists, describing the sights of China.

China's Neighbors

CONNECTIONS

Taiwan is known for the production of many small products. Can you name any products in your home that were made in Taiwan?

TERMS

arable, buffer state

FOCUS

How are Taiwan, Hong Kong, and Mongolia different from China?

A. Taiwan, "the Other China"

A Nationalist Island Less than 100 miles (160 km) off the southern coast of China is an island nation that is often called "the other China." This is the nation of Taiwan, or as it is formally called, the Republic of China. The language and religion of the Taiwanese are similar to those of the People's Republic of China. Indeed, their island, sometimes called Formosa, was inhabited by the Chinese and belonged to the Chinese empire for hundreds of years.

The governments of Taiwan and China are different. China is controlled by the Chinese Communist party, which began to form in 1911. At that time, many people who did not agree with the ideas of the Communists formed a different political party, called the Nationalists. The Communists and Nationalists fought for control of China for several decades. Finally, in 1949, the Communists won control of China, and the Nationalists fled to the island of Taiwan, where they formed their own government.

With money and political support from the United States, the Nationalists built a modern country on their island. This was difficult, because Taiwan has few mineral resources or fuels. The eastern half of the island is mountainous and is covered with dense forests. In the west there is a broad coastal plain, a flat area along the coast of the Taiwan Strait. The map on page 420 shows that the Taiwan Strait is a body of water that separates Taiwan and China.

The farms on the coastal plain are small but highly productive. The most common crop is rice, but farmers there also grow wheat, tea, sweet potatoes, sugarcane, and tropical fruits. Irrigation, rice paddy farming, and terracing allow Taiwan's farmers to produce surplus foods to export to other countries.

Most of Taiwan's 20 million people live and work on the western coastal plain. Taipei (tye PAY), the capital city of Taiwan, is located at the northern end of the coastal plain. Smaller cities have grown up along the foothills of the mountains. Factories in these cities use hydroelectric power generated from the rivers that tumble out of the mountains and empty into the Taiwan Strait.

An Export Economy Taiwan's industries are similar to Japan's. The Taiwanese import raw materials such as iron ore, petroleum, minerals, and cotton. They manufacture these materials into machinery, clothing, calculators, radios, televisions,

Taiwan's capital, Taipei, has modern department stores.
▶ How are such stores a sign of a high standard of living?

and plastic goods such as toys. These products are then exported around the world. As in the country of South Korea, shipbuilding is another important and profitable industry in Taiwan.

Taiwan is much smaller than China, only 13,887 square miles (35,967 sq km) in area, which is somewhat larger than the states of Massachusetts and Connecticut combined. Taiwan, however, has a higher standard of living than China and more goods and food available for its citizens. It has also moved toward having a democratic form of government.

Taiwan's government continues to claim that it is the rightful ruler of mainland China. Most nations of the world—including the United States—recognize China's Communist government as the legitimate government of mainland China.

B. Hong Kong, the Tiny Dynamo

A British Colony At the mouth of China's Xi Jiang is the British colony of Hong Kong. Most of Hong Kong's population is of Chinese ancestry, and most of the people speak Chinese and practice Chinese religions. Like Taiwan, Hong Kong was part of China for many centuries. But unlike Taiwan, which is controlled by Chinese Nationalists, Hong Kong came under the control of Great Britain in the nineteenth century, but it has been given some control over its own affairs.

Hong Kong has three main areas, altogether covering about 400 square miles (1,036 sq km). As you can see from the map on this page, the colony stretches across the tiny island of Hong Kong, the mainland area called Kowloon Peninsula, and a large coastal zone called the New Territories. People and businesses are spread over this entire area. Huge apartment buildings, office complexes, and factories crowd almost every corner of the tiny island of Hong Kong.

HONG KONG: POLITICAL

Hong Kong consists of islands and a peninsula attached to mainland China.
▶ What two cities are on opposite sides of Victoria Harbor?

Hong Kong's population is about 6 million. Less than one tenth of the land in Hong Kong is **arable**, or useful for agriculture. This means that most of Hong Kong's food is imported, much of it from China and Japan. However, Hong Kong has one of the strongest export economies in East Asia.

A Busy Economy Hong Kong's busy factories produce textiles, electronics, clocks, toys, and cameras, which are sold around the world. Most of these goods are produced with raw materials that must be imported from other countries. The finished products are sold to industrialized countries, such as the United States, the nations of the United Kingdom, and France.

437

China and the United Kingdom have agreed that all of Hong Kong will be returned to China in 1997. China has said that it will allow Hong Kong to have special political and economic rights that will allow its economy to continue to prosper.

C. Mongolia, a Buffer State

Between Two Nations Few countries in the world are located between two powerful nations. Mongolia, or the Mongolian People's Republic, has been one such country. In the past, Mongolia was sandwiched between two enemies—China and the Soviet Union.

It might seem that the Mongolian people should have been in constant fear of war between China and the Soviet Union. But Mongolia's location actually helped to keep that from happening. The Soviet Union would never have allowed China to take over Mongolia. And China would never have allowed the Soviet Union to invade Mongolia and approach the Chinese border. So Mongolia is a country that kept these two

countries separated. We call such a country a **buffer state**.

Deserts and Grasslands Mongolia is a large country of deserts, grasslands, and forested mountains. The total area of Mongolia is 604,247 square miles (1, 564,395 sq km), which makes it about twice the size of Texas. But its population is only 1.9 million, about one-eighth the population of Texas.

The Gobi Desert covers eastern and southern Mongolia. The southern part of the Gobi is covered by grasslands on which herds of cattle, sheep, goats, and horses feed. For centuries, nomadic herders have moved their livestock across the Gobi's grasslands from season to season, searching for grass and water.

The nomads depend on their animals for almost everything. For example, the sheep wool is made into *felt*, a tough woolen fabric used to make clothing and to make the herders' tents, which are called *yurts*.

Even in villages, Mongolians have a

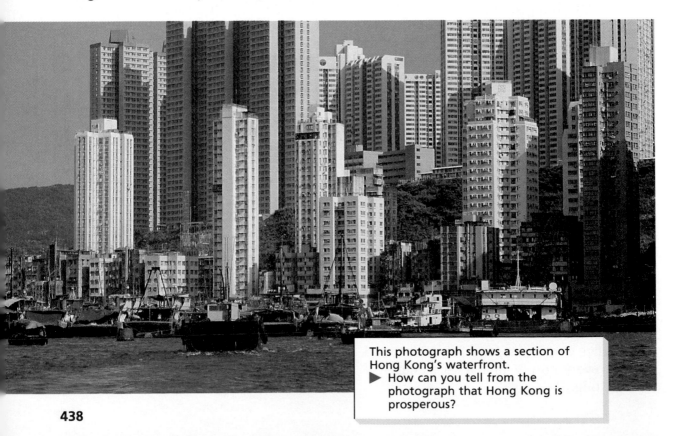

This photograph shows a section of Hong Kong's waterfront.
▶ How can you tell from the photograph that Hong Kong is prosperous?

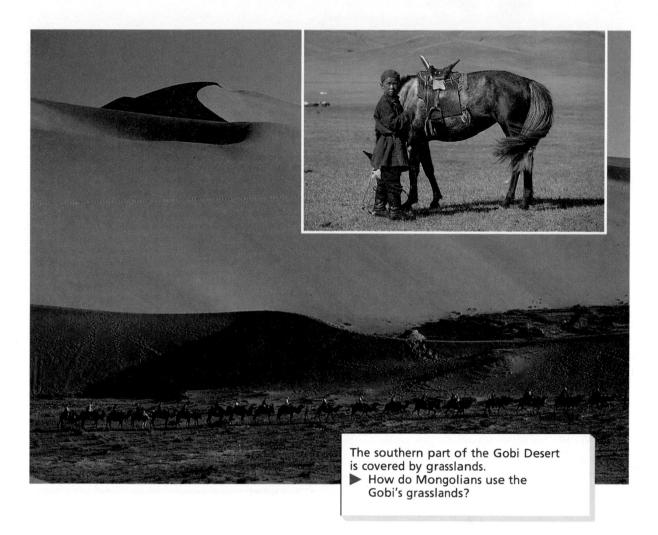

The southern part of the Gobi Desert is covered by grasslands.
▶ How do Mongolians use the Gobi's grasslands?

difficult life. Dry, cold winds blow constantly, and fresh fruits and vegetables are in short supply. Some people believe that the harsh environment made Mongolians into tough warriors in the past. One of these warriors was Genghis Khan, who ruled an empire that stretched into Russia and Eastern Europe. Genghis, his son, and his grandson, Kubla Khan, conquered much of China and the Middle East.

Today, Mongolia is building modern roads, railways, and industries with the help of other countries. In the capital city of Ulan Bator, factories produce wool products, cement, leather goods, soap, and machinery. Most of Mongolia's exports still come from its livestock and from products made from their milk and hides.

LESSON 4

Review

REVIEWING MAIN IDEAS

A. Why is Taiwan called "the Other China?"
B. What are Hong Kong's main industries?
C. Why is Mongolia called a buffer state?

SKILLS CHECK

MAP SKILL

Use the Gazetteer on pages 707–720 to find the latitude and longitude of each of the following cities. Then determine which city is farthest west:

Ulan Bator   Taipei   Hong Kong

REVIEWING TERMS

On a separate sheet of paper, write the letter of the term that best matches each numbered statement.

a. alpine
b. tableland
c. triple cropping
d. loess
e. alluvial soil
f. dynasty
g. commune
h. arable
i. buffer state

1. A country that separates two powerful countries
2. A continuous method of planting and harvesting crops that allows farmers to get more food from their land
3. Rock fragments and silt deposited on the land when a river floods during the rainy season
4. A plateau that is level and flat
5. A family that ruled China for many generations
6. A huge farm owned by the state
7. Land that is useful for agriculture
8. Mountainous
9. A powdery, fertile soil

REVIEWING THE FACTS

On a separate sheet of paper, answer the following questions in complete sentences.

1. What is the official name of China?
2. What rivers cross the North China Plain?
3. What mountains are located in the western interior region of China?
4. Why are yaks important to the people of the Tibetan plateau?
5. Why is the Gobi sparsely populated?
6. Why have the Chinese built canals?
7. How is the city of Beijing organized into different sections?

8. What Chinese philosopher taught that people should do good deeds and treat others as they would like to be treated?
9. How is the government of Taiwan different from the government of China?
10. What country currently controls the colony of Hong Kong?

WRITING ABOUT CULTURE

Like the yak herders of the Tibetan plateau, other groups of people also depend on animals to help them in many ways. Write several paragraphs describing how people in other parts of the world use animals.

THINKING CRITICALLY

On a separate sheet of paper, answer the following questions in complete sentences.

1. What are some advantages to using bicycles for transportation in the streets of Beijing?
2. Why, do you think, did the Mongol's culture not influence Chinese culture?
3. What reasons might explain why the communes of China did not produce much more food than the old system of agriculture produced?
4. What other countries, like China, face the problem of feeding their growing populations?
5. Why, do you think, was the United States willing to give money and political support to help the Nationalists make Taiwan a strong nation?

On a separate sheet of paper, draw a graphic organizer like the one shown here. Copy the information from this graphic organizer to the one you have drawn. Under the main idea for each lesson, write three statements that you think best support it.

CHAPTER THEME

China, a large country with varied landscapes, has undergone important social changes. Its smaller neighbors offer many contrasts.

Lesson 1 The western part of China is different from the eastern part of China.

1. _____
2. _____
3. _____

Lesson 2 China has three different regions.

1. _____
2. _____
3. _____

Lesson 3 The people living in the desert and mountain areas of China have different languages and religions from other Chinese.

1. _____
2. _____
3. _____

Lesson 4 Taiwan, Hong Kong, and Mongolia are different from China.

1. _____
2. _____
3. _____

CHAPTER **18**

SOUTHEAST ASIA

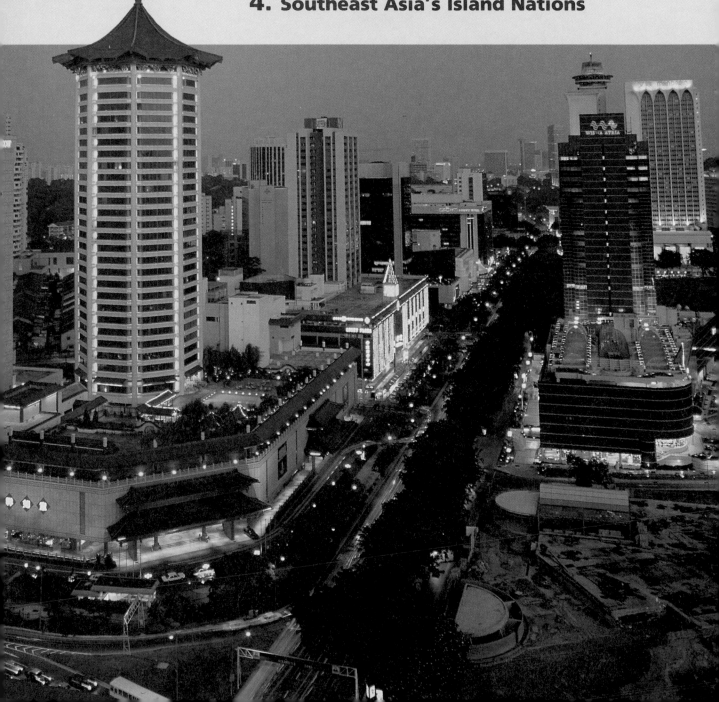

Mainland Nations and Island Nations

CONNECTIONS

Many countries in Southeast Asia have an equatorial climate. List the words you would use to describe such a climate.

TERMS

equatorial climate, ebony

FOCUS

How does Southeast Asia's location affect the region's economy?

A. Mainland Nations and Island Nations

A Green, Lush Land An ancient tale describes how two men from China traveled to Southeast Asia to seek their fortune. If you look at the map on page 444, you can see the route they took. They sailed from China across the South China Sea and the Gulf of Siam toward the city of Bangkok, which is now the capital of Thailand. This is what the men saw during their trip.

> As the [boat] sailed lazily along the coast, they saw in the distance the wealth of bright green rice-fields and all around the spreading trees welcoming them with outstretched arms, and they conjured up in their own minds a vision of abundance and prosperity such as they had never heard or dreamt of before. Never had they seen cultivable land so suited to their nimble minds and hands. . . .

Southeast Asia today is still a land of beauty and of fertile farmland. And like the Chinese travelers, many other Chinese have migrated to Southeast Asia, where they have hoped to live a prosperous life.

Mainland and Islands Using the map on page 444, you can see that seven Southeast Asian countries are located near each other on the mainland of Asia. These are the countries of Myanmar, Malaysia, Singapore,

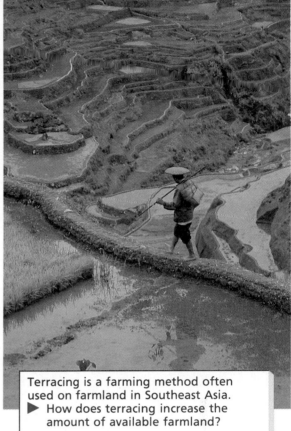

Terracing is a farming method often used on farmland in Southeast Asia.
▶ How does terracing increase the amount of available farmland?

Thailand, Cambodia, Laos (LAY ahs), and Vietnam. These mainland countries occupy about 46 percent of the area of Southeast Asia. About 44 percent of Southeast Asia's people live in the mainland countries.

The other Southeast Asian countries are located on islands. These are Indonesia, the Philippines, and Brunei (broo NYE). Part of Malaysia is also located on an island. The largest country in Southeast Asia is Indonesia. Indonesia's total area of 779,675 square miles (2,019,358 sq km) makes it about one-fifth the area of the United States. But if you could place the islands on a map of the United States, you would find that they would stretch from the West Coast to the East Coast. Indonesia's population, over 177 million people, is one of the largest in the world, and the largest in Southeast Asia. About 40 percent of all the people of Southeast Asia live on the islands that make up Indonesia. Yet less than half of Indonesia's 13,600 islands are inhabited.

▶ An evening view of the shopping area along Orchard Road in Singapore.

National capitals

Elevations

Feet	Meters
10,000	3,000
5,000	1,500
2,000	600
1,000	300
0	0

0   400   800 miles

0   400   800 kilometers

CHINA

TAIWAN

Tropic of Cancer

INDIA

BANGLADESH

MYANMAR LAOS Hanoi

Vientiane

Bay of

Rangoon

THAILAND

Bengal   Bangkok

CAMBODIA

Phnom
Penh

MALAY
PENINSULA

MALAYSIA

Kuala Lumpur

Singapore

SINGAPORE

SUMATRA

Equator

Jakarta

JAVA

BALI

South
China
Sea

Chao
Praya R.

VIETNAM

Gulf
of Siam

BRUNEI

BORNEO

LUZON

Manila

MINDORO

PANAY

PALAWAN

NEGROS

Bandar Seri
Begawan

CELEBES

CEBU

SAMAR

PHILIPPINES

MINDANAO

Celebes
Sea

MOLUCCAS

INDONESIA

TIMOR

PACIFIC   OCEAN

NEW
GUINEA

IRIAN JAYA

GUINEA

Arafura
Sea

PAPUA
NEW
GUINEA

AUSTRALIA

INDIAN OCEAN 90°E   100°E   110°E   120°E   130°E

Rain Forest, Vietnam

Many of the countries of Southeast Asia are islands or peninsulas. Rain forests are found throughout Southeast Asia because of heavy daily rainfall and consistently warm temperatures.
▶ Which country extends from about longitude 95°E to about longitude 141°E?

B. Southeast Asia's Many Cultures

Migrations The Chinese travelers you read about earlier were only two individuals in a steady stream of migrants to Southeast Asia. As you can see from the map above, anyone wishing to travel from the Indian Ocean to the Pacific Ocean along the shortest route would have to pass through the waters of Southeast Asian countries.

Beginning about 2,000 years ago, people from India began moving into Southeast Asia. Many of them introduced their religion, Hinduism, to Southeast Asia, and as a result, today there are many Hindus in this region. India's artistic styles were also adopted by Southeast Asians. Many traditional paintings, drawings, and sculptures in both India and Southeast Asia have a similar style.

In the fifth, sixth, and seventh centuries, Buddhists moved into Southeast Asia and converted many people to Buddhism. This is still the main religion of Thailand, Myanmar, and Cambodia.

As you read earlier, many Chinese migrated to Southeast Asia. Most became traders and merchants, and their descendants quickly grew in number. Today the Chinese are the largest minority group in most Southeast Asian countries.

Arabs and Europeans Arab traders also sailed into Southeast Asia's harbors. Most of the Arab traders were Muslims, and they converted many people in the island nations of Southeast Asia to Islam. Today, Muslims make up a large part of the populations of Indonesia and Malaysia. In fact, the country with the world's largest Muslim population is not in the Middle East—it is Indonesia. More than 100 million Muslims live in Indonesia.

Beginning in the 1500s, Europeans became interested in buying Southeast Asia's silks, spices, jewels, and coffee. The British, French, Dutch, and Spanish established many trading ports and cities, such as Manila and Jakarta (juh KAHR tuh). Only Thailand remained an independent kingdom. After World War II the people of Southeast Asia gradually gained independence from the Europeans. This means that most Southeast Asian countries have been independent less than fifty years.

C. Southeast Asia's Climate

The green rice fields and thick forests described by the Chinese travelers are typical of most of Southeast Asia and other areas of the world located near the Equator. As you can see from the map on page 444, the Equator crosses through Southeast Asia. Because of their location, the nations of Southeast Asia are said to have an **equatorial climate**.

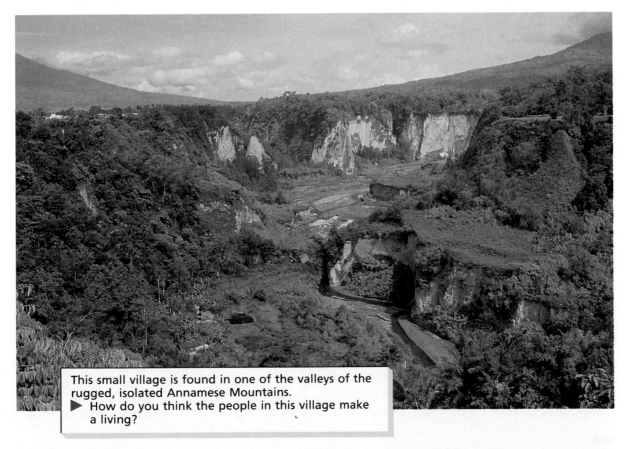

This small village is found in one of the valleys of the rugged, isolated Annamese Mountains.
▶ How do you think the people in this village make a living?

Climograph:
SINGAPORE

Singapore's equitorial climate gives this city-state high temperatures and constant rainfall throughout the year.
► Which month receives the most precipitation?

Places with low elevations along the Equator usually have much higher temperatures all year round than do other parts of the world. Most of these warm areas near the Equator also receive heavy rainfall. The air near the earth's surface heats up, and then it rises and cools. Cooler air cannot hold as much moisture as warm air, so warm air that rises and cools usually drops some of its moisture as precipitation. This happens almost all year round in the island nations of Southeast Asia. The weather is both warm and rainy almost every day. In fact, you could say that it is always like summer in an equatorial climate.

The climograph for Singapore on this page shows how little temperature and precipitation vary in an equatorial climate. Temperatures vary by only 2° or 3° at the least, and 7° or 8° at the most. Equatorial climates have the least change in annual temperature range. Rainfall is heavy throughout the year. It is also humid almost every day. Regions that are at a higher elevation, of course, escape some of this heat and humidity.

The abundant rainfall and warm temperatures produce thick vegetation throughout Southeast Asia. Forests provide valuable woods, such as **ebony**. Ebony is a hard, dark, strong wood that comes from various trees found in tropical areas such as Southeast Asia. Ebony wood is used to make the black keys on expensive pianos.

Another plant that grows especially well in an equatorial climate is bamboo. There are more than 700 different kinds of this tall, sturdy plant that is actually a giant form of grass. Bamboo has hundreds of uses and can be used to make items ranging from chairs to food containers.

Farmers' lands produce rich harvests of rice, tea, fruits, vegetables, and sugarcane. No wonder the Chinese travelers felt sure they could make a fortune by moving to Southeast Asia.

LESSON 1

Review

REVIEWING MAIN IDEAS
A. Which countries are located on the mainland of Southeast Asia?
B. What are the three principal religions found in Southeast Asia?
C. How is it always like summer in an equatorial climate?

SKILLS CHECK

MAP SKILL
Use the map on page 444 to name the Southeast Asian countries that have coastlines on these bodies of water:

South China Sea   Pacific Ocean
Gulf of Siam   Strait of Malacca

The Mainland Nations of Vietnam, Laos, and Cambodia

CONNECTIONS

Many people from Vietnam and Cambodia have come to live in the United States because of wars in their countries. How do you think their lives changed when they arrived in the United States?

TERMS

delta, teak, refugee

FOCUS

How have recent wars affected the mainland nations of Southeast Asia?

A. Vietnam, a Land of Mountains and Coasts

Indochina Lisa Bennett, a young American student, excitedly unwrapped a package of photographs from Southeast Asia. Lisa's aunt, a photographer for a newspaper in Vietnam, had sent the photos.

Lisa was curious about these photos because her mother was born and raised in Vietnam. In 1968, Lisa's mother had married Lisa's father, an American soldier who had been sent to Vietnam. Lisa's older brother and sister were born in Vietnam and came to the United States with her parents in 1972. Lisa was born in California, and she had never seen Vietnam or any of the other countries that make up the region called Southeast Asia. So she was fascinated by her aunt's photos.

Lisa separated the photos, making one group for each country. Her mother told her that the mainland countries of Vietnam, Laos, and Cambodia had once been united as a French colony called Indochina. So she decided to put those photos into a single group.

The Annamese Mountains Some of the photos of Vietnam showed rugged mountains. Her aunt had written their name, the Annamese Mountains, on the photos. The Annamese run almost the entire length of western Vietnam along its western border and reach into Laos, Vietnam's western neighbor. These isolated mountains are sparsely populated. Dense forests cover the slopes, and small villages fill the valleys. Most farmers practice subsistence farming.

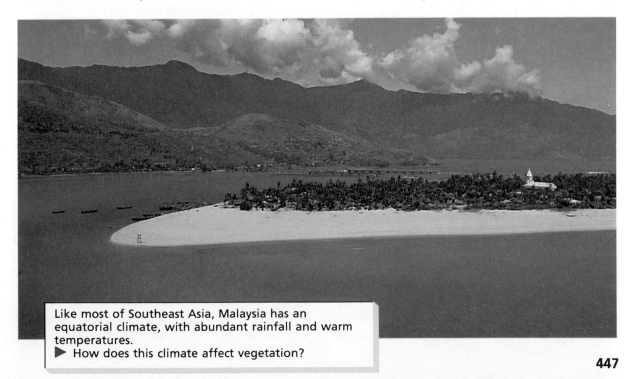

Like most of Southeast Asia, Malaysia has an equatorial climate, with abundant rainfall and warm temperatures.
▶ How does this climate affect vegetation?

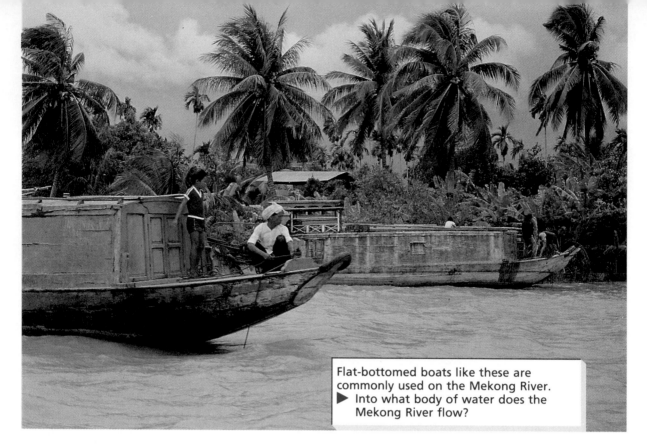

Flat-bottomed boats like these are commonly used on the Mekong River.
▶ Into what body of water does the Mekong River flow?

Some of the photos of Vietnam showed farms and cities on level land. They were taken along the Red River, the Mekong River, and the coast of the South China Sea. The Red River begins in China and flows along the northern part of Vietnam to empty into the Gulf of Tonkin.

The Mekong River The Mekong River begins in China and flows 2,600 miles (4,183 km) toward the southeast, where it forms most of the border between Laos and Thailand. The Mekong River then cuts across Cambodia and southern Vietnam to empty into the South China Sea.

Both the Red River and the Mekong River deposit rich alluvial soils along their banks. Villages and rich farmlands prosper along these rivers. But even more valuable are the lands at the mouths of the rivers, where they empty into the sea.

Delta Cities The Red River and the Mekong River both flow more slowly as they enter the sea, just as you slow down when you hit the water after zipping down a slide and splashing into a swimming pool. As the rivers slow, they deposit the heavy loads of sand and soil that they carried down from the Annamese Mountains. This sediment has built up over the centuries and has created a **delta**, which is new land formed at the mouth of a river.

On the delta of the Red River in northern Vietnam is the country's capital city, Hanoi, with over 2 million people. On the delta of the Mekong River in southern Vietnam is Vietnam's largest city, Ho Chi Minh City, with almost 3 million people. With a long coastline and rich deltas, Vietnam is not only larger than Laos and Cambodia, but it is also much more densely populated.

B. The Two Vietnams

Two Countries Hanoi and Ho Chi Minh City were the capitals of two different countries at one time. How did this happen? In 1954, an international conference decided that Vietnam should be divided into two countries along the line of latitude at 17°N. This border was needed because two different groups, the Communists in the north of Vietnam and the non-Communists in the south, both claimed to be the leaders of the country. Elections were to be held to decide which group should govern the entire peninsula of Vietnam.

North Vietnam, including Hanoi, was made up of the area to the north of this boundary and was controlled by a Communist government. South Vietnam included the land to the south of the border. Its capital city was in what is now Ho Chi Minh City. At that time, however, it was called Saigon. South Vietnam had a non-Communist government.

The Vietnam War Five years after the border was drawn, guerrillas from North Vietnam began to invade South Vietnam. In 1965 the United States sent troops to help South Vietnam defend itself against the Communist troops from the north. More than 50,000 United States soldiers died in the fighting, which continued until 1973. In that year the United States, North Vietnam, and South Vietnam signed an agreement to end the conflict. United States troops returned home. But the war continued. By 1975, North Vietnam had conquered South Vietnam.

Resources Most of the people who experienced the terror and destruction of the war lived along Vietnam's coast and in its two largest cities. Today these people are rebuilding the irrigation canals and fields that help them produce Vietnam's main food crop, rice.

Northern Vietnam has coal deposits, along with small amounts of iron ore, bauxite, and other minerals. Most of Vietnam's manufacturing centers are in the north, in and around Hanoi. These factories produce textiles, motorcycles, and processed foods.

The Boat People After North Vietnam took control of South Vietnam, many Vietnamese left the country. Lisa's mother told her about many friends and relatives who fled from Vietnam during this time. Perhaps 1 million Vietnamese escaped in small, dangerous boats and crossed the South China Sea to other countries. They were called "Boat People." About one million more crossed the mountains and fled to Thailand and Laos, hoping to someday find a permanent home. Many came to the United States.

C. Laos, a Landlocked Country

Several of Lisa's photos from Laos showed people in traditional dress, with elaborate embroidery and unusual headpieces. These people lived in the Annamese Mountains, which cover most of the country of Laos. Small tribes of people with different languages and customs lived in villages in the basins and valleys in the mountains. One group, called the Hmong (hmawng), fought with the United States against Communist guerrillas in Laos. When Communists gained control of Laos, many of the Hmong came to the United States.

A large group of South Vietnamese people struggle to board the last American helicopter to leave Saigon.
▶ What is Saigon called today?

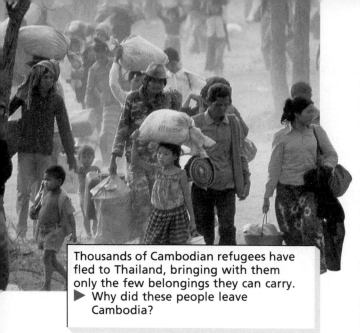

Thousands of Cambodian refugees have fled to Thailand, bringing with them only the few belongings they can carry.
▶ Why did these people leave Cambodia?

The Mekong River runs along the western border of Laos. Most of the population of Laos lives in the Mekong River valley. The capital city, Vientiane, is located in this valley. The country's only railroad runs from Vientiane across the Mekong River into Thailand.

The farmers in the Mekong River valley grow rice, cotton, and corn. These are Laos's main agricultural products. But its main exports are timber and electricity, both of which come from the mountains. The heavy forests of the mountain slopes contain many **teak** trees. Teak is a hard, yellowish-brown wood that can be used for carving and to make furniture. Teak contains a great deal of oil, which makes it water resistant, so it is also used for shipbuilding.

D. Cambodia, a Nation Torn by War

Cambodia, the third country in the area called Indochina, is different from Vietnam and Laos because it is a mainly flat land with only a few mountains on its southern border.

Lisa's aunt had sent her photographs of people in the capital city of Phnom Penh (puh NAWM pen), located on the Mekong River. Most of the people in these photo-

graphs looked quite sad, perhaps because their country has undergone bloody conflicts and invasions for many years. In 1975, Communists called the Khmer Rouge (kuh MER roozh) took over Cambodia and killed hundreds of thousands of Cambodians. Thousands of other Cambodians fled across the western border into Thailand and became **refugees**. A refugee is a person who is forced to leave his or her country. In 1978, Vietnam invaded Cambodia, and forced the Khmer Rouge out of power. The Khmer Rouge continued to fight the Vietnamese. In 1989, Vietnamese soldiers left Cambodia. The Khmer Rouge have continued to fight the Cambodian government despite recent efforts by the United Nations to negotiate peace for this war-torn country.

Cambodia has fertile soils and large forests. The forests supply firewood and lumber for construction, but roads and railroads are needed to bring these resources out of the forest areas. Farmers grow rice, soybeans, and corn, and raise some cattle. They need fertilizers, modern machinery, roads, and storage facilities in order to produce more food. There is little manufacturing in Cambodia. Some factories produce cement, paper, and textiles.

LESSON 2

Review

REVIEWING MAIN IDEAS
A. How are Vietnam's two most important rivers used?
B. Why was Vietnam once divided into two countries?
C. What are the two most important exports from Laos?
D. How has Cambodia been affected by war?

SKILLS CHECK

THINKING SKILL
Why, do you think, did the United States send soldiers to fight in South Vietnam?

The Countries of the Malay Peninsula

CONNECTIONS

What kinds of economic activities would you expect to find in a country with few natural resources but with a good harbor and port?

TERMS

pagoda, isolationism, latex, city-state

FOCUS

Why are the Malay Peninsula's main cities located on water routes?

A. The Ancient Nation of Thailand

A Growing Country Lisa Bennett, the young American student you read about earlier, watched photos from Thailand tumble through her hands. Scenes of hamburger stands on busy city streets, small fishing boats crowded along rivers, and huge traffic jams caught her eye. Thailand is a country with a long and rich history, but it is growing and modernizing quickly today.

Thailand, along with Myanmar, Malaysia, and Singapore, is part of the long, narrow Malay Peninsula. Most of Thailand is a flat plain crossed by rivers. The Mekong River flows along the edge of this plain, following Thailand's eastern border with Laos. Thailand's most important river is the Chao Phraya (CHOU prah YAH) River. As you can see from the map on page 444, this river flows out of the mountains of Laos and empties into the Gulf of Siam.

Bangkok Thailand's capital city, Bangkok, is located near the mouth of the Chao Phraya River. With over four million residents, Bangkok is a busy, crowded city. Its population is growing quickly, and could triple in the next twenty years.

What makes Bangkok so special? For one thing, it is a primate city. As you remember, a primate city is the only city in a nation where almost everything important is found. Almost all of Thailand's businesses, factories, hotels, schools, government offices, and hospitals are located in Bangkok. The concentration of such important services in one place can be a problem for people who live in small towns or in the countryside. They must travel to the primate city for practically everything they need. Living in the primate city itself is much more convenient. So people move into a primate city like Bangkok by the thousands.

Thailand's Products How did Bangkok become so prosperous? Many Bangkok businesses grew wealthy by exporting Thailand's products. For example, Thailand's farmers produce large quantities of food, especially rice. In fact, Thailand is the world's largest exporter of rice. Most of Thailand's rice is grown in paddies similar to the rice paddies of Japan and China.

Thailand's farmers also raise corn, sugarcane, and tobacco. And they grow cassava, a small shrub with roots that can be ground up and eaten or used to make puddings such as tapioca.

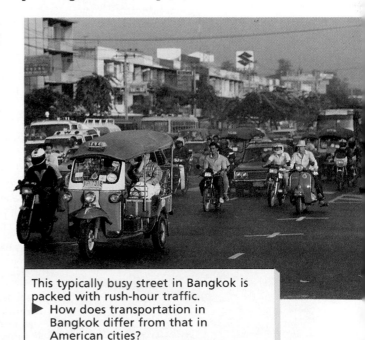

This typically busy street in Bangkok is packed with rush-hour traffic.
► How does transportation in Bangkok differ from that in American cities?

451

Thailand has deposits of tin, iron ore, lead, bauxite, and tungsten. These are shipped down the Chao Phraya to Bangkok, where they are used to manufacture steel, electronic goods, and automobiles.

B. Myanmar, Land of the Golden Pagodas

The Irrawaddy River Like a horseshoe, mountains ring Myanmar on three sides. Between the mountains, long river valleys reach like fingers toward the south. The Irrawaddy River is the most important of these rivers. It stretches to the south across Myanmar and forms a huge delta before it empties into the sea. The capital city of Myanmar, Rangoon, is located near the mouth of the Irrawaddy River.

Most people of Myanmar live in the Irrawaddy River valley. Mandalay, near the country's center, once was Myanmar's largest and most important city. Today, Mandalay is second to Rangoon in size and importance. When the British began trading in Myanmar in the middle 1800s, they built rice paddies on the delta of the Irrawaddy. They also turned the small settlement near Rangoon into a major trading station and port. Today, Rangoon has over 3 million inhabitants and is growing quickly.

Roads, railways, and the Irrawaddy River connect Myanmar's two main cities of Mandalay and Rangoon. Rice, grown in paddies along the river, is sent by boat to Rangoon, where it is milled and then packaged before it is sold.

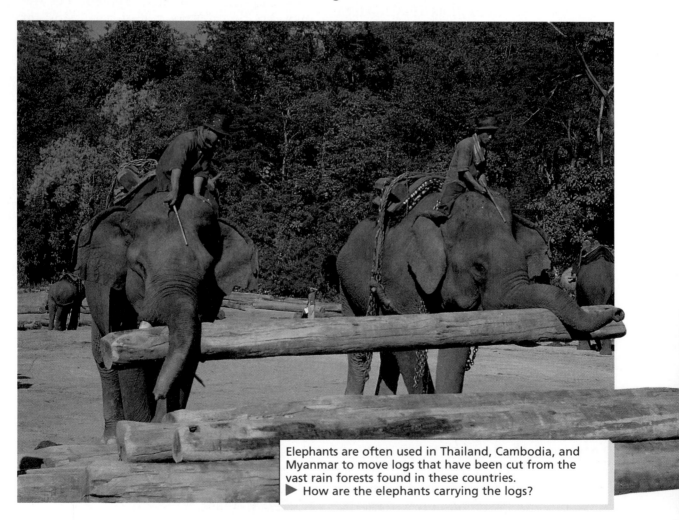

Elephants are often used in Thailand, Cambodia, and Myanmar to move logs that have been cut from the vast rain forests found in these countries.
▶ How are the elephants carrying the logs?

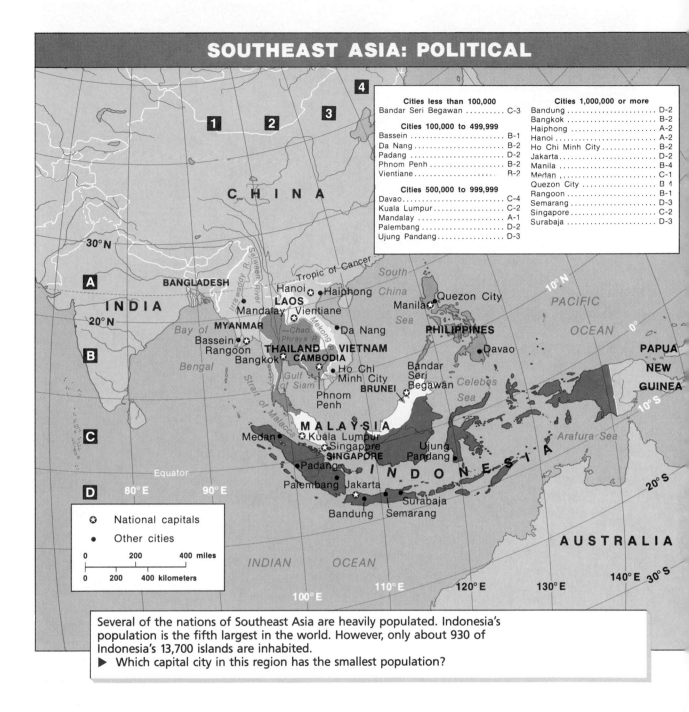

SOUTHEAST ASIA: POLITICAL

Cities less than 100,000	
Bandar Seri Begawan	C-3

Cities 100,000 to 499,999	
Bassein	B-1
Da Nang	B-2
Padang	D-2
Phnom Penh	B-2
Vientiane	B-2

Cities 500,000 to 999,999	
Davao	C-4
Kuala Lumpur	C-2
Mandalay	A-1
Palembang	D-2
Ujung Pandang	D-3

Cities 1,000,000 or more	
Bandung	D-2
Bangkok	B-2
Haiphong	A-2
Hanoi	A-2
Ho Chi Minh City	B-2
Jakarta	D-2
Manila	B-4
Medan	C-1
Quezon City	B-1
Rangoon	B-1
Semarang	D-3
Singapore	C-2
Surabaja	D-3

National capitals

Other cities

0   200   400 miles
0   200   400 kilometers

Several of the nations of Southeast Asia are heavily populated. Indonesia's population is the fifth largest in the world. However, only about 930 of Indonesia's 13,700 islands are inhabited.
▶ Which capital city in this region has the smallest population?

Sugarcane, wheat, cotton, and corn are also sent down the Irrawaddy to Rangoon. Huge rafts carry teak logs, which grow in Myanmar's tropical forests, to Rangoon for processing.

A Land of Pagodas Lisa saw several photos of graceful, rounded buildings that reached a point at their tops. Her aunt labeled these **pagodas**, the name for the Buddhist shrines that are found all over Myanmar and the other Buddhist regions of Southeast Asia. Myanmar has so many pagodas, which are decorated with gold, that is is often called "The Land of the Golden Pagodas."

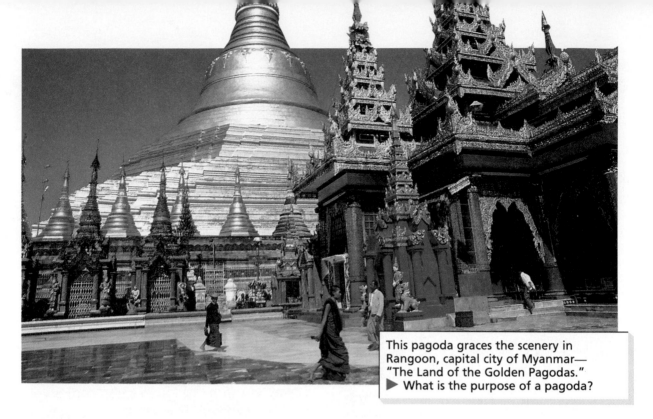

This pagoda graces the scenery in Rangoon, capital city of Myanmar— "The Land of the Golden Pagodas."
► What is the purpose of a pagoda?

Isolation Myanmar gained its independence from the United Kingdom in 1948. Shortly after, Myanmar's leaders decided to follow a policy of **isolationism**, or cutting off contact with foreign countries. Without information and funds from people in other countries, Myanmar's industries have not grown. Only basic goods such as textiles, soap, cement, glass, and paper are produced in their factories. Recently, Myanmar's government has opened the doors to outsiders. It hopes they will bring capital to modernize Myanmar's industries.

C. Malaysia's Many Cultures

A Divided Country From the map on page 444, you can see that Malaysia has a very interesting shape. It includes the southern tip of the Malay Peninsula and part of the island called Borneo. Malaysia shares the island of Borneo with Indonesia and with Brunei.

You might also notice from the map that Malaysia's capital city, Kuala Lumpur, is located along a narrow channel of water called the Strait of Malacca. This strait has been an important passageway for ships traveling between India and China. Kuala Lumpur and other coastal cities became important trading centers because of the strait's location.

Through the centuries, ships brought many different kinds of people to Malaysia. Today, the descendants of the original Malays make up about 59 percent of Malaysia's population. Most Malaysians are Muslim. About 32 percent of Malaysians are of Chinese ancestry, and most of them are Buddhists. And about 9 percent of Malaysia's people are descendants of Indians, who are mostly Hindus. Other religious and ethnic groups are also found in Malaysia.

Rubber Plantations A photo showing dozens of perfectly straight rows of trees puzzled Lisa. Trees don't usually grow in lines! Her aunt's label said this was a picture of a rubber tree plantation in Malaysia. Malaysia, along with Indonesia, Cambodia, and Thailand, is a major world producer and exporter of rubber.

Rubber trees grow naturally in tropical forests, and workers carry buckets from tree to tree to collect a liquid called **latex**. This latex is then boiled and processed and sent to factories to be made into tires and other rubber products. Wild rubber trees are scattered in the forest, so workers waste valuable time searching for them. They work more efficiently when the rubber trees are planted and cared for on a plantation.

Malaysia's economy is strong and growing because of its other products. One of these products, palm oil, is also produced on plantations. A special type of palm tree grown here produces nuts containing oil that is used as a cooking oil. Palm oil is a major export of Malaysia. If you look at the list of ingredients on a box of cookies you might see palm oil on the list.

Malaysia is also fortunate to have huge deposits of tin. Malaysia produces more tin than any other country in the world. Tin can be made into cans, and a layer of tin can prevent steel from rusting.

D. Singapore, a City-State on an Island

The Strait of Malacca between Malaysia and Indonesia is such an important sea route that in 1819 the British decided to build a new port city on this channel, at the tip of Malaysia. They called the new city Singapore.

Today, Singapore is an independent nation and a powerful center of trade and commerce. Singapore is also one of the wealthiest countries in Southeast Asia. This is amazing, because Singapore is small, crowded, and has no natural resources.

Singapore's total area is only 225 square miles (583 sq km), which is a bit smaller than the District of Columbia in the United States. Singapore occupies one large island, which is connected to Malaysia by a causeway. As you have learned, a causeway is a road running along a ridge of land. Other tiny islands surround the main island.

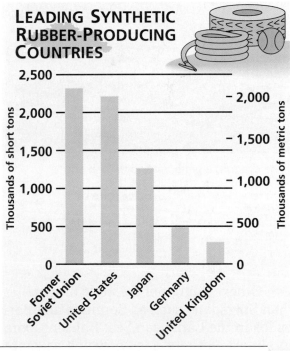

Products such as radial tires require natural and synthetic rubber.

► Which nations produce more rubber, natural or synthetic, than Thailand?

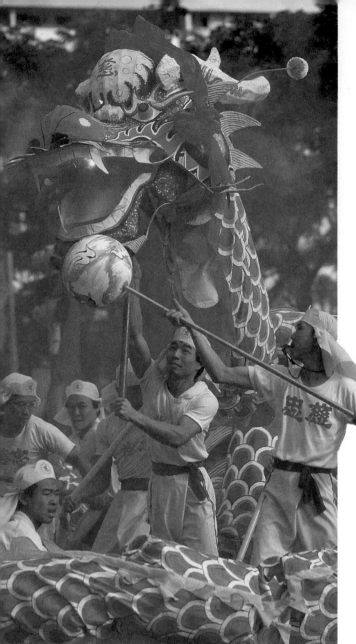

The dragon, a symbol of good luck and wealth, is used to celebrate the Chinese New Year in the city-state of Singapore.
▶ Why is Singapore called a city-state?

people, Singapore has one of the highest population densities in the world, with at least 12,000 people per square mile (4,633 per sq km).

How did Singapore become so wealthy? Like the Japanese, the people of Singapore learned to import raw materials and manufacture them into goods for export. Singapore's businesses import lumber, food, cotton, petroleum, and rubber. The country's factories then manufacture paper, flour, canned fruits and vegetables, textiles, clothing, plastics, chemicals, and tires for export to other countries.

Singapore's rapid growth into a major economic power in the Pacific Ocean region has attracted the attention of other countries. Many governments in poorer countries would like to follow Singapore's example.

They would also like to follow the economic examples of South Korea, Taiwan, and Hong Kong. These three lands, along with Singapore, have been called the Four Tigers because of their growing economic power.

LESSON 3

Review

REVIEWING MAIN IDEAS

A. Why is Bangkok Thailand's primate city?

B. Why is the Irrawaddy River so important in Myanmar?

C. What products are grown on plantations in Malaysia?

D. How did Singapore become a wealthy country?

SKILLS CHECK

WRITING SKILL

Write a short letter to an imaginary friend in Southeast Asia, asking for photographs of life in that region. Describe what kinds of things you would like to see in the photographs.

Other countries of the world are smaller than Singapore, such as Bermuda and Barbados in the Caribbean Sea. But Singapore is almost entirely a city, which is quite unique. Singapore is called a **city-state** because the whole nation of Singapore is really one huge city. With over 2.7 million

Southeast Asia's Island Nations

CONNECTIONS

Find the countries of Indonesia and the Philippines on the map on page 453. Make a list of the problems you think a government might have when its territory is made up of thousands of islands.

TERMS

tsunami, green revolution

FOCUS

What are the natural resources of Southeast Asia's island nations?

A. Indonesia, the Giant of Southeast Asia

A Nation of Islands   With over 177 million people, Indonesia has nearly three times as many people as the Philippines, the second most populated country of Southeast Asia. Indonesia has over three times as much territory as Myanmar, the second largest country of Southeast Asia.

Indonesia's huge territory is spread across more than 13,000 small islands and two large islands, called Sumatra and Java. Indonesia includes part of the island of Borneo and shares another island, called New Guinea, with the nation of Papua New Guinea.

These islands and many others of Southeast Asia belong to the Ring of Fire that you read about in the chapter on Japan. Many of Indonesia's islands are really the peaks of volcanos that have grown up from the ocean floor. Some of these peaks reach 10,000 feet (3,084 m) in elevation.

Volcanic eruptions and earthquakes are quite common in this part of the world. One of the largest eruptions the world has ever seen occurred on the island of Krakatau (krah kah TOU) in 1883. This island was located between the islands of Java and Sumatra. The volcanic explosion was so powerful that it blew the island to pieces. Thousands of people were killed in **tsunamis** (tsoo NAH meez), or tidal waves, huge walls of water set in motion by an earthquake or a volcano. Tsunamis washed over many coasts of Southeast Asia and wiped out buildings and farms.

A Resourceful Country   Volcanos can be destructive, but nature has been kind to Indonesia, too. Nickel, copper, coal, and bauxite are found in Indonesia's mountains. These resources are exported or are used in manufacturing tools, machinery, household appliances, and bicycles.

Most of Indonesia's industry is concentrated in the capital city, Jakarta. Jakarta is quickly becoming one of the largest cities of the world, with over 10 million inhabitants. Jakarta, like Bangkok, is also a primate city.

Agriculture and Oil   Indonesia is mainly an agricultural country. More than half of its people work in agriculture. Most Indonesians work on or own plantations that produce rice, spices, sugarcane, coffee, and rubber. The Dutch, who colonized Indonesia in the 1600s, traded Indonesia's coffee all over the world. Today, coffee is one

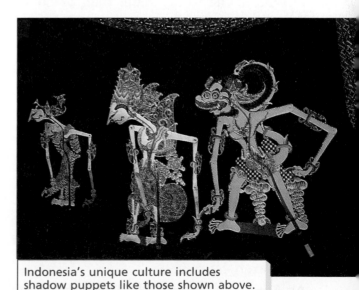

Indonesia's unique culture includes shadow puppets like those shown above.
▶ How are these puppets different from American puppets?

457

of Indonesia's main exports. Because it uses so much land for export crops, Indonesia must import huge amounts of food, including rice.

Indonesia has large petroleum fields and exports oil to many countries. This is perhaps a great source of wealth for the future. But for now, Indonesia is still a poor, overcrowded country without enough education or decent jobs for most of its huge population.

B. Brunei and Papua New Guinea

Brunei As you read earlier, Brunei is the tiny state that shares the island of Borneo with Malaysia and Indonesia. It is surrounded by land belonging to Malaysia.

Brunei has two things in common with Indonesia. First, most of Brunei's people are Muslims, as are most Indonesians. And second, Brunei has petroleum fields, like Indonesia. But Brunei has only 2,226 square miles (5,765 sq km) of area, which makes it a little larger than the state of Delaware. And Brunei has less than half a million people. The earnings they receive from their oil have made many of them quite wealthy. In fact, Brunei has the highest per capita income in the world: more than $20,000 per person.

Papua New Guinea Another neighbor of Indonesia is Papua New Guinea, which shares the island of New Guinea with Indonesia. Papua New Guinea is a dramatic contrast to Brunei. Nearly 4 million people inhabit its mountains. Over 80 percent of its land is blanketed in dense forests. Most people there live in small villages or rural towns with few schools, hospitals, or industries.

C. The Philippines: A Nation of Scattered Islands

An American Colony The Philippines was a colony of Spain until Spain lost the

Spanish-American War to the United States in 1898. Spain was forced to turn the Philippines over to the United States, which controlled it until independence in 1946. Because of these events, three languages are spoken widely in the Philippines. They are Spanish, English, and Tagalog, a native language.

The Republic of the Philippines is made up of over 7,000 islands in the South China Sea. The two largest islands are Luzon (loo ZAHN) and Mindanao (mihn duh NOU). Luzon has the capital city, Manila. Most of the people in Luzon are Catholic. Mindanao has a smaller population, and most of its people are Muslims. There has been conflict between the Muslims and the Catholics. Some Muslims on Mindanao would like to form their own country, and they have fought a guerrilla war with the government.

The Economy The Philippines has been able to build a strong agricultural economy. Plantations, especially on the flat coastlands, grow sugarcane and coconut palm trees. Coconuts produce an oil used in soap, shampoos, and prepared foods such as breakfast cereal. The fleshy part of the coconut is dried and used in cooking. Coconut products and sugarcane are the Philippines' main agricultural products that are exported.

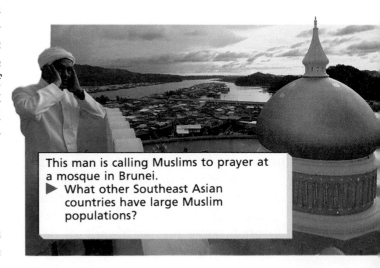

This man is calling Muslims to prayer at a mosque in Brunei.
▶ What other Southeast Asian countries have large Muslim populations?

The Green Revolution Subsistence farmers in valleys and mountainous areas raise rice, corn, tobacco, and fruits. Many of these farmers have very little land and are trying to take advantage of the **green revolution**, which is modern ways of farming rice, wheat, and corn.

The green revolution began in the 1960s when scientists working in the Philippines and in other countries, such as India, invented new kinds of seeds that would produce more food on each acre of land. In addition, experts helped farmers by providing information about fertilizers and new methods of farming. The government helped by giving farmers loans to buy new tools and equipment. Farmers soon were producing twice as much food, and the green revolution spread to many other countries.

The Philippines has become an important manufacturing center in Southeast Asia. Factories produce clothes, shoes, electronic equipment, and chemicals. Some of the Philippines' copper, silver, and nickel deposits are used in manufacturing. The Philippines uses its earnings from exports to import goods such as machinery and petroleum.

A Special Relationship The Philippines has had a special relationship with the United States. For decades, thousands of American soldiers had been stationed at two giant United States military bases in the Philippines. And the United States is the Philippines' largest trading partner.

The United States has also played a role in the Philippines' return to democracy. From 1965 to 1986, the country was ruled by Ferdinand Marcos. Marcos did not allow the Philippine people political freedoms. In 1986, the Philippine people removed Marcos from power. The United States supported the removal of Marcos and gave economic aid to the new president of the country, Corazon Aquino.

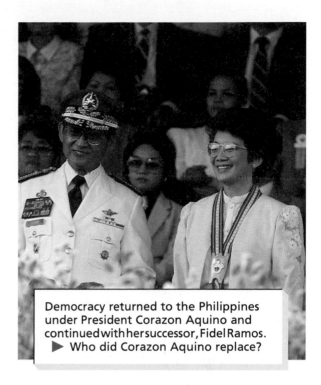

Democracy returned to the Philippines under President Corazon Aquino and continued with her successor, Fidel Ramos.
► Who did Corazon Aquino replace?

Aquino returned the Philippines to democracy. When her term ended in 1992, Fidel V. Ramos was elected president. Mr. Ramos had been one of Corazon Aquino's strongest supporters. He was one of the leaders who removed Marcos from power and he had fought off several coup attempts against Aquino's government.

LESSON 4

Review

REVIEWING MAIN IDEAS
A. Why is Indonesia considered a poor country?
B. How are Brunei and Papua New Guinea different from each other?
C. How did the green revolution help farmers in the Philippines?

SKILLS CHECK

MAP SKILL
Use the map on page 453 and name the countries that occupy the following islands:
Borneo, Java, New Guinea, Sumatra, Luzon, Mindanao

REVIEWING TERMS

On a separate sheet of paper, write the term that best matches each numbered statement.

ebony	isolationism
delta	latex
teak	tsunamis
refugee	city-state
pagodas	green revolution

1. A person who is forced to leave his or her country
2. A country's policy of cutting off contacts with foreign countries
3. New land formed at the mouth of a river
4. Huge walls of water set in motion by an earthquake or a volcano
5. A hard, dark, strong wood found in tropical areas that can be used to build ships
6. Buddhist shrines found in Myanmar
7. Where a whole nation is one city.
8. Modern ways of growing rice, wheat, and corn
9. A hard, yellowish-brown wood used for carving and furniture
10. A liquid from certain trees used to make tires and other rubber products

REVIEWING THE FACTS

On a separate sheet of paper, answer the following questions in complete sentences.

1. How did the people from India who moved into Southeast Asia influence the region?
2. Why did Europeans establish trading ports in Southeast Asia?

3. What two important cities in Vietnam are located on deltas?
4. Why were some Vietnamese people referred to as "boat people?"
5. What are the main exports of Laos?
6. What three countries are in the area that was once called Indochina?
7. What country exports more rice than any other country in the world?
8. What did the British do that helped Rangoon become such a large and important city?
9. Why is Singapore called a city-state?
10. What two things does Brunei have in common with Indonesia?

WRITING ABOUT GEOGRAPHY

If you were a photographer like Lisa's aunt, what pictures would you take of Southeast Asia? Maybe you would choose to photograph people at work, the varied landscapes, or the resources of the region such as rice paddies, or forests. Write several paragraphs describing what you would photograph.

THINKING CRITICALLY

On a separate sheet of paper, answer the following questions in complete sentences.

1. Why, do you think, did the "boat people" want to leave Vietnam?
2. What are some possible reasons to explain why the Cambodian government has not built roads, or supplied its farmers with modern machinery, or developed industries in the country?

3. What other country have you read about that, like Myanmar, had a policy of isolationism at one time in its history?
4. What reasons can you give to support the statement that Thailand has very fertile soil?
5. Why is Indonesia mainly an agricultural country?

SUMMARIZING THE CHAPTER

On a separate sheet of paper, draw a graphic organizer like the one shown here. Copy the information from this graphic organizer on the one you have drawn. Under the main idea of each lesson, write three statements that you think best support that idea.

CHAPTER THEME → Southeast Asia, an area of great ethnic diversity, suffers from political and economic instability.

Lesson 1 The location of Southeast Asia affects the region's economy.

1. _____
2. _____
3. _____

Lesson 2 Recent wars have affected the mainland nations of Southeast Asia.

1. _____
2. _____
3. _____

Lesson 3 The main cities of the Malay Peninsula are located on water routes.

1. _____
2. _____
3. _____

Lesson 4 The island nations of Southeast Asia have many natural resources.

1. _____
2. _____
3. _____

INDIA AND ITS NEIGHBORS

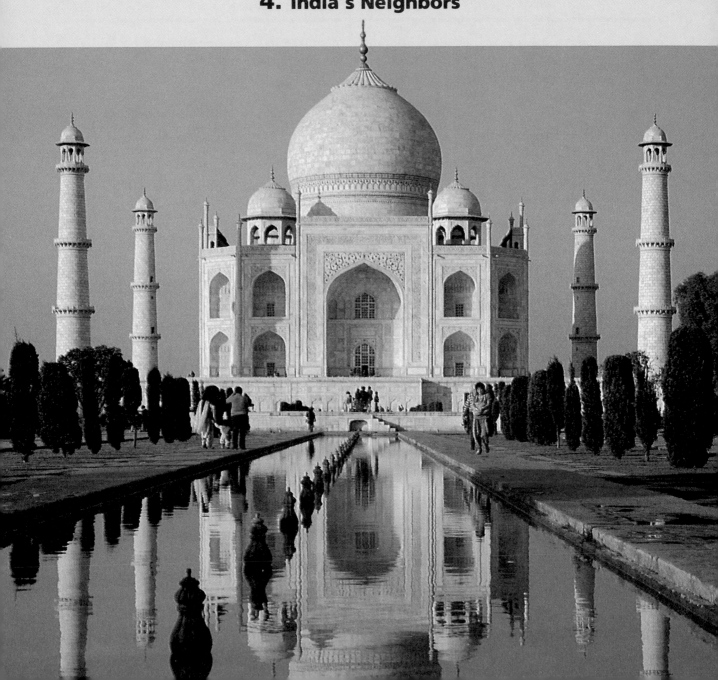

The Region of South Asia

CONNECTIONS

Look at the photograph on the opposite page. What do you think this building was constructed for, and what do you think it is used for today?

TERMS

subcontinent

FOCUS

What are South Asia's principal physical features?

A. The Subcontinent of Asia

The Taj Mahal In a small town in northern India stands one of the world's most beautiful monuments—the Taj Mahal (tahz muh HAHL). This tomb was built in the early 1600s by Shah Jahan, a great emperor of India. Shah Jahan built the Taj Mahal to honor his young wife, who had died shortly after they were married.

Jahan spared no expense in building this magnificent structure. It is built of the world's finest marble and is surrounded by pools and fountains. Marble and ivory archways lead into courtyards lined with balconies of marble that are carved into delicate, lacy patterns.

The Taj Mahal displays two important characteristics of India and the surrounding region. First, the monument serves as evidence that this is a region where great civilizations have thrived for centuries. The people who have lived here have developed advanced techniques of architecture, engineering, and crafts such as weaving and silver working.

Second, the Taj Mahal shows that the people of this region have long conducted trade with other nations. For centuries, traders have brought treasures such as the pearls, ivory, silver, and marble used to decorate the Taj Mahal. Merchants leaving India and neighboring lands have carried cotton, jewels, and precious spices such as pepper to China or Europe. Travelers who have passed through India by land or by sea also have brought philosophies, religions, and languages from other parts of the world.

The Subcontinent India and its neighboring countries form a huge triangle that juts into the Indian Ocean. The Arabian Sea stretches along the western coast of this gigantic triangle. The eastern coast faces the Bay of Bengal. At the southern-most tip of the triangle is the island nation of Sri Lanka (sree LAHNG kuh). Much of the northern edge of the triangle runs through the Himalayas.

This huge triangle of land is cut off from the rest of Asia because it has coasts and high mountains along its borders. Sometimes this triangle of land is called a **subcontinent**. A subcontinent is a landmass that belongs to a larger continent. The term *South Asia* is also used to describe this huge triangle of land. South Asia includes India and most of the countries on its *perimeter*, or edges. These neighboring countries are Pakistan, Nepal (nuh PAWL), Bhutan, Bangladesh, and the island nations of Sri Lanka and the Maldives. India is the largest country on the subcontinent. Its total area is 1,229,424 square miles (3,184,208 sq km). This makes it about one-third the size of the United States.

A Rural Population India's population of over 800 million people is one of the largest in the world. Only China has a larger population than India. As in China, most of the people in India and the rest of South Asia live in small villages and rural areas. Less than one fourth of South Asia's population lives in cities.

Nevertheless, India and its neighbors have some of the largest cities of the world, such as Karachi in Pakistan, and Bombay,

▶ The magnificent Taj Mahal, in Agra, is a symbol of India's great civilizations.

SOUTH ASIA: PHYSICAL

Mount Everest

Mt. Everest
29,028 ft.
(8,848 m)

IRAN
THE PAMIRS
HINDU KUSH
AFGHANISTAN
Islamabad
PAKISTAN
THAR DESERT
Sutlej
HIMALAYAS
CHINA
NEPAL
Brahmaputra
New Delhi
Ganges
River
Katmandu
Thimbu
BHUTAN
Dacca
INDIA
BANGLADESH
MYANMAR
Arabian
Narmada
DECCAN PLATEAU
Gulf of
Cambay
Godavari
WESTERN GHATS
EASTERN GHATS
Sea
Bay of
Bengal
Tropic of Cancer
SRI LANKA
Colombo
Male
MALDIVES
Equator
INDIAN OCEAN

50° N
40° N
30° N
20° N
10° N
0°
10° S

70° E
80° E
90° E
100° E
110° E
120° E
130° E

○ National capitals
▲ Mountain peak

Elevations
Feet   Meters
10,000 ----3,000
5,000 ----1,500
2,000 ----600
1,000 ----300
0 ----0

0   400   800 miles
0   400   800 kilometers

India is the largest country in South Asia. It
forms a peninsula that is separated from the rest
of Asia by mountain ranges in the north.
▶ In which countries is Mt. Everest located?

Madras, and Calcutta in India. Most South
Asian cities are crowded and busy. A visitor
might see "streetcars. . . bulging with twice
as many passengers as they were built to
carry—the last few people to have boarded
them. . . just dangling from the back plat-
form like a bunch of human bananas."

B. The Mountains and Plains of South Asia

Landforms South Asia has three major
landforms. The first of these landforms is
the Deccan Plateau. This huge, rugged
plateau forms the core of the peninsula of
India. On the eastern and western edges of

the Deccan Plateau are mountain ranges called the Eastern Ghats and the Western Ghats.

The Ganges (GAN jeez) River and its plain are South Asia's second major landform. The Ganges is a wide river that flows across northern India from west to east for 1,560 miles (2,670 km).

The Himalayas are the third major landform of South Asia. The Himalayas cross through northern Pakistan, northern India, Nepal, and Bhutan. Between the high mountain peaks are valleys and basins where towns, villages, and farms are found.

The Indus River The Indus River and its valley are an important part of the South Asian landscape. The Indus River begins in the Himalayas and flows south across Pakistan. It is 1,976 miles (3,179 km) in length, which makes it longer than the Ganges River. The water of the Indus River is extremely valuable because the area around the river is desert.

South Asia's other important river is the Brahmaputra (brah muh POO truh). This river has both a long name and a long route,

1,802 miles (2,883 km), which is about the same length as the Rio Grande in North America. You can see from the map on page 464 that most of the nation of Bangladesh is located in the broad valley and deltas of the Brahmaputra River.

C. The Importance of Religion

Religion and Politics South Asia has an amazing variety of religions. Hinduism, India's principal religion, has the largest number of followers in South Asia. Islam has the second largest number of followers. There are also many smaller religious groups, such as the Sikhs (seeks) and the Tamils (TAM ulz). Each of these groups has its own beliefs and its own shrines or temples.

Many of South Asia's conflicts and political problems are based on religious differences. For example, some of the borders of South Asia's nations were created because of a past conflict between Muslims and Hindus. In 1947, when the British gave the people of India independence, the Muslims and Hindus faced a difficult problem.

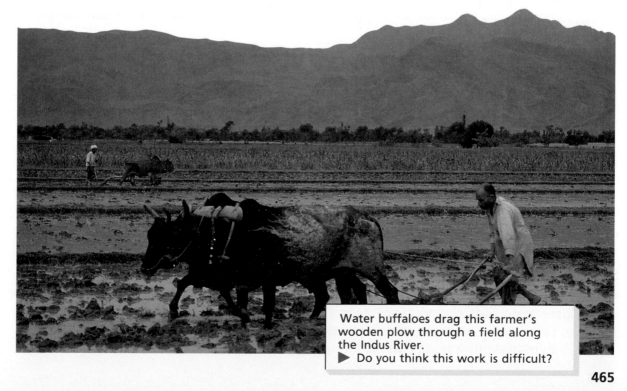

Water buffaloes drag this farmer's wooden plow through a field along the Indus River.
▶ Do you think this work is difficult?

465

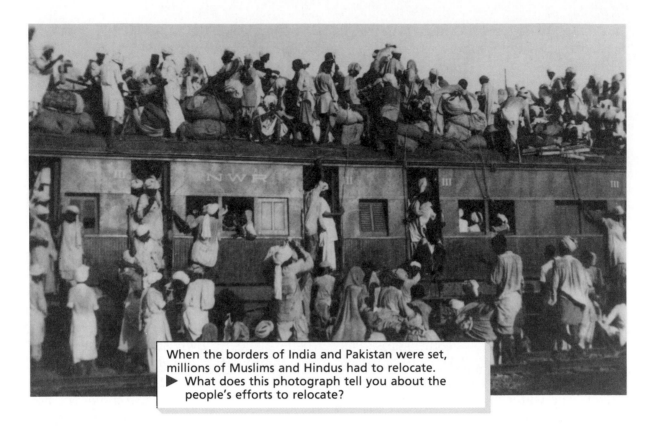
When the borders of India and Pakistan were set, millions of Muslims and Hindus had to relocate.
▶ What does this photograph tell you about the people's efforts to relocate?

They did not want to form a single independent nation because their beliefs were so different. So two separate countries were formed, India and Pakistan.

A Violent Beginning The results of this decision were dramatic. If the Hindus and the Muslims had lived in completely separate areas, the boundaries of the new countries could have been drawn between them. This would have been simple and efficient. But the Hindus and Muslims lived in the same villages and towns. When the national borders were established, millions of Muslims living in the new country of India fled across the border into Pakistan, where Muslims were to be the majority of the population. And going in the other direction, millions of Hindus who found themselves living in Pakistan fled to India to live with other Hindus.

There were riots and violence as millions of people tried to move their families and belongings as quickly as possible. Many were farmers who had to leave their land behind. When they arrived in their new country, these farmers had no land and no way to earn a living. This caused terrible hardship and suffering for many people.

LESSON 1

Review

REVIEWING MAIN IDEAS

A. Why are India and its neighbors sometimes considered a separate region?
B. What are the three main rivers of South Asia?
C. Why was India divided into two separate nations?

SKILLS CHECK

MAP SKILL

Use the map on page 464 to name the countries that border the following South Asian nations: Pakistan, Nepal, Bhutan.

India and Its Regions

CONNECTIONS

What are the ways in which we can describe a country's geography?

TERMS

domestic, monsoon, precipice

FOCUS

Which of India's regions produce agricultural products?

A. India's Regions

Geographers have a method for sorting out what they see of the land and people of a country and for learning about the country in an organized way. They study the special features of each region within a country. You have already done this before in studying China's regions, and we can use the same method to study India's vastly different regions.

India's three regions center around the country's major landforms. In the first of these regions, the Ganges River plain, are rolling hills and many shrines and religious sites. Green farmland stretches out alongside rivers and streams, and villages are grouped near clumps of trees. Women walk carefully along narrow paths with big pots or bundles balanced on their heads.

Buses traveling to India's second region, the Deccan Plateau, sputter and groan as they climb up zigzag roads. At the top of the plateau are forests, grasslands, and plantations on which tea and coffee are grown for export.

India's third region is the Himalayas. Dense jungle covers the foothills of the mountains. The jungle has been cut away in many places to allow the building of huge tea plantations and resort towns.

B. The Ganges River and Its Plain

The Sacred Ganges For Indians, the most important river on earth is the Ganges. The Ganges begins high in the Himalayas, where Hindus believe their gods live. Hindus believe the gods send the river through India, so they consider the entire length of the Ganges River holy.

The Ganges provides a valuable re-

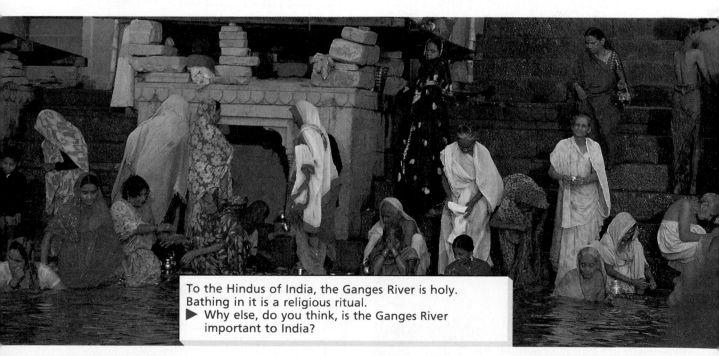

To the Hindus of India, the Ganges River is holy. Bathing in it is a religious ritual.
▶ Why else, do you think, is the Ganges River important to India?

source for farmers who live along its banks. Every year this river floods during the rainy season, leaving rich soils on the surrounding farmlands. For thousands of years, farmers have used these rich soils to grow crops, such as wheat, cotton, and rice.

The population of the Ganges River plain has grown considerably over the years, and today this region of India is one of the most densely populated parts of the world. Many areas have more than 1,800 people per square mile. Most of these people live in farm villages and make their living from agriculture.

The Ganges River plain also has large cities. Delhi, which is more than 700 years old, is located on a tributary of the Ganges River in the western part of the plain. Over 6 million people live in Delhi, making it the third largest city in India. New Delhi, the capital city of India, is also located on the Ganges River plain.

The Western Plain We usually think of a plain as an area of flat land where there is little variation in climate from place to place. But the Ganges River plain is different from most plains. The climate of the western end of the Ganges Plain is much

Daily life continues in India during the monsoon rains. The heavy downpour floods the streets of most cities.
▶ What is the monsoon?

drier than that at the eastern end. As a result the crops and methods of farming are different in these two areas.

In the western Ganges River plain, farmers grow corn, barley, and wheat, which is the main food crop. India is a major world producer of wheat, growing nearly as much as the United States. Most of the wheat produced in India is for **domestic** use, which means that it is used in India and is not exported to other countries.

Farmers in the western part of the Ganges River plain also grow cotton and sugarcane. India is the world's fourth largest producer of cotton, and the world's second largest producer of sugarcane. The Ganges River and its tributaries provide irrigation water to grow these crops. Hydroelectric power is generated from huge dams built recently along the Ganges River.

The Eastern Plain The eastern part of the Ganges River plain receives far more rainfall than the western area. Rice is the major crop grown here. Only China produces more rice than India, and both countries consume most of the rice they produce. Tropical fruits, such as bananas and oranges, and other crops such as tea and sugarcane are also grown in the eastern plain.

The difference in rainfall in eastern and western India is dramatic. In the western Ganges Plain near Delhi, the total amount of rain that falls during a year is about 25 inches (64 cm). Calcutta, at the eastern end of the Ganges River, receives over 63 inches (160 cm) of rain per year.

C. India's Monsoonal Climate

The Monsoon Why is the eastern part of India so much rainier than the western part? The **monsoon**, a seasonal wind, is responsible for India's climate. From November until March, monsoon winds blow from the northeast and bring dry air from the Himalayas. The winter months are dry throughout most of India. Almost all of

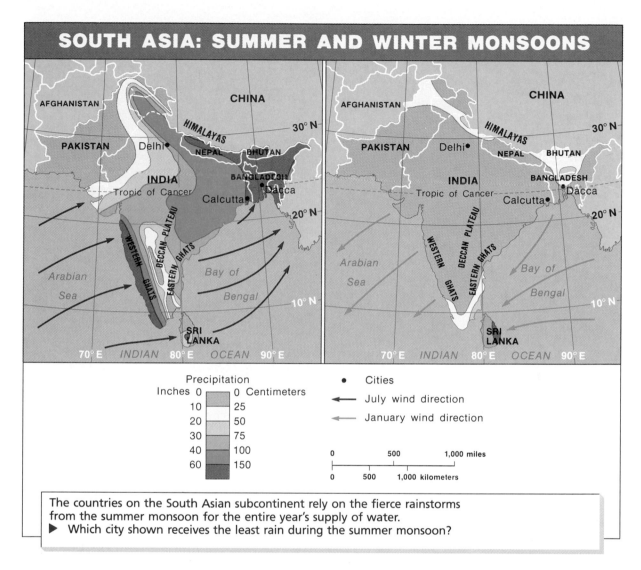

SOUTH ASIA: SUMMER AND WINTER MONSOONS

Precipitation

Inches		Centimeters
0		0
10		25
20		50
30		75
40		100
60		150

- Cities
← July wind direction
← January wind direction

0   500   1,000 miles
0   500   1,000 kilometers

The countries on the South Asian subcontinent rely on the fierce rainstorms from the summer monsoon for the entire year's supply of water.
▶ Which city shown receives the least rain during the summer monsoon?

India receives less than one inch (2.54 cm) of rainfall per month during the dry season.

In June, July, and August, monsoon winds blow from the southwest to the northeast, carrying moisture from the Indian Ocean and dropping it over the land. Everywhere in India, summer is a rainy season. But some places receive more rain during the summer than others do.

Using the maps of India on this page, you can see that moist air from the Bay of Bengal moving from southwest to northeast must blow along the eastern edge of India. This moist air drops heavy rainfall near the mouth of the Ganges River and in Bangladesh. Calcutta and the eastern part of the Ganges River plain receive a drenching in the summer, with up to 13 inches (33 cm) of rainfall per month.

Moist winds from the Arabian Sea also carry rainfall toward India. But when these winds arrive at India's west coast, they immediately climb up to the Deccan Plateau. These winds leave their rain along the western coast, so they are dry by the time they reach the western part of the Ganges River plain. As a result, Delhi receives only about 7 inches (18 cm) of rain per month in the rainy season.

Calcutta   In the early 1700s the British built a port and trading center in Calcutta.

This made the eastern Ganges Plain as important as the western part and Delhi. Today, Calcutta is India's largest city, with over 10 million inhabitants. Calcutta is also the main port for exporting the farm products of the Ganges Plain. Tea, rice, and wheat are processed in Calcutta. Textile mills there turn cotton into clothing and fabrics for export.

India's main coal and iron ore deposits are located to the west of Calcutta. These resources are used to make steel and some of the iron ore is exported. Calcutta is India's main industrial city for producing metals, machinery, tools, and chemicals.

D. The Rugged Deccan Plateau

The Deccan Plateau The Deccan Plateau, India's second region, is a level area cut by **precipices**, or sharp drop-offs. Swirling rivers wind their way between cliffs and steep valleys, and many deep, narrow chasms cut across the plateau.

Most of the Deccan Plateau is at an elevation of 2,000 feet (610 m) or less. Some areas of the plateau are densely forested. Most of it is sparsely populated, with only a few scattered villages. Farmers raise cotton, a few vegetables, and millet. Millet is a wheatlike grain that can be ground up into flour. It is then usually made into bread.

The tableland of the Deccan Plateau drops to sea level along the coasts of the Arabian Sea and the Bay of Bengal. The side of the plateau is steep and nearly vertical along these coasts. The coastal plains at the base of the plateau are narrow and are densely populated.

The coastal plain along the western edge of the Deccan Plateau is called the Malabar Coast. This coastal plain receives heavy rainfall during the rainy season. Farmers along the Malabar Coast produce crops such as rice, rubber, tea, coffee, coconuts, and pepper.

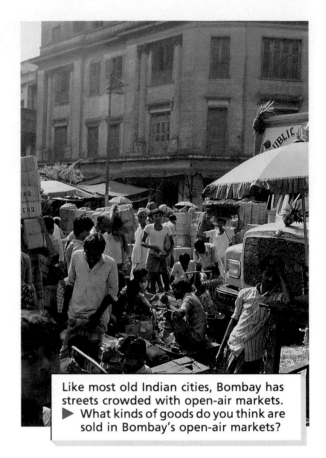

Like most old Indian cities, Bombay has streets crowded with open-air markets.
▶ What kinds of goods do you think are sold in Bombay's open-air markets?

Bombay Bombay is the principal city on the western coast, and it is also India's second largest city. Over 8 million people live in Bombay. They work in many different industries, including textiles. Bombay's textile industry uses cotton grown in western and central India.

Other industries in Bombay manufacture leather goods, process foods, and produce chemicals and railway equipment. Many of Bombay's factories use hydroelectric power generated from the rivers that drop off the Deccan Plateau along the western coast. India has some petroleum fields along the coast of Bombay, but there is not enough oil to provide power for all the country's factories.

Madras The eastern coast of the Deccan Plateau is called the Coromandel (kor uh MAN dul) Coast. Here, farmers grow rice, sugarcane, citrus fruits, cashew nuts, and

GROWING UP IN INDIA

Shiv is a young boy who lives in a small village in northern India. Shiv, his brothers, and his younger sister all attend school from 7:00 A.M. until 1:00 P.M. in the summertime. After school they return home and spend about one hour and a half doing homework. They also help out with the housework and farm chores. In the wintertime, they attend school from 9:00 A.M. until 4:00 P.M.

Shiv's family grows most of the food the family eats. Rice is the main dish. It is often flavored with curry, which is a combination of many spices. The family also has vegetables and chapatis (chuh PAHT eez), flat disks of bread that look like pancakes.

In the past, Shiv could look forward to a life of farming. In fact, farming was the occupation of all the males in his family. When Shiv's grandfather grew too old to continue farming, the family followed tradition and divided up the farm among Shiv's father and uncles. But when Shiv's father dies, the land will not be split among Shiv and his brothers. If it was split among the family sons, each would receive only a tiny piece of land. This would not be enough to make a living. Instead, Shiv and his brothers are studying to learn a craft or trade someday. Farming alone will not provide a livelihood for their future families.

Villages everywhere in India are modernizing and changing, but progress is slow. Shiv's village is small, with only 64 houses. It has a population of 500 people. Unlike most villages, Shiv's has a small hospital, electricity, and a school.

Even as the village modernizes, people have kept many customs. For example, Hinduism plays an important role in Shiv's family and village. There are portraits of Hindu gods and goddesses in Shiv's house, and the adults pray every morning.

Shiv's parents hope that a good education will help their children lead healthier, more prosperous lives.

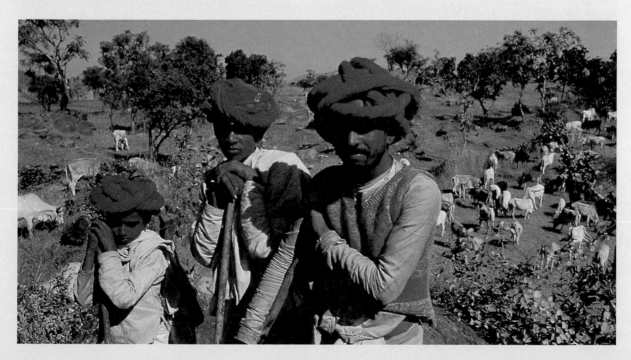

peanuts. These crops grow quickly in the warm, rainy climate. The largest city on the Coromandel Coast is the port city of Madras. Madras is India's fourth largest city, with over 5 million residents.

Fort St. George is in the oldest part of Madras. This fort was built by the British in 1640, only 20 years after the Pilgrims landed at Plymouth Rock in the American colonies. From Madras the British gained control of trade up and down the coast and later established Calcutta and Bombay.

E. The Himalayan Region

The Northern Border The Himalayas run along the northern border of India. India's territory includes some of the highest peaks of the Himalayas, but lower foothills are also found along India's northern border. These foothills are lower than the Himalayas themselves, but the land is still steep. The city of Darjeeling is built on the steep sides of these foothills. Houses perch on the hillsides or nestle in protected nooks.

In the east the lower foothills have a rainy climate. Here grow thick forests of valuable woods such as teak, which is used for making fine furniture. Large areas of these foothills have been cleared for huge tea plantations. The state of Assam and the city of Darjeeling, both in eastern India, have given their names to teas that are considered to be among the best teas in the world.

Workers on tea plantations must keep an eye on tea plants and cultivate them with care as they grow. The tea plants are trimmed and kept to a height of about 2 or 3 feet (61 or 91 cm). At times they are even cut back down to the ground to begin growing again. This keeps the tea leaves fresh and young, making them the best kind for brewing tea. After the tea leaves are picked, they are weighed, dried, and sifted before being packed.

Kashmir Kashmir is a state in India in the highest and most western reaches of the Himalayas. Although small, it is well

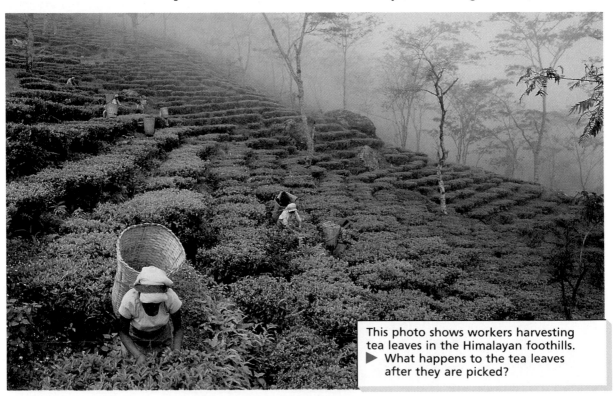

This photo shows workers harvesting tea leaves in the Himalayan foothills.
▶ What happens to the tea leaves after they are picked?

PROCESSING TEA LEAVES

1 Picking tea leaves from tea plants

2 Spreading the leaves on withering racks to remove excess moisture

3 Crushing the leaves to release juices

4 Fermenting the leaves, using high humidity

5 Drying the leaves in drying machines

6 Sorting the leaves by size

7 Packing the tea into waterproof chests for shipment

8 Shipping the tea to other countries

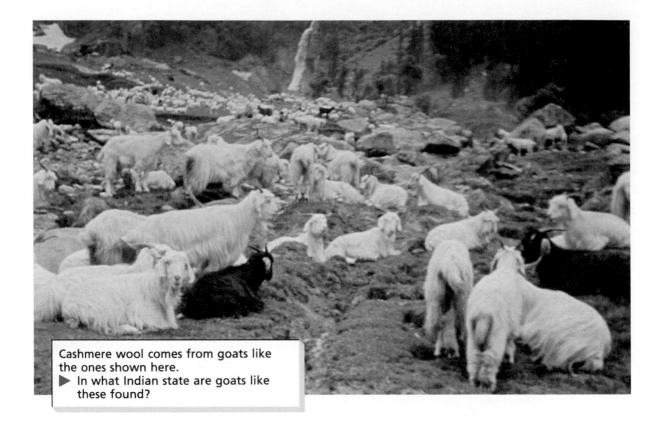

Cashmere wool comes from goats like the ones shown here.
▶ In what Indian state are goats like these found?

known for two reasons. One is that its goats produce a soft, luxurious wool called *cashmere* in English. A cashmere coat or sweater is an expensive item in the United States.

The second reason for Kashmir's fame is that India and Pakistan have fought over this territory for several decades. Most of the people in Kashmir are Muslim, but their rulers throughout history have usually been Hindu. When the new nations of India and Pakistan were formed, there was much disagreement about whether Kashmir should be part of Pakistan or part of India.

Because the majority of Kashmir's population is Muslim, it seemed reasonable for this state to join Pakistan. But the Hindu rulers preferred to join India. This disagreement erupted into violence until the United Nations sent troops to Kashmir to maintain peace.

Even today, Pakistan and India continue to disagree about Kashmir. This region is important to both countries because many rivers begin here. Control of river water is important during the dry season.

LESSON 2

Review

REVIEWING MAIN IDEAS

A. What are India's three main regions?
B. Why is the Ganges River plain so important to India?
C. How do monsoons affect the climate of the Ganges River plain?
D. Describe the land of the Deccan Plateau.
E. What valuable products come from the foothills of the Himalayas?

SKILLS CHECK

THINKING SKILL

On a separate sheet of paper, list the three regions of India. Now list, under each region's name, the products grown in that region.

Ways of Life in Modern India

CONNECTIONS

Name as many different religions of the United States as you can and describe some of the different beliefs or traditions of those religions.

TERMS

caste, Aryans, autonomy

FOCUS

How did past migrations of people help to create the variety of religions in India today?

A. Old and New in India's Cities

Delhi and New Delhi In every Indian city, people practice both ancient ways and modern lifestyles. The differences between Delhi and New Delhi are especially surprising. Delhi is one of the most important cities in India's history. For centuries, Delhi was the capital city of huge empires that stretched across most of South Asia. In 1912, the British established their colonial government just outside of Delhi, in a newly built city named New Delhi.

Although Delhi and New Delhi are near each other, they have different landscapes. New Delhi, with its long, straight concrete roads and vast open lawns, has a neat and efficient appearance. Few people stroll in the streets, and the buildings seem large and cold. New Delhi was built as a showcase for the British, and it was laid out to provide plenty of space and room for growth.

In contrast, Delhi has crooked, narrow streets and is filled to the brim with busy people. The older part of Delhi is similar to the older parts of most Indian cities. Vast mazes of narrow alleyways crisscross through marketplaces. Fruit stands, tailors, watch-repair shops, shoemakers, and bread sellers are almost overrun by bicyclists, running children, beggars, and women carrying bundles of purchases.

Indian Dress Most Indian men wear pants and shirts, or a suit and tie. Many Indian women still wear the traditional *sari*, a dress made by draping graceful lengths of material over the shoulders and around the waist. The beautiful colors of the saris—"mustard-yellow and scarlet and petunia," and many shades of blue and green—swish elegantly as women walk through the streets of India's big cities and tiny villages.

Modern shops and businesses are also found in Delhi. Army officers in crisp uniforms and businessmen in well-pressed suits stroll through the streets. Policemen direct traffic, which often includes both ox-drawn carts and luxury cars. Boutiques, cafes, and movie theaters line the spacious streets of newer neighborhoods. Many of these businesses have English names, because English became a widely used language when India was a British colony.

Today many Indian children learn English in school or while traveling in the United States. Many Indian doctors, engineers, teachers, and scientists study in North America or Europe and then return to India to practice their professions.

B. Hinduism, India's Main Religion

Sacred Animals Another unforgettable sight when first visiting India is the respectful behavior Indians show toward animals. Hindus believe that every living creature has a soul and that killing or injuring an animal is a terrible thing. Cattle are especially sacred to Hindus and Hindus are not allowed to eat beef. In many places, cattle roam freely, and traffic stops to let them pass in the streets.

Hinduism is a religion of many gods. It does not have just one written holy book such as the Bible. Instead, Hindu teachings are recorded in poems and stories written in the ancient language of Sanskrit.

Benares (buh NAH reez), on the Ganges River, is a famous holy city. Hindus journey to Benares to bathe in the Ganges. They believe that this will purify, or make clean, their souls. Lining the river's banks are huge steps that lead down into the water of the Ganges. Elaborate Hindu temples and Hindu people dressed in many colors add excitement to the scenery.

Hindus believe that the soul of each living being returns after death in the body of another animal or person. This process is called *reincarnation*. At the time a person is born, his or her place in society is determined for a lifetime. This is how each person becomes a member of a **caste**, or group of people with a similar standing in society.

The Indian government has banned the use of caste to determine a person's social standing, but it is still widely practiced in India. The highest caste is the Brahmans; the lowest is the Untouchables.

The Aryans How did Hindus come to dominate India, while Muslims and Buddhists are common in other parts of South Asia? The answer is found in India's history. Hinduism was brought to South Asia about 1750 B.C. At that time, farming people living on the Ganges Plain were overrun by invaders called **Aryans**. The Aryans were warriors from the northwest who introduced many gods to India. The Aryans' beliefs gradually formed a new religion, Hinduism. All across northern India, people began to practice Hinduism.

The Aryans also introduced their languages into South Asia. Hindi is the most widespread of these languages, but many other languages are also spoken in India.

The Aryans settled across northern India but found the Deccan Plateau, farther south, rugged and difficult to farm. Because of this, the Aryans had only moderate influence on the people of the Deccan Plateau, whose culture and language are called Dravidian. However, most of the people on the Deccan Plateau added Hindu beliefs to their own beliefs and are now considered Hindus.

C. Other Religions of India

Buddhism In the sixth century B.C., a prince named Siddhartha Gautama (sihd-DAHR tuh GOUT uh muh), who lived in northern India, left his life of luxury and began to teach a new religion that became known as Buddhism. Over many centuries, people in South Asia, Southeast Asia, China, and Japan adopted Buddhism. But Hinduism was still strong in India, and relatively few people there became Buddhists.

Islam's Influence Arab traders from North Africa and the Middle East began arriving at ports on India's western coast in the

Elaborately carved figures are part of this Hindu temple's exterior.
▶ Which group of people brought Hinduism to India?

FROM: **The Bhagavad Gita**

Translated and Interpreted by Franklin Edgerton

Hinduism teaches that a person's soul is immortal. When a person dies, his or her soul is reincarnated in a new body. Hinduism allows its followers to break free from this cycle of death and reincarnation and attain *nirvana*, or heaven. The way to reach *nirvana* is described in "The Song of the Blessed One", a poem which is part of the *Bhagavad Gita*. The poem is one of the most important religious works of the Hindu religion.

*L*et the disciplined man ever discipline
Himself, abiding in a secret place,
Solitary, restraining his thoughts and soul,
Free from aspirations and without possessions.

In a clean place establishing
A steady seat for himself.
That is neither too high nor too low,

. . . .

There fixing the [mind] on a single object,
Restraining the activity of his mind and senses,
Sitting on the seat, let him practice
Discipline unto self-purification.
[Straight] body, head, and neck
Holding motionless, steady,
Gazing at the tip of his own nose,
And not looking in any direction,

. . . .

Thus ever disciplining himself,
The man of discipline, with controlled mind,
. . . attains [nirvana].

The Golden Temple of Amritsar is the most holy place in the Sikh religion.
▶ In what Indian state is the city of Amritsar located?

fifth century. In the eleventh century, Arab warriors invaded the Hindu kingdoms of India and took over the land. The Arabs introduced Islam into their new empire. Most people in what are today Pakistan and Bangladesh became Muslims, and a large number of people in India follow this new religion as well.

The empire built in India by the Muslim Arabs was known as the Mogul (MOH-gul) Empire. Mogul emperors ruled a large area of South Asia from the 1500s until the middle 1800s. The Moguls were not successful in converting most Indians to Islam. But in the far north of India, in a state called the Punjab, the Muslims left a legacy that still causes conflict today. This legacy was the Sikh religion, which is based on both Hindu and Muslim beliefs. The Sikhs built their own empire and held fiercely to their customs for centuries.

The most holy place in the Sikh religion is the Golden Temple in the city of Amritsar. This beautiful marble building has a solid gold dome and a copper base.

The Sikhs consider themselves different from the Hindus and Muslims of South Asia. Their religion and culture are unique, and their homeland in the Punjab has a higher standard of living than most areas of South Asia. In recent years they have campaigned for special status and **autonomy**, or self-government, for their state. Their campaign has been bloody because the Sikhs have resorted to using terrorism.

LESSON 3

Review

REVIEWING MAIN IDEAS

A. In what ways are Delhi and New Delhi different?
B. Why is Hinduism the main religion of India?
C. How did Buddhism, Islam, and Sikhism develop in India?

SKILLS CHECK

WRITING SKILL

Imagine that you have been chosen to visit India as an exchange student. Write a short letter to the principal of your new Indian school, explaining whether you would prefer to live in Delhi or New Delhi, and why.

478

India's Neighbors

CONNECTIONS

What special precautions would you take if you lived in an area that flooded regularly?

TERMS

jute, sediment

FOCUS

In what ways are India's neighbors different from India?

A. Pakistan and the Indus River

A Desert Country A huge white concrete dam is supported by 66 arches and stretches for 1 mile (1.6 km) across the Indus River of Pakistan. This huge dam holds back the waters of the Indus. The water is released slowly during the dry winter months. The dam is a reminder that the waters of the Indus River are Pakistan's lifeline.

The rains carried by the summer monsoon to India and Bangladesh almost never reach Pakistan. In fact, they never even reach the westernmost stretch of India along the border of Pakistan. The dry zone along this border is called the Thar Desert. With less than 20 inches (51 cm) of rainfall per year, it is one of the driest places in South Asia.

Pakistan's population of over 100 million people is spread out over 310,403 square miles (803,944 sq km). This is about twice the size of California. Its population density of 356 people per square mile (137 per sq km) is much lower than that of India. Most of Pakistan's people, cities, factories, and farms are located along the banks of the Indus River.

Pakistan's farmers continually face the same problem: getting enough water to grow crops. Pakistan's government has built many canals and dams to carry water for irrigation to farmers' fields.

The government began this program of building dams and canals more than a hundred years ago. It was only in recent years, however, that the construction of dams and canals was accelerated, or sped up, as the government began to modernize Pakistan's agriculture.

Besides building these new water-control systems, the government also began to introduce Pakistani farmers to the benefits of the Green Revolution. The new seeds and the new methods of growing crops have helped Pakistan's farmers rapidly increase the amount of food they produce. In fact, Pakistan has experienced an incredible increase in the output of crops such as wheat.

Sugarcane, wheat, cotton, and corn are

The *minarets*, or towers of Muslim mosques are a common sight in the cities and villages of Pakistan.
► Why are mosques a common sight?

also important agricultural products. Where farmers have an adequate supply of water, rice is grown as well. Pakistan is one of the world's leading producers of both cotton and rice.

Karachi Karachi, which is located on the Arabian Sea, is Pakistan's largest city, with over 6 million inhabitants. It is also Pakistan's main industrial city. Steel is produced here, using some of Pakistan's small iron ore deposits, which are located in the central part of the country. A factory that assembles automobiles from imported parts is also located in Karachi. But Pakistan's main industry is manufacturing cotton textiles. Plants that produce cotton cloth, yarn, and clothing are important to Pakistan's economy.

Karachi was once the capital city of Pakistan, but today Islamabad is the capital city. Government leaders felt that Islamabad was closer than Karachi to the heartland of Pakistan's culture in central and northern Pakistan.

B. Bangladesh, a Young Nation

When the Muslim nation of Pakistan was formed in 1947, it was divided into two parts. The area that is today the nation of Pakistan was called West Pakistan. The area that is now the nation of Bangladesh was called East Pakistan. Together the people of West Pakistan and East Pakistan belonged to one country, called Pakistan.

In 1971 the people of East Pakistan decided to separate from West Pakistan and form the country of Bangladesh. Why did this happen? And what results did this division create? To answer these questions, we need to compare Pakistan and Bangladesh.

Pakistan and Bangladesh are very different geographically and economically. You have already read about Pakistan's dry climate. Pakistan receives less than 10 inches (25 cm) of rainfall per year. Bangladesh, in contrast, has a rainy climate, with over 80 inches (203 cm) of rainfall per year. Farmers in Bangladesh usually have a problem with too much water in their fields. Their fields

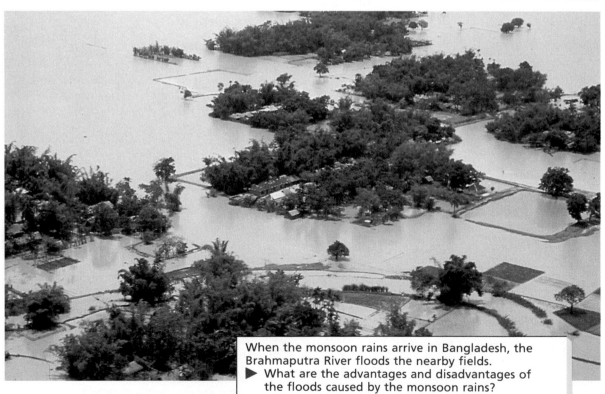

When the monsoon rains arrive in Bangladesh, the Brahmaputra River floods the nearby fields.
▶ What are the advantages and disadvantages of the floods caused by the monsoon rains?

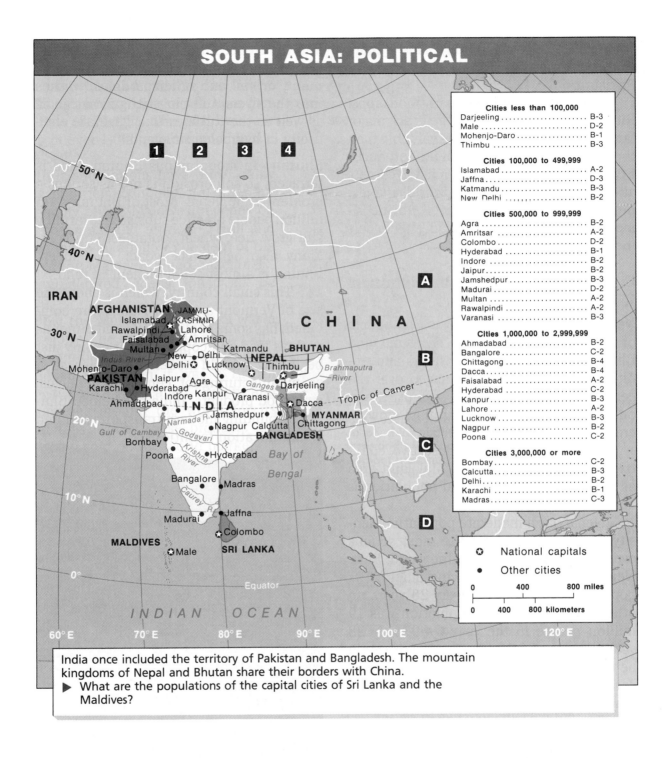

SOUTH ASIA: POLITICAL

Cities less than 100,000
Darjeeling B-3
Male D-2
Mohenjo-Daro B-1
Thimbu B-3

Cities 100,000 to 499,999
Islamabad A-2
Jaffna......................... D-3
Katmandu B-3
New Delhi B-2

Cities 500,000 to 999,999
Agra B-2
Amritsar A-2
Colombo....................... D-2
Hyderabad B-1
Indore B-2
Jaipur......................... B-2
Jamshedpur B-3
Madurai....................... D-2
Multan A-2
Rawalpindi.................... A-2
Varanasi B-3

Cities 1,000,000 to 2,999,999
Ahmadabad B-2
Bangalore..................... C-2
Chittagong B-4
Dacca......................... B-4
Faisalabad A-2
Hyderabad C-2
Kanpur B-3
Lahore........................ A-2
Lucknow B-3
Nagpur B-2
Poona......................... C-2

Cities 3,000,000 or more
Bombay C-2
Calcutta....................... B-3
Delhi.......................... B-2
Karachi B-1
Madras........................ C-3

⊘ National capitals
• Other cities

0   400   800 miles
0   400   800 kilometers

India once included the territory of Pakistan and Bangladesh. The mountain kingdoms of Nepal and Bhutan share their borders with China.
▶ What are the populations of the capital cities of Sri Lanka and the Maldives?

are only a few feet above sea level when the monsoon rains arrive. With the rains, the Brahmaputra and its tributaries quickly flood and wash over the farmers' fields.

Almost every inch of land in Bangladesh is covered with crops and fields. Bang-

ladesh has an area of 55,126 square miles (142,776 sq km), which means that it is about the same size as the state of Wisconsin. Over 114 million people are crowded onto this land, giving the country a population density of over 2,081 people per

THE BALANCE BETWEEN FOOD AND POPULATION

Famine, flood, drought, starvation: Reports of these catastrophes appear often in newspapers and in television news broadcasts. But because of two global changes that have begun to take place, these reports may become more infrequent. These two global changes are the green revolution and the control of population growth.

The Green Revolution

A dramatic revolution in agriculture began in the 1960s. At that time, experts predicted that as a result of increasing populations and decreasing food supplies, the world would run out of food within a few decades. These predictions led scientists working in laboratories in countries such as India, Zimbabwe, the Philippines, and Mexico to step up their efforts to find new ways of producing greater amounts of food.

The scientists developed new varieties of seeds for growing food grains, such as rice and wheat. These new types of seeds were called miracle seeds. Compared with the old varieties of seeds, the new seeds produced much more food on each plant. For example, with the new rice seeds, farmers could grow up to three times as much rice as they could with older types of seeds. Even farmers with small plots of land could grow more food with the miracle seeds.

The scientists' development of miracle seeds was only the first step toward increasing the world's food supply. The second step was to convince farmers in India and other countries to try the new seeds. Many farmers, especially those with small family farms, were reluctant to experiment with new technology. If the new seeds did not work, a farm family could lose its entire harvest and not have enough to eat. In India, for example, few farm families had savings accounts or government welfare, so the families could starve if their farms did not provide most

Scientists in India and other countries developed new types of seeds to produce larger harvests of grains, such as wheat.
▶ What do you think the wheel shown in the right-hand photo is used for?

of the household food. For many farmers the risk was too great. They continued to follow the old ways of farming.

For the farmers who were willing to take the risk and try the new seeds, government leaders had to take another step. They had to spend money and effort to help the farmers use the new seeds correctly to get the best results. Miracle seeds require special treatment. They need large quantities of fertilizers and irrigation water. Miracle seeds are also easily ruined by plant diseases and insects, so the farmers had to learn to use chemicals such as pesticides and insecticides.

Government advisors traveled to farms and showed farmers how to get the most out of their miracle seeds. The advisors also helped farmers get loans to buy the seeds, fertilizers, chemicals, and equipment needed to produce good crops. These efforts paid off in India, where many farmers began using the new seeds and new technology. In northern India, for example, farmers who received government help in using the new seeds quickly increased their wheat harvest. Wells were drilled to provide irrigation water for wheat fields, and farmers learned to use fertilizers. In the state called Punjab, over 75 percent of the wheat farms began using miracle seeds.

India is an example of a country that has had success with the *green revolution.* This term refers to the worldwide effort to increase food production through the use of high-yielding seed varieties, pesticides and other chemicals, and improved land management. In India, food production gradually increased, and the world's image of the country began to change. National pride increased, for India evoked images not of starving children but of

Irrigated fields in the Indus River valley produce wheat and other crops.
▶ In what part of India is the Indus River valley located?

local farmers using modern techniques to plant fertile, well-irrigated fields.

Future Food Supplies

By the 1980s, India's farmers were producing twice as much food as they did in the 1950s. In fact, the country was producing more food than it needed and was able to begin exporting grains such as rice and wheat. But in looking toward India's future, experts explain that these food increases are not a permanent solution to India's food shortages. Droughts, floods, or plant diseases could cause a major disaster. If one or two years go by with small harvests, people will have to use their food reserves, or the surplus crops from previous years. Once these reserves are gone, even miracle seeds will not produce enough food quickly enough to feed everyone. India and other countries will then have to turn to the rest of the world for help and food donations.

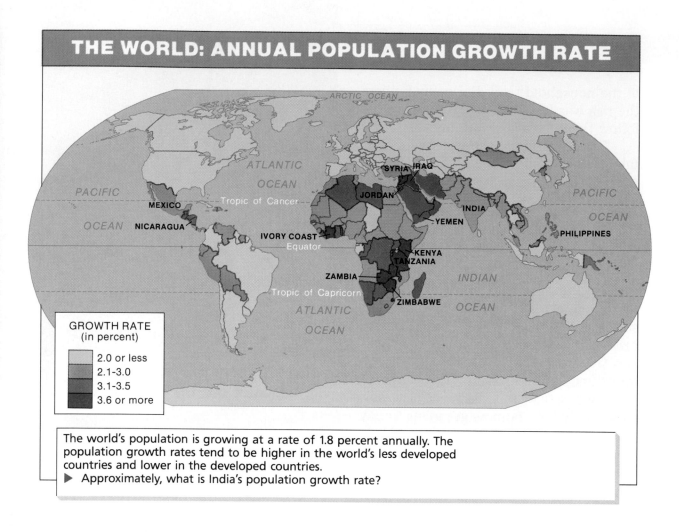

THE WORLD: ANNUAL POPULATION GROWTH RATE

GROWTH RATE
(in percent)

- 2.0 or less
- 2.1–3.0
- 3.1–3.5
- 3.6 or more

The world's population is growing at a rate of 1.8 percent annually. The population growth rates tend to be higher in the world's less developed countries and lower in the developed countries.
▶ Approximately, what is India's population growth rate?

Another factor that threatens the success of the green revolution is the continuing population growth. Although farmers have learned to produce more food, the number of mouths to feed has grown even more quickly. Miracle seeds are barely able to keep up with current population increases. What, then, can India and other countries do to produce enough food to feed their future populations?

A Plan for Producing More Food

The strategy for feeding all the world's people involves two parts: raising even more food and controlling population growth. To raise more food, Indian government leaders plan to continue to take advantage of the research and technology of the green revolution. For example, rice farmers in eastern and southern India have had problems with the miracle seeds. The new rice plants became infected with diseases and insects more often than wheat plants do. More research is needed to help these farmers get good results from miracle seeds and improve their rice harvests.

India's government wants to provide loans and education to farmers who still use the old farming methods and types of seeds. In addition, more food can be produced by encouraging farmers to use land that has never been farmed before. Thus the government wants to build more irrigation canals to allow farming in new areas, and more roads, bridges, and storage facilities for moving and storing farm products.

Another way to increase food production is to reorganize farm boundaries. For example, India's government would like to redraw property boundaries of tiny farms so that each family would own a larger piece of farmland and would produce more crops.

Plans for Limiting Population Growth

The second part of the strategy for feeding all the world's people involves slowing population growth. The populations of countries around the world are growing quickly because modern medicine helps to save lives. Diseases can be prevented or cured more easily than ever before. Also, as a result of the green revolution, people have more food, better nutrition, and healthier lives, so more people live longer and fewer people die. The end result is rapid increases in population.

Many countries, including India, have decided to try to limit population growth by decreasing their birthrates. India's government is encouraging all the country's people to participate in the population control effort. Projects have been organized to convince families that they should have fewer children. For example, thousands of small clinics in the countryside now provide basic medical care for children to ensure that they survive. In this way, healthy children are able to help out on farms and at home, and their families do not need to have as many children as before.

India's leaders have also found that education plays an important role in controlling population. In southern India many more children are being sent to school to learn valuable skills. Then when

India's leaders have found that education plays a role in controlling population.
▶ What subject do you think these schoolchildren are studying?

they become adults, they can work part time or full time to help support their families. With this extra income, the families do not need to have as many children.

The world is watching and waiting to see the results of the green revolution and population control efforts in India. Many countries are only beginning to experiment with these two strategies. India's success could encourage more countries to look ahead and help ensure that our future food supplies will feed all the people of the world.

THINKING CRITICALLY

1. To what countries of the world do you think the green revolution and population control are especially important issues, and why?
2. What problems might some farming techniques of the green revolution present?
3. In what other ways might education be a useful tool in helping to control population growth?

REVIEWING TERMS

From the list below, choose a term that could be used in place of the underlined words in each sentence. Rewrite the sentences on a separate sheet of paper.

> subcontinent
> monsoon
> caste
> jute
> sediment

1. The people of Bangladesh make carpets and rope from <u>a plant that produces a coarse, tough fiber.</u>
2. The huge triangle formed by India and its neighbors is a <u>landmass that belongs to a larger continent.</u>
3. In the Ganges and Brahmaputra rivers, <u>soil and other particles</u> washes into the rivers and clog irrigation canals.
4. In traditional Indian culture, each person belongs to a particular <u>group of people of similar standing in society.</u>
5. India's climate is affected by the <u>seasonal wind</u> that blows through the country.

REVIEWING THE FACTS

On a separate sheet of paper, answer the following questions in complete sentences.

1. What two important characteristics of India and the surrounding region does the Taj Mahal display?
2. What two geographical features cut the subcontinent of South Asia off from the rest of Asia?
3. In what ways are India and China similar countries?
4. What are the three major landforms of South Asia?

5. How have religious differences caused problems for South Asia?
6. How is the western part of the Ganges River plain different from the eastern part of the Ganges River plain?
7. What are some beliefs of Hinduism, India's main religion?
8. What nations are neighbors of India?
9. How do the climates of Pakistan and Bangladesh differ?
10. What problems in Nepal are caused by deforestation?

WRITING ABOUT GOVERNMENT

If you were a member of the United Nations you might become involved in a debate about whether the state of Kashmir should remain part of India or become part of Pakistan. Write a paragraph that explains why you think Kashmir, which has a largely Muslim population, should be a part of India or Pakistan.

THINKING CRITICALLY

On a separate sheet of paper, answer the following questions in complete sentences.

1. Why is jute a more valuable crop to the economy of Bangladesh than rice, tea, or sugarcane?
2. What problems could be caused by over-population?
3. Why do you think the Indian government outlawed the caste system?
4. What steps could Nepal take to decrease its soil erosion?
5. Why do you think the people of Nepal and Bhutan live according to customs and traditions that have changed very little?

On a separate sheet of paper, draw a graphic organizer like the one shown here. Copy the information from this graphic organizer to the one you have drawn. Fill in the blanks for each region with important facts about that region. Answers may include the region's landforms, climates, cities, agricultural products, industries, religions, ethnic groups, or other facts that you think are important.

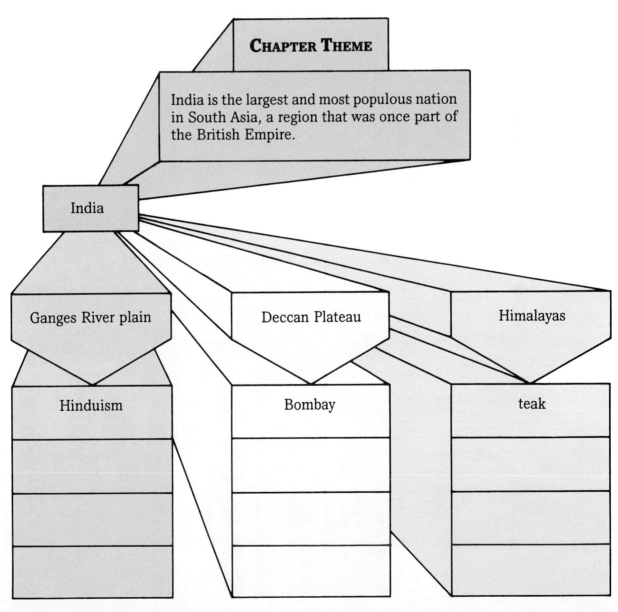

CHAPTER THEME

India is the largest and most populous nation in South Asia, a region that was once part of the British Empire.

India

Ganges River plain

Deccan Plateau

Himalayas

Hinduism

Bombay

teak

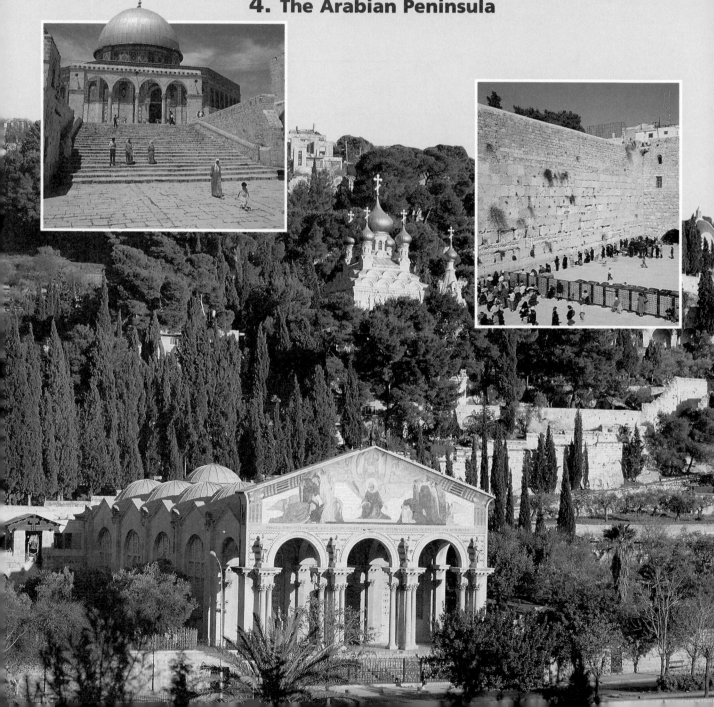

CHAPTER **20**

THE MIDDLE EAST

The Middle East: Crossroads of the World

CONNECTIONS

Look at the photographs in this lesson. What are some of the words that you would use to describe the Middle East?

TERMS

ethnocentrism, oasis, Fertile Crescent

FOCUS

How has the Middle East played an important role in ancient and modern history?

A. The Middle East: A Strategic Region

A Violent Region On the morning of October 24, 1983, Americans woke up to morning newspaper stories similar to this one from the *New York Times*.

> *WASHINGTON, Oct. 23—President Reagan, voicing outrage over the "despicable" destruction of the Marine Corps headquarters in Lebanon, called on the nation today to be more determined than ever to keep a force in that country and resist "the bestial [fierce] nature of those who would assume power."*
>
> *The President, plunging into a day of emergency strategy meetings... denounced the unidentified forces behind the attack and said the nation "must be more determined than ever that they [the unidentified forces] cannot take over that vital and strategic area of the earth."*

The terrible act the President was referring to was the bombing of the United States Marine barracks in Beirut, Lebanon. Over 200 Marines were killed in the bombing. President Reagan had sent the Marines to Lebanon to help end the conflict between groups trying to gain control of Lebanon.

Americans and the Middle East Why would the United States be interested in trying to end fighting in Lebanon, one of the smallest countries in the Middle East? Like all important world powers in history, the United States realizes that Lebanon, and all of the Middle East, is in a strategic location. It is here that three of the world's continents—Africa, Asia, and Europe—meet. It is here that by way of the Suez Canal, ships can cross from the Mediterranean Sea to the Red Sea and eastward to India and China. And most important, it is here that more than half of the world's known oil reserves are found.

The United States is also interested in the Middle East for another reason: Israel. This small country on the eastern edge of the Mediterranean Sea is the United States' most important ally, or friend, in the Middle East.

B. The Geography of the Middle East

What is the Middle East? In the previous chapters, we have looked at what was once called the Far East: Japan, China, the countries of Southeast Asia, and India and its neighbors. The countries that stretch from the eastern edge of the Mediterranean Sea down the Arabian Peninsula and all the way west to Afghanistan are called the Middle East. The name Middle East was given to the region by British geographers during the nineteenth century.

The people of the region, however, do not consider themselves to be in the "middle" of the East. Both the terms *Far East* and *Middle East* are examples of **ethnocentrism**. Ethnocentrism is looking at the rest of the world and making judgments about it based only on your own cultural background and experience. Because the British considered themselves to be the center of the world, they thought all other parts of the earth were either east or west of the United Kingdom.

491

▶ Three of the world's major religions consider Jerusalem a holy city.

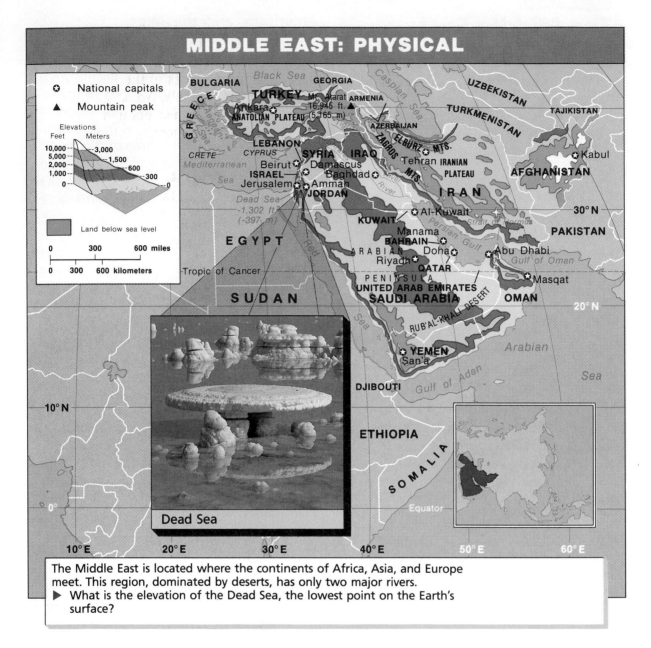

MIDDLE EAST: PHYSICAL

Legend:
- ✪ National capitals
- ▲ Mountain peak

Elevations
Feet	Meters
10,000	3,000
5,000	1,500
2,000	600
1,000	300
0	0

Land below sea level

Scale:
0 — 300 — 600 miles
0 — 300 — 600 kilometers

**Map labels:**
Black Sea, BULGARIA, GEORGIA, GREECE, TURKEY, Ankara, Mt. Ararat 16,945 ft. ▲ (5,165 m), ARMENIA, ANATOLIAN PLATEAU, Caspian Sea, AZERBAIJAN, UZBEKISTAN, TURKMENISTAN, TAJIKISTAN, LEBANON, CYPRUS, CRETE, Mediterranean Sea, SYRIA, Beirut, Damascus, IRAQ, ELBURZ MTS., Tehran, IRANIAN PLATEAU, Kabul, AFGHANISTAN, ISRAEL, Baghdad, ZAGROS MTS., Jerusalem, Amman, JORDAN, Dead Sea -1,302 ft. (-397 m), IRAN, EGYPT, KUWAIT, Al-Kuwait, 30° N, PAKISTAN, Manama, BAHRAIN, Doha, Abu Dhabi, Gulf of Oman, ARABIAN PENINSULA, Riyadh, QATAR, UNITED ARAB EMIRATES, Masqat, Tropic of Cancer, SUDAN, SAUDI ARABIA, OMAN, 20° N, RUB'AL-KHALI DESERT, Red Sea, Arabian Sea, YEMEN, San'a, DJIBOUTI, Gulf of Aden, 10° N, ETHIOPIA, SOMALIA, Equator, Persian Gulf, Strait of Hormuz

Dead Sea

The Middle East is located where the continents of Africa, Asia, and Europe meet. This region, dominated by deserts, has only two major rivers.
▶ What is the elevation of the Dead Sea, the lowest point on the Earth's surface?

The Highlands The countries of the Middle East can be divided into three geographic regions: the highlands, the Arabian Peninsula, and the Fertile Crescent. The highland region includes Turkey, Iran, and Afghanistan. As you can see from the map above, a series of mountain ranges stretches across these countries. The rugged Taurus Mountains rise in Turkey, where they are more than 8,000 feet (2,438 m) high. The Zagros Mountains cross the southern reaches of Iran. The Elburz Mountains cross the northern part of Iran and border the Caspian Sea. The mountains of Iran are often the site of devastating earthquakes. The quake that occurred in the northern mountains in June 1990 killed more than 35,000 people, injured more than 100,000, and left more than 500,000 homeless.

Afghanistan is home to the towering peaks of the Hindu Kush, a range of desolate mountains that form the western edge of the Himalayas. The Hindu Kush and the Himalayas come together in a rugged part of Afghanistan known as the Pamir Knot. The Pamir Knot gets its name because it is the meeting point, or knot, that ties together the Himalayas and the Hindu Kush.

The Arabian Peninsula   The Arabian Peninsula, the second region of the Middle East, is the easiest to find on a map. Bordered by the Red Sea, the Persian Gulf, and the Arabian Sea, this giant peninsula is about 1 million square miles (3 million sq km) in area. The largest country in the Middle East, Saudi Arabia, occupies most of the peninsula. Much of the Arabian Peninsula is covered by three deserts. One of these, which is called the Empty Quarter, or the Rub 'al-Khali in Arabic, covers 250,000 square miles (648,000 sq km). Here in this desolate, barren region, mountains of sand

reach heights of over 900 feet (300 m). Only a few adventurers have dared to cross this dry, hot desert. Most people live in the cities along the coasts of the Arabian Peninsula or near an **oasis**. An oasis is a place in the desert that has enough water for plants and trees to grow.

The Fertile Crescent   The map on page 492 shows an area north of the Persian Gulf that includes the countries of Iraq, Syria, Lebanon, Israel, and Jordan. This is the **Fertile Crescent**. The Fertile Crescent is a 1,000-mile- (1,600-km-) long area of flat, fertile land shaped like a crescent moon and wrapped around the northern end of the deserts of the Arabian Peninsula. Three major rivers flow through the Fertile Crescent: the Tigris, the Euphrates, and the Jordan. With irrigation water from these

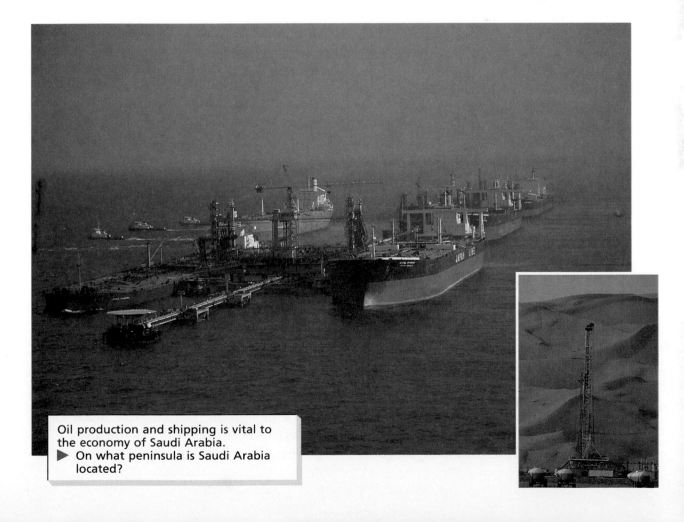

Oil production and shipping is vital to the economy of Saudi Arabia.
▶ On what peninsula is Saudi Arabia located?

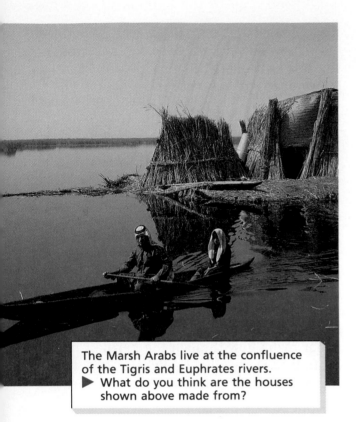

The Marsh Arabs live at the confluence of the Tigris and Euphrates rivers.
▶ What do you think are the houses shown above made from?

rivers, farmers grow crops that include wheat, barley, rye, carrots, onions, and garlic.

C. The People of the Middle East

A Mixture of Many Peoples The Middle East is sometimes called the Arab World. Yet while Arabs make up the largest part of the population of the Middle East, they are not the only people who live here. Many other ethnic groups, including Turks, Israelis, Iranians, Armenians, and Kurds, are found throughout the Middle East.

Cultural Influences The people of the Middle East have made many contributions to the world. During the day, you and your family may make use of them. In the morning, your parents may drink *qahwa*, or coffee, which was first roasted by the Arabs. At school, you study *al-jabr*, or algebra. In the evening, you may sit on the *suffa*, or sofa, and read a *makhzan*, or magazine.

At bedtime you put on *pa-jameh* and sleep on your *matrah*, or mattress.

The people of the Middle East have also made use of many Western ideas and inventions. During the time that Europe was plunged into the Dark Ages, Arab scholars and writers preserved the writings of the ancient Greeks and Romans. They studied the ideas and the practices of these ancient Western civilizations concerning medicine, mathematics, and astronomy, and helped to develop them further.

Three Important Religions The Middle East is known as the birthplace of three of the world's religions: Christianity, Islam, and Judaism. Each religion considers Jerusalem, the capital city of Israel, a holy city. Christians make special pilgrimages to the city to visit the site where Jesus Christ was crucified. Followers of Islam believe that the founder of Islam, Muhammad, ascended to heaven from here. For Jews, Jerusalem is a very special city; it was here that the first temple was built. A visitor to Jerusalem would find churches, mosques, and temples throughout this ancient and historic city.

LESSON 1

Review

REVIEWING MAIN IDEAS

A. Why is the Middle East important to the United States?

B. What are the major landforms of the three regions that make up the Middle East?

C. How is religion an important part of Middle Eastern culture?

SKILLS CHECK

MAP SKILL

Turn to the map on page 492. List the Middle Eastern countries that touch the borders of the following continents:

Africa   Asia   Europe

494

The Highlands of the Middle East

CONNECTIONS

What are some of the ways in which religion can influence the way a country is governed?

TERMS

strait, qanat, Shiite, Sunni, theocracy

FOCUS

In what ways is Turkey different from Iran and Afghanistan?

A. Turkey, Between East and West

The Straits If you look at the map on page 492, you can see that the northern tip of Turkey is split off from the rest of the country by two of the world's most strategic **straits**—the Bosporus and the Dardanelles. A strait is a narrow waterway that connects two larger bodies of water. These two straits connect the Black Sea with the Mediterranean Sea. In the past, these narrow straits provided the main crossing points between Europe and Asia for traders and armies. Today Russia, Ukraine, and many other countries depend on passage through the Bosporus and Dardanelles to transport goods and people.

The tip of Turkey, north of the straits, borders on Bulgaria and Greece. Turkey's southern border faces Iran, Iraq, and Syria. The country's northern boundary is on the Black Sea. Georgia and Armenia, former republics of the Soviet Union, are located to the northeast.

Most of Turkey's territory is south of the straits. This area, which is called the Anatolian Peninsula, is home to the country's major cities and economic regions.

The Taurus Mountains form the northern border of the Anatolian Peninsula. These mountains force the winds to drop their moisture on the peninsula. The rains that fall allow Turkish farmers to grow wheat,

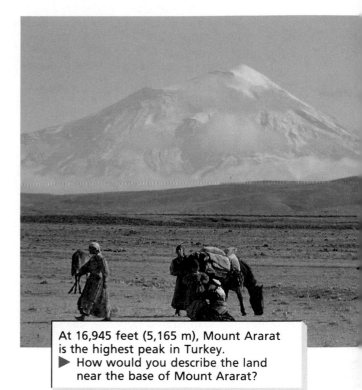

At 16,945 feet (5,165 m), Mount Ararat is the highest peak in Turkey.
▶ How would you describe the land near the base of Mount Ararat?

cotton, tobacco, and hazelnuts. The Taurus Mountains also hold important deposits of coal, chromium, and other minerals. Turkey has the Middle East's largest nonfuel mineral deposits. The country has worked hard to use these minerals to develop industries.

The Ottomans The modern country of Turkey was once the heart of the Ottoman Empire. This empire stretched from Egypt in North Africa, through the Middle East, and north into Romania and southern Russia. The Ottomans, who were Muslim Turks, ruled their empire for over 600 years. The ancient city of Constantinople, which is now named Istanbul, was the capital of the Ottoman Empire.

The end of the Ottoman Empire came after World War I. During the war the Ottomans fought on the side of Germany. The Ottomans and the Germans were defeated, and in 1918 the winning nations, which included France, Italy, and the United

The ancient city of Constantinople, now called Istanbul, was the capital of the Ottoman Empire in what is now Turkey.
▶ What is the capital of Turkey today?

Kingdom, carved the empire into many smaller countries. The area now known as Turkey is all that is left of the former empire.

Modern Turkey The collapse of the Ottoman Empire brought about enormous changes in Turkey. Most of these changes were the result of one man: Mustafa Kemal. Kemal, who became Turkey's leader, changed the way the Turks were ruled and how they lived. Turkey was proclaimed a republic, with Kemal as its president. The capital was moved to a new city, Ankara, which was in the center of the country's new boundaries.

Kemal was determined to modernize Turkey and to make it more like the countries of Europe. People had to wear European-style clothing, and the Turkish alphabet was changed from Arabic letters to Roman letters. Women were given the right to vote and to receive an education. Because of his enormous influence, Kemal was given the name *Atatürk*, which means "the father of modern Turkey."

Today, Turkey is a member of NATO and considers itself more a part of Europe than a part of the Middle East. The country is poor, however. Millions of Turks in search of jobs have migrated to Western European countries such as Germany. Turkey has also suffered from military dictatorships. But the new democratic government hopes that it can join the European Community and make Turkey into a strong, prosperous nation.

B. Iran: The Land of Ancient Persia

An Arid Land Like Turkey, Iran was once the heart of an empire. This was the Persian Empire, which ruled parts of the Middle East more than 2,000 years ago. The Persian language is still used in Iran, although it is now called Farsi (FAHR see).

The geography of Iran is quite different from that of Turkey. Northern Iran is bounded by the Elburz Mountains. To the east and south are the Zagros Mountains. The center of the country is the Plateau of Iran. The Plateau of Iran consists mainly of flat areas that are actually dried up lake beds. The plateau is an arid region, with few towns and people.

Qanats The ruins of the Persian Empire's magnificent capital city, Persepolis, are found on the dry Plateau of Iran. How did the people of this large city find water in such a dry part of the country? The answer lies in a system of irrigation that has been used throughout the Middle East and North Africa for thousands of years.

Rain and snow that fall on the Zagros Mountains form small streams that run off the mountains and seep, or slowly flow, into the ground to form ground water. Digging wells to pump the ground water into irrigation canals is not useful in the desert; most of the water would evaporate before it flowed to where it was needed. The ancient Persians avoided this problem by developing an ingenious system of un- derground tunnels called **qanats** (kah NATS). The qanats allow the ground water to flow underground until it reaches a flat area with fertile soils.

The qanat system allows farming along the dry edges of the Plateau of Iran. Crops are also grown in the foothills of the Zagros Mountains. There is also farming along the Zayandeh River, which flows out of the Zagros Mountains. This is Iran's largest river, and it is in the most fertile part of the country. Most of Iran's 50 million people live in the foothills of the mountain ranges and along the irrigated sections of the plateau.

The Kurds The mountain regions of Iran are home to an ethnic group called the Kurds. There are about 13 million Kurds throughout the Middle East. Large Kurdish populations are found in the mountains of

A QANAT IRRIGATION SYSTEM

Well

Air Holes

Tunnel

Opening

Farmland

Canal

Groundwater Level

A qanat is one of the oldest methods of bringing ground water to the surface. The water can be used for either drinking or irrigation.
▶ What do you think the canal water is used for?

497

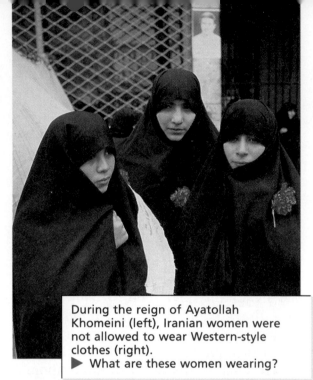

During the reign of Ayatollah Khomeini (left), Iranian women were not allowed to wear Western-style clothes (right).
▶ What are these women wearing?

Turkey and Iraq. Most Kurds make a living by herding sheep and goats.

The Kurds have not been treated well by the governments of the countries they live in. For this reason, many Kurds would like to see their traditional homeland, which stretches through the mountains of Turkey and Iraq, become an independent country.

C. Oil, Revolution, and War

Oil and the Shah Iran's economy depends almost entirely on the export of oil. Pipelines carry oil from the huge oilfields near the Zagros Mountains to ports on the Persian Gulf. Supertankers from around the world fill up with the oil.

Iran has used the money from the sale of oil to develop the country's economy. One of the most ambitious efforts to turn Iran into a modern, industrial nation occurred under the shah Mohammed Reza Pahlavi. *Shah* is the Farsi word for "ruler." The shah introduced land reform, giving larger pieces of land to farmers. His government built new factories in the country's cities. Like Turkey's Atatürk, the shah also tried to make Islam less powerful. Women were allowed to vote and to attend school.

Islamic Revolution The shah's reforms were not met with approval, especially by

Iran's **Shiites** (SHEE yts). The Shiites make up one of the two main branches of Islam. The other branch is made up of **Sunnites** (SOON yts). The Shiites and the Sunnites have different beliefs about how to practice their religion.

Over 90 percent of all Iranians are Shiites. A growing number of Iran's Shiites grew dissatisfied with the shah's attempts to make Iran a more secular nation. In 1979 they staged a revolution against the shah. Led by a man called Ayatollah Ruhollah Khomeini (eye yuh TOH luh roo HOH luh koh MAY nee), the Shiite revolutionaries turned Iran into a **theocracy**, a nation ruled according to religious laws instead of laws passed by the people. Strict Islamic laws were to be followed; women were no longer allowed to vote, and Western-style clothes, especially for women, were considered improper.

Attacks on the United States The new revolutionary government also changed Iran's policies toward the United States. Under the shah, Iran and the United States had been good friends. The Ayatollah and his supporters believed that the United

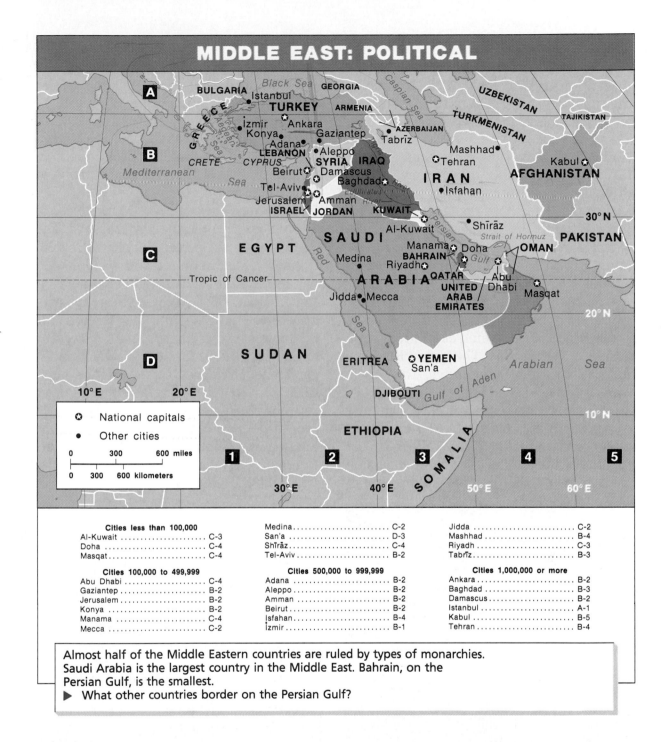

MIDDLE EAST: POLITICAL

| | | National capitals |
| | • | Other cities |

| 0 | 300 | 600 miles |
| 0 | 300 | 600 kilometers |

Cities less than 100,000
Al-Kuwait	C-3
Doha	C-4
Masqat	C-4

Cities 100,000 to 499,999
Abu Dhabi	C-4
Gaziantep	B-2
Jerusalem	B-2
Konya	B-2
Manama	C-4
Mecca	C-2

Medina	C-2
San'a	D-3
Shīrāz	C-4
Tel-Aviv	B-2

Cities 500,000 to 999,999
Adana	B-2
Aleppo	B-2
Amman	B-2
Beirut	B-2
Isfahan	B-4
İzmir	B-1

Jidda	C-2
Mashhad	B-4
Riyadh	C-3
Tabrīz	B-3

Cities 1,000,000 or more
Ankara	B-2
Baghdad	B-3
Damascus	B-2
Istanbul	A-1
Kabul	B-5
Tehran	B-4

Almost half of the Middle Eastern countries are ruled by types of monarchies. Saudi Arabia is the largest country in the Middle East. Bahrain, on the Persian Gulf, is the smallest.

▶ What other countries border on the Persian Gulf?

States helped keep the shah in power. When he was overthrown, the new government showed its hostility toward the United States by taking Americans hostage and engaging in terrorism in the Middle East.

A few years later a war broke out between Iran and its neighbor, Iraq. Hundreds of thousands of Iranians and Iraqis were killed in the fighting, and Iran's economy suffered drastically. The war ended in 1988. A year later the leader of Iran's revolution, Ayatollah Khomeini, died. The new leader of Iran has made some changes in the way the country is governed.

D. Afghanistan: Gateway to the East

A Landlocked Country East of Iran is the nation of Afghanistan. Afghanistan, which is about the size of the state of Texas, is one of the largest landlocked countries in Asia. For more than 20 centuries, invaders and traders have swept through Afghanistan on their way to and from India. They have made their way into India through the Khyber (KYE bur) Pass, which allows passage through the mountains that make up Afghanistan's eastern border.

Almost two thirds of Afghanistan is mountainous. The highest mountain range is the Hindu Kush, which cuts through the middle of the country. The Hindu Kush are rugged, barren, dry mountains. The people who live here are herders.

But Afghanistan is not only a country of dry mountains. Oases on the dry desert plains and rainfall on the valleys of the mountain ranges have made Afghanistan famous for its fruit orchards. Crops grown by Afghan farmers include grapes, apples, cherries, wheat, and cotton.

Invasion and War In 1979 the Soviet Union invaded Afghanistan because of fighting between members of Afghanistan's Communist government. The Soviet Union set up a new Communist government in the capital city of Kabul. Afghans living in the rugged mountain areas refused to accept the new government. Many began a guerrilla war against the Soviet troops. The United States supported the guerrillas with millions of dollars in aid and weapons.

In 1988 the Soviet Union's soldiers left Afghanistan. The Afghan guerrillas continued to fight, hoping to replace the Communist government put in power by the Soviet Union. In 1992 the Communist government resigned as the Afghan guerrillas captured the capital city. Fighting between rival guerrilla groups has continued over leadership of the country. Even if the fighting ends soon, it will take many years to repair the damage caused by the invasion and the guerrilla war.

Many Afghan children attend schools set up by people who fight their government.
▶ How is this school different from the school you attend?

LESSON 2

Review

REVIEWING MAIN IDEAS

A. How did Atatürk modernize Turkey?

B. Why are qanats used in the deserts of Iran?

C. How did Iran's Shiites react to the shah's program to modernize Iran?

D. What effects did the Soviet invasion have on Afghanistan?

SKILLS CHECK

THINKING SKILL

The Constitution of the United States says that there should be a separation between religion and government. Why, do you think, did the Iranian Shiites not want to separate religion from public life?

The Fertile Crescent

CONNECTIONS

What are some of the ways in which countries can try to solve conflicts that they have with each other?

TERMS

monotheism, Palestinian, Bedouin

FOCUS

Why is there conflict between Israel and the Arab countries of the Middle East?

A. Syria and Lebanon

Two Countries from One   The Ottoman Empire included the region that extended along the eastern coast of the Mediterranean Sea. When the European powers divided up the Ottoman Empire, they created several new territories in this region. At first these territories were under the control of the United Kingdom and France. By the 1940s, however, the Europeans had granted them independence. One of these territories under the control of France was divided into the independent countries of Syria and Lebanon.

Syria   Unlike most Middle Eastern countries, Syria has few oil deposits. But Syria, which is about the size of North Dakota, is rich in water and agricultural lands. Between 25 and 40 inches (63 and 102 cm) of rain fall along Syria's Mediterranean coast. This is a large amount of rain by Middle Eastern standards, and the farmers along the coast can easily grow wheat, citrus fruits, and olives. Two rivers, the Euphrates in the east and the Orontes in the west, allow irrigated farming in other parts of the country. The abundant crops that grow in the farmland watered by these rivers allow almost 12 million people to live in Syria. Southern Syria is mainly dry, barren desert.

An Ancient City   Damascus, the country's largest city, is also the capital. Damascus

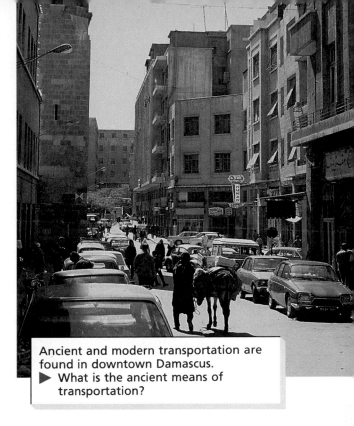

Ancient and modern transportation are found in downtown Damascus.
▶ What is the ancient means of transportation?

is an ancient city; it is considered to be the oldest continuously inhabited city in the entire world. Damascus sits on the site of an ancient oasis that is fed by the Barada River.

City life in Damascus is similar to that found in many other desert cities of the Middle East. Here is how one visitor described a typical day in Damascus.

> *The day begins in the cool dawn, when the streets surrounding the Old City become a vast open-air market, with thousands of carts displaying fresh vegetables and fruit. By ten or so, the shops have opened, both in the darkened souk [bazaar] and narrow streets of the Old City and in the modern downtown. (Even there, the tradition of the small merchant remains the rule; there are no department stores in Damascus.) Until about one o'clock in the afternoon, commerce is intense. . . . As the heat approaches its peak, the shopkeepers lower their shutters. . . . The city naps through the afternoon, waking again as the sun descends and the temperature. . . begins to drop.*

501

At five or so, the shops and most of the business office are open again, but now the city seems less devoted to commerce than to play. Promenading families tour the downtown streets, window-shopping, nibbling pastries from trays in bake shops, sipping coffee in the cafés. . . . At eight, when the offices close, secretaries and clerks pour out onto the streets . . . and by ten, when bright lights are switched off in the store windows, parents have their children in hand and are headed home for bed. . . .

Damascus is located in the southwestern corner of Syria, near a range of mountains. On a clear day a person can stand on these mountains and see into the lands of Syria's neighbor, Lebanon.

Lebanon Compared with Syria, Lebanon is much smaller and has many more problems. Until about 1975, however, Lebanon and its beautiful capital city of Beirut were considered to be "gems" in the Middle East.

Part of Lebanon's appeal comes from its climate and geography. A mild Mediterranean climate makes Beirut somewhat like southern California. In the past, tourists from the surrounding desert countries came to Lebanon's beaches during the hot summers to enjoy the cool sea breezes.

The Lebanon Mountains abruptly rise from the Mediterranean coast. They range upward to 9,000 feet (2,743 m) in height and are snow-covered during the winter. The Lebanon Mountains form the center of Lebanon, and continue almost its entire length. To the east of the Lebanon Mountains is the Bekáa (bih KAH) Valley, where wheat and citrus fruits are raised.

Civil War The Middle East is sometimes called the World of Islam, but that name does not accurately describe all of the Middle East. In Lebanon, for example, over one third of the population is Christian

Large parts of the city of Beirut have been destroyed in the civil war between Lebanese Christians and Muslims.
▶ In what year did the civil war begin in Lebanon?

rather than Muslim. For many years after independence, the members of these two religions lived together peacefully. In 1975, however, a civil war erupted between the Christians and the Muslims in Lebanon.

Various Muslim and Christian groups fought for control of the countryside and Beirut, the capital city. The war continued for 16 years. In 1991 the different fighting groups surrendered their weapons to the Lebanese army as a new government was formed. Peace may come yet to this country as its people begin to rebuild the beautiful capital city that had been called "the Paris of the Middle East."

B. Israel, the Land of Milk and Honey

The Promised Land Four thousand years ago, a group of nomadic herders traveled from the desert and entered the land they believed their God had promised them. The Hebrews, as these nomads were called, described this new, promised land as "flowing with milk and honey." Part of that land is known today as Israel.

The Hebrews, who were the ancestors of the Jews, practiced **monotheism**. Monotheism is the belief in only one God. The Hebrews were the first people to practice monotheism. Their beliefs were simple, as shown in this passage from the Hebrew Bible.

> *It has been shown to you, O man, what is good*
> > *and what the Lord requires of you;*
> *Only to do justice*
> > *and to love loyally*
> > *and to walk humbly with your God*

Exile and Return By about 900 B.C., the Jewish people had built a great kingdom in their promised land. The capital was Jerusalem, which was the site of a huge temple built of stone and gold. The temple and the kingdom were destroyed when the Romans conquered this region in A.D. 72.

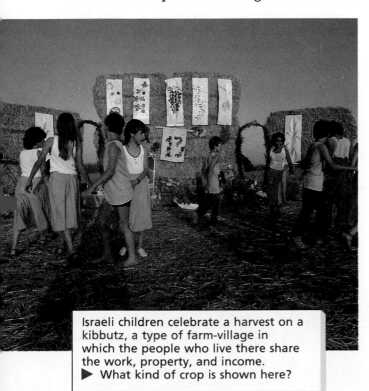

Israeli children celebrate a harvest on a kibbutz, a type of farm-village in which the people who live there share the work, property, and income.
▶ What kind of crop is shown here?

The Romans forced most of the Jews to leave their land, which the Romans called Palestine. Over the next 1,900 years, Palestine was conquered by many peoples. Among the last to occupy Palestine were the Arabs and the Turks. During all this time, there was always a small Jewish population in Palestine.

In the nineteenth century, Jews who were scattered throughout the world began to dream of returning to their ancient homeland. Fleeing persecution, numbers of Jews, especially from Eastern Europe, came to Palestine. They either bought or rented land from the Arabs and Turks and began to try to rebuild the land of milk and honey. The movement for a modern Jewish homeland grew, and finally, in 1948, the independent state of Israel was established.

Transforming the Land In the years since independence, Israel has become one of the Fertile Crescent's most prosperous, modern countries. But this nation, which is only about the size of Massachusetts, has few natural resources, has a small population, and shares borders with hostile neighbors. What, then, accounts for its growth?

One factor has been Israel's climate and land. Israel's main geographic features are a coastal plain, some hills and mountain highlands, and the deep Jordan River valley. Much of the coastal region and the northern hills around Lake Tiberias receive enough rainfall for agriculture. The southern part of the country is a desert known as the Negev. The Israelis have built a pipeline to transport the water from the Jordan River to irrigate farmland in the Negev.

The major reason for Israel's success, however, has been the hard work and energy of the Israeli people. By the early twentieth century, Israel was as one writer said, "a country whose valleys were largely malarial swamps, whose pastures had been grazed down to the ground and turned into dust-bowls, whose hills had been [stripped] of forests.'' By the mid-1960s, the Israeli settlers had changed this landscape to make the desert bloom with fruit orchards and cropland.

Industry Aid from other countries, especially the United States, and funds from Jewish people around the world, have helped Israel develop some thriving industries. These industries produce electronic goods, metal products, and beverages. Israel also has a large armaments industry. The guns, missiles, and planes made in Israel have been used to defend the country against its Arab neighbors.

Another important industry is diamond-cutting, which is centered in the city of Tel Aviv. This city is also home to most of Israel's other industries. Located on the Mediterranean Sea, Tel Aviv is the largest city in Israel, with more than 1 million people. It is a modern city with skyscrapers, sidewalk cafes, and crowded beaches.

Israel's other main city is the ancient religious center of Jerusalem, with a population of almost 500,000. Jerusalem is located in the dry highlands that make up central Israel.

C. The Arab-Israeli Conflict

The Conflict's Beginning Israel has faced intense hostility from the neighboring Arab states from the day it became an independent nation. As the map on page 506 shows, Israel and the Arab states have fought several wars. The wars have occurred because the land of Israel is claimed by two peoples: the Israelis and the Arab **Palestinians**.

The Palestinians lived in most of what now is Israel until 1948. In that year the United Nations decided Palestine should be divided between the Jews who wanted to return to their homeland and the Palestinians. The neighboring Arab countries believed the Jews did not have a right to a homeland in the Middle East and began the first of many wars with Israel.

Israel won the wars fought with the Arab nations. It also won large areas of new territory from the Arab states, especially after the 1967 war. In 1979, one Arab country, Egypt, decided to make peace with Israel.

The West Bank After the 1967 war, Israel gained a large section of land claimed by

In 1993, Prime Minister Yitzhak Rabin of Israel (left) and Yasir Arafat, leader of the Palestinian Liberation Army, (right) met in Washington, D.C.
► Why did the two leaders meet?

504

ANWAR SADAT'S SPEECH BEFORE THE ISRAELI PARLIAMENT

On November 20, 1977, an Arab named Anwar Sadat, the President of Egypt, made history. On that day, Sadat stood before the Israeli Parliament and said he wanted to live in peace with Israel.

I come to you on solid ground to shape a new life and to establish peace. . . .

Any life that is lost in war is a human life, be it that of an Arab or an Israeli. A wife who becomes a widow is a human being entitled to a happy life, whether she be an Arab or an Israeli.

Innocent children who are deprived of the care and compassion of their parents are ours. They are ours, be they living on Arab or Israeli land. . . .

You want to live with us, in this part of the world.

In all sincerity I tell you we welcome you among us, with full security and safety. This in itself is a tremendous turning point, one of the landmarks of a decisive historical change. We used to reject you. We had our reasons and our fears, yes. . . .

Yet today I tell you, and I declare it to the whole world, that we accept to live with you in permanent peace based on justice. . . .

What is peace for Israel? It means that Israel lives in the region with her Arab neighbors in security and safety. . . .

Peace is not a mere endorsement of written lines. Rather it is a rewriting of history.

This is Egypt, whose people have entrusted me with their sacred message. A message of security, safety, and peace to every man, woman and child in Israel. I say, encourage your leadership to struggle for peace.

1. What consequences of war are shared by Arabs and Israelis according to Sadat?
2. How does President Sadat define peace?
3. Why, do you think, haven't other Arab countries made peace with Israel?

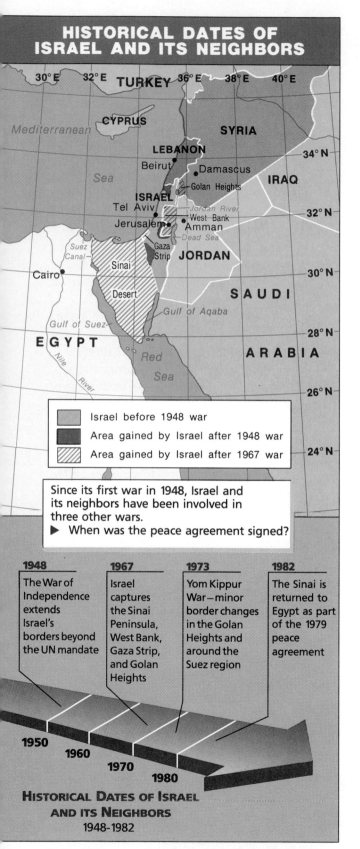

HISTORICAL DATES OF ISRAEL AND ITS NEIGHBORS

Israel before 1948 war

Area gained by Israel after 1948 war

Area gained by Israel after 1967 war

Since its first war in 1948, Israel and its neighbors have been involved in three other wars.

▶ When was the peace agreement signed?

1948
The War of Independence extends Israel's borders beyond the UN mandate

1967
Israel captures the Sinai Peninsula, West Bank, Gaza Strip, and Golan Heights

1973
Yom Kippur War—minor border changes in the Golan Heights and around the Suez region

1982
The Sinai is returned to Egypt as part of the 1979 peace agreement

1950 1960 1970 1980

HISTORICAL DATES OF ISRAEL AND ITS NEIGHBORS
1948-1982

Jordan and called the West Bank. The West Bank is home to the majority of the Palestinians. In 1993, Israel and the Palestinians signed a peace accord, or agreement. They agreed to work together to create an independent country for the Palestinians with land from the West Bank. The Palestinians have also held peace talks with Syria, Jordan, and Lebanon to try to resolve their differences.

D. The Arab Kingdom of Jordan

A Desert Land Jordan is about the size of the state of Indiana, and almost all of the country is desert. Much of Jordan's most productive land is along the east side of the Jordan River valley. This extensively irrigated region makes agriculture the most important part of Jordan's economy.

Jordan also held the land west of the Jordan River until 1967. The West Bank was Jordan's most fertile land.

The Dead Sea The Jordan River flows south along Jordan's border and empties into the Dead Sea. This body of water is called the Dead Sea because there is almost no life in or around it. But the waters of the sea are useful because they contain many minerals, such as phosphates. These phosphates are Jordan's most important mineral export.

The Bedouins Most of Jordan's land east of the Jordan River is sparsely populated. This region of desert and patchy grassland is home to a nomadic people called the **Bedouins** (BED oo ihnz). *Bedouin* is an Arabic word that means "people who live in open country." The Bedouins move with their herds of sheep, camels, and goats among the oases, towns, and villages of the desert. They camp wherever they find pasture for their animals.

The Bedouins have kept alive many of the traditions of the Middle East. They dress in long robes and wear *footas*, or turbans, around their heads. This long, loose clothing protects them from the hot daytime sun, the cool desert nights, and the blowing sand of desert sandstorms.

E. Iraq, a Nation Between Rivers

The Land and Its People Much of the nation of Iraq lies between the Tigris and Euphrates rivers. In ancient times this region was called Mesopotamia, which means "between the rivers." The Tigris and Euphrates begin in the Taurus Mountains of Turkey and flow south toward the Persian Gulf. About 120 miles (193 km) from the gulf, the waters merge into a channel, named the Shatt-al-Arab, and flow southeasterly into the Persian Gulf.

Most of Iraq's 18 million people live in the cities and villages built on the lowlands along the Tigris and Euphrates. Iraq's most important cities are here—Baghdad, the capital, which has a population of 3.8 million, and Basra. Basra is Iraq's main port for its largest export: oil. It makes up about 90 percent of Iraq's exports.

War with Kuwait Following the war between Iran and Iraq, (1980–1988), which you read about on page 499, Iraq was heavily in debt. In 1990, Iraq attacked Kuwait, its neighbor to the south, and quickly seized control of that oil-rich country. Iraq's President Saddam Hussein accused Kuwait of plotting with the United States to keep oil prices low. He also insisted that Kuwait settle a long-standing border dispute in Iraq's favor.

The United Nations Security Council and the United States strongly condemned the Iraqi invasion and demanded the immediate withdrawal of Iraqi troops from Kuwait. Saddam Hussein refused to back off. Early in 1991 an international force led by the United States launched air and missile attacks on Iraq and Iraqi-occupied Kuwait. The war against Saddam Hussein was called the Persian Gulf War. General H. Norman Schwarzkopf, Jr., commanded the United States forces in the offensive known as Operation Desert Storm. Within six weeks the Iraqi army was defeated.

The Bedouins move across the desert of Jordan in search of pasture for their herds of sheep, camels, and goats.
▶ What does the word *Bedouin* mean?

LESSON 3

Review

REVIEWING MAIN IDEAS

A. What caused Lebanon's continuing civil war?

B. How have the Israelis changed their land since 1948?

C. Why is there conflict between the Israelis and the Palestinians?

D. What is the source of Jordan's mineral wealth?

E. Why did United States troops participate in a war against Iraq in 1991?

SKILLS CHECK

WRITING SKILL

Write several paragraphs explaining how you think the Israelis and the Palestinians might end their fighting.

The Arabian Peninsula

CONNECTIONS

List some uses of oil. How would daily life and activities be affected if oil were not available?

TERMS

Koran, hajj

FOCUS

How have most of the countries on the Arabian Peninsula benefited from oil?

A. Saudi Arabia: Desert, Sand, and Oil

A Huge Tilted Landform The Arabian Peninsula is like a giant tabletop that tilts downward toward the east and the north. The physical map of the Middle East, which is found on page 492, shows that the peninsula has this tilt because of high elevations in the south. The highest points are along the Hejaz Mountains. The land north of the mountains gradually slopes downward toward the Persian Gulf. Here, at its northern edge, the Arabian Peninsula is flat, dry, and sandy.

The Desert Country Saudi Arabia, the largest country on the Arabian Peninsula, is about the size of Alaska and Texas combined. But Saudi Arabia has a total population of only about 15 million people. Why do so few people live in this large country?

Most of Saudi Arabia is covered by desert. The southern part of the country is mainly the huge desert called the Empty Quarter, which you read about in Lesson 1. No one lives in the Empty Quarter, and few people have ever traveled through this huge "sea" of sand dunes.

Life in the other parts of this desert country is centered around oases. Here are the country's towns and villages. Some oases have grown into large cities. One of these is Riyadh, the capital city of Saudi Arabia. This growing, modern city is in the center of the country.

Along the Persian Gulf are towns and cities that have grown because of the large oil fields located near them. This area is dry and has few sources of water, so the government has built *desalination plants* to produce fresh water from the salt water of the Persian Gulf. Creating fresh water this way is expensive, but it is the only way Saudi Arabia can supply water to the work-

Riyadh, the capital of Saudi Arabia, is one city that grew around an oasis.
▶ What vegetation shown in this photo is typical of an oasis?

THE WORLD: CRUDE OIL PRODUCTION

Production per year
(in millions of short tons)

- 0-34
- 35-100
- 101-150
- 151-350
- 351 or more

Much of the world's crude oil is produced in the Middle East. However, seven of the ten leading crude oil producers are in other regions of the world.
▶ Which country is the leading crude oil producer in the Middle East?

ers and other people who support the country's vital oil industry.

The Region's Oil Leader Saudi Arabia is the world's third largest oil producer and the world's largest oil exporter. The Saudi Arabian government has used the profits from oil sales to build new schools, hospitals, and highways. It has also built two new cities to refine oil, produce chemicals, and make cement and steel. One of these cities, Yenbo, is on the Red Sea coast; the other, Jubail, is on the Persian Gulf. Many people from other countries, such as Pakistan, Egypt, and South Korea, have come to Saudi Arabia to work in the new cities and in the oil fields.

B. The Persian Gulf States

The Benefits of Oil The countries that spread along the Persian Gulf coast of the Arabian Peninsula are small. However, they are among the world's most important countries, since they hold the largest known supplies of oil reserves in the world.

The second largest of these countries is Kuwait, which forms a wedge of land between Iraq and Saudi Arabia. Kuwait is slightly smaller than the state of New Jersey. This flat, sandy desert country has little fresh water and no forests. But Kuwait does have oil—lots of it. In fact, this small country is situated on top of the richest single oil deposit in the world.

On page 507 you read that Kuwait was attacked by Iraq in 1990. Toward the end of the Persian Gulf War, Iraqi troops set afire hundreds of oil wells in Kuwait. The damage to the Kuwaiti oil industry was enormous. Burning oil consumed about 6 million barrels of oil per day. That represented a daily loss of nearly $100 million.

In addition to the damage to the oil industry, the fires caused monstrous damage to the environment. Dense smoke from burning oil wells blocked out sunlight for long periods of time. Oil spurting from wells that were damaged created huge flammable lakes of petroleum. Some wells released poisonous gas.

Shortly after the war had ended, a delegate from the United Nations Environment Program compared the situation to Chernobyl, the 1986 disaster at a Soviet nuclear power plant. It was estimated that the consequences of the damages would be felt for years.

The Other Gulf States Bahrain, Qatar (ke-TAHR), and the United Arab Emirates are also wealthy because of oil. Bahrain consists of one large island and many smaller islands. It has a population of about 500,000. Before it became an oil exporter, Bahrain was an important trading port. It was also well known for its pearls, which come from the surrounding waters of the gulf.

Qatar, too, was best known for its pearls before oil became an important export. This peninsular nation juts out into the Persian Gulf. About 400,000 people, most of whom are foreign oil workers, live here.

The United Arab Emirates is actually composed of seven small city-states that have formed a political union. The total population of the United Arab Emirates is about 1.7 million. As in Qatar, most of the population is made up of workers from other countries.

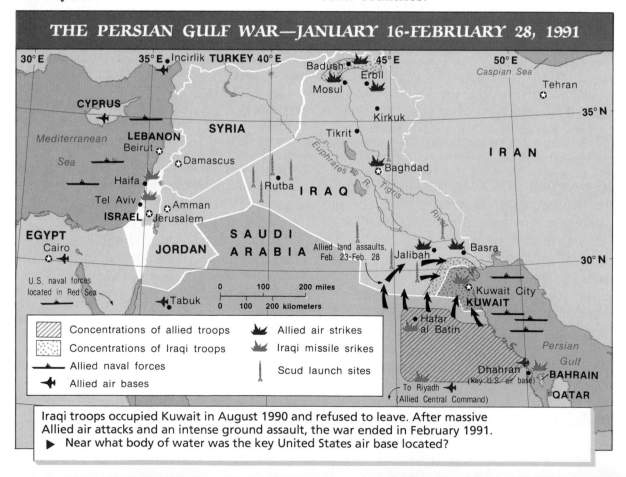

THE PERSIAN GULF WAR—JANUARY 16-FEBRUARY 28, 1991

Iraqi troops occupied Kuwait in August 1990 and refused to leave. After massive Allied air attacks and an intense ground assault, the war ended in February 1991.
▶ Near what body of water was the key United States air base located?

OPEC The nations of the Persian Gulf and 13 other leading oil-producing nations all belong to the Organization of Petroleum Exporting Countries. This group is often referred to as OPEC. It decides how much oil the members will produce and controls the prices other countries pay for the oil.

C. Oman and Yemen

Oman Along the southern end of the Arabian Peninsula are two countries that do not have as much oil as other countries in the Middle East. One of these countries is Oman. This ancient coastal nation is about the size of our state of Kansas. Unlike most of the other countries on the Arabian Peninsula, farming is possible in some parts of Oman. This is because of the monsoon rains that cross the Indian Ocean each year.

Yemen Along the southern and western coasts of the Arabian Peninsula is Yemen, a country with almost no natural resources. Yemen was formerly two countries—North Yemen and South Yemen. In 1990 the leaders of both countries agreed on unification for economic reasons. San'a (sah NAH), once the capital of North Yemen, was made the new capital.

Yemen has a narrow plain all along its coastline. This gives way to a chain of low-lying mountains. Farther inland, in the north and west, is the high interior section. More than 3 times as many people live in the higher part of the country than in the lower.

Most people in Yemen are farmers or herders of cattle and sheep. Farmers in the north grow wheat, vegetables, grapes, and coffee. Only a few crops grow well in the hot, dry south. Most people in the south live near the port of Aden. Ships moving between the Gulf of Aden and the Red Sea use the port for refueling, transferring cargo, and making repairs.

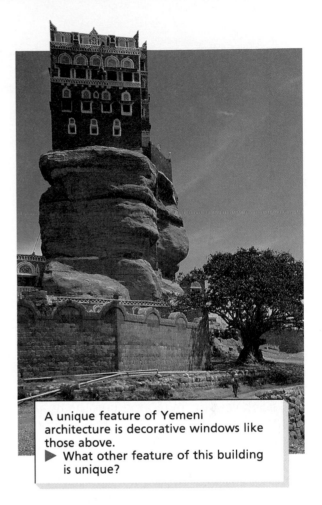

A unique feature of Yemeni architecture is decorative windows like those above.
▶ What other feature of this building is unique?

D. The Birthplace of Islam

Islam's Holy Land The countries on the Arabian Peninsula are known for their oil, and so they are of interest to many industrial countries. But Saudi Arabia, in particular, has a special interest to Muslims, since it is the location of Mecca and Medina. These two cities make up the holy land of Islam. Mecca and Medina are considered to be holy because they were important in the life of Muhammad, the man who spread the religion of Islam.

Muhammad, an Arab, was born in the oasis town of Mecca in A.D. 570. He taught that people should submit to the will of Allah, or God. On the next page, you can read an example of Muhammad's teachings, which are written in Islam's holy book, called the **Koran**.

When a [courteous] greeting
is offered you, meet it
with a greeting still more
Courteous, [at least]
Of equal courtesy.
Allah takes careful account
Of all things.

Because of his beliefs, Muhammad was forced to move to Medina. From there his followers quickly spread the religion of Islam from Arabia westward across North Africa and into Spain. Islam also spread eastward as far as the Philippines.

The Hajj Muslims are required to visit Mecca once during their lifetime if they can afford it. This trip is called the **hajj** (haj), or pilgrimage. A pilgrimage is a journey made for religious purposes.

Each year during Ramadan, the holiest month of the year in Islam, thousands of Muslims from across the world make the hajj. They travel by train, boat, and plane to the holy city of Mecca. Many first arrive at Jidda, a port city located to the west of Mecca.

Abdul, a teenager who lives in Oman, recently made the hajj with his family. They were not able to afford the plane trip to Mecca, so they made the journey by *dhow* (dou). A dhow is an Arab sailboat that has a distinctive triangular sail.

Abdul and his family left the harbor at Muscat and then followed the coast of the Arabian Peninsula as they sailed southwest toward the Gulf of Aden. Then they sailed northward through the Red Sea until they reached the port of Jidda. There the family joined thousands of other Muslims who were beginning the 46-mile (74-km) walk over the Hejaz Mountains to Mecca.

Finally reaching Mecca, Abdul and his family and the other Muslim pilgrims entered the central mosque in the city. Once inside the mosque, they went to the courtyard. Here they circled seven times

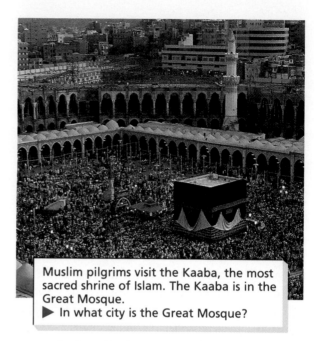

Muslim pilgrims visit the Kaaba, the most sacred shrine of Islam. The Kaaba is in the Great Mosque.
▶ In what city is the Great Mosque?

around the Kaaba (KAH buh), the sacred shrine of Islam.

While in Mecca, Abdul's family stayed at a modern hotel. The hotel and all the other sights and sounds of Mecca were new and exciting to Abdul. It was the first time he had traveled away from Masqat. He told himself that he would always remember the experience.

LESSON 4

Review

REVIEWING MAIN IDEAS

A. How have Saudi Arabia's cities changed because of oil?
B. Why are the small Persian Gulf states important to the world today?
C. How are Oman and Yemen different from the Persian Gulf states?
D. Why is Saudi Arabia considered to be the holy land of Islam?

SKILLS CHECK

THINKING SKILL

Turn to the bar graph of world petroleum producers on page 737. Which leading oil-producing countries are not in the Middle East?

20 REVIEW

REVIEWING TERMS

On a separate sheet of paper, write the letter of the term that best matches each numbered statement.

a. ethnocentrism
b. oasis
c. Fertile Crescent
d. strait
e. qanat
f. theocracy
g. monotheism
h. Bedouins
i. Koran
j. hajj

1. The belief that there is only one God
2. A place in the desert that has enough water for plants and trees to grow
3. A nation ruled according to religious laws instead of laws that have been passed by the people
4. A system of underground tunnels that is used in the Middle East to supply water to dry areas
5. A nomadic group of people who live on the Arabian Peninsula
6. The pilgrimage to Mecca that every Muslim is required to try to make at least once during his or her lifetime
7. A way of looking at the world and making judgments about it based only on your own cultural background and your own experience
8. Islam's holy book that contains the teachings of Muhammad
9. A long, flat, fertile area north of the Persian Gulf that includes the countries of Iraq, Syria, Lebanon, Israel, and Jordan
10. A narrow waterway that connects two larger bodies of water

REVIEWING THE FACTS

On a separate sheet of paper, answer the following questions in complete sentences.

1. Why is the Suez Canal in a strategic location?
2. Why is it incorrect to refer to the Middle East as the "Arab World"?
3. How did the Ottoman Empire come to an end?
4. What natural resource supports most of Iran's economy?
5. How did the revolutionary government of the Ayatollah Khomeini show its hostility toward the United States?
6. How does Syria differ from most other Middle Eastern countries?
7. Why has Israel fought many wars with the neighboring Arab countries?
8. What Arab country has made peace with Israel?
9. What is OPEC?
10. What impact did the Persian Gulf War have on the environment and economy of the Arabian Peninsula?

WRITING ABOUT ECONOMICS

Imagine that OPEC has decided to cut back the amount of oil produced by its members and wants to substantially raise the selling price of its oil. Write several paragraphs explaining how the economies of many nations around the world might be affected by these decisions.

THINKING CRITICALLY

On a separate sheet of paper, answer the following questions in complete sentences.

1. Where does the water come from that supplies an oasis?
2. Why would a visitor find churches, mosques, and temples in Jerusalem?
3. What reasons can you give to defend the statement that a nation should be ruled by laws passed by the people and not by religious laws?
4. What effect, do you think, did losing the West Bank have on Jordan's economy?
5. Why, do you think, did the nations of the Persian Gulf and other leading oil-producing nations join together to form OPEC?

SUMMARIZING THE CHAPTER

On a separate sheet of paper, draw a graphic organizer like the one shown here. Copy the information from this graphic organizer to the one you have drawn. Under the main idea for each lesson, write three statements that you think support the main idea.

CHAPTER THEME

The Middle East is a region that is experiencing rapid change, mainly because of oil and ethnic or religious conflict.

Lesson 1 The Middle East has played an important role in ancient and modern history.

1. _____
2. _____
3. _____

Lesson 2 Turkey is different from Iran and Afghanistan in several ways.

1. _____
2. _____
3. _____

Lesson 3 There is conflict between Israel and the Arab countries of the Middle East.

1. _____
2. _____
3. _____

Lesson 4 Many of the countries on the Arabian Peninsula have benefited from oil.

1. _____
2. _____
3. _____

COOPERATIVE LEARNING

In this unit you learned about important places in Japan, China, Southeast Asia, India, and the Middle East. Sometimes people and places are the basis for works of literature, such as plays. How could you write a play about a certain event in a country?

PROJECT

Work with a group of classmates to plan, write, and perform a play about a real place from Unit 5. For example, a play could be written about Japan's economic miracle. The setting could be in a corporation. A group of Japanese sales people are talking about a new kind of product they could invent. The plot could tell how their invention made the corporation successful.

Meet as a group and look through the chapters to select a subject for your play. Be sure to discuss each other's ideas politely and try to stay on the job.

Once you have chosen the subject for your play, discuss specific ideas for the characters, setting, and plot. Take notes to record each group member's ideas.

Once you have planned your play, the group is ready to begin writing. Divide the play's characters among the group members. Each group member should suggest what lines his or her assigned character or characters might say. You may want to have a narrator introduce and explain the action of the play. Decide together which group member will play each role.

PRESENTATION AND REVIEW

Rehearse your play. When you are ready, present your play in front of your classmates.

Meet again with your group to evaluate your project. How well did your group members work together? How could your play have been improved?

REMEMBER TO:
- Give your ideas.
- Listen to others' ideas.
- Plan your work with the group.
- Present your project.
- Discuss how your group worked.

SKILLBUILDER

HYPOTHESIZING FROM TABLES AND GRAPHS

WHY DO I NEED THIS SKILL?

Hypothesizing is an intellectual skill used in explaining facts or solving problems. The skill involves forming a *hypothesis*, a possible explanation or solution. A hypothesis is an "educated guess" based on information that is already available. When you form hypotheses, you are interpreting information and proposing conclusions that may be drawn from that information. One way to hypothesize is to use information presented in tables and graphs.

LEARNING THE SKILL

The table and pie graph on these pages present facts about Japan's imports and ex-

ports in one year. The table lists different categories of products and the amount of import and export trade for each category. For example, the table tells you that Japan imported $19,432,000,000 worth of food and food product, and exported $1,567,000,000 worth. The last two columns of the table give percentages of the total import and export dollars for each category. Here you can see that food and food products made up 15 percent of Japan's total import dollars and 1 percent of its total export dollars.

The pie graph on the next page presents the same import percentages presented in the table. But the pie graph is easier to understand at a glance because it gives you proportions in pictures.

The information in the table and graph can be used to make various hypotheses

JAPAN'S IMPORTS AND EXPORTS

Products	Imports (in millions of dollars)	Exports (in millions of dollars)	Percentage of total import dollars	Percentage of total export dollars
Food and food products	19,432	1,567	15	1
Fuels and raw materials	54,196	2,002	43	1
Chemicals	9,733	9,484	8	4
Machinery and transportation equipment	13,283	133,326	10	62
Other manufactured goods	21,023	60,725	17	29
Miscellaneous products	8,742	2,048	7	1
Total	126,409	209,152	100	100

JAPAN'S IMPORTS

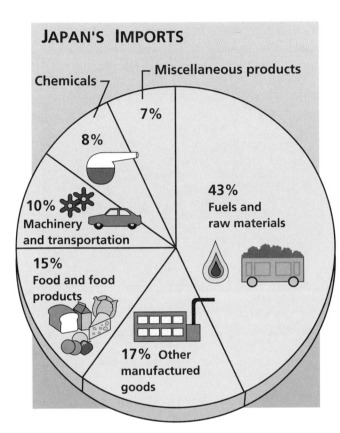

- **Miscellaneous products** 7%
- **Chemicals** 8%
- **Machinery and transportation** 10%
- **Food and food products** 15%
- **Other manufactured goods** 17%
- **Fuels and raw materials** 43%

Japan uses imported fuels and raw materials in its manufacturing industries.

PRACTICING THE SKILL

Use the table and graph in this Skillbuilder to answer the following questions.

1. What product category accounts for the greatest percentage of Japanese trade, either import or export?
2. Based on what you already know about Japan, what specific types of products do you think are included in the category called "Machinery and transportation equipment"?
3. What other types of products do you think are included in the category "Other manufactured goods"?
4. For which product category is there the greatest difference between the percentage of total import dollars and the percentage of total export dollars?
5. In what kinds of jobs do you think many people in Japan are employed?

about Japan's economy. For example, the information provided shows that Japan imported more than $54 billion in fuels and raw materials but exported only about $2 billion. Based on this information, you might hypothesize that Japan has limited amounts of fuels and raw materials and must rely on imported supplies.

How do you think Japan used many of the fuels and raw materials that it imported? You could look at the data for the country's exports to get an idea. You can see that Japan exported almost $200 billion in machinery, transportation equipment, and other manufactured goods. You might hypothesize that

APPLYING THE SKILL

As you continue reading your geography textbook, form hypotheses by using information in tables, graphs, photographs, maps, and other visuals. Use all the related information in the chapters to see if your hypotheses are correct and you have drawn the right conclusions. You can also use the hypothesizing skill in other subject areas—such as in science, in which hypothesizing is an important part of the scientific method.

USING THE *READERS' GUIDE TO PERIODICAL LITERATURE*

WHY DO I NEED THIS SKILL?

It is necessary to learn how to gather information by using many sources. You may have questions that are not answered in your social studies book. If you know how to do additional research, you can find the information you need to answer those questions.

One important source of information is magazines, which are also called *periodicals*. A valuable reference tool to help you find information in magazines is the *Readers' Guide to Periodical Literature*. The *Readers' Guide* is an index that will tell you the names of magazines in which articles on specific topics are located. Knowing how to use the *Readers' Guide* is an important research skill, for it will allow you to use magazines as sources of information for reports and for answering questions.

LEARNING THE SKILL

The *Readers' Guide* lists articles that are found in about 185 popular magazines. It is published each year in a large volume and in smaller supplements for recent months. The *Readers' Guide* lists entries by authors and by subjects. Usually, you will be looking for information on a specific topic, so this Skillbuilder will focus on finding subject entries in the *Readers' Guide.*

Imagine that your teacher has asked everyone in your class to prepare an oral report about current events in an Asian country. You have selected Japan. You have decided to begin your research with the 1987 *Readers' Guide to Periodical Literature*. You can then work forward by looking in more recent volumes. When you locate the entry *Japan*, you will find a long list that looks like this.

> **Japan**
>   *See also*
>   Airports—Japan
>   Architecture—Japan
>   Baseball, Professional—Japan
>   Billionaires—Japan
>   Opera—Japan
>   Space research—Japan
>   Television advertising—Japan
>   Tokyo—Japan
>   Volcano—Japan

These are just a few of the many cross-references for *Japan*.

Cross-references give you other entries in the *Readers' Guide* where you will find information about Japan. For example, if you wanted to learn about professional baseball in Japan, you would look under *Baseball, Professional—Japan*.

Following the cross-references is a long list of articles on Japan. However, you have now become interested in Japan's largest city, Tokyo. You would use the cross-reference information and find the entry for *Tokyo—Japan*. There you will find entries such as the following.

> East meets West, postmodern style [traveling exhibit entitled Tokyo: form and spirit]. R. Silberman, il *Art Am* 75:13–15+ My '87

To conserve space in the *Readers' Guide*, you will notice that the editors use various abbreviations for things such as magazine titles (*Art Am = Art in America*), dates (My '87 = May 1987), and other information (*il* = illustrated). Sometimes the title does not explain what an article is about, so the editors add information in brackets. For example, in the entry above we learn that the article is about a traveling art exhibit.

PRACTICING THE SKILL

On a sheet of paper, answer these questions about the following *Readers' Guide* entries on Japan.

Adventures in travel. T. Assenza. il
  Car Driv 33:27 N '87
How to win over a Japanese boss.
  J. B. Copeland. il *Newsweek* 109:
  46–8 F 2 '87
Japan Air Lines begins four-year
  expansion plan. *Aviat Week Space
  Technol* 126:34 Mr 2 '87
Strangers in a strange land (Miami),
  four Japanese baseball players find
  it tough getting to first base [playing
  for the Marlines in the minor
  leagues]. P. Jordan. il *People Wkly*
  28:46–8 Jl 13 '87

1. What article would give you information about the Japanese airline industry?
2. How many pages long is the article by P. Jordan?
3. Which articles have illustrations?

4. Where could you go to learn something about Japanese baseball players?
5. In what volume of *Car and Driver* will you find the article by T. Assenza?
6. Who wrote the article in *Newsweek*?
7. When was the *People Weekly* article published?

APPLYING THE SKILL

Use the *Readers' Guide* when you need to research any topic. Important information can be found in magazines. By using the articles referenced in the main entries and by looking under cross-references, you should be able to find the information you need.

You can also use the *Readers' Guide* to locate information on events that happened in the distant past. For example, if you want to find out about the 1972 Winter Olympic Games that were held in Sapporo, Japan, you could look in the 1972 *Readers' Guide* under *Olympic Games* to find where articles on that subject appeared. Your public library keeps back issues of many of the periodicals listed in the *Readers' Guide*, and the librarian will help you locate the articles you need.

CONNECTIONS

What are some of the ways in which a rich country can help poor countries?

TERMS

savanna

FOCUS

What are Africa's main geographic regions?

Peace Corps is Widening Its Role in Africa
By James Brooke

NDJAMENA, Chad—At 24, Lori Leonard is younger than most of her students at Chad University.

But discipline is rarely a problem. After losing school years to civil war and Libyan invasion, Chadians are serious students. They are also delighted that an American has come all the way from La Crescent, Minn., to teach them English.

Miss Leonard is a volunteer with the Peace Corps, an enduring aid program that . . . is poised for a new spurt of growth.

A. The United States and Africa

The Peace Corps is a United States-sponsored group of volunteers who work in other countries. These volunteers—often young people—teach new skills to people in developing countries. These skills include using new farming methods, building fisheries, using forests wisely, and developing water supplies.

The countries of Africa have the largest number of Peace Corps volunteers. Many African countries are struggling to develop their economies and need the help of groups like the Peace Corps.

B. A Huge Continent

Over 50 countries are found in Africa. With about 12 million square miles (31 million sq km) of total area, Africa is the world's second largest continent. It is so big that all the United States except Hawaii and Alaska would fit into Africa nearly four times.

Almost all of this huge continent is a vast plateau, high above sea level. Only a few small areas could be called coastal plains. Near the coastline of the continent, the plateau drops off to the narrow coastal plains. This sharp drop in elevation is marked around the edge of the African continent by a series of mountain ranges and cliffs.

The coastline of Africa is fairly smooth, with few natural indentations that would make good harbors. Just a few

Much of Africa is located on a plateau that is 1,000 feet (300 m) above sea level. Deserts stretch across the northern part of the continent. Many large lakes are found in the eastern region.
▶ What is the average elevation along the coasts of Africa?

AFRICA: PHYSICAL

Elevations

Feet	Meters
10,000	3,000
5,000	1,500
2,000	600
1,000	300
0	0

Land below sea level

● Cities

▲ Mountain peaks

0   400   miles
0   400   kilometers

EUROPE

ASIA

ATLANTIC OCEAN

Mediterranean Sea

Strait of Gibraltar

Casablanca

ATLAS MOUNTAINS

Tripoli

Gulf of Sidra

Cairo

S A H A R A

Red Sea

TIBESTI MASSIF

Senegal River

Niger

Lake Chad

Benue

Khartoum

Blue Nile

Gulf of Aden

ETHIOPIAN HIGHLANDS

Shebele

Gulf of Guinea

Ubangi River

ZAIRE BASIN

Zaire River

Lake Albert

White Nile

Equator

Kampala

Mt. Kenya 17,058 ft (5,199 m)

0°

Lake Victoria

GREAT RIFT VALLEY

Kinshasa

Mt. Kilimanjaro 19,340 ft (5,895 m)

Lake Tanganyika

ATLANTIC OCEAN

Lake Malawi

10° S

Zambezi

Mozambique Channel

NAMIB DESERT

KALAHARI DESERT

20° S

Tropic - - - of - - - Capricorn

Vaal River

Orange River

DRAKENSBERG MTHS.

INDIAN OCEAN

30° S

Cape of Good Hope

Cape Town

Cape Agulhas

Kalahari Desert

10° W   0°   10° E   20° E   30° E   40° E   50° E miles upstream on Africa's major rivers, there are waterfalls and rapids. These natural barriers prevented early explorers and traders from traveling to the continent's interior. Because of this lack of exploration, the interior of Africa remained virtually unknown to outsiders for many years. As recently as the mid-1800s, maps of Africa showed large blank spaces in the interior.

C. Africa's Climates

Most people know that the Equator passes through Africa, and many automatically associate the region with hot, humid conditions and dense jungle vegetation. Yet in some places just a few miles from the Equator, there are mountains that are covered with snow year-round. There are some areas of tropical forests along the Gulf of Guinea.

But most of the continent is covered by extensive grasslands. Scattered around the grassland regions are clumps of trees and bushes. These areas of tall natural grasslands found in tropical regions are called **savannas.** These savanna regions cover about two fifths of Africa.

Much of Africa's population lives in the area north of the Equator, where the savanna is like the steppes of the Soviet Union. In recent years, this region has been hit by many droughts.

Across the northern part of the continent, and extending almost 4,000 miles (6,436 km) from the Atlantic Ocean to the Red Sea, is the world's largest desert—the Sahara. Desert climates extend southward along the Red Sea and down the eastern coast of the continent as far as the country of Kenya.

The highest mountain in Africa is Mount Kilamanjaro. Find its elevation on the map on page 523. Mount Kenya, at more than 17,000 feet (5,182 m), is right on the Equator and is covered with snow year-round. Two huge lakes, Lake Victoria and Lake Tanganyika, are found to the west of these mountains.

D. Africa's Resources

Unlike many mountains in other places, the mountains in Africa do not hold mineral resources. But a huge crescent-shaped region that extends from Central Africa to Southern Africa is rich in mineral resources, such as copper, coal, iron ore, gold, and diamonds.

Africa's other resources include tropical plantation products, such as cacao, palm oil, rubber, coffee, and tea. Most of these come from a region that extends from the rain forests of West Africa across to the highlands of East Africa.

Review

REVIEWING MAIN IDEAS

A. How do Peace Corps volunteers help people in developing countries?

B. What prohibited the exploration of Africa by Europeans?

C. What vegetation zone covers two fifths of Africa?

D. Where are Africa's mineral resources found?

SKILLS CHECK

MAP SKILL

Look at the map of Africa on the next page. Use the scale on the map to determine how wide Africa is from its farthest western and eastern points.

30° W   20° W

EUROPE

AFRICA: POLITICAL

⊛ National capitals
• Other cities

| 0 | 400 | 800 miles |
| 0 | 400 | 800 kilometers |

40° N

MADEIRA
ISLANDS
(PORTUGAL)

CANARY
ISLANDS
(SPAIN)

Strait of Gibraltar

Mediterranean   Sea

⊛ Algiers   ⊛ Tunis

TUNISIA

⊛ Rabat
• Casablanca

MOROCCO

• Tripoli

Gulf of Sidra

ASIA

Alexandria ⊛⊛ Cairo
        • Giza   ⊛ Cairo

30° N

WESTERN
SAHARA
(MOROCCO)

ALGERIA

LIBYA

EGYPT

Nile River

Red Sea

0° N

MAURITANIA

⊛ Nouakchott

MALI

Niger

NIGER

Niamey ⊛

CHAD

Lake
Chad

• N'Djamena

Khartoum •

SUDAN

ERITREA
⊛ Asmara

DJIBOUTI
• Djibouti

Gulf of Aden

Dakar ⊛
SENEGAL
⊛ Banjul

GAMBIA

Bamako •

⊛ Ouagadougou

SOMALIA

⊛ Mogadishu

GUINEA-BISSAU

Bissau ⊛ GUINEA

⊛ Conakry

BURKINA FASO

BENIN
TOGO

NIGERIA

• Abuja ⊛

Addis Ababa •

ETHIOPIA

SIERRA
Freetown ⊛ LEONE

IVORY
COAST

GHANA

Lomé ⊛
Accra ⊛

• Ibadan
⊛ Lagos
Porto-
Novo

CAMEROON

• Bangui

CENTRAL
AFRICAN
REPUBLIC

• Monrovia ⊛

LIBERIA

• Abidjan

Niger
River

Malabo ⊛

⊛ Yaoundé

UGANDA

KENYA

EQUATORIAL GUINEA

• Douala

SÃO TOMÉ E PRÍNCIPE

⊛ São Tomé

Equator

⊛ Libreville

GABON

CONGO

Zaire   River

⊛ Kampala

• Nairobi ⊛

RWANDA
Kigali ⊛

Lake
Victoria

0°

Brazzaville ⊛

ZAIRE

Bujumbura ⊛ BURUNDI

ATLANTIC

Cabinda
(Angola)

Kinshasa ⊛

TANZANIA

ZANZIBAR

Dar es Salaam •

10° S

OCEAN

• Luanda ⊛

ANGOLA

COMOROS
⊛ Moroni •

MAYOTTE
ISLAND
(FRANCE)

MALAWI

ZAMBIA

Lilongwe ⊛

Lusaka ⊛

River

Harare •

MOZAMBIQUE

Zambezi

NAMIBIA

ZIMBABWE

Antananarivo •

MADAGASCAR

20° S

• Windhoek ⊛

BOTSWANA

Mozambique   Channel

Walvis Bay
(South
Africa)

Gaborone •

Pretoria •

Maputo ⊛
• Mbabane

INDIAN

Tropic of Capricorn

SOUTH AFRICA

Maseru •

SWAZILAND

30° S

There are 53 independent countries on
the continent of Africa.
▶ Name the countries in Africa through
which the Equator passes.

LESOTHO

• Durban

OCEAN

• Cape Town

	FLAG AND PRINCIPAL LANGUAGE(S)	POPULATION AND LANDMASS	PRINCIPAL PRODUCTS EXPORT	IMPORT

ALGERIA

Algiers

Arabic, French, Berber

POPULATION
24,000,000
26 per sq mi/10 per sq km

LANDMASS
919,591 sq mi/2,381,741 sq km

Crude Oil

Food

ANGOLA

★Luanda

Portuguese, Bantu

POPULATION
8,500,000
18 per sq mi/7 per sq km

LANDMASS
481,351 sq mi/1,246,699 sq km

Crude Oil

Machinery

BENIN

Porto-Novo
★

French

POPULATION
4,700,000
108 per sq mi/40 per sq km

LANDMASS
43,483 sq mi/116,621 sq km

Footwear

Textiles

BOTSWANA

Gaborone
★

English, Setswana

POPULATION
1,200,000
5 per sq mi/2 per sq km

LANDMASS
219,916 sq mi/569,582 sq km

Diamonds

Food

BURKINA FASO

★
Ouagadougou

French, Sudanic languages

POPULATION
8,700,000
82 per sq mi/32 per sq km

LANDMASS
105,869 sq mi/274,201 sq km

Cotton

Food

BURUNDI
Bujumbura
★

French, Kirundi

POPULATION
5,500,000
511 per sq mi/197 per sq km

LANDMASS
10,759 sq mi/27,866 sq km

Coffee

Petroleum

CAMEROON

★Yaoundé

French, Ewondo, English, Donala

POPULATION
10,800,000
59 per sq mi/23 per sq km

LANDMASS
183,591 sq mi/475,501 sq km

Crude Oil

Machinery

CAPE VERDE ISLANDS

★Praia

Portuguese

POPULATION
400,000
257 per sq mi/99 per sq km

LANDMASS
1,557 sq mi/4,033 sq km

Fish

Food

CENTRAL AFRICAN REPUBLIC
Bangui
★

French, Sango

POPULATION
2,800,000
12 per sq mi/4 per sq km

LANDMASS
240,533 sq mi/622,980 sq km

Diamonds

Vehicles

	FLAG AND PRINCIPAL LANGUAGE(S)	POPULATION AND LANDMASS	PRINCIPAL PRODUCTS EXPORT	IMPORT
CHAD N'Djamena	French, Massa, Sara, Arabic, Kanembou	**POPULATION** 4,900,000 10 per sq mi/4 per sq km **LANDMASS** 495,752 sq mi/1,283,998 sq km	Cotton	Machinery
COMOROS ★Moroni	French, Arabic, Swahili	**POPULATION** 400,000 463 per sq mi/179 per sq km **LANDMASS** 863 sq mi/2,235 sq km	Cloves	Rice
CONGO Brazzaville	French, Lingala, Kokongo	**POPULATION** 2,200,000 17 per sq mi/6 per sq km **LANDMASS** 132,012 sq mi/342,000 sq km	Crude Oil	Food
DJIBOUTI Djibouti	Arabic, French, Afar, Somali	**POPULATION** 400,000 45 per sq mi/17 per sq km **LANDMASS** 8,800 sq mi/22,999 sq km	Livestock	Food
EGYPT Cairo	Arabic	**POPULATION** 52,000,000 134 per sq mi/52 per sq km **LANDMASS** 386,660 sq mi/1,001,449 sq km	Crude Oil	Food
EQUATORIAL GUINEA ★Malabo	Spanish, Fang, Bubi	**POPULATION** 300,000 28 per sq mi/11 per sq km **LANDMASS** 10,825 sq mi/28,037 sq km	Cocoa	Food
ETHIOPIA [1] Addis Ababa	Amharic, Galligna, Tigrigna	**POPULATION** 49,800,000 106 per sq mi/41 per sq km **LANDMASS** 471,775 sq mi/1,221,897 sq km	Coffee	Crude Oil
GABON ★Libreville	French, Bantu	**POPULATION** 1,100,000 11 per sq mi/4 per sq km **LANDMASS** 103,347 sq mi/267,667 sq km	Crude Oil	Machinery
GAMBIA ★Banjul	English, native languages	**POPULATION** 800,000 200 per sq mi/77 per sq km **LANDMASS** 4,003 sq mi/10,368 sq km	Groundnuts	Food

[1] Eritrea declared itself free from Ethiopia and an independent nation in 1993. See political map of Africa on page 698.

AFRICA

	FLAG AND PRINCIPAL LANGUAGE(S)	POPULATION AND LANDMASS	PRINCIPAL PRODUCTS EXPORT	IMPORT
GHANA Accra 	 English, Twi, Fanti, Ga, Ewé, Dagbani	**POPULATION** 14,600,000 159 per sq mi/61 per sq km **LANDMASS** 92,100 sq mi/238,539 sq km	Cocoa	Crude Oil
GUINEA Conakry 	 French, Malinké, Susu, Fulani	**POPULATION** 7,100,000 75 per sq mi/29 per sq km **LANDMASS** 94,925 sq mi/245,856 sq km	Bauxite	Machinery
GUINEA-BISSAU Bissau 	 Portuguese, Crioulo	**POPULATION** 1,000,000 72 per sq mi/28 per sq km **LANDMASS** 13,948 sq mi/36,125 sq km	Groundnuts	Food
IVORY COAST Abidjan	 French	**POPULATION** 12,100,000 97 per sq mi/38 per sq km **LANDMASS** 124,503 sq mi/322,463 sq km	Coffee	Food
KENYA Nairobi	 Swahili, English, Kikuyu	**POPULATION** 24,100,000 107 per sq mi/41 per sq km **LANDMASS** 224,960 sq mi/582,646 sq km	Coffee	Crude Oil
LESOTHO Maseru 	 English, Sesotho	**POPULATION** 1,700,000 145 per sq mi/56 per sq km **LANDMASS** 11,716 sq mi/30,344 sq km	Diamonds	Food
LIBERIA Monrovia 	 English, tribal dialects	**POPULATION** 2,500,000 58 per sq mi/22 per sq km **LANDMASS** 43,000 sq mi/111,370 sq km	Iron Ore	Food
LIBYA Tripoli 	 Arabic	**POPULATION** 4,100,000 6 per sq mi/2 per sq km **LANDMASS** 679,358 sq mi/1,759,537 sq km	Crude Oil	Machinery
MADAGASCAR Antananarivo 	 Malagasy, French	**POPULATION** 11,600,000 51 per sq mi/20 per sq km **LANDMASS** 226,657 sq mi/587,042 sq km	Spices	Crude Oil

TABLE OF COUNTRIES

	FLAG AND PRINCIPAL LANGUAGE(S)	POPULATION AND LANDMASS	PRINCIPAL PRODUCTS EXPORT	IMPORT

▶ MALAWI

Lilongwe

Chichewa, English, Nyanja, Yao

POPULATION
8,700,000
193 per sq mi/74 per sq km

LANDMASS
45,193 sq mi/117,050 sq km

 Tobacco

 Chemicals

▶ MALI

★Bamako

French

POPULATION
8,900,000
19 per sq mi/7 per sq km

LANDMASS
478,652 sq mi/1,239,709 sq km

 Cotton

 Machinery

▶ MAURITANIA

Nouakchott
★

French, Arabic, Tucolor

POPULATION
2,000,000
5 per sq mi/2 per sq km

LANDMASS
397,955 sq mi/1,030,703 sq km

 Iron Ore

 Food

▶ MAURITIUS

Port Louis

English

POPULATION
1,100,000
1,528 per sq mi/590 per sq km

LANDMASS
720 sq mi/1,865 sq km

 Sugar

 Food

▶ MOROCCO

★Rabat

Arabic, Berber, French, Spanish

POPULATION
25,600,000
148 per sq mi/57 per sq km

LANDMASS
172,413 sq mi/446,550 sq km

  Phosphates

  Crude Oil

▶ MOZAMBIQUE

Maputo

Portuguese, Bantu, English

POPULATION
15,200,000
51 per sq mi/20 per sq km

LANDMASS
297,846 sq mi/771,421 sq km

  Fish

Food

▶ NAMIBIA

Windhoek
★

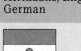
Afrikaans, English, German

POPULATION
1,000,000
3 per sq mi/1 per sq km

LANDMASS
317,887 sq mi/823,327 sq km

  Diamonds

N/A

▶ NIGER

★Niamey

French, Fulani

POPULATION
7,400,000
16 per sq mi/6 per sq km

LANDMASS
459,073 sq mi/1,188,999 sq km

  Uranium

 Cereals

▶ NIGERIA

★
Abuja

English, Hausa, Yoruba, Ibo

POPULATION
115,300,000
323 per sq mi/125 per sq km

LANDMASS
356,669 sq mi/923,773 sq km

 Crude Oil

 Machinery

AFRICA

	FLAG AND PRINCIPAL LANGUAGE(S)	POPULATION AND LANDMASS	PRINCIPAL PRODUCTS EXPORT	IMPORT
RWANDA Kigali ★	French, Kinyarwanda	**POPULATION** 7,000,000 688 per sq mi/266 per sq km **LANDMASS** 10,169 sq mi/26,338 sq km	Coffee	Machinery
SÃO TOMÉ E PRÍNCIPE São Tomé ★	Portuguese	**POPULATION** 100,000 269 per sq mi/104 per sq km **LANDMASS** 372 sq mi/963 sq km	Cocoa	Food
SENEGAL ★Dakar	French, Wolof, Serer	**POPULATION** 7,200,000 95 per sq mi/37 per sq km **LANDMASS** 76,124 sq mi/197,161 sq km	Petroleum	Food
SEYCHELLES ★Victoria	English, French, Creole	**POPULATION** 100,000 571 per sq mi/221 per sq km **LANDMASS** 175 sq mi/453 sq km	Petroleum	Petroleum
SIERRA LEONE ★Freetown	English, Krio	**POPULATION** 4,100,000 148 per sq mi/57 per sq km **LANDMASS** 27,699 sq mi/71,740 sq km	Diamonds	Crude Oil
SOMALIA Mogadishu ★	Somali, Arabic, English	**POPULATION** 8,200,000 33 per sq mi/13 per sq km **LANDMASS** 246,154 sq mi/637,539 sq km	Livestock	Machinery
SOUTH AFRICA Pretoria ★	Afrikaans, English, Bantu	**POPULATION** 38,500,000 82 per sq mi/32 per sq km **LANDMASS** 471,445 sq mi/1,221,043 sq km	Gold	Machinery
SUDAN ★ Khartoum	Arabic, English, tribal dialects	**POPULATION** 24,500,000 25 per sq mi/10 per sq km **LANDMASS** 967,500 sq mi/2,505,825 sq km	Cotton	Food
SWAZILAND Mbabane ★	English, Siswati	**POPULATION** 681,000 102 per sq mi/36 per sq km **LANDMASS** 6,705 sq mi/17,366 sq km	Sugar	Machinery

	FLAG AND PRINCIPAL LANGUAGE(S)	POPULATION AND LANDMASS	PRINCIPAL PRODUCTS EXPORT	IMPORT

TANZANIA

Dar es Salaam

English, Swahili, Bantu, Arabic

POPULATION
26,300,000
72 per sq mi/28 per sq km

LANDMASS
364,943 sq mi/945,202 sq km

 Coffee

 Crude Oil

TOGO

Lomé

French, Ewé, Mina, Kabyé, Cotocoli

POPULATION
3,400,000
156 per sq mi/60 per sq km

LANDMASS
21,853 sq mi/56,599 sq km

 Phosphates

 Food

TUNISIA
Tunis

Arabic, French

POPULATION
7,900,000
125 per sq mi/48 per sq km

LANDMASS
63,170 sq mi/163,610 sq km

 Crude Oil

 Machinery

UGANDA

Kampala

English, Swahili, Luganda, Ateso, Luo

POPULATION
17,000,000
187 per sq mi/72 per sq km

LANDMASS
91,134 sq mi/236,037 sq km

 Coffee

 Machinery

ZAIRE

★Kinshasa

French, Ishiluba, Kikongo, Lingala

POPULATION
34,900,000
39 per sq mi/15 per sq km

LANDMASS
905,063 sq mi/2,344,113 sq km

Copper

 Machinery

ZAMBIA

Lusaka

English, Bantu

POPULATION
8,100,000
28 per sq mi/11 per sq km

LANDMASS
290,585 sq mi/752,615 sq km

 Copper

 Machinery

ZIMBABWE

Harare

English, Chishona, Sindebele

POPULATION
10,100,000
67 per sq mi/26 per sq km

LANDMASS
150,820 sq mi/390,624 sq km

 Tobacco

 Machinery

THE COUNTRIES OF NORTH AFRICA

North Africa: A Desert Region

CONNECTIONS

The Sahara Desert covers much of North Africa. Imagine that you are in the Sahara. What do you see around you? What is it like to be in the desert?

TERMS

erg, desert pavement, hammada, diffusion

FOCUS

What are the differences between the three main physical features of North Africa?

A. North Africa's Physical Features

The Mystery Plane During the Second World War, airplanes called B-24's flew from North Africa to Italy to drop bombs on enemy positions there. In 1943, one of these B-24 bombers, named the *Lady Be Good* by its crew, took off from Benghazi, Libya. After many hours, when all the other airplanes had returned, the *Lady Be Good* was missing. Everyone thought that it had probably crashed in the Mediterranean Sea.

Sixteen years later an exploration team was searching for new oil fields in remote areas of southern Libya. Unexpectedly they came upon the *Lady Be Good*.

The *Lady Be Good* had crash-landed on a giant sea of sand, 450 miles (724 km) south of Benghazi. Canteens of water and some food were found in the plane, and the radio still worked! However, there was no sign of the eight crew members.

About 75 miles (121 km) north of the crash site, the skeletons of five of the crew were found. With the skeletons was a diary that told the crew's story.

The crew had parachuted out of the plane when it ran out of fuel. They started walking north, mistakenly thinking they were close to the Mediterranean Sea. The men traveled only at night and rested during the 130°F (54°C) days beneath shelters made out of their parachutes. They shouldn't have lasted more than three or four days in the harsh desert. But they rationed their tiny water supply and trekked on for eight days, through the Sahara.

The five men whose bones were found had decided to stop. The three strongest men pushed on northward in search of help. Entries in the diary during the next couple of days ranged from "all want to die" to "have hope for help very soon." The last entry read, "no help yet, very cold nite." The bodies of the three men who went on have never been found.

Three Main Regions As the story of the *Lady Be Good* shows, there are huge empty areas in the Sahara. In the Arabic language the word *Sahara* means "emptiness." It is a vast desert that stretches across the northern end of the continent of Africa. Only the Red Sea separates northeastern Africa from Asia, which begins on the Arabian Peninsula. Together the nations of Egypt, Libya, Tunisia, Algeria, Morocco, and the territory of Western Sahara form the area referred to as North Africa.

There are two other physical regions of North Africa besides the Sahara—the Atlas Mountains and the coastal margin. The Atlas Mountains are found in Morocco, as well as in parts of Algeria, Tunisia, and the Western Sahara. The coastal margin is the land between the Atlas Mountains and the coastline of the Atlantic Ocean and the Mediterranean Sea.

B. The Sahara

Landscape Features It is the Sahara's 3 million square mile area (8 million sq km) that dominates North Africa. This makes the Sahara about the same size as the United States.

Some parts of the Sahara are giant sand seas like the one in which the *Lady*

▶ The Sphinx and the Pyramids at Giza, near Cairo, Egypt.

Be Good crashed. These large areas called **ergs** are what most people picture when they think of a desert—loose sand blown into tall dunes by the wind. But most of the Sahara is made up of **desert pavement** and **hammadas**. Desert pavements are vast plains of gravel and boulders, and hammadas are rocky plateaus. Both surfaces are the result of the erosion of the soil due to the wind.

Located in the center of the Sahara are huge clusters of mountains. These mountains are actually the high peaks of extinct volcanoes. The highest peak in the Ahaggar Mountains, which are found in southern Algeria, has an elevation of 9,852 feet (3,003 m).

Not all of the Sahara is barren land. Oases are found scattered throughout the desert wherever water is available. Oases are the key to living in the Sahara because the oasis land is arable, or suitable for growing crops. The Nile River valley in Egypt is the largest oasis area found in the region of North Africa.

A Wet Sahara? The Sahara has not always been as dry as it is today. It is believed that 10,000 years ago much of the region was once covered with grass, like the Great Plains of the United States. A huge lake once covered much of the central Sahara, and large animals, such as elephants and hippopotamuses, roamed the grasslands. Ancient carvings of elephants and other types of animal life have been discovered throughout the region of the central Sahara.

About 5,000 years ago the climate of the Sahara started becoming drier, which slowly created the desert. Animals could no longer survive there and either died or moved south. Many scientists believe that this process is still continuing. The Sahara is slowly becoming larger as the grasslands to the south of this desert gradually get drier.

C. The Atlas Mountains and the Coastal Margin

Atlas Mountains The second major geographical feature of North Africa is the Atlas Mountains. The Atlas Mountains stretch 1,500 miles (2,414 km) along the northwest coast of the African continent. The name Atlas comes from the ancient

DESERT LANDSCAPE

Sand dune

Oasis

DESERT PAVEMENT

Wadi

ERG

HAMMADA

The landscape of the Sahara is made up of (from left to right) ergs, desert pavements, and hammadas.
▶ What are hammadas?

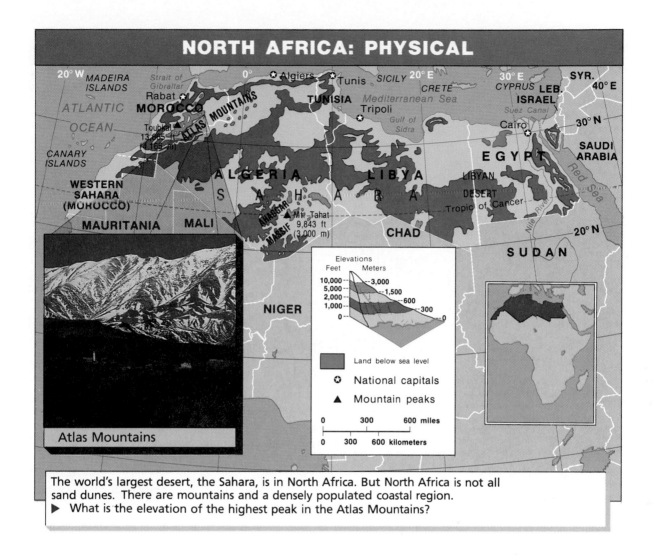

NORTH AFRICA: PHYSICAL

Elevations

Feet	Meters
10,000	3,000
5,000	1,500
2,000	600
1,000	300
0	0

Land below sea level

✪ National capitals

▲ Mountain peaks

0   300   600 miles

0   300   600 kilometers

Atlas Mountains

The world's largest desert, the Sahara, is in North Africa. But North Africa is not all sand dunes. There are mountains and a densely populated coastal region.

▶ What is the elevation of the highest peak in the Atlas Mountains?

Greeks, who told a myth about a giant named Atlas. For his part in a revolt against the gods, Atlas was condemned to hold up the heavens above the earth. To the Greeks, this range of mountains literally rose high enough to support the heavens. Tunisia, Algeria, Morocco, and Western Sahara benefit from the mineral resources of this mountain range.

The Coastal Margin The coastal margin is the region north of the mountains that slopes down to the sea. The height of the Atlas Mountains acts as a barrier to the moist air flowing in off the Atlantic Ocean

and Mediterranean Sea. The air flows up the mountain slopes and cools enough so that clouds form and some rain falls. The valleys in the mountains and the foothills north of the range receive about 30 inches (76 cm) of rain per year. With the exception of the Nile River valley, this area is the best watered and the most populated region of North Africa.

D. North Africa and the Middle East

Much in Common Some geography books put the Middle East and North Africa together in the same chapter because they

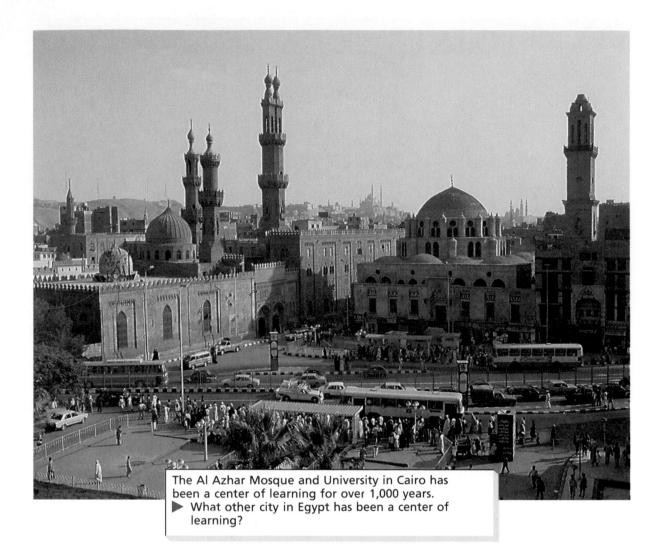

The Al Azhar Mosque and University in Cairo has been a center of learning for over 1,000 years.
▶ What other city in Egypt has been a center of learning?

have much in common. Both the Middle East and North Africa have a desert environment. The people who live in the deserts of both regions depend on oases. The majority of the people of these two regions also have the same religion and culture.

The Berbers, a nomadic people, are the oldest surviving inhabitants of the western part of the Sahara. The biggest change in their way of life came when the Arab people spread into North Africa from the Middle East. The Arabs moved across North Africa early in the eighth century A.D., converting people to Islam. Many of the Berbers were gradually absorbed into the

Arab culture. The mixture of Arabs and Berbers created a new ethnic group—the Moors. Over time the Moors crossed the Strait of Gibraltar into Spain.

Arabs Preserved Knowledge While the Moors made their way across Spain, Europe was in the midst of the Dark Ages. This was a time when the knowledge and learning of the Greek and Roman empires was forgotten in Europe. European civilization collapsed under the weight of barbarian invasions. Greek and Roman discoveries about mathematics, science, geography, and literature were lost to the Europeans.

TABLE OF NUMERALS

Hindu	Arabic	Modern
o	o	0
/	/	1
ว	ح	2
३	३	3
४	ン	4
५	८	5
६	५	6
)	∨	7
८	∧	8
८	9	9
/o	/o	10

The writing of numbers has changed over time as it has passed from culture to culture.
► How would you write the current year with each type of numeral?

However, the Arab world of North Africa carried on that body of knowledge and merged it with their own. The Arabs had inherited this knowledge from the ancient Greek and Roman education centers, such as Alexandria, in Egypt. The Arabs preserved that tradition of learning and took it with them as they spread their people and culture across North Africa.

Diffusion The Moors carried the knowledge with them on into Spain. It was from there in the fifteenth and sixteenth centuries that the Europeans finally began to rediscover the knowledge of the classical Greek and Roman world. This spread of knowledge from one group of people to another is known as **diffusion**.

Look at the table of numerals on this page. Numerals are the written symbols of mathematical numbers. Notice the similarity between the three types of numerals. Which numbers were written the same way?

Some of them appear the same because they passed by diffusion from Hindu to Arab to European society.

The way we write numbers today can be traced back to Hindu and Arabic origins. Arab merchants and armies reached India and learned the Hindu numeral system. The use of this system spread throughout the Arab world. Contact with Europeans brought the Arabic system into Europe. Arabic numerals, like the ones shown in the table, were first used in a European book in the tenth century A.D. Modern numerals first appeared in a book in the year 1202. This book was a translation of an Arabic book on mathematics written four centuries earlier.

The Berbers, Arabs, and other inhabitants of North Africa have learned how to live in the region's desert environment. Just as the religion and culture of North Africans are like those of people in the Middle East, so too is their way of making a living.

LESSON 1

Review

REVIEWING MAIN IDEAS
A. What are the three main regions of North Africa's physical geography?
B. What are the physical features of the Sahara's surface?
C. How do the Atlas Mountains affect the weather of the western part of North Africa?
D. What do North Africa and the Middle East have in common?

SKILLS CHECK
MAP SKILL
During World War II, American warplanes like the *Lady Be Good* flew from North Africa to Italy. Using the map on page 547, calculate the distance from the southern coast of Italy to the following cities: Benghazi, Tripoli, Cairo, and Tunis.

Living and Working in North Africa

CONNECTIONS

How, do you think, is making a living in North Africa similar to or different from making a living in the Middle East?

TERMS

fellahin, bazaar, caravan

FOCUS

How do people in North Africa make a living from their desert environment?

A. Life in a North African Oasis Village

Oasis Farmers Life in North Africa can be studied by looking at three ways in which people have lived through the centuries—as villagers, as city dwellers, and as nomads. About three fourths of the people in North Africa are farmers. As in the Middle East, these farmers are often called **fellahin** (FEL uh heen), which is an Arabic word that means "peasant." Most fellahin live in small villages. In areas such as the Nile River valley, where there is abundant water available, there are many villages located close together. But across the vast Sahara region, a village is located wherever there happens to be enough water for an oasis.

Oasis Economy Some oases of the Sahara are fed by underground springs that supply enough water to support small towns and villages. The value of each oasis is determined by the number of date palm trees it supports. The number of date palm trees surrounding an oasis can reach as high as 300,000. The date palms are the heart of the desert oasis economy because of the variety of goods that can be made from these trees.

Every part of the date palm tree is useful. The fruit is eaten and also used to make sugar. The leaves are used to make baskets and mats, while other parts of the

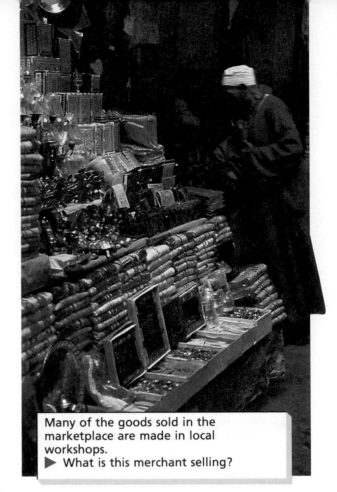

Many of the goods sold in the marketplace are made in local workshops.
▶ What is this merchant selling?

tree are used to make rope, sandals, cooking oil, and even medicine.

In addition to raising date palm trees, oasis farmers grow almonds, apricots, oranges, lemons, pomegranates, and some wheat and millet. Millet is a grass similar to hay and is used for its grain. Farmers may also raise a few goats and chickens, and maybe even a water buffalo or two. The chief foods of the villagers are fruits, nuts, bread, and goat cheese.

B. Life in a North African City

The North African City Most North Africans are Arabs who are followers of Islam. Therefore the Islamic mosque is one of the dominant features of any North African city. The mosque is the center of religious life. The people of the city live in housing quarters, or districts, located around the mosque and **bazaar**. The bazaar is the central marketplace.

The bazaar is almost like a huge shopping center where you can buy almost anything you need or want. Many bazaars are a series of small shops or stands lined up along very narrow streets. You can see all kinds of merchandise for sale—from pots and pans to camel saddles; from leather goods and cloth to chickens; from books and religious jewelry to carpets. In the bazaar the nomads and the people from the villages can buy sugar, coffee, tea, glassware, and many other things. The workshops of the craftspeople who make many of the items for sale are often located behind the merchants' stalls.

C. A Nomadic Way of Life

Nomads The nomads lead a third way of life in North Africa. They move from place to place, searching out watering holes and grasses for their herds of goats, sheep, and camels. Nomads sell and trade wool and animal hides to the city dwellers in return for the things the nomads need. Craftspeople and merchants in the city make finished items from the wool and hides. Wool, for example, is made into carpets that are sold in the bazaar.

Caravans For centuries, goods such as ivory, gold, salt, and even slaves were moved overland across the Sahara to the grasslands located south of the desert. The only way to cross the desert safely was to go by camel **caravan**. A caravan is a group of people traveling together, usually on animals or in vehicles.

Caravan trading routes connected the scattered oasis villages in the region. Expert caravan leaders would guide their train of camels by relying on landmarks in the desert. Camels are sometimes called "ships of the desert" because they move cargo across the desert like ships move across the sea. Camels adapt well to the dry environment. A camel's body can store enough water and food to survive for long periods of time in the desert.

One tribe of nomads that has been involved in the caravan trade lives in the western part of the Sahara. These nomads are the Tuaregs (TWAH regz). The Tuaregs

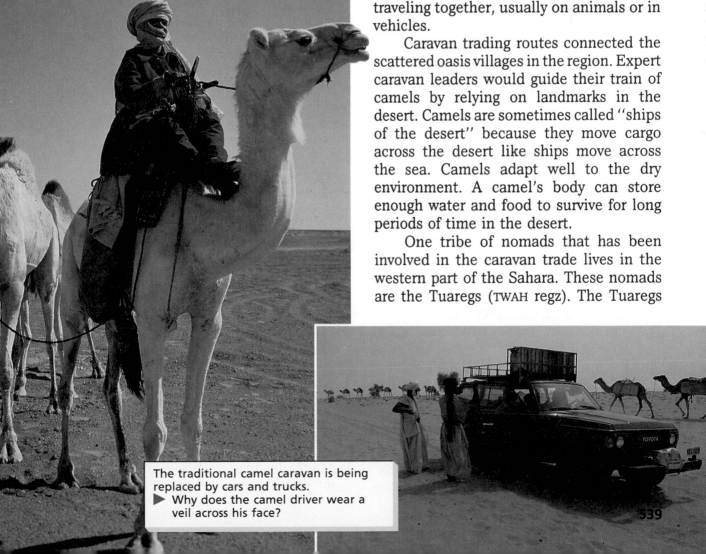

The traditional camel caravan is being replaced by cars and trucks.
► Why does the camel driver wear a veil across his face?

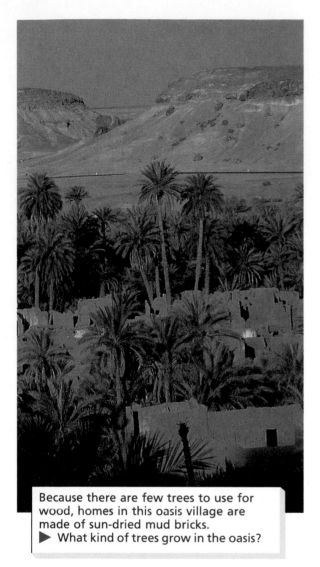

Because there are few trees to use for wood, homes in this oasis village are made of sun-dried mud bricks.
▶ What kind of trees grow in the oasis?

live in tents, often made of leather. In Tuareg societies, all men over the age of 15 or 16 wear a long scarf wrapped around their head as a turban. It also serves as a veil and hides all but their eyes from others. The turban-veil provides cover that keeps the mouth from drying out during hot caravan trips. Also, the dark color of the turbans helps to cut down on the glare of the bright sun. Through the years the turban-veil has become a symbol for the well-dressed Tuareg male.

A Vanishing Way of Life In the past the Tuaregs and other nomads traveled across the Sahara. But the nomadic way of life is

disappearing in the modern world. To continue trading along the old caravan routes, nomads would have to ignore political boundaries. The governments of modern nations, however, do not like people freely crossing their borders. Today most of the trade is carried on by sea. Also, roads for cars and trucks now cross the desert, replacing the need for caravans. Therefore, many nomads have moved to urban areas to find work.

Three Ways of Life North Africa's three ways of life are distinctively different, yet they are closely interrelated. Villagers are mostly peasant farmers who raise food crops. Wool and hides are produced by the nomads. For their part, the city dwellers collect and process the crops and other raw materials, and in turn sell certain necessary items to the villagers and the nomads. This three-way interrelationship is found all over North Africa, and it is typical of the way of life in the Middle East. This shows another strong cultural connection between the Middle East and North Africa.

LESSON 2

Review

REVIEWING MAIN IDEAS
A. How do the fellahin make a living?
B. What would you be likely to see in a North African city?
C. How has the nomadic way of life changed?

SKILLS CHECK

WRITING SKILL
Experienced caravan leaders relied on landmarks in the desert to guide their way. Imagine that you are a caravan leader traveling from the southern tip of Algeria to Cairo, Egypt. Using the map on page 535, describe the route you will take and the landmarks you will use to guide the caravan.

Egypt

CONNECTIONS

What difficulties would a heavily populated country experience if there were very little arable land available for its people to use?

TERMS

distributary, ecology

FOCUS

What influence has the Nile River had on the country of Egypt?

A. The Nile Valley

The Gift of the Nile The ancient Greek historian Herodotus (hih RAHD uh tus) once wrote, "Egypt is an acquired country, the gift of the river." How right Herodotus was! Without the Nile River there would be no Egypt. The 4,187-mile-(6,737-km-) long Nile is the only major river in North Africa. For thousands of years, Egypt has been dependent on the Nile River. The ancient Egyptian civilization emerged and flourished along the narrow gash of green that the Nile cut across the Sahara. In most places the Nile River valley is less than 10 miles (16 km) wide.

Just north of Cairo the river breaks into two main **distributaries**, the Rosetta Mouth and the Damietta Mouth. A distributary is a river branch flowing away from the main stream. It is the opposite of a tributary, which, as you read in Chapter 12, flows into the main stream.

As a major river reaches a flat region, its speed slows, and the silt and sand that it is carrying settles to the bottom of the river. The silt and sand eventually create sandbars and new islands, which cause the river to divide into two or more separate channels of water.

Each of these newly formed channels becomes a distributary. In other words, they distribute the river's flow across the delta and into the sea or ocean. The delta is the land that is formed by the mud and sand deposited at the mouth of the river.

Population Density Almost all of Egypt's 52 million people live in the Nile's narrow river valley and its triangular-shaped delta. Only a few Egyptians live elsewhere, in scattered desert oases. Egypt has about 386,660 square miles (1,001,449 sq km) of territory. That works out to a population

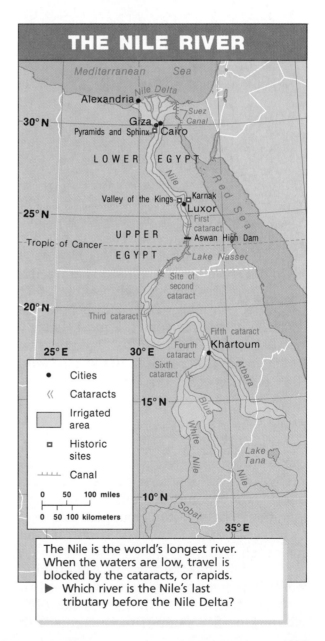

THE NILE RIVER

The Nile is the world's longest river. When the waters are low, travel is blocked by the cataracts, or rapids.
▶ Which river is the Nile's last tributary before the Nile Delta?

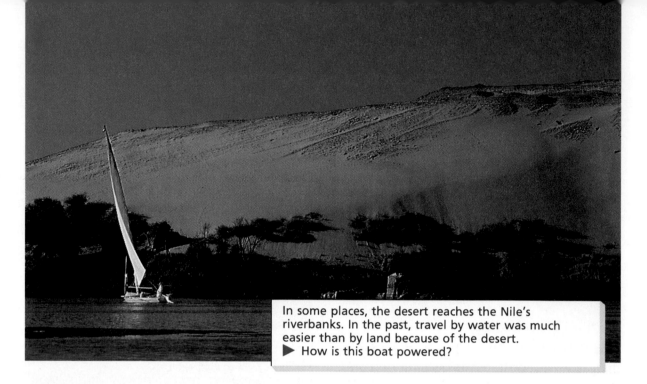

In some places, the desert reaches the Nile's riverbanks. In the past, travel by water was much easier than by land because of the desert.
► How is this boat powered?

density of 134 people per square mile (52 people per sq km).

However, about 96 percent of Egypt's land is barren desert and wasteland. Nothing will grow there because there is no water. This leaves only 15,466 square miles (40,057 sq km) of land that is usable for farms, villages, cities, and so on. If we only count the usable land in calculating the population density, then the result is 3,362 people per square mile (1,298 people per sq km). In comparison, the most densely populated state in the United States is New Jersey, with 1,006 people per square mile (389 people per sq km).

A Dry Land Because Egypt is one of the driest countries in the world, it is dependent on the Nile. The most rainfall, about 8 inches (20 cm) per year, occurs along the Mediterranean Sea near the city of Alexandria. The amount of rainfall decreases as you move inland; for example, south of Cairo, less than 2 inches (5 cm) of rain falls each year.

The Nile has the advantage of drawing water from two sources that get rain at two different times. One tributary is the Blue Nile, which flows out of the mountains of Ethiopia. The other tributary is the White Nile, which gathers its waters from the much wetter regions near the rain forests of central Africa.

B. Irrigation from the Nile

The Nile God The ancient Egyptians worshipped more than one god. Among their gods the Nile god was very important because the river was their source of water. Also, every year the Nile would overflow its banks. As the water receded, it deposited new fertile silt onto the farms of the valley. The Egyptians knew the exact day of the year when the Nile would overflow. They also had elaborate systems of gauges and measurements so that they could predict just how high the flood waters would get.

The Aswan High Dam The rulers of Egypt long desired to store the Nile's water and use it to create and irrigate more farmland. In the nineteenth century the first large dams were built along the river. In 1970 the huge Aswan High Dam was completed in the southern part of Egypt. This dam created a huge new reservoir, or artificial lake, called Lake Nasser. The lake is so long that it backs the Nile's waters up into a section of the country of Sudan called Nubia. Many Nubian people and their villages had to be relocated when the dam was built.

The Aswan High Dam provides hydroelectric power, and Lake Nasser gives Egypt an assured year-round water supply for irrigation. Egyptian leaders had hoped that many of their problems would be solved by the Aswan Dam. But that was not to be. Egypt's population continued to increase very rapidly, so that any gains made in new lands for farming were quickly offset by many new mouths to feed.

The Aswan High Dam created a number of disastrous side effects for which no one was prepared. All the rich silt that used to provide natural fertilizer to the farmers' fields was now blocked by the dam and deposited on the bottom of Lake Nasser. Egyptian farmers are now forced to rely on expensive artificial fertilizers that they cannot afford. Also, below the dam the river now flows faster because it is not laden with its load of silt. Many water-lifting devices, like the one shown on this page, have been washed away by the swift current.

The **ecology** of the coastal region has been affected. Ecology refers to the balance between living things and their environment. Silt no longer reaches the coast, and the coastal beaches along the delta are eroding. The sardine industry along the Mediterranean coast has suffered because of the change in the content of the Nile water. Egypt has learned the hard way about how human interference can sometimes cause major changes in the ecological balance of a place.

C. Egypt's Economic Growth

Lower and Upper Egypt As you can see on the map on page 699, the Nile River flows from the mountains in the south and empties through its delta into the Mediterranean Sea in the north. The Nile delta area has traditionally been referred to as Lower Egypt, and farther south on the map is Upper Egypt. These region names might confuse you because often when giving

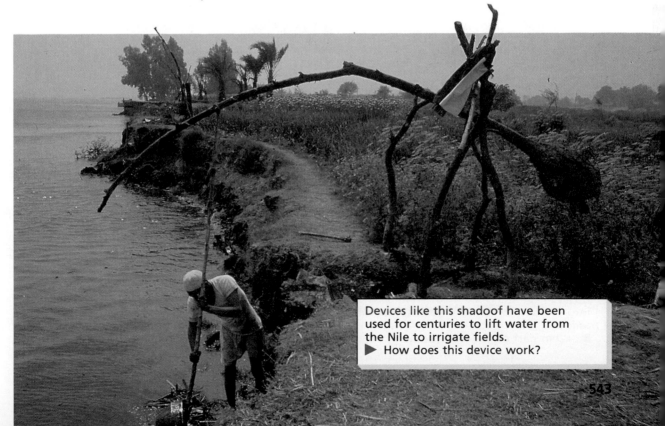

Devices like this shadoof have been used for centuries to lift water from the Nile to irrigate fields.
► How does this device work?

543

directions on a map we wrongly use *up* and *down* instead of *north* and *south*. The terms *upper* and *lower* refer to the flow of a river as it relates to elevation, not placement on the map. All rivers flow downhill, to lower elevations. So the higher elevations of a river are often referred to as its upper end and the delta of a river is often called its lower end.

Rice and wheat are grown in the delta of Lower Egypt. Lower Egypt is also where long-staple cotton is grown. This kind of cotton has long, very fine fibers and is highly prized for making cloth. Sugarcane is grown farther upstream, in the region known as Upper Egypt. Upper Egypt's farmers also harvest fruits, including apricots, nectarines, oranges, lemons, figs, grapes, and olives. For many centuries, agriculture has been Egypt's main source of income.

Suez Canal Another source of income for Egypt is the Suez Canal. Originally built by the French in 1869, the canal was controlled by French and British companies. The Egyptians took control of the canal in 1956. The tolls collected from foreign ships using this 107-mile-long (172-km-long) strategic waterway are an important source of income for Egypt.

Tourism Tourism provides another major source of income for Egypt. Every year thousands of people travel to Egypt to see its historic monuments. The Great Pyramid and the Sphinx at Giza, and the huge temple ruins of Karnak at Luxor are some of the biggest attractions. Also, across the Nile from Luxor is the famous Valley of the Kings, where many of the ancient Egyptian pharaohs, or kings, were buried along with their riches.

COTTON PLANT AND PRODUCTS

FIBERS   **LINT**   **SEEDS**

Boll
Flower
Seeds
Lint
Fibers
Stem
Leaves

Different products are made from each part of the cotton plant. Fibers are made into a variety of textile products, from fine fabrics to typewriter ribbons and sailcloth.
▶ What part of the plant would be used to feed livestock?

544

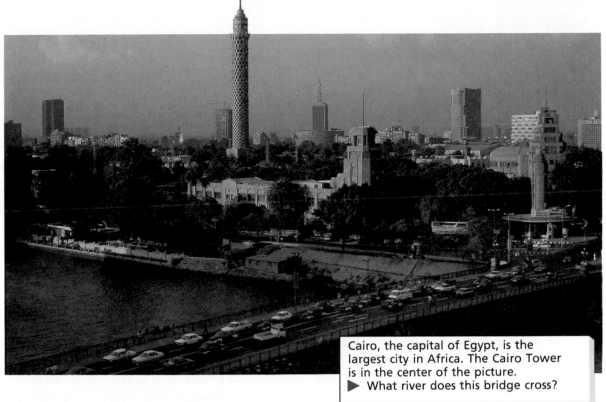

Cairo, the capital of Egypt, is the largest city in Africa. The Cairo Tower is in the center of the picture.
▶ What river does this bridge cross?

D. Rapid Population Growth

A Giant Metropolis Cairo is a huge, rapidly growing city. The metropolitan area has a population of over 14 million people, making it by far the largest city in Egypt as well as the largest city in Africa. Cairo is an old city, and it has long been one of the leading centers of the Islamic world. The Al Azhar Mosque of Cairo is one of the largest mosques in all of Islam.

Growth Problems Egypt, like other rapidly growing areas of the world, is running into the problem of not having enough space. Thousands of homeless people in Cairo actually live in the large city cemetery because they can find no other space to live in. The population of Egypt continues to increase by about 1 million people per year, or about 2,740 people per day.

All these people have to live somewhere, and cities such as Cairo continue to expand. But Egypt cannot afford the luxury of building more cities on its little, narrow ribbon of irrigated land. Egypt needs this land just as desperately for farming.

This is one of the problems that Egypt will continue to face into the next century.

LESSON 3

Review

REVIEWING MAIN IDEAS

A. What effect does the Nile River have on Egypt's population density?
B. What are some of the benefits and drawbacks of the Aswan High Dam?
C. What are some of the major sources of income for Egypt?
D. What are some of the problems caused by Egypt's rapid population growth?

SKILLS CHECK

MAP SKILL

Locate the Suez Canal on the map on page 547. What two seas does the canal connect? Before the canal was made, what route did ships have to follow to travel between these two seas?

545

Libya and the Maghreb

CONNECTIONS

A part of North Africa has a climate like that in Southern Europe because both border the Mediterranean Sea. What crops would you expect to find in this climate?

TERMS

Maghreb, Tell, phosphate

FOCUS

Where do most of the people of the western part of North Africa live and why do they live there?

A. The Heart of Arid North Africa

Libya   Libya is big. With 679,359 square miles (1,759,540 sq km), it is equal to about one fifth of the continental United States. However, it has no major rivers. The only moisture supply other than a few oases is some rainfall along the Mediterranean coast. The rainfall there ranges from 8 inches (20 cm) per year in the east to 24 inches (61 cm) per year in the west.

Libya is so dry that only about 4 million people live there, and almost all of them live within 50 miles (80 km) of the coast. Over half the people of Libya live in two cities—Tripoli, which is the capital, and Benghazi. The population density of Libya is only 6 people per square mile (2 people per sq km), and there are huge areas of empty desert land in Libya's interior where no one can live. No wonder that the *Lady Be Good* was not found for 16 years, and then only by accident!

Libya's Resource   Those oil explorers who found the *Lady Be Good* also found the answer to Libya's future. Rich oil fields were discovered in 1959, and the Libyans have used the income from oil production to build up their nation. They have a fairly high per capita income, and they are using oil profits to build irrigation systems to increase farmland. At this time, Libya imports about three fourths of its food, a situation that its leaders would like to change in the future.

Leadership   Throughout the 1970s and 1980s, Muammar Al-Qaddafi (MOO uh mahr al kuh DAH fee) tried to make Libya a leader among the Arab nations. He also tried to have a strong influence on other nations. For example, Qaddafi sent troops into Chad, Uganda, and other countries. By doing so, he caused problems with his Arab neighbors, especially Egypt, Tunisia, and Chad. Libya also came into conflict with the United States, which accused Qaddafi of supporting terrorist attacks throughout the world.

Much of Qaddafi's power comes from the money Libya earns from the oil business. Libya's oil industry is owned by the government, which is a dictatorship run by Qaddafi. He has put some of the profit from oil sales into improving farming and into building new schools, houses, and hospitals. His government has also provided free social services to Libya's citizens. Still, many Libyans would like their country to be run democratically.

B. Western North Africa

The Maghreb   Tunisia, Algeria, and Morocco form the region of North Africa known as the **Maghreb** (MUH grub). *Maghreb* is an Arabic word meaning "western isle." The

Muammar Al-Qaddafi became the ruler of Libya in 1969.
▶ How has he caused conflict with neighboring countries?

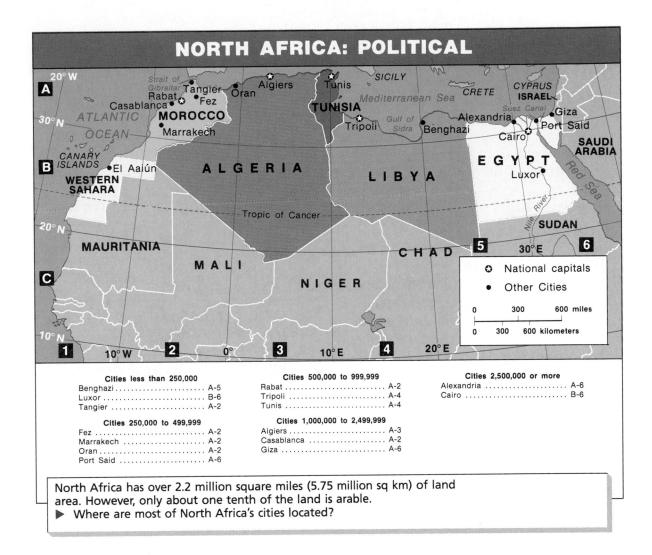

NORTH AFRICA: POLITICAL

		National capitals
	●	Other Cities

Cities less than 250,000		
Benghazi	. . . .	A-5
Luxor	. . . .	B-6
Tangier	. . . .	A-2

Cities 250,000 to 499,999		
Fez	. . . .	A-2
Marrakech	. . . .	A-2
Oran	. . . .	A-2
Port Said	. . . .	A-6

Cities 500,000 to 999,999		
Rabat	. . . .	A-2
Tripoli	. . . .	A-4
Tunis	. . . .	A-4

Cities 1,000,000 to 2,499,999		
Algiers	. . . .	A-3
Casablanca	. . . .	A-2
Giza	. . . .	A-6

Cities 2,500,000 or more		
Alexandria	. . . .	A-6
Cairo	. . . .	B-6

North Africa has over 2.2 million square miles (5.75 million sq km) of land area. However, only about one tenth of the land is arable.

▶ Where are most of North Africa's cities located?

name most likely refers to the fact that here the Atlas Mountains rise like an island out of the western part of the Sahara.

The Atlas mountain range protects the coast along the Atlantic Ocean and Mediterranean Sea from the dry climate of the Sahara. On the coast side of the mountain range there is plentiful rainfall and arable land. On the other side there is useless desert sand.

This land pattern is the same for the entire Maghreb. Along the coast is a hilly region called the **Tell**. *Tell* is an Arabic word meaning "hill." Adjacent to the Tell is a steppe-like plateau, where nomads raise their flocks of sheep. This grassy plateau

region and the coastal Tell are actually parts of the lower elevations of the Maghreb's Atlas Mountains.

Maghreb Economy As with the people of Libya, the people of the Maghreb live on the hills and plains along the coast. These people benefit from the warm, wet winters and hot, dry summers of the Mediterranean climate. Wheat, olives, grapes, and citrus fruits are grown in this climate. Industries that have developed from these crops include wine making, olive oil production, and fruit canning. Fishing and fish canning is another Maghreb industry.

Tourists are also attracted to the sunny North African coast. Algeria receives about

714,000 visitors per year. Tunisia and Morocco each receive more than 2 million tourists a year.

The Atlas Mountains supply Tunisia, Algeria, and Morocco with mineral resources. These countries mine **phosphates**, iron ore, zinc, lead, and copper. Phosphate is a vital mineral used in making fertilizers for the farmers of the world.

C. Tunisia, Algeria, and Morocco

Tunisia Tunisia is the smallest of the countries of North Africa. With an area of 63,170 square miles (163,610 sq km), it is about the size of New England. Tunis, the capital city, has a population of about 1 million, and is the largest city in this nation of 8 million people. Tunis is located next to the ruins of the city of Carthage.

In ancient times, Carthage competed with Rome for power. After a series of wars,

LEADING PHOSPHATE-PRODUCING COUNTRIES

Morocco is the world's third largest phosphate producer. Yet, it is the largest exporter of phosphates.
► About how many tons of phosphates does Morocco produce?

Carthage was conquered by the Romans and destroyed. Today, along the coast of Tunisia, the ruins of the ancient Roman Empire are visited by tourists.

Algeria Algeria is located in the middle part of the Maghreb. It is the largest country in North Africa. About three fourths of Algeria's 919,591 square miles (2,381,741 sq km) is desert.

Like Libya, Algeria has tremendous reserves of oil and natural gas. Natural gas is exported to Europe from the Algerian port cities of Oran and Algiers in two ways. Some of it is changed from a gas into a liquid and shipped out by tanker. The other way it is transported is through a gas pipeline that goes beneath the waters of the Mediterranean Sea to Italy.

Algeria was a French colony until 1962, when after a bloody revolution that lasted eight years, the Algerians won their independence. Almost 1 million French settlers left Algeria at that time and returned to France. Today Algeria has a population of 24 million, most of whom live in the northern part of the country.

Morocco The High Atlas range slices across the middle of Morocco, the westernmost country of the Maghreb. About the size of the state of California, Morocco has an area of 172,413 square miles (446,550 sq km).

Almost all of Morocco's 24 million people live between the coast and the Atlas Mountains. Marrakech, a city nestled at the base of the Atlas range, is an inland trading center and resort city. It has long been a place that has attracted tourists and other visitors. Here also is Casablanca, the largest city of the Maghreb, with a population of over 3 million. The capital city of Rabat is on the Atlantic coast, about 60 miles (97 km) northeast of Casablanca.

Morocco has a fairly large fishing industry, which is based on the abundance of fish found off the Atlantic coast. Tuna

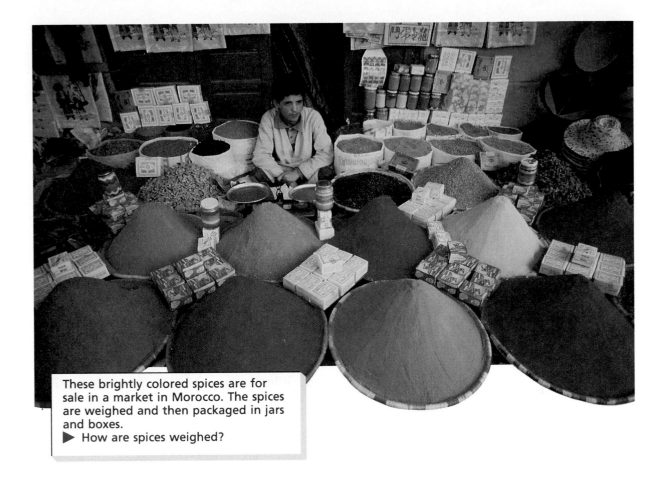

These brightly colored spices are for sale in a market in Morocco. The spices are weighed and then packaged in jars and boxes.
▶ How are spices weighed?

and sardines are the most important catches. Much of the catch is processed by Morocco's cannery industry.

Most of Morocco's wealth comes from one mineral resource, phosphates. With over half the world's supply, Morocco has become the world's leading exporter of phosphates.

Western Sahara In 1975, Morocco claimed the region along its southern border. This area, which is called the Western Sahara, was a Spanish colony. In 1975, Spain gave up its claim to the Western Sahara. When Spain pulled out, Morocco's government allowed 350,000 Moroccan people to march into the Western Sahara and claim the land for Morocco. No other nations recognize Morocco's claim to the Western Sahara.

LESSON 4

Review

REVIEWING MAIN IDEAS

A. What is meant when it is said that Libya's economy is heavily dependent on one resource?

B. What do the countries of the Maghreb have in common?

C. What are some sources of income for Tunisia, Algeria, and Morocco?

SKILLS CHECK

THINKING SKILL

Create a bar graph comparing the population density of the countries of North Africa. Population and land area figures to calculate the population density can be found in Lesson 4. Egypt's population density can be found in Lesson 3.

REVIEWING TERMS

Use the following terms to complete the sentences below. Write your answers in sentence form.

erg	caravan
hammada	distributary
diffusion	ecology
fellahin	Maghreb
bazaar	phosphate

1. From the edge of the _____, a vast stretch of desert could be seen below.

2. The Rosetta Mouth is a main _____ that flows away from the Nile River.

3. The _____ of the Hindu numeral system to Europe occurred because of the Arabs.

4. The _____ raise their crops in an oasis.

5. Our tour traveled through the _____ countries of Tunisia, Algeria, and Morocco.

6. I bought a copper bracelet from a vendor in the _____.

7. The *Lady Be Good* crashed in the middle of a giant _____, or sea of sand.

8. The Aswan High Dam has affected the _____ of the Nile River.

9. A _____ is a vital mineral that is used in making fertilizers.

10. The _____ of camels could be seen in the distance, moving across the top of a sand dune.

REVIEWING THE FACTS

On a separate sheet of paper, answer the questions in complete sentences.

1. Why are oases the key to living in the desert?

2. What barrier creates abundant rainfall in the coastal margin?

3. What influence did the Moors have on the people of Europe in the fifteenth and sixteenth centuries?

4. Why are date palm trees the heart of the desert oases economy?

5. Why do Tuareg men wear turban-veils?

6. How is a delta formed?

7. What are the two sources of the Nile River?

8. How has Libya spent the profits it has received from the sale of oil?

9. What attracts tourists to the Maghreb region?

10. What are the two ways natural gas is exported from Algeria to Europe?

WRITING ABOUT GEOGRAPHY

Sahara is the Arabic word for "emptiness." In a paragraph, describe how this emptiness is filled with life at an oasis.

THINKING CRITICALLY

On a separate sheet of paper, answer the following in complete sentences.

1. How has water influenced where people live in North Africa?
2. How can the diffusion of knowledge help create a better life for people?

3. In what ways has technology changed the lifestyles of the North Africans?
4. Some people consider the Sahara an empty place. What do you think?
5. Why is it important for North Africans to make good use of their arable lands?

SUMMARIZING THE CHAPTER

On a separate sheet of paper, draw a graphic organizer that is like the one shown here. Copy the information from this graphic organizer to the one you have drawn. For each country, write a plus sign (+) if the country has the characteristic listed. Write a minus sign (−) if the country does not have the characteristic.

CHAPTER THEME — The Sahara Desert has strongly influenced the culture, economy, and lifestyles of the people of North Africa.

CHARACTERISTIC	EGYPT	LIBYA	TUNISIA	ALGERIA	MOROCCO
Atlantic Ocean					
Atlas Mountains					
Coastal margin					
Maghreb					
Mediterranean Sea					
Nile River					
Sahara Desert					

CHAPTER 22
THE COUNTRIES OF WEST AFRICA

West Africa: A Varied Region

CONNECTIONS
West Africa has four different tropical climates. Describe the climates of tropical areas that you have studied.

TERMS
mangrove, Sahel

FOCUS
In what ways is West Africa a varied region?

A. A Disease Under Control

Looking carefully at the ground, the young boy walks along the pathway, avoiding tree roots or stones. If he were alone, he could easily walk around or jump over any object in his way. But he is not alone. The boy holds on to one end of a stick, leading his father, who holds the other end. On this path the boy must be the eyes for his father. His father is blind.

In West Africa, it is common to see a young person guiding someone who suffers from river blindness. River blindness is a disease given to humans by the bite of a fly called the black fly. The name of the disease comes from the fact that it is commonly found in people who live near rapidly flowing rivers where the flies reproduce in great numbers.

When the black fly bites, it transmits a microscopic-sized worm into the human body. In the body, the worm produces millions of smaller worms. When these smaller worms die, they accumulate under the skin and in the eyes of the victim. Under the skin, they cause itching so severe that some people commit suicide. In the eyes, they block vision to the point of total blindness.

One black fly bite can cause a little itching, but it takes repeated exposure to the flies to create a severe condition. The disease can be controlled by eliminating the flies. It is important to put an end to the disease because people cannot live near rivers where there is fear of the black fly. One result of the fear is that good farmland next to the rivers is not being used.

Since the 1970s, scientists have led the battle against the black fly by spraying pesticides on rivers where the flies breed. The spraying has been a great success. In 90 percent of the area being treated, there have been no new cases of river blindness. Thanks to the efforts against the disease, almost all of the 16 countries of West Africa have opened up new farmland without risk of infection and blindness. Gaining new farmland is important because West Africa is the most populated area on the continent. An estimated 200 million people, or about one third of Africa's total population, live there.

A young boy leads a person from his village who suffers from river blindness.
▶ What causes river blindness?

▶ Thousands of slaves were shipped from Elmina Castle in Ghana.

553

WEST AFRICA: PHYSICAL

Elevations
Feet   Meters
10,000---3,000
5,000---1,500
2,000---600
1,000---300
0---0

National capitals

0   300   600 miles
0   300   600 kilometers

Many rivers of West Africa flow directly towards the Atlantic Ocean. The Niger River traces a circular route through several countries.
▶ Through which countries does the Niger River pass?

Sahel, Niger

As you can see from the map on this page, four of West Africa's 16 countries— Mali, Burkina Faso (bur KEE nuh FAH soh), Niger(NYE jur), and Chad—are landlocked. The remaining 12 countries have coastlines on the Atlantic Ocean. One other country is sometimes included with West Africa. The Republic of Cape Verde is a group of fifteen islands located in the Atlantic Ocean 375 miles (600 km) west of Cape Verde.

Cape Verde is the westernmost point in the continent of Africa.

B. Landforms of West Africa

Coastal Lowland On the map above, you can see that West Africa can be divided into coastal and inland regions. The coastal lowland is one of the largest in Africa. At its western end, in Mauritania (mor uh TAY nee uh), it is part of the Sahara. This is also the coastal lowland's widest point, and it includes nearly all of the country of Senegal.

Mangrove swamps are found along the coast, especially in the delta of the Niger River and other places where rivers reach the sea. The mangrove is a tree that has a very unusual root system. Part of the roots are above the water and look like bare branches. These roots hold the main part of the plant above the water. The rest of the roots go deep into the soil below the water. A mangrove swamp in Nigeria is pictured below.

Inland Plateaus Much of West Africa is made up of plateaus that are between 500 feet (150 m) and 2,000 feet (610 m) in elevation. In the west a highland zone called the Fouta Djallon (FYOOT uh juh LOHN) rises above the plateaus. These highlands are rarely higher than 6,000 feet (1,829 m), but they are where most of the important rivers of West Africa begin. The Senegal, Gambia, and Niger rivers all originate here.

The Niger River is one of Africa's great rivers. From the Fouta Djallon, the Niger River flows north into the country of Mali.

From Mali, the Niger turns southeast to flow for over 1,000 miles (1,600 km) through the countries of Niger and Nigeria (nye JIHR ee uh) before it reaches the sea.

The Tibesti Mountains are located at the eastern end of West Africa in Chad. The elevation of the highest of its five peaks is 11,204 feet (3,415 m). Near the Tibesti Mountains is Lake Chad, West Africa's largest lake. The Chari River feeds into Lake Chad. The lake has no outlet to the sea, so it slowly evaporates in the dry climate. Depending on the season, the size of the lake can vary by as much as 6,000 square miles (15,540 sq km).

C. The Climates of West Africa

From Desert to Rain Forest If you look at the world climate map in the Atlas, you can see that West Africa has four climate zones that stretch from east to west across the region. Most of the territory of Mauritania, Mali, Niger, and Chad extends into the Sahara. These desert lands have little vegetation and are mainly the home of groups of nomadic herders.

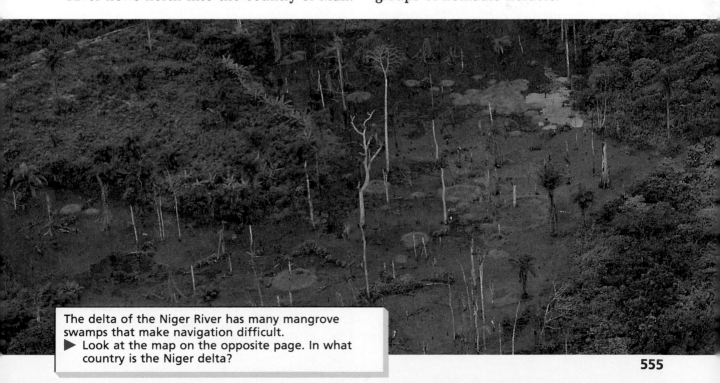

The delta of the Niger River has many mangrove swamps that make navigation difficult.
▶ Look at the map on the opposite page. In what country is the Niger delta?

Scattered trees cover this savanna in Burkina Faso. The grasslands of the savanna are used to graze cattle.
▶ What is the savanna climate like?

Along the coast of the Gulf of Guinea (GIHN ee) is the equatorial climate. As you have learned, the hot, humid, and rainy equatorial climate creates the rain forest environment. Rainfall can exceed 135 inches (343 cm) per year in southern Nigeria, which is in this climate zone.

Transition Zones There are two zones that form a transition between the desert and the rain forest. The first of these two zones has a semidesert climate. This land is known as the **Sahel**, an Arabic word that means "border." The Sahel forms the border between the desert and the more humid lands to the south. In the Sahel, enough rain normally falls to grow the short grasses and scattered trees that support grazing animals. Farming is not usually possible without irrigation.

The second transitional zone has a savanna climate. As you read earlier, the savanna is a grassland that contains scattered trees. The savanna climate has a long rainy season and a long dry season. Farming is possible during the rainy season in the savanna climate. As one moves south through the savanna toward the Equator, the rainfall increases and forest begins to replace the savanna climate grassland.

People who live in each of the four climate zones of West Africa have different ways of life. Since nearly all the countries of West Africa extend across two or more of these climate zones, their people are highly varied in their ways of living.

LESSON 1

Review

REVIEWING MAIN IDEAS

A. How has river blindness affected the countries of West Africa?
B. What are the main landforms of West Africa?
C. In what ways is West Africa a region of contrasts?

SKILLS CHECK

MAP SKILL

Turn to the world climate map in the Atlas. Locate the areas that have the same climates as West Africa. List two countries for each of the four climate types found in West Africa.

Living and Working in West Africa

CONNECTIONS

Think about ways of making a living in your community. What effect do these jobs have on the environment?

TERMS

forage, desertification, drought

FOCUS

How has the environment been affected by the various ways in which people make their living in West Africa?

A. West African Cities

Important Cities West African countries have modern cities with many of the same conveniences found in cities throughout the world. Most West African cities are growing rapidly. The most important cities in West Africa are Lagos and Ibadan in Nigeria, and Dakar, Senegal, and Abidjan, in the Ivory Coast. Lagos, the largest city in West Africa, has over 3 million people.

Ibadan has over 1 million people. Dakar, too, has more than 1 million inhabitants, and Abidjan has over 1.5 million.

If you visited one of these West African cities, you would find it similar to large cities in the United States. You would see large buildings with government and business offices in the downtown areas. You would find wealthy neighborhoods and poor neighborhoods. You would see people dressed in business suits or in traditional African clothing. They would be going to work in offices as well as heading to work in factories. These people might be riding on the many buses going up and down the city streets, especially during rush hours. You might also notice vendors along the street selling newspapers, candy, and many other items to passersby.

Markets If you explored a bit, you would eventually find a market where people from farming areas bring food to sell. You would find people selling many different kinds of fruit and vegetables. Some of the things you would see would be familiar, like oranges, bananas, pineapples, and corn. But you would surely see many things for sale that you did not recognize. For example, there might be many different kinds of palm fruit and products like palm oil for cooking and palm wine, which is made

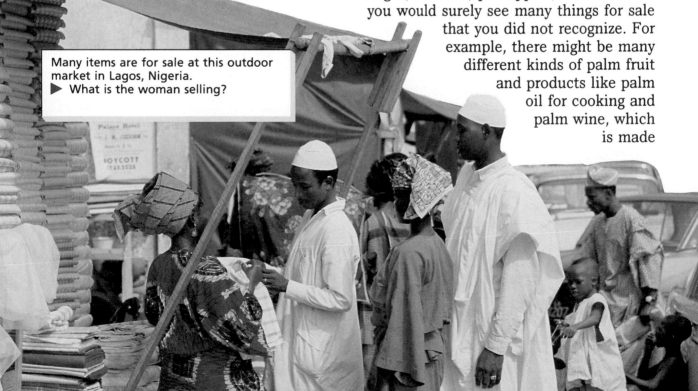

Many items are for sale at this outdoor market in Lagos, Nigeria.
▶ What is the woman selling?

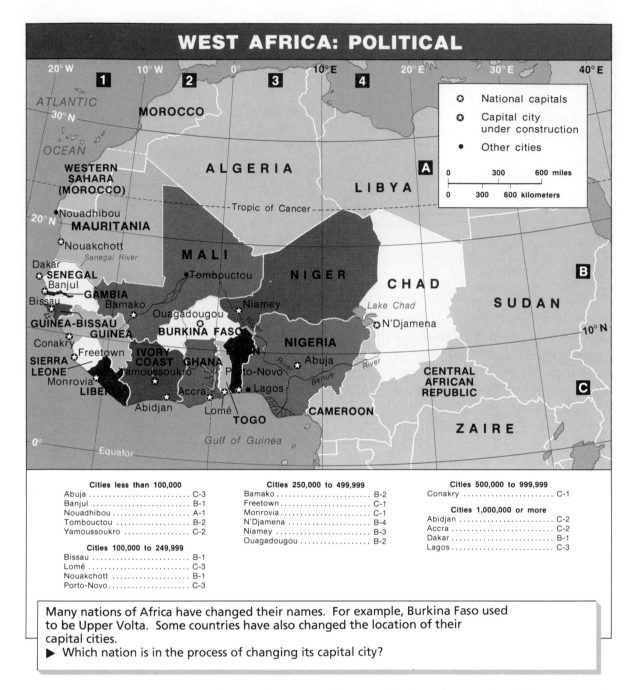

WEST AFRICA: POLITICAL

Legend	
⊘	National capitals
⊘	Capital city under construction
●	Other cities

0 300 600 miles
0 300 600 kilometers

Cities less than 100,000

Abuja	C-3
Banjul	B-1
Nouadhibou	A-1
Tombouctou	B-2
Yamoussoukro	C-2

Cities 100,000 to 249,999

Bissau	B-1
Lomé	C-3
Nouakchott	B-1
Porto-Novo	C-3

Cities 250,000 to 499,999

Bamako	B-2
Freetown	C-1
Monrovia	C-1
N'Djamena	B-4
Niamey	B-3
Ouagadougou	B-2

Cities 500,000 to 999,999

Conakry	C-1

Cities 1,000,000 or more

Abidjan	C-2
Accra	C-2
Dakar	B-1
Lagos	C-3

Many nations of Africa have changed their names. For example, Burkina Faso used to be Upper Volta. Some countries have also changed the location of their capital cities.

▶ Which nation is in the process of changing its capital city?

from the sap of the palm oil tree. Cacao beans, kola nuts, mangoes, and many different kinds of yams and sweet potatoes would also be common. The sweet-flavored kola nuts are used in soft drinks like Coke and Pepsi.

In the coastal cities, you might find a fish market near the water. The fishers often bring their catch to sell as soon as they reach the shore. The fish are usually sold whole. Inland cities might have an animal market where you could see sheep, goats, and camels offered for sale.

B. Farming in West Africa

A Traditional Village Despite the rapid growth of cities, most people in West Africa still live in small villages. In the traditional

African village the houses are round, with cone-shaped straw thatch roofs. The walls of the house are made of mud mixed with dried straw.

The village probably would not have straight streets. Instead, there would be paths that wander between the houses. Aside from the houses, in smaller villages there might be a small health center, a school, and a building for the police and the local government officials.

Houses in most villages do not have electricity, running water, or indoor plumbing. Every day, the women and children go to the nearest well or stream for water. They also have to spend many hours looking for firewood to build cooking fires.

Subsistence Farming Most of the villagers make their living by subsistence farming. As you have learned, subsistence farmers are only able to grow enough food for their family's use. Shifting agriculture is the most common kind of subsistence farming in rain forest areas. Shifting agriculture means that the farmers relocate their fields when the soil is no longer fertile enough to grow crops. Even in the savanna areas, farmers often change fields every few years if they can. If the farmers had fertilizers to use, they could plant the same land year after year. Unfortunately, most poor subsistence farmers have trouble getting enough money to buy chemical fertilizers.

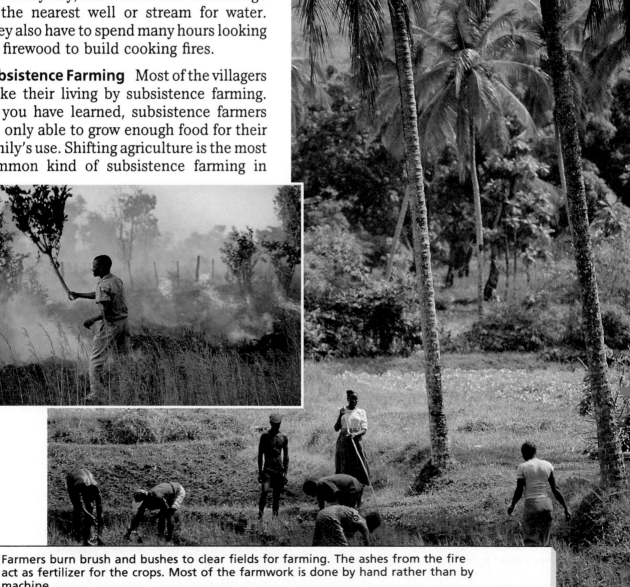

Farmers burn brush and bushes to clear fields for farming. The ashes from the fire act as fertilizer for the crops. Most of the farmwork is done by hand rather than by machine.
▶ What, do you think, is the man doing with the tree branch?

In the rain forest areas, the farmers raise crops that include yams, sweet potatoes, corn, rice, and manioc, which is also called cassava. Cassava is a root crop similar to a potato. It can be made into flour for bread or used in a type of pudding called tapioca. In the savanna areas you would see peanuts, millet, sorghum, and sesame being grown. Millet and sorghum are types of grain that grow well with little rain.

Cash Crops West Africa has become a world leader in the production of coffee, cacao, rubber, and palm oil. These crops are raised on plantations. The plantations are mainly in the rain forest, where the climate is suitable for growing these crops. A plantation is the opposite of a subsistence farm. Instead of raising just for their own use, the plantation farmer raises one or two main crops to be sold. These crops are called cash crops and are usually exported to bring income into the country.

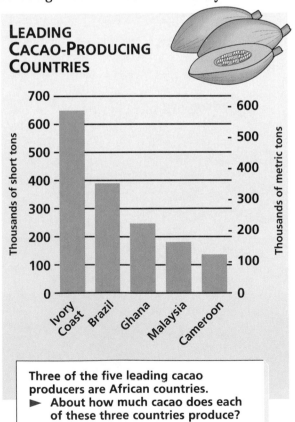

LEADING CACAO-PRODUCING COUNTRIES

Three of the five leading cacao producers are African countries.
► About how much cacao does each of these three countries produce?

In some cases, land that had been used to grow food is now used to grow cash crops. This has led to food shortages that have caused some countries to begin importing food to feed the people in towns and cities. Despite the problems, the income brought into some West African countries by cash crops is greater than the income received from any other products.

C. Herding in West Africa

Herding In the Sahara, the Sahel, and the drier parts of the savanna, livestock herding is the main occupation. Livestock such as sheep, goats, cattle, and camels feed on the **forage** that grows in these areas. Forage is plants such as grass and shrubs that serve as food for livestock.

Once, most of the herders were nomadic, moving their herds in search of green forage. Today nomadic herding is not as common in many parts of West Africa for several reasons.

Governments have built irrigation projects in some of the drier areas so that farmers can use the land. When the land is turned into farms, nomads can no longer use it for their animals. Some governments have dug wells so there is water in one place for animals. This eliminates some of the need for herders to move, but it has caused new problems. When the wells were dug, the herders used the new water to expand their herds. And because the animals stayed close to the wells where there was water, the forage quickly became used up. The area around the wells soon began to look like desert.

Throughout the Sahel, livestock herders have allowed their flocks to overgraze the land. The livestock eat the natural seeds of the grasses and shrubs, so the plant life does not grow back. Without plants, nothing is left to prevent the soil from blowing away. As a result, vegetation disappears completely. The land changes into desert.

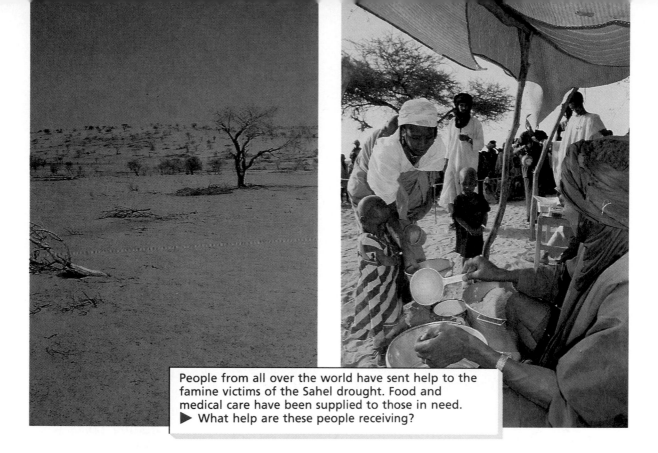

People from all over the world have sent help to the famine victims of the Sahel drought. Food and medical care have been supplied to those in need.
▶ What help are these people receiving?

Often, the word **desertification** is used to describe this process.

The Expanding Desert Perhaps you have read in the newspaper or have seen stories on television about **drought** in the Sahel. A drought is an extreme shortage of water. Droughts are common in the Sahel and are part of a natural cycle of wet years followed by dry years. In the 1960s an unusually long period of adequate rainfall allowed more people to move into the Sahel. New farms were started and the number of livestock increased because there was more water and forage.

When the drought came, between 1968 and 1973, disaster occurred. Rivers dried up, crops failed, and millions of cattle died. Over 250,000 people died of starvation. Millions more migrated southward in search of food. A similar drought occurred between 1980 and 1984, driving still more people from the Sahel.

The combination of natural drought and overgrazing has totally destroyed once productive parts of the Sahel. Desertification is an especially important problem along the southern parts of the Sahara. Desertification has quickened the slow natural advance of the Sahara into the Sahel. If farming and grazing continue to expand in the Sahel, the desertification process will make even more land useless.

LESSON 2

Review

REVIEWING MAIN IDEAS

A. In what ways are West African cities different from American cities?
B. How have cash crops affected West African village life?
C. Why are deserts expanding into the Sahel?

SKILLS CHECK

THINKING SKILL

What solutions do you propose to solve the problems discussed in this lesson?

561

West Africa's Past: From Empires to Independence

CONNECTIONS
The European colonies in West Africa were broken into many small countries after independence. In what other areas of the world did this happen?

TERMS
imperialism, enclave

FOCUS
What changes have occurred in the countries of West Africa since independence?

A. Trade Changes West Africa

Trading Empires Today the Sahel suffers from drought and an expanding desert. In the past, however, it was a region of productive farmland. Yet the Sahel's main source of income did not come from farming—it came from trade. The people in the Sahel were located on the trade route between the people in the rain forest and the people in the desert. Market towns emerged in the Sahel and grew into large trading cities.

One of the leading trade cities was Tombouctou (tohn book TOO), or Timbuktu, on the Niger River at the southern edge of the Sahara Desert. Trading cities like Tombouctou became wealthy by placing a tax on camel caravans that passed through the city. They used this tax money to pay for powerful armies. These cities became the centers of a series of trading empires in the savanna region.

The savanna trade empires began around the year 300. The earliest one was Ghana (GAH nuh). Following the decline of Ghana, Mali became the most important trade empire. Two modern African nations are named after these trading empires. After Mali, Songhai became the major trading empire. Songhai declined around 1500, just as the first European trading posts were established in the coastal areas.

Unknown Continent Portuguese sailors had explored the African coast before Columbus made his famous voyage to America in 1492. Still, European knowledge of the

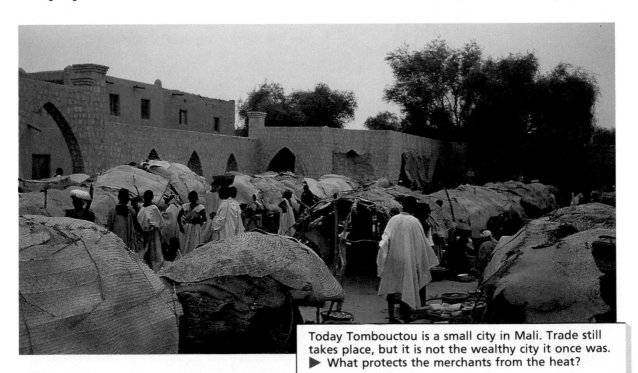

Today Tombouctou is a small city in Mali. Trade still takes place, but it is not the wealthy city it once was.
▶ What protects the merchants from the heat?

interior of Africa was limited up until about 100 years ago. People in Europe knew little about Africa, so they called Africa the "dark continent."

Why were Europeans, who quickly explored and colonized large parts of North and South America, so slow to explore and colonize Africa, which is much closer to Europe than are North and South America?

A Portuguese historian named João de Barros (zhoo OUN day BAHR roosh), writing about 1540, tells one of the reasons why Europeans didn't explore beyond the coast of Africa.

> *It seems that for our sins, or for some inscrutable [mysterious] judgement of God, in all the entrances of [the coast of West Africa] that we sail along, He has placed a striking Angel with a flaming sword of deadly fevers, who prevents us from penetrating into the interior. . . .*

Africa is the home of some of the most dreaded diseases known to humans. The Europeans who dared to attempt exploration of this continent suffered from many diseases that weakened or killed them. Even their horses and other animals sickened and died. Africa quickly gained a reputation for being the graveyard of Europeans. Many of the young Europeans who were sent to protect or work in the trading posts along the coast never expected to see their relatives or friends again.

Hostile Lands and Independent People

In addition to the diseases that plagued Africa, this large and mysterious continent offered other barriers to European colonization and settlement. The great rivers that flow out of the continent, the Nile, the Niger, the Zaire, the Zambezi, and others, have waterfalls, swampy deltas, or other barriers that make it impossible to sail ships far in from the coast. Another important reason that exploration and colonization were so long delayed was that the

This early map of Africa shows how little Europeans knew about the interior of Africa.
▶ What animals are shown on the map?

native people of Africa were fiercely independent and resisted efforts to bring them under European rule.

The Europeans who wanted to benefit from the many products found in Africa set up trading posts along the coast. From these posts, they traded with the native people for the things they wanted. In this way, they did not have to face the dangers that awaited those who dared to travel beyond the coast.

The Slave Trade The Europeans named sections of the coast based on each section's main export product. The modern country of Ghana was the British colony called the Gold Coast. The former French colony that was known as the Ivory Coast still uses that name. It earned this name because of the ivory elephant tusks that were shipped from this coast.

The Atlantic coast of the modern countries of Togo (TOH goh), Benin (be NEEN), and Niger was once called the Slave Coast. Although many slaves were shipped from

563

The Granger Collection

there, most of the slaves were not native to West Africa. The slave trade had been going on for centuries in Africa before the Europeans became involved. But, once they were involved, the Europeans took millions of slaves from Africa and sent them to the Americas and Europe.

Since the Europeans traded for slaves rather than capturing the slaves, the Europeans cared little where the slaves came from. Many of the slaves were captured far inland and marched to the Atlantic coast by slave traders. Most of the people who became slaves were unlucky people who were caught by the slave traders. Some slaves were criminals or prisoners of war that were sold to the slave traders.

In his book *The Africans*, David Lamb describes Goree Island, located off the coast of Senegal. This island is one of the places where slaves were gathered before being sold and put in ships for the Americas or other destinations.

For millions of West Africans . . . this is where freedom ended and serfdom [slavery] began. It was here, in the dark, dank [damp] slave house, that Arab traders bartered and bickered with European shippers, here that the Africans spent the last weeks in their homeland, chained to a wall in underground cubicles, awaiting a buyer, a boat and, at the end of a long, harrowing voyage, a master.

In the weighing room below the trading office, the men's muscles were examined, . . . the children's teeth checked. Those were the qualities . . . on which human worth was judged. The slaves were fattened like livestock up to what was considered an ideal shipping weight, 140 pounds, and those who remained sickly or fell victim to pneumonia or tuberculosis, were segregated [separated] from the rest . . . , led into a corridor whose open door overlooked the ocean and tossed out for the sharks.

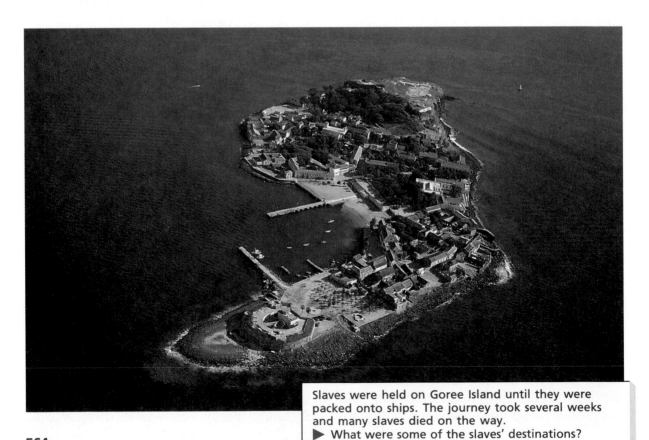

Slaves were held on Goree Island until they were packed onto ships. The journey took several weeks and many slaves died on the way.
▶ What were some of the slaves' destinations?

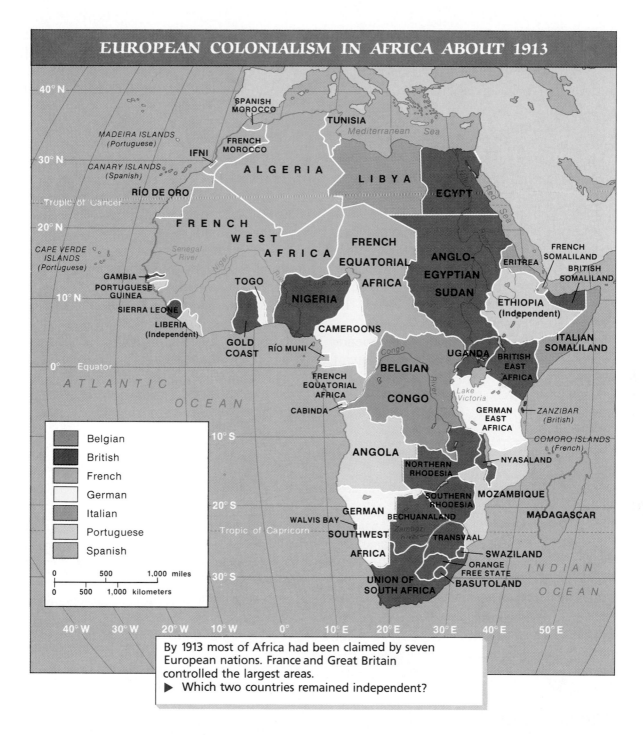

EUROPEAN COLONIALISM IN AFRICA ABOUT 1913

Belgian
British
French
German
Italian
Portuguese
Spanish

0   500   1,000 miles
0   500   1,000 kilometers

By 1913 most of Africa had been claimed by seven
European nations. France and Great Britain
controlled the largest areas.
▶ Which two countries remained independent?

B. From Colonies to Independence

In the late 1800s, Great Britain, France, Portugal, Spain, Belgium, and Germany extended their control from the coast toward the interior of Africa. These European countries followed a policy of **imperialism**. Imperialism is a policy of conquering new lands to build an empire. Africa was divided into separate European-controlled territories. As you can see from the map above, by 1913 almost the entire continent belonged to the Europeans.

After several decades of European control, the people of West Africa began to

565

demand the right to rule themselves. In 1957, Ghana became the first country in West Africa to gain independence from a colonial power. Independence did not come easily. Kwame Nkrumah (KWAH mee un KROO muh) led the struggle for independence and became Ghana's first president. At the independence celebration, Nkrumah wore the clothing of a prisoner because he had been jailed by the British several years earlier for demanding independence.

By 1965, all the countries of West Africa were independent except for Guinea-Bissau (GIHN ee bih SOU) and the Cape Verde Islands. These two Portuguese colonies gained their independence in the mid-1970s.

Today, there are almost 50 independent countries south of the Sahara. Many of these countries, including those in West Africa, have ties to their former colonial owners. The language and customs of the Europeans are still used, and Europe is a leading trade partner.

C. The French-Speaking Countries

Export Economies All the West African countries of the Sahel as well as Guinea, the Ivory Coast, Togo, and Benin were once colonies of France. These former colonies have maintained close ties with France, and they have kept French as the official national language.

In colonial times, the French encouraged farmers to grow cash crops such as cacao, coffee, and bananas for European markets. Today these products are still among the main exports of these countries.

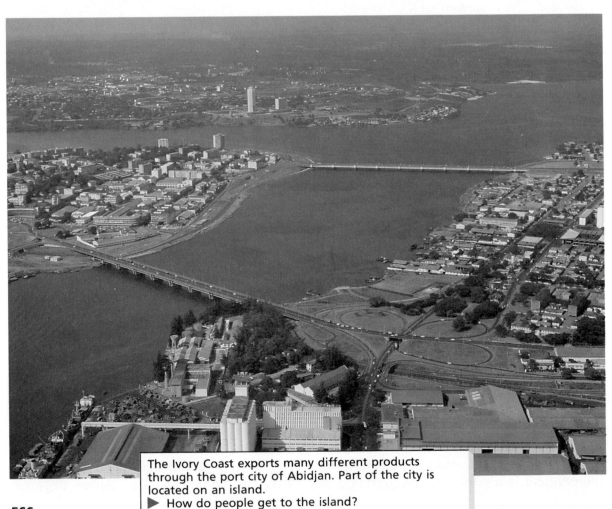

The Ivory Coast exports many different products through the port city of Abidjan. Part of the city is located on an island.
▶ How do people get to the island?

PRODUCTS OF PEANUTS

More than 300 uses for the peanut have been found. The fruit is in the form of a pod, or shell, with the seeds, or peanuts, inside. Growing peanuts and making products from them is a major part of the economy of West Africa.
▶ Where does the fruit grow?

The French-speaking countries on the coast are smaller than most of the Sahel countries, but they are more prosperous. The most prosperous of these countries and one of the wealthiest countries in Africa is the Ivory Coast. The Ivory Coast is a world leader in the production of cacao, leads Africa in the production of coffee, and is Africa's second largest producer of palm oil. The country also produces bananas, coconuts, rubber, cotton, and sugarcane. In the 1980s, oil and natural gas were discovered offshore in the Gulf of Guinea. Crude oil and petroleum products play a part in the Ivory Coast's economy.

Isolation In contrast, the countries of the Sahel are among the poorest countries in the world. One cause of their poverty is their isolated location. Of the countries of the Sahel, only Senegal and Mauritania have a seacoast. Mali, Burkina Faso, Niger, and Chad are landlocked. They must bring in food, machinery, and motor vehicles over long routes through neighboring countries. The additional time and distance adds to the cost of the products. Being landlocked also increases the amount of time it takes to export goods to foreign countries.

Transportation Guinea, Ivory Coast, Togo, and Benin all have coastal locations, so they are not isolated in the same sense as the landlocked countries of the Sahel. Still, isolation is a problem.

The French built railroads in Guinea, to bring minerals and agricultural products such as peanuts and cotton from the interior. Similar railroads were built in Ivory Coast, Togo, and Benin. These railroads

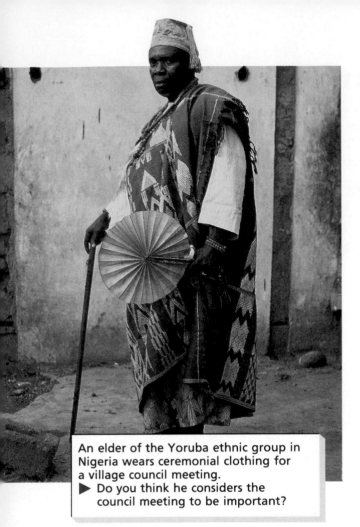

An elder of the Yoruba ethnic group in Nigeria wears ceremonial clothing for a village council meeting.
▶ Do you think he considers the council meeting to be important?

were intended to bring export goods from the interior of each colony to coastal ports. From these ports, goods could be shipped to France. So, the rail lines extend inland from the coast like delicate threads.

The French were not interested in using the railroads to connect places within each colony, nor did they care about connecting the coastal colonies with each other. Later, roads followed the rail lines into the interior, but none were built along the coast between the newly independent countries. Because of this, the transportation systems do not help to unite these countries which share a common colonial language and colonial heritage.

The isolation of these countries from each other is made even greater by the fact that they have continued to depend on trading one or two goods with the countries of Europe. If the economies of these countries were better linked, they might be able to develop trade among themselves. In this way, they could reduce their dependence on Europe.

D. The English-Speaking Countries

Isolation Four former British colonies lie scattered along the coast of West Africa. They include Sierra Leone (see ER uh lee OHN), Ghana, Nigeria, and the tiny country of Gambia. A fifth English-speaking country is Liberia. Liberia was settled by American slaves who were freed before and after the American Civil War.

As with the other countries of West Africa, isolation is a problem for the English-speaking countries. They also have transportation systems that were designed to bring goods to the coast for export rather than to *integrate*, or bring together, the different countries. This problem is made greater by the fact that the English-speaking countries are widely separated from each other. This makes it hard for them to take advantage of their common language and colonial heritage.

Diversity Another problem is the great diversity in size and resources of the English-speaking countries. Tiny Gambia, smaller than the state of Connecticut, and with fewer than one million people, is an **enclave**. An enclave is a country that is completely surrounded by another country. Except for its tiny seacoast, Gambia is completely surrounded by the much larger Senegal.

Because of the enclave, Gambia and Senegal have joined in a confederation called Senegambia. The confederation agreement between Gambia and Senegal makes it possible for the governments of the two countries to work together for economic development.

At the other extreme is Nigeria, one of the larger countries in West Africa. Nigeria is also the most populous country in Africa, with about 115 million people. Some experts say that Nigeria's population will more than double by the year 2020 because of that country's high birthrate.

Nigeria is a prosperous country compared with its neighbors. It has some of the best farmland in West Africa. In addition to this, Nigeria has valuable oil reserves and is the largest oil producer in sub-Saharan Africa. The government has used part of the money it has earned from petroleum exports to develop industry. These industries include textile manufacturing, food processing, oil refining, metal processing, and automobile assembly. These industries produce goods mainly for the large population within Nigeria. If the countries of West Africa were less isolated from each other it

might be possible for Nigeria to sell manufactured goods to its neighbors and have even more industry.

Setting Boundaries The countries of West Africa did not exist before European colonization. The Europeans extended their control along the coast from the trading posts until they came to the territory of another European power. In this way, the coast was divided up into separate European-controlled territories. Later, as Europeans extended their influence away from the sea, the coastal boundaries were simply pushed inland.

The native people of West Africa belonged to hundreds of different ethnic groups or tribes. Each of these groups had its own language, territory, and way of life. The boundaries drawn by the Europeans paid no attention to the territories of the native people. Later, when the West African colonies became independent, the new countries kept their colonial boundaries. These new countries included many different culture groups, some of which might have been long-time enemies or rivals. This made it very hard to govern the new countries.

A mountain of peanuts is prepared for shipment from a plantation in Senegal.
▶ What are the steps made from?

LESSON 3

Review

REVIEWING MAIN IDEAS
A. In what ways has trade changed in West Africa?
B. How have the European countries affected West African countries?
C. In what ways are the countries of West Africa isolated?
D. What type of economic diversity is found in West Africa?

SKILLS CHECK
WRITING SKILL
Write an article for a newspaper, describing the problems of the modern countries of West Africa.

REVIEWING TERMS

mangrove   imperialism
forage   enclave
drought

On a separate sheet of paper, match the word with its correct definition. Write your answers in sentence form.

1. Plants such as grasses and shrubs that livestock eat
2. A tree with an unusual root system, usually found in swamps
3. An extreme shortage of water
4. A country enclosed within another country
5. A policy of conquering new lands to build an empire

REVIEWING THE FACTS

On a separate sheet of paper, answer the questions in complete sentences.

1. Why is the Fouta Djallon important?
2. What are the four climate zones of West Africa?
3. In what ways are West African cities similar to cities in the United States?
4. What is the difference between subsistence crops and cash crops?
5. How did Tombouctou become a wealthy city?
6. Why was West Africa difficult to explore and settle?

7. What products are exported by the French-speaking countries?
8. Who settled the country of Liberia?
9. Why did Senegal and Gambia form a confederation?
10. How has Nigeria used the profits from oil exports?

WRITING ABOUT GEOGRAPHY

Independence for most West African countries came about during the 1950s and 1960s. Imagine you are a leader of a West African country at the time of independence. Write a speech outlining the major problems of your country and possible solutions to these problems.

THINKING CRITICALLY

On a separate sheet of paper, answer the following in complete sentences.

1. What are the causes of desertification in West Africa?
2. How has slavery hurt the development of West Africa?
3. Compare the economies of the French-speaking and English-speaking countries. Which countries have experienced the greatest development?
4. What effect has disease had on West Africa?
5. Compare the West African trading empires with European trade in West Africa.

SUMMARIZING THE CHAPTER

Many events discussed in this chapter caused other events to occur. On a separate sheet of paper, draw a graphic organizer that is like the one shown here. Copy the information from this graphic organizer on the one you have drawn. Fill in the missing effects.

CHAPTER THEME

The influence of the Europeans has affected the economic, political, and cultural growth of West Africa.

LESSON 1 The environment affects how people make their living.

Cause	Effect
1. People will not live next to rivers because of the black fly.	1. _____
2. Desert areas in Mauritania, Mali, Niger, and Chad have little vegetation.	2. _____ _____
3. The savanna climate has a long rainy season and a long dry season.	3. _____ _____

LESSON 2 The environment of West Africa has been affected by the way people make a living.

Cause	Effect
1. Governments have built irrigation projects in drier areas.	1. _____
2. Nomads expanded the size of their herds because new wells were built.	2. _____ _____
3. Throughout the Sahel, herders have allowed their livestock to overgraze the land.	3. _____

LESSON 3 Former European control has influenced the development of the modern West African countries.

Cause	Effect
1. Europeans encouraged farmers to grow cash crops.	1. _____ _____
2. Europeans built railroads from coastal ports of each colony to the interior.	2. _____
3. Newly independent African countries have boundaries set by European countries.	3. _____ _____

THE COUNTRIES OF CENTRAL AFRICA

Central Africa: The Rain Forest

CONNECTIONS

Look at the picture of the rain forest on this page. What, do you think, is it like under that sea of green?

TERMS

canopy, jungle

FOCUS

What are Central Africa's environment and landforms?

A. The Rain Forest

Anyone who has stood in the silent emptiness of a tropical rain forest [feels] overpowered by the heaviness of everything—the damp air, the gigantic water-laden trees that are constantly dripping, never quite drying out between the violent storms that come with monotonous regularity. . . . And, above all, . . . people feel overpowered by the silence . . . and loneliness of it all.

But these are the feelings of outsiders, of those who do not belong to the forest. If you [live in] the forest it is a very different place . . . a cool, restful, shady world with light filtering through the tree tops that meet high overhead and shut out the direct sunlight. . . .

There are a multitude of sounds, but most of them are as joyful as the brightly colored birds that chase one another through the trees, . . . or the chatter of the handsome black-and-white Colobus monkeys as they leap from branch to branch. . . . And the most joyful sound of all . . . is the sound of the voices of the forest people as they sing . . . praise to this wonderful world of theirs.

The author of this description is Colin Turnbull. For several years he lived in the rain forest that is located in the center of Africa. This rain forest region is outlined by the long, curving course of the Zaire (zah IHR) River and its tributaries. The rain forest covers the countries of Gabon, Equatorial Guinea, Congo, and Zaire. It is also found in the southern portions of Cameroon and the Central African Republic. All these countries and the island nation of São Tomé and Príncipe (soun toh ME and PRIHN suh pee) are included in the region that is called Central Africa.

The Canopy From an airplane the rain forest looks like a vast sea of dark green covering the landscape. The surface of this "green sea" is called the **canopy**. The canopy is formed by thousands of leafy, umbrellalike treetops. Some of the trees can reach heights of 200 feet (61 m).

Much of the life of the rain forest is found in the canopy layer. Birds, insects, snakes, small rodents, and monkeys live out most of their lives high above the floor of the forest.

When most people think of a rain forest, they imagine vegetation so thick that you cannot walk through it without cutting a path. But this description of an overgrown, thick tangled mass of tropical

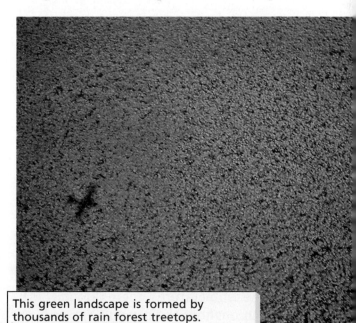

This green landscape is formed by thousands of rain forest treetops.
► What shadow appears in the photograph?

► A farm village in the Ruwenzori Mountains of Zaire

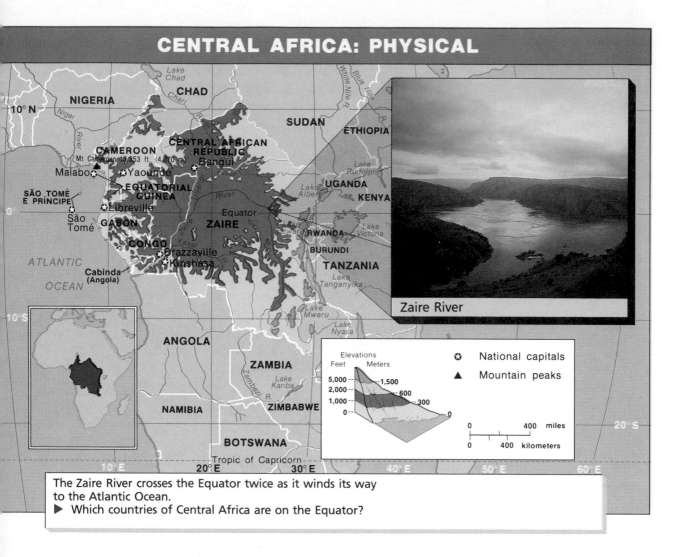

Zaire River

Elevations	
Feet	Meters
5,000	1,500
2,000	600
1,000	300
0	0

✪ National capitals
▲ Mountain peaks

0   400 miles
0   400 kilometers

The Zaire River crosses the Equator twice as it winds its way to the Atlantic Ocean.
▶ Which countries of Central Africa are on the Equator?

vegetation characterizes a **jungle**. Wherever sunlight reaches into the rain forest, a jungle is present. For example, jungles appear along river banks or where fields have been cleared and abandoned. A rain forest is different—the canopy is so thick that sunlight cannot easily penetrate. As a result, the ground remains relatively clear of plants.

B. Climate of Central Africa

Central Africa has an equatorial climate. All year long the temperature remains high. The temperature remains around 80°F (27°C) throughout the day and the air does not cool off much when the sun goes down.

Away from the Equator, in Cameroon and the Central African Republic, the rain forest gives way to savanna. Unlike the rain forest, which has a yearlong wet climate, the savanna has alternating wet and dry seasons. The savanna extends along the coast. Because of the cool ocean water, the climate is cooler along the coast than the equatorial climate.

C. Landforms of Central Africa

The Zaire River Basin The landscape of Central Africa is dominated by the Zaire River basin. The Zaire River drains an area covering 1,425,000 square miles (3,690,750 sq km) in five countries. The river's eight

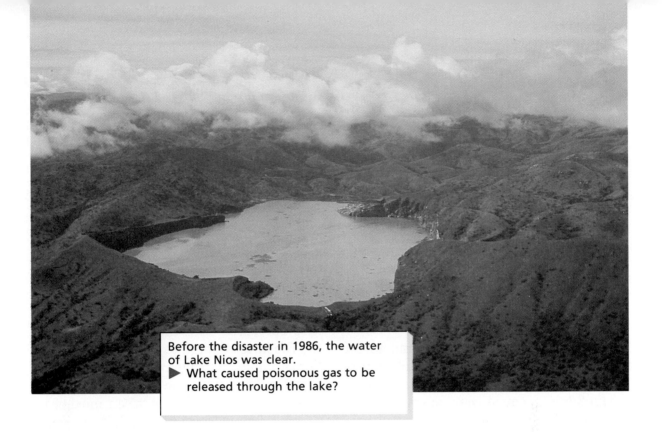

Before the disaster in 1986, the water of Lake Nios was clear.
▶ What caused poisonous gas to be released through the lake?

major tributaries make it second only to the Amazon River in the volume of water that it carries. The Zaire is Africa's second longest river and the world's seventh longest, at 2,716 miles (4,370 km).

Look at the map on page 574. Around the Zaire River basin are highland regions that form its rim. To the east are the Mitumba (mih TOOM buh) and Ruwenzori (roo un ZOR ee) mountains. The peaks of the Ruwenzori Mountains reach heights above 16,750 feet (5,105 m).

Plateaus are located to the north and south of the basin. At the western end of the northern plateau is Mount Cameroon. This mountain is located in Cameroon, near the coast of the Gulf of Guinea.

Volcanic Region Mount Cameroon is a volcano that had its last volcanic eruption in 1959. In 1986 deadly poisonous gases were released from deep underground through the waters of Lake Nios. About 1,700 people who lived on the mountain slopes surrounding the lake were killed.

This lake, near the town of Wum, is located in a dormant volcano crater. Scientists who investigated the disaster believe that the gas was a result of volcanic activity. A similar incident occurred in 1984 when 37 people were killed by gas released from a lake located near Lake Nios.

LESSON 1

Review

REVIEWING MAIN IDEAS

A. What is the difference between a rain forest and a jungle?
B. What different types of climates are found in Central Africa?
C. In what way does the Zaire River basin dominate Central Africa?

SKILLS CHECK

WRITING SKILL

Colin Turnbull described the rain forest environment as he came to see it from living in it. Write a description of the environment where you live.

Living and Working in Central Africa

CONNECTIONS

If you could carry only five items on an expedition into a rain forest, what would you take?

TERMS

Bantu, leaching, humus, tsetse fly

FOCUS

What are the main economic activities in Central Africa?

A. Life in the Rain Forest

Hunters and Gatherers In the rain forest of Central Africa live a group of people known as Pygmies. They are called Pygmies by outsiders because their average height is only 4.5 feet (1.4 m). These people consider the name Pygmy to be offensive and prefer to be called by the name of their ethnic group. One of these ethnic groups is called the Efe (AY fay).

The Efe are nomadic and survive as hunters and gatherers. The men skillfully hunt small animals, using bows and arrows or spears and nets. Efe women search the forest to gather vegetables, roots, berries, fruits, and nuts.

The women also take care of the children and build the small huts in which the families live. These huts are made of bent branches that are tied together and covered with leaves to make them waterproof. The huts are abandoned when the Efe move to a new part of the forest in search of food.

The Efe's way of life seems very primitive compared with the way we live. But the Efe have adapted to their environment. For example, starting a fire in the wet rain forest is difficult. So the Efe keep their fires constantly burning—even when moving to a new location. They carry embers, glowing hot pieces of wood, wrapped in waterproof leaves from one campsite to another. In this way they are able to move their continuously burning campfires with them.

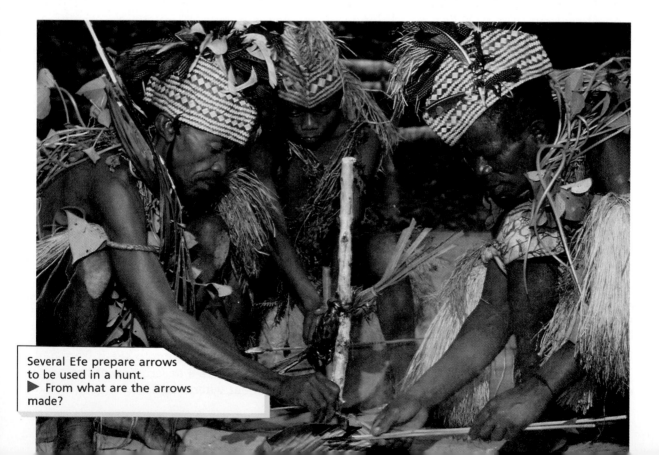

Several Efe prepare arrows to be used in a hunt.
▶ From what are the arrows made?

There are approximately 175,000 people in Central Africa who live as hunters and gatherers. Frequently, hunters and gatherers have close ties to their farming neighbors. The farmers exchange what they grow for the meat that the hunters get in the forest. Honey gathered in the forest is a highly prized item in both groups. Trading is possible between the two groups because they speak the same language and desire each other's products.

The Bantu The majority of the farmers are Bantu-speaking Africans. **Bantu** is a family of African languages. Today there are more than 200 languages and dialects related to Bantu.

The Bantus probably originated in the area of modern Cameroon more than 2,000 years ago. They were farmers who used iron tools. As their population grew, groups of Bantus migrated in search of more farmland. By A.D. 300 the Bantus had spread to eastern and southern Africa.

Many Bantus moved into the rain forest of Central Africa. They cleared the forest for farming and built permanent villages. Today much of the land is farmed the same way it has been farmed for centuries.

B. A Rain Forest Family

Amosa and his family live in the rain forest of Zaire in a small village on the Ikelemba River, a tributary of the Zaire River. The village huts are small, made of sticks and grass, and have cone-shaped roofs. All around Amosa's village are small clearings in the rain forest, where the villagers grow their food crops. Amosa's mother does the farming at the clearing. In Amosa's tribe it is the custom that the women do the farming and the men hunt and fish to provide meat for the village.

Amosa's mother and the other women of the village use simple hoes and pointed digging sticks to prepare the soil for plant-

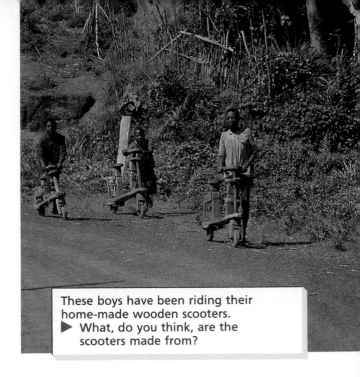

These boys have been riding their home-made wooden scooters.
► What, do you think, are the scooters made from?

ing and to dig the weeds out of the clearing. The yields from the clearings around Amosa's village are very low because of the poor soil. For this reason, the villagers practice shifting agriculture.

Because of the heat, the people of Amosa's village cannot store food very long before it spoils. There are no refrigerators, freezers, or even electricity in Amosa's village, so gathering food is a daily task. Some of the men, like Amosa's father, leave the village for several weeks or months at a time to work on plantations. In this way, they can earn some money to help buy extra food and other things that the people of the village may need.

C. Farming in Central Africa

Infertile Soil The main difficulty farmers face in Central Africa is infertile soil. Because of almost daily rainfall, **leaching** occurs. Leaching is a process in which nutrients in the top layers of the soil are washed down into the lower soil layers. Farm crops have shallow root systems that cannot reach the nutrients. Trees can survive because their roots reach deep into the soil.

The rain forest also lacks **humus** (HYOO mus). Humus is a very fertile layer of

A swarm of locusts descends on a village in Central Africa.
► What is a locust?

decayed plant material that forms slowly. Leaves that fall off trees, and other vegetation that dies, lie upon the surface of the soil and decay. This decaying process creates a new humus layer. In cooler climate regions, the decay occurs gradually, allowing the humus layer to form. Because of the very hot and humid conditions of the rain forest, the decay occurs very rapidly. As a result, the vegetation does not lie on the surface long enough to form a new layer of humus.

Sleeping Sickness Another major problem facing farmers is disease. One disease found in Central Africa is known as sleeping sickness. Symptoms, or signs of the disease, include fever, weakness, and sleepiness. The result is often a coma followed by death. This dreaded disease is passed by the bite of the **tsetse** (TSET see) **fly.** The tsetse fly also bites livestock, causing cattle to die. The farmer can lose his or her own life as well as cattle and crops.

Locusts The crops are also at risk from swarms of locusts. A locust is a large grasshopper. In Africa giant hordes of millions of locusts swarm every few years. These insects eat almost all the vegetation in their path including farmer's crops. The following is a description of a locust swarm by Nigerian author Chinua Achebe in his book *Things Fall Apart*.

> [Q]uite suddenly a shadow fell on the world, and the sun seemed hidden behind a thick cloud. Okonkwo looked up from his work and wondered if it was going to rain at such an unlikely time of the year. . . .
>
> At first, a fairly small swarm came. They were the harbingers [advance group] sent to survey the land. And then appeared on the horizon a slowly-moving mass like a boundless sheet of black cloud drifting towards [the village]. Soon it covered half the sky, and the solid mass was now broken only by tiny eyes of light like shining star dust. It was a tremendous sight, full of power and beauty. . . .
>
> [A]t last the locusts did descend. They settled on every tree and on every blade of grass; they settled on the roofs and covered the bare ground. Mighty tree branches broke away under them, and the whole country became the brown-earth color of the vast, hungry swarm.

LESSON 2

Review

REVIEWING MAIN IDEAS
A. In what ways have the Efe adapted to life in the rain forest?
B. How does Amosa's family make a living?
C. What difficulties do farmers face in the rain forest?

SKILLS CHECK

THINKING SKILL
Draw a diagram that shows the sequence of events in the leaching process and in the creation of a humus layer.

Zaire and Its Neighbors

CONNECTIONS
Why do we need transportation systems?

TERMS
islet, exploitation

FOCUS
What problems do the countries of Central Africa face?

A. Zaire

Zaire River Basin Zaire is the second largest country south of the Sahara. With an area of 905,063 square miles (2,344,113 sq km), it is slightly larger than Alaska and Texas combined. Zaire's population of 30 million is the fourth largest in Africa. However, because of Zaire's vast size, the population density is only 33 people per square mile (13 per sq km). Most of the land consists of the sparsely populated rain forest of the Zaire River basin.

Before Europeans arrived in Africa, the Africans called the Zaire River the Nzere. *Nzere* means the "river that swallows all rivers." The earliest Europeans to explore the coast called the river the Zaire, after the African word. The Europeans later changed the name to Congo, after the Kongo tribe that lived near the mouth of the river. The region became known as the Belgian Congo because the area was claimed by Belgium. Today the name has come full circle, with Zaire now used for the country and the river for which it was named.

The name change was one of the first acts of Joseph Mobutu (moh boo too), a military officer who took control of the government in 1965. Mobutu changed the name of the capital city from Leopoldville to Kinshasa. He also ordered the people to change their names and style of dress. Even Mobutu changed his first and middle names from Joseph Désiré (day zee ray) to Sese Seko (SES ay SEK oh) to set an example. Business suits and ties were forbidden because they were part of a style of clothing that was not African. By replacing the European colonial names and customs, Mobutu restored his people's pride in their African heritage.

The Inga Dam is one of several dams producing hydroelectricity on the Zaire River. The inset photograph shows the dam being built in 1972.
▶ What were previous names of the Zaire River?

Great Potential Zaire is often described as a nation with great potential. With the Zaire River and its many tributaries, Zaire probably has the ability to generate more hydroelectric power than does any other country in the world. It also has tremendous mineral wealth. Zaire is a world leader in the production of copper, cobalt, and industrial diamonds. Southern Zaire has rich deposits of lithium, silver, gold, tin, and manganese, and it has some oil. Lithium is a soft silver-white element that is the lightest metal known. Most of Zaire's mineral wealth has been untapped.

Zaire is unable to exploit some of its vast resources, because it cannot afford to build hydroelectric plants or to mine its minerals. The rain forest makes it difficult to reach these resources. Because of the expense of building roads and railroads, few have been built to tie the different parts of Zaire together.

Railroads and roads have been built to improve transportation on the Zaire River. Entire sections of the river are not navigable; that is, they are not able to be traveled by boat or ship. From Kinshasa to the port city of Matadi, the river drops almost 1,500 feet (457 m) through a series of waterfalls and rapids that river boats cannot pass. A railroad is used to move goods between the two cities. This means that cargo must be transferred between boats and trains at both ends of the rapids. Every time the cargo has to be loaded and unloaded, the cost of transportation increases.

Although some factories have been built near the mines and in the major cities, farming is the main occupation in Zaire. More than 70 percent of the people are farmers. Most of the agricultural production is from plantations. Coffee is a leading export, and cotton is a major product, which has led to a growing textile industry. Food production is limited because much of the farmland is used for cash crops.

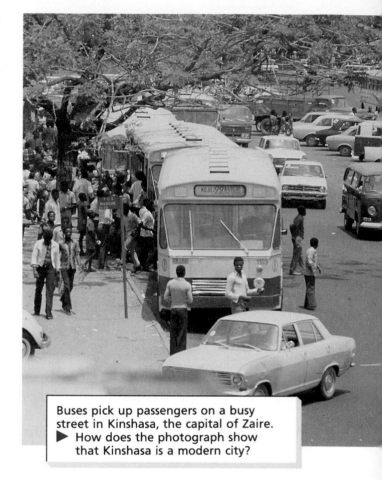

Buses pick up passengers on a busy street in Kinshasa, the capital of Zaire.
▶ How does the photograph show that Kinshasa is a modern city?

Kinshasa, Zaire's Capital As you can see on the map on page 582, Kinshasa is located in western Zaire on the southern bank of the Zaire River. Kinshasa is Zaire's largest city and it is the country's national capital. The first settlement that was built on the site of Kinshasa dates back more than 500 years.

Most of the government buildings are in a section of the city located along the river. These are modern high-rise buildings on wide tree-lined streets. Most of Zaire's wealthy citizens live in spacious bungalows. Foreign visitors to Kinshasa stay in modern hotels. But, there are many poor people who work and live in the city. These people live in buildings made from dried mud bricks with thatched roofs.

B. Former French Colonies

Congo Across the Zaire River from Kinshasa is Brazzaville, the capital of the Congo. The Congo is one of four nations, along with Gabon, the Central African Republic, and Cameroon, that were created from the breakup of the former colony called French Equatorial Africa.

With 132,012 square miles (342,000 sq km) of territory, the Congo is about the size of the state of Montana. Nearly 2 million people live in the Congo, which serves mainly as a link for its neighboring countries to the outside world. The reason is the rail network that connects the Congo's port of Pointe-Noire (pwant nuh WAHR) with the interior of Central Africa. One rail line goes to the border with Gabon, and the other goes inland to Brazzaville, where it picks up trade coming down the Zaire River. The Congo's main resources are oil and timber.

Gabon Gabon, with an area covering 103,347 square miles (267,667 sq km), is about the size of Colorado and has a population of about 1 million. Most of the people live near the capital city of Libreville, located on the Atlantic coast. The Equator passes through Gabon. Most of the country is covered by rain forest. Very little land has been cleared for farming, and the country has to import food. Gabon has some large reserves of oil. Other resources include manganese and iron ore.

Central African Republic Another former French colony in Central Africa is named the Central African Republic. With a total area of 240,533 square miles (622,980 sq km), it is almost as big as the state of Texas. The Central African Republic is landlocked. It is a good example of how a landlocked geographic location causes problems of movement. Its capital, Bangui, is located on the Ubangi River. Goods are shipped down river on the Ubangi to where

LEADING DIAMOND-PRODUCING COUNTRIES

Most of the world's diamonds are used by industry. Zaire is the world's largest producer of these diamonds.
► What other African countries are diamond producers?

it merges with the Zaire River, which borders Zaire and the Congo. Then the goods continue down river to Brazzaville, where they have to be transferred to a railroad to go across the Congo to the port city of Pointe-Noire.

Most of the Central African Republic's nearly 3 million people are subsistence farmers who raise cotton, peanuts, and coffee. The country's major known resource is industrial diamonds, which are found by digging in the gravel of dry stream beds.

There is hope that more resources will be discovered, since the country is located on a highland plateau that is geographically similar to the mineral-rich region of southern Zaire.

Cameroon The northernmost of the Central African countries is Cameroon. Cameroon was originally a German colony that

CENTRAL AFFICA: POLITICAL

National capitals

Other Cities

0   400   miles

0   400   kilometers

Cities less than 100,000		Kisangani	A-3
Kolwezi	C-3	Libreville	A-1
Malabo	A-1	Lubumbashi	C-3
São Tome	A-1	Yaoundé	A-2
Cities 100,000 to 249,999		Cities 500,000 to 999,999	
Matadi	B-2	Douala	A-1
Pointe-Noire	B-2	Kananga	B-3
Cities 250,000 to 499,999		Cities 1,000,000 or more	
Bangui	A-2	Kinshasa	B-2
Brazzaville	B-2		

Zaire, the largest country in central
Africa, has many natural borders.
▶ What types of natural borders does
Zaire have?

extended northward from the Atlantic coast
to Lake Chad. After Germany was defeated
in World War I, four fifths of the colony
was controlled by the French and the re-
mainder was divided into two British sections. In 1960 the French section became
independent Cameroon. During 1961, one
British section joined independent Cameroon and the other joined Nigeria.

In Cameroon the soils are rich and
fertile. As you read earlier, Mount Cameroon, which is located here, is an active
volcano. Soil near a volcano is often very
rich and fertile because of the fresh layers
of volcanic ash that are periodically deposited. In Cameroon, bananas, coffee, and
rubber trees grow on large plantations.

C. Island Countries

Volcanic Islands South of Cameroon, in
the Atlantic Ocean, are a series of islands
that are a part of the volcanic mountain
chain that includes Mount Cameroon. Like
Cameroon, these islands have fertile volcanic soil. Coconut, coffee, and cacao are
the cash crops that are grown on plantations
in these islands.

Two major islands and several **islets**
form the nation of São Tomé and Príncipe.
An islet is a very small island, usually
uninhabited. For four centuries the two
islands of São Tomé and Príncipe were
owned by the Portuguese. The Portuguese
prospered from the slave trade. After the
slave trade ended, more prosperity came
from cocoa and from coffee plantations.

However, the residents of the islands
were victims of **exploitation**. Large profits
were taken from the islands, but very little
was left for the people who lived there.
When independence was granted in 1975,
the Europeans departed, leaving nothing
behind. Since then, São Tomé and Príncipe
has struggled economically.

The island of Bioko is also a part of
the volcanic mountain chain mentioned
above. Bioko, four islets, and the territory
of Río Muni, on the mainland, form Equatorial Guinea. This country of about 300,000
people was a Spanish colony, but it has
had ties to other countries, especially France.
Since gaining independence in 1968, Equatorial Guinea has experienced political
problems and economic failure. By establishing trade with France and former French
colonies, Equatorial Guinea hopes to improve its economy.

In 1985, the people of a western province in Cameroon celebrated the fiftieth year of their king's reign. Pictured here are the king's musicians leading the celebration.
▶ What type of instruments are the musicians playing?

Looking at Problems The problems in Equatorial Guinea and in São Tomé and Príncipe are also found in the Congo, the Central African Republic, and other developing nations of Africa. Although there have been nations in Africa for centuries, many of the modern countries of Africa are less than 30 years old. Compared with the ages of other countries throughout the world, these African nations are toddlers. They are only now beginning to stand and walk.

These countries lack political stability, education, and literate populations. They need to develop agriculture and manufacturing. Even the forces of nature are working against development. Disease, locusts, and poor soil fertility in the rain forest contribute to the difficulties.

These nations, especially Zaire, have tremendous potential. Because of the possibility of great hydroelectric power, mineral wealth, and the greatest resource—a growing population—these Central African countries will increase in importance in the future.

LESSON 3

Review

REVIEWING MAIN IDEAS
A. What is Zaire's untapped potential?
B. What are the transportation problems of Central Africa?
C. What problems are the Central African countries working on?

SKILLS CHECK
MAP SKILL
Using the maps on pages 574 and 582, calculate the distance covered by cargo that is moved from Bangui to Pointe-Noire by the route described on Page 581.

REVIEWING TERMS

On a separate sheet of paper, write the term that best completes each sentence.

leaching
humus
tsetse fly
islet
exploitation

1. An _____ is a very small island, usually uninhabited.
2. The rain forest of Central Africa lacks _____, a fertile layer of decayed plant material that forms slowly.
3. The process in which nutrients in the top layers of the soil are washed down into the lower soil layers is called _____.
4. The _____ is an insect found in Central Africa that causes the disease known as sleeping sickness.
5. The residents of the island countries of Central Africa were victims of _____ when the Europeans took large profits from the islands but left very little for the people who lived there.

REVIEWING THE FACTS

On a separate sheet of paper, answer the following questions in complete sentences.

1. Why is the climate of the savanna along the coast of Central Africa cooler than the climate of the rain forest?
2. What has been the main economic activity of Bantu-speaking Africans for a long time?

3. Why do trees rather than farmers' crops survive better in the rain forest?
4. What conditions in the rain forest cause vegetation to decay rapidly?
5. What disease in Central Africa can affect both people and cattle?
6. Why do the farmers of Central Africa fear locusts?
7. Why did Joseph Mobutu force many changes upon the people of Zaire?
8. What natural resources are found in Zaire?
9. What makes the soils of Cameroon rich and fertile?
10. What four countries were created from the breakup of the former colony of French Equatorial Africa?

WRITING ABOUT CULTURE

Recall what you have read about other groups of people, beside the Efe, who have successfully adapted to their environment. Describe some of these groups and give examples of how they have adapted to their environment.

THINKING CRITICALLY

On a separate sheet of paper, answer the following questions in complete sentences.

1. Why is much of the life of the rain forest found in the canopy layer and not on the ground of the forest?
2. Why, do you think, did the Africans give the Zaire River a name that means "river that swallows all rivers?"

3. Why does Zaire need to import so much of its food?
4. Why does it seem likely that the Central African Republic may possess the same minerals as those that are found in Zaire?
5. Why might a growing population be considered a valuable resource for a developing country?

SUMMARIZING THE CHAPTER

On a separate sheet of paper, draw a graphic organizer that is like the one shown here. Copy the information from this graphic organizer to the one you have drawn. Complete the chart by writing statements that will support the chapter theme. The first one has been done for you.

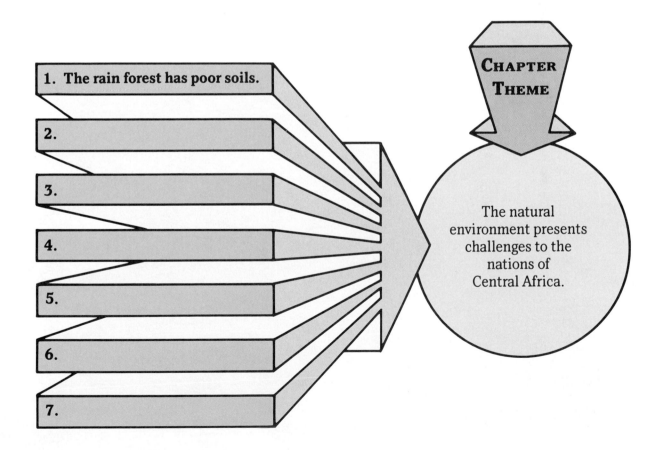

1. The rain forest has poor soils.
2.
3.
4.
5.
6.
7.

CHAPTER THEME

The natural environment presents challenges to the nations of Central Africa.

CHAPTER **24**

THE COUNTRIES OF EAST AFRICA

The Lands of East Africa

CONNECTIONS

You have learned that there are hot, humid rain forests in regions near the Equator. How, then, could a person in a region near the Equator get frostbite?

TERMS

Swahili, rift valley, sisal

FOCUS

What are the landforms and climates of East Africa?

A. East African Wildlife

Two black hairy arms circled the tree trunk. A moment later a furry head appeared. Bright eyes peered at me through a lattice [framework] of ferns. . . . The face was familiar, not only by its features but by its impish expression; it belonged to Peanuts.

The person who had this curious encounter was a woman named Dian Fossey. An American zoologist, Fossey spent nearly 18 years living among and studying mountain gorillas in the highlands of Rwanda (roo AHN duh). Peanuts was one of Fossey's favorite gorillas.

Rwanda is home to one of the largest populations of mountain gorillas in Africa. These gorillas are found in forests of the Virunga Mountains, which form the border between Rwanda and Zaire. The Virunga Mountains extend northward into the country of Uganda, and mountain gorillas live there as well. Rwanda, Uganda, and the other nations shown on the map on page 588 make up the region that is known as East Africa.

Dian Fossey set up a research center to study the rare mountain gorillas. She focused her efforts on protecting these animals from *poachers*, or people who hunt illegally, and on preserving the gorillas' mountain habitats. Fossey described her work in the book *Gorillas in the Mist*, which was later made into a movie. Her research helped to make people more aware of the rich wildlife heritage of East Africa.

Endangered Species Mountain gorillas are not the only endangered wildlife species in East Africa. For example, the African elephant—found throughout Kenya, Tanzania, Sudan, Ethiopia, Somalia, and Uganda—faces the danger of extinction. In one week, poachers kill an average of 1,000 elephants for their valuable ivory tusks. The tusks are sold to merchants in Asia, where the ivory is carved into piano keys, jewelry, and decorative figures. A poacher can live for a year on the money from the sale of just one elephant tusk.

Many countries around the world have banned the sale of ivory to try to stop the slaughter of elephants. However, not all countries have agreed to the ban, so the profitable ivory trade has not been eliminated. Many African countries have set aside land as game reserves and national parks in an effort to protect gorillas, elephants, and other important wildlife resources found on this continent.

African Safaris The protection of wildlife is an especially important issue in East Africa. One of the major sources of income in this region, particularly in Kenya, is the safari. *Safari* is the **Swahili** (swah HEE lee) word for "journey." Swahili, a mixture of Arabic and African languages, is spoken throughout much of East Africa.

Since Europeans first came to Africa, people have gone on safaris to hunt the animals of the continent. People have wanted to bring home trophies of the hunt, such as lion heads, zebra hides, and elephant tusks. Today, however, a different kind of safari has become a key part of the East African economy: the photographic safari.

587

▶ Mount Kilimanjaro, the highest peak in Africa

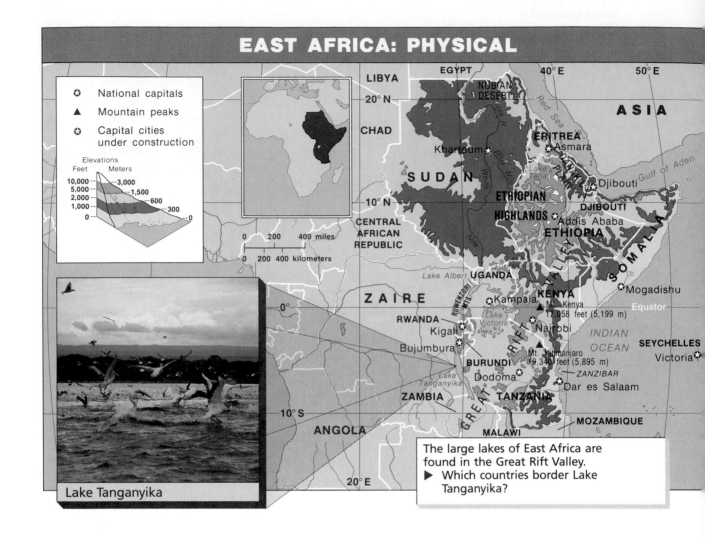

EAST AFRICA: PHYSICAL

National capitals
▲ Mountain peaks
Capital cities under construction

Elevations
Feet   Meters
10,000 — —3,000
5,000 —
2,000 — —1,500
1,000 — —600
0 — —300
 — —0

0   200   400 miles
0   200 400 kilometers

LIBYA
EGYPT
20° N
CHAD
NUBIAN DESERT
Khartoum
SUDAN
10° N
Red Sea
ASIA
ERITREA
Asmara
Djibouti
Gulf of Aden
ETHIOPIAN HIGHLANDS
Addis Ababa
DJIBOUTI
ETHIOPIA
CENTRAL AFRICAN REPUBLIC
Lake Tana
Blue Nile
White Nile
Nile
SOMALIA
ZAIRE
0°
Lake Albert
UGANDA
RUWENZORI MTS.
Kampala
Mt. Kenya 17,058 feet (5,199 m)
KENYA
Mogadishu
Equator
RWANDA
Kigali
Lake Victoria
Nairobi
INDIAN OCEAN
SEYCHELLES
Victoria
Bujumbura
BURUNDI
Mt. Kilimanjaro 19,340 feet (5,895 m)
ZANZIBAR
10° S
Lake Tanganyika
Dodoma
Dar es Salaam
ZAMBIA
TANZANIA
ANGOLA
MALAWI
MOZAMBIQUE
20° E

Lake Tanganyika

The large lakes of East Africa are found in the Great Rift Valley.
▶ Which countries border Lake Tanganyika?

People from all around the world travel to East Africa to photograph zebras, rhinos, gazelles, giraffes, and the other wildlife found in the region's national parks and game reserves. These safaris are particularly profitable to Kenya and Tanzania.

Although wildlife safaris are an important source of income, not all East Africans favor spending so much effort and large amounts of money to protect wildlife. Some Africans argue that valuable land set aside as game reserves could be put to better use as farmland. This feeling is particularly strong in areas of East Africa that do not have enough land or a climate suitable for farming.

B. The Diverse Climates of East Africa

Desert and Savanna Like most of North Africa, much of northern East Africa has a desert climate. This desert region extends southward along the coast of the Red Sea, the Gulf of Aden, and the Indian Ocean. The area receives less rainfall than might be expected in a coastal region. This is because monsoon winds blow parallel to the coastline and thus do not carry moist air over the land.

South of East Africa's desert region, the landscape changes to savanna, grassy plains with no trees or with some scattered trees and bushes. The savanna region has wet and dry seasons. Rainfall is heavy in winter and very light in summer. The temperatures, however, are high year-round in the savanna region.

Highland Climates Farther south the East African landscape changes abruptly from the savanna plains to the rugged Ethiopian highlands and, still farther south, the highlands of the East African plateau. Scattered around the plateau are mountain ranges with elevations well over 10,000 feet (3,048 m). These high mountains and other landforms of the region contribute to the diversity of East Africa's climates.

Parts of the East African highlands lie along the Equator and receive more rain than other areas. Around Lake Victoria, for example, thunderstorms may occur on 200 or more days a year.

Lower elevations in the East African highlands have enough rainfall to support some forest growth, but much of the region is savanna. At higher elevations, tempera-

tures are colder and vegetation is more scarce. Mountain peaks at the highest elevations are snowcapped year-round. Here it is cold enough that mountain climbers trying to reach the summit of one of these peaks could get frostbite.

The cooler climate in the East African highlands makes living conditions there more comfortable than in the savanna or forests found at lower elevations. In addition, the highland savanna of the East African plateau is ideal for the herding of cattle because many disease-carrying insects cannot live at the higher, colder elevations. For example, highland areas above 4,000 feet (1,220 m) are safe from the tsetse fly, which carries the dreaded sleeping sickness.

C. Africa's Great Valley and Highest Peak

Rift Valley Slicing through East Africa from north to south is a gigantic **rift valley**. A rift valley is a deep, trenchlike valley with

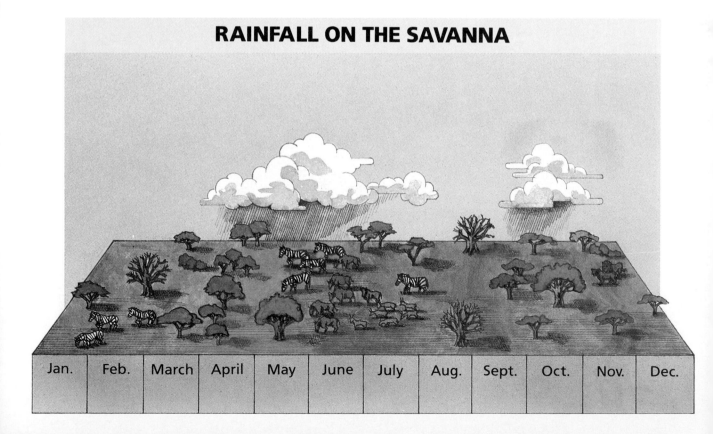

RAINFALL ON THE SAVANNA

| Jan. | Feb. | March | April | May | June | July | Aug. | Sept. | Oct. | Nov. | Dec. |

steep walls. It is caused by the shifting of the earth's crust. The huge East African rift valley, shown on the map on page 523, is called the Great Rift Valley. It begins in the Jordan River valley of the Middle East, extends through the floor of the Red Sea, and then enters the African landmass at Ethiopia. The Great Rift Valley continues south to Lake Victoria. There the valley divides into two sections, one to the east of the lake, the other to the west. South of Lake Victoria the Great Rift Valley continues into Southern Africa.

Many lakes fill parts of the 5,000-mile-long (8,045-km-long) Great Rift Valley. One of these lakes is the Dead Sea, which you learned about in Chapter 20. Other lakes located in the Great Rift Valley include Lake Malawi and Lake Tanganyika. Both of these lakes are found in East Africa. With a depth of 4,710 feet (1,436 m), Lake Tanganyika is the second deepest lake in the world.

In some places, such as at the Dead Sea, the Great Rift Valley is below sea level. In other places, especially in East Africa, the floor of the valley is at an elevation of 6,000 feet (1,829 m). In most places the walls of the Great Rift Valley are cliffs from several hundred to several thousand feet high.

Volcanoes Many volcanoes—some active, some dormant, some extinct—are found along both sides of the Great Rift Valley. The volcanic mountains of the Ethiopian highlands reach elevations of about 13,000 feet (3,962 m). Mount Kilimanjaro is an extinct volcano. Its peak, at 19,340 feet (5,895 m), is the highest point in Africa. Find Kilimanjaro on the physical map on page 588. Another extinct volcano in this region is Mount Kenya, which has an elevation of 17,058 feet (5,199 m). Both Kilimanjaro and Mount Kenya are snowcapped throughout the year.

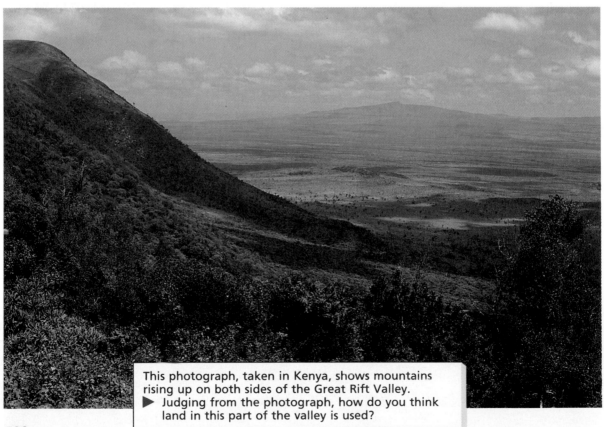

This photograph, taken in Kenya, shows mountains rising up on both sides of the Great Rift Valley.
▶ Judging from the photograph, how do you think land in this part of the valley is used?

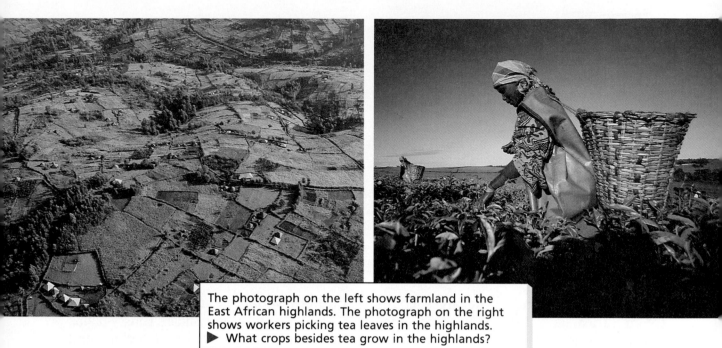

The photograph on the left shows farmland in the East African highlands. The photograph on the right shows workers picking tea leaves in the highlands.
► What crops besides tea grow in the highlands?

D. Farming in East Africa

Lowland Crops East Africa's varied climate allows people to raise many different kinds of crops here. In Sudan, for example, over 2 million acres (809,389 ha) of low, flat land between the Blue Nile and the White Nile is irrigated and used to raise cotton and sugarcane. Water is taken from the Blue Nile and channeled across the fields toward the White Nile.

Highland Crops The fertile volcanic soils and cool temperatures in the highlands around Lake Victoria and the Ethiopian highlands make these among the best farming regions of East Africa. One of the main cash crops raised on large farms throughout the highlands is coffee. Tea, tobacco, sugarcane, and rice are other important highland crops.

Coastal Crops The crop **sisal** is one of several crops grown primarily along the East African coast south of the desert region. Sisal is a fibrous plant used to make rope, string, and bags. Cashew nuts and coconuts also come from this East African coastal region. The two islands of Zanzibar and Pemba are world centers for growing cloves, a spice often used in baking. If you have eaten pumpkin pie, you may have tasted cloves from Zanzibar or Pemba.

LESSON 1

Review

REVIEWING MAIN IDEAS

A. Why is the protection of wildlife important to the countries of East Africa?

B. What are the climate regions of East Africa?

C. How do landforms affect the climates of East Africa?

D. What are the major crops grown in East Africa?

SKILLS CHECK

MAP SKILL

Reread Section B, and use the map on page 588 to identify the East African countries that have a desert climate.

591

Sudan, Ethiopia, and the Horn of Africa

CONNECTIONS
What factors do you think have an effect on how long people live?

TERMS
life expectancy

FOCUS
What are the lands and peoples of Sudan, Ethiopia, and the Horn of Africa like?

A. Sudan—Two Climates, Two Cultures

Northern Sudan Sudan, the largest country in Africa, is a little more than one-fourth the size of the United States. About 25 million people live in Sudan. The northern and southern halves of the country, and the people who live there, are distinctly different from each other.

People in the northern half of the country share the same desert heritage as the people of North Africa. Most people in northern Sudan are Arab Muslims. And as in the desert nations of North Africa, nomadic herding is an important way of life in northern Sudan. Herds of livestock can be found wherever oases or small farming villages are located.

Most people in northern Sudan, however, make their living by farming along the narrow band of fertile land near the Nile River. The population center of the north is found where the Blue Nile and the White Nile meet. Sudan's capital city, Khartoum, and its second largest city, Omdurman, are located in this population center.

Southern Sudan Southern Sudan is very different from northern Sudan. Grassy plains cover much of the southern region, and there is a small area of forest growth along Sudan's border with Uganda.

Sudan's best farmland is in this southern region. The leading crop is cotton. Other agricultural products include sorghum, wheat, groundnuts, and sesame, a plant

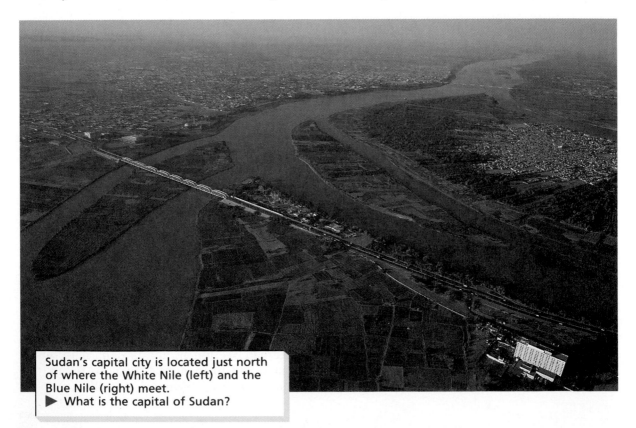

Sudan's capital city is located just north of where the White Nile (left) and the Blue Nile (right) meet.
▶ What is the capital of Sudan?

whose seeds are used to flavor breads. Sudan also produces 80 percent of the world's supply of gum arabic, a product that is used in adhesives, candy, medicines, and other products.

The culture of southern Sudan is more closely related to that of Central Africa than to that of northern Sudan and North Africa. For example, most people in southern Sudan follow either the Christian religion or traditional African religions rather than the Islamic religion.

Conflict Sudan was formerly called Anglo-Egyptian Sudan, when it was ruled jointly by Great Britain and Egypt. Since 1956, when Sudan became independent, a series of civil wars has hurt the country. The southerners have tried to break away from the Arabic northerners and start a separate nation. The rulers in the north have kept trying to impose an Islamic government on the whole country.

Rebellion on the part of the southern Sudanese has blocked Sudan's economic development. Petroleum has been discovered in the south, but rebel attacks on oil wells have stopped production. Rebel attacks have also slowed the construction of a canal that Sudan is building with Egypt. When completed, the canal will divert water from the White Nile to irrigate more land for farming.

Sudan has suffered from the same drought and famine that has affected the Sahel of West Africa. Because of the turmoil and poor economic development caused by civil wars, the Sudanese have had to rely on foreign help to deal with the famine.

B. Ethiopia

An Independent Land Ethiopia is a country of about 50 million people. For more than 2,000 years, Ethiopians have prided themselves on their independence. Their country was not claimed by Europeans

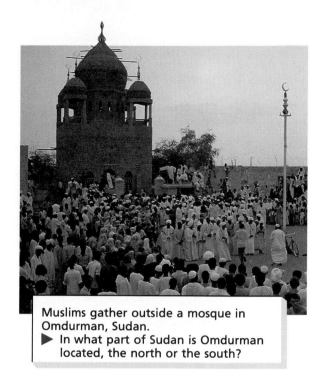
Muslims gather outside a mosque in Omdurman, Sudan.
▶ In what part of Sudan is Omdurman located, the north or the south?

during the period of colonialism in Africa. Except for during the period from 1935 to 1941, when Italy invaded and occupied the country, Ethiopia has remained an independent land.

Among the nations of East Africa, Ethiopia has had a unique history. According to Ethiopian tradition, part of the northern region of the country was the rich kingdom known as Sheba. Legend has it that the first emperor of Ethiopia was the son of the Biblical Queen of Sheba and King Solomon of Israel. Many later Ethiopian rulers claimed to be descendants of this king and queen.

Since the fourth century the majority of Ethiopians have been Coptic Christians. They are members of a branch of Christianity that was centered in Alexandria, Egypt. When Muslims conquered lands to the north of Ethiopia in the seventh century, the country's Coptic Christians became isolated. It wasn't until 1490 that ties to other Christians were restored.

The geography of Ethiopia has contributed to its independence and isolation. It is extremely difficult to travel across

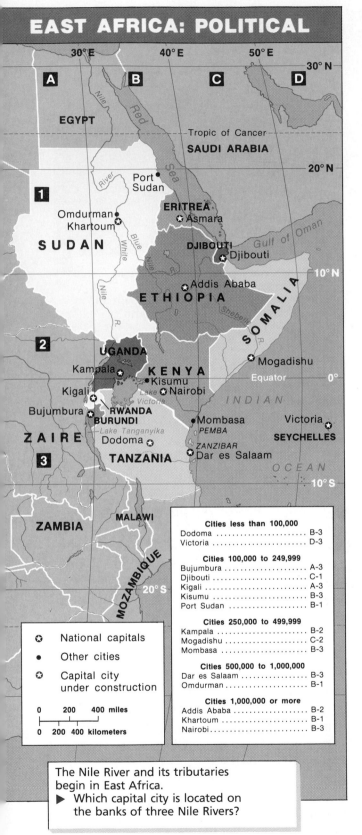

EAST AFRICA: POLITICAL

Cities less than 100,000
Dodoma B-3
Victoria D-3

Cities 100,000 to 249,999
Bujumbura A-3
Djibouti C-1
Kigali A-3
Kisumu B-3
Port Sudan B-1

Cities 250,000 to 499,999
Kampala B-2
Mogadishu C-2
Mombasa B-3

Cities 500,000 to 1,000,000
Dar es Salaam B-3
Omdurman B-1

Cities 1,000,000 or more
Addis Ababa B-2
Khartoum B-1
Nairobi B-3

The Nile River and its tributaries begin in East Africa.
▶ Which capital city is located on the banks of three Nile Rivers?

Ethiopia's landscape. The rugged Ethiopian highlands cover most of the country. The highest peak in the highlands is Ras Dashen, at 15,158 feet (4,620 m). The highlands are chopped into sections by the Great Rift Valley. Several rivers, including the Awash and tributaries of the Nile, have cut deep gorges through the region.

Danakil Plain   The Danakil Plain, near the Red Sea, is so hot and dry that any water that flows into the area quickly evaporates. The region is named for the Danakil people who make their home in this desert. For years the Danakil believed that to protect their water supply, they had the right to kill strangers who ventured into this barren land.

Some areas of the Danakil Plain are below sea level. In places, water from the Red Sea slowly seeps up through rock layers below the desert surface. However, the sea water quickly evaporates, leaving behind a layer of salt. The Danakil people cut blocks of this salt from the desert floor. They carry the salt inland by camel or mule caravan to trade for the things they need.

Famine and War   People throughout the world have heard of Ethiopia because of the famine and civil wars that have occurred there. Several years of drought caused a massive famine in Ethiopia in the 1970s and 1980s. The famine killed hundreds of thousands of people.

The people of Ethiopia are very aware of the threat that drought and disease pose to **life expectancy** in their country. Life expectancy is the average number of years a person can expect to live. In Ethiopia, life expectancy is about 40 years; in the United States it is more than 70 years.

For years the people of Eritrea (er uh TREE uh), an Ethiopian province along the Red Sea coast, fought to gain their independence from Ethiopia. In 1991 the Eritreans defeated the Ethiopian forces who controlled

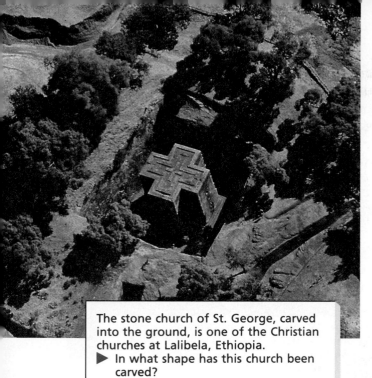

The stone church of St. George, carved into the ground, is one of the Christian churches at Lalibela, Ethiopia.
► In what shape has this church been carved?

the area. Two years later, Eritrea declared itself a free and independent nation.

Eritrea is a trumpet-shaped country that is about the size of the state of Indiana. Its most valuable natural resources are gold, iron, and copper. The capital city, Asmara, is located in the country's highlands.

C. Somalia and Djibouti: On the Horn of Africa

Somalia Wrapping around the Horn of Africa is the desert country of Somalia. The name Horn of Africa refers to the eastern-most part of Africa, which is shaped like the horn of a rhinoceros. Rainfall in Somalia rarely exceeds 20 inches (50 cm) per year. Only a few inches of rain fall each year along the Indian Ocean coast. Mogadishu, the capital city, is located in Somalia's dry coastal region.

Somalia is a poor country. Because it is so dry, it has little land suitable for agriculture. Most of Somalia's 8 million people are Muslims, who have traditionally practiced nomadic herding. For centuries, Somalia's herders have migrated from coastal pastures to inland pastures, according to the season of the year.

Today, herding provides a living to 75 percent of the people in Somalia. Eighty percent of the country's export income comes from livestock. The main exports are skins, canned meat, butter, and live animals. The rest of Somalia's export income is from bananas, sugarcane, and cotton. These crops are grown using irrigation water from the Juba and Shebelle rivers.

Djibouti To the north of the Horn of Africa is the small nation of Djibouti (jih BOOT-ee). With an area of about 8,880 square miles (23,000 sq km), it is slightly larger than the state of Massachusetts. Approximately half of Djibouti's 400,000 people live in the capital city, which is also called Djibouti. A railroad connects this city with Addis Ababa, Ethiopia. Most of Ethiopia's trade goes through the port in the capital city of Djibouti.

Like Somalia, Djibouti is a dry, poor country. The average amount of rainfall is less than 5 inches (13 cm) per year. Farming here is difficult, so livestock herding is the only major agricultural activity.

LESSON 2

Review

REVIEWING MAIN IDEAS

A. In what ways is Sudan a divided country?
B. How has the geography of Ethiopia helped the country maintain its independence?
C. How do the people of Somalia and Djibouti make a living in their dry climates?

SKILLS CHECK

THINKING SKILL

Create a bar graph showing a comparison of the populations of Sudan, Ethiopia, Somalia, and Djibouti.

Kenya and Uganda

CONNECTIONS

You have already read about countries that have had political turmoil. How do countries recover from the problems that political turmoil creates?

TERMS

pyrethrum

FOCUS

How do the lands and peoples of Kenya differ from those of Ugandа?

A. Kenya

Kenyans Pull Together   Kenya was a British colony for many years. In the late 1800s the British built a railroad from the port of Mombasa (mahm BAH suh) inland to Lake Victoria. The British then began to move to the highlands of Kenya's interior to establish coffee and tea plantations.

The largest African ethnic group in the highlands at that time was the Kikuyu people. Many of the Kikuyus resented the British farmers who were now living where the Kikuyus herded cattle. The bad feelings built up over many years and finally grew into a freedom movement.

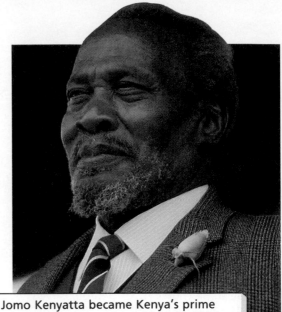

Jomo Kenyatta became Kenya's prime minister in 1963 and president in 1964.
▶ What was the theme of Kenyatta's presidency?

After several years of turmoil, Kenya gained its independence from Great Britain in 1963. Kenya struggled at first, but it had a strong president named Jomo Kenyatta. Kenyatta had been a leader in the freedom movement. As president he earned respect by working for equal rights for all Kenyans. The theme of his presidency was the call "Harambee!" This is a Swahili word that means "Let us all work together!"

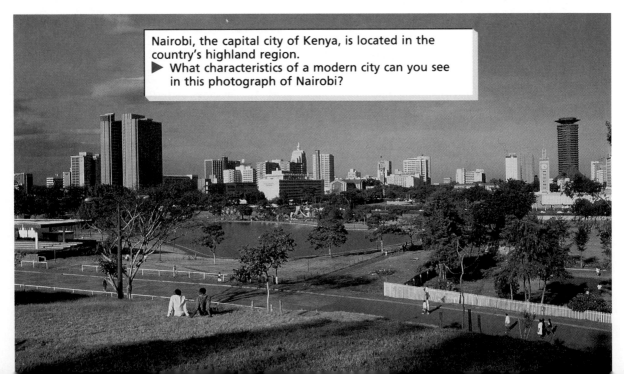

Nairobi, the capital city of Kenya, is located in the country's highland region.
▶ What characteristics of a modern city can you see in this photograph of Nairobi?

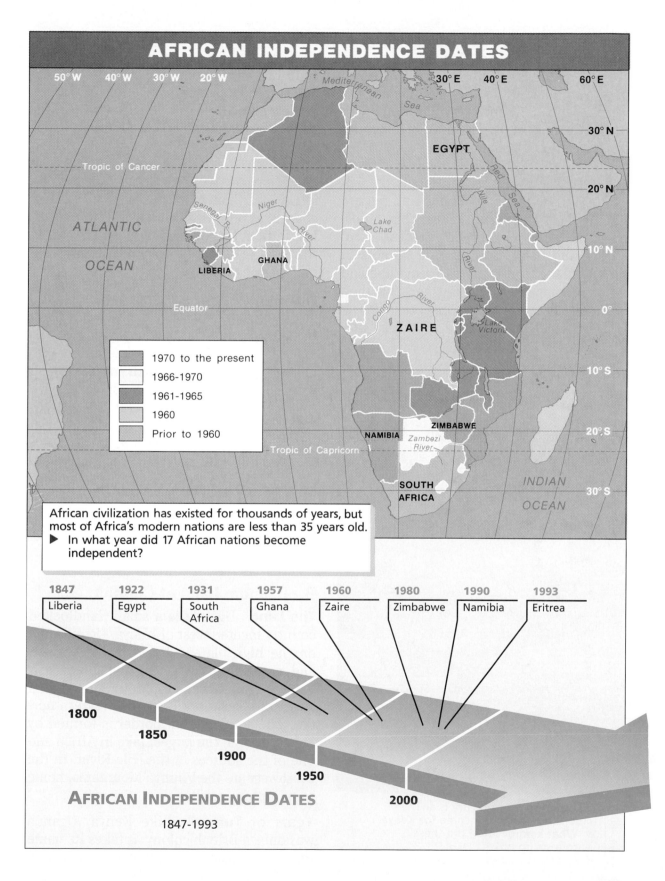

AFRICAN INDEPENDENCE DATES

50°W 40°W 30°W 20°W   30°E 40°E 60°E

Mediterranean Sea

EGYPT

Tropic of Cancer   30°N

20°N

Senegal R.   Niger   Lake Chad   Nile   Red Sea

ATLANTIC   River   10°N

OCEAN

LIBERIA   GHANA

Congo River   River

Equator   0°

ZAIRE   Lake Victoria

10°S

1970 to the present
1966–1970
1961–1965
1960
Prior to 1960

ZIMBABWE

NAMIBIA   Zambezi River   20°S

Tropic of Capricorn

INDIAN   30°S

SOUTH AFRICA   OCEAN

African civilization has existed for thousands of years, but most of Africa's modern nations are less than 35 years old.
▶ In what year did 17 African nations become independent?

1847	1922	1931	1957	1960	1980	1990	1993
Liberia	Egypt	South Africa	Ghana	Zaire	Zimbabwe	Namibia	Eritrea

1800

1850

1900

1950

2000

AFRICAN INDEPENDENCE DATES

1847–1993

Kenya's Economy Most of the land in northern and eastern Kenya is semiarid steppe and desert. The southwestern part of the country, however, is highland savanna. Most of Kenya's 24 million people live in the highlands. The mile-high capital city of Nairobi is located there.

The highland region and the coastal lands around Mombasa are areas of high economic productivity. Coffee and tea are the main crops raised in the highlands. Highland farms also produce wheat, corn, millet, and dairy cattle. Some farmers in the highlands grow **pyrethrum**, a small flower that is dried and crushed and then used to make a natural insecticide. The fertile coastal land around Mombasa produces coconuts and sisal.

The safari-tourist industry is an important source of income for Kenya.
▶ What kind of safari did these tourists go on?

Kenya's highland region, with its parks and game reserves, is the center of the country's large and highly profitable safari-tourist industry. Kenya also has industries that process the country's agricultural products. These industries include sugar refining, textile production, and coffee bean processing.

Many of these industries are located in Nairobi. This modern capital city is the country's commercial and industrial center. In addition, Nairobi's railway system makes the city the center of Kenya's shipping and transportation industries.

Future Challenges Kenya is one of the most economically developed countries in East Africa. But the country has its problems. For example, Kenya has one of the highest population growth rates in the world—almost 4.1 percent per year. With this high growth rate, experts predict that by the year 2010, Kenya's population will be about twice what it was in 1990.

Although Kenya has a productive agricultural system, the country today still has to rely on imported food to feed all its people. In the future, Kenya must find better ways to use its land and resources to support its growing population.

B. Uganda, Land of Conflict

The Land Uganda is a small, landlocked country located west of Kenya. Uganda sits on the high plateau between the eastern and western branches of the Great Rift Valley. The Ruwenzori Mountains and a string of lakes mark Uganda's western border. The southeastern border is formed by Lake Victoria, the largest lake in Africa and one of the sources of the Nile River. In the southwest are the Virunga Mountains, home to mountain gorillas.

Years of Turmoil Like Kenya, Uganda was once a British colony. It takes its name from the *Buganda* people who live around

The Ruwenzori Mountains and a string of lakes mark the western border of Uganda.
► The Ruwenzori Mountains are part of what major landform of East Africa?

Kampala, the capital city. The British used the Buganda people as administrators in the colony. This caused resentment among some of the other ethnic groups who live in Uganda.

After independence was granted, in 1962, Uganda experienced much turmoil and instability. In a military coup in 1971, a soldier named Idi Amin was made president of Uganda. Amin was a brutal dictator who killed his opponents. Nearly 300,000 people were killed while he was in power. Many others were forced to leave the country or fled to safety in neighboring Sudan and Zaire. Amin was finally removed from power in 1979, but Uganda's government has continued to be unstable.

Uganda's Economy The political turmoil and violence of the 1970s and 1980s has had a lasting effect on Uganda's economy. The country has some minerals, including copper and cobalt, but has not fully developed those resources. Coffee is the leading export crop in Uganda, but most of the country's farmers are subsistence farmers who raise crops such as cassava, beans, and corn. These farmers must use their crops to feed themselves and their families.

Uganda has a great deal of potential. The climate and soils are ideal for agricultural development, and mineral resources are available. Hydroelectricity from the waters of the White Nile River could be used to power industries. Perhaps if the people of Uganda work together, their country could surpass Kenya in successful economic development.

LESSON 3

Review

REVIEWING MAIN IDEAS

A. What threat does a high population growth rate pose to the economy of Kenya?

B. Why has Uganda had difficulty developing its resources?

SKILLS CHECK

MAP SKILL

Using the scale of miles on the map on page 594, find the distance between Nairobi, the capital of Kenya, and Kampala, the capital of Uganda.

Tanzania and Its Neighbors

CONNECTIONS

Based on what you have already learned about other East African countries, what problems do you think might affect the countries of Tanzania, Rwanda, and Burundi?

TERMS

kraal

FOCUS

What different ethnic groups influence the cultures of Tanzania, Rwanda, and Burundi?

A. Tanzania

Land and Population Tanzania is a large nation about the size of Texas and Colorado combined. The country stretches westward across the East African plateau from the Indian Ocean to Lake Tanganyika and Lake Victoria. Tanzania also includes the islands of Zanzibar and Pemba. The capital and main port of Tanzania is Dar es Salaam, an Arabic name that means "harbor of peace."

Much of the land in central Tanzania is dry savanna. As a result, most of the population is scattered around the outside edge of the country in a few economically productive areas. This geographic distribution of the population makes it difficult to unite the various regions of Tanzania. This in turn has been a hindrance to the country's economic development.

Tanzania is made up of two former colonies, Tanganyika and the island of Zanzibar. The population of the country is mainly African, but the presence of other ethnic groups reflects the history of the region. Many Arabs still live along the coast and on the islands of Zanzibar and Pemba, where they once practiced the slave trade. There are also Europeans and Indians.

Herders of East Africa On the high plateau of East Africa, many of the people are traditionally cattle herders. In Kenya and northern Tanzania lives one of these groups, called the Masai (mah SYE). The Masai are nomadic people who practice transhumance. They keep their cattle on the plateau grazing lands during the wetter months of the year. During the dry season, the herds are moved to the grassier pastures found in the mountains.

Sometimes a Masai kraal is surrounded by a barrier made of thorny branches.
▶ What purpose do you think the thorny barrier serves?

Some of the Masai live in small, round huts made of thatch. The huts are arranged in a large circle with only one entrance, forming a settlement called a **kraal** (krahl). At night the cattle are kept in pens inside the kraal. During the day the Masai lead the cattle out onto the grazing lands.

A Need for Conservation Mount Kilimanjaro and the Serengeti Plain are located in Tanzania. You have already learned that Kilimanjaro is the highest peak in Africa. The Serengeti Plain is world famous for its wildlife. Many tourists go on photographic safaris in Serengeti National Park.

Tanzania, like the other nations of East Africa, must be cautious in caring for its wildlife resources. If wildlife starts disappearing, then a large, healthy source of income for East Africa will also disappear.

B. The Landlocked Countries of Rwanda and Burundi

Land Use Rwanda and Burundi are two of the smallest countries in Africa. They are also the most crowded nations on the African mainland. Rwanda has a population density of about 688 people per square mile (266 people per sq km). Burundi has a population density of about 511 people per square mile (197 people per sq km).

Almost every piece of available land in Rwanda and Burundi is used for farming. Even so, if drought occurred, these countries would face problems. The potential for famine is high because of the dense populations. Because both countries are landlocked, it would be difficult to get relief supplies to where they are needed.

Ethnic Disputes Like neighboring Uganda, the small countries of Rwanda and Burundi have faced ethnic disputes and rivalries. Over 80 percent of the people of both countries are members of the Hutu ethnic group. The rest of the people belong to the Tutsi ethnic group.

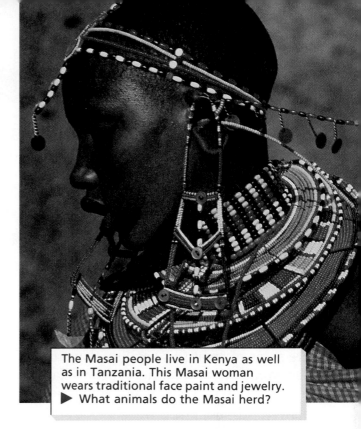

The Masai people live in Kenya as well as in Tanzania. This Masai woman wears traditional face paint and jewelry.
▶ What animals do the Masai herd?

For hundreds of years the Tutsi minority ruled over the Hutu majority. But during the African independence movement of the 1950s and 1960s, the Hutus began to fight to gain control. The resulting conflicts left thousands of people, both Hutus and Tutsis, dead. Today the leaders of Rwanda and Burundi are trying to bring stability and order back to their nations.

LESSON 4

Review

REVIEWING MAIN IDEAS
A. How do the Masai people use their land?
B. Why is the threat of famine so great in Rwanda and Burundi?

SKILLS CHECK

WRITING SKILL
Write a paragraph describing how the countries of East Africa could protect their wildlife resources and still support growing human populations.

601

GLOBAL ISSUES

PROTECTING THE EARTH'S WILDLIFE

In many semiarid regions of the world, huge seas of grass provide a rich environment for many kinds of human activity. Grasslands cover about one fourth of the earth's land surface. Because grasses die almost every year, new organic material is continually added to the soil. As a result, grasslands are areas of great soil fertility. Some of the world's richest farming regions have developed in grasslands, including the Wheat Belt in the United States, the steppes in Ukraine, and the Pampas in Argentina.

On the African continent the high plateaus are covered with extensive grasslands. The African grasslands provide lush grazing for hundreds of kinds of wildlife. In turn, the grazing animals provide food for the many types of predatory animals that live on the grasslands. But how do human populations affect the grasslands and other environments, and the wildlife these environments support?

East Africa's Wildlife Habitats

The plateau grasslands in the East African nations of Kenya and Tanzania are among the largest natural habitats for wildlife left in the world today. Both countries have established large national parks and game reserves to try to preserve some of the natural grasslands and the wildlife that lives there. The Serengeti Plain of Tanzania is home to one of Africa's largest parks, Serengeti National Park. This magnificent nature reserve covers an area of about 5,600 square miles (14,504 sq km) and continues across

Tanzania's border into Kenya, where it is known as the Masai Mara Game Reserve.

This part of Africa inspires a feeling of unlimited open space and awe. Across the gently rolling grasslands of the Serengeti Plain are literally thousands of animals and birds. As far as the eye can see are vast herds of wildebeests, zebras, giraffes, and gazelles and other types of antelopes. The list could go on and on. Scattered here and there are groups of lions and elephants. Together they create an impression of an animal paradise.

This grassland environment of East Africa has existed for thousands of years. The balance of nature has been at work here to ensure the survival of the healthiest, strongest animals. But the balance of nature has been upset by the influence of humans.

Dian Fossey (bottom right) studied mountain gorillas, one of the many rare and beautiful animal species found in Africa.
▶ In what country did Fossey study the gorillas?

Human Interaction with the Environment

In the 1950s and 1960s, anthropologists Louis and Mary Leakey discovered fossils of early humans in this part of East Africa. In Olduvai (AWL doo vye) Gorge, on the eastern edge of the Serengeti Plain, the Leakeys unearthed human bones that were almost 2 million years old. These and other fossils and artifacts found in the region have allowed anthropologists to paint a picture of how humans have changed over the years. For example, scientists have learned that because of the ability to use tools and weapons, humans eventually became hunters and began to dominate this part of Africa.

In the twentieth century, rapid human population growth and the search for new lands to settle have led people to invade land that once belonged only to wildlife. Some of these people are nomadic herders who move around the grasslands in search of water and better pastures for their livestock. Others are farmers who have moved farther into the grasslands in search of new, fertile land.

As little as 30 years ago, there were largely unsettled zones surrounding nature reserves like Serengeti. These zones protected the reserves from the pressures of farming and grazing. But as the need for more food and more grazing land and cropland increased, many people moved closer to the reserves.

The Threat to Wildlife

Hunting is illegal in East Africa's parks and reserves, which have been set up

603

THE WORLD: ENDANGERED SPECIES

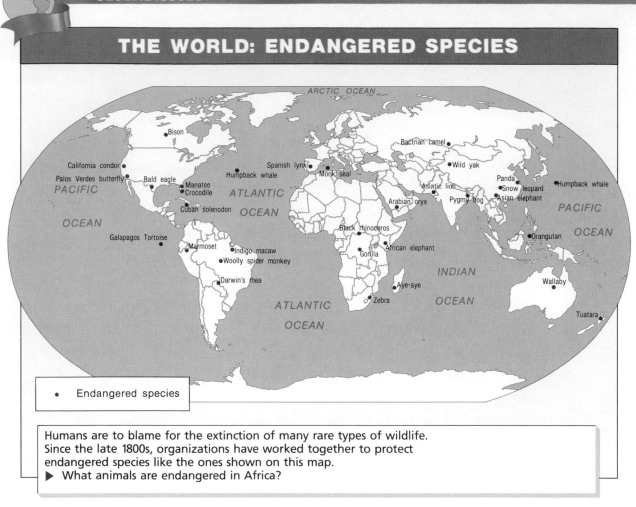

Bison

California condor
Palos Verdes butterfly
Bald eagle
PACIFIC
OCEAN
Manatee
Crocodile
Cuban solenodon
Galapagos Tortoise
Marmoset
Indigo macaw
Woolly spider monkey
Darwin's rhea

ARCTIC OCEAN

Spanish lynx
Humpback whale
ATLANTIC
OCEAN
Monk seal

ATLANTIC
OCEAN

Bactrian camel
Wild yak
Asiatic lion
Arabian oryx
Pygmy hog
Panda
Snow leopard
Asian elephant
Humpback whale
PACIFIC
OCEAN
Orangutan

Black rhinoceros
Gorilla
African elephant
Aye-aye
Zebra

INDIAN
OCEAN
Wallaby
Tuatara

• Endangered species

Humans are to blame for the extinction of many rare types of wildlife.
Since the late 1800s, organizations have worked together to protect
endangered species like the ones shown on this map.
▶ What animals are endangered in Africa?

largely to protect gorillas, elephants, and other wildlife. But many people in this region of Africa live in poverty, and some turn to poaching as a way to survive. Each year, poachers kill thousands of animals. As you have already learned, elephants are hunted for their ivory tusks. Rhinoceroses are hunted for their horns, which are ground into medicines that are considered valuable in some parts of the world. Some types of animals are caught illegally and sold to zoos, and some are killed for their meat or to be sold as trophies to collectors around the world.

What are some of the results of poaching? In the past 20 years, the number of elephants in Kenya has decreased from over 130,000 to fewer than 20,000. During the same period, the rhinoceros

population has fallen from over 20,000 to fewer than 600. Many African animals are now endangered—that is, their numbers are greatly reduced. Unless strong measures are taken to protect these animals, they will die out.

People are part of nature and part of the grassland environment of East Africa. Like the animals here, the people are trying to survive in this semiarid region. but as you can see from the map showing endangered species, above, people pose a serious threat to the survival of wildlife in Africa and, indeed, around the world.

Solutions in East Africa and Beyond

National parks and game reserves rich in wildlife can be an important source of income for a country, as they are for Kenya and Tanzania. Tourism is worth millions of dollars to these two countries—and the tourists go there primarily to see the African wildlife. If the animals were to die out, the countries would be hurt financially as well as ecologically.

Realizing the importance of wildlife to their national economies, the governments of Kenya and Tanzania have created a strong force of park rangers and game wardens to catch and arrest poachers. Kenya's government is considering building fences around some of the most important wildlife habitats to protect the wildlife by keeping the animals in and the poachers out.

Kenya and Tanzania are actively promoting tours and safaris in their national parks and game reserves. With more money from tourism coming in, more people can be hired to protect wildlife. Also, the tourist dollars help to raise the income levels of the people living in these countries. Perhaps in the future, poverty will decrease to the point where poaching will be eliminated—that is, people will no longer need to illegally hunt animals to survive.

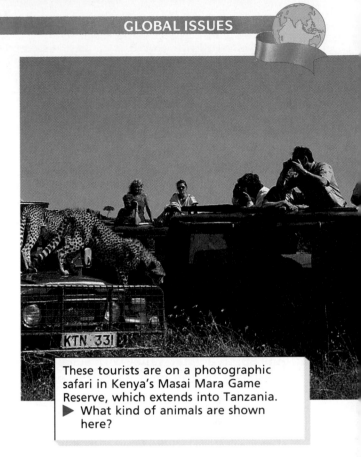

These tourists are on a photographic safari in Kenya's Masai Mara Game Reserve, which extends into Tanzania.
▶ What kind of animals are shown here?

The protection of wildlife is of worldwide concern. People around the world must cooperate with efforts to protect wildlife if these efforts are to be successful. For example, governments must help to enforce the worldwide ban on the sale of ivory. Zoos must purchase animals from sources that follow strict regulations regarding the types and number of animals that can be removed from their natural habitats. Individuals can support international organizations formed for the purpose of raising money to help protect wildlife. Through these and other efforts, we can protect wildlife around the world.

THINKING CRITICALLY

1. Why have humans moved closer to areas where African wildlife lives?
2. What is the connection between poverty and poaching?
3. How could *you* help to protect wildlife in Africa or somewhere else in the world?

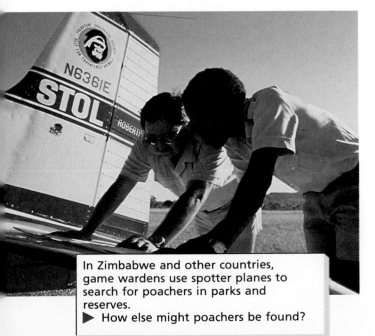

In Zimbabwe and other countries, game wardens use spotter planes to search for poachers in parks and reserves.
▶ How else might poachers be found?

605

24 REVIEW

REVIEWING TERMS

From the list below, choose a term that could be used in place of the underlined words in each sentence. Rewrite the sentences on a separate sheet of paper.

Swahili   **life expectancy**
rift valley   **pyrethrum**
sisal

1. The people of the East African coast make rope, string, and bags from <u>a fibrous plant</u>.
2. <u>A deep, trenchlike valley with steep walls</u> is caused by the shifting of the earth's crust.
3. <u>A mixture of Arabic and African languages</u> is spoken throughout much of East Africa.
4. Some farmers in the highlands of Kenya make a natural pesticide from <u>a small flower that is dried and crushed</u>.
5. In Ethiopia the <u>average number of years a person can expect to live</u> is about 40 years.

REVIEWING THE FACTS

On a separate sheet of paper, answer the following questions in complete sentences.

1. Why is the African elephant in danger of extinction?
2. What geographic region is located south of East Africa's desert region?
3. What is Africa's highest peak?
4. In what ways do the people of northern Sudan make a living?
5. What religions are practiced in Sudan?

6. Where is the Danakil Plain located?
7. What desert country is located on the Horn of Africa?
8. Why is Nairobi Kenya's most important city?
9. What two major problems does Kenya face today?
10. What ethnic groups live in Tanzania?

WRITING ABOUT GEOGRAPHY

Pretend you are the leader of an East African country. Write a speech giving reasons why your country's land should be used for game preserves instead of farming.

THINKING CRITICALLY

On a separate sheet of paper, answer the following questions in complete sentences.

1. How might the civil wars in Sudan be partly responsible for the famine that occurs in that country?
2. In the statement "Ethiopia is an independent land," what does *independent* mean?
3. How might the history of Ethiopia have been different if its geography did not include rugged highlands?
4. Why, in your opinion, is life expectancy so much higher in the United States than it is in Ethiopia?
5. Why does Kenya still rely on imported food to feed its people even though it has a productive agricultural system?

On a separate sheet of paper, draw a graphic organizer like the one shown. Copy the information from this graphic organizer to the one you have drawn. Under the main idea for each lesson, write three statements that support the main idea.

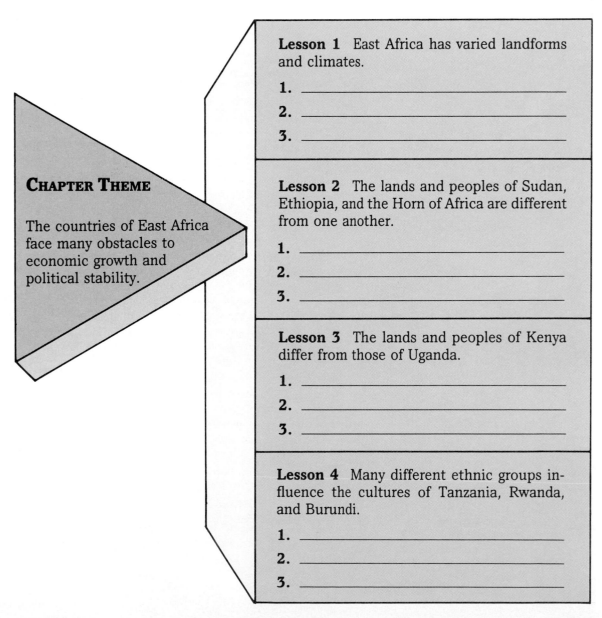

CHAPTER THEME

The countries of East Africa face many obstacles to economic growth and political stability.

Lesson 1 East Africa has varied landforms and climates.

1. _____
2. _____
3. _____

Lesson 2 The lands and peoples of Sudan, Ethiopia, and the Horn of Africa are different from one another.

1. _____
2. _____
3. _____

Lesson 3 The lands and peoples of Kenya differ from those of Uganda.

1. _____
2. _____
3. _____

Lesson 4 Many different ethnic groups influence the cultures of Tanzania, Rwanda, and Burundi.

1. _____
2. _____
3. _____

THE COUNTRIES OF SOUTHERN AFRICA

The Lands of Southern Africa

CONNECTIONS

The plateau that covers much of East Africa also covers much of Southern Africa. Knowing this, what type of climate would you expect to find in the plateau region of Southern Africa?

TERMS

escarpment, High Veld, Afrikaans

FOCUS

What are the landforms and climates of Southern Africa?

A. A Region of Independent Nations

The date was March 21, 1990. The place was a sports stadium in a capital city called Windhoek. The time was just past midnight. As thousands of people looked on, the blue, white, and orange flag of South Africa was taken down and a new blue, red, green, and gold flag was raised. And with that, an independent African nation was officially born: the nation of Namibia (nuh MIHB ee uh).

For more than 70 years, Namibia had been under the control of the country of South Africa, its neighbor to the southeast. Before independence, Namibia was often referred to as South-West Africa, a name that symbolized both the country's location and its political standing in relation to South Africa.

For more than 20 years, a strong nationalist movement had been fighting for Namibia's independence. Now, in the early morning hours of that day in March, the moment had arrived. Sam Nujoma, a major leader of the movement, was sworn in as the country's first president. He proclaimed before the cheering crowd, "In the name of our people, I declare that Namibia is forever free, sovereign, and independent."

Cape Town, South Africa, was built near the edge of the Southern African plateau.
▶ How do you think people might travel to the top of the plateau?

Namibia and South Africa are just two of the independent nations that make up the region known as Southern Africa. The different peoples, landforms, climates, and cultures of these nations, which are shown on the map on page 610, make Southern Africa unique.

B. The Plateau of Southern Africa

The Plateau's Edge In some ways, the southern region of the African continent is similar to the other parts of Africa that you have already read about. The same high plateau that dominates much of East Africa extends into the countries of Southern Africa. The plateau in Southern Africa is surrounded by mountains, hills, and valleys. This rugged landscape forms a barrier between the narrow coastal plain and the gently rolling plain atop the plateau.

In many places there are sudden changes in elevation and you can see the great **escarpments** that form the edge of the plateau. An escarpment is a steep slope or cliff formed by erosion or by movements of the earth's rock layers. Not too far inland from the Atlantic coast of Angola, for example, the land abruptly rises up in a series of giant steps to the top of the Southern African plateau.

Mountain Ranges Along the southern coast of Africa, a region called the Karroo separates the narrow coastal plain from the plateau. In this region, several major mountain ranges run from east to west. Separated by valleys, each of these mountain ranges

SOUTHERN AFRICA: PHYSICAL

Cape Agulhas is Africa's southernmost point. Its line of longitude is the dividing line between the Atlantic and Indian Oceans.
▶ What is the longitude of Cape Agulhas?

Cape Agulhas

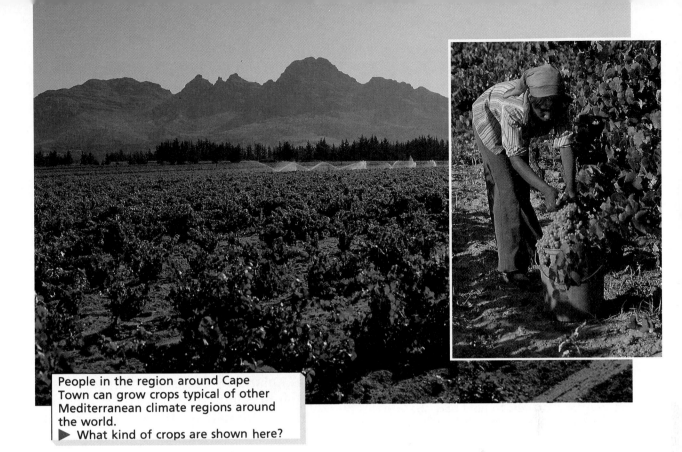

People in the region around Cape Town can grow crops typical of other Mediterranean climate regions around the world.
▶ What kind of crops are shown here?

becomes successively higher in steplike fashion as you move northward from the coast to the top of the plateau.

Farther east and extending north along the edge of the continent is the Drakensberg Mountain range. These and the many other mountains in the southern third of Africa make it difficult to travel from the coast to the interior plateau.

C. A Variety of Climates

High Veld Because of its southerly location and high elevations, much of the plateau of Southern Africa is grassland. This is the type of climate and vegetation found in Kansas and other places in the central United States. In Southern Africa this high plateau grassland is called the **High Veld**. The word *veld* means "grassland" in the **Afrikaans** language. Afrikaans, a language that is widely used in South Africa, is a variation of Dutch influenced by various African languages.

Mediterranean There are other types of climates in different parts of Southern Africa. A small coastal region around the city of Cape Town, South Africa, has a Mediterranean climate. This is one of the more comfortable climates in all of Africa. The winter season is rainy but mild, and the summer is sunny and dry. Residents and tourists alike can be almost certain of beautiful weather all summer long. As in other Mediterranean climate regions of the world, such as Greece, Italy, and southern California, people in this region of Southern Africa can grow crops such as wheat, barley, oats, apricots, plums, citrus fruit, and grapes.

Subtropical Another kind of climate is found along the coast of the Indian Ocean in southeastern Africa. A region of humid subtropical climate, it has warm and humid summers, mild winters, and year-round rainfall. People in this region can grow a variety of crops, including pineapples,

611

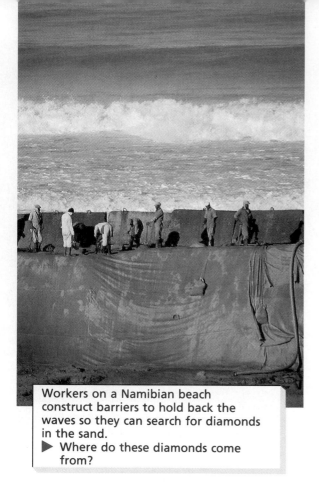

Workers on a Namibian beach construct barriers to hold back the waves so they can search for diamonds in the sand.
▶ Where do these diamonds come from?

interior, and the gravel that washes downstream includes millions of tiny diamonds no bigger than large grains of sand. Much of this gravel washes all the way into the Atlantic Ocean.

The Benguela Current, a cool current shown on the map on page 199, sweeps the gravel northward and deposits it and the tiny diamonds on the beaches of the Namib desert region. These beaches are fenced off and patrolled by armed guards. Diamond-mining companies have developed large machines to sort the tiny diamonds from the sand. Larger diamonds are used as gem stones; smaller diamonds are used industrially, for example, to make strong, hard drill bits.

The Kalahari The second major desert region in Southern Africa is the Kalahari, which is located on the interior plateau. The Kalahari is actually a semidesert region. It does receive a little rain, and grass and scrub grow in some areas. The Kalahari is mostly in the country of Botswana and is home to the San people, an ethnic group of Southern Africa.

bananas, and citrus fruits. However, the most important cash crop raised in this part of Southern Africa is sugarcane.

D. The Dry Regions of Southern Africa

The Namib Stretching up the coast of southwestern Africa from the mouth of the Orange River into Angola is a dry, barren landscape covered with sand and gravel. This arid part of Africa is the Namib Desert. Like Chile's Atacama Desert, the Namib is a coastal desert. It extends about 60 miles (97 km) inland to the escarpments that mark the edge of the African plateau.

The Namib Desert, however, is not a useless wasteland. It is the site of profitable diamond mines. In addition, millions of dollars worth of diamonds are found in the sand of its beaches. The Orange River erodes mineral-rich areas of South Africa's

LESSON 1

Review

REVIEWING MAIN IDEAS
A. When did Namibia become independent?
B. What is the High Veld?
C. What different types of climates are found in Southern Africa's coastal regions?
D. What valuable resource is found in the Namib Desert?

SKILLS CHECK

MAP SKILL
Using the map on page 610, find the lines of latitude between which the countries of Southern Africa are located.

Zimbabwe and Its Neighbors

CONNECTIONS

You have already read about European colonialism. What European countries had colonies in Africa?

TERMS

Malagasy

FOCUS

What are the lands and peoples of the northern half of Southern Africa like?

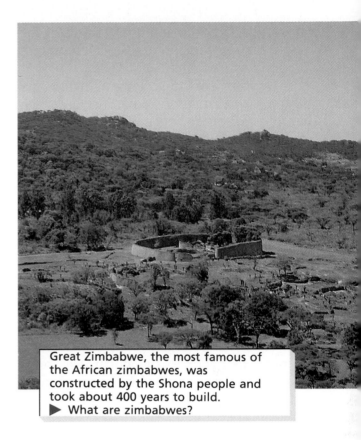

Great Zimbabwe, the most famous of the African zimbabwes, was constructed by the Shona people and took about 400 years to build.
▶ What are zimbabwes?

A. Zimbabwe: From Colony to Country

Zimbabwe's History Zimbabwe was once a British colony called Southern Rhodesia (roh DEE zhuh). It and another British colony, Northern Rhodesia, were named for Cecil Rhodes, a British colonizer and businessman. Rhodes acquired land for Britain and played a major role in governing its empire in Southern Africa. Southern Rhodesia was an important part of that empire.

When the first British colonizers moved into Southern Rhodesia in the late 1800s, they found a land inhabited by various African ethnic groups. The country today has a population of more than 9 million people, about 96 percent of whom are black. In the 1960s, Great Britain had said that it would grant independence to Southern Rhodesia only if the black majority there were allowed to rule. However, the white minority in the country refused to agree to the British plan. They declared independence in 1965 and governed the country under their own rules.

After years of turmoil caused by protests from other countries and an all-out civil war, Southern Rhodesia's white minority finally agreed to give control of the nation to the black majority in 1980. The country was renamed after *zimbabwes*, great stone communities built for the kings of an ancient trading kingdom that dominated this part of Africa in the twelfth to fifteenth centuries.

Zimbabwe's Resources Zimbabwe, a landlocked country about the size of Montana, is agriculturally productive. It has a humid subtropical climate that receives enough rainfall for people to be able to raise crops. These include tobacco, corn, cotton, wheat, sugarcane, vegetables, and the country's leading export crop, tobacco.

Zimbabwe is also part of the mineral-rich crescent of Southern Africa. Beginning near the country's capital city, Harare, and running southwest toward the industrial city of Bulawayo is what is called the Great Dyke. This mineral-rich rock formation is from 3 to 6 miles (5 to 10 km) wide and about 320 miles (516 km) long. It is a source of gold, copper, coal, iron ore, and nickel. In addition, about two thirds of the world's supply of chromite, a chromium ore, comes from the Great Dyke.

Another of Zimbabwe's major resources is the mighty Zambezi River, which forms the border between Zimbabwe and Zambia. One of the main scenic attractions in Africa, the impressive Victoria Falls, is located on the Zambezi. Several hundred miles downstream is Kariba Dam, which Zimbabwe and Zambia jointly built and own. The hydroelectric power plant at this dam provides almost all of the electricity used by the two countries.

B. Zambia and Malawi, Former British Colonies

Zambia   The country of Zambia, Zimbabwe's neighbor to the north, was once the British colony called Northern Rhodesia. It is a country that is rich in mineral deposits. The Copper Belt, part of Southern Africa's mineral crescent, extends from Zaire into Zambia, and copper is the major mineral resource of Zambia. The country also produces gold, silver, and cobalt.

Zambia is about the size of Texas and West Virginia combined. The country is similar to Zimbabwe in that it is also landlocked and sits on the high African plateau. About 7 million people live in Zambia, mostly in the capital city, Lusaka, and in mining and manufacturing cities such as Ndola (en DOH luh) and Kitwe, which are located in the Copper Belt.

Malawi   The country of Malawi, Zambia's neighbor to the east, used to be a British colony called Nyasaland. It gained independence in 1964.

Malawi is a small country, about the size of Mississippi. Like Zimbabwe and Zambia, Malawi is landlocked. However, it is more mountainous than either Zambia or Zimbabwe because it is located along

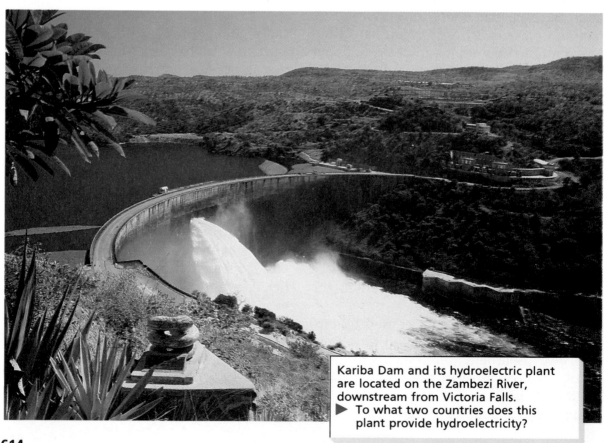

Kariba Dam and its hydroelectric plant are located on the Zambezi River, downstream from Victoria Falls.
▶ To what two countries does this plant provide hydroelectricity?

the Great Rift Valley, with its bordering ranges of volcanic peaks. Because of the rich volcanic soils found here, the people of Malawi can grow and export many kinds of crops, including rice, corn, sugarcane, tea, cotton, and tobacco.

C. Madagascar and the Comoro Islands

A Mixed Heritage Just off the Southern African coast is the world's fourth largest island, Madagascar. It is about as big as Colorado and New Mexico combined. Running down the middle of Madagascar is a high plateau where many of the country's 11 million people live. Here in the island's center is the capital city, which is called Antananarivo (an tuh nan uh REE voh).

Madagascar's central plateau divides the island into eastern and western halves, which have different cultural backgrounds. On the western side of the island, across from the African coast, the people are descendants of black Africans who spoke traditional African languages.

In many parts of eastern Madagascar, you can see rice fields up and down terraced hillsides. This part of the island reflects the influence of Southeast Asia. Many of Madagascar's people trace their ancestry back to Malay and Polynesian peoples who sailed here in outrigger canoes about 2,000 years ago.

A third major ethnic influence in Madagascar is French. For many years the island was a French colony. Many of Madagascar's people are Christians as a result of this French-European heritage, and many still speak the French language. However, the island's chief language is **Malagasy** (mal-uh GAS ee), an Asian language.

Agriculture Madagascar's climate is mostly tropical, and a variety of agricultural products grow here. In addition to rice, the island's farmers raise coffee, sugarcane,

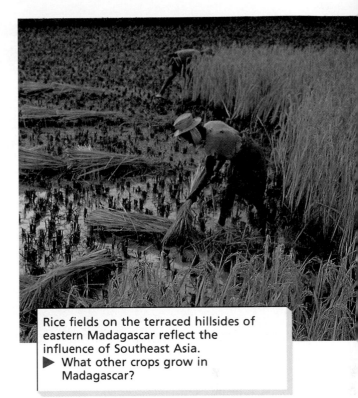

Rice fields on the terraced hillsides of eastern Madagascar reflect the influence of Southeast Asia.
▶ What other crops grow in Madagascar?

peppers, and cloves. Two specialty crops also grown here are vanilla beans and ylang-ylangs (EE lahng EE lahngz). Madagascar grows over half of the world's natural vanilla. If you have ever eaten vanilla ice cream with real vanilla beans ground into it, you have probably tasted vanilla from Madagascar. Ylang-ylangs are trees with fragrant flowers. The oil from these greenish-yellow flowers is used to scent perfumes. Madagascar also has some mineral resources, including coal, iron ore, chromite, graphite, and mica.

Comoro Islands The original settlers of the Comoro Islands were Muslims who came from the African mainland and who spoke Swahili. Later the Comoros, like Madagascar, became a French colony. In fact, one of the four main islands in this archipelago still belongs to France. The other islands, however, make up a fully independent nation.

615

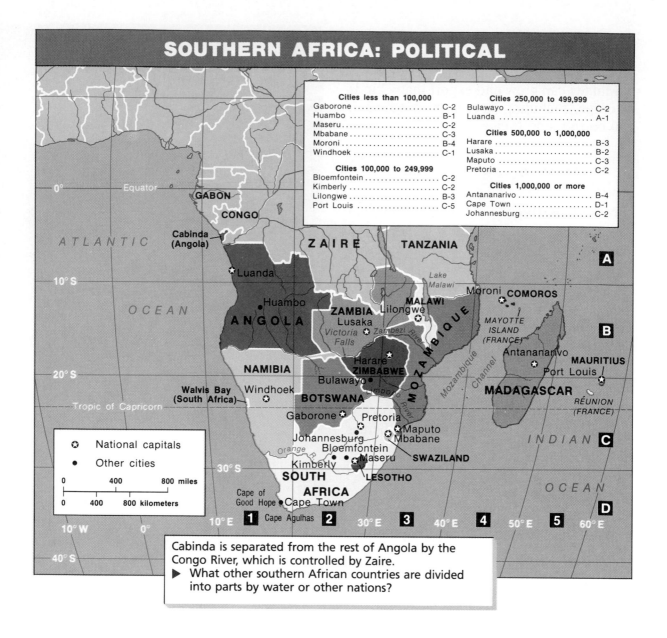

SOUTHERN AFRICA: POLITICAL

Cities less than 100,000
Gaborone	C-2
Huambo	B-1
Maseru	C-2
Mbabane	C-3
Moroni	B-4
Windhoek	C-1

Cities 100,000 to 249,999
Bloemfontein	C-2
Kimberly	C-2
Lilongwe	B-3
Port Louis	C-5

Cities 250,000 to 499,999
Bulawayo	C-2
Luanda	A-1

Cities 500,000 to 1,000,000
Harare	B-3
Lusaka	B-2
Maputo	C-3
Pretoria	C-2

Cities 1,000,000 or more
Antananarivo	B-4
Cape Town	D-1
Johannesburg	C-2

⊗ National capitals
• Other cities

0   400   800 miles
0   400   800 kilometers

Cabinda is separated from the rest of Angola by the Congo River, which is controlled by Zaire.
▶ What other southern African countries are divided into parts by water or other nations?

The Comoro Islands are volcanic in origin and, like Madagascar, have a mostly tropical climate. Much of the land here supports abundant tropical vegetation. The main agricultural products of the islands are rice, maize, and tropical fruits. Fishing is another important industry.

D. Botswana, Land of the San

Land and Resources Botswana, a former British colony, is a country about the size of New Mexico and Nevada combined. The capital city, Gaborone, and most other towns are located near the railroad running along Botswana's eastern border. This railroad connects Zimbabwe to South Africa.

Only about a million people live in Botswana. Most live in the eastern part, where the African plateau is higher in elevation and so there is enough rainfall to allow cattle herding. However, most of Botswana's income is from minerals, including copper, diamonds, and nickel.

People of the Desert A large part of Botswana is covered by the Kalahari Desert, which forms the dry interior of Southern Africa. Here live most of the San people of Africa. This ethnic group, formerly called Bushmen, leads a traditional and vanishing way of life on the desert plateau.

Once the San people roamed over much of Southern Africa. But in the 1600s, Europeans began pushing into the region from the south and other African peoples from the north began moving south with their cattle. The San tried to hold their ground, but many were killed and others were eventually forced to move. Finally the San retreated into the Kalahari Desert. Here they found a place that no one else wanted. The heat and scarcity of water offered the San some protection from their enemies.

Today about 5,000 San still lead a traditional life in the desert. They do not practice farming or herding but use hunting and gathering to survive. The San people have learned how to find water underground and to extract moisture and food from the few plants they can gather in the desert, such as roots, berries, and nuts. The San people also hunt game with bows and arrows or spears.

These San live in family groups of anywhere from a dozen people to more than 50. When they use up the resources of a part of the desert, they gather their few belongings and move on. The nomadic San travel light because they move around the desert on foot.

About 55,000 San people still live in the Kalahari region. Most are no longer nomadic hunters and gatherers. Many work as laborers on farms and ranches or in villages. To many people in the modern world, the life of the still-nomadic San people is primitive. But they know the secrets of survival in a harsh desert land that seems as if it could not possibly support human life.

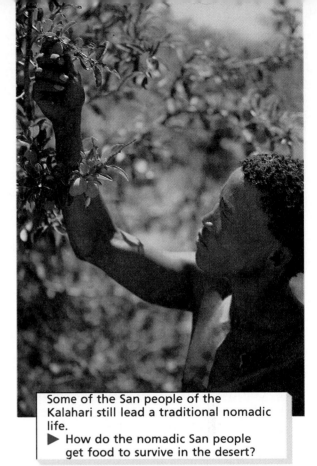

Some of the San people of the Kalahari still lead a traditional nomadic life.
▶ How do the nomadic San people get food to survive in the desert?

LESSON 2

Review

REVIEWING MAIN IDEAS
A. What are some of Zimbabwe's valuable resources?
B. Historically, what do Zambia and Malawi have in common?
C. Which ethnic groups have had an influence on the culture of Madagascar?
D. How do the San people of Botswana survive in the Kalahari Desert?

SKILLS CHECK

THINKING SKILL

Suppose you were going to the Kalahari Desert to spend a month studying the San way of life. Make a list of the things you would want or need to take with you to survive in the desert. Also make a list of the things the San use to survive. Then compare the two lists.

Angola and Mozambique

CONNECTIONS
Why did European countries establish colonies in Africa?

TERMS
exclave

FOCUS
What characteristics do Angola and Mozambique have in common?

A. Angola and Its Resources

Portuguese Colonies The Southern African countries of Angola and Mozambique (moh zum BEEK) were once part of Portugal's colonial empire. Portugal's official policy toward its colonies could best be described as exploitation, the use of something or someone purely for profit. Portugal wanted all the resources and raw materials that it could possibly get from its colonies. The country did almost nothing to develop or improve the colonies but merely took their cash crops, such as sugar and cotton, and used their people as slaves and laborers.

Portugal finally bowed to world pressure and granted independence to Angola and Mozambique in 1975. Since then, both countries have been plagued by civil war, with several different groups of people seeking power.

Angola Today Angola, the largest nation in Southern Africa, is about the size of Arizona, Nevada, New Mexico, and Alabama combined. About 8 million people live in Angola, mostly scattered across the high plateau country, away from the plain along the Atlantic coast.

Angola's narrow coastal plain is the site of the capital city, Luanda. However, the plain is sparsely populated because it is so dry. The cold Benguela Current that

flows offshore has an effect on Angola's coastal region. One benefit is that the cool ocean water is rich in nutrients that fish feed on, so fish are abundant in this region. Therefore, fishing is an important industry along the coast of Angola.

The northern part of Angola receives more rainfall than the rest of the country does and even has a few areas of dense tropical forest. During the colonial period the Portuguese had tried to establish their own agricultural industry in this part of Angola, but those efforts were largely unsuccessful. However, in the mid-twentieth century, the northern coffee plantations began to make a profit. Coffee is now Angola's main export crop.

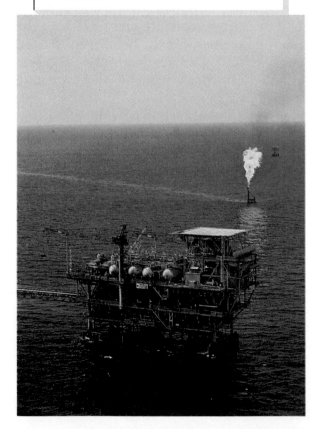

Oil is Angola's main export. The country's offshore oil fields are vital to its economy.
▶ Where are Angola's oil fields located?

B. Mozambique and Its Resources

On the Indian Ocean coast of Southern Africa is the nation of Mozambique, which is about the size of Texas and South Carolina combined. Like Angola, Mozambique has some mineral resources, including coal, iron ore, bauxite, and tungsten. There is a variety of crops, including cotton, sugarcane, tea, and cashew nuts. This coastal country also has a profitable fishing industry, with catches of tuna, lobster, and shrimp.

Mozambique has been able to develop some of its other resources. An example is the massive Cabora Bassa Dam project on the Zambezi River. This dam produces hydroelectricity for use in Mozambique and also for export to the neighboring country of South Africa.

Another source of income for Mozambique is its ports. This country has a fairly wide coastal plain with some major rivers, including the Zambezi and the Limpopo, emptying across it. The major port cities of Beira and Maputo, serve not only Mozambique but also the landlocked nations of Southern Africa. Railroads connect these port cities to the countries of Malawi, Zimbabwe, Zambia, and Botswana.

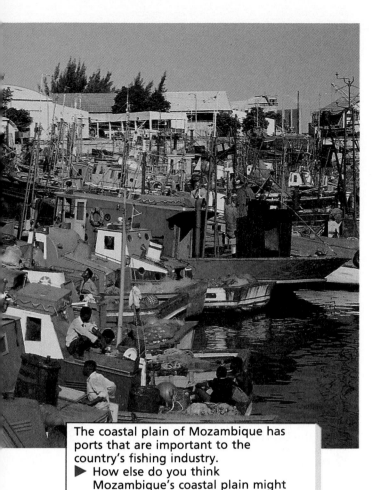

The coastal plain of Mozambique has ports that are important to the country's fishing industry.
▶ How else do you think Mozambique's coastal plain might be used?

Mineral Resources One small but very important coastal territory of Angola is separated from the rest of this large country. If you look at the map on page 616, you will see that part of Zaire protrudes, or extends, west to the Atlantic. Above this protrusion is the Angolan **exclave** (EHKS-klayv) of Cabinda. An exclave is a territory surrounded or nearly surrounded by the territory of another country. Cabinda is important to Angola because oil fields are located offshore. Oil is Angola's most important resource and its main export. The other major mineral resources found in Angola include diamonds, iron ore, gold, manganese, and copper.

LESSON 3

Review

REVIEWING MAIN IDEAS
A. What important resources does Angola have?
B. Why are waterways a valuable source of income for Mozambique?

SKILLS CHECK
WRITING SKILL

Write a paragraph or two explaining why you think Portugal would have wanted to establish colonies on opposite coasts of Southern Africa.

South Africa and Its Neighbors

CONNECTIONS

What country gave up control of Namibia in 1990?

TERMS

Boer, Great Trek, apartheid, homeland

FOCUS

What lasting effect has European colonialism had on the southernmost countries of Africa?

A. Europeans in South Africa

At the end of a long peninsula just south of Cape Town is a cape named the Cape of Good Hope. Many people mistakenly believe that the Cape of Good Hope is the southern tip of the African continent. This is probably because people learn in school that the Portuguese explorer Vasco da Gama sailed around this cape in 1498 on his voyage to discover a sea route to India. Actually, the southernmost point in Africa is Cape Agulhas, which lies about 100 miles (161 km) southeast of the Cape of Good Hope.

The Portuguese had been the first Europeans to see the South African coast when they discovered the Cape of Good Hope. But until the first Dutch colonizers arrived in 1652, South Africa was inhabited only by several different African ethnic groups. Among these groups were the Hottentots, San, Zulus, Swazis, and Basutos.

In 1652 the Dutch landed at Table Bay, the inlet that forms the harbor at Cape Town. There the Dutch East India Company established a supply station for their ships that were sailing back and forth between the Netherlands and the East Indies, a source of such valuable spices as pepper, cloves, nutmeg, and ginger. The Dutch who settled at Table Bay began to set up farms

After the British took control of Cape Town and the surrounding area, many of the Dutch settlers began to move to the South African interior.
▶ What were the Dutch settlers called?

and ranches. Soon other Europeans— French, German, and British—also settled at Table Bay. Many Europeans used the African peoples as slaves on their farms and ranches.

B. Growth of Colonies in South Africa

The Great Trek In 1806 the British decided they needed Table Bay as part of their African empire. They took control of the area and established the city of Cape Town as the capital of their new Cape Colony. The British began to force their way of life on the Dutch settlers, who were generally called the **Boers**. Many Boers decided it was time to seek out new lands in the South African interior. And thus

THE WORLD: GOLD PRODUCTION

**Production per year
(in thousands of pounds)**

- 0-10
- 11-50
- 51-100
- 101-200
- 201 or more

Throughout history, gold has been a highly prized metal. In the past, it was used for jewelry and coins. Today it is also used in electronics and dentistry.
▶ Which countries are the world's two leading gold producers?

began the **Great Trek**, the mass migration of thousands of Boers to the High Veld between 1835 and 1838.

Many of the Boers settled between the Orange and Vaal rivers. Find this area on the map on page 610. Here the Boers established an independent republic called the Orange Free State. By the mid-1800s they had established another republic, the Transvaal, farther to the northeast.

Dutch-British Conflict In 1867, diamonds were discovered along the Vaal River near where it joins the Orange River. Within four years the town there, Kimberley, had become the second largest town in South Africa as people rushed to the Orange Free State to search for diamonds.

During this "diamond rush," many British moved to the region around Kimberley. Then the British changed the official boundary of their colony to put Kimberley and its diamond riches within the borders of the Cape Colony, not within the Orange Free State. Many of the Boers, feeling cheated by the British, were outraged.

The tension between the Boers and the British increased with a second valuable mineral discovery. In the 1880s, gold was discovered in the Transvaal, another region that had been settled by the Boers. The gold rush that resulted here created the largest city in South Africa, Johannesburg. It also brought more British and other Europeans to the Transvaal region.

Eventually the tension between the

FROM: **Kaffir Boy** by Mark Mathabane

In his autobiography, *Kaffir Boy,* Mark Mathabane describes the story of a black youth's childhood in apartheid South Africa.

Mathabane spent the first eighteen years in Alexandra, a black ghetto of Johannesburg. Mark writes about the feelings of hate, bitterness, hunger, pain, and terror he experienced as he grew up.

. . . *W*hereas in the past I had been more or less conscious of their [the police's] presence in black life—as they stopped people in the streets and demanded passes, as they chased after *tsotsis* [gangsters] and other hoodlums, as they raided shebeens [places where liquor is sold without a license] in search of illicit liquor, and they launched an occasional pass raid into the neighbourhood—they now moved permanently into my consciousness. Scarcely a week passed without the neighbourhood being invaded by waves of black and white policemen.

They always came unannounced, at any time of day or night, and gradually I came to accept, and to dread, their presence as a way of life. They haunted me in real life and in my dreams, to the extent that I would often wake up screaming in the middle of the night, claiming that the police were after me with dogs or flashlights, trying to shoot me down. Word had it that our neighbourhood, because of the increasing presence of people whose papers were not in order, had been designated a "hot spot," which meant that it had to

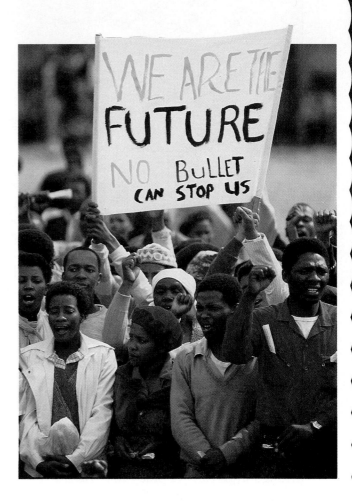

be raided constantly. So, barely six years old, I was called upon to deal with constant terror. . . .

Mark was an especially talented tennis player, and it was this ability that allowed him to escape the system of apartheid. In 1978, he received his passport to freedom when he was granted a tennis scholarship to an American college. Because of his experiences in America, Mark came to understand the meaning of human rights and a life without fear.

Boers and the British led to the Anglo-Boer War, which lasted from 1899 to 1902. The British won this war and, in 1910, created the new nation of South Africa, which united the Cape Colony, the Orange Free State, the Transvaal, and the eastern colony of Natal.

C. South Africa Today

A Modern Nation South Africa today has two capital cities. The main government offices are in Pretoria, which was the capital of the former Boer republic of Transvaal. The parliament meets in Cape Town, which was the capital of the British Cape Colony.

South Africa has developed into the most modern, industrialized nation in Africa because of its tremendous mineral riches. About 65 to 70 percent of all the gold in the world comes from South Africa. A large proportion of the world's gem diamonds also comes from this country, and it also has iron ore, coal, and other valuable minerals. Most of these minerals lie in the Witwatersrand area, near Johannesburg. This region is the southern end of the mineral-rich crescent that extends through much of Southern Africa.

Racial Conflict The government of South Africa is controlled by the country's white minority. The whites have tried to enforce **apartheid**, a policy of social control. *Apartheid* is an Afrikaans word that means "separateness." Basically, apartheid calls for the complete separation of South Africa's racial groups.

South Africa has a population of almost 38 million. It is divided into four main racial groups. The whites, descendants of the Europeans, only make up about 16 percent of the population. The largest population group is the black African group, who make up about 72 percent. About 3 percent of the population is Asian, primarily from India. Another 9 percent are people of mixed race. They are called Coloreds.

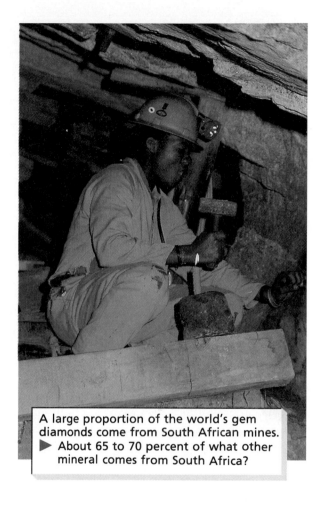

A large proportion of the world's gem diamonds come from South African mines.
▶ About 65 to 70 percent of what other mineral comes from South Africa?

The apartheid policy does not provide for the equality of all people. Apartheid has resulted in separate jobs, transportation, schools, communities, and other facilities for the different ethnic groups. The whites are the privileged group; the nonwhites are denied many basic freedoms. Many South African blacks have been forced to move to special reserves called **homelands**.

Opposition Nonwhites in South Africa have struggled for years to end apartheid and to gain equal rights. The United Nations has asked South Africa to end apartheid, and among people who believe apartheid violates human rights, there is a worldwide movement to abolish the policy. Even some white South Africans spoke out against the apartheid policy.

Stephen Ndotshoni is 15-years-old. He lives with his father, mother, and three little brothers in a one-room shack in South Africa. His father built the shack from old metal roofing panels, old boards, and pieces of cardboard.

The sleeping arrangements are simple. Stephen's mother sleeps on a small cot in the corner of the room. Stephen, his father, and his brothers sleep on mats and bedding on the dirt floor of the hut. During the day, the bedding is folded and stuffed into the corner to make room for other daily activities.

Every day Stephen has to walk a half mile to the nearest water source to fill the family's water containers. Stephen often has to wait in long lines because several thousand families use the same source of water.

Black families in South Africa do not have many modern luxuries. There are few televisions, toasters, washing machines, or microwave ovens; most of the shacks do not even have electricity.

The South African government's policy of apartheid makes it very difficult for blacks and other ethnic groups to improve their standard of living. Many blacks cannot make a living inside their homeland, but if they want to leave the homeland they often cannot take their families. Also, educational opportunities are far from equal among these groups.

Stephen lives with his family in the South African township of Leauadi. Many families live in poor, overcrowded conditions because they have no choice. The South African government forced the black people to live in designated homelands.

One of the bright spots in Stephen's day is school. He is in the seventh grade at the Number 3 school in Leauadi. The school is in an old wooden building with four classrooms. There is one teacher for both the sixth and seventh grades.

A few years ago, a government official tried to enforce a law that required the schools in black homelands to teach the Afrikaans language instead of the English language. Afrikaans is the language of the people in the government who have forced apartheid on the community. The residents in the black homelands protested. English was ruled to be the official language. Since the language dispute was won by the community, Stephen and his family believe that there will eventually be more victories over the apartheid system. Recent events in South Africa indicate that the system of apartheid may soon be changing. Black South Africans are hoping for a brighter future.

The 1993 Nobel Peace Prize was awarded to South African President Frederik de Klerk (left) and African National Congress President Nelson Mandela (right). They were honored for their efforts to bring peace and democracy to South Africa.
► Why were the efforts of both leaders needed to end apartheid?

The South African government has made some changes in response to outside pressure. The government lifted its ban on the African National Congress, a group that works to gain economic and political equality for Africans. Nelson Mandela, a leader of the black freedom movement in South Africa, who had been in jail for nearly 30 years, was released in 1990. And in 1991 the Population Registration Act, which classified Africans by race from birth, was eliminated. This law was the legal basis for apartheid.

A Yes Vote The South African government began to negotiate with the African National Congress and other nonapartheid groups to end white minority rule. But not all white South Africans want to end their control over the country. These people want things to remain as they were in the past.

In 1992 the government decided to put the matter to a vote to determine how the majority of whites felt about the issue. All whites who were eligible to vote were asked to answer the question: "Do you support continuation of the reform process?" Almost 70 percent voted "yes".

D. South Africa's Neighbors

Namibia The country of Namibia is large, about the size of Texas and North Carolina combined. However, only about a million people live in Namibia; more than 24 million people live in Texas and North Carolina. Only about 75,000 of Namibia's people are white, and since the country has become independent, many of them who are Afrikaners have moved to South Africa.

You have already read about the Namib Desert. This coastal desert covers most of Namibia. Inland is a high, arid plateau. The country's capital, Windhoek, is located on the plateau. Recall that the sports stadium in Windhoek was the site of Namibia's independence celebration.

Besides having diamonds in mines and along the beaches of the Namib Desert, Namibia has some copper and uranium. And as in the country's neighbor to the north, Angola, fishing is an important industry. Tuna and sardines are harvested from the cool waters of the Atlantic. In addition, some areas of Namibia have enough grazing land to support livestock, and both cattle and sheep are raised.

Swaziland Nestled between South Africa and Mozambique is the tiny country of Swaziland. About the size of Connecticut, Swaziland has a population of about 800,000. Located where the High Veld descends over an escarpment to a low hilly area, the country has generally good soils. Many kinds of agricultural products grow here. Forest products, sugarcane, cotton, pineapples, cattle, and dairy products are Swaziland's chief sources of income. In addition, Swaziland and its capital, Mbabane (em bah BAH nay), are important tourist centers. Many South Africans travel to Swaziland to see certain movies and find other types of entertainment banned in their own country.

Lesotho As you can see on the map on page 616, the small nation of Lesotho (le-SUT hoh) is within the country of South Africa. How has this black African country managed to survive where it is, completely surrounded by the white-controlled country of South Africa?

Many years ago the Basuto ethnic group moved to the Drakensberg Mountains of Southern Africa to escape hostile enemies to the north. Later, when the Boers started moving closer to this area, the Basutos asked the British government in the Cape Colony for protection. The British established a colony called Basutoland.

When the nation of South Africa was formed, Basutoland remained a British colony. Because the land here is so mountainous and the soils are so poor, there was nothing here that South Africa wanted. When Britain granted the colony its independence, it was renamed Lesotho.

Lesotho is only about the size of the state of Maryland, and the country's population is about 2 million. The capital city is Maseru. The country provides many workers for the industries of South Africa. People from Lesotho can commute across the border daily to work in the South African factories. And in this way, Lesotho—like Namibia and Swaziland—is tied to its large neighbor, South Africa.

The people of Swaziland celebrate their independence day, September 6, 1968, at a ceremony in the capital city.
▶ What is the capital of Swaziland?

LESSON 4

Review

REVIEWING MAIN IDEAS

A. Who were the main groups of people living in South Africa when the Europeans first arrived?
B. Why did the Boers move to the South African interior?
C. What is apartheid?
D. What country is found within South Africa?

SKILLS CHECK

WRITING SKILL

Write an editorial describing how you think apartheid could be eliminated in South Africa.

CHAPTER

25 REVIEW

REVIEWING TERMS

On a separate sheet of paper, rewrite the sentences using the term from the list that best completes each sentence.

escarpment
exclave
Great Trek
apartheid
homeland

1. A territory that is surrounded or nearly surrounded by the territory of another country is called an _____.
2. The _____ began in South Africa when thousands of Boers migrated to the High Veld between 1835 and 1838.
3. The policy of _____ calls for the complete separation of South Africa's racial groups.
4. In South Africa each special area reserved for blacks to live in is called a _____.
5. An _____ is a steep slope or cliff formed by erosion or by movements of the earth's rock layers.

REVIEWING THE FACTS

On a separate sheet of paper, answer the following questions in complete sentences.

1. How is the southern region of Africa similar to the other parts of Africa?
2. What two deserts are found in Southern Africa?
3. Where is Madagascar located?
4. What nation colonized Madagascar and the Comoro Islands?
5. What ethnic group inhabits the Kalahari Desert?

6. Why is Mozambique important to the landlocked nations of South Africa?
7. Why did the Dutch East India Company establish a colony at Table Bay?
8. What conflicts eventually led to the Anglo-Boer War?
9. What natural resource found in South Africa has allowed it to develop into the most modern, industrialized nation in Africa?
10. What is the largest population group in South Africa?

WRITING ABOUT ECONOMICS

Colonialism has a long history, not only in South Africa but in other areas of the world. Write several paragraphs that give examples of colonization in other areas of the world and explain why those areas were valuable.

THINKING CRITICALLY

On a separate sheet of paper, answer the following questions in complete sentences.

1. Why, do you think, would a country be an independent nation rather than a colony?
2. Why don't the San people of the Kalahari Desert practice farming or herding?
3. What actions could a country take to avoid exploitation of its colonies?
4. What mineral "rush" took place in the United States in 1849 that was similar to the "diamond rush" that took place in the Orange Free State?
5. How does the geography of Madagascar help explain why the island has a mixed cultural heritage?

On a separate sheet of paper, draw a graphic organizer that is like the one shown here. Copy the information from this graphic organizer to the one you have drawn. Complete the chart by writing in the appropriate item for each box. Some of the boxes have been done for you.

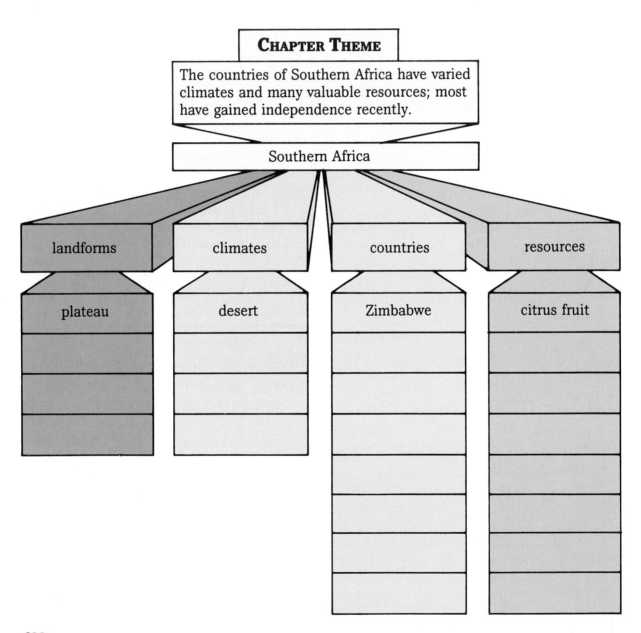

CHAPTER THEME

The countries of Southern Africa have varied climates and many valuable resources; most have gained independence recently.

Southern Africa

landforms	climates	countries	resources
plateau	desert	Zimbabwe	citrus fruit

COOPERATIVE LEARNING

In Unit 6 you learned about the continent of Africa. The regions of northern, western, central, eastern, and southern Africa will be the subjects of your class project.

PROJECT

Your teacher will assign one of the regions you studied in Unit 6 to your group. This region will be the name of your group. There must be five groups. Each group will be responsible for a different region of Africa.

Your group's project is to create a television game show similar to the famous game show "Jeopardy." The teacher will be the host of the game show, which will be called "Africa." He or she will choose a scorekeeper.

The game will have a point system of 10, 20, 30, 40 and 50-point questions. Each group must write two questions about their region of Africa for each point category. The 10-point questions will be the easiest to answer, while the 50-point questions will be the most difficult.

Meet with your group to choose a leader. The leader will distribute the type of questions each member will write. Each group will write 10 questions.

Use the information in your chapter to write questions. Questions can be asked about the physical features, farming, economy, ways of life, and living and working conditions in a region of Africa.

The teacher will help you understand how the game is to be organized. He or she will draw the game on the blackboard for you and answer any questions you may have.

PRESENTATION AND REVIEW

Each group will give 10 questions to the teacher. The teacher will distribute the questions in the 10-, 20-, 30-, 40-, or 50-point pile. There will be piles of 10 to 50 point questions for the teacher to ask each group.

Each group will take turns and choose a box on the board. For example, one of the groups may want to try to answer a 30-point question. After the teacher asks the question, the group will try to come up with an answer. If the answer given by the group leader is correct, the group will receive 30 points and an *X* will be placed in the box by the scorekeeper. The points will be added on the scoreboard. At the end of the game, the points will be added up and a winner will be determined.

After the game is over, your group should meet to evaluate your project. How well did your group's members work together? How could your project have been improved?

REMEMBER TO:
- Give your ideas.
- Listen to others' ideas.
- Plan your work with the group.
- Present your project.
- Discuss how your group worked.

SKILLBUILDER

ANALYZING AND INFERRING FROM A POPULATION DENSITY MAP

WHY DO I NEED THIS SKILL?

Analyzing information and making inferences from it are two important thinking skills. They help you "get more out of" the information. You can develop the skills of analyzing and inferring by using a population density map. Population density maps show how people are distributed throughout an area of the world.

LEARNING THE SKILL

The term *population density* refers to the average number of people per square mile or square kilometer in a particular place, such as a state, country, or region. To find population density, you divide the number of people living in a place by the area—that is, by the size of the place in square miles or square kilometers.

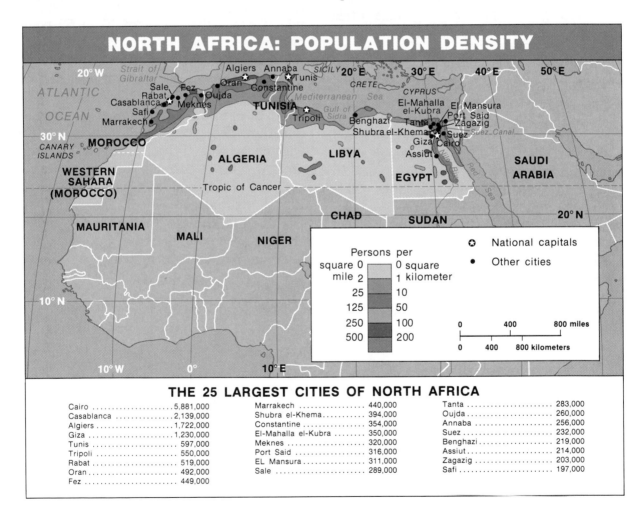

NORTH AFRICA: POPULATION DENSITY

Persons per	
square mile 0	0 square kilometer
2	1
25	10
125	50
250	100
500	200

✪ National capitals
● Other cities

THE 25 LARGEST CITIES OF NORTH AFRICA

Cairo 5,881,000	Marrakech 440,000	Tanta 283,000
Casablanca 2,139,000	Shubra el-Khema. 394,000	Oujda 260,000
Algiers 1,722,000	Constantine 354,000	Annaba 256,000
Giza 1,230,000	El-Mahalla el-Kubra 350,000	Suez 232,000
Tunis 597,000	Meknes 320,000	Benghazi 219,000
Tripoli 550,000	Port Said 316,000	Assiut 214,000
Rabat 519,000	EL Mansura 311,000	Zagazig 203,000
Oran 492,000	Sale 289,000	Safi 197,000
Fez 449,000		

For example, the area of the country of Egypt is 386,660 square miles (1,001,449 sq km). The population of the country is 52,000,000. By dividing the population by the area, you find that the population density of Egypt is about 134 people per square mile (52 people per sq km). This means about 142 people live in each square mile of land.

Of course, each square mile or kilometer does not have exactly the same number of people. Population density refers to the *average* number of people per square mile or square kilometer. The higher the average number of people per square mile or kilometer, the higher the population density.

A population density map shows the variation of population density within an area. For example, the population density map of North Africa shows the variation of population density from place to place within that region. The various colors show the degree of population density in the different parts of the region. As the key indicates, areas shown in beige have between 0 and 2 people per square mile (0 and 1 person per sq km). Areas shown in purple have the highest population densities, 500 people per square mile (200 people per sq km) or more.

This population density map also has a table that lists the 25 largest cities in North Africa. Notice that in Egypt, for example, the largest cities are located where the highest population density is found. On most population density maps, you will find that the largest cities are usually located in the more densely populated areas. Thus, even when a population density map does not list the largest cities in a table, you can usually infer that the largest cities are located in the more densely populated areas.

PRACTICING THE SKILL

Use the population density map of North Africa to answer the following questions.

1. How many different population density areas does the map show?
2. What geographical characteristic do you think the most densely populated areas have in common?
3. What is the population density in the area along the Nile River?
4. What is the population density in the area around the city of Tripoli, Libya?
5. What city in Morocco has a population density between 250 and 500 people per square mile (100 and 200 people per sq km)?
6. What is the population density around the capital city of Algeria?
7. Why, do you think, is the population density in Western Sahara so low?
8. In which country is the fifth largest city in North Africa located?
9. How many of the 25 largest cities are located along the Mediterranean?
10. How many areas shown on the map have population densities between 125 and 250 people per square mile (50 and 100 people per sq km)?

APPLYING THE SKILL

You can analyze and make inferences from the information presented in all the maps in your geography textbook. Use the specific map skills you have just learned when you study the population density map of Australia and New Zealand, which is found on page 651 of Chapter 26.

SKILLBUILDER

UNDERSTANDING CAUSE AND EFFECT

WHY DO I NEED THIS SKILL?

The connection between events or actions is called a *cause-and-effect relationship*. It can help to explain why events occur or why people act as they do. The *cause* is an event or action that results in the *effect*, another event or action. Recognizing and understanding cause-and-effect relationships will help you comprehend and learn from your geography book and other textbooks.

LEARNING THE SKILL

Some causes and effects are simple. For example, think about the story you read in Chapter 21 of the World War II bomber *Lady Be Good*.

Cause:	Effect:
Lady be Good ran out of fuel	Crash-landed in the Sahara.

Sometimes there are signal words, such as *because, so, since, therefore, as a result*, to suggest that there might be a cause-and-effect relationship.

Cause:	Effect:
Because they rationed their water and traveled at night	Crew of the *Lady Be Good* lasted eight days

Some cause-and-effect relationships are more complex. For example, one cause could have multiple effects.

C1: Plane ran out of fuel

E1: Fliers parachuted out
E2: Plane crashed
E3: Fliers ultimately died

Sometimes, multiple causes contribute to one effect.

C1: Lack of water
C2: Extreme heat
C3: Exhaustion

E1: Fliers died

Often, causes and effects overlap and result in a cause-and-effect chain:

C1: Crew was lost

E1 (C2): Plane ran out of fuel
E2 (C3): Plane crashed (and so on)

PRACTICING THE SKILL

On pages 542–543 of Chapter 21, you read about the construction of the Aswan High Dam in Egypt. The dam was the cause of many different effects, some of them good and some of them bad.

Copy the partially completed cause-and-effect diagram shown on the next page and fill in the missing causes and effects. Draw additional boxes to represent other causes and effects. Use arrows to show the cause-and-effect relationships.

CAUSE-AND-EFFECT RELATIONSHIPS

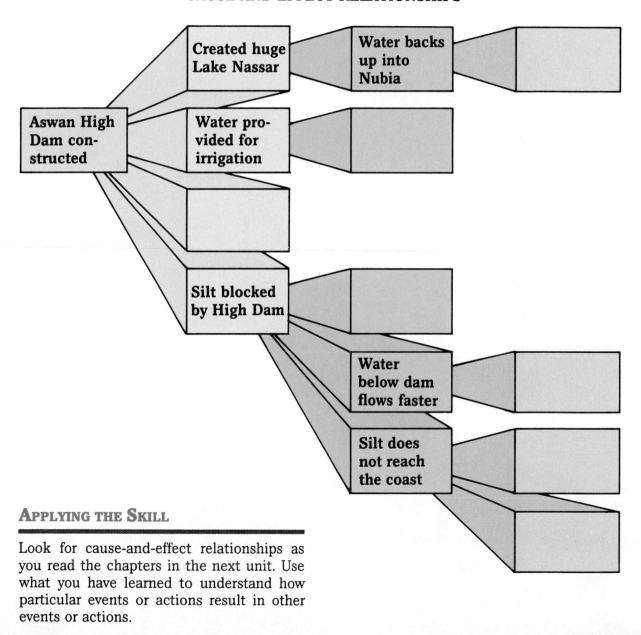

APPLYING THE SKILL

Look for cause-and-effect relationships as you read the chapters in the next unit. Use what you have learned to understand how particular events or actions result in other events or actions.

UNIT 7

AUSTRALIA, NEW ZEALAND, AND THE PACIFIC ISLANDS

CONTINENTAL HANDBOOK

TABLE OF COUNTRIES

CONNECTIONS

Look at the map on page 637. Why would the United States want to have island territories in the Pacific Ocean?

TERMS

typhoon

FOCUS

How has Oceania changed in recent years?

Australian Reassures Reagan of Commitment to Alliance
By Gerald M. Boyd

WASHINGTON, April 17—Administration officials said today that Prime Minister Bob Hawke of Australia had assured President Reagan that Australia would continue a security pact with the United States, even if the alliance did not include New Zealand.

A. The United States in the Pacific

In 1986 the United States and New Zealand had a disagreement about the defense treaty the two countries had signed. The treaty, which was also signed by Australia, was designed to protect Australia, New Zealand, and the United States. Problems occurred when New Zealand said it would not allow a ship to dock in New Zealand unless the ship's captain first announced whether the ship held nuclear weapons. The United States said that American ships would not follow New Zealand's request, since the request violated United States military policy. When New Zealand refused to make any exceptions, the United States decided to break its treaty commitments with New Zealand. The United States and New Zealand are still on good terms, however, and both countries continue to trade with each other.

The defense treaty with Australia is only one example of how important the countries and territories of the Pacific Ocean are to the United States. Our fiftieth state—Hawaii—is located in the Pacific Ocean. Two United States territories are also located here. American Samoa lies south of the Equator in the region called Polynesia. Guam, in the region called Micronesia, is west of the International Date Line. When it is Monday afternoon on the American mainland, it is Tuesday morning in Guam.

The people of Guam are American citizens. American Samoans are American nationals but not citizens. Both territories elect their own governors and legislatures. Their voters also send a nonvoting delegate to the United States Congress.

AUSTRALIA, NEW ZEALAND, AND OCEANIA: POLITICAL

Map legend:
- ⊙ National capitals
- ⊙ Capitals of free association nations
- • Other cities

0   500   1,000 miles
0   500   1,000 kilometers

AUST. —AUSTRALIA
FR. —FRANCE
N.Z. —NEW ZEALAND
U.K. —UNITED KINGDOM
U.S. —UNITED STATES

Some Pacific islands are territories of other countries. Other islands are independent or have a free association, which means they have self-rule but choose to leave foreign policy to a larger country.
▶ What islands have a free association with New Zealand?

The United States possesses several very small islands in the Pacific. Wake and Midway islands are little more than landing fields for airplanes. Johnson Atoll and Howland Island each have an area of only 1 square mile (2.6 sq km). Tiny Baker Island is even smaller.

After World War II the United States took over a number of islands in the region called Micronesia. It was agreed that the peoples of these islands would decide their own future. These islands now have separate governments: the Commonwealth of the Northern Marianas, the

Federated States of Micronesia, the Republic of the Marshall Islands, and the Republic of Palau.

B. The World's Largest Ocean

Oceans and seas cover about 70 percent of the earth's surface. The Pacific Ocean with its marginal, or bordering, seas makes up half of the earth's watery cover. The Pacific is nearly twice as large as the Atlantic Ocean.

The Pacific is the deepest of the world's oceans. A depth of over 36,000 feet (10,973 m) has been measured east of the Mariana Islands. That is almost 7 miles (11 km) deep. If Mount Everest, the world's tallest mountain, rose from the floor of the Pacific, its top would still be more than a mile below the surface.

The name Pacific means "peaceful" or "calm." Ferdinand Magellan, the first European to sail across the great ocean, in 1520, gave the Pacific its name. When he first saw the open sea after a storm-tossed voyage around the tip of South America, the ocean appeared peaceful and calm. But do not let the name mislead you, because the Pacific Ocean is not always peaceful. During certain seasons, tropical storms called **typhoons** sweep over the Pacific and its islands. Typhoons are similar to the Atlantic storms called hurricanes.

C. Oceania: Scattered Islands in the Ocean

Scattered across the Pacific Ocean are thousands of islands. They range in size from Australia, the world's smallest continent and largest island, to tiny islets, islands so small that no one has ever lived on them. Most of the islets are too small to be shown on a map.

Some of the islands in the Pacific, such as Japan, Indonesia, and the Philippines, are so close to Asia that they are usually considered part of that continent. However, Australia and other Pacific Islands differ so greatly from Asia that they are considered a separate region of the world. Years ago a geographer thought that this region of scattered islands should have a name. He decided that since it was located in the greatest of oceans, he would call it Oceania.

D. The Countries of Oceania

The political map of Oceania has changed greatly since 1959. Earlier maps showed only two independent countries: Australia and New Zealand. All other lands were shown as possessions or territories of outside countries.

Since 1959 a number of islands have formed independent countries. These new countries include the ones you read about earlier in this lesson. Others include the former Gilbert and Ellice islands. Once a British colony, these islands divided and became two countries, Kiribati and Tuvalu.

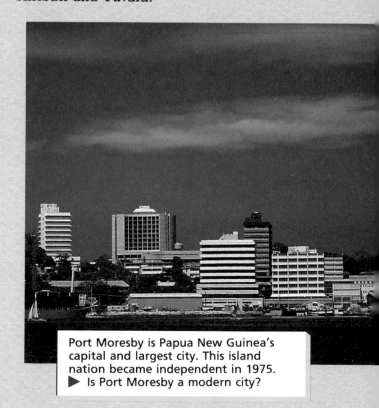

Port Moresby is Papua New Guinea's capital and largest city. This island nation became independent in 1975.
▶ Is Port Moresby a modern city?

Huge stone statues mark the landscape of Easter Island. Scientists think that the statues were carved by early explorers from the Pacific Islands.
► What were these statues carved from?

Fiji and the Solomon Islands have kept the same names, but they are now independent countries rather than parts of the British Empire. So, too, is Tonga, which the British at one time called the Friendly Islands. The New Hebrides, once controlled by both Britain and France, is now the country of Vanuatu.

Papua New Guinea is one of the largest countries of the Pacific Islands. It consists of New Guinea plus New Britain, Bougainville, and other small islands. Australia once controlled this land as well as tiny Nauru, which has an area of only 8 square miles (21 sq km). Western Samoa, now independent, was formerly governed by New Zealand.

French Polynesia and New Caledonia remain French. An independence movement exists in New Caledonia, but 40 percent of the people are of French descent and have opposed separation from France in the past.

Review

REVIEWING MAIN IDEAS

A. What agreement did the United States and Micronesia have?
B. Why is the Pacific Ocean's name misleading?
C. How did Oceania get its name?
D. How has the political map of Oceania changed in recent years?

SKILLS CHECK

MAP SKILL

Turn to the map on page 637. What line of longitude does the International Date Line run parallel to?

AUSTRALIA, NEW ZEALAND & OCEANIA

	FLAG AND PRINCIPAL LANGUAGE(S)	POPULATION AND LANDMASS	PRINCIPAL PRODUCTS EXPORT	IMPORT

AUSTRALIA

Canberra ★

English

POPULATION
16,800,000
6 per sq mi/2 per sq km

LANDMASS
2,967,909 sq mi/7,686,884 sq km

Coal   Machinery

FEDERATED STATES OF MICRONESIA

Kolonia ★

English

POPULATION
87,000
105 per sq mi/41 per sq km

LANDMASS
825 sq mi/2,137 sq km

Food   Coconut Oil

FIJI

★ Suva

English, Fijian,
Hindustani

POPULATION
800,000
115 per sq mi/45 per sq km

LANDMASS
6,938 sq mi/17,969 sq km

Sugar   Petroleum

KIRIBATI

Bairiki ★

English

POPULATION
63,848
192 per sq mi/74 per sq km

LANDMASS
332 sq mi/860 sq km

Copra   Food

MARSHALL ISLANDS

Majuro ★

English

POPULATION
31,041
7 per sq mi/3 per sq km

LANDMASS
439,735 sq mi/1,138,914 sq km

Coconut Oil   Food

NAURU

Yaren ★

Nauruan, English

POPULATION
8,042
946 per sq mi/365 per sq km

LANDMASS
9 sq mi/22 sq km

Phosphates   Food

NEW ZEALAND

Wellington ★

English, Maori

POPULATION
3,400,000
33 per sq mi/13 per sq km

LANDMASS
103,736 sq mi/268,676 sq km

Meat   Machinery

	FLAG AND PRINCIPAL LANGUAGE(S)	POPULATION AND LANDMASS	PRINCIPAL PRODUCTS EXPORT	IMPORT

NORTHERN MARIANAS

★Saipan

English

POPULATION
19,000
103 per sq mi/40 per sq km

LANDMASS
184 sq mi/477 sq km

Coconut Oil   N/A

PAPUA NEW GUINEA

Port Moresby

Pidgin English,
Chinese

POPULATION
3,900,000
21 per sq mi/8 per sq km

LANDMASS
182,700 sq mi/473,193 sq km

Gold   Machinery

SOLOMON ISLANDS

Honiara ★

English,
Pidgin English

POPULATION
300,000
20 per sq mi/8 per sq km

LANDMASS
6,938 sq mi/17,969 sq km

Copra   Petroleum

TONGA

Nukualofa ★

Tongan, English

POPULATION
96,448
357 per sq mi/138 per sq km

LANDMASS
270 sq mi/699 sq km

Coconut Oil   Food

TUVALU

Funafuti ★

Tuvaluan, English

POPULATION
8,229
914 per sq mi/353 per sq km

LANDMASS
9 sq mi/23 sq km

Copra   Food

VANUATU

★Port Vila

English, French

POPULATION
200,000
35 per sq mi/14 per sq km

LANDMASS
109,483 sq mi/283,561 sq km

Copra   Food

WESTERN SAMOA

★Apia

Samoan, English

POPULATION
200,000
182 per sq mi/70 per sq km

LANDMASS
1,097 sq mi/2,841 sq km

Coconut Oil   Food

26 AUSTRALIA AND NEW ZEALAND

Australia: Continent and Country

CONNECTIONS

What are the benefits of being located a great distance from other places on the earth?

TERMS

outback, marsupial, coral, reef, Aborigine, anthropologist

FOCUS

What is the landscape of Australia, and how was the continent settled?

A. The Southern Continent

The Mystery In 1768, Captain James Cook and his crew set sail aboard the *Endeavour* in search of the solution to a mystery. From the time of the ancient Romans to the travels of Marco Polo, geographers believed in the existence of a southern continent. Clues to the existence of this southern land were gained by Spanish, Portuguese, Dutch, and English explorers.

The Clues From the beginning of the 1500s, brave ship captains led sailing expeditions throughout the vast unknown waters of the Pacific Ocean. Spanish ships searched in vain for the continent. It is believed that one expedition passed within several miles of the continent, but no crew members sighted it. The Portuguese may have landed on the shore but kept it a secret from their rivals, the Spanish.

In 1605 a Dutch ship exploring New Guinea headed south and discovered the northern tip of Australia, which would later be named Cape York. Within the next forty years, more clues came in from other Dutch ships that found parts of the coastline. One expedition, led by Abel Tasman, missed the mainland but discovered New Zealand and the island that would later be named Tasmania.

The Answer The British sent Captain Cook and the *Endeavour* after several British explorations also failed to find the continent. By March of 1770, Cook and his crew had decided to return home. After sailing for almost two years, they were ready to give up their search. They had explored various islands, including New Zealand, but had not found the missing continent. It was during the voyage home on April 19 that the Australian coast was sighted. Ten days later, they went ashore in a smaller boat called a longboat.

It was time to land. A young midshipman [naval officer] named Isaac Smith was in the bow [front of the boat]. Years later, after many promotions, Admiral Smith . . . would proudly tell how the greatest navigator in history hesitated before quitting the longboat, touched him on the shoulder and said, "Isaac, you shall land first." The lad sprang into the green bottle-glass water . . . and waded ashore. Cook and the others followed, and the seal of distance and space that had protected the east coast of Australia . . . was broken.

A Land Close to Asia Because it takes so long to get to Australia from Europe and North America, most people think of Australia as being a long way from anywhere. But Australia is not far from Asia. It is only about 100 miles (161 km) from the northern tip of Australia to the island of New Guinea. From there, it is relatively easy to travel through the islands of East Asia to mainland Asia. People from Indonesia, Japan, or China don't think of Australia as being far away and isolated.

You might expect that a country that is so close to Asia would have many people from densely populated China or Japan. But there are few Asians in Australia. Today, most Australians are of European origin, especially from Great Britain and Ireland. For many years, Australia had laws that made

▶ One of Sydney, Australia's, most prominent landmarks is the Sydney Opera House.

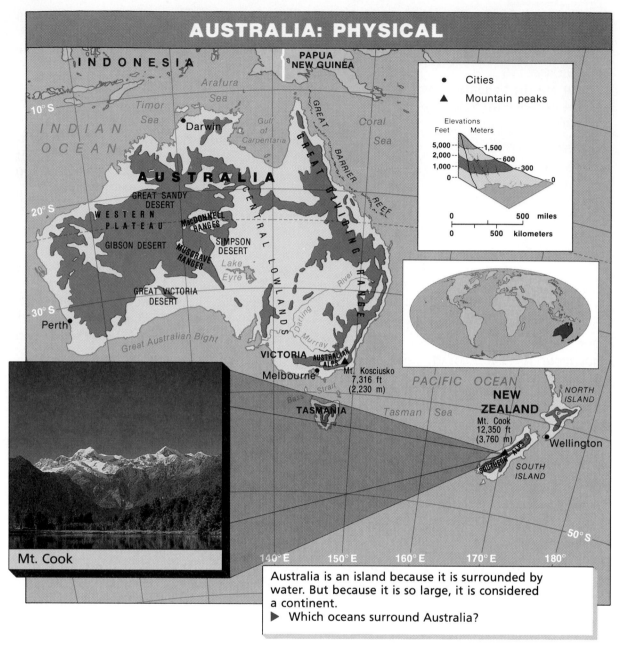

AUSTRALIA: PHYSICAL

- • Cities
- ▲ Mountain peaks

Elevations
Feet — Meters

5,000—	—1,500
2,000—	—600
1,000—	—300
0—	—0

INDONESIA

PAPUA NEW GUINEA

Arafura Sea

Timor Sea

Darwin

Gulf of Carpentaria

Coral Sea

INDIAN OCEAN

GREAT BARRIER REEF

AUSTRALIA

GREAT SANDY DESERT

WESTERN PLATEAU

MacDONNELL RANGES

GIBSON DESERT

MUSGRAVE RANGES

SIMPSON DESERT

CENTRAL LOWLANDS

GREAT DIVIDING RANGE

Lake Eyre

River

GREAT VICTORIA DESERT

Darling

Murray

Perth

Great Australian Bight

VICTORIA

AUSTRALIAN ALPS

Melbourne

Mt. Kosciusko 7,316 ft (2,230 m)

Bass Strait

TASMANIA

Tasman Sea

PACIFIC OCEAN

NEW ZEALAND

Mt. Cook 12,350 ft (3,760 m)

SOUTHERN ALPS

NORTH ISLAND

Wellington

SOUTH ISLAND

50° S

10° S

20° S

30° S

140° E 150° E 160° E 170° E 180°

Mt. Cook

Australia is an island because it is surrounded by water. But because it is so large, it is considered a continent.
▶ Which oceans surround Australia?

---

it almost impossible for people from Asian countries to move there. Those laws were changed during the 1950s and 1960s to allow small numbers of people from Asia to immigrate to Australia, and the number of Asians is growing.

B. The Island Continent

The Smallest Continent Australia is so small compared to the other continents that you might wonder why it isn't called an island instead of a continent. The answer is that Greenland, the largest island in the world, is just over 839,999 square miles (2,175,597 sq km) in area. By comparison, Australia is 2,967,909 square miles (7,686,884 sq km) or roughly four fifths the size of the United States. Even though Australia is the smallest continent, it is still much closer in size to Europe, the second smallest continent, than it is to the world's largest island.

A Land with Few Mountains Australia does not have any very tall mountains. The highest point in Australia, Mount Kosciusko (kahs ee US koh) in the Snowy Mountains, reaches an elevation of only 7,310 feet (2,228 m). Even the name *Snowy Mountains* is misleading, since the mountains have snow only in the winter. The Snowy Mountains are part of a highland area called the Great Dividing Range that extends most of the length of Australia's east coast. This highland area is the only part of Australia that has mountains.

The rest of the continent is rather low and flat. The western half of Australia is a large plateau with elevations of 1,000 to 1,600 feet (305 m to 488 m). Between the plateau and the mountains of the east is a low plain. The southern part of this plain near the cities of Adelaide (AD ul ayd) and Melbourne is one of Australia's best farming areas.

Australian Climates Australia's six climate zones can be seen on the world climate map in the Atlas. Most of the continent is dry. The **outback**, as the interior of the continent is known, is desert and semidesert grassland. Only about 10 percent of the country, mostly in the southeast, can be considered well watered. This area is where most of the Australian people live.

The northern section of Australia has a tropical climate. This area has scattered tropical forests and savannas. The southern areas around Perth and Adelaide have a Mediterranean climate that is similar to that of Southern Europe.

Little Land for Farming With a dry climate throughout much of the country, it is not surprising that Australia has little land that is good for farming. Only about one fourth of Australia's land gets enough rain for farming. Most of that land is in the mountains, where it is too rugged for farming. This leaves less than 10 percent of the land of the continent suitable for farming. However, that is more than enough land to

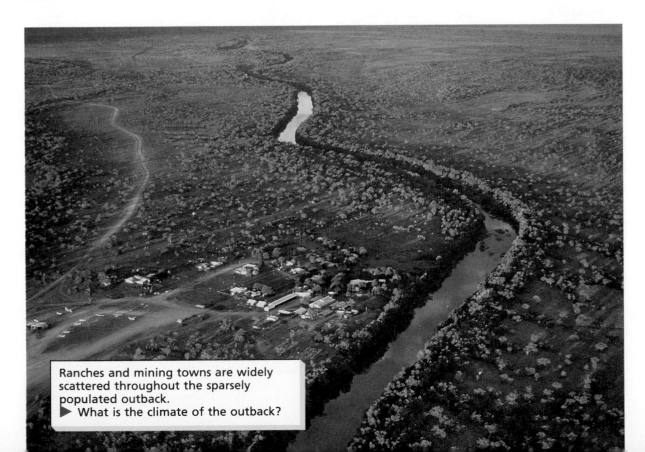

Ranches and mining towns are widely scattered throughout the sparsely populated outback.
▶ What is the climate of the outback?

provide food for Australia's people and for export to other countries.

The Animals of Australia There are many unusual animals that are native only to Australia. You may have seen kangaroos or koala bears, two of Australia's unique animals. The koala and kangaroo are **marsupials**. These are mammals that carry their young in a pouch. There is a greater variety of marsupials in Australia than in any other continent. Europe has none and North America only has the opossum.

Perhaps the most unusual Australian animal is the duck-billed platypus. This little animal looks as if it can't make up its mind what it wants to be. It has a large, flat bill and webbed feet like a duck. But it is a mammal with a furry body like a beaver. And, even stranger, the duck-billed platypus lays eggs like a bird, something that mammals do not normally do.

The Great Barrier Reef The largest structure ever built by living creatures was not made by human hands. It is made of **coral**. Coral is a hard, chalky, rocklike material that is made of the shells of sea animals called coral polyps. Polyps are tiny sea animals that live in warm seawater. They have hard outer skeletons, somewhat like hard cups, into which their bodies fit.

When coral polyps are alive, they fasten to each other. When the polyps die, they leave their connected shells behind as a rocky covering on the sea floor. Then new polyps attach to this covering. When billions of polyps mass together over a long

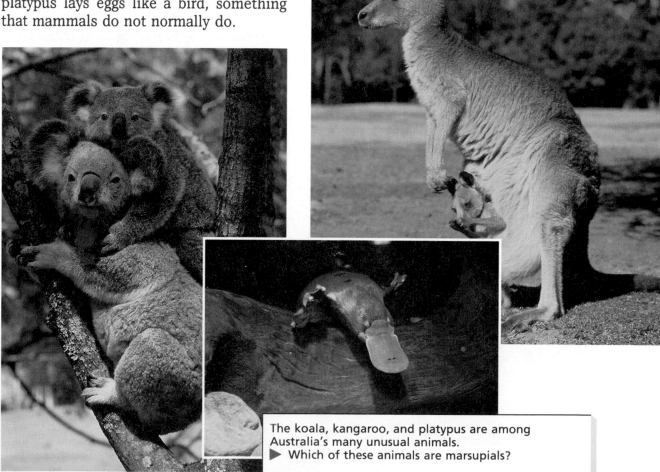

The koala, kangaroo, and platypus are among Australia's many unusual animals.
▶ Which of these animals are marsupials?

Scuba divers from around the world travel to the Great Barrier Reef to view its beautiful wonders. In some places, the water is shallow enough to see the coral from the water's surface.
▶ What is the length of the Great Barrier Reef?

period of time, they form rocklike ridges or mounds in the water called **reefs**.

The world's largest coral reef stretches 1,250 miles (2,011 km) along the northeast coast of Australia. The Great Barrier Reef, as it is known, is made up of thousands of individual coral reefs and islets. In 1979, Australia set aside part of the Great Barrier Reef as a marine park. In doing this, the government hoped to protect this remarkable coral structure and the different creatures that live there.

C. The People of Australia

The First Australians Australia's first human inhabitants, the **Aborigines** (ab uh RIHJ uh neez), probably migrated from Asia over 30,000 years ago. The Aborigines crossed over a land bridge that connected Asia and Australia. Later, the sea level rose, and the land bridge was flooded, ending the migration.

For thousands of years, the Aborigines lived by nomadic hunting and gathering. They used only simple tools, such as spears and the boomerang. The boomerang is a flat curved stick shaped somewhat like a bent wing. When thrown, the boomerang will sail out toward its target. If it misses, it curves back to land near the feet of the person who threw it.

The British explorers who first met the Aborigines thought the Aborigines were very primitive people. It wasn't until later that **anthropologists** learned about the Aborigines' rich and complex spiritual life and folklore. An anthropologist studies humans and their culture. Anthropologists study both the past and the present cultures of a people.

There may have been over 300,000 Aborigines living in Australia when James Cook first landed. Today, there are only about 145,000 Aborigines left which is about 1 percent of Australia's 16 million people. Just like the Indians of the Amer-

THE JOURNALS OF JAMES COOK

The following excerpt is a passage from the journal of James Cook. In it he gives an account of the Aborigines, whom Cook often referred to as Indians.

. . . From what I have said of the natives of New Holland they may appear to some to be the most wretched people upon earth; but in reality they are far more happier than we Europeans, being wholly unacquainted not only with the superfluous [unnecessary] but the necessary conveniences so much sought after in Europe; they are happy in not knowing the use of them. They live in a tranquility which is not disturbed by the inequality of their condition. The earth and sea of their own accord furnishes them with all things necessary for life. They covet [desire] not magnificent houses, household stuff, etc.; they live in a warm and fine climate, and enjoy every wholesome air, so that they have very little need of clothing; and this they seem to be fully sensible of, for many to whom we gave cloth, etc., left it carelessly upon the sea beach and in the woods, as a thing they had no manner of use for. In short, they seemed to set no value upon anything we gave them, nor would they ever part with anything of their own for any one article we could offer them. This, in my opinion, argues that they think themselves provided with all the necessaries of life.

1. Why might the Aborigines have appeared to some people as the "most wretched people upon earth"?

2. According to Captain Cook, in what ways were Aborigines different from Europeans?

3. What were some of the necessities of life that the earth and the sea provided for the Aborigines?

Several Aborigines watch convicts being taken ashore. The first group of convicts, which numbered more than 700, reached Australia in 1788. They were accompanied by about 300 soldiers who guarded the prisoners.
▶ Why was Australia used as a prison colony?

icas, many were killed or died of diseases brought by European colonists.

Australia Becomes a Colony The British claimed Australia because of James Cook, but they did not have much use for it. Australia was far from England and it did not seem to have many natural resources that the British could use. Still, England wanted to keep its colony. So, the British used Australia as a prison colony. Both prisoners and free settlers were sent to Australia.

From Colonies to Country It was nearly impossible for the convicts to get back to England when they finished their prison sentences. Before long, more people who were not convicts began to move to Australia, looking for land to settle. As the population grew, the continent was divided into seven English colonies. In 1901 the colonies became the six states and one territory of the independent country of Australia. Today, there is a second territory, the Australian Capital Territory, where Canberra, the capital of Australia, is located.

LESSON 1

Review

REVIEWING MAIN IDEAS

A. What efforts were made to discover the southern continent?
B. How has Australia's climate affected its population?
C. How is Australia's history reflected in its population?

SKILLS CHECK

MAP SKILL

Turn to the map on page 657. Use the scale of the map to calculate the distance from Australia's capital, Canberra, to each of the state capitals.

Living and Working in Australia

CONNECTIONS

At least once during the school day, you may take a drink of water from a water fountain or faucet. What is the source of that water?

TERMS

core, aquifer, station

FOCUS

What are Australia's most important resources?

A. Southeastern Australia

The Heart of a Nation When geographers talk about countries, they often use the word **core**. The word *core* refers to the part of a country that has the largest population, the largest cities, the most productive economy, and the best transportation facilities and other services.

It might help to think of the core area as the heart of the nation. But this does not mean that the core area will be found in the center of the country. In fact, usually, the core of a country is located in or near a coastal area so that goods can be shipped in and out easily.

Australia's Core In the case of Australia, the core is easy to identify. If you look at the population density map on page 651, you can pick out the core very easily. It is the area that lies along the eastern and southern coasts of Australia between the cities of Brisbane and Adelaide. Over 11 million of Australia's 16 million people live in this region.

Four of Australia's five largest cities—Sydney, Melbourne, Adelaide, and Brisbane—are in the core area. The city of Perth in southwestern Australia is the only large city in Australia that lies outside of the core. The core has most of the industry, roads, railroads, electrical plants, schools, hospitals, and other services that are demanded by a large urban population. In fact, Australia is a very urban country. About 85 percent of Australians live in cities. Because so many of Australia's people live in cities, the rural population density is low—less than one person per square mile or kilometer.

B. Farming in Australia

Little Land for Farming The best land for farming lies in the east, and nearly all of that land is in or close to the core. In Lesson 1 you read that only about 10 percent of Australia's land is good for farming. Still, farming is one of the most important parts of Australia's economy. The farms are mechanized, and some of the machines that are used have been invented just for use on Australia's large farms.

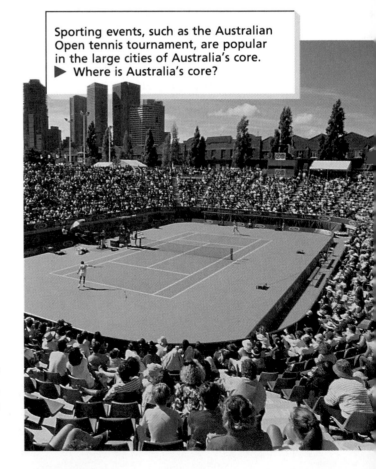

Sporting events, such as the Australian Open tennis tournament, are popular in the large cities of Australia's core.
▶ Where is Australia's core?

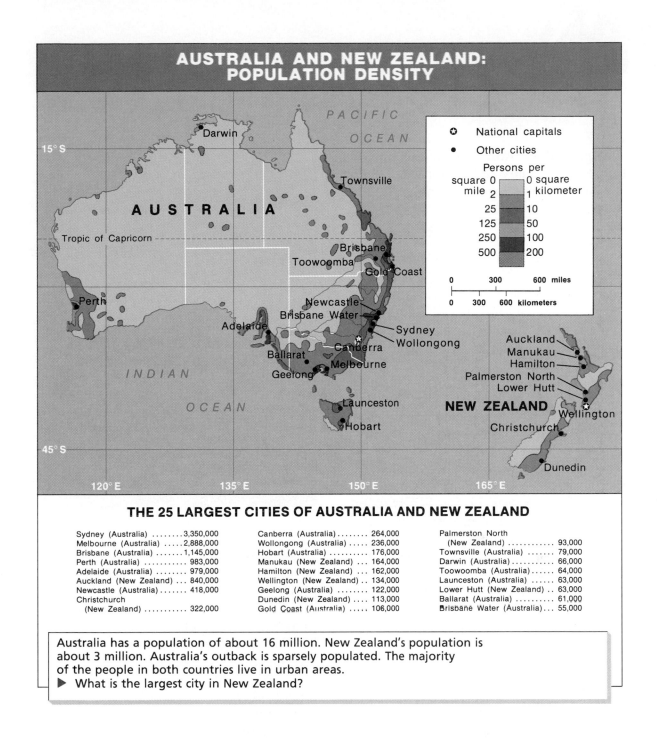

AUSTRALIA AND NEW ZEALAND: POPULATION DENSITY

National capitals

Other cities

Persons per

square mile	0	0	square kilometer
	2	1	
	25	10	
	125	50	
	250	100	
	500	200	

THE 25 LARGEST CITIES OF AUSTRALIA AND NEW ZEALAND

Sydney (Australia) 3,350,000
Melbourne (Australia) 2,888,000
Brisbane (Australia) 1,145,000
Perth (Australia) 983,000
Adelaide (Australia) 979,000
Auckland (New Zealand) ... 840,000
Newcastle (Australia).......418,000
Christchurch
   (New Zealand) 322,000

Canberra (Australia)........264,000
Wollongong (Australia) 236,000
Hobart (Australia) 176,000
Manukau (New Zealand) ... 164,000
Hamilton (New Zealand) ... 162,000
Wellington (New Zealand) .. 134,000
Geelong (Australia) 122,000
Dunedin (New Zealand) 113,000
Gold Coast (Australia) 106,000

Palmerston North
   (New Zealand) 93,000
Townsville (Australia) 79,000
Darwin (Australia)........... 66,000
Toowoomba (Australia)...... 64,000
Launceston (Australia) 63,000
Lower Hutt (New Zealand) .. 63,000
Ballarat (Australia) 61,000
Brisbane Water (Australia)... 55,000

Australia has a population of about 16 million. New Zealand's population is about 3 million. Australia's outback is sparsely populated. The majority of the people in both countries live in urban areas.
▶ What is the largest city in New Zealand?

Wheat Farms Australia's most important crop is wheat. The main wheat growing belt extends across the southeastern part of the country in the states of Victoria and South Australia. Australia does not have many rivers, so irrigation is often difficult. The longest and most important rivers of the continent—the Murray and its tributary, the Darling—pass through Australia's wheat belt. The Murray and the Darling are each about 1,650 miles (2,655 km) long. However, the Murray is more important than the Darling because it has more flat land that is good for farming along its banks.

GROWING UP IN AUSTRALIA

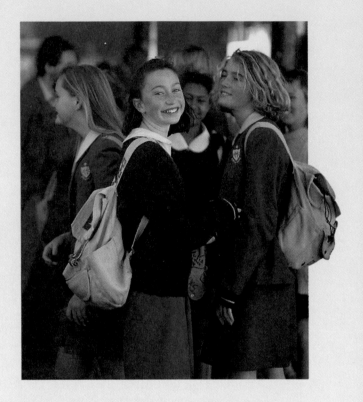

Imagine what it would be like to have summer in January and winter in July. That is what you could expect if you grew up in Australia. Because Australia lies south of the Equator, its seasons are opposite to those in the United States.

December comes in the middle of the summer, when the temperatures in Sydney and other Australian cities reach as high as 90° F (32°C) or even higher. Yet Christmas decorations still show snowy scenes of Santa Claus.

In July and August, Australians go to ski areas in the Snowy Mountains to enjoy winter sports. This happens while people in the Northern Hemisphere are going to the beach to swim and enjoy the hot summer weather.

There are other differences that you would notice if you grew up in Australia. For example, the school year is very different from that of North America. Summer vacation is only about six weeks, from the week before Christmas to the end of January. Australian students are dismissed from school for two weeks in May and about two weeks in September.

About half the students in Australia attend private schools, most of which are operated by churches. Many students go to schools that are for all girls or all boys. Australians take courses similar to those of North American students, except that everyone is required to take a second language beginning in the sixth grade. Latin and French are the two most popular languages.

All students in Australia wear uniforms to school. In the summer, boys wear a shirt and tie with slacks. The girls wear a blouse, tie, and skirt along with a wide-brimmed hat for shade. In the winter, sweaters and blazers are added to the uniforms. Each school has its own uniform colors and style.

Food is different in Australia. Australians eat lamb as often as we eat beef. Tropical fruits are enjoyed here. Kiwi fruit, pineapple, or pomegranates are eaten at breakfast. A pomegranate is a fruit that has a hard rind and looks similar to an orange. It has a deep, yellow-red color.

Australia's wildlife is also different. It is not unusual to see "Kangaroo Crossing" signs on the highway. Trucks and buses are equipped with sets of heavy steel bars on the front and back called "kangaroo bars." These bars protect vehicles that run into wild kangaroos. Sometimes panic-stricken kangaroos run into the back of slow moving trucks and buses.

Another important wheat-producing area is located on the west coast around Perth. About 60 percent of Australia's farmland is used to grow wheat. Some of the wheat is used in Australia, but most is exported to other countries. Australia is the world's fourth largest wheat exporter.

Other Crops Wheat is not the only important farm product of Australia. Sugarcane is also grown on farms in Queensland, where the climate is warm all year round. Most of Australia's sugar is exported to its main trade partner, Japan.

Australia's farms also produce barley, rice, oranges, grapes, and a variety of other fruits and vegetables. Much of this produce is sold in the grocery stores and supermarkets of Australia's cities, but some is exported to Europe and Asia.

C. Sheep and Cattle Ranching

The Great Artesian Basin Australia's outback is too dry for farming. There is a lack of both rainwater and surface water, such as lakes and rivers, to irrigate the land. But the scrubby grasses that grow in the outback are good for sheep and cattle ranching. Yet cattle, like plants, need water to survive. The lack of water has been overcome by drilling wells into the Great Artesian Basin, a vast underground water supply.

The Great Artesian Basin is beneath an area covering 670,000 square miles (1,735,300 sq km). The water from rains that fall on the highlands in the eastern part of Australia slowly seeps westward through the ground. The water collects underground in huge **aquifers**, layers of rock, sand, or gravel that can absorb or collect water. The ranchers drill deep holes to tap into the water to supply their cattle. The aquifers are so deep that the water brought out through a bore is very hot. The water has to run through a ditch above ground for at least 1 mile (1.6 km) to cool enough for cattle to drink it.

A helicopter, instead of a cowboy on a horse, does the job of rounding up the cattle on this ranch in Australia.
▶ Why, do you think, would a helicopter be used to round up cattle?

You may be wondering, why isn't the water used for farming? The problem is that the water is generally too salty for farming. Although the salty water does not harm cattle, the salt content of the water would cause problems if used to grow crops. After the water evaporates, the salt would be left, making the land unsuitable for future farming. So, the Great Artesian Basin region is used mostly to raise millions of sheep and cattle.

Sheep for Meat and Wool Sheep are raised mainly for their wool, and as you can see on the graph on page 659, Australia is the world's leading producer of wool. Meat is another product of sheep. The meat of young sheep is called lamb, and the meat of older sheep is called mutton. Mutton is a popular meat in Australia. Australians eat far more mutton than they do beef. Frozen lamb and mutton are also important exports from Australia.

PRODUCTS FROM COAL

Electricity

Coal-fired power station

Coking plant

Coke for steel

Coal gas

Chemicals

Light oils

Coal tar

COAL TAR BY-PRODUCTS

Soap and detergents

Linoleum

Perfume

Battery electrolyte

Nylon

Fertilizers

Adhesives

Plastics

Paint

Ink

Coal products come from different stages of processing coal. The production of electricity and coke are the main uses of coal. By-products of the coking process such as coal tar are used to produce goods like the ones shown.
▶ Which coal products can be used in the home?

Large Ranches Cattle and sheep are raised on large ranches that the Australians call **stations.** Some stations are huge, covering up to 12,000 square miles (31,080 sq km), an area larger than the entire state of Maryland! Large stations use helicopters and planes to track the thousands of sheep and cattle that graze on the ranch.

Dairy cattle are raised in southeast Australia and on the island of Tasmania. Those areas have enough rain for good pastures. Dairy cattle are also raised near the large cities where there are good markets for milk and other dairy products, such as cheese and butter.

D. Australia's Mineral Resources

Gold Opens the Way Australia's lack of good land for farming is made up for by the country's vast mineral riches. In 1851, a gold rush similar to the one in California in 1848 and 1849 brought thousands of miners to this continent. Life was hard and few people grew rich. As one miner at the gold diggings wrote in a poem,

> I've come back all skin and bone
> From the diggins-oh.
> And I wish I'd never gone
> To the diggings-oh.
> Believe me, 'tis no fun, . . .
> At the diggins-oh!

The gold rush ended quickly, but many of the migrants who came seeking their fortune stayed to help build a country. Gold mining today is much different than it was in the mid-1800s. Today, large companies own the mines and the mining is done with machines. Also gold is no longer Australia's most important mineral resource.

Other Minerals Australia is the world's leading producer of bauxite and lead. These minerals are among Australia's most valuable resources. Australia is one of the world's top producers of iron ore, manganese, nickel, zinc, tungsten, silver, gold, and coal.

Australia uses some of these minerals in its own manufacturing industry. About 25 percent of Australia's workers have jobs in manufacturing. The main industries include food processing and manufacturing different kinds of machinery.

Steel is made at this plant in New South Wales.
▶ What are Australia's main industries?

LESSON 2

Review

REVIEWING MAIN IDEAS

A. Why is Australia's core important?
B. What are Australia's most important agricultural products?
C. What products does Australia get from sheep?
D. What minerals are mined in Australia?

SKILLS CHECK

WRITING SKILL
A larger population is needed in order to have Australia's industry grow. Write a paragraph explaining the problems that might occur if Australia's government encouraged many people to move to Australia.

New Zealand: Land of the Kiwi

CONNECTIONS

New Zealand is even more isolated than Australia. What, do you think, do these two countries have in common?

TERMS

emblem, Maori

FOCUS

How is New Zealand different from Australia?

A. Getting to Know New Zealand

A Strange Bird New Zealand is a small country in the southern part of the Pacific Ocean. New Zealanders call themselves Kiwis (KEE weez). Why did they choose such an unusual nickname for themselves? The name comes from a strange bird called a kiwi. Kiwis cannot fly and they are nocturnal, meaning they hide during the day and come out to hunt for food at night. Because of this, kiwis are hard to find. This distinctive bird is New Zealand's national **emblem**, or symbol. Its picture is on New Zealand's seal and money and on some of its postage stamps.

Like Australia, New Zealand has many unique animals and plants. In fact, Australia and New Zealand have much in common. However, there are differences between them, beginning with the landscape.

Larger Than It Looks New Zealand is about 1,200 miles (1,935 km) from Australia. Usually, when we look for New Zealand on a map, we look at a world map or a map of the Pacific Ocean. Because the world and the Pacific Ocean are such large areas, they must be greatly reduced to fit on a small map. Islands like New Zealand look very tiny on such maps.

In reality, the two main islands of New Zealand combined—North Island and South Island—are about 10 percent larger than the United Kingdom. They only look small because they have been included on a map of such a large area.

Two Islands The two main islands are both mountainous. South Island, however, has higher and more rugged mountains than North Island. The mountains of South Island are called the Southern Alps. They are snow-capped and have glaciers, much like the western part of Canada and the state of Alaska. North Island has many volcanos, some of which are active. North Island has many geysers and hot springs, like those found in Yellowstone National Park in the United States.

A Temperate Climate New Zealand has a cool, rainy climate, much like the climate of the northwestern part of the United States. Snow is common in the Southern Alps but not elsewhere. The mountain ranges greatly affect rainfall, particularly on South Island. Rainfall on the western side of the range may average from 60 to more than 100 inches (152 to 254 cm) a year. The east side averages less than 30 inches (76

The kiwi uses its long, narrow, curved bill to poke into the ground to find worms to eat.
▶ How is the kiwi used as an emblem?

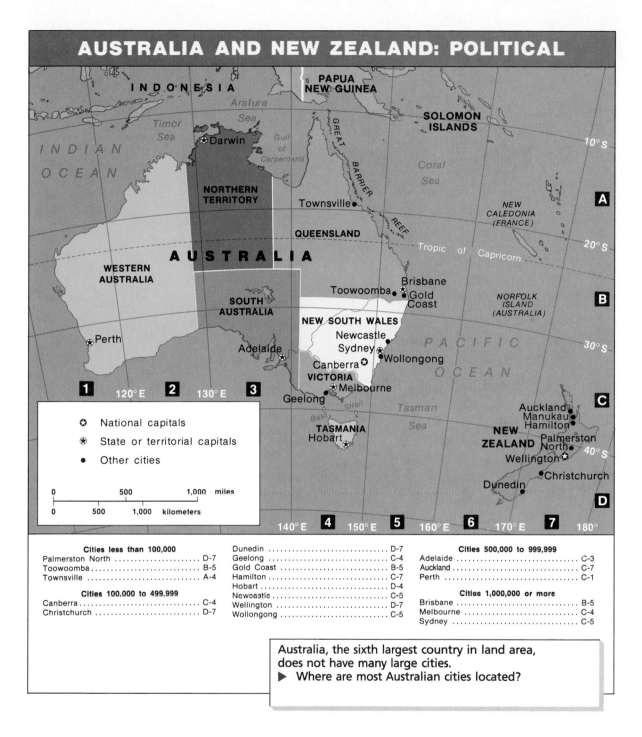

AUSTRALIA AND NEW ZEALAND: POLITICAL

Legend:
- ✪ National capitals
- ✺ State or territorial capitals
- • Other cities

0   500   1,000   miles
0   500   1,000   kilometers

Australia, the sixth largest country in land area, does not have many large cities.
▶ Where are most Australian cities located?

cm) a year. This is another example of the rain shadow effect.

New Zealand's Largest Cities Auckland, on the North Island, is the largest city in the country. It has a population of over 800,000 people. Auckland is located on a narrow neck of land at the base of the long northern peninsula. The city covers the whole width of the peninsula between two deep bays, so it is nearly surrounded by water. This peninsula of New Zealand extends over 200 miles (320 km) north from Auckland.

Sheep are raised on the hills below Mount Cook.
▶ How many sheep are in New Zealand?

Wellington, New Zealand's capital, is at the southern tip of North Island. Visitors to Wellington enjoy driving to the top of Mount Victoria, a high peak in the city. From there visitors can see the whole city of Wellington spread out below. On a clear day, you can even see the northern tip of the South Island, only 20 miles (32 km) away.

Christchurch, the largest city on South Island, has about 300,000 people. It lies on the eastern side of the island, in the middle of New Zealand's best farming area. Because New Zealand lies close to Antarctica, Christchurch has long been a headquarters for Antarctic explorers.

B. The People of New Zealand

The First New Zealanders The first people to settle in New Zealand were not Europeans. About 600 years ago, sailors from small Pacific islands far to the northeast sailed to New Zealand in giant canoes.

These people are called the **Maoris** (MAH oh reez). No one is sure from what island they sailed for New Zealand, but it may have been one of the islands near Tahiti.

Europeans Find New Zealand European explorers didn't find New Zealand until 1642, when Abel Tasman, the Dutch sea captain, sailed there. The Maoris, who were skilled warriors, were not friendly to Tasman, who sailed away without landing.

It was over 100 years later, in 1769, when Captain Cook's expedition aboard the *Endeavour* claimed the islands for England. For four months he explored the coastline, mapping every detail. But England had little interest in these distant islands, and no effort was made to colonize them for many years.

Over several decades some settlers from Britain did move to New Zealand. The settlers cleared forests to create pastures

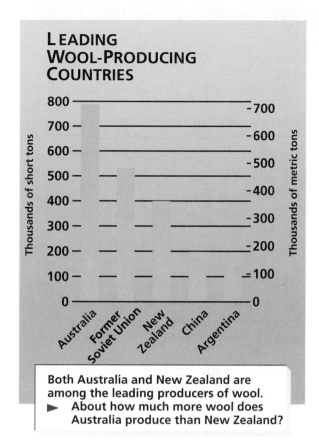

LEADING WOOL-PRODUCING COUNTRIES

Thousands of short tons / Thousands of metric tons

Australia, Former Soviet Union, New Zealand, China, Argentina

Both Australia and New Zealand are among the leading producers of wool.
► About how much more wool does Australia produce than New Zealand?

New Zealand has a pastoral economy and raising sheep and cattle is the most important part of the economy.

New Zealand accounts for over 40 percent of the world's wool exports. It is also a major exporter of lamb, mutton, beef, butter, cheese, and dried milk. You may have seen frozen New Zealand lamb in a grocery store near where you live. But most of New Zealand's meat exports go to the United Kingdom. Wool and meat account for 75 percent of New Zealand's income earned from exports.

Productive Farms   Only 3 percent of New Zealand's land is farmed, but that land produces enough wheat, vegetables, and fruit to feed the country's population. New Zealand's farms also produce hay and grain to feed its many millions of cattle and sheep. The best farmland is located on the Canterbury Plain, a large, flat area near Christchurch.

New Zealand has few mineral resources. There is some coal and iron ore, and a steel mill was opened in the 1980s near Auckland. The most important industries are textiles, wood products, fertilizers, cement, and building materials.

and farmland. Because of the islands' growing population, Britain made New Zealand a colony in 1840. The Maoris didn't like the settlers moving into their land. Fierce battles were fought until 1872, when the Maoris were finally defeated.

A Proud Heritage   Today, about 10 percent of New Zealand's more than 3 million people are Maori. The New Zealanders are proud of their Maori heritage and have built many museums to display crafts such as wood carving, for which the Maori are famous. But the dominant culture of New Zealand is British. New Zealanders speak English, and they have many other customs that have come from England.

C. Earning a Living in New Zealand

Sixty-eight Million Sheep   Just over 3 million people live in New Zealand, but the islands are home to over 68 million sheep!

LESSON 3

Review

REVIEWING MAIN IDEAS

A. What are the differences in the physical landscapes of New Zealand's two main islands?

B. How have the Maoris and the British influenced life in New Zealand?

C. How do New Zealanders earn a living?

SKILLS CHECK

THINKING SKILL

Look at the world political map in the Atlas. Why is New Zealand sometimes called "the land where the day begins"?

26 REVIEW

REVIEWING TERMS

On a separate sheet of paper, write the letter of the term that best matches each numbered statement.

    a. outback
    b. marsupial
    c. coral
    d. reef
    e. Aborigine
    f. anthropologist
    g. aquifer
    h. station
    i. emblem
    j. Maori

1. A symbol
2. A layer of rock, sand, or gravel that can absorb or collect water
3. A mammal that carries its young in a pouch
4. A scientist who studies humans and their past and present cultures
5. The name of the first people to settle in New Zealand
6. The interior of Australia, which is largely desert and semidesert grassland
7. A large ranch in Australia on which sheep and cattle are raised
8. A rocklike ridge or mound in the water made of the connected shells of coral polyps
9. A hard, chalky, rocklike material made of the shells of sea animals
10. The name of Australia's first human inhabitants

REVIEWING THE FACTS

On a separate sheet of paper, answer the following questions in complete sentences.

1. Why is it incorrect to say that Australia is isolated and far away from other lands?
2. Why is so little of Australia's land good for farming?
3. Where is the Great Barrier Reef located?
4. Why are there so few Aborigines living in Australia today?
5. Why did the British use Australia as a prison colony?
6. Why is the core of a country usually located near a coastal area?
7. What animals are raised on the ranches of Australia?
8. What are the two main islands that make up the country of New Zealand?
9. What is the mixed heritage of New Zealand?
10. Why are sheep and cattle so important to the economy of New Zealand?

WRITING ABOUT GEOGRAPHY

Imagine that you are a member of Captain Cook's crew and that you are going ashore to visit Australia for the first time. Write several paragraphs describing what you see.

THINKING CRITICALLY

On a separate sheet of paper, answer the following questions in complete sentences.

1. What could be some possible reasons to explain why Australia has so many unusual animals?
2. Why, do you think, did the British explorers think that the Aborigines were a very primitive people?
3. What reasons could the European colonists have had for killing Aborigines?
4. Why would many people prefer to live in the core area of a country?
5. How might the history of New Zealand have been different if the Maoris had been friendly to Abel Tasman in 1642?

SUMMARIZING THE CHAPTER

On a separate sheet of paper, draw a graphic organizer like the one shown here. Copy the information from this graphic organizer to the one you have drawn. Next to the main idea for each lesson, write three statements that you think best support the main idea.

CHAPTER THEME — Australia and New Zealand each have a unique geography, economy, and history.

Lesson 1 — Australia has varied landforms, climates, and wildlife.
1. _____
2. _____
3. _____

Lesson 2 — Australia has important mineral resources.
1. _____
2. _____
3. _____

Lesson 3 — There are differences between New Zealand and Australia.
1. _____
2. _____
3. _____

PACIFIC ISLAND NATIONS AND ANTARCTICA

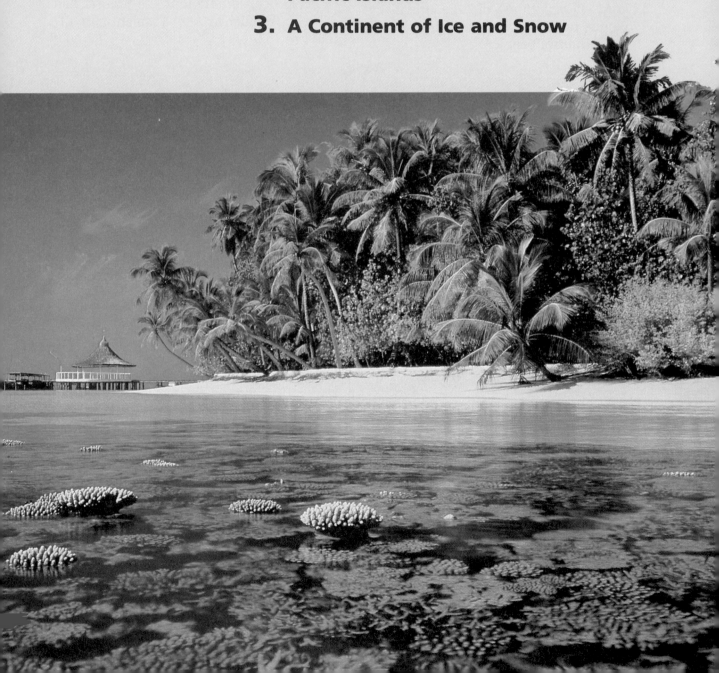

Locating the Pacific Islands

CONNECTIONS

How would you describe the physical landscape of an island in the Pacific?

TERMS

catamaran, continental island, atoll, lagoon

FOCUS

Why are the Pacific Islands considered isolated locations?

A. A Vast Area

A Perilous Voyage There were tearful farewells as the men and women loaded their few belongings into the **catamaran**. This catamaran was made of two large canoes that had been fastened together with wooden boards, making one raftlike boat that would not tip over easily in rough seas. There was enough space on the catamaran for 30 people and for some of the food and water the travelers would need on their long voyage. They carried dried and green bananas, sugarcane, coconuts, and sweet potatoes. The travelers also were taking along some dried fish, but they expected to be able to catch fresh fish along the way.

Soon everything was ready. The men paddled the catamaran from the shore into the open sea. Then they opened the sail to catch the wind and began to travel north. Their destination was about 1,800 miles (2,900 km) away. With good winds and no storms, it would take about two weeks of steady sailing for the group to complete their voyage.

These people were leaving their home in the Marquesas (mahr KAY zuz) Islands to sail to islands that had been discovered far to the north. There they would plant crops from the seeds they also carried with them. What were the islands that these brave voyagers were sailing to more than 1,000 years ago? Today we know them as the Hawaiian Islands.

Many of the thousands of islands that are scattered across the Pacific Ocean were settled by other small groups of people looking for new homes and a new life. The islands of the Pacific were the last places on earth that people discovered and occupied. In order to travel to these islands to settle them, people had to learn to make seagoing canoes. They also had to discover how to navigate over hundreds of miles of open ocean. When the people of the Pacific mastered these skills, they were able to make the long voyages that were necessary to cross the vast Pacific.

The Largest Ocean The Pacific Ocean covers nearly one third of the earth's surface, or an area of about 70 million square miles (181 million sq km). The world map on pages 688–689 seems to show that most of the Pacific Ocean between Australia and the United States is empty. However, there are thousands of islands strewn across the Pacific, many of them separated by hundreds of miles of ocean.

Four Kinds of Islands There are four kinds of islands in the Pacific. The largest islands, such as New Guinea (noo GIHN ee) and the islands of New Zealand, are the kind called **continental islands**. They are connected to a continent by land that has been flooded by the sea. Some continental islands are large enough to have many different landforms and climates, like continents.

Many of the smaller islands are volcanic islands, such as the Caribbean islands you studied in Chapter 6. A volcanic island forms when a volcano extends from the floor of the sea to above the water's surface. The Hawaiian Islands, Tahiti (tuh HEET ee), and Fiji (FEE jee) are examples of volcanic islands in the Pacific Ocean.

Coral islands are the third kind of

▶ A coral reef off a tropical island

THE MAKING OF A CORAL ATOLL

Coral reef

Barrier reef

Lagoon

Coral island

An atoll is a chain of coral islands that surrounds a lagoon.
▶ How does a coral reef become a coral island?

island found in the Pacific. Coral islands are actually coral reefs, like the Great Barrier Reef you studied in Chapter 26, that have been pushed above the ocean's surface. Only a few of the Pacific Islands were formed in this way.

Shifts in the ocean floor can also create **atolls**. An atoll is a circular coral island that encloses or partly encloses an area of shallow water. An atoll begins as a coral

reef around a volcanic island. Shifts in the ocean floor may cause the center of the island to sink. As it sinks, a shallow body of water, which is called a **lagoon**, forms inside the reef.

B. Island Groups of the Pacific

Polynesia Look at the map on page 637. The Pacific Islands are divided into three large areas—Polynesia, Micronesia, and Melanesia. Different groups of people live in each of these areas. The inhabitants of the islands in the central part of the Pacific Ocean are Polynesians. The name *Polynesia* means "many islands." A triangle drawn to connect Hawaii in the north with Easter Island in the southeast and New Zealand in the southwest would include most of the thousands of islands of Polynesia. The area encompassed by the Polynesian triangle is over 8 million square miles (21 million sq km), an area nearly as large as North America. But the total land area of Polynesia is only a tiny fraction of the total surface of the Polynesian triangle.

Polynesians speak similar languages. Because of this similarity, anthropologists believe that all Polynesians may have originated from one culture. It is believed that people from this single culture migrated across the Pacific. The story of the catamaran voyage at the beginning of this lesson is an example of such a migration.

Micronesia To the west of Polynesia there are several groups of small islands. Together, these island groups are known as Micronesia. The name *Micronesia* means "small islands." This name relates to the fact that the islands of Micronesia are all very small; some are less than 1 square mile (3 sq km) in area.

Probably the best-known island of Micronesia is Guam, a territory of the United States. Guam is only 210 square miles (544 sq km) in area, but it is the largest island of Micronesia. It is part of a group of islands

In 1925, a famous anthropologist named Margaret Mead set sail for the islands of the Pacific. She planned to study the people of Samoa and to describe their culture. She was especially interested in how Samoans raise children and teenagers.

When she first arrived in Samoa, Dr. Mead had to learn the language and many customs of the Samoans. She lived like the Samoans, eating Samoan food and participating in the life of the village. Several years later she described some of her experiences.

The life of the day begins at dawn. . . . Restless little children roll out of their sheets, and wander drowsily down to the beach to freshen their faces in the sea. Boys, bent upon an early fishing, start collecting their tackle. . . . The whole village, sheeted and frowsy, stirs, rubs its eyes, and stumbles toward the beach. . . .

. . . Families who will cook today are hard at work. . . . The children are scuttling back and forth, fetching sea water, or leaves to stuff the pig. . . . Those whose excursions have been short return to the village. . . .

It is high noon. The sand burns the feet of the little children . . . as they creep into the shade of the houses. The women who must go [outdoors] carry great banana leaves as sun-shades or wind wet cloths about their heads. . . . The fishermen beach their canoes, weary and spent from the heat. . . .

Finally the sun sets. . . . Children straggle home, dark little figures etched against the sky; lights shine in the houses, and each household gathers for its evening meal.

. . . Again quiet settles upon the village, as first the head of the household, then the women and children, and last of all the patient boys, eat their supper. After supper the old people and little children are bundled off to bed. . . .

. . . Sometimes sleep will not descend upon the village until long past midnight; then at last there is only the mellow thunder of the reef . . . as the village rests until dawn.

1. Why, do you think, did Dr. Mead try to speak and live as the Samoans did?
2. Why was the sea important to the people of Samoa?
3. What observations made by Dr. Mead about life in Samoa do you find most interesting?

A tropical forest grows in this volcano crater on Krakar Island in Papua New Guinea. The crater is about 7 miles (11 km) wide.
▶ Of which island group is New Guinea a part?

called the Marianas. The map on page 637 shows that most of the islands in Micronesia form groups of islands. Besides the Marianas, other island groups of Micronesia include the Caroline Islands and the Marshall Islands.

Unlike the Polynesians, Micronesians speak many different languages. Often the people of one island group cannot understand the language of people from another Micronesian island group.

Melanesia South of Micronesia is the large island of New Guinea—the second largest island in the world, after Greenland. Stretching south and east of New Guinea is a string of middle-size and small islands that includes the Solomon Islands, New Caledonia, Vanuatu (vahn wah TOO), and Fiji. These are the main island groups that make up Melanesia, the third group of Pacific Islands. It was named *Melanesia*, which means "islands of black-skinned people," because the first inhabitants of these islands had very dark skin and hair.

The ways people in Melanesia make their living vary from farming in New Guinea to fishing in the small islands of Fiji. As in Micronesia, different languages are spoken in Melanesia. Neighboring ethnic groups on New Guinea may not understand each other's languages.

LESSON 1
Review

REVIEWING MAIN IDEAS
A. Why did it take so long for humans to settle the Pacific Islands?
B. What similarities are there between the three different population groups that live on the Pacific Islands?

SKILLS CHECK

MAP SKILL
Use the map on page 637 to find the distance between the following Pacific Islands.
1. Fiji and New Guinea
2. Tahiti and Fiji
3. Guam and Hawaii
4. Palau and Hawaii

Living and Working in the Pacific Islands

CONNECTIONS

How do you think you might earn a living if you lived on one of the Pacific Islands?

TERMS

copra, trust territory, compact

FOCUS

In what ways are the lives of Melanesians, Micronesians, and Polynesians similar?

A. Melanesia

The Countries of Melanesia The islands of Melanesia make up about 70 percent of the total land area of the Pacific Islands. These islands are divided into several countries. The island of New Guinea is split into two nearly equal halves. The western half is called Irian Jaya. It is part of Indonesia. The eastern half of New Guinea is the country of Papua New Guinea. It was once a colony of Australia, but it became independent in 1975. Other independent countries of Melanesia are the Solomon Islands, Vanuatu, and Fiji.

Working in Melanesia The countries of Melanesia do not have much industry. Many people are subsistence farmers who raise pigs and grow crops of yams and plantains, or cooking bananas. Some farmers grow cash crops such as sugarcane, coconuts, cassava, and bananas.

In the coastal areas, Melanesian people catch turtles, fish, shellfish, and other sea animals to eat and to sell. In the past, seashells were made into beads and other ornaments that could be sold. Today, food processing is one of the leading industries in Melanesia.

Fiji If you look at the map on page 637, you can see that Fiji is centrally located in the southwest Pacific. Fiji is a major refueling stop for airplanes traveling between North America and Australia or New Zealand. This has made Fiji an important tourist center and the most prosperous country in Melanesia.

Fiji is the only country in Melanesia in which Melanesians are not a majority of the population. About 50 percent of Fiji's population is of Indian origin. Most of these people were brought from India by the British, Fiji's former colonial rulers, to work on the island's sugar plantations.

Papua New Guinea Papua New Guinea is the largest country in Melanesia. It is about the same size as California. Volcanic mountains that reach elevations of over 16,000 feet (4,879 m) make this a rugged land. Navigable rivers wind their way across the country's swampy coastal lowlands.

Papua New Guinea has mineral resources such as gold, silver, copper, and natural gas. Coffee, coconuts, and cacao are important agricultural products. However, only small amounts of these crops are grown for export.

As on many Melanesian islands, fishing is an important industry on Fiji.
▶ In what related, important industry are these workers employed?

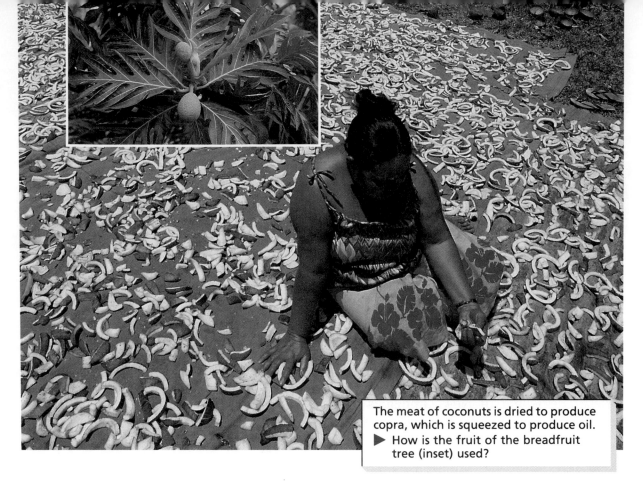

The meat of coconuts is dried to produce copra, which is squeezed to produce oil.
► How is the fruit of the breadfruit tree (inset) used?

B. Micronesia

Atolls Micronesia provides a striking contrast to Melanesia. Unlike Melanesia, which is made up of large islands with mountains and other landforms, Micronesia is made up of groups of tiny islands. Most of these islands are atolls.

Travel posters that advertise trips to islands in the Pacific often include pictures that make atolls look very attractive. There are white sandy beaches with rows of palm trees and thatched huts. All of these can be found on an atoll. But to the people who live there, an atoll is a hard place to survive on.

Some of the atoll islands barely rise above the waves of the Pacific. Because these islands are low in elevation, there isn't much rain. Think about the way the rain shadow effect relates to mountains. Without higher elevations, there is little rain. On an atoll, water for drinking and for irrigation is often hard to find.

In addition, the atolls' sandy soils are not very fertile, making farming difficult. Because of the lack of water and the difficulty of farming, only a few people live on most atolls. Often the entire population of an atoll may be no more than several hundred people.

Sources of Food Two kinds of trees have adapted to the sandy soils of the atolls—the breadfruit and the coconut palm. In the past, these trees provided much of the food and material that islanders needed. Both trees are still widely used today, but imported foods have been added to the islanders' meals.

Breadfruit can be baked, roasted, or dried into flour. It is called breadfruit because it resembles baked bread. A single full-grown breadfruit tree produces enough fruit to feed a family. These tall trees also provide lumber, and breadfruit juice is made into glue and caulking for canoes.

The coconut tree was and still is another major source of food on the islands. The uses for the coconut palm tree are similar to those of the date palm tree, which you read about in Chapter 21. The inside of a ripe coconut contains a sweet, watery juice that people drink. The coconut provides food in the form of *coconut meat*, which is squeezed to get coconut milk and cream. This milk is used the way we use cow's milk. And oil is squeezed from **copra** (KAH pruh), or dried coconut meat.

Trust Territory   Nearly all of the islands of Micronesia were turned over to the United States as a **trust territory** after World War II. A trust territory is a land that is temporarily held by a larger country. The larger country administers the area until the people are ready to rule themselves.

The former member islands of the United States Trust Territory have now reached various levels of independence. The Commonwealth of the Northern Marianas has its own elected government, but its people are citizens of the United States, like the people of Puerto Rico. They have most of the rights of citizens in the 50 states except the right to vote for President.

The Commonwealth of the Northern Marianas does not include Guam, the largest island of the Marianas. Guam is a United States territory that is working toward commonwealth status.

The Republic of the Marshall Islands, the Federated States of Micronesia, and the Republic of Palau are independent. Both the Marshall Islands and the Federated States of Micronesia have chosen to remain associated with the United States by signing **compacts,** or agreements, with the United States. These compacts provide that the United States is responsible for these islands' military defense. The Republic of Palau did not approve a compact but may do so in the future.

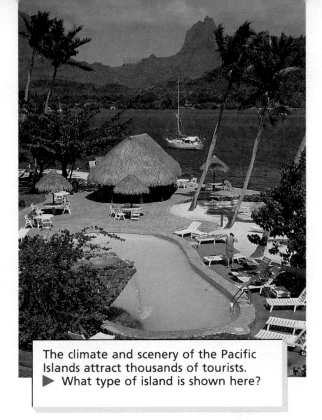

The climate and scenery of the Pacific Islands attract thousands of tourists.
▶ What type of island is shown here?

C. Polynesia

Scattered Islands   The islands of Polynesia, like those of Micronesia, include atolls as well as volcanic islands. However, there are more volcanic islands in Polynesia. Volcanic islands are good for farming because of the rich volcanic soils. These islands can support many crops. The crops grown in Polynesia are similar to those grown in Micronesia and Melanesia. A popular crop in Polynesia is taro. Taro is a plant with a starchy root that can be cooked whole or ground up into a paste that is used as food. The Hawaiians call it poi. As in other Pacific regions, the economy of the Polynesian islands is based on tourism and farming.

If you look at the map on page 637, you can see that some islands of Polynesia are independent and others belong to different countries. Two island groups, Tonga and Western Samoa, are independent countries. The islands in the center of Polynesia, including Tahiti and the Marquesas Islands, are territories of France. Other islands of

669

FROM: **Tales of the South Pacific**

by James A. Michener

The author James Michener describes the unusual features of a cacao tree which is found on the islands of the South Pacific. The cacao is an evergreen tree whose seeds, or beans, are used to make chocolate and cocoa. The beans also supply cocoa butter, which is used in candies and medicines.

. . . The cacao is small, hardly more than a bush, reaching at most twenty feet in height. It has a sturdy trunk, thick branches about five feet from the ground, and grows symmetrically [balanced]. Its leaves are brilliantly glistened like poison ivy, only more shimmering. And they are of myriad [varied] color! Some are pale green, others darkest green, some purple, some almost blue, or gray or bright yellow. And on most trees at least fifty leaves are brilliant vermillion [red pigment], shading off to scarlet and deep red. Each leaf is iridescent [rainbowlike], and dead leaves drop immediately from the tree.

. . . In late January and February the cacao puts out buds that will later grow into pods. They appear without reason at the strangest places! Two inches from the ground on a barren, stiff trunk, a pod will suddenly appear. On one branch there may be a dozen pods. On another, none. In the crevice [crack] formed where a branch leaves the trunk a cluster of pods may appear and the branch itself may be bare. A mature cacao in full season looks as if someone had stood at a distance and flung a huge handful of random pods upon it.

At first the miniature pods are light purple. Then as they grow to full size, they become a weird greenish purple, . . . Next they are all green, and from then on they become the chameleons [lizards] of the jungle. On one tree mature pods, which now look like elongated cantaloupes seven and eight inches long, will be bright green, golden yellow, reddish yellow, red, purple, and greenish purple. And on each tree a few will be dead, charred, black, ugly, with small holes where rats had eaten out the sweet seeds, which, when toasted and ground, become cocoa.

Many people who work at the military base at Pearl Harbor (inset) use sophisticated equipment like that shown here.
▶ What do you think this equipment is used for?

Polynesia belong to Australia, England, New Zealand, Chile, and the United States.

Many of the islands of Polynesia continue to be territories because they are small, scattered far apart, and lightly populated. American Samoa is a United States territory that includes several small volcanic islands. American Samoa's population is only about 34,000 people. The islands' main occupation is canning fish, especially tuna caught by fishing ships from the United States, South Korea, and Taiwan. Tourism is important. The islands are connected by local airlines to Hawaii, New Zealand, and Fiji.

Strategic Locations Why would countries such as the United States and France want to control tiny islands in the middle of the Pacific? One reason is that the Pacific Islands have strategic locations. Airplanes that fly across the Pacific Ocean often stop at Hawaii, Fiji, and Tahiti. These and other islands are also important naval ports and army bases for the countries that control them. So for countries that want to control transportation and trade across the Pacific, these tiny islands can be very important.

Strategic location was one of the main reasons for settlement of the Hawaiian Islands. Russian, British, French, and American merchants, whalers, and missionaries competed during the 1800s for control of the islands. Finally, in 1959, they became the United States' fiftieth state.

Hawaii is still a very strategic location. There are several military bases on the islands, such as Pearl Harbor. Hawaii is the headquarters of the Pacific Command, which is responsible for all United States military in the Pacific and Indian ocean areas.

LESSON 2

Review

REVIEWING MAIN IDEAS
A. How do people make a living in Melanesia?
B. Why is life on an atoll difficult?
C. Why do many of the islands of the Pacific still belong to some large countries?

SKILLS CHECK
WRITING SKILL
The tourist industry in the Pacific Islands has grown in recent years. In a paragraph, explain what might be the advantages or disadvantages of this growth.

A Continent of Ice and Snow

CONNECTIONS

Make a list of things you might need if you went to Antarctica.

TERMS

ice shelf, crevasse, whiteout

FOCUS

Why are so many countries interested in Antarctica?

A. The Race to the South Pole

Exploring Antarctica Early explorers who sailed into the southern waters of the Pacific Ocean looking for land found huge cliffs of ice blocking their way. These cliffs were the edge of giant **ice shelves**. An ice shelf is a mass of ice that floats on the water but is attached to a glacier—that is, the ice on the land. The Ross ice shelf, which can be seen on the map on page 675, covers about 130,000 square miles (336,700 sq km) during the winter. Around the Antarctic coast, large pieces of ice called icebergs continually break off from the ice shelves. These icebergs can be quite large and can drift hundreds of miles or kilometers, making ship travel difficult.

In 1820, explorers discovered the continent that lay beyond the icebergs and ice shelves. As you might guess, exploring this giant, frozen land was not an easy task. But at the beginning of the twentieth century, there was a race to see who would be first to reach the South Pole.

The Amundsen Expedition A Norwegian expedition, led by Roald Amundsen (ROH ahl AH moon sun), reached the South Pole on December 14, 1911. Amundsen's words here describe what it was like to finally arrive at the goal after almost eight weeks of walking across the vast Antarctic ice and snow.

We reckoned now that we were at the Pole. Of course, every one of us knew that we were not standing on the absolute spot; it would be an impossibility with the time and the instruments at our disposal to ascertain [locate] that exact spot. But we were so near it that the few miles which possibly separated us from it could not be of the slightest importance. . . .

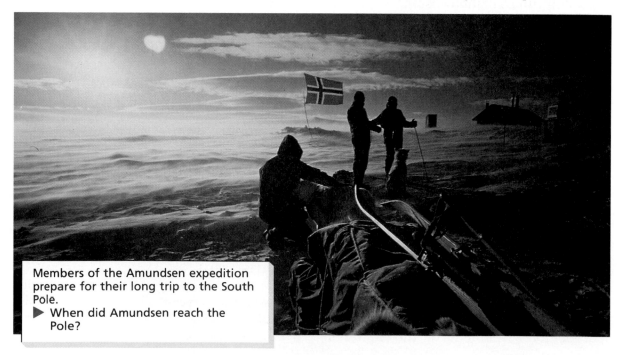

Members of the Amundsen expedition prepare for their long trip to the South Pole.
▶ When did Amundsen reach the Pole?

After we had halted we . . . congratulated each other. . . . After this we proceeded to the greatest and most solemn act of the whole journey—the planting of our flag. Pride and affection shone in the five pairs of eyes that gazed upon the [Norwegian] flag, as it unfurled itself with a sharp crack, and waved over the pole. . . . Five weather-beaten, frostbitten fists they were that grasped the pole, raised the waving flag in the air, and planted it as the first at the geographical South Pole.

The Scott Expedition A month later a British expedition, led by Robert Scott, reached the Pole only to find that Amundsen had arrived there first. They were bitterly disappointed and exhausted after nearly ten weeks of struggling over glaciers and snowfields. Scott and his four companions began the long, hard trip back to the coast, where the rest of their expedition waited.

Two months later, they were nearly out of supplies and confronted by constantly worsening weather. One man had died and another was near death, suffering from severely frostbitten feet. Scott wrote the following entry in his journal.

Friday, March 16 or Saturday March 17. Lost track of dates, but think the last correct. Tragedy all along the line. At lunch, the day before yesterday, poor Titus Oates said he couldn't go on; he proposed we should leave him in his sleeping bag. That we could not do, and we induced him to come on, on the afternoon march. In spite of its awful nature for him he struggled on and we made a few miles. At night he was worse and we knew the end had come.

[Oates] slept through the night before last, hoping not to wake; but he woke in the morning—yesterday. It was blowing a blizzard. He said 'I am just going outside and may be some time.' He went out into the blizzard and we have not seen him since.

We knew that poor Oates was walking to his death, but though we tried to dissuade him, we knew it was the act of a brave man and an English gentleman. We all hope to meet the end with a similar spirit, and assuredly the end is not far.

Two days later the three survivors were trapped in their tent by a blizzard. Their bodies were found there in November 1912 by a search party. Scott and his companions died only 11 miles from a store of supplies that might have saved their lives.

B. Antarctica: the Frozen Continent

A Land of Ice and Snow As you can see on the map on page 675, Antarctica faces three oceans—the Indian, Atlantic, and Pacific. Nearly all of Antarctica lies south of the Antarctic Circle. All but a small part of the continent—the northern tip of the Antarctic Peninsula—is covered with ice and snow. The ice that covers the continent reaches a maximum thickness of about 14,000 feet (4,267 m). Antarctica has about 90 percent of all the world's ice. If this ice

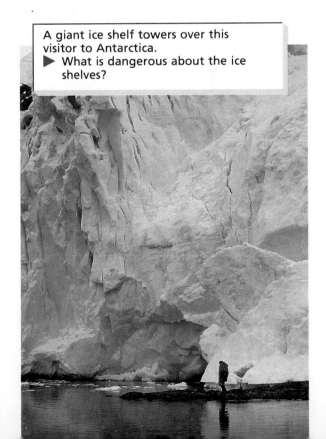

A giant ice shelf towers over this visitor to Antarctica.
▶ What is dangerous about the ice shelves?

melted, the resulting water would raise the sea level around the world by about 200 feet (61 m)!

Antarctica has the highest average elevation of any continent, 8,000 feet (2,438 m). The high elevation adds to the polar cold, making Antarctica the coldest place on earth. Temperatures as low as -128.6°F (-89.2°C) have been recorded during the intense polar winter. During the summer the temperature has reached 59°F (15°C) at the northern end of Antarctic Peninsula. But temperatures rarely rise above freezing elsewhere on the continent.

A Desert Although there is a tremendous supply of water in its ice, Antarctica is considered to be a frozen desert. The interior receives only about 2 inches (5 cm) of precipitation per year. Because of the intense cold, there is no liquid water, so people must melt snow for drinking water. Without fuel to melt the ice, explorers could face the ironic situation of dying of thirst while sitting on top of thousands of feet of frozen water. Of course, without fuel, they would most likely freeze to death long before they died of thirst.

C. Modern Polar Exploration

Why Go to Antarctica? Why would anyone want to go to a place like Antarctica? The answer is that scientists want to learn about the world's coldest and most remote landmass. They have learned that Antarctica has an important influence on the weather and climate of the entire world. Scientists have also discovered that Antarctica may possess valuable mineral deposits. Among the minerals that lie under the ice and snow of Antarctica are coal, oil, gold, and iron.

People have also gone to Antarctica to hunt and fish. The interior has no animals or plants except for some mosses and bacteria. But near the coast, one can find seals, whales, penguins, porpoises, dolphins, and about 45 types of birds.

Modern Equipment The story of the race for the Pole tells something of how hard it was to live in Antarctica. Today, life is much different for people who live and work in Antarctica. Expeditions that visit Antarctica are supplied with the most modern equipment. They have airplanes, helicopters, large snow tractors, and the best communications equipment that can be acquired. The scientists live in buildings that are designed for the intense cold.

Still, Antarctica is a dangerous place for humans. Temperatures at the South Pole are so cold that simply touching a metal object with bare hands can instantly freeze a person's fingers to it. People must wear several layers of clothing, including thermal underwear, thickly padded trousers and jackets, and waterproof parkas and pants for the outer layer. Of course, they must also wear several layers of socks under insulated boots and insulated gloves under mittens. However, people rarely stay outdoors for long because it is very easy to

There are about 50 permanent research stations in Antarctica for scientists from all over the world.
▶ What clothing do the scientists wear?

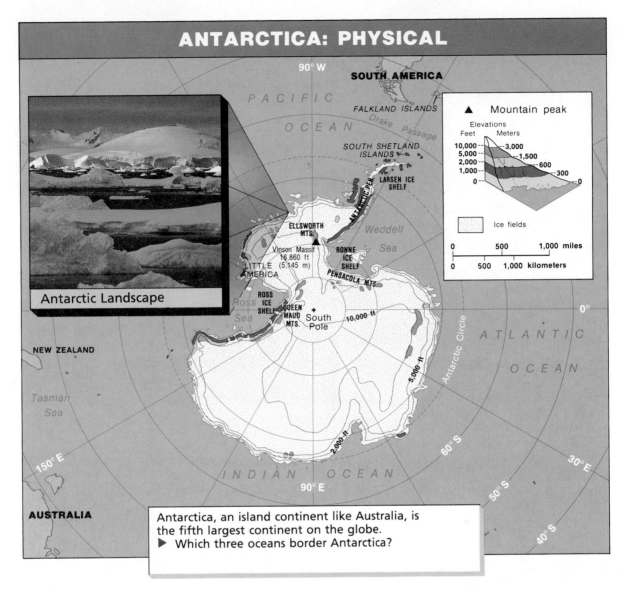

ANTARCTICA: PHYSICAL

Antarctic Landscape

▲ Mountain peak

Elevations
Feet   Meters

Feet	Meters
10,000	3,000
5,000	1,500
2,000	600
1,000	300
0	0

Ice fields

0   500   1,000 miles
0   500   1,000 kilometers

SOUTH AMERICA

PACIFIC OCEAN

FALKLAND ISLANDS

Drake Passage

SOUTH SHETLAND ISLANDS

ANTARCTIC PEN.

LARSEN ICE SHELF

Weddell Sea

ELLSWORTH MTS.

Vinson Massif
16,860 ft
(5,145 m)

LITTLE AMERICA

RONNE ICE SHELF

PENSACOLA MTS.

ROSS ICE SHELF

Ross Sea

QUEEN MAUD MTS.

South Pole

10,000 ft

5,000 ft

2,000 ft

ATLANTIC OCEAN

Antarctic Circle

NEW ZEALAND

Tasman Sea

INDIAN OCEAN

AUSTRALIA

90° W

0°

90° E

150° E

30° E

60° S

50° S

40° S

Antarctica, an island continent like Australia, is
the fifth largest continent on the globe.
▶ Which three oceans border Antarctica?

become frostbitten, even through all the insulated clothing.

Dangers Any outdoor activity in Antarctica requires great care. In many areas, especially on the glaciers that flow from the center of the continent to the coast, there are deep cracks in the ice called **crevasses** (kruh VAS ihz). Many times these deep cracks get covered with snow. A hiker could easily walk across the thin snow and fall through into the crevasse.

Another danger is the **whiteout**. Sometimes the white snow-covered ground blends with the white sky, making it impossible to see shadows or even the horizon. People who are caught in a whiteout are unable to locate directions and can become hopelessly lost in a world without landmarks.

For these reasons, people who live in Antarctica almost always travel in pairs or in larger groups. That way, if one person gets into trouble, someone else will be there to help out.

D. The Continent We All Own

Who Owns Antarctica? Over the years, many nations, including Argentina, Australia, Norway, and the United Kingdom,

These chinstrap penguins are just one type of animal found in Antarctica's coastal areas.
▶ What other animals are found there?

have claimed parts of Antarctica. On the other hand, a large section of the continent called Marie Byrd Land has not been claimed by any country. Some countries, like the United States, have permanent research stations in Antarctica. Yet these countries do not claim any land there.

Many people believe that Antarctica should not belong to any country. They think it should belong to all the world's people and that its resources should not be used for the benefit of any single country.

A Place to Protect Antarctica is a unique place in the world. It was the last continent on earth to be discovered, and it is the only continent that has no land suitable for farming, herding, or any other common way of earning a living. But as people explore Antarctica and use its resources, there is a need to take care of its environment. Governments and private groups are working together to protect the unspoiled beauty of

this remote land. Many people consider this a unique opportunity to study and care for a land that is somewhat untouched by humans.

LESSON 3

Review

REVIEWING MAIN IDEAS

A. What difficulties did Amundsen and Scott face while racing for the Pole?

B. Why are scientists interested in Antarctica?

C. What precautions must people take when living in Antarctica?

D. Why is it important to protect Antarctica?

SKILLS CHECK

THINKING SKILL

Australia, New Zealand, Argentina, and Chile claim land in Antarctica. Look at the map on pages 688–689. What do you think is the explanation for their claims?

GLOBAL ISSUES

GLOBAL WARMING AND THE GREENHOUSE EFFECT

In 1958, a young scientist named Charles Keeling was hired by a scientific organization to test how much carbon dioxide was in the atmosphere. Carbon dioxide is the colorless, odorless gas that humans and other animals exhale when they breathe. It is also created by cars and other machines powered by fossil fuels.

Keeling set up special equipment to monitor the atmosphere at the South Pole and on Mount Loa, in Hawaii. He soon was able to confirm what other scientists had thought: the amount of carbon dioxide in the atmosphere was increasing.

Continued monitoring at Mount Loa from 1958 to 1984 showed a continued increase in the amount of carbon dioxide in the atmosphere. Keeling's initial work and the later observations at Mount Loa have helped make the issue of carbon dioxide in the atmosphere a global concern.

Why is the amount of carbon dioxide in the atmosphere a global concern? Because carbon dioxide strongly influences the world's climates. Too little carbon dioxide in the atmosphere leads to cooler temperatures on earth. Too much carbon dioxide in the atmosphere, scientists believe, will lead to warmer temperatures throughout the world. And that could have dramatic consequences. Water shortages, farmland unable to support crops, rising sea levels, and creeping deserts are only a few of the effects that could occur.

What Is the Greenhouse Effect?

The possible consequences of the buildup of carbon dioxide and other gases in the atmosphere are the result of what

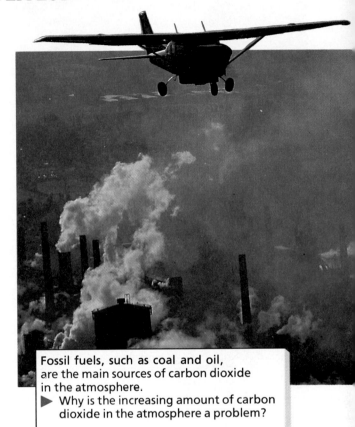

Fossil fuels, such as coal and oil, are the main sources of carbon dioxide in the atmosphere.
▶ Why is the increasing amount of carbon dioxide in the atmosphere a problem?

scientists call the greenhouse effect. A greenhouse is a building made of clear plastic or glass that is used to grow plants. The heat from the sun penetrates the glass of the greenhouse, where it is trapped inside.

The earth's atmosphere acts like the glass in a greenhouse. The atmosphere allows heat from the sun to pass through and continue on to the earth. And like the glass in the greenhouse, the atmosphere traps much of the heat that is on the earth.

The greenhouse effect itself is not bad. In fact, without it, life on earth could not occur. The greenhouse gases keep the earth at a livable temperature. The problem scientists now see is that the

THE GREENHOUSE EFFECT

Escaping heat

Incoming sunlight

Greenhouse gases

Trapped heat

Reflected sunlight

Industry

Deforestation

Farming

Automobiles

The earth's atmosphere acts like a greenhouse by absorbing sunlight and retaining heat. Carbon dioxide contributes to the greenhouse effect.
▶ What are the sources of greenhouse gases?

increasing amount of carbon dioxide and other gases may be making the greenhouse effect stronger. Carbon dioxide and other gases in the atmosphere also absorb or trap heat as it tries to escape the earth. More heat trapped in the atmosphere means higher temperatures. And higher temperatures could have a tremendous impact on the world's climates.

You may remember the difference between climate and weather. The weather is the way the atmosphere of a place is on any given day. It may be sunny one day and stormy the next. As a result, the daily weather is hard to predict in advance.

Climate, however, is more predictable. Climate is the pattern of weather over a period of time. We know that a place with an equatorial climate will usually have daily rainfall and consistently high temperatures. An area with a humid continental climate will have cold winters and hot, humid summers.

The climate of a place can change, however. The change, though, is usually slow and gradual. An example of the most recent change in climate is the last Ice Age the earth experienced.

The Consequences

The scientists studying the greenhouse effect are not sure how higher temperatures will affect climate. This is because climate is affected by more than temperature. Ocean currents and clouds are among the factors that also determine climate. Because of this uncertainty, there is disagreement among scientists about the consequences of global warming.

Some scientists believe global warming might cause an increase in the earth's sea level. This could occur for two reasons. One would be the result of ice sheets melting near the North and South poles as temperatures increased. As they melted, the ice sheets would drop into the ocean. This would force the world's sea levels upward.

Many scientists have adopted a second theory to explain why the earth's sea level may rise. As temperatures across the globe rise, the world's oceans could become warmer and expand. This would occur because warm water takes up more room than cold water. If global temperatures increased by the amount predicted, the seas would rise by about 1 foot (31 cm).

One foot does not seem like much of an increase, but it could have immense consequences. The Maldive Islands, for example, are only 2 feet (61 cm) above sea level. An increase of only 1 foot would leave the island at the mercy of storms that would push high tides far inland.

Carbon Emissions from Fossil Fuels, Selected Countries, 1960 and 1987

Country	Carbon 1960	Carbon 1987	Country	Carbon 1960	Carbon 1987
	(million tons)			(million tons)	
United States	791	1,224	France	75	95
Canada	52	110	South Korea	3	44
Australia	24	65	Mexico	15	80
Former Soviet Union	396	1,035	China	215	594
Saudi Arabia	1	45	Egypt	4	21
Poland	55	128	Brazil	13	53
Germany	149	182	India	33	151
United Kingdom	161	156	Indonesia	6	28
Japan	64	251	Nigeria	1	9
Italy	30	102	Zaire	1	1
			World	2,547	5,599

The table shows the amount of carbon that various countries have produced in the years 1960 and 1987.
► Which five countries have had the largest increases in carbon emissions?

In 1988, President Bush visited farmers after the drought in the Midwest. Many people thought the drought was a sign of the greenhouse effect.
▶ What is a drought?

International Solutions to an International Problem

Scientists are unsure about many of the issues concerning the greenhouse effect. They are all united, however, in concluding that carbon dioxide has increased in the atmosphere and could cause global warming. As a result, many countries throughout the world have taken notice of the possible consequences of the greenhouse effect and have pledged to decrease their output of carbon dioxide.

It will be difficult for the industrial countries to cut back on carbon dioxide output. Fossil fuels power the factories that have made these countries industrial powers. There is no easy way to change over to fuels that do not produce carbon dioxide, such as solar power or even nuclear power.

The same problem holds true with cutting back on carbon dioxide emissions from cars. Governments would have to invest heavily in mass transit and other means of allowing people to commute, or travel, to their workplaces.

However, the broad solutions are in place at this time: cut back on carbon dioxide emissions. If the countries of the world continue to cooperate on this issue, global warming may be avoided.

Scientists continue to debate the extent of other changes that might be caused by global warming. They do agree that temperatures in equatorial climates would increase dramatically. Droughts, such as the one that occurred in the midwestern United States in 1988, might happen more often. This could force farmers in the Great Plains to give up wheat farming because of decreased rainfall.

Not all predictions of global warming see harmful results to the planet. Warmer temperatures would mean that parts of northern Canada and Russia would be warm enough for farming. These countries could then increase their grain output. Other countries might receive more rainfall than they do now, which would cut down on water shortages they now face.

THINKING CRITICALLY
1. How has the creation of a modern, manufacturing economy contributed to the greenhouse effect?
2. How could countries work together to decrease the creation of gases that lead to the greenhouse effect?
3. Some people have argued that nuclear power could be used instead of coal-powered plants to produce electricity. Do you think the risks of nuclear power plants are less than the risks of increasing global warming because of the use of coal-powered plants?

REVIEWING TERMS

On a separate sheet of paper, write the term that best matches each numbered statement.

catamaran

continental island

atoll

lagoon

copra

trust territory

compact

ice shelf

crevasse

whiteout

1. A _____ happens when the white snow-covered ground blends with the white sky, making it impossible to see shadows or even the horizon.
2. A _____ is made of two canoes that have been fastened together to make one boat that will not tip over in rough seas.
3. _____ is dried coconut meat.
4. A circular coral island, called an _____, encloses or partly encloses an area of shallow water.
5. A _____ is connected to a continent by land that has been flooded by the sea.
6. A _____ is a land that is temporarily held by a larger country.
7. The shallow body of water inside a reef is called a _____.
8. The Marshall Islands and the Federated States of Micronesia have each signed a _____, or agreement, with the United States.
9. An _____ is a mass of ice that floats on the water but is attached to a glacier.
10. A deep crack in the ice of a glacier is called a _____.

REVIEWING THE FACTS

On a separate sheet of paper, answer the following questions in complete sentences.

1. What skills did people need to master in order to travel to the islands of the Pacific Ocean?
2. New Guinea and the islands of New Zealand are what kind of island?
3. What islands in the Pacific are volcanic islands?
4. Of what island group is Guam a part?
5. Why is Fiji the most prosperous country in Melanesia?
6. What are two major sources of food for the people of Micronesia?
7. What are the two major activities that support the economy of Polynesia?
8. Why is Hawaii's location important to the United States today?
9. Why is Antarctica considered a frozen desert?
10. What are three minerals that lie under the ice and snow of Antarctica?

WRITING ABOUT GEOGRAPHY

Imagine four travel posters. Each poster shows the climate and scenery of a different island in the Pacific Ocean. Write a caption for each poster that includes the name of the island and tells why tourists should visit the island.

On a separate sheet of paper, answer the following questions in complete sentences.

1. Why would you have wanted to or not wanted to be one of the travelers who sailed a thousand years ago in search of islands on which to make a new home?

2. What evidence might lead you to believe that the people of Micronesia come from many different cultures?
3. How are atoll islands and Antarctica alike?
4. Why, in your opinion, do animals live near the coast of Antarctica and not in the interior of the continent?
5. What do you think should happen to Antarctica in the future?

SUMMARIZING THE CHAPTER

On a separate sheet of paper, draw a graphic organizer like the one shown. Copy the information from this graphic organizer to the one you have drawn. Under the main idea for each lesson, write three statements that you think best support the main idea.

CHAPTER THEME

The Pacific Islands are scattered over a vast area of the Pacific Ocean. Antarctica, with no permanent inhabitants, is a base for scientific study.

Lesson 1 The Pacific Islands are isolated nations.

1. _____
2. _____
3. _____

Lesson 2 The lives of the Melanesians, Micronesians, and Polynesians are similar to one another.

1. _____
2. _____
3. _____

Lesson 3 Many countries are interested in Antarctica.

1. _____
2. _____
3. _____

COOPERATIVE LEARNING

In Unit 7 you learned about Australia, New Zealand, the Pacific Island nations, and Antarctica. Each area has unique characteristics.

A report is a beneficial way for your group to learn more about a country or island.

PROJECT

Work with a group of classmates to write a report about a country or island in Unit 7. The purpose of the report will be to learn more about a certain place and to help your classmates learn about it also.

The first step in the project will be brainstorming. Hold a group meeting to talk about all the interesting material that you would like to focus on in your report. Try to come up with at least ten different ideas. Choose one member to write down all your group's ideas. When you are finished brainstorming, that person should read the list aloud and ask group members to vote on what they think are the five best ideas to research.

After you have decided on the five best ideas, divide the following tasks among group members.

- One group member will be the leader. This leader will gather all the information from the others and present the report to the class. Each member in the group will gather information. Information can be found in your textbook and different encyclopedias.
- One person should draw and label the location studied. This could be the cover for the report.
- One group member will be responsible for writing or typing the report.
- One person should gather interesting photographs for the report.

PRESENTATION AND REVIEW

The group leader will present the report to the class. The students in other groups should ask questions based on the report. The members of the group will answer these questions.

Finally, hold another group meeting to evaluate your project. Did everyone in your group have a job to do? Did the group work well together? Did the class think your report was well organized?

REMEMBER TO:
- Give your ideas.
- Listen to others' ideas.
- Plan your work with the group.
- Present your project.
- Discuss how your group worked.

SKILLBUILDER

UNDERSTANDING A CARTOGRAM

WHY DO I NEED THIS SKILL?

A *cartogram* is one type of special-purpose map. Like all maps, a cartogram is a tool that can help you understand a particular characteristic of a geographic area. Like a graph, a cartogram presents data visually. Most cartograms use different sizes to illustrate data. What do *all* cartograms have in common? They are dramatic, visual tools that can help you understand data quickly and easily.

LEARNING THE SKILL

Suppose you want to find out how the states in the United States rank according to population. The unusual map of the United States on page 685 could help you do that quickly. As you can see, all 50 states are shown in their usual shapes, but their sizes are different. Compare this map with the political map of the United States on page 692. How are the sizes of the states different between the two maps, and what do the differences mean?

The states on the cartogram on page 685 are drawn according to population size, not according to land area. How much larger or smaller a state is drawn depends on the proportion of its population in relation to the population of other states. If each state had the same number of people, all the states would be the same size on the cartogram. A state that has twice the population of another state is twice as large on the cartogram.

A cartogram has a map key to tell you how to interpret the cartogram. The key for the United States cartogram has different size boxes. Each box represents a certain number of people. To estimate the population of California, for example, you would determine about how many times the largest box would fit into the state and multiply that number by the population that the box represents.

PRACTICING THE SKILL

Use the cartogram of the United States and the political map on page 692 to answer the following questions.

1. Which western states have populations of less than 1 million people?
2. What eastern state has a population about the same as or greater than that of Texas?
3. Which state has the largest population?
4. Which half of the United States has the greater population, the eastern half or the western half?
5. Which southern state has about twice as many people as Virginia?

APPLYING THE SKILL

You can make your own cartogram to illustrate data for a geographic area. For example, you can draw a cartogram to show the student population of an area of your school. First, select a section of the school and do a survey to determine how many students there are in each classroom. In the key for your map, draw a small box to represent 2 students. Next, draw a box about five times larger to represent 10 students. Then draw a box twice as large as the 10-student box to represent 20 students.

Now you are ready to make your cartogram. Draw each classroom in the correct location and shape on your map, but use the scale in the key to draw the classroom size according to the number of students. Check the sizes of the classrooms you draw by comparing the populations they repre-sent. For example, a classroom that has 40 students should be drawn twice as large as a classroom that has 20 students. Any classrooms that have the same number of students are drawn the same size.

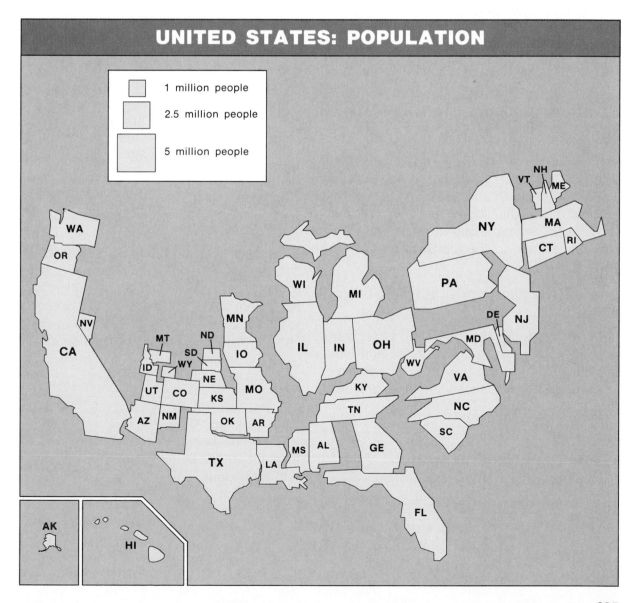

UNITED STATES: POPULATION

1 million people

2.5 million people

5 million people

SKILLBUILDER

EVALUATING FACTS AND OPINIONS

WHY DO I NEED THIS SKILL?

Some things that people write or say are facts. *Facts* are statements that can be proved to be true. People also express *opinions*, which express thoughts or beliefs. Opinions cannot be proved to be true or false. Understanding the difference between facts and opinions will help you to become a more critical listener and reader.

LEARNING THE SKILL

Facts can be evaluated to see if they are true.

- Australia is roughly four-fifths the size of the United States.

You can verify this statement by comparing the areas of Australia and the United States, which are found in the tables on pages 69–71 and 640–641.

Opinions express what someone thinks or believes.

- It was wrong for the English to send their convicts to Australia. When the convicts were released from prison, they were unable to return to England, their homeland.

- It was a good idea for the English to send prisoners to Australia, since the growing population there prevented other countries from challenging England's claim to the Australian land.

These two opinions are different, but they are both based on facts. It was difficult for released prisoners to find ships that would take them on the long journey back to England. And England was able to maintain its claim to the land of Australia. Based on these facts, you can decide if you agree with either one of the opinions.

Sometimes, opinions include false statements or illogical arguments.

- It was all right for the English to use Australia as a prison colony because the only English people who went to Australia were convicts.

This opinion includes the false statement that only convicts went to Australia. You read in Chapter 26 that free settlers also went to Australia. Therefore this statement might be an opinion you would disagree with.

PRACTICING THE SKILL

Use the information in Lesson 3 of Chapter 26 to evaluate each statement in the table on the next page. Copy the table on a separate sheet of paper. Then put a check in the appropriate column to indicate whether each statement is a fact or an opinion. In the last column, write facts or information from the lesson to support your evaluation of each statement as a fact or an opinion.

APPLYING THE SKILL

The ability to distinguish opinions from facts is an important skill that you should use whenever you read. The ability to evaluate opinions—to decide whether they are based on facts or on false statements or faulty arguments—is another important skill. Both skills will help you be an informed and critical reader, listener, and thinker.

EVALUATING OPINIONS

Statement	Fact	Opinion	Why?
1. Kiwi birds are hard to find.			
2. The country of New Zealand is not as small as it seems.			
3. The city of Christchurch is a good jumping-off point for explorations of Antarctica.			
4. It was wrong for Captain Cook to claim New Zealand for England in 1769 because the Maori people were already living there.			
5. It is a good thing that New Zealanders are proud of their Maori heritage, since virtually all inhabitants have some Maori blood.			
6. New Zealand has few minerals, so it is not highly industrialized.			

THE WORLD: PHYSICAL

Elevations
Feet   Meters
10,000 ---- 3,000
5,000 ---- 1,500
2,000
500 ---- 600
0 ---- 150
---- 0

Land below sea level

Land under ice

PACIFIC

OCEAN

40° N

NORTH
AMERICA

ROCKY MOUNTAINS

APPALACHIAN MTS.

ATLANTIC

Tropic of Cancer

20° N

OCEAN

160° E   180°   160° W   140° W   120° W   100° W   40° W

0°

ANDES MTS.

SOUTH
AMERICA

20° S

Tropic of Capricorn

ANDES MOUNTAINS

PACIFIC

OCEAN

40° S

60° S

Antarctic Circle

A N

Nor
ARCT

So

ole

CEAN

Arctic Circle

EUROPE

ALPS

URAL MOUNTAINS

ASIA

KUN LUN SHAN

HIMALAYAS

PACIFIC

OCEAN

AFRICA

0° W   0°   60° E   80° E   140° E

Equator

ATLANTIC

INDIAN

AUSTRALIA

OCEAN   OCEAN

A R C T I C A

le

THE UNITED STATES: POLITICAL

⊛ National capital
⊛ State capitals
• Other cities

200 miles
200 kilometers

692

THE UNITED STATES: PHYSICAL

Abbreviations

Mt. —MOUNT
MTS. —MOUNTAINS
I. —ISLAND

CANADA

ATLANTIC OCEAN

St. Lawrence River
Cape Cod
LONG ISLAND
Boston
Hudson R.
New York
Cape May
Cape Charles
Washington, D.C.
Baltimore
Philadelphia
Chesapeake Bay
Cape Hatteras
ADIRONDACK MTS.
L. Ontario
Lake Erie
Lake Huron
Lake Superior
Lake Michigan
Detroit
Columbus
Ohio River
Indianapolis
Wabash River
Illinois R.
Milwaukee
Chicago
Mississippi R.
St. Louis
Kansas City
APPALACHIAN
ALLEGHENY MTS.
BLUE RIDGE
MOUNTAINS
Mt. Mitchell 6,684 ft. (2,037 m)
Atlanta
Cumberland
Nashville
Tennessee River
Memphis
Mississippi River
ATLANTIC COASTAL PLAIN
Cape Fear
Cape Canaveral
Cape Sable
FLORIDA KEYS
Straits of Florida
Jacksonville
Cape San Blas
Gulf of Mexico
Mississippi Delta
New Orleans
Houston
GULF COASTAL PLAIN
OZARK PLATEAU
GREAT PLAINS
Arkansas River
Red River
Oklahoma City
Canadian River
Brazos River
Rio Grande
Pecos R.
LLANO ESTACADO
Platte River
North Platte River
S. Platte R.
Missouri River
Yellowstone River
BLACK HILLS
Cheyenne R.
Longs Peak 14,256 ft. (4,345 m)
Denver
Pikes Peak 14,110 ft. (4,301 m)
Blanca Peak 14,317 ft. (4,364 m)
Mt. Elbert 14,433 ft. (4,399 m)
Albuquerque
CONTINENTAL DIVIDE
ROCKY MOUNTAINS
Grand Teton 13,766 ft. (4,196 m)
Green River
Colorado River
COLORADO PLATEAU
GREAT BASIN
Phoenix
DEATH VALLEY
MOJAVE DESERT
Los Angeles
Snake River
Columbia River
COLUMBIA PLATEAU
Humboldt River
SIERRA NEVADA
CENTRAL VALLEY
Sacramento
Mt. Whitney 14,495 ft. (4,418 m)
Point Conception
CASCADE RANGE
COAST RANGES
Mt. Rainier 14,410 ft. (4,392 m)
Seattle
Portland
Cape Flattery
Cape Blanco
Cape Mendocino
PACIFIC OCEAN
MEXICO

Elevations
Feet / Meters
12,000 / 3,658
9,000 / 2,743
5,000 / 1,524
2,000 / 610
1,000 / 305
500 / 152
0 / 0

0 100 200 miles
0 100 200 kilometers

CANADA
RUSSIA
ARCTIC OCEAN
Barrow
BROOKS RANGE
Yukon River
ALASKA RANGE
Mt. McKinley 20,320 ft. (6,194 m)
Anchorage
Gulf of Alaska
KODIAK I.
Bering Sea
0 200 miles
0 200 kilometers

HAWAII
KAUAI
OAHU
Honolulu
Pearl Harbor
MOLOKAI
MAUI
HAWAII
0 100 miles
0 100 kilometers

CUBA

693

ASIA

ARCTIC OCEAN

Barrow

ALASKA (U.S.)

Bering Sea

Fairbanks

Anchorage

Yukon R.

Dawson

Beaufort Sea

Thule

Greenland (Den.)

ICELAND

Pond Inlet

Baffin Bay

Gulf of Alaska

150° W

50° N

Juneau

Port Radium

Great Bear Lake

Arctic Circle

Great Slave Lake

Godthaab

PACIFIC

OCEAN

40° N

Edmonton

Vancouver

Victoria   Seattle

Portland

Columbia

Calgary

CANADA

Missouri

Churchill

Hudson Bay

Goose Bay

Labrador Sea

130° W

Spokane

Regina

Lake Winnipeg

Winnipeg

Seven Islands

Gander
St. John's

San Francisco

Salt Lake City

Great Salt Lake

Minneapolis   St. Paul

Quebec

Montreal

Ottawa

Halifax

Denver

Omaha

Milwaukee

Great Lakes

Toronto

Detroit   Buffalo

Boston

30° N

Los Angeles

San Diego

Phoenix

UNITED STATES OF AMERICA

Kansas City

Chicago

Cleveland   New York

St. Louis

Cincinnati

Pittsburgh

Ohio R.

Washington   Philadelphia

Baltimore

Norfolk

ATLANTIC

Arkansas R.

Mississippi R.

Memphis

El Paso

Dallas

Atlanta

BERMUDA IS. (U.K.)

OCEAN

San Antonio

Houston

New Orleans

GUADALUPE I. (MEX.)

Gulf of California

Monterrey

MEXICO

Gulf of Mexico

Miami

GRAND BAHAMA I.

GREAT ABACO I.

ELEUTHERA I.

THE BAHAMAS

Nassau

ANDROS I.

CAT I.

Tropic of Cancer

Havana

CUBA

GREAT EXUMA I.

LONG I.

ACKLINS I.

MAYAGUANA I.

GREAT INAGUA I.

PUERTO RICO (U.S.)

VIRGIN IS. (U.S.&U.K.)

Guadalajara

Mexico City

Orizaba

Santiago-de-Cuba

CAYMAN IS. (U.K.)

JAMAICA

Kingston

HAITI

Port-au-Prince

DOMINICAN REPUBLIC

Santo Domingo

ANTIGUA & BARBUDA

NORTH AMERICA: POLITICAL

⊛ National capitals

• Other cities

0   250   500 miles

0   250   500 kilometers

Belmopan

BELIZE

GUATEMALA

Guatemala

San Salvador

EL SALVADOR

HONDURAS

Tegucigalpa

NICARAGUA

Managua

San José

COSTA RICA

Caribbean Sea

ST. KITTS-NEVIS

GUADELOUPE (FR.)

DOMINICA

MARTINIQUE (FR.)

ST. LUCIA

NETH. ANTILLES (NETH.)

ST. VINCENT AND THE GRENADINES

ARUBA (NETH.)

GRENADA

Panama Canal

Panamá

PANAMA

TRINIDAD AND TOBAGO

0°

Equator

100° W

90° W

SOUTH AMERICA

NORTH AMERICA: PHYSICAL

ASIA

Bering Strait

ARCTIC OCEAN

ST. LAWRENCE ISLAND
60° N
NUNIVAK ISLAND
Point Barrow
Beaufort Sea
QUEEN ELIZABETH ISLANDS
ELLESMERE ISLAND
KNUD RASMUSSEN LAND
70° N

Alaska Peninsula
BROOKS RANGE
ALASKA RANGE
Mt. McKinley 20,320 ft. (6,194 m)
KODIAK ISLAND
Gulf of Alaska
YUKON PLATEAU
Barrow Strait
VICTORIA ISLAND
Great Bear Lake
Mackenzie River
Arctic Circle
BAFFIN ISLAND
Baffin Bay
GREENLAND
Davis Strait
ICELAND

50° N
Alexander Archipelago
QUEEN CHARLOTTE ISLANDS
COAST MTS.
Peace River
Great Slave Lake
Athabasca R.
SOUTHAMPTON ISLAND
Cape Farewell
60° N

PACIFIC OCEAN
VANCOUVER ISLAND
ROCKY MOUNTAINS
North Saskatchewan R.
CANADIAN SHIELD
Hudson Bay
Labrador Sea

40° N
Mt. Rainier 14,410 ft. (4,392 m)
CASCADE RANGE
Columbia River
South Saskatchewan R.
GREAT
LABRADOR
50° N
NEWFOUNDLAND

Cape Mendocino
SIERRA NEVADA
Snake River
Great Salt Lake
Missouri River
BLACK HILLS
Lake Winnipeg
Lake Superior
LAURENTIAN HIGHLANDS
St. Lawrence River
Montreal
NOVA SCOTIA

San Francisco
GREAT BASIN
Mt. Elbert 14,433 ft. (4,399 m)
North Platte R.
PLAINS
Lake Michigan
Lake Huron
Lake Ontario
L. Erie
Detroit
Cape Cod

Point Conception
Mt. Whitney 14,495 ft. (4,418 m)
COLORADO PLATEAU
South Platte R.
Chicago
CENTRAL
LONG IS.
40° N

Los Angeles
LOWLANDS
New York
Philadelphia
Washington, D.C.

GUADALUPE ISLAND
OZARK PLATEAU
Ohio R.
APPALACHIAN MTS.
Mt. Mitchell 6,684 ft. (2,037 m)
Cape Hatteras

Eugenia Point
LOWER CALIFORNIA
Rio Grande
Red River
Mississippi River
COASTAL
BERMUDA ISLANDS
30° N

Abbreviations
Mt. —MOUNT
MTS. —MOUNTAINS

False Cape
Gulf of California
C O A S T A L   P L A I N
Houston
Cape Canaveral
Florida Peninsula
ATLANTIC OCEAN

120° W
SIERRA MADRE OCCIDENTAL
Gulf of Mexico
BAHAMA ISLANDS
Tropic of Cancer

Guadalajara
SIERRA MADRE ORIENTAL
Mexico City
Citlaltépetl 18,700 ft. (5,700 m)
Yucatan Peninsula
FLORIDA KEYS
CUBA
W E S T   I N D I E S
GREATER ANTILLES
HISPANIOLA
LEEWARD IS.
WINDWARD IS.
LESSER ANTILLES

Elevations
Feet	Meters
10,000	3,000
5,000	1,500
2,000	600
1,000	300
0	0

0   250   500 miles
0   250   500 kilometers

CENTRAL AMERICA
Caribbean Sea
70° W

80° W
90° W

SOUTH AMERICA

695

110° W   100° W

30° N   40° N   50° N   60° N   70° N

Barranquilla
Cartagena
Valencia
Maracaibo
Caracas
Barquisimeto
Cúcuta
San Cristóbal
Medellín
Bucaramanga

VENEZUELA

Georgetown
Paramaribo
Cayenne

GUYANA

SURINAME

French Guiana (Fr.)

10° N

MALPELO I.
(COL.)

Cali
Bogotá

COLOMBIA

0°
Quito

ECUADOR

Guayaquil

Iquitos

Equator

Belém
São Luis

Manaus

Fortaleza

P E R U

B R A Z I L

Trujillo

Recife
Maceió

10° S

Callao
Lima
Cuzco

Lake Titicaca

Arequipa

BOLIVIA

La Paz

Brasília
(Federal District)

Salvador

PACIFIC

Sucre

Belo Horizonte

20° S

OCEAN

Chuquicamata

PARAGUAY

Rio de Janeiro
São Paulo
Niterói

Asunción

Antofagasta

Curitiba
Santos

Tropic of Capricorn

SAN FELIX I.—*SAN AMBROSIO I.*
(CHILE)   *(CHILE)*

**C
H
I
L
E**

Tucumán

River

ATLANTIC

Pôrto Alegre

30° S

Córdoba
Santa Fe
Paraná

URUGUAY

OCEAN

Valparaíso
Santiago

Rosario
Buenos Aires

Montevideo

JUAN FERNÁNDEZ IS.
(CHILE)

Concepción

La Plata

Río de la Plata

ARGENTINA

Bahía Blanca
Mar del Plata

40° S

FALKLAND IS. (U.K.)
(MALVINAS IS.)

Strait of Magellan

50° S
696

Punta Arenas

90° W   80° W   60° W   50° W

40° W   30° W

Caribbean Sea

Guajira Pen.

MARGARITA I.

Caracas

Orinoco River Delta

10° N

Orinoco R.

Angel Falls

DEVILS I.

C. Orange

G. of Panama

Mt. Tolima
18,425 ft
(5,616 m)

Bogotá

MALPELO I.

Meta R.

Caquetá

Orinoco Rio

LLANOS

GUIANA HIGHLANDS

Negro R.

Amazon River Delta

0°

Mt. Chimborazo
20,561 ft.
(6,267 m)

Japura

AMAZON

MARAJÓ I.

Equator

Gulf of Guayaquil

Marañón

Juruá

R.

BASIN

Amazon R.

Tapajós R.

Xingu

Tocantins R.

Parnaíba R.

C. São Roque

Aguja Pt.

Ucayali

Purus

Madeira

Araguaia

Tocantins

São Francisco R.

Mt. Huascarán
22,205 ft.
(6,768 m)

10° S

Beni R.

Mamoré R.

Lima

MATO

Lake Titicaca

ANDES

Mt. Ancohuma
20,958 ft
(6,388 m)

Potosí

GROSSO

PLATEAU

Brasília

BRAZILIAN

HIGHLANDS

20° S

Mt. Bandeira
9,495 ft
(2,894 m)

Tropic of Capricorn

ATACAMA DESERT

GRAN CHACO

Pilcomayo R.

Paraguay R.

Paraná R.

São Paulo

C. Frio

Rio de Janeiro

SAN FELIX I.

SAN AMBROSIO I.

Salado R.

R.

R.

ATLANTIC

30° S

Mt. Aconcagua
22,834 ft
(6,960 m)

Santiago

PACIFIC

JUAN FERNÁNDEZ IS.

OCEAN

PAMPAS

Paraná R.

Uruguay R.

Buenos Aires

Montevideo

Rio de la Plata

OCEAN

40° W

30° W

Colorado R.

Blanca Bay

San Matías Gulf

40° S

CHILOÉ I.

Valdés Pen.

CHONOS ARCH.

Gulf of San Jorge

SOUTH AMERICA: PHYSICAL

Taitao Pen.

C. Tres Puntas

Elevations
Feet   Meters

PATAGONIA

10,000 — 3,000
5,000 — 1,500
2,000 — 600
1,000 — 300
0 — 0

FALKLAND IS. (U.K.)
(MALVINAS IS.)

Grande Bay

Strait of Magellan

697

0   500 miles

0   500 kilometers

50° S

Strait of Magellan

TIERRA DEL FUEGO

Cape Horn

90° W

80° W

60° W

50° W

50° N

30° W   20° W

EUROPE

40° N

MADEIRA
ISLANDS
(PORTUGAL)

Mediterranean

Tangier   Algiers Tunis   Sea   ASIA
        Rabat Oran
Casablanca   TUNISIA   Benghazi
MOROCCO   Tripoli
        Marrakesh   Alexandria   Cairo

CANARY
ISLANDS
(SPAIN)

30° N

El Aaiún   ALGERIA   LIBYA   EGYPT

WESTERN
SAHARA
(MOROCCO)   Tropic of Cancer

MAURITANIA   Port
        Nouakchott   Sudan
                    MALI   NIGER   CHAD   Asmara
Dakar   Tombouctou   Khartoum   ERITREA
SENEGAL   Niamey   Lake   SUDAN
Banjul   Bamako   Chad   DJIBOUTI
GAMBIA   NIGERIA N'Djamena   Djibouti
GUINEA-BISSAU BURKINA FASO   SOMALIA
Bissau GUINEA   BENIN   CENTRAL   Addis Ababa
    Conakry   TOGO River Abuja   AFRICAN   ETHIOPIA
SIERRA IVORY GHANA   REPUBLIC
Freetown LEONE COAST Lomé   CAMEROON Bangui   Mogadishu
Monrovia   Accra Porto-   Yaoundé   UGANDA KENYA
LIBERIA   Abidjan   Novo Malabo   Kampala
                              EQUATORIAL GUINEA   Zaire River   Nairobi
                        SÃO TOMÉ E PRÍNCIPE   RWANDA
Equator   São Tomé   Libreville CONGO   Kigali Lake
                            GABON   Bujumbura Victoria
                        Brazzaville   ZAIRE   BURUNDI Mombasa
                    Cabinda   Kinshasa   ZANZIBAR
                    (Angola)   TANZANIA Dar es Salaam

ATLANTIC

OCEAN
                            Luanda   COMOROS
                                                            ISLANDS Moroni
10° S   ANGOLA   MAYOTTE
                                          MALAWI   ISLAND
                                  ZAMBIA Lilongwe   (FRANCE)
AFRICA: POLITICAL   Lusaka   River
                                          Zambezi   MOZAMBIQUE   Antananarivo
    National capitals   Harare
                                  ZIMBABWE   MADAGASCAR
    Other cities

    0   400   800 miles
                                  NAMIBIA   20° S
    0   400   800 kilometers   BOTSWANA
20° S   Walvis Bay   Gaborone
                    (South Windhoek
                    Africa)   Pretoria Maputo
    Tropic of Capricorn   Johannesburg SWAZILAND
                                      Mbabane   INDIAN
                              SOUTH Maseru Durban
                              AFRICA LESOTHO   OCEAN
698   Cape Town Umtata
                        Port Elizabeth   30° S

20° W   10° W   0°   10° E   20° E   30° E   40° E

EUROPE

ATLANTIC

OCEAN

AZORES

40°N

50°N

30°W   20°W   10°W

Strait of Gibraltar

Mediterranean Sea

Gulf of Sidra

ASIA

Casablanca

MADEIRA IS.

30°N

CANARY IS.

ATLAS MOUNTAINS

S A H A R A

LIBYAN DESERT

Alexandria

Cairo

Suez Canal

Sinai Pen.

Tropic of Cancer

Cape Blanco

AHAGGAR PLATEAU

TIBESTI MASSIF

NUBIAN DESERT

Red Sea

Senegal River

Cape Verde

Niger River

Niger River

Lake Chad

Blue Nile

White Nile

Gulf of Aden

Somali Peninsula

ETHIOPIAN HIGHLANDS

Shabelle River

Benue

Niger River

GRAIN COAST

IVORY COAST

GOLD COAST

SLAVE COAST

Cape Palmas

FERNANDO PO

Gulf of Guinea

SÃO TOMÉ

Cape Lopez

0°   Equator

ZAIRE

BASIN

Ubangi

Zaire River

Congo River

Lake Albert

Lake Turkana

Mt. Kenya 17,058 ft. (5,199 m)

Mt. Kilimanjaro 19,340 ft. (5,895 m)

Lake Victoria

ATLANTIC

OCEAN

Kinshasa

Kasai River

Lake Tanganyika

MASAI STEPPE

ZANZIBAR

Cape Delgado

Abbreviations

Mt. —MOUNT

Pen. —PENINSULA

10°S

SHABA

BIÉ PLATEAU

Lake Malawi

COMORO IS.

AFRICA: PHYSICAL

Elevations

Feet   Meters

10,000 --- 3,000

5,000

2,000 --- 1,500

1,000 --- 600

--- 300

0 --- 0

Land below sea level

0   400   miles

0   400   kilometers

NAMIB DESERT

Zambezi

Victoria Falls

Okavango Swamp

Limpopo River

20°S

Mozambique Channel

MADAGASCAR

Tropic of Capricorn

KALAHARI DESERT

Johannesburg

INDIAN

OCEAN

Orange River

Vaal River

DRAKENSBERG

30°S

Cape of Good Hope   Cape Agulhas

20°W   10°W   0°   10°E   20°E   30°E   40°E

ATLANTIC OCEAN

ARCTIC OCEAN

IRELAND
Dublin
Glasgow

SPITSBERGEN (NOR.)
NORTH LAND

MADEIRA IS. (PORT.)
Lisbon
PORTUGAL
Madrid
SPAIN
Valencia
Barcelona
Marseille
BALEARIC IS. (SP.)
CORSICA
SARDINIA

UNITED KINGDOM
London
The Hague
Brussels
NETH.
BELG.
LUXEMBOURG
FRANCE
Bordeaux
ANDORRA
Bern
SWITZ.
LIECH.
Munich
MONACO
Nice
Milan
ITALY
SAN MARINO
Rome
Naples
Palermo
SICILY
MALTA

Bergen
NORWAY
Oslo
North Sea
Amsterdam
DENMARK
Hamburg
Hannover
GERMANY
Berlin
Prague
CZ. REP.
AUSTRIA
Vienna
Bratislava
SLOVAKIA
Budapest
HUNGARY
2
3
4
Tirane
ALBANIA
5
Sofia
BULGARIA

Göteborg
SWEDEN
Stockholm
Copenhagen
Kaliningrad
POLAND
Warsaw
LITHUANIA
Vilnius
BELARUS
Minsk

Narvik
NORWAY
Murmansk
Barents Sea
NOVAYA ZEMLYA

FINLAND
Helsinki
Tallinn
ESTONIA
Riga
LATVIA
St. Petersburg

Archangel

RUSSIA

Moscow
Perm
Kazan
Yekaterinburg
Chelyabinsk
Ufa
Samara
Magnitogorsk
Omsk
Tomsk
Novosibirsk
Saratov
Orenburg
Volgograd
Krasnodar

Yenisei R.
Ob River

1-SLOVENIA
2-CROATIA
3-BOSNIA AND HERCEGOVINA
4-YUGOSLAVIA
5-MACEDONIA

Danube River
UKRAINE
Kiev
ROMANIA
Bucharest
MOLDOVA
Chisinau
Odessa
Kharkov

Volga R.

GREECE
Athens
CRETE (GR.)
Mediterranean Sea

Istanbul (Constantinople)
Izmir
Ankara
TURKEY
Nicosia
CYPRUS

Black Sea

Aral Sea

KAZAKHSTAN

GEORGIA
Tbilisi
ARMENIA
Yerevan
Baku
AZERBAIJAN

Caspian Sea

Urumqi

Alma-Ata
Bishkek
KYRGYZSTAN

Abbreviations

BAH. —BAHRAIN
BELG. —BELGIUM
CZ. REP. —CZECH REPUBLIC
LIECH. —LIECHTENSTEIN
NETH. —THE NETHERLANDS
SWITZ. —SWITZERLAND

GR. —GREECE
IND. —INDIA
NOR. —NORWAY
PORT. —PORTUGAL
SP. —SPAIN
U.K. —UNITED KINGDOM
U.S. —UNITED STATES

LEBANON
Beirut
ISRAEL
Jerusalem
SYRIA
Damascus
Amman
JORDAN
IRAQ
Baghdad
Basra
Abadan
Kuwait
KUWAIT
Euphrates R.
Tigris R.

Tehran

IRAN

UZBEKISTAN
Tashkent
TURKMENISTAN
Ashkhabad
Dushanbe
TAJIKISTAN

SINKIANG

Kabul
AFGHANISTAN
Islamabad
Lahore
JAMMU AND KASHMIR
TIBET

AFRICA

Red Sea
SAUDI ARABIA
Riyadh
Manama
BAH.
QATAR
Doha
Abu Dhabi
UNITED ARAB EMIRATES
Empty Quarter
Mecca
Persian Gulf

Masqat
OMAN

PAKISTAN
Indus R.
Karachi
Hyderabad
Delhi
New Delhi
NEPAL
Katmandu

Ganges R.
Ahmadabad

INDIA

San'a
YEMEN
Madinat ash Sha'b

Arabian Sea
Bombay
Hyderabad

SOCOTRA (YEMEN)

10°N

LACCADIVE IS. (IND.)

Madras

SRI LANKA

0°
Equator

MALDIVES
Male

Colombo

INDIAN OCEAN

10°S

700

40°N

50°E
60°E
70°E
80°E

NEW
SIBERIAN
IS.

Bering Sea

ALEUTIAN IS.
(U.S.)

40° N

30° N

SIBERIA

Magadan

Kamtchatka
Peninsula

Yakutsk

Sea of
Okhotsk

Lena R.

RUSSIA

SAKHALIN

KURIL IS.

20° N

rasnoyarsk

Amur R.

Khabarovsk

Irkutsk

MANCHURIA

Harbin

Vladivostok

Sapporo

JAPAN

Ulan Bator

MONGOLIA

Fushun

Shenyang

INNER
MONGOLIA

Dalian

N. KOREA

Pyongyang

Seoul

Beijing

S. KOREA

Pusan

Sea
of
Japan

Tokyo
Yokohama

Kyoto

Kōbe

Nagoya

Ōsaka

Great Wall

Tianjin

Qingdao

Taiyuan

Huang He

Lanzhou

Xi'an

CHINA

Nanjing

Shanghai

Kitakyūshū

East
China
Sea

Wuhan

Chengdu

Chang Jiang

Chongqing

RYUKYU IS. (JAPAN)

Tropic of Cancer

10° N

Lhasa

Taipei

TAIWAN

HUTAN
Thimbu

Brahmaputra R.

Kunming

Guangzhou

Macao
(Port.)

Hong Kong
(U.K.)

PACIFIC

OCEAN

BANGLADESH

Dacca

Mandalay

Calcutta

Hanoi

MYANMAR

LAOS

Hue

Vientiane

Da Nang

South
China
Sea

Manila

PHILIPPINES

FEDERATED STATES OF MICRONESIA

0°

Rangoon

THAILAND

VIETNAM

Equator

Bay
of
Bengal

Bangkok

CAMBODIA

Phnom
Penh

Ho Chi Minh
City

Davao

ANDAMAN
IS. (IND.)

Bandar
Seri
Begawan

Djajapura

Lae

PAPUA NEW GUINEA

NICOBAR
IS. (IND.)

BRUNEI

Manado

IRIAN
JAYA

NEW GUINEA

Port Moresby

Medan

MALAYSIA

BORNEO

Samarinda

CELEBES

Kuala Lumpur

Singapore

Pontianak

Bandjermasin

Ujung
Pandang

Coral Sea

Arafura Sea

SUMATRA

INDONESIA

TIMOR

701

Palembang

Jakarta

JAVA

Surabaja

Bandung

AUSTRALIA

90° E

100° E

EURASIA: POLITICAL

✪ National capitals

• Other cities

0   400   800 miles

0   400   800 kilometers

Laptev
Sea

NEW
SIBERIAN
ISLANDS

Peninsula

ALEUTIAN ISLANDS

40° N

30° N

CHERSKI RANGE

VERKHOYANSK RANGE

KOLYMA RANGE

CENTRAL RANGE

Bering
Sea

Kamtchatka
Peninsula

C E N T R A L

S I B E R I A N

P L A T E A U

Lena
River

Aldan
River

Sea of
Okhotsk

Tropic of Cancer

Lower
Tunguska R.

Angara
River

Lake
Baikal

Shilka
River

S I B E R I A

KURIL ISLANDS

SAKHALIN

SAYAN
MTS.

Yenisei
River

Amur
River

River

HOKKAIDŌ

MONGOLIAN
PLATEAU

GREAT KHINGAN MTS.

MANCHURIA
PLAIN

Harbin

HONSHŪ

Sea of
Japan

Tokyo

Mt. Fuji
12,388 ft.
(3,776 m)

THE GOBI

Shenyang

Kyōto

EURASIA: PHYSICAL

Elevations
Feet   Meters

10,000 ---- --- 3,000
5,000 ---- --- 1,500
2,000 ----
1,000 ---- --- 600
0 ---- --- 300
--- 0

Land below sea level

0   400   800 miles
0   400   800 kilometers

MTS.

Great Wall

Beijing

Tianjin

Dalian

SHIKOKU

KYŪSHŪ

Korea Strait

NAN SHAN

NORTH
CHINA
PLAIN

Yellow
Sea

Huang He

SHAN

OF

Chang Jiang

Shanghai

East
China
Sea

OKINAWA

10° N

RYUKYU ISLANDS

Chongqing

BOREA HILLS

Philippine

Sea

P A C I F I C

Brahmaputra R.

Calcutta

Xi River

Guangzhou

Hong
Kong

TAIWAN

Luzon Strait

PHILIPPINE ISLANDS

O C E A N

0°

HAINAN

LUZON

Manila

Irrawaddy R.

Salween R.

Mekong

River

South
China Sea

MINDORO

SAMAR

PANAY

NEW
IRELAND

ADMIRALTY
ISLANDS

Bay of
Bengal

Indochina

Peninsula

Ho Chi
Minh City

NEGROS

PALAWAN

MINDANAO

NEW
BRITAIN

ANDAMAN
ISLANDS

Gulf
of
Siam

Celebes

Sea

HALMAHERA

MOLUCCAS

NEW GUINEA

SNOW
MTS.

Andaman
Sea

NICOBAR
ISLANDS

Strait of Malacca

NATUNA
ISLANDS

CERAM

ARU
ISLANDS

Coral
Sea

BORNEO

BURU

Arafura

Sea

SUMATRA

CELEBES

MENTAWAI ISLANDS

BANGKA

S U N D A   I S L A N D S

FLORES

TIMOR

703

Java Sea

SUMBAWA

SUMBA

A U S T R A L I A

Jakarta

BALI

JAVA

LOMBOK

90° E

100° E

704

INDONESIA

INDIAN OCEAN

Banda Sea

Timor Sea

Arafura Sea

BISMARCK ARCHIPELAGO

NEW BRITAIN (P.N.G.)

PAPUA NEW GUINEA

Port Moresby

Torres Strait

Coral Sea

Great Barrier Reef

SOLOMON ISLANDS

Honiara

VANUATU

Port-Vila

NEW CALEDONIA (FR.)

NORFOLK ISLAND (AUSTRAL.)

PACIFIC OCEAN

FIJI

Suva

Tropic of Capricorn

Gulf of Carpentaria

Cape York Peninsula

Darwin

NORTHERN TERRITORY

Alice Springs

MacDONNELL RANGES

MUSGRAVE RANGES

Simpson Desert

Lake Eyre

Townsville

Mount Isa

QUEENSLAND

GREAT ARTESIAN BASIN

Rockhampton

Toowoomba

Ipswich

Brisbane

GREAT DIVIDING RANGE

Newcastle

Sydney

Wollongong

Port Kembla

NEW SOUTH WALES

Canberra

Bathurst

Wagga Wagga

Broken Hill

Murray River

Darling River

DARLING RIVER

AUSTRALIA

WESTERN AUSTRALIA

GREAT SANDY DESERT

GIBSON DESERT

GREAT VICTORIA DESERT

Kalgoorlie

NULLARBOR PLAIN

SOUTH AUSTRALIA

Port Augusta

Whyalla

Spencer Gulf

Adelaide

Great Australian Bight

VICTORIA

Bendigo

Ballarat

Geelong

Melbourne

Mt. Kosciusko (7,316 ft; 2,230 m)

AUSTRALIA

Bass Strait

TASMANIA

Launceston

Hobart

North West Cape

Carnarvon

Geraldton

Perth

Albany

Tasman Sea

NEW ZEALAND

NORTH ISLAND

North Cape

Whangarei

Auckland

Hamilton

Gisborne

Napier

Wellington

Cook Strait

SOUTH ISLAND

Mt. Cook (12,349 ft.; 3,764 m)

Southern Alps

Christchurch

Dunedin

Invercargill

Equator

10° S

20° S

30° S

10° S

20° S

30° S

170° E

160° E

170° E

160° E

150° E

140° E

150° E

140° E

20° S

30° S

180°

170° W

40° S

30° S

20° S

170° E

160° E

AUSTRALIA AND NEW ZEALAND: POLITICAL – PHYSICAL

State or Territorial boundaries

✪ National capitals

⊛ State or Territorial capitals

• Other cities

0   150   300 miles

0   150   300 kilometers

Elevations
Feet   Meters
5,000 — 1,500
2,000 — 600
1,000 — 300
0 — 0

THE WORLD: AVERAGE ANNUAL PRECIPITATION

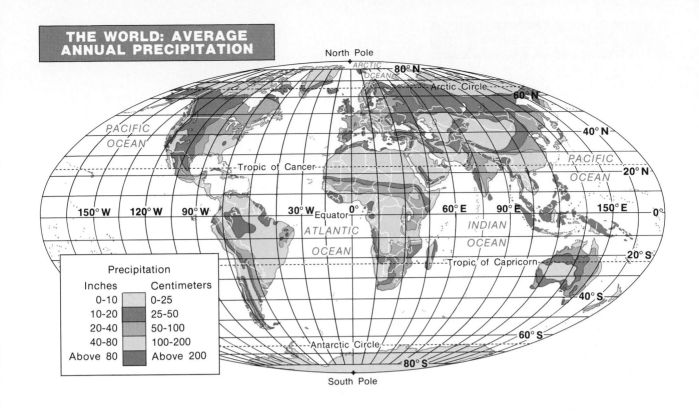

North Pole

ARCTIC OCEAN

80° N

Arctic Circle

60° N

40° N

PACIFIC OCEAN

Tropic of Cancer

20° N

PACIFIC OCEAN

150° W   120° W   90° W

30° W   Equator   0°

60° E   90° E   150° E   0°

ATLANTIC OCEAN

INDIAN OCEAN

20° S

Tropic of Capricorn

40° S

Precipitation

Inches	Centimeters
0-10	0-25
10-20	25-50
20-40	50-100
40-80	100-200
Above 80	Above 200

60° S

Antarctic Circle

80° S

South Pole

THE WORLD: AVERAGE ANNUAL TEMPERATURES

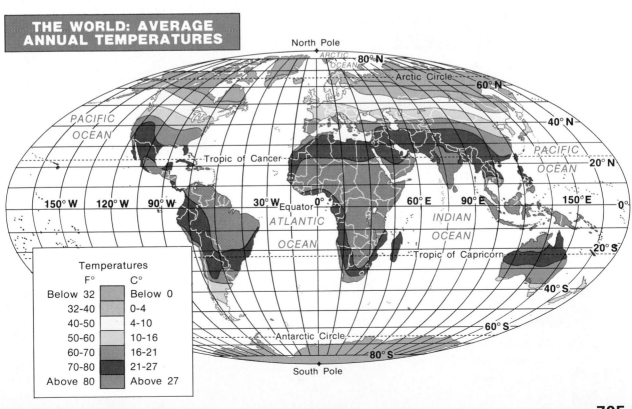

North Pole

ARCTIC OCEAN

80° N

Arctic Circle

60° N

40° N

PACIFIC OCEAN

Tropic of Cancer

20° N

PACIFIC OCEAN

150° W   120° W   90° W

30° W   Equator   0°

60° E   90° E   150° E   0°

ATLANTIC OCEAN

INDIAN OCEAN

20° S

Tropic of Capricorn

40° S

Temperatures

F°	C°
Below 32	Below 0
32-40	0-4
40-50	4-10
50-60	10-16
60-70	16-21
70-80	21-27
Above 80	Above 27

60° S

Antarctic Circle

80° S

South Pole

THE WORLD: CLIMATE ZONES

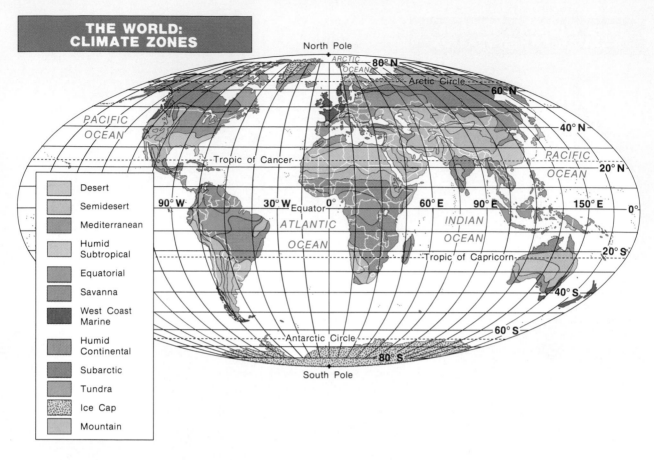

Desert
Semidesert
Mediterranean
Humid Subtropical
Equatorial
Savanna
West Coast Marine
Humid Continental
Subarctic
Tundra
Ice Cap
Mountain

North Pole
ARCTIC OCEAN
80° N
Arctic Circle
60° N
40° N
PACIFIC OCEAN
20° N
PACIFIC OCEAN
Tropic of Cancer
90° W
30° W
Equator
0°
60° E
90° E
150° E
0°
ATLANTIC OCEAN
INDIAN OCEAN
Tropic of Capricorn
20° S
40° S
Antarctic Circle
60° S
80° S
South Pole

THE WORLD: VEGETATION ZONES

Equatorial rain forest
Savanna
Desert and semidesert
Mediterranean
Grasslands
Broad-leaved forest
Coniferous forest
Tundra
Ice

North Pole
ARCTIC OCEAN
80° N
Arctic Circle
60° N
40° N
PACIFIC OCEAN
20° N
PACIFIC OCEAN
Tropic of Cancer
150° W
120° W
90° W
30° W
Equator
0°
60° E
90° E
150° E
0°
ATLANTIC OCEAN
INDIAN OCEAN
Tropic of Capricorn
20° S
40° S
Antarctic Circle
60° S
80° S
South Pole

706

The Gazetteer is a geographical dictionary. It shows latitude and longitude for cities and certain other places. Latitude and longitude are shown in this form: 9°N/39°E. This means "9 degrees north latitude and 39 degrees east longitude." The page reference tells where each entry may be found on a map.

Some words in this book may be new to you or difficult to pronounce. Those words have been spelled phonetically in parentheses. The syllable that receives stress in a word is shown in small capital letters.

For example: **Chicago** (shuh KAH goh)

Most phonetic spellings are easy to read. In the following Pronunciation Key, you can see how letters are used to show different sounds.

PRONUNCIATION KEY

a	after	(AF tur)	oh	flow	(floh)	ch	chicken	(CHIHK un)
ah	father	(FAH thhur)	oi	boy	(boi)	g	game	(gaym)
ai	care	(kair)	oo	rule	(rool)	ing	coming	(KUM ing)
aw	dog	(dawg)	or	horse	(hors)	j	job	(jahb)
ay	paper	(PAY pur)	ou	cow	(kou)	k	came	(kaym)
						ng	long	(lawng)
e	letter	(LET ur)	yoo	few	(fyoo)	s	city	(SIHT ee)
ee	eat	(eet)	u	taken	(TAY kun)	sh	ship	(shihp)
				matter	(MAT ur)	th	thin	(thihn)
ih	trip	(trihp)	uh	ago	(uh GOH)	thh	feather	(FETHH ur)
eye	idea	(eye DEE uh)				y	yard	(yahrd)
y	hide	(hyd)				z	size	(syz)
ye	lie	(lye)				zh	division	(duh VIHZH un)

Abidjan (ab uh JAHN). Capital of the Ivory Coast. Located on the Gulf of Guinea. (5°N/4°W) p. 525.

Abuja (ah BOO juh). Officially replaced Lagos as the capital of Nigeria in 1992. Located in central Nigeria. (9°N/7°E) p. 525.

Acapulco (ah kuh POOL koh). Seaport and international resort located in Mexico, on the Pacific Ocean. (17°N/100°W) p. 132.

Accra (uh KRA). Capital of and most populated city in Ghana. Port city located on the Atlantic Ocean. (6°N/0° long.) p. 525.

Addis Ababa (AD ihs AB uh buh). Capital of and most populated city in Ethiopia. Located at an elevation of 7,900 ft (2,408 m). (9°N/39°E) p. 525.

Adelaide (AD ul ayd). Capital of the Australian state of South Australia. (35°S/139°E) p. 657.

Aden (AHD un). City in Yemen. Located on the Gulf of Aden. (13°N/45°E) p. 389.

Adriatic Sea (ay dree AT ihk see). Arm of the Mediterranean Sea located between Italy and the Balkan Peninsula. p. 257.

Aegean Sea (ee JEE un see). Part of the Mediterranean Sea located between the eastern coast of Greece and the western coast of Turkey. Bounded on the north by the Greek mainland and on the south by Crete. p. 257.

Ahaggar Mountains (uh HAHG ur MOUNT unz). High plateau region in the central Sahara. p. 535.

Alexandria (aligh AZN dree uh). Second most populated city in Egypt. Located in the Nile Delta. (31°N/30°E) p. 547.

Algiers (al GIHRZ). Capital of Algeria. Located on the Mediterranean Sea. (37°N/3°E) p. 525.

Alma-Ata (al muh uh TAH). Capital of Kazakhstan. Located near the borders of Kyrgyzstan and China. (43°N/77°E) p. 372.

Alps (alps). Mountain system extending in an arc from the Mediterranean coast between Italy and France through Switzerland and Austria. p. 255.

Amazon River (AM uh zahn RIHV ur). Second longest river in the world. Tributaries rise in the Andes Mountains and Guiana Highlands. Flows into the Atlantic near Belém, Brazil. p. 171.

American Samoa (uh MER ih kun suh MOH uh). Group of islands of Samoa. Located in the southwestern Pacific Ocean. (14°S/171°W) p. 637.

Amman (AH mahn). Capital of Jordan. (32°N/36°E) p. 389.

Amritsar (ahm RIHT sur). City in northern India. Holy city in the Sikh religion. (31°N/75°E) p. 481.

Amsterdam (AM stur dam). Capital of and most populated city in the Netherlands. Connected to the North Sea by canals. (52°N/5°E) p. 257.

Anatolia (an uh TOH lee uh). Peninsula on which Asian Turkey is located. Lies between the Black and Mediterranean seas. p. 499.

Andes (AN deez). High mountains that stretch north to south along the western part of South America. Highest peak is Mount Aconcagua, with an elevation of 22,834 ft (6,960 m). p. 171.

Angel Falls (AYN jul fawlz). World's highest waterfall, 3,212 ft (979 m) high. Located in southeastern Venezuela. (6°N/63°W) p. 178.

Ankara (ANG kuh ruh). Capital of Turkey. (40°N/33°E) p. 492.

Annamese Mountains (an uh MEEZ MOUNT unz). Range of mountains that runs almost the entire length of western Vietnam and into Laos. p. 444.

Antananarivo (an tuh nan uh REE voh). Capital of Madagascar. (19°S/48°E) p. 525.

Antarctic Peninsula (ant AHRK tihk puh NIHN suh luh). Peninsula in Antarctica that extends toward South America. p. 675.

Antofagasta (ahn taw fuh GAHS tuh). Port city located in northern Chile. (24°S/70°W) p. 219.

Antwerp (ANT wurp). Chief port of Belgium. Located on the Schelde River, about 50 miles (80 km) from the North Sea. (51°N/4°E) p. 296.

Apennines (AP uh nynz). Mountains in Italy. Extend from northwestern Italy to the southern tip of the Italian peninsula. p. 255.

Appalachian Mountains (ap uh LAY chun MOUNT unz). Chain of mountains stretching from Canada to Alabama. p. 65.

Arabian Peninsula (uh RAY bee un puh NIHN suh luh). Large peninsula located east of the Red Sea. p. 387.

Arctic Ocean (AHRK tihk OH shun). Large body of water north of the Arctic Circle. p. 65.

Arequipa (ah ruh KEE puh). Important city in southern Peru. (16°S/72°W) p. 204.

Ashkhabad (ASH kuh bad). Capital of Turkmenistan. Located near the country's southern border with Iran. (38°N/58°E) p. 372.

Asunción (ah soon SYOHN). Capital of Paraguay. Located on the Paraguay River. (25°S/58°W). p. 219.

Aswan (ahs WAHN). Egyptian city known in ancient times as Syene. Located on the Nile River. Site of Aswan High Dam. (24°N/33°E) p. 541.

Atacama Desert (ah tah KAH mah DEZ urt). Very dry area that covers about one third of Chile. Major source of nitrates. p. 212.

Athens (ATH unz). City-state in ancient Greece. Capital of and largest city in modern Greece. (38°N/24°E) p. 257.

Atlantic Ocean (at LAN tihk OH shun). Large body of water separating North America and South America from Europe and Africa. pp. 688-689.

Atlas Mountains (AT lus MOUNT unz). Mountain system located in Morocco, Algeria, and Tunisia, along the northern edge of the Sahara. p. 523.

Auckland (AWK lund). Seaport in northern New Zealand. (37°S/175°E) p. 657.

Baghdad (BAG dad). Capital of and most populated city in Iraq. Located on the Tigris River. (33°N/44°E) p. 389.

Baku (bah KOO). Capital of Azerbaijan. Located on a peninsula in the Caspian Sea. (40°N/50°E) p. 372.

Balkan Peninsula (BAWL kun puh NIHN suh luh). Peninsula in southeastern Europe. Usually thought to consist of Greece, Albania, Bulgaria, Romania, the former Yugoslavia, and European Turkey. p. 255.

Baltic Sea (BAWL tihk see). Part of the Atlantic Ocean, south and southeast of Sweden. p. 257.

Bangkok (BANG kahk). Capital of and most populated city in Thailand. Located on the Chao Phraya River. (14°N/101°E) p. 389.

Bangui (bahng GEE). Capital city of the Central African Republic. Located on the Ubangi River. (4°N/19°E) p. 525.

Barcelona (bahr suh LOH nuh). Important Mediterranean port city in northeastern Spain. (41°N/2°E) p. 325.

Barents Sea (BAR unts see). Part of the Arctic Ocean north of Norway and of the European portion of Russia. p. 257.

Basel (BAH zul). City in Switzerland. Located on both sides of the Rhine River. (48°N/8°E) p. 302.

Basra (BUS ruh). City in Iraq. Country's main port for oil exportation. (31°N/48°E). p. 510.

Bavaria (buh VER ee uh). Region in the foothills of Germany. The capital is Munich. p. 302.

Bay of Bengal (bay uv ben GAWL). Part of the Indian Ocean between the eastern coast of India and the Malay Peninsula. p. 389.

Beijing (BAY jing). Capital of China. Formerly known as Peking. (40°N/116°E) p. 389.

Beira (BAY ruh). Seaport on the southeastern coast of Mozambique. (20°S/35°E) p. 616.

Beirut (bay ROOT). Capital of Lebanon. Located on the eastern shore of the Mediterranean Sea. (34°N/35°E) p. 389.

Belfast (BEL fast). Port city on the eastern coast of Northern Ireland. (55°N/6°W). p. 270.

Belgrade (BEL grayd). Capital of Serbia and the former Yugoslavia. Located where the Sava River joins the Danube River. (45°N/21°E) p. 350.

Belo Horzionte (BAY loh hor uh ZAHN tee). Large industrial city in eastern Brazil. (20°S/44°W) p. 235.

Benares (buh NAH reez). Indian holy city. Located on the Ganges River. Now called Varanasi. (25°N/83°E) p. 481.

Benghazi (ben GAH zee). Port city in Libya. Located on the shore of the Gulf of Sidra. (32°N/20°E) p. 547.

Bering Sea (BER ing see). Part of the North Pacific Ocean bounded on the east by the Alaskan mainland and on the south and southeast by the Aleutian Islands. p. 65.

Bering Strait (BER ing strayt). Narrow body of water connecting the Arctic Ocean and the Bering Sea. Between Russia and Alaska. p. 65.

Berlin (bur LIHN). The capital city of Germany. Berlin is located on the North European Plain. It is the most populated city in Germany. (53°N/13°E) p. 302.

Bern (burn). Capital of Switzerland. (47°N/7°E) p. 257.

Birmingham (BUR ming ham). Second most populated city in the United Kingdom. (53°N/2°W) p. 270.

Bishkek (BISH kek). Capital of Kyrgyzstan. Formerly called Frunze. Located near the border of Kazakhstan. (43°N/75°E) p. 372.

Black Sea (blak see). Large sea bounded by the Ukraine on the north, Russia and Georgia on the east, Turkey on the south, and Bulgaria and Romania on the west. p. 356.

Blue Nile (bloo nyl). River that flows from northern Ethiopia and joins with the White Nile at Khartoum, Sudan. p. 541.

Bogotá (boh guh TAH). Capital of and most populated city in Colombia. Located at 8,563 ft (2,610 m) on a plateau in the Andes Mountains. (5°N/75°W) p. 173.

Bombay (bahm BAY). Indian port city on the Arabian Sea. (19°N/73°E) p. 481.

Bonn (bahn). City in Germany. Located on the Rhine River. (51°N/7°E) p. 257.

Borneo (BOR nee oh). Large island in the East Indies, southwest of the Philippines. p. 389.

Bosporus (BAHS puh rus). Narrow body of water separating European Turkey from Asian Turkey. Connects the Black Sea and the Sea of Marmara. p. 499.

Boston (BAWS tun). Capital of and most populated city in Massachusetts. Important port city. (42°N/71°W) p. 67.

Brahmaputra River (brahm uh POO truh RIHV ur). River that rises in southwestern Tibet and flows south into Bangladesh. Joins the Ganges River near Dacca, India, and flows into the Bay of Bengal. p. 387.

Brasília (bruh ZIHL yuh). Capital of Brazil. Located at the southern edge of the Brazilian Highlands. (16°S/48°W) p. 173.

Brazilian Highlands (bruh ZIHL yun HYE lundz). Highland area located in southeastern Brazil. p. 171.

Brazzaville (BRAH zuh vihl). River port and capital of the Congo. Located on the Zaire River. (4°S/15°E) p. 525.

Brisbane (BRIHZ bayn). Capital of the Australian state of Queensland. Port city located on the eastern coast. (28°S/153°E) p. 657.

Brussels (BRUS ulz). Capital of Belgium. Located on the Senne River. (52°N/4°E) p. 257.

Bucharest (boo kuh REST). Capital of Romania. Located on a tributary of the Danube River. (44°N/26°E) p. 257.

Budapest (BOOD uh pest). Capital of Hungary. Located on both sides of the Danube River. (48°N/19°E) p. 257.

Buenos Aires (BWAY nus ER eez). Capital of and most populated city in Argentina. Located on the estuary of the Río de la Plata. (35°S/58°W) p. 173.

Buffalo (BUF uh loh). City in New York. Located on Lake Erie and the Niagara River. (43°N/79°W) p. 84.

Bulawayo (boo luh WAH yoh). Industrial city in southwestern Zimbabwe. (20°S/29°E) p. 616.

Cabinda (kuh BIHN duh). Territory of Angola, located on the western coast of Africa. Separated from Angola by part of Zaire. p. 525.

Cairo (KYE roh). Capital of Egypt. Most populated city in Africa. Located on the eastern side of the Nile River. (30°N/31°E) p. 525.

Calcutta (kal KUT uh). Port city in northeastern India. (23°N/88°E) p. 481.

Calgary (KAL guh ree). City in the province of Alberta in the prairie region of southwestern Canada. Third largest city in Canada. (51°N/114°W) p. 81.

Callao (kuh YAH oh). Seaport in western Peru. (12°S/77°W) p. 204.

Canadian Shield (kuh NAY dee un sheeld). Upland region of western Canada that extends in a horseshoe shape from the Labrador coast to the Arctic Ocean west of Victoria Island. p. 74.

Canary Islands (kuh NER ee   EYE lundz). Islands off the northwest coast of Africa that belong to Spain. p. 525.

Canberra (KAN bur uh). Capital of Australia. Located in the southeast. (35°S/149°E) p. 637.

Cancún (kan KOON). Large tourist resort located at the eastern tip of the Yucatan Peninsula in Mexico. (21°N/87°W) p. 132.

Cape Agulhas (kayp   uh GUL us). Southernmost point of Africa. Located at 20°E longitude, which serves as the dividing line between the Indian and Atlantic oceans. (35°S/20°E) p. 523.

Cape of Good Hope (kayp uv good hohp). Cape located on the southwestern coast of South Africa. (34°S/18°E) p. 523.

Cape Town (kayp   toun). Port city on the southwestern coast of South Africa. (34°S/18°E) p. 616.

Caracas (kuh RAHK us). Capital of and most populated city in Venezuela. (11°N/67°W) p. 173.

Caribbean Sea (kar uh BEE un see). Part of the Atlantic Ocean that is bounded by South America on the south, Central America on the west, and Cuba, Puerto Rico, and other islands on the north and east. p. 67.

Carpathian Mountains (kahr PAY thee un   MOUNT unz). Mountain range that stretches from the Alps in the west to the Balkans in the east. p. 255.

Casablanca (kas uh BLANG kuh). Seaport in northwestern Morocco. Located on the Atlantic Ocean. (34°N/8°W) p. 547.

Caspian Sea (KAS pee un see). Largest inland body of water in the world. Surrounded by Azerbaijan, Russia, Kazakhstan, Turkmenistan, and Iran. p. 356.

Caucasus Mountains (KAW kuh sus MOUNT unz). Mountains located between the Caspian Sea and Black Sea. Highest peak is Mount Elbrus, with an elevation of 18,481 ft (5,633 m). p. 356.

Cayenne (kye EN). Capital of French Guiana. Located on an island in the Cayenne River. (5°N/52°W) p. 173.

Central America (SEN trul uh MER ih kuh). Area that is made up of the countries of Guatemala, El Salvador, Honduras, Nicaragua, Costa Rica, Panama, and Belize. p. 159.

Chaco (CHAH koh). Semiarid plains of the Paraná and Paraguay rivers. p. 171.

Chang Jiang (chahng jee AHNG). Longest river in China. Starts in the central part of the country. Winds eastward before it empties into the East China Sea. p. 420.

Chao Phraya River (CHOU prah YSH RIHV ur). Thailand's most important river. Flows out of the mountains of Laos and empties into the Gulf of Thailand. p. 444.

Chicago (shuh KAH goh). Third most populated city in the United States. Located in Illinois, at the southern tip of Lake Michigan. (42°N/88°W) p. 67.

Chihuahua (chih WAH wah). Capital city of the state of Chihuahua, in northern Mexico. (29°N/106°W) p. 132.

Chisinau (kee shih NOU). Romanian form of name for capital of Moldova. The Russian form is Kishinev. (47°N/29°E) p. 372.

Christchurch (KRYST CHURCH). City in New Zealand. Located on South Island. (44°S/173°E) p. 657.

Ciudad Guayana (syoo DAHD gwuh YAHN uh). City in eastern Venezuela. Located where the Orinoco and Caroní rivers join. (8°N/63°W) p. 188.

Cologne (kuh LOHN). Manufacturing and commercial city in Germany. Located on the western bank of the Rhine River. (51°N/7°E). p. 302.

Colombo (kuh LUM boh). Capital and seaport of Sri Lanka. Located near the mouth of the Kelani River, on the Indian Ocean. (7°N/80°E) p. 389.

Columbia River (kuh LUM bee uh   RIHV ur). River that rises in the Rocky Mountains in Canada and flows into the Pacific Ocean along the Washington-Oregon boundary. p. 65.

Comoros (KAHM uh roh). Country of volcanic islands located in the Indian Ocean off the southeastern coast of Africa. p. 525.

Congo River (KAHNg goh   RIHV ur). River that rises in southeastern Zaire as the Lualaba River. Flows into the Atlantic Ocean at Matadi, Zaire. Now called the Zaire River. p. 523.

Copenhagen (koh pun HAY gun). Capital of and largest city in Denmark. An important port. (56°N/13°E) p. 257.

Córdoba (KOR doh buh). Second most populated city in Argentina. Located on the western edge of the Pampas. (31°S/164°W) p. 219.

Crete (kreet). Largest island in Greece. Located in the Mediterranean Sea. p. 334.

Cuzco (KOOS koh). City in the Andes of Peru. Was the capital of the Inca Empire. (14°S/72°W) p. 204.

Dacca (DAHK uh). Capital of Bangladesh. Located in west central Bangladesh. (24°N/90°E) p. 389.

Dakar (duh KAHR). Capital and port city of Senegal. Located in western Africa. (15°N/17°W) p. 525.

Damascus (duh MAS kus). Capital of and most populated city in Syria. (33°N/36°E) p. 389.

Danakil Plain (DAN uh kihl playn). Desert region located in East Africa, mostly in the Great Rift Valley. Inhabited by the Danakil people. p. 588.

Danube River (DAN yoob   RIHV ur). Second longest river in Europe. Begins in the Alps and flows into the Black Sea in Romania. p. 255.

Dardanelles (dahr duh NELZ). Narrow straight in Turkey, connecting the Sea of Marmara and the Aegean Sea. p. 499.

Dar es Salaam (dahr es suh LAHM). Capital of Tanzania. Located on the Indian Ocean. (7°S/39°E) p. 525.

Darling River (DAHR ling). River in southeastern Australia. Flows southwest into the Murray River. p. 644.

Darwin (DAHR wihn). Capital of Northern Territory, Australia. Port city located on the Timor Sea. (12°S/131°E) p. 657.

Dead Sea (ded see). Salt lake located on the border between Israel and Jordan. (32°N/36°E) p. 492.

Deccan Plateau (DEK un pla TOH). Peninsula of India, between the Eastern Ghats and Western Gahts. p. 464.

Delhi (DEL ee). City in India. Once the capital of Mogul India. (29°N/77°E) p. 481.

Denver (DEN vur). Capital of and most populated city in Colorado. (40°N/105°W) p. 67.

Detroit (dih TROIT). Important industrial city in Michigan. Located on the Detroit River, near Lake Erie. (42°N/83°W) p. 67.

Dinaric Alps (dih NAR ihk alps). Range of the eastern Alps that runs along the Adriatic coast of the former Yugoslavia and northern Albania. p. 340.

Djibouti (jih BOOT ee). Capital of the country of Djibouti. Located on the Gulf of Aden. (12°N/43°E) p. 525.

Dnieper River (NEE pur RIHV ur). River in Europe. Rises in the Valdai Hills of Russia and flows through Belarus and Ukraine and into the Black Sea. p. 356.

Donets Basin (duh NETS BAYS un). Important coal producing and industrial area in the lower valley of the Donets River. The river flows mostly in the Ukraine. p. 373.

Don River (dahn RIHV ur). River in Russia. Connected by canal to the Volga River. p. 356.

Drakensberg Mountains (DRAH kenz burg MOUNT unz). Range of mountains that extends north along the southeastern edge of Africa. Located in the Karroo region. p. 523.

Dresden (DREZ dun). Industrial city in Germany. Located on the Elbe River. (51°N/14°E) p. 302.

Dublin (DUB lun). Capital and port city of Ireland. Located on the Irish Sea. (53°N/6°W) p. 270.

Dushanbe (doo SHAM buh). Capital of Tajikistan. Located near border of Uzbekistan. (39°N/69°E) p. 372.

Eastern Ghats (EES turn gawts). Mountains located along eastern coast of India. p. 464.

Ebro River (AY broh RIHV ur). River in northern Spain. Flows southeast and empties into the Mediterranean. p. 325.

Edinburgh (ED un bur uh). Capital of Scotland. Located in the southeastern part of the country. (56°N/3°W) p. 270.

Edmonton (ED mun tun). Capital of the province of Alberta. (54°N/113°W) p. 81.

Elbe River (el buh RIHV ur). River in Europe rises in the Czech Republic, flows through Germany, and empties into the North Sea. p. 255.

Elburz Mountains (el BOORZ MOUNT unz). Mountains in northern Iran that separate the Iranian Plateau from the Caspian Sea. Highest peak is Mount Damavand, with an elevation of 18,934 ft (5,771 m). p. 492.

English Channel (ING glihsh CHAN ul). Narrow body of water separating the southern edge of the island of Great Britain from France. p. 255.

Equator (ee KWAYT ur). Line drawn on maps at 0° latitude. Circles the earth halfway between the North pole and the South Pole. p. 6.

Euphrates River (yoo FRAYT eez RIHV ur). River that rises in the mountains of eastern Turkey and flows through Syria into Iraq. Joins with the Tigris River to form the Shatt-al-Arab, which flows into the Persian Gulf. p. 492.

Falkland Islands (FAWK lund EYE lundz). Located in the South Atlantic Ocean, east of the southern tip of South America. p. 173.

Fertile Crescent (FURT ul KRES unt). Stretch of land from Jericho to Ebla through Mesopotamia. p. 36.

Fiji (FEE jee). Country formed by a group of islands north of New Zealand, in the southwestern Pacific (between 16° and 19°S and 178°W and 177°E). p. 637.

Florence (FLOR uns). City in Italy. Located on the Arno River at the base of the Apennines. (44°N/11°E). p. 330.

Fraser River (FRAY zur RIHV ur). River that rises in the Canadian Rockies and flows into the Pacific Ocean near Vancouver, British Columbia. p. 74.

Gaborone (gah buh ROH nay). Capital of Boswana. Located in the southeastern part of the country. (25°S/26°E) p. 525.

Ganges River (GAN jeez RIHV ur). Sacred river of India. Rises in the Himalayas. Joined by the Brahmaputra River near Dacca before flowing into the Bay of Bengal. p. 464.

Gdańsk (guh DAHNSK). Important port city in Poland. Located on the Baltic Sea. Formerly called Danzig. (45°N/19°E) p. 350.

Genoa (JEN uh wuh). City in Italy. One of the most important Italian seaports. (44°N/8°E) p. 330.

Georgetown (JORJ toun). Capital and chief port of Guyana. (7°N/58°W) p. 173.

Giza (GEE zuh). City in northern Egypt, near Cairo. Site of the Grat Pyramid. (30°N/31°E) p. 547.

Glasgow (GLAS koh). Most populated city in Scotland. Important port located in the west-central part of the country. (56°N/4°W) p. 270.

Gobi Desert (GOH bee DEZ urt). Dry area located in the country of Mongolia and in the Inner Mongolian region of northern China. p. 387.

Gold Coast (gohld kohst). Coast of the Gulf of Guinea between the Ivory Coast and the Slave Coast. Named for large amounts of gold once mined in the area. p. 565.

Grand Canyon (grand KAN yun). Gorge in the Colorado River where the river flows across the northwstern corner of Arizona. More than 1 mi (2 km) deep in places. (36°N/112°W) p. 99.

Great Barrier Reef (grayt BAR ee ur reef). World's largest deposit of coral. Located in the Coral Sea off the northeastern coast of Australia. p. 644.

Great Dividing Range (grayt duh VYD ing raynj). Mountain area of Australia. Extends from north to south along most of the eastern coast. Highest peak is Mount Kosciusko, at 7,316 ft (2,230 m). p. 644.

Greater Antilles (GRAYT ur an TIHL eez). Group of islands in the West Indies. Includes the islands of Cuba, Jamaica, Puerto Rico, and Hispaniola. p. 146.

Great Lakes (grayt layks). Chain of five large lakes—Superior, Michigan, Huron, Erie, and Ontario. Located in central North America, mostly along the border between Canada and the United States. p. 67.

Great Plains (grayt playnz). Elevated plains region east of the Rockies. Extends from northeastern British Columbia and northwestern Alberta in Canada south to western Texas. p. 65.

Greenland (GREEN lund). Large island belonging to Denmark. Located off the northeastern coast of North America. Largest island in the world except for the continent of Australia. p. 67.

Greenwich (GREN ihch). A borough of Greater London in southeastern England. The Prime Meridian, which divides the globe into the Eastern and Western hemispheres, passes through this city. (51°N/0° long.) p. 6.

Guadalajara (gwah duh uh HAHR uh). Second most populated city in Mexico. Located in central Mexico. (21°N/103°W) p. 132.

Guam (gwahm). Largest of the Mariana Islands. Located in the western Pacific Ocean. Territory of the United States. (13°N/145°E) p. 637.

Guanajuato (gwah nah HWAH toh). Rich mining center, especially for silver, in Mexico. (21°N/101°W) p. 132.

Guangzhou (GUAHNG joh). Major port city in southeastern China. Located near the mouth of the Xi Jiang (West River). (23°N/113°E) p. 423.

Guatemala City (gwah tuh MAH luh SIHT ee). Capital city of Guatemala. Largest city in Central Amercia. (15°N/91°W) p. 159.

Guayaquil (gwye ah KEEL). Most populated city and chief port of Ecuador. (2°S/80°W) p. 204.

Guiana Highlands (gee AN uh HYE lundz). Area of low mountains and hills in northern South America. Stretches from eastern Venezuela across northern Brazil, Guyana, Suriname, and French Guiana. p. 171.

Gulf of Aden (gulf uv AHD un). Part of the Arabian Sea located between Africa's Somalia and the Arabian Peninsula. p. 387.

Gulf of Mexico (gulf uv MEKS ih koh). Body of water bordered by the United States, Mexico, and Cuba. p. 67.

Gulf of Thailand (gulf uv TYE land). Inlet of South China Sea. Mostly in Thailand, although its southeastern shore is formed by Cambodia and Vietnam. Often called the Gulf of Siam. p. 444.

Gulf of Tonkin (gulf uv TAHN kihn). Arm of the South China Sea, east of Vietnam. p. 389.

Halifax (HAL uh faks). Capital of Nova Scotia, Canada. Located on the Atlantic Ocean. (45°N/64°W) p. 81.

Hamburg (HAM burg). Port city on the Elbe River in Germany. The country's second largest city. (54°N/10°E) p. 296.

Hanoi (hah NOI). Capital of Vietnam. (21°N/106°E) p. 389.

Harare (hah RAH ree). Capital of Zimbabwe. (18°S/31°E) p. 525.

Havana (huh VAN uh). Capital of Cuba and most populated city in the West Indies. (23°N/82°W) p. 67.

Hawaiian Islands (huh WAH ee un EYE lundz). Group of islands in the North Pacific. State of the United States. Largest island is Hawaii. p. 99.

Helsinki (HEL sing kee). Capital and seaport of Finland. Located on the Gulf of Finland. (60°N/25°E) p. 257.

Hermosillo (er moh SEE yoh). City in northwestern Mexico. (29°N/111°W) p. 132.

Himalayas (hihm uh LAY uz). World's highest mountain system. Located in central Asia. Mount Everest—at 29,028 ft (8,848 m), the highest peak in the world—is located in the Himalayas. p. 387.

Hindu Kush (HIHN doo kush). Mountain range located mostly in Afghanistan. p. 387.

Hiroshima (hihr uh SHEE muh). Industrial city in Japan. City was destroyed by an atomic bomb on August 6, 1945, the first time an atomic bomb was ever used in warfare. (34°N/132°E) p. 413.

Hispaniola (hihs pun YOH luh). Second largest island in the West Indies. p. 695.

Hobart (HOH burt). Capital of the Australian state of Tasmania. (43°S/147°E) p. 657.

Ho Chi Minh City (HOH CHEE MIHN SIHT ee). City formerly called Saigon. Name was changed in 1975 after the Communist takeover of South Vietnam. (11°N/107°E) p. 389.

Hokkaido (hoh KYE doh). Northernmost of the four main islands of Japan. p. 398.

Hong Kong (HAHNG KAHNG). British colony in southeastern China. Hong Kong will return to China in 1997. (22°N/114°E) p. 423.

Honshu (HAHN shoo). Largest of Japan's four major islands. Site of many of the country's most populated cities, including Tokyo, Osaka, and Yokohama. p. 398.

Houston (HYOOS tun). Most populated city in Texas and fourth most populated city in the United States. (30°N/95°W) p. 67.

Huancavelica (wahn kuh vuh LEE kuh). Town in Peru, southeast of Lima. (13°S/75°W) p. 204.

Huang He (HWAHNG HIH). Chinese river sometimes called the Yellow River. Rises in the mountains of Xijang and flows into the Yellow Sea. p. 420.

Hudson Bay (HUD sun bay). Large body of water in Canada that is connected with the Atlantic Ocean by the Hudson Strait. p. 67.

Hungarian Plain (hung GER ee un playn). Large plain located mostly in Hungary. The Danube River crosses it. p. 340.

Ibadan (ee BAH dahn). City in southwestern Nigeria. (7°N/4°E) p. 525.

Iberian Peninsula (eye BIHR ee un puh NIHN suh luh). European peninsula southeast of the Pyrenees. Spain and Portugal are on this peninsula. p. 325.

Indian Ocean (IHN dee un OH shun). Large body of water between Africa and Australia. p. 387.

Indus River (IHN dus RIHV ur). River that rises in the Himalayas in Tibet. Flows northwest through the northern tip of India and then southwest through Pakistan to the Arabian Sea. p. 387.

Iquitos (ee KEE tohs). City and port located on the Amazon River, in northeastern Peru. (4°S/73°W) p. 204.

Irian Jaya (ihr ee AHN JAH yuh). Province of Indonesia that covers the western half of New Guinea and some nearby small islands. p. 444.

Irkutsk (ihr KOOTSK). City in Siberia. Located near Lake Baikal and the Lena River. (52°N/104°E) p. 389.

Irrawaddy River (ihr uh WAH dee RIHV ur). River that forms in upper Myanmar. Flows south through Myanmar into Bay of Bengal, near Rangoon. p. 387.

Islamabad (ihs LAHM uh bahd). Capital of Pakistan. Located in the northeastern part of the country. (34°N/73°E) p. 389.

Istanbul (ihs tan BOOL). Most populated city in Turkey. Located on both sides of the Bosporus River. Part of the city is in Europe and part is in Asia. Formerly called Constantinople. (41°N/29°E) p. 499.

Jakarta (juh KAHR tuh). Capital of Indonesia. One of the world's most populated cities. Located on the northwestern coast of Java. (6°S/107°E) p. 453.

Japanese Alps (jap uh NEEZ alps). Highest mountain range in Japan. Located near the center of the island of Honshu. Mount Fuji, the range's highest peak, rises 12,388 ft (3,776 m) above sea level. p. 398.

Java (JAH vuh). Most populated island in Indonesia. Located between the Java Sea and the Indian Ocean. p. 444.

Jerusalem (juh ROOZ uh lum). Capital of Israel. Holy city for Jews, Christians, and Muslims. (32°N/35°E) p. 499.

Jidda (JIHD uh). Port city in Saudi Arabia. Located on the Red Sea. (22°N/39°E) p. 499.

Johannesburg (joh HAN ihs burg). Most populated city in South Africa. (26°S/28°E) p. 616.

Jordan River (JORD un RIHV ur). River that rises in Syria. Flows south through the Sea of Galilee into the Dead Sea. p. 506.

Juba River (JOO buh RIHV ur). River that rises in the mountains of south-central Ethiopia. Flows south across southwestern Somalia and empties into the Indian Ocean. p. 588.

Jura Mountains (JOOR uh MOUNT unz). Mountains along the border between France and Switzerland. p. 288.

Jutland Peninsula (JUT lund puh NIHN suh luh). Peninsula located between the North and Baltic seas. Denmark and part of Germany are located on the peninsula. p. 264.

Kabul (KAH bool). Capital and most populated city in Afghanistan. (35°N/69°E) p. 389.

Kalahari Desert (kal uh HAHR ee DEZ urt). Dry plateau region located in Botswana, South Africa, and Namibia. p. 523.

Kampala (kahm PAH luh). Capital of Uganda, in East Africa. (0° lat./32°E) p. 525.

Kansas City (KAN zus SIHT ee). Second largest city in Missouri. (39°N/95°W) p. 115.

Karachi (kuh RAH chee). Most populated city in Pakistan. Formerly the capital. Port city located on the Arabian Sea. (25°N/67°E) p. 481.

Katmandu (kaht mahn DOO). Capital of Nepal. Located in the Himalayas. (28°N/85°E) p. 389.

Khartoum (kahr TOOM). Capital of Sudan. Located where the Blue Nile and White Nile join. (15°N/32°E). p. 525.

Kiev (kee EV). Capital of Ukraine. Located on the Dnieper River. (50°N/31°E) p. 372.

Kingston (KINGZ tun). Capital and chief seaport of Jamaica. (18°N/77°W) p. 67.

Kinshasa (keen SHAH sah). Capital city of Zaire. Located on the Zaire River. Formerly known as Leopoldville. (4°S/15°E) p. 582.

Kjølen Mountains (CHUL un MOUNT unz). Mountains that stretch along the border between northeastern Norway and northwestern Sweden. p. 264.

Kobe (KOH bee). City in the foothills of the Japanese Alps. (35°N/135°E) p. 413.

Korea Strait (kuh REE uh strayt). Channel between South Korea and southwestern Japan. Connects the Sea of Japan with the East China Sea. p. 398.

Kourou (koo ROO). Port city in French Guiana. (5°N/53°W) p. 188.

Kraków (KRA kou). Poland's main industrial city. Located in the southern part of the country, on the Vistula River. (50°N/20°E) p. 350.

Kuala Lumpur (KWAH luh loom POOR). Capital of Malaysia. Located along the Strait of Malacca. Important trading center. (3°N/102°E). p. 389.

Kyushu (kee oo shoo). Southernmost of the four islands of Japan. p. 398.

Lagos (LAY gahs). Capital of and most populated city in Nigeria. Located on the Gulf of Guinea. (6°N/4°E) p. 525.

Lake Baikal (layk bye KAWL). World's deepest lake, 5,715 ft (1,742 m) deep. Located in Russia. p. 356.

Lake Chad (layk chad). Lake located at the borders of Niger, Chad, Nigeria, and Cameroon. p. 523.

Lake Malawai (layk muh LAH wee). Lake located between Malawi, Tanzania, and Mozambique. Formerly known as Lake Nyassa. p. 523.

Lake Tanganyika (layk tan gun YEE kuh). Lake in east central Africa. Four nations—Tanzania, Zaire, Zambia, and Burundi—have coastlines on this lake, which is 4,710 ft (1,436 m) deep. p. 523.

Lake Victoria (layk vihk TOR ee uh). One of the largest bodies of fresh water in the world. Located in East Africa. Kenya, Uganda, and Tanzania all have coastlines on this lake. p. 523.

La Paz (lah pahs). Capital of and most populated city in Bolivia. Third highest city in the world, at 12,001 ft (3,658 m). (17°S/68°W) p. 173.

Larnaca (LAHR nuh kuh). Important port city in Cyprus. (35°N/34°E) p. 320.

Le Havre (luh HAHV ruh). Major port city in France. Located on the English Channel. (50°N/0° long.) p. 294.

Leipzig (LYP sihg). Industrial city in Germany. Country's tenth largest city. (51°N/12°E) p. 302.

Lesser Antilles (LES ur an TIHL eez). Group of islands in the West Indies. Includes the Virgin Islands, the Leeward Islands, and the Windward Islands. p. 146.

Lhasa (LAH suh). Major city in Xizang, at 11,830 ft (3,606 m). (30°N/30°E) p. 257.

Libreville (LEE bruh veel). Capital and seaport of Gabon. Located on the Gulf of Guinea. (0 ° lat./9°E) p. 525.

Lima (LEE muh). Capital of and most populated city in Peru. (12°S/77°W) p. 173.

Limpopo River (lihm POH poh RIHV ur). River that rises near Johannesburg, South Africa. Flows across Mozambique and empties into the Indian Ocean. p. 616.

Lisbon (LIHZ bun). Capital of Portugal. Mainland Europe's westernmost port city. (39°N/9°W) p. 325.

Liverpool (LIHV ur pool). Port city in northwest England. Hometown of the rock group the Beatles. (53°N/3°W) p. 270.

Ljubljana (lee uh blee AHN uh). Capital of Slovenia. Located on Sava River. (46°N/15°E) p. 350.

London (LUN dun). Capital of and most populated city in the United Kingdom. Located along the Thames River. Major industrial and financial center. (52°N/0° long.) p. 270.

Los Angeles (laws AN juh lus). City in southern California. Located on the pacific Ocean. Second most populated city in the United States; only New York City has more people. (34°N/118°W) p. 67.

Luanda (loo AHN duh). Capital and seaport of Angola on the Atlantic Ocean. (9°S/13°E) p. 525.

Lusaka (loo SAH kah). Capital of Zambia. Located in central Zambia, in the center of a farming region. (15°S/28°E) p. 525.

Luzon (loo ZAHN). Chief island of the Philippines. Manila is located on this island. p. 444.

Macao (muh KOU). Portuguese colony located in the southern part of China, on the South China Sea. (22°N/113°E) p. 423.

Macdonnell Ranges (muk DAHN ul raynj ihs). Mountains in central Australia. p. 644.

Mackenzie River (muh KEN zee RIHV ur). Canadian river. Source in the Northwest Territories. p. 74.

Madagascar (mad uh GAS kur). Island nation located in the Indian Ocean, off the southeastern coast of Africa. World's fourth largest island, excluding Australia. p. 525.

Madras (muh DRAS). City in India. Main port on the country's southeastern coast. (13°N/80°E) p. 481.

Madrid (muh DRIHD). Capital of Spain. Second most-populated city in Western Europe. (40°N/4°W) p. 325.

Malay Peninsula (MAY lay puh NIHH suh luh). Peninsula located in Southeast Asia. Parts of Malaysia and Thailand are on this peninsula. p. 444.

Managua (mah NAH gwah). Capital of and most populated city in Nicaragua. (12°N/86°W) p. 159.

Manaus (mah NOUS). City in rain forest of Brazil. Located on the Negro River, a branch of the Amazon River. (3°S/60°W) p. 235.

Manila (muh NIHL uh). Capital of and most populated city in the Philippines. (15°N/121°E) p. 444.

Maracaibo (mar uh KYE boh). Seaport in northwestern Venezuela. Located between Lake Maracaibo and the Gulf of Venezuela. (11°N/72°W) p. 188.

Marianas (mer ee AN uz). Group of islands located in the western Pacific, east of the Philippines. Except Guam, a commonwealth of the United States. p. 637.

Marquesas Islands (mahr KAY zuhz EYE lundz). Group of islands in the eastern South Pacific. p. 637.

Marseilles (mahr SAY). Important port city in southern France. Located on the Mediterranean Sea. (43°N/5°E) p. 294.

Marshall Islands (MAHR shul EYE lundz). Group of islands in the western Pacific, east of the Caroline Islands. Since 1947, part of the United States Trust Territory of the Pacific Islands. p. 637.

Maseru (MAZ uh roo). Capital of Lesotho, a country located within South Africa. (29°S/27°E) p. 616.

Masqat (mus KAT). Capital city of Oman. (24°N/59°E) p. 499.

Matadi (mah TAH dee). Zaire's major port city. Located on the Atlantic Ocean. (6°S/13°E) p. 582.

Mbabane (em buh BAHN). Capital of Swaziland. Located in southeastern Africa. (26°S/31°E) p. 616.

Mecca (MEK uh). City in Saudi Arabia. Birthplace of the prophet Muhammad and a holy city for Muslims. (21°N/40°E) p. 499.

Medellín (may day YEEN). Second most populated city in Colombia. Once the heart of a gold-mining region and an important coffee-growing center. (6°N/76°W) p. 188.

Medina (muh DEE nuh). Holy city in Saudi Arabia. (25°N/40°E) p. 499.

Mediterranean Sea (med ih tuh RAY nee un see). Large body of water surrounded by Europe, Africa, and Asia. p. 255.

Mekong River (MAY kahng RIHV ur). River in Southeast Asia. Rises in Tibet and forms most of the boundary between Thailand and Laos. Flows into the South China Sea. p. 44.

Melanesia (mel uh NEE zhuh). Group of islands in the South Pacific, northeast of Australia. Includes New Guinea, the Solomon Islands, New Caledonia, Vanuatu, and Fiji. p. 637.

Melbourne (MEL burn). Capital of the Australian state of Victoria. Located on Port Phillip Bay on the southeastern coast. (38°S/145°E) p. 657.

Mendoza (men DOH zuh). City located in northwestern Argentina. Important wine-producing and industrial center. (33°S/69°W) p. 219.

Mesopotamia (mes uh puh TAY mee uh). One of the earliest centers of civilization. Located between the Tigris and Euphrates rivers. p. 36.

Meuse River (myooz RIHV ur). River that rises in northeast France. Flows north through Belgium and the Netherlands into the North Sea. p. 288.

Mexico City (MEKS ih koh SIHT ee). Capital of Mexico. Most populated city in the Western Hemisphere. (19°N/99°W) p. 67.

Micronesia (mye kruh NEE zhuh). Several groups of small islands located east of the Philippines. Some of the island groups include the Marianas, the Caroline Islands, and the Marshall Islands. p. 637.

Milan (mih LAN). Important industrial city in northern Italy. Country's second most populated city. (45°N/9°E) p. 330.

Mindanao (mihn duh NOU). Largest and second most populated island in the Philippines. p. 444.

Minneapolis (mihn ee AP ul ihs). Most populated city in Minnesota. (45°N/93°W) p. 67.

Minsk (MIHNSK). Capital of Belarus. Official location for the government of the Commonwealth of Independent States. (54°N/28°E) p. 372.

Mississippi River (mihs uh SIHP ee RIHV ur). Second longest river in the United States. Rises in northern Minnesota and flows into the Gulf of Mexico, near New Orleans, Louisiana. p. 65.

Mogadishu (moh gah DEE shoo). Capital and seaport of Somalia. Located on the Indian Ocean. (2°N/45°E) p. 525.

Mombasa (mahm BAH suh). Port city on the eastern coast of Kenya. (40°S/40°E) p. 594.

Monclova (mawng KLOH vuh). Town in northeastern Mexico. Site of copper, silver, and zinc mines. (27°N/101°W) p. 132.

Mont Blanc (mohn BLAHN). Located in the French Alps, near the border with Italy. Highest peak in the Alps, at 15,781 ft (4,810 m). p. 288.

Monterrey (mahn tuh RAY). Industrial city in Mexico (26°N/100°W) p. 132.

Montevideo (mahnt uh vuh DAY oh). Capital of and most populated city in Uruguay. Located on the Río de la Plata. (35°S/56°W) p. 173.

Montreal (mahn tree AWL). Second most populated city in Canada. Located in the province of Quebec, on Montreal Island in the St. Lawrence River. (46°N/74°W) p. 81.

Moscow (MAHS koh). Capital of Russia and former capital of the Soviet Union. Most populated city in Europe. Located on both sides of the Moskva River. (56°N/38°E) p. 257.

Moselle River (moh ZEL RIHV ur). River in northeastern France and western Germany. Flows into the Rhine River. p. 255.

Mount Aconcagua (mount ah kawn KAH gwuh). Highest mountain in the Western Hemisphere, 22,834 ft (6,960 m) high. Located in the Andes Mountains in Chile. (33°S/70°W) p. 212.

Mount Everest (mount EV ur ihst). Highest peak in the world, with an elevation of 29,028 ft (8,848 m). Located in the Himalayas. (28°N/87°E) p. 387.

Mount Fuji (mount FOO jee). Highest peak in the Japanese Alps, rising 12,388 ft (3,776 m) above sea level. (35°N/139°E) p. 398.

Mount Kenya (mount KEN yuh). Located in central Kenya. Second highest point in Africa, with an elevation of 17,058 ft (5,199 m). (0° lat./37°E) p. 588.

Mount Kilimanjaro (mount kihl uh mun JAHR oh). Highest mountain peak in Africa, at 19,340 ft (5,895 m). Located in northeast Tanzania, near the Kenyan border. (3°S/37°E) p. 588.

Mount Kosciusko (mount kahs ee US koh). Highest peak in the Australian Alps, at 7,316 ft (2,230 m). Located in southeastern Australia. (36°S/148°E) p. 644.

Mount McKinley (mount muh KIHN lee). Highest mountain peak in the United States, 20,320 ft (6,194 m) high. Located in Alaska. (63°N/151°W) p. 65.

Mount Vesuvius (mount vuh SOO vee us). Active volcano in southern Italy. About 4,203 ft (1,281 m) high. Erupted and buried the city of Pompeii in A.D. 79. (41°N/14°E) p. 320.

Munich (MYOO nihk). Industrial city in Germany. (48°N/12°E) p. 302.

Murray River (MUR ee RIHV ur). Most important river in Australia. Rises in the Great Dividing Range. Flows into the Indian Ocean near Adelaide. p. 644.

Nagasaki (nah guh SAH kee). Industrial city and seaport in Japan. Located on the island of Kyushu. Destroyed by an atomic bomb near the end of World War II. (33°N/130°E) p. 413.

Nairobi (nye ROH bee). Capital of and most populated city in Kenya. (1°S/37°E) p. 525.

Namib Desert (NAHM ihb DEZ urt). Dry area along coast of Namibia. p. 523.

Naples (NAY pulz). Important port city in Italy. Located on the Mediterranean Sea. (40°N/15°E) p. 330.

New Caledonia (noo kal uh DOHN yuh). French island in the southwestern Pacific, east of Australia. p. 637.

New Delhi (noo DEL ee). Capital of India. (29°N/77°E) p. 389.

New Guinea (noo GIHN ee). Large island located north of Australia. Western half is part of Indonesia; Eastern half is the country of Papua New Guinea. p. 637.

New York City (noo york SIHT ee). Most populated city in the United States. Located at the mouth of the Hudson River, in the southern part of New York State. One of the world's most important ports. (41°N/74°W) p. 67.

Niagara Falls (nye AG uh ruh fawlz). Great falls of the Niagara River, on the United States-Canada border. Divided by Goat Island into Horseshoe (or Canadian) Falls, 158 ft (48 m) high and 2,600 ft (792 m) wide; and American Falls, 167 ft (51 m) high and 1,000 ft (305 m) wide. p. 65.

Nicosia (nihk oh SEE uh). Capital of Cyprus. (35°N/33°E) p. 334.

Niger River (NYE jur RIHV ur). Rises in Guinea, near Sierra Leone border. Flows into Gulf of Guinea in Nigeria. p. 554.

Nile River (nyl RIHV ur). Longest river in the world at 3,473 miles (5,588 km). Flows into the Mediterranean Sea at Alexandria, Egypt. p. 541.

North European Plain (north yoor uh PEE un playn). Large area of flat land curving from southwestern France through Belgium, the Netherlands, Germany, and Poland, then stretching into the former Soviet Union. p. 255.

North Island (north EYE lund). Northernmost of the two major islands of New Zealand. p. 644.

North Pole (north pohl). Most northern place on the earth. Located at 90° north latitude. p. 6.

North Sea (north see). Part of the Atlantic Ocean between Great Britain and the European continent. p. 255.

Ob River (ohb RIHV ur). River in Russia that flows north into the Arctic Ocean. p. 356.

Oder River (OH dur RIHV ur). River that rises in the Czech Republic and flows north through Poland. Flows north to the Baltic Sea, forming the boundary between Poland and Germany. p. 257.

Odessa (oh DES uh). Seaport in Ukraine. Located on the Black Sea. (46°N/31°E) p. 365.

Ohio River (oh HYE oh RIHV ur). River that forms in Pittsburgh, Pennsylvania, by the joining of the Allegheny and Monongahela rivers. Flows into the Mississippi River. p. 99.

Oporto (oh POHR too). Important port city in Portugal. (41°N/9°W) p. 325.

Oran (oh RAN). Seaport in northern Algeria. Located on the Mediterranean Sea. (36°N/1°W) p. 547.

Orange River (OR inj RIHV ur). Longest river in South Africa. Part of it forms the boundary between South Africa and Namibia. Flows into the Atlantic Ocean. p. 610.

Orinoco River (or uh NOH koh RIHV ur). River located in Venezuela. Rises in the Guiana Highlands and flows into the Atlantic Ocean near Trinidad and Tobago. p. 178.

Orlando (or LAN doh). City in east-central Florida. (29°N/81°W) p. 692.

Orontes River (oh RAHN teez RIHV ur). Unnavigable river in western Syria. Flows into the Mediterranean Sea. p. 492.

Osaka (OH sah kah). Second most populated city in Japan. Major seaport, located on Osaka Bay, on Honshu Island. (35°N/136°E) p. 400.

Ottawa (AHT uh wuh). Capital of Canada. Located in southeastern Ontario. (45°N/76°W) p. 67.

Pachuca (pah CHOO kah). City in east-central Mexico. (20°N/99°W) p. 132.

Palau (pah LOU). A group of islands and islets in the western Pacific Ocean. p. 637.

Pampas (PAHM puz). Fertile agricultural plains area in Argentina and Uruguay. p. 171.

Panama Canal (PAN uh mah kuh NAL). Artificial waterway that cuts across the Isthmus of Panama and links the Atlantic and Pacific oceans. p. 159.

Papua New Guinea (PAP yoo uh noo GIHN ee). Country that occupies the eastern half of the island of New Guinea and nearby islands. Capital is Port Moresby. p. 637.

Paraguay River (PAR uh gway RIHV ur). River that flows from southern Brazil through Paraguay. Empties into the Paraná River. p. 171.

Paramaribo (par uh MAR ih boh). Port city and capital of Suriname. (6°N/55°W) p. 173.

Paraná River (pah rah NAH RIHV ur). Forms in Brazil. Flows into the Río de la Plata. p. 212.

Paris (PAR ihs). Capital of and most populated city in France. Located on the Seine River. (49°N/2°E) p. 257.

Patagonia (pat uh GOH nee uh). Barren plains area in southern Argentina. p. 212.

Pearl Harbor (purl HAHR bur). Inlet on the island of Oahu, in Hawaii. Site of the United States naval base attacked by the Japanese on December 7, 1941. (21°N/158°W) p. 693.

Pemba (PEM buh). Island belonging to Tanzania. Located in the Indian Ocean off the coast of East Africa, north of the island of Zanzibar. (13°S/41°E) p. 594.

Pennine Mountains (PE nyn MOUNT unz). Mountain range that runs from north to south through Great Britain. p. 264.

Persian Gulf (PUR zhun gulf). Arm of the Arabian Sea. Separates Iran and Saudi Arabia. Connected with the Gulf of Oman and the Arabian Sea by the Strait of Hormuz. p. 387.

Perth (purth). Capital of the Australian state of Western Australia. Located on the west coast of Australia. (32°S/116°E) p. 657.

Philadelphia (fihl uh DEL fee uh). City at the point where the Delaware and Schuylkill rivers join. The most populated city in Pennsylvania, and the fifth most populated city in the United States. (40°N/75°W) p. 67.

Phnom Penh (puh NAHM PEN). Capital of Cambodia. Located on the Mekong River. (12°N/105°E) p. 444.

Pikes Peak (pyks peek). High mountain located in the Rockies in east-central Colorado. Altitude of 14,110 ft (4,301 m). (39°N/105°W) p. 693.

Pindus Mountains (PIHN dus MOUNT unz). Mountain range in western Greece. p. 320.

Piraeus (pye REE us). Important port city in Greece. (38°N/24°E) p. 320.

Podgorica (PAHD guh reet sah). Capital of Montenegro, a region in the Republic of Yugoslavia. Formerly called Titograd. (42°N/19°E) p. 350.

Pointe-Noire (pwant nuh WAHR). Port city of the Congo. (5°S/12°E) p. 582.

Polynesia (pahl uh NEE zhuh). Groups of scattered islands in the central and south Pacific. It includes Hawaii and Tahiti. p. 637.

Pompeii (pahm PAY ee). Ancient city in southern Italy. It was completely buried under volcanic ash and lava from Mt. Vesuvius. (41°N/14°E) p. 332.

Po River (poh RIHV ur). Longest river in Italy. Starts in the Alps and flows into the Adriatic Sea south of Venice. p. 330.

Prague (prahg). Capital of and most populated city in the Czech Republic. Located on the Vltava River. (50°N/14°E) p. 257.

Pretoria (pree TOR ee uh). Capital of South Africa. Located on a tributary of Limpopo River. (26°S/28°E) p. 525.

Puerto Rico (PWER tuh REE koh). Self-governing commonwealth in union with the United States. An island of the West Indies. (18°N/65°W) p. 67.

P'yongyang (PYUNG yahng). Capital of North Korea. (39°N/126°E) p. 389.

Pyrenees (PIHR uh neez). Mountains along the border between France and Spain. p. 288.

Quebec (kwee BEK). City in Canada, on the north side of the St. Lawrence River. It was founded in 1608 by Samuel de Champlain. Today, it is the capital of the province of Quebec. (47°N/71°W) p. 81.

Queensland (KWEENZ land). State located in northeastern Australia. Its capital city is Brisbane. p. 657.

Quito (KEE toh). Capital city of Ecuador. Lies almost on the Equator, at an altitude of over 9,000 ft (2,743 m). (0° lat./79°W) p. 173.

Rabat (ruh BAHT). Capital city of Morocco. (34°N/7°W) p. 525.

Rangoon (ran GOON). Capital of and most populated city in Myanmar. Located on the Rangoon River. (17°N/96°E) p. 389.

Red Sea (red see). Large inland sea between the Arabian Peninsula and northeast Africa. p. 492.

Rhine River (ryn RIHV ur). Starts in the Alps in Switzerland. Flows north through Germany and then west through the Netherlands, where it empties into the North Sea at Rotterdam. p. 255.

Rhone River (rohn RIHV ur). Starts from a glacier in the Alps in Switzerland and flows south through France, emptying into the Mediterranean Sea at Marseilles. p. 255.

Riga (REE guh). Capital of Latvia and port on the Baltic Sea. Located on the Western Dvina River. (57°N/24°E) p. 372.

Rio de Janeiro (REE oh day zhuh NER oh). The second most populated city in South America. Major port of Brazil. Located on the Atlantic coast. (23°S/43°W) p. 235.

Río de la Plata (REE oh de lah PLAH tah). An estuary of the Paraná and Uruguay rivers. p. 219.

Riyadh (ree YAHD). Capital of Saudi Arabia. (25°N/47°E) p. 499.

Rome (rohm). Capital of an most populated city in Italy. Located on the Tiber River. Most important city in the Roman Empire. (42°N/12°E) p. 330.

Rotterdam (RAHT ur dam). City in the Netherlands. Located on the Nieuwe Maas, about 15 mi (24 km) from the North Sea. An important port city. (52°N/4°E) p. 296.

Ruhr River (roor RIHV ur). Small tributary of the Rhine River. p. 255.

Ruwenzori Mountains (roo un ZOR ee MOUNT unz). Mountains located in central Africa, on the boundary of between Uganda and Zaire. p. 574.

St. John's (saynt jahnz). Capital of Newfoundland, Canada. Located on the southeast coast of Newfoundland Island, on the Atlantic Ocean. (48°N/53°W) p. 81.

St. Lawrence River (saynt LAHR uns RIHV ur). Flows northeast out of lake Ontario into the Gulf of St. Lawrence. Forms the boundary between New York State and the Canadian province of Ontario, then passes through southern Quebec province. p. 84.

St. Petersburg (saynt PEET urz burg). Second most populated city in Russia. Located on the Gulf of Finland. Formerly Leningrad and former capital of Russia. (60°N/30°E) p. 257.

San'a (sah NAH). Capital city of Yemen. (15°N/44°E) p. 389.

San Francisco (san frun SIHS koh). Seaport city situated on the north-central coast of California, between San Francisco Bay and the Pacific Ocean. (38°N/122°W) p. 159.

San José (san hoh ZAY). Capital city of Costa Rica. (10°N/84°W) p. 159.

San Juan (san hwahn). Capital of and largest city in the Commonwealth of Puerto Rico. A major seaport city, located on the north side of the island, on San Juan Bay. (18°N/66°W) p. 151.

San Luis Potosí (san LWEES poh toh SEE). Major industrial city in Mexico. (23°N/101°W) p. 132.

San Salvador (san SAL vuh dor). Capital city of El Salvador. (14°N/89°W) p. 159.

Santiago (sahn tee AH goh). Capital of and most populated city in Chile. (33°S/71°W) p. 173.

Santo Domingo (SAHN toh doh MING goh). Capital city of the Dominican Republic. (18°N/70°W) p. 151.

São Paulo (soun POU loo). The most populated city in South America. Located in southeastern Brazil. (24°S/47°W) p. 235.

Sapporo (SAH poh roh). Industrial city on the island of Hokkaido in Japan. (43°N/141°E) p. 400.

Sarajevo (sar uh YAY voh). Capital of Bosnia and Hercegovina. Located near the Bosna River. (44°N/18°E) p. 350.

Sea of Japan (see uv juh PAN). Body of water that separates the island of Japan from the mainland of Asia. p. 398.

Seine River (sayn RIHV ur). Starts in eastern France, flows westward through Paris, and then empties into the English Channel at Le Havre. p. 288.

Seoul (sohl). Capital of South Korea. Located on the Han River. One of the world's most populated cities. (38°N/127°E) p. 389.

Serengeti Plain (ser un GET ee playn). A region in northern Tanzania noted for its wildlife. The location of the Serengeti National Park. p. 594.

Shanghai (SHANG HYE). World's most populated city. Located on the delta of the Chang Jiang in China on the East China Sea. (31°N/121°E) p. 427.

Shatt-al-Arab (shat ul AH rahb). Channel in southeastern Iraq formed by the merger of the Tigris and Euphrates rivers. Flows southeasterly into the Persian Gulf. p. 492.

Shikoku (SHEE koh koo). The smallest of Japan's four main islands. p. 398.

Siberia (sye BIHR ee uh). Part of Russia, covering much of the area between the Ural Mountains and the Pacific Ocean. p. 356.

Sierra Nevada (see ER uh   nuh VAD uh). High mountain range located mostly in eastern California. Mount Whitney, with an elevation of 14,494 ft (4,418 m), is located in this range. It is the highest peak in the continental United States. p. 65.

Singapore (SING uh por). Capital of the island nation of Singapore. One of the world's busiest ports. Located on Singapore Strait. (1°N/104°E) p. 444.

Skopje (SKAHP yay). Capital of Macedonia. Located on Vardar River. (42°N/21°E) p. 350.

Snowy Mountains (SNOH ee   MOUNT unz). Part of the Great Dividing Range, located in eastern Victoria and southeastern New South Wales, in Australia. An important hydroelectric power project is located there. p. 644.

Sofia (SOH fee uh). Capital of Bulgaria. (43°N/23°E) p. 350.

Solomon Islands (SAHL uh mun   EYE lundz). Group of islands that includes both the country of Solomon Islands and Bougainville, Buka, and other islands belonging to Papua New Guinea. p. 637.

South Australia (south   aw STRAYL yuh). State located in the south-central part of Australia. The capital city is Adelaide. p. 657.

South China Sea (south   CHYE nuh   see). Part of the Pacific Ocean, enclosed by eastern China, the Indochina and Malay peninsulas, Borneo, the Philippines, and Taiwan. Often called the China Sea. p. 387.

Southern Alps (SUTH urn   alps). Range of mountains on South Island, New Zealand. Highest peak is Mount Cook, with an elevation of 12,349 ft (3,764 m). p. 644.

South Island (south   EYE lund). Southern island of the two main islands of New Zealand. p. 644.

South Pole (south   pohl). The most southern place on the earth. Located at 90° south latitude. p. 6.

Stockholm (STAHK hohm). Capital of and most populated city in Sweden. Located on the country's east coast, on the Baltic Sea. (59°N/18°E). p. 276.

Strait of Gibraltar (strayt   uv   jih BRAWL tur). Narrow passageway connecting the Atlantic Ocean and the Mediterranean Sea. p. 320.

Strait of Malacca (strayt   uv   muh LAK uh). A narrow channel of water in Malaysia that is an important passageway for ships traveling between India and China. p. 387.

Sucre (SOO kray). The official capital city of Bolivia. (19°S/65°W) p. 173.

Sumatra (SOO MAH truh). The westernmost of the main islands of Indonesia. Divided into two almost equal parts by the Equator. p. 444.

Sydney (SIHD nee). Capital of the Australian state of New South Wales. Most populated city in Australia. (34°S/151°E). p. 651.

Taipei (tye PAY). Capital of and most populated city in Taiwan. (25°N/122°E) p. 389.

Taiwan Strait (tye WAHN   strayt). Body of water that separates Taiwan and China. p. 387.

Tajumulco (tah hoo MOOL koh). Volcano in Guatemala. It is the highest point in Central America, standing 13,845 ft (4,220 m) high. p. 146.

Tallinn (TAL un). Capital of Estonia. Baltic Sea port on the Gulf of Finland. (59°N/25°E). p. 372.

Tampico (tam PEE koh). Port city in Mexico. (22°N/98°W). p. 132.

Tashkent (tash KENT). Capital of Uzbekistan. Located on border with Kazakhstan. (41°N/69°E). p. 372.

Tasmania (taz MAY nee uh). Island off the coast of Australia. Also one of Australia's states. p. 657.

Tbilisi (tuh BIHL uh see). Capital of Georgia. Located on the Kura River. Founded in A.D. 455. For centuries, served as an important trade center between Asia and Europe. (42°N/45°E). p. 372.

Tel Aviv (tel   uh VEEV). Most populated city in Israel. Located on the Mediterranean Sea. (32°N/35°E) p. 499.

Thames River (temz   RIHV ur). Flows east across south central England. Passes through London before emptying into the North Sea. p. 270.

Thessalonica (thes uh LAHN ih kuh). Busy port city in Greece. Located on the Aegean Sea. Greece's second most populated city. (41°N/23°E) p. 334.

Tianjin (tyen JIHN). Important port city in northeastern China. (39°N/117°E). p. 423.

Tiber River (TYE bur   RIHV ur). River in Italy. Rises in the Apennines and flows through Rome to the Mediterranean Sea. p. 330.

Tigris River (TYE grus   RIHV ur). Rises in the mountains of southeastern Turkey. Flows through Iraq, where it unites with the Euphrates River to form the Shatt-al-Arab, which flows into the Persian Gulf. p. 492.

Tiranë (tuh RAHN uh). Capital of Albania. (41°N/20°E) p. 350.

Tokyo (TOH kee oh). Capital of Japan. Located on Tokyo Bay, on the island of Honshu. Second most populated city in the world. (36°N/140°E) p. 389.

Toronto (tuh RAHNT oh). Most populated city in Canada. Capital of the province of Ontario. Located on the northeastern end of Lake Ontario. Is also a port. (44°N/79°W) p. 81.

Tripoli (TRIHP uh lee). Capital of Libya. Port city on the Mediterranean Sea. (33°N/13°E). p. 525.

Tunis (TOO nihs). Capital city of Tunisia. (37°N/10°E) p. 525.

Turin (TOOR ihn). Industrial city located on the Po River, in northwestern Italy. (45°N/8°E) p. 330.

Ulan Bator (oo lahn bah TOR). Capital of Mongolia. (48°N/107°E) p. 389.

Ural Mountains (YOOR ul MOUNT unz). Located in Russia. They form the division between Asia and Europe. p. 356.

Vancouver (van KOO vur). City in British Columbia, Canada. Canada's most important seaport on the Pacific Ocean. (49°N/123°W). p. 81.

Vanuatu (vahn uh WAH too). Island nation in the Pacific Ocean. (16°S/167°W). p. 637.

Victoria (vihk TOR ee uh). State located in the southeastern part of Australia. The capital city is Melbourne. p. 657.

Vienna (vee EN uh). Capital of and largest city in Austria. Located on the Danube River. (48°N/16°E) p. 257.

Vientiane (vyen TYAHN). Capital of Laos. Located in the Mekong River valley. (18°N/103°E) p. 444.

Vilnius (VIHL nee us). Capital of Lithuania. Located near border of Belarus. (55°N/25°E). p. 372.

Vistula River (VIHS choo luh RIHV ur). Poland's most important river. Rises in the Carpathian Mountains, flows north through Warsaw, then empties into the Baltic Sea at Gdańsk. p. 340.

Vladivostok (vlad ih VAHS tahk). City in Russia, at the eastern end of the Trans-Siberian Railway. Located on the Sea of Japan. (43°N/132°E) p. 389.

Volga River (VAHL guh RIHV ur). Most important river in Russia, and the longest river in Europe. Empties into the Caspian Sea. p. 356.

Warsaw (WOR saw). Capital of Poland. Located on the Vistula River. (52°N/21°E). p. 350.

Washington, D.C. (WAWSH ing tun dee see). Capital of the United States. Located between Maryland and Virginia, on the east bank of the Potomac River. (39°N/77°W) p. 65.

Wellington (WEL ing tun). Capital of New Zealand. Located on North Island and Cook Strait. (41°S/175°E) p. 657.

West Indies (west IHN deez). Group of islands stretching about 2,500 mi (4,023) km) from near Florida to near Venezuela. p. 151.

White Nile (hwyt nyl). River rises in Lake Victoria and flows north through Uganda and Sudan, where it joins the Blue Nile. p. 541.

Windhoek (VIHNT hook). Capital of Namibia. (23°S/17°E) p. 525.

Winnipeg (WIHN uh peg). Capital of Manitoba, Canada. Located on the Red River. (50°N/97°W) p. 81.

Xizang (SHEE ZANG). High mountainous area in China, near border with India and Nepal. Formerly called Tibet. p. 423.

Yerevan (yer uh VAHN). Capital of Armenia. Located on Razdan River. (40°N/45°E) p. 372.

Yokohama (yok kuh HAHM uh). Japanese seaport city on the island of Honshu. Located on the western shore of Tokyo Bay. (35°N/140°E) p. 413.

Yucatán Peninsula (yoo kah TAHN puh NIHN suh luh). Located in southeastern Mexico and in Belize and northern Guatemala in Central America. Separates the Gulf of Mexico from the Caribbean Sea. p.126.

Zagreb (ZAH greb). Capital of Croatia. Located on the Sava River. (46°N/16°E) p. 350.

Zambezi River (zam BEE zee RIHV ur). River that rises in Angola. Flows into the Indian Ocean at Mozambique. Forms boundary between Angola and Zimbabwe. p. 610.

Zanzibar (ZAN zuh bahr). Island belonging to Tanzania. Located in the Indian Ocean, off the coast of Tanzania. Also the name of the chief city on the island. (6°S/39°E) p. 594.

Aborigine (ab uh RIHJ uh nee). A member of the earliest group of people known to inhabit Australia. p. 647.

absolute location (AB suh loot loh KAY shun). The latitude and longitude of a place. p. 45.

adobe (uh DOH bee). A building material that is made of sun-dried mud and straw. p. 129.

Afrikaans (af rih KAHNZ). A language that is widely used in South Africa. p. 611.

alloys (AL oiz). Mixtures of metals that are harder or stronger than the individual metals from which they are made. p. 37.

alluvial soil (uh LOO vee ul soil). Rock fragments and silt deposited on the land when a river floods during the rainy season. p. 428.

alpine (AL pyn). Mountain areas above the highest elevation where trees grow. p. 419.

anthropologist (an throh PAHL uh jihst). A person who studies humans and their cultures. p. 647.

antimony (AN tuh moh nee). A mineral used to make a metal harder. p. 207.

apartheid (uh PAHR tayt). The forced separation, by law, of whites and nonwhites in South Africa. p. 623.

aqueduct (AK wuh dukt). An artificial channel for carrying a large quantity of flowing water. p. 108.

aquifer (AK wuh fur). A layer of rock, sand, or gravel that can absorb or collect water. p. 653.

arable (AR uh bul). Suitable for growing crops. p. 437.

archipelago (ahr kuh PEL uh goh). A group or chain of islands. p. 147.

arid (AR ihd). Very dry, usually due to insufficient rainfall, making agriculture difficult. p. 332.

Aryans (ar EE unz). A people who invaded India and introduced their language and their religion. p. 476.

atmosphere (AT mus fihr). The blanket of air that covers the earth. p. 28.

atoll (A tawl). A ring-shaped coral island enclosing or partly enclosing a lagoon. p. 664.

autobahn (AWT oh bahn). West Germany's superhighway system. p. 303.

autonomy (aw TAHN uh mee). Self-government for a state or other political entity. p. 478.

avalanche (AV uh lanch). A giant snowslide that occurs in high mountain areas when too much snow builds up on steep slopes. p. 196.

axis (AK sihs). An imaginary line that goes through the earth from the North Pole to the South Pole. p. 104.

Bantu (BAN too). A family of African languages. p. 577.

basin (BAYS un). A low area almost entirely surrounded by higher land. p. 125.

bazaar (buh ZAHR). The central marketplace in Middle Eastern and North African cities. p. 538.

Bedouins (BED oo ihnz). A nomadic group of people who live in many of the countries of the Arabian peninsula. p. 506.

bilingual (bye LING gwel). Expressed in or using two languages. p. 82.

Boers (boorz). Early Dutch settlers in South Africa; Dutch word for "farmers." p. 620.

bog (bahg). A small marsh or swamp, comprised of wet spongy ground. p. 270.

buffer state (BUF ur stayt). A country that separates two or more countries that are hostile to each other. p. 438.

canopy (KAN uh pee). The interlocking leaves that form the top of a rain forest. p. 573.

canton (KAN tun). A small territorial division of a

country, which functions as a separate political unit. A canton corresponds to a state in the United States. Switzerland is divided into cantons. p. 310.

capital (KAP ut ul). Money used to develop a country's economy. p. 207.

caravan (KAR uh van). A group of people traveling together, usually on animals or in vehicles. p. 539.

cartography (kahr TAHG ruh fee). The making of maps. p. 16.

cash crop (kash krahp). A crop that is sold, usually for export. p. 181.

caste (kast). A system that separates people into groups, or classes, based on birth. p. 476.

catamaran (kat uh muh RAN). Two canoes fastened together to make one boat. Sometimes planks fastened on the framework serve as the deck. p. 663.

causeway (KAWZ way). A raised way or road across wet ground or water. p. 134.

censor (SEN sur). To control the content of publications, radio and television broadcasts, and other forms of free speech. p. 339.

channel (CHAN ul). A strait or a narrow sea between two large areas of land that are close together. p. 265.

chernozem (CHER nuh zem). A rich black soil, which is common in cool or temperate semiarid climates. p. 372.

chromium (KROH mee um). A blue-white mineral that is used to make steel harder. p. 351.

cinder cone (SIHN dur kohn). A small volcano that looks like a cone-shaped hill. p. 130.

city-state (SIHT ee stayt). A self-governing state consisting of a city and its surrounding territory. p. 456.

climate (KLYE mut). The pattern of weather that a place has over a period of time. Temperature and precipitation are two important parts of climate. p. 28.

coastal plain (KOHS tul playn). An area of flat land that borders a coast. p. 98.

commercial farm (kuh MUR shul fahrm). A farm on which crops are raised for sale rather than for home use. p. 137.

commodity (kuh MAHD uh tee). A product that is bought and sold in commerce. p. 224.

Commonwealth of Nations (KAHM un welth uv NAY shunz). An organization of 48 former British colonies with special defense and economic ties. p. 266.

commune (KAHM yoon). A community, often rural, in which labor, decision making, and profits are shared. p. 435.

communism (KAHM yoo nihz um). A social system in which property and goods are owned in common, or the theory that favors such a system. p. 372.

compact (KAHM pakt). An agreement between nations. p. 669.

compass rose (KUM pus rohz). A small drawing on a map, used to show direction. p. 4.

confederation (kun fed ur AY shun). A union comprised of many different states. p. 310.

confluence (KAHN floo uns). The place where two or more streams or rivers join. p. 212.

conquistador (kahn KWIHS tuh dor). A Spanish soldier of the sixteenth century in the Americas. p. 134.

constitutional monarchy (kahn stuh TOO shuh nul MAHN ur kee). A government in which the monarch, or ruler, serves as head of state and has only those powers given to the ruler by the constitution and laws of the nation. p. 77.

consumer (kun SOOM ur). A person who buys and uses many types of goods. p. 52.

consumer goods (kun SOOM ur goodz). Things

that are grown or made by producers and are used by people. p. 369.

continental island (kahn tuh NENT ul   EYE lund). An island that was once part of a continent. It is now separated from the continent by a stretch of water. p. 663.

contour lines (KAHN toor   lynz). Lines on a map connecting the points that have the same elevation on a land surface. p. 12.

cooperative (koh AHP ur uh tihv). A cooperative is a plantation or other business that is owned by its workers. p. 137.

copra (KAH pruh). Dried coconut meat from which coconut oil is made. p. 669.

coral (KOR ul). A hard, chalky, rocklike material that is made of the shells of sea animals called coral polyps. p. 646.

core (kor). The part of the country that has the largest population, the largest cities, the most productive economy, and the best transportation facilities and other services. p. 650.

coup d'état (koo   day TAH). A sudden overthrowing of a government by a small group. p. 198.

crevasse (kruh VAS). A deep crack in the ice. p. 675.

crop rotation (krahp   roh TAY shun). The practice of growing first one crop and then another type of crop on the same land, which preserves the ability of the soil to produce crops. p. 107.

culture (KUL chur). The way of life of a people. p. 31.

czar (zahr). The title given to the rulers of Russia. p. 364.

Czech (chek). A person born or living in the Czech Republic. p. 345.

deforestation (dee for ihst AY shun). The large-scale cutting down of forests. p. 179.

delta (DEL tuh). The land that is formed by mud

and sand deposited at the mouth of the river. p. 448.

demilitarized zone (dee MIHL uh tuh ryzd   zohn). An area free of military control, where there are no troops or weapons. p. 412.

desert pavement (DEZ urt   PAYV munt). Vast plains of gravel and boulders in the desert. p. 534.

desertification (dih zurt uh fih KAY shun). The process by which livestock eat the seeds of grasses and shrubs, causing vegetation to disappear and the land to change to desert. p. 561.

diffusion (dih FYOO zhun). The spread of knowledge from one group of people to another. p. 537.

dike (dyk). A wall or bank built to control or hold back the water of a river or sea. p. 188.

distortion (dih STOR shun). A twisting or stretching out of shape. p. 16.

distributary (dih STRIHB yoo ter ee). A river branch flowing away from the main stream. p. 541.

distribution map (dihs trih BYOO shun   map). A map that shows the range of people, crops, or resources in a country or region. p. 13.

domestic (doh MES tihk). A product that is used in one country and not exported to another. p. 468.

domesticate (doh MES tih kayt). To tame wild animals to live with humans. p. 27.

drought (drout). A long, dry period with no rain. p. 561.

dynasty (DYE nus tee). A family of rulers. p. 430.

ebony (EB uh nee). A hard, dark, strong wood that comes from various trees found in tropical areas. p. 446.

ecology (ee KAHL uh jee). The balance between living things and their environment. p. 543.

ejido (ay HEE doh). Communal farmland in Mexico

that is owned and worked on by several families or by an entire village. p. 129.

emblem (EM blum). A symbol or sign, such as the flag or the seal of a country. p. 656.

emigrate (EM ih grayt). To leave one country or region in order to permanently settle in another. p. 321.

enclave (EN klayv). A country that is completely surrounded by another country. p. 568.

equatorial climate (ee kwuh TOR ee ul KLYE mut). A place with a very warm, humid climate that is near the Equator. p. 445.

equinox (EE kwih nahks). Either of the two times in the year when the sun's direct rays are over the Equator and day and night are of equal length. p. 104.

erg (urg). A large sea of sand in the desert, highlighted by wind-swept dunes. p. 534.

erosion (ee ROH zhun). The process by which the soil blows away in the wind or washes down the slopes of the hills when it rains. p. 333.

escarpment (e SKAHRP munt). The steep slope, or drop, at the edge of a plateau. p. 610.

estuary (ES tyoo er ee). The mouth of a river into which ocean water flows, mixing fresh water and seawater. p. 211.

ethnocentrism (eth noh SEN trihz um). The process of looking at the rest of the world and making judgments about it based only on your own cultural background and experience. p. 491.

Eurasia (yoo RAY zhuh). The landmass made up of the continents of Europe and Asia. p. 254.

European Community (yoor uh PEE un kuh MYOO nuh tee). An organization comprised of 12 Western European countries whose purpose is to make trade easier among them. p. 300.

exclave (EKS klayv). A territory surrounded or nearly surrounded by the territory of another country. p. 619.

exploitation (eks ploi TAY shun). Taking large profits from a country, leaving very little for the people who live there. p. 582.

expropriate (eks PROH pree ayt). To take over the property of another. p. 150.

fallow (FAL oh). Not cultivated or planted for a season or more. p. 187.

famine (FAM ihn). An extreme shortage of food. p. 274.

federation (fed ur AY shun). A government in which the national government and the governments of the provinces share certain powers. p. 77.

fellahin (FEL uh heen). A group of crop-raising farmers in the Arab countries of North Africa and the Middle East. p. 538.

Fertile Crescent (FURT ul KRES unt). A 1,000-mile-long crescent-shaped region of the Arabian peninsula that is made up of green, flat, fertile land. The Fertile Crescent stretches across Iraq, Syria, Lebanon, Israel, and Jordan. p. 493.

fjord (fyord). A long, narrow, often deep inlet of the sea lying between steep cliffs. p. 79.

flax (flaks). A plant whose fiber can be used to make linen. Oil and livestock feed are obtained from its seed. p. 299.

Fleming (FLEM ing). One of a group of Dutch-speaking people inhabiting Flanders, a region of northern Belgium. p. 299.

forage (FOR ihj). Plants such as grass and shrubs that serve as food for livestock. p. 560.

foreign debt (FOR ihn det). Money a government owes to banks in another country. p. 237.

foreign policy (FOR ihn PAHL uh see). The decisions a country makes about how it will work with other countries. p. 64.

futon (FOO tahn). A heavy padded quilt that is commonly used in Japan. p. 411.

Gaelic (GAYL ihk). Of, relating to, or being the Celtic speech of persons born or living in Ireland, the Isle of Man, and the Scottish Highlands. p. 273.

gasohol (GAS uh hawl). A fuel made by mixing gasoline with alcohol that is made from sugarcane and used to power cars and trucks. p. 234.

geography (jee AHG ruh fee). The science that deals with location of living and nonliving things on the earth and the way they affect one another. p. 25.

geologic hazard (jee uh LAHJ ihk HAZ urd). A natural event involving the land, such as an earthquake, volcanic eruption, landslide, or flood, that causes problems for people. p. 196.

geyser (GYE zur). A fountain of steam and water that has been heated by hot lava and forced above ground by volcanic gases. p. 279.

glacial till (GLAY shul tihl). The soil and silt deposited by glacial ice sheets as they melted and retreated northward. p. 92.

glacier (GLAY shur). A large mass of ice formed from snow on high ground and moving very slowly down a mountainside or along a valley. p. 44.

great circle (grayt SUR kul). Any circle on the earth's surface that divides the earth into equal parts. The Equator is a great circle. A great circle is the shortest possible distance between any two places on the surface of the earth. p. 18.

Great Trek (grayt trek). The mass migration of thousands of Boers to the High Veld of Southern Africa. The trek began in 1835 and continued into the 1840s. p. 621.

green revolution (green rev uh LOO shun). The growing of more crops on the same amount of land, due to the development of new types of grain by agricultural scientists. p. 459.

grid system (grihd SIHS tum). A network of horizontal lines of latitude and vertical lines of longitude that aids in the location of places on a map. p. 6.

ground water (ground WAWT ur). Rainwater that collects in underground rocks. p. 51.

guerrilla (guh RIHL uh). A person who fights against a government. p. 158.

hacienda (hah see EN duh). A large estate in Spanish-speaking countries. p. 129.

hajj (haj). A pilgrimage that every Muslim must make to Mecca at least once in his or her life if he or she can afford it. p. 512.

hammada (huh MAH duh). A rocky plateau in the desert. p. 534.

harbor (HAHR bur). A protected body of water that is safe for ships. p. 66.

heavy industry (HEV ee IHN dus tree). The production of goods such as tractors, mining equipment, and factory machinery. p. 367.

hemisphere (HEM ih sfihr). Half the earth or the globe. p. 18.

High Veld (hye velt). The upland grassland area of Southern Africa. p. 611.

high-technology industries (hye tek NAHL uhjee IHN dus treez). Industries that produce electronics, computers, and other goods that are extremely complex and specialized. p. 113.

Hispanic (hih SPAN ihk). A Spanish-speaking American. p. 103.

homeland (HOHM land). A special reserve in South Africa where many South African blacks have been forced to move. p. 623.

humid continental (HYOO mihd kahn tuh NENT ul). A climate that has a wide range of temperatures, with warm to unpleasantly hot summers and cold to very cold winters. Precipitation also varies considerably in this climate. p. 104.

humid subtropical (HYOO mihd sub TRAHP ih kul). A climate that has very hot temperatures in the summer and mild temperatures in the winter. There is plenty of rain all year but very little snow. p. 105.

humus (HYOO mus). The product of the partial decay of plant or animal matter that forms the organic portion of soil. p. 577.

hydroelectricity (hye droh ih lek TRIHS ih tee). Electricity made from the force of flowing water. p. 87.

ice shelf (eyes shelf). A mass of ice that floats on the water but is attached to a glacier. p. 672.

immigrant (IHM uh grunt). A person who comes into one country from another country to settle permanently. p. 103.

imperialism (ihm PIHR ee ul ihz um). A policy of conquering new lands to build an empire. p. 565.

import (IHM port). A product one country buys from another. p. 52.

industry (IHN dus tree). The manufacturing of goods. p. 109.

inflation (ihn FLAY shun). The decline in the value of money accompanied by an increase in prices. p. 141.

irrigation (ihr uh GAY shun). The watering of crops or other plants by pipes, canals, or ditches. p. 51.

in-migration (IHN mye gray shun). Movement into a region or community. p. 332.

islet (eye liht). A very small island, usually uninhabited. p. 582.

isolationism (eye suh LAY shun ihz um). A national policy of avoiding international political and economic relations. p. 454.

isthmus (IHS mus). A narrow strip of land that connects two larger land areas. p. 148.

jungle (JUNG gul). A thick tangled mass of tropical vegetation. p. 574.

jute (joot). A plant, raised mostly in the Ganges River delta, from which the fiber for burlap and twine is obtained. p. 482.

key (kee). A device on a map that tells what real things and places the symbols on a map stand for. p. 4.

kilometer (KIL uh meet ur). A measure of distance in the metric system. p. 9.

Koran (kuh RAN). A book of sacred writings accepted by Muslims as revealed to Muhammad by Allah. p. 511.

kraal (krahl). A village commonly found in eastern and southern Africa. p. 600.

lagoon (luh GOON). A shallow channel or pond near or connected with a larger body of water. p. 664.

land bridge (land brihj). A narrow piece of land that connects two larger land masses. p. 76.

landform (LAND form). A feature of the earth's surface, such as a mountain, hill, river, lake, or ocean, that is made by nature. p. 10.

landlocked (LAND lahkt). Not having a seacoast. p. 195.

language family (LANJ gwihj FAM uh lee). A group of languages that all come from one ancestor language. p. 31.

Lapps (laps). A group of people who live in the far north of the Scandinavian Shield, near the Arctic Ocean. p. 278.

latex (LAY teks). A mixture of water and fine particles of rubber or plastic, used especially in paints and adhesives. p. 455.

latitude (LAT uh tood). Distance, measured in degrees, north and south of the Equator. Lines of latitude are used to locate places on a map or globe. p. 5.

lava (LAH vuh). The melted rock forced out of a volcano. p. 66.

leaching (LEECH ing). A process in which nutrients in the top layers of the soil are washed down into the lower layers of soil. p. 577.

life expectancy (lyf ek SPEK tun see). The average number of years a person can expect to live. p. 594.

light industry (lyt IHN dus tree). The production of goods such as textiles, clothing, furniture, and the processing of grains and vegetables. p. 367.

lignite (LIHG nyt). A usually brownish black coal of low quality, sometimes called brown coal. p. 305.

literacy rate (LIHT ur uh see rayt). The percentage of people who know how to read and write. p. 160.

lock (lahk). An enclosed area of a canal, with gates on both sides, used for raising or lowering ships as they go from one water level to another. p. 84.

loess (LOH es). A fine, light silt that is very fertile. p. 428.

longitude (LAHN juh tood). Distance, measured in degrees, east and west of the Prime Meridian. Lines of longitude are imaginary circles that go around the earth and pass through the North Pole and South Pole. p. 6.

Maghreb (MUH grub). The region of Morocco, Tunisia, and Algeria. It receives more rain than any other part of North Africa. p. 546.

magma (MAG muh). Melted rock beneath the earth's surface. p. 66.

Magyars (MAG yahrz). The group of people who settled originally in what is now Hungary. p. 346.

Malagasy (mal uh GAS ee). The language of Madagascar, which is a combination of Malay and Indonesian. p. 615.

mangrove (MANG grohv). A tropical tree whose wood is used for fuel and whose bark is a source of tannin. Mangroves grow in swamps and along riverbanks. p. 555.

Maori (MAH oh ree). A descendant of the first inhabitants of New Zealand. p. 658.

maritime (MAR ih tym). Of, relating to, or bordering on the sea. p. 265.

marsupial (mahr SOO pee ul). An animal, such as a kangaroo, that carries its young in a pouch until the young are fully developed. p. 646.

Mediterranean climate (med ih tuh RAY nee un KLYE mut). A climate that has hot, dry summers and cool, rainy winters. p. 320.

mesa (MAY suh). A large, flat-topped mountain with steep sides. p. 177.

mestizo (mes TEE zoh). A person of Spanish and Native American ancestry. p. 131.

meteorologist (meet ee ur AHL uh jihst). A scientist who studies and forecasts the weather. p. 46.

metropolitan area (me troh PAHL ih tun ER ee uh). An area made up of a large city and the surrounding towns, smaller cities, and other communities. p. 114.

modernize (MAHD ur nyz). To develop the economy of a country. p. 293.

monotheism (MAHN oh thee ihz um). The belief in only one God. p. 503.

monsoon (mahn SOON). A seasonal wind that blows from the land to the water in one season and from the water to the land in the other season. p. 468.

Moors (moorz). A group of people who invaded North Africa and conquered the Iberian Peninsula. p. 327.

mosque (mahsk). An Islamic place of worship. p. 33.

mulatto (muh LAHT oh). A person who is born of one black and one white parent. p. 148.

mural (MYOOR ul). A painting drawn on a wall or ceiling. p. 136.

natural resource (NACH ur ul REE sors). A material made by nature that people can use. p. 28.

navigable (NAV ih guh bul). A lake or river that is deep and wide enough to be traveled by ships and boats. p. 97.

navigator (NAV uh gayt ur). A person who is responsible for directing the course of a ship or airplane. p. 45.

neutral (NOO trul). Not favoring either side in a quarrel, conflict, or war. p. 283.

nitrate (NYE trayt). A mineral that can be used to make fertilizers, explosives, and other products. p. 224.

nomads (NOH madz). People who have no permanent home and who move from place to place p. 35.

nonrenewable resource (nahn rih NOO uh bul REE sors). A resource that, once used, cannot be replaced by nature or people. p. 111.

oasis (oh AY sihs). A place in the desert that has enough water for plants and trees to grow. p. 493.

ore (or). A mineral mined to obtain a substance that it contains. p. 36.

outback (OUT bak). The interior of the continent of Australia. p. 645.

overgrazing (OH vur grayz ing). Allowing livestock to eat too much of the natural vegetation. p. 333.

Pacific Rim (puh SIHF ihk rihm). The nations bordering the Pacific Ocean. p. 390.

paddy (PAD ee). A rice field, particularly a field in which irrigated rice is raised. p. 402.

pagoda (puh GOH duh). A Buddhist shrine that has upward-curving roofs and a pyramidlike shape. p. 453.

Palestinian (pal us TIHN ee un). A person who has a strong commitment to the creation of an independent Palestinian state. p. 504.

Pampas (PAHM puz). The large, fertile grassy plain that covers parts of Argentina, Uruguay, and Paraguay. p. 170.

Parliament (PAHR luh munt). The supreme legislative body of countries that have a parliamentary system of government. p. 273.

pass (pas). A low place in a mountain range. p. 289.

pastoralism (PAS tur ul ihz um). The practice of herding animals for a living. p. 35.

peat (peet). Plant matter used as a fertilizer or fuel. It is made of partially rotted plants and moss. p. 270.

per capita income (per KAP ih tuh IHN kum). The total amount of money that a nation's people earn in a year divided by the total population. p. 152.

permafrost (PUR muh frawst). Permanently frozen ground, sometimes extending to great depths below the earth's surface in very cold regions. p. 75.

petrochemical (pe troh KEM ih kul). A chemical or synthetic material made from petroleum or natural gas. p. 115.

phosphate (FAHS fayt). A vital mineral used in making fertilizers and detergents. p. 548.

physical map (FIHZ ih kul map). A map that shows physical features, such as mountains, plains, and other forms that land and water take. p. 12.

planned city (pland SIHT ee). A city that has been built according to a plan. p. 234.

plantation (plan TAY shun). A large commercial farm that grows only one specific crop. p. 25.

polder (POHL dur). A piece of land reclaimed from the water, usually by building dikes and pumping the water out of the area enclosed by the dikes. p. 297.

population density (pahp yoo LAY shun DEN suh tee). The average number of people who live in a square mile or square kilometer of a state, country, or other area. p. 76.

potash (PAHT ash). A type of mineral salt that is mined from deposits found below the earth's surface. p. 304.

prairie (PRER ee). A large area of level or rolling land that is covered by tall grass and has fertile soil. p. 85.

precipice (PRES ih pihs). A very steep and high face of a rock or mountain. p. 470.

primate city (PRYE mayt SIHT ee). A city that is far more important than any other city in a country. p. 198.

projection (proh JEK shun). The representation on a map of all or part of the earth. p. 16.

pyrethrum (pye RETH rum). A small flower that is dried and crushed and then used to make a natural insecticide. p. 598.

qanat (kah NAT). A tunnel system that allows ground water to flow underground until it reaches a flat area with fertile soils. p. 497.

rain forest (rayn FOR ihst). A large, very thick growth of tall trees that usually have large, broad leaves. Rain forests are found only in areas with an equatorial climate. p. 179.

rain shadow (rayn SHAD oh). An area that does not get much rain, because it is on the protected side of a mountain. p. 217.

reef (reef). A narrow ridge of coral, rocks, or sand at or near the surface of the water. p. 647.

refuge (REF yooj). A safe place that provides shelter or protection from danger. p. 273.

refugee (ref yoo JEE). A person who flees for safety in a time of persecution, war, or disaster. p. 450.

region (REE jun). A part of the earth that has one or more common characteristics. p. 41.

regional specialization (REE jun ul spesh uh lyz AY shun). An economic activity that is the specialty of a particular region. p. 108.

relative location (REL uh tihv loh KAY shun). Gives the location of a place according to some known landmark. p. 46.

relief (rih LEEF). The difference in the elevation or height of the land. p. 43.

renewable resource (rih NOO uh bul REE sors). A resource that once used can be replaced by nature or by people. p. 88.

reserve (rih ZURV). A supply of a resource (such as fuel) that is available or that has been set aside for future use. p. 132.

reservoir (REZ ur vwahr). A place where water is collected and stored for use. p. 51.

rift valley (rihft VAL ee). A canyonlike hollow formed by the sinking of the earth's crust between two parallel faults. p. 589.

Ring of Fire (ring uv fyr). An area of earthquakes and volcanoes in the mountain ranges on the coasts around the Pacific Ocean, including Japan. p. 399.

rural population (ROOR ul pahp yoo LAY shun). People who live outside an urban zone. p. 218.

Sahel (sah HEL). A semidesert area in Africa that lies south of the Sahara. p. 556.

sand dune (sand doon). A mountain of sand that has been formed by the wind. p. 127.

savanna (suh VAN uh). A treeless grassland, or a grassland with scattered trees and bushes, especially in tropical lands that have seasonal rains. p. 524.

scale (skayl). The relationship between distance on a map and distance on the earth. Also, the

729

line drawn on maps that shows this relationship. p. 9.

scrub forest (skrub FOR ihst). A place where trees do not grow very high because of a dry climate. p. 229.

sediment (SED uh munt). The soil, silt, and other material in a river or stream that settles to the bottom. p. 482.

seedbed (SEED bed). The place where seeds are planted. p. 402.

shifting agriculture (SHIHFT ing AG rih kul chur). The process by which subsistence farmers clear plots of forest land to plant crops. p. 187.

Shiites (SHEE yts). Followers of the second largest branch of the Islamic religion. About one fifth of the world's Muslims are Shiite Muslims. Most people in present-day Iran and Iraq are Shiites, followers of the Shi'ah faith. p. 498.

sisal (SYE sul). A fibrous plant used to make rope, string, and bags. p. 591.

Slavs (slahvz). A group of people who were among the first people to live in what is now Eastern Europe. p. 304.

Slovaks (SLOH vahks). A Slavic people who live in Slovakia, which was the eastern region of the former Czecholovakia. p. 345.

smelting (SMELT ing). An extraction process that separates ore from rock. p. 89.

smorgasbord (SMOR gus bord). A self-service luncheon or supper that offers a large variety of foods and dishes. p. 281.

smuggling (SMUG ul ing). The act of exporting or importing goods secretly and unlawfully. p. 182.

Solidarity (sahl uh DAR uh tee). A Polish labor organization and political party that is independent of the Communist party in Poland. p. 343.

solstice (SAHL stihs). Either of the two times in the year when the sun's most direct rays are as far north or south of the Equator as they will ever be. p. 104.

squatter settlement (SKWAHT ur SET ul munt). A settlement filled with people, known as squatters, who have taken over land they do not own. p. 197.

station (STAY shun). A large ranch in Australia where cattle and sheep are raised. p. 654.

steppe (step). Land in regions of wide temperature range that is dry, usually rather level, and covered with grass. Steppes are found in southeastern Europe, parts of Asia, Africa, and South America. p. 372.

strait (strayt). A narrow waterway that connects two larger bodies of water. p. 495.

strike (stryk). A stopping of work by a group of workers to force an employer to meet demands. p. 343.

subcontinent (SUB kahnt un unt). A landmass of great size but smaller than the continents. p. 463.

subsistence (sub SIHS tuns). An economy in which the people collect only enough food to feed themselves. p. 35.

subsistence agriculture (sub SIHS tuns AG rih kul chur). A family or similar group's practice of growing food chiefly for itself. p. 131.

summit (SUM iht). The highest point of a mountain. p. 289.

Sunnites (SOON yts). The largest branch of the Islamic religion. Most Muslims are Sunnites. p. 498.

superpower (SOO pur pou ur). A large and powerful country that plays a leading role in world affairs. p. 355.

Swahili (swah HEE lee). A language of eastern and central Africa. Swahili contains many Arabic, Persian, and Indian words. p. 587.

synthetic material (sihn THET ihk muh TIHR ee ul). A product that is made from materials that are produced by people, not by nature, and is often made from chemicals. p. 406.

tableland (TAY bul land). A level, flat plateau. p. 421.

taiga (TYE guh). The great coniferous forest region of Canada and the southern part of Siberia in Russia. p. 367.

tannin (TAN ihn). A plant extract used to cure leather. p. 217.

tariff (TAR ihf). A tax on imports, or in some countries, on exports. p. 300.

tatami (tuh TAH mee). A soft woven floor mat. p. 411.

teak (teek). A hard yellowish-brown wood that is often used for carving and for furniture. p. 450.

technology (tek NAHL uh jee). The knowledge and skill people use to make things. p. 50.

tell (tel). An Arabic word meaning "hill." p. 547.

terrace (TER us). A flat shelf of land, arranged like wide steps on a mountainside, where crops are grown. p. 200.

theocracy (thee AHK ruh see). A nation that is ruled according to religious laws instead of laws passed by the people. p. 498.

transhumance (trans HYOO muns). The seasonal migration of livestock between lowlands and adjacent mountains. p. 309.

tributary (TRIHB yoo ter ee). A stream or river that flows into a larger body of water. p. 305.

triple cropping (TRIHP ul KRAHP ing). The process of harvesting one crop and then immediately planting another type of crop on the same land. p. 425.

tropics (TRAHP ihks). The zone between the Tropic of Capricorn and the Tropic of Cancer. p. 156.

trust territory (trust TER uh tor ee). A territory, region, or small country administered by another country for the United Nations. p. 669.

tsetse fly (TSET see flye). A kind of fly found mostly in Africa south of the Sahara desert. Some forms of the tsetse fly pass on a one-celled animal that causes a fatal sickness in cattle and sleeping sickness in humans. p. 578.

tsunami (tsoo NAH mee). A great sea wave produced by an earthquake or volcano eruption under the sea. p. 457.

tundra (TUN druh). A rolling plain without trees, found in the Arctic area of the high latitudes. p. 75.

tungsten (TUNJ stun). A mineral that is used to harden steel and to make the filaments in light bulbs. p. 328.

typhoon (TYE foon). A tropical storm accompanied by strong winds and heavy rain. p. 638.

urban population (UR ban pahp YOO LAY shun). People who live in or near cities or towns. p. 218.

vineyard (VIHN yurd). A field of grape vines. p. 293.

volcano (vahl KAY noh). An opening in the earth, usually at the top of a cone-shaped hill or mountain, out of which gases, rock, ashes, and lava may erupt. p. 66.

Walloon (wah LOON). One of a group of French-speaking people inhabiting the southern part of Belgium. p. 299.

weather (WETHH ur). The condition of the air at a certain time, in terms of precipitation, temperature, and other factors. p. 28.

west coast marine (west kohst muh REEN). A climate with temperatures that are warm in the summer and cool in the winter. There is precipitation all year round. p. 105.

whiteout (HWYT out). A condition that occurs when the white snow-covered ground blends with the white sky, making it impossible to see shadows or even the horizon. p. 675.

wood pulp (wood pulp). A wet, soggy mass of ground-up wood chips. p. 89.

GRAPH APPENDIX

THE WORLD: LARGEST COUNTRIES IN AREA

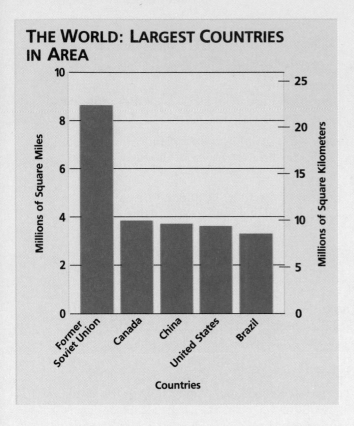

Millions of Square Miles / Millions of Square Kilometers

Former Soviet Union, Canada, China, United States, Brazil

Countries

THE WORLD: LARGEST COUNTRIES BY POPULATION

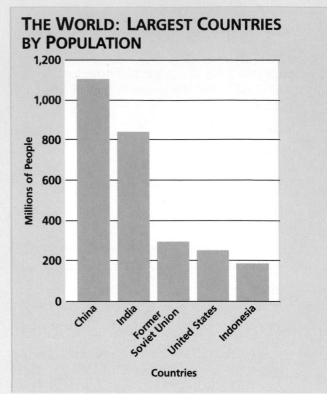

Millions of People

China, India, Former Soviet Union, United States, Indonesia

Countries

THE WORLD: LAND AREA

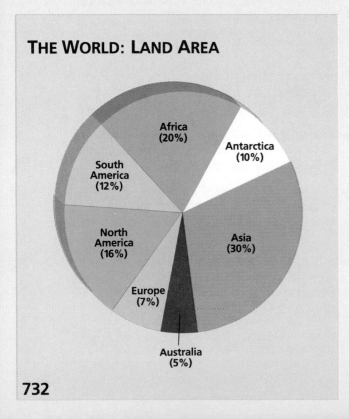

Africa (20%)
Antarctica (10%)
South America (12%)
North America (16%)
Asia (30%)
Europe (7%)
Australia (5%)

THE WORLD: POPULATION

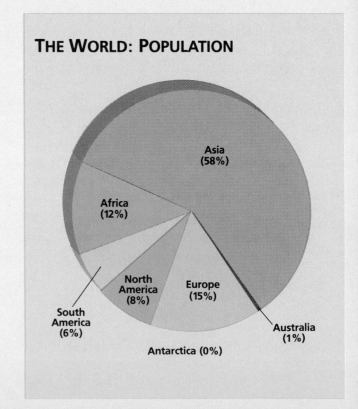

Asia (58%)
Africa (12%)
North America (8%)
Europe (15%)
South America (6%)
Australia (1%)
Antarctica (0%)

THE WORLD: HIGHEST ELEVATIONS BY CONTINENT

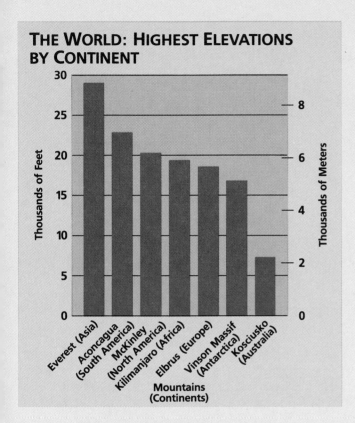

THE WORLD: LONGEST RIVERS BY CONTINENT

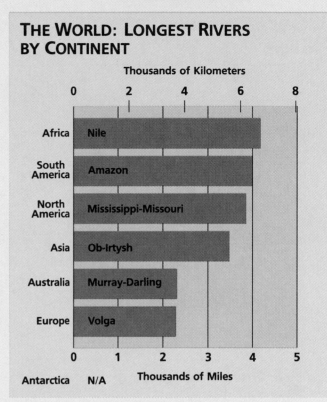

THE WORLD: FIVE HIGHEST ELEVATIONS

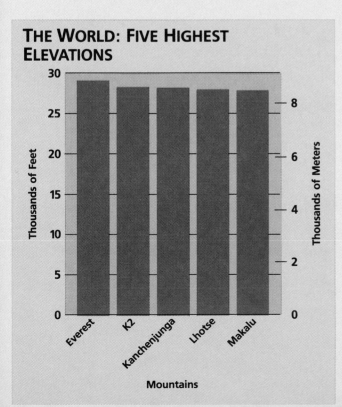

THE WORLD: LONGEST RIVERS

LEADING BARLEY-PRODUCING COUNTRIES

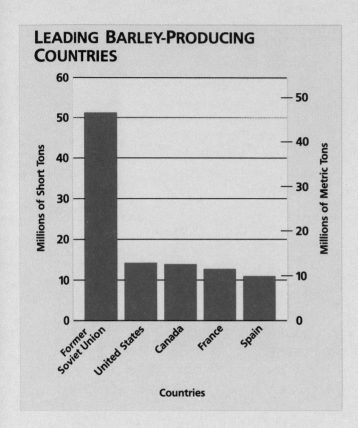

Millions of Short Tons

Millions of Metric Tons

Former Soviet Union, United States, Canada, France, Spain

Countries

LEADING CATTLE-PRODUCING COUNTRIES

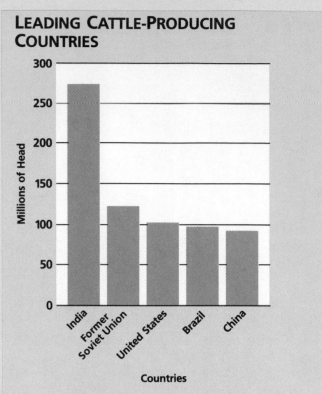

Millions of Head

India, Former Soviet Union, United States, Brazil, China

Countries

LEADING COTTON-PRODUCING COUNTRIES

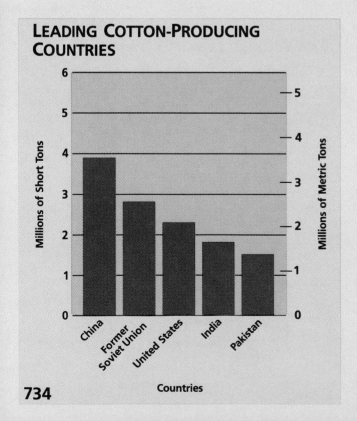

Millions of Short Tons

Millions of Metric Tons

China, Former Soviet Union, United States, India, Pakistan

Countries

LEADING PALM-OIL-PRODUCING COUNTRIES

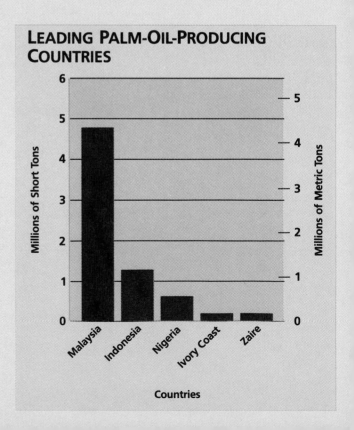

Millions of Short Tons

Millions of Metric Tons

Malaysia, Indonesia, Nigeria, Ivory Coast, Zaire

Countries

LEADING POTATO-PRODUCING COUNTRIES

LEADING RYE-PRODUCING COUNTRIES

LEADING SOYBEAN-PRODUCING COUNTRIES

LEADING TOBACCO-PRODUCING COUNTRIES

735

LEADING BAUXITE-PRODUCING COUNTRIES

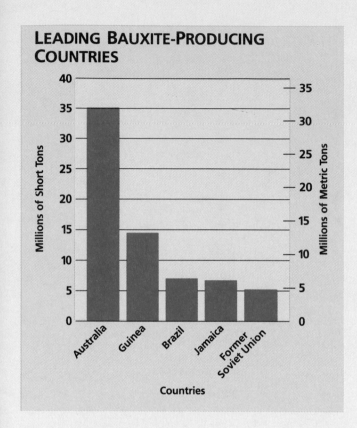

Millions of Short Tons / Millions of Metric Tons

Countries: Australia, Guinea, Brazil, Jamaica, Former Soviet Union

LEADING IRON ORE-PRODUCING COUNTRIES

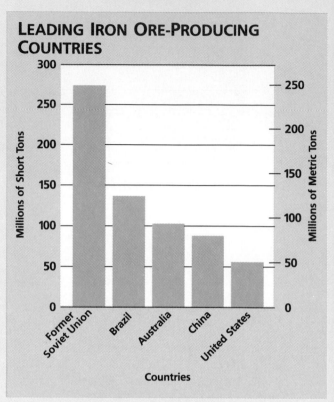

Millions of Short Tons / Millions of Metric Tons

Countries: Former Soviet Union, Brazil, Australia, China, United States

LEADING LEAD-PRODUCING COUNTRIES

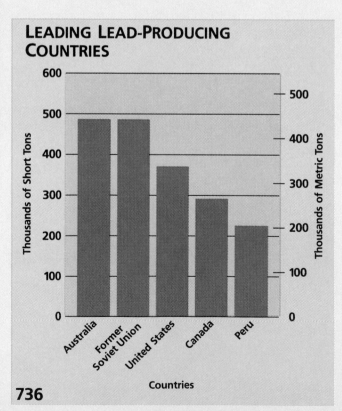

Thousands of Short Tons / Thousands of Metric Tons

Countries: Australia, Former Soviet Union, United States, Canada, Peru

LEADING NICKEL-PRODUCING COUNTRIES

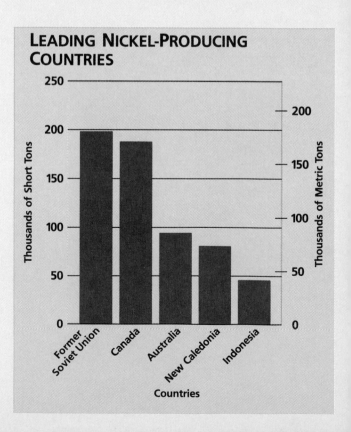

Thousands of Short Tons / Thousands of Metric Tons

Countries: Former Soviet Union, Canada, Australia, New Caledonia, Indonesia

Leading Petroleum-Producing Countries

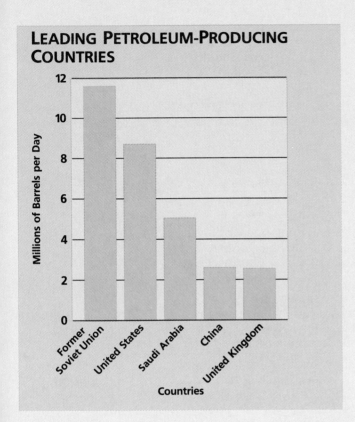

Millions of Barrels per Day

| Former Soviet Union | United States | Saudi Arabia | China | United Kingdom |

Countries

Leading Silver-Producing Countries

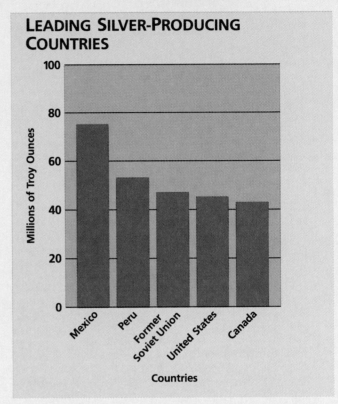

Millions of Troy Ounces

| Mexico | Peru | Former Soviet Union | United States | Canada |

Countries

Leading Steel-Producing Countries

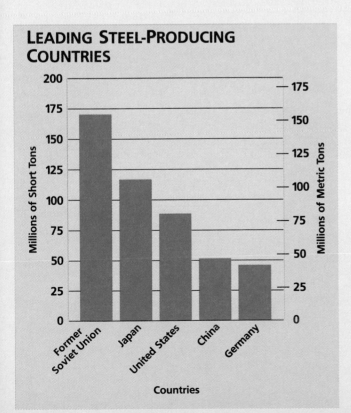

Millions of Short Tons — Millions of Metric Tons

| Former Soviet Union | Japan | United States | China | Germany |

Countries

Leading Uranium-Producing Countries

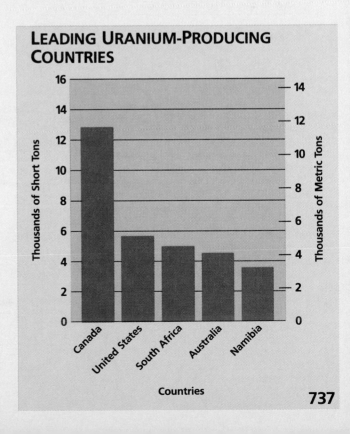

Thousands of Short Tons — Thousands of Metric Tons

| Canada | United States | South Africa | Australia | Namibia |

Countries

THE WORLD:
25 LARGEST CITIES BY POPULATION

	CITY	POPULATION
1.	Mexico City, Mexico	15,669,000
2.	Cairo, Egypt	13,000,000
3.	Seoul, South Korea	9,501,000
4.	Moscow, Russia	8,527,000
5.	Sao Paulo, Brazil	8,494,000
6.	Tokyo, Japan	8,355,000
7.	Bombay, India	8,227,000
8.	New York, United States	7,353,000
9.	Jakarta, Indonesia	7,348,000
10.	Shanghai, China	6,881,000
11.	London, United Kingdom	6,768,000
12.	Beijing, China	5,755,000
13.	Tehran, Iran	5,734,000
14.	Istanbul, Turkey	5,495,000
15.	Tientsin, China	5,312,000
16.	Karachi, Pakistan	5,103,000
17.	Rio de Janeiro, Brazil	5,093,000
18.	Bangkok, Thailand	5,018,000
19.	Delhi, India	4,884,000
20.	St. Petersburg, Russia	4,359,000
21.	Santiago, Chile	4,225,000
22.	Los Angeles, United States	3,353,000
23.	Calcutta, India	3,305,000
24.	Berlin, Germany	3,063,000
25.	Chicago, United States	2,978,000

UNITED STATES:
25 LARGEST CITIES BY POPULATION

	CITY	POPULATION
1.	New York, New York	7,353,000
2.	Los Angeles, California	3,353,000
3.	Chicago, Illinois	2,978,000
4.	Houston, Texas	1,698,000
5.	Philadelphia, Pennsylvania	1,647,000
6.	San Diego, California	1,070,000
7.	Detroit, Michigan	1,036,000
8.	Dallas, Texas	987,000
9.	San Antonio, Texas	941,000
10.	Phoenix, Arizona	924,000
11.	Baltimore, Maryland	751,000
12.	San Jose, California	738,000
13.	San Francisco, California	732,000
14.	Indianapolis, Indiana	727,000
15.	Memphis, Tennessee	645,000
16.	Jacksonville, Florida	635,000
17.	Washington, D.C.	617,000
18.	Milwaukee, Wisconsin	599,000
19.	Boston, Massachusetts	578,000
20.	Columbus, Ohio	570,000
21.	New Orleans, Louisiana	532,000
22.	Cleveland, Ohio	521,000
23.	El Paso, Texas	511,000
24.	Seattle, Washington	502,000
25.	Denver, Colorado	492,000

CLIMATE TABLES

			J	F	M	A	M	J	J	A	S	O	N	D
								MONTHS						
EQUATORIAL: Rangoon, Myanmar	Temperature	°F	77	79	84	87	84	81	80	80	81	82	80	77
		°C	25	26	29	31	29	27	27	27	27	28	27	25
	Precipitation	in.	.2	.2	.3	1.4	12.1	18.4	21.5	19.7	15.4	7.3	2.8	.3
		cm	.5	.5	.8	3.6	30.7	46.7	54.6	50.0	39.1	18.5	7.1	.8
SAVANNA: Darwin, Australia	Temperature	°F	84	83	84	84	82	79	77	79	83	85	86	85
		°C	29	28	29	29	28	26	25	26	28	30	30	30
	Precipitation	in.	15.9	12.9	10.1	4.1	.7	.1	.1	.1	.5	2.2	4.8	10.3
		cm	40.4	32.8	25.7	10.4	1.8	.3	.3	.3	1.3	5.6	12.2	26.2
SEMIDESERT: Tehran, Iran	Temperature	°F	34	42	48	61	71	80	85	83	77	66	51	42
		°C	1	6	9	16	22	27	30	28	25	19	11	6
	Precipitation	in.	1.6	1.0	1.9	1.4	.5	.1	.2	0	.1	.3	1.0	1.3
		cm	4.1	2.5	4.8	3.6	1.3	.3	.5	0	.3	.8	2.5	3.3

CLIMATE TABLES
Continued

MONTHS

			J	F	M	A	M	J	J	A	S	O	N	D
DESERT: Baghdad, Iraq	Temperature	°F	49	54	61	71	81	90	95	94	88	80	63	53
		°C	10	12	16	22	27	32	35	35	31	27	17	12
	Precipitation	in.	1.2	1.3	1.3	.9	.2	0	0	0	0	.1	.8	1.2
		cm	3.0	3.3	3.3	2.3	.5	0	0	0	0	.3	2.0	3.0
MEDITERRANEAN: Rome, Italy	Temperature	°F	45	47	51	57	64	71	76	76	70	62	53	46
		°C	7	8	11	14	18	22	25	25	21	17	12	8
	Precipitation	in.	3.2	2.7	2.9	2.6	2.2	1.6	.7	1.0	2.5	5.0	4.4	3.9
		cm	8.1	6.9	7.4	6.6	5.6	4.1	1.8	2.5	6.4	12.7	11.2	9.9
HUMID SUBTROPICAL: Montevideo, Uruguay	Temperature	°F	72	72	69	63	57	51	51	51	55	58	65	69
		°C	22	22	21	17	14	11	11	11	13	15	18	21
	Precipitation	in.	2.7	2.8	3.2	4.5	3.5	3.2	2.5	3.6	3.4	2.6	3.2	3.6
		cm	6.9	7.1	8.1	11.4	8.9	8.1	6.4	9.1	8.6	6.6	8.1	9.1
WEST COAST MARINE: Portland, United States	Temperature	°F	39	42	46	51	57	61	67	66	61	54	46	41
		°C	4	7	8	11	14	16	20	19	16	12	8	5
	Precipitation	in.	6.7	5.5	4.8	3.1	2.3	1.6	.6	.6	1.9	3.3	6.5	6.9
		cm	17.0	14.0	12.2	7.9	5.8	4.1	1.5	1.5	4.8	8.4	16.5	17.5
HUMID CONTINENTAL: Vienna, Austria	Temperature	°F	29	33	40	50	59	65	68	67	60	50	39	32
		°C	-2	1	4	10	15	18	20	20	16	10	4	0
	Precipitation	in.	1.5	1.3	1.8	2.0	2.8	2.7	3.1	2.7	2.0	1.9	1.8	1.8
		cm	3.8	3.3	4.6	5.1	7.1	6.9	7.9	6.9	5.1	4.8	4.6	4.6
MOUNTAIN: Mexico City, Mexico	Temperature	°F	54	57	61	64	65	64	62	62	61	59	56	54
		°C	12	14	16	18	18	18	17	17	16	15	13	12
	Precipitation	in.	.2	.2	.5	.8	1.9	3.9	4.5	4.6	3.9	1.6	.5	.2
		cm	.5	.5	1.3	2.0	4.8	9.4	11.4	11.7	9.9	4.1	1.3	.5
SUBARCTIC: Okhotsk, Russia	Temperature	°F	-11	-7	7	21	35	45	55	55	46	27	6	-8
		°C	-24	-22	-14	-6	2	7	13	13	8	-3	-15	-22
	Precipitation	in.	.1	.1	.1	.2	.5	1.1	.5	1.8	2.1	.7	.2	.2
		cm	.3	.3	.3	.5	1.3	2.8	1.3	4.6	5.3	1.8	.5	.5
TUNDRA: Point Barrow, United States	Temperature	°F	-19	-13	-14	-2	21	35	40	39	31	16	0	-15
		°C	-28	-25	-26	-19	-6	2	4	4	-1	-9	-18	-26
	Precipitation	in.	.3	.2	.2	.3	.3	.3	1.1	.8	.5	.8	.4	.4
		cm	.8	.5	.5	.8	.8	.8	2.8	2.0	1.3	2.0	1.0	1.0
ICE CAP: Little America, Antarctica	Temperature	°F	22	9	-7	-24	-27	-29	-34	-34	-29	-14	9	24
		°C	-6	-13	-22	-31	-33	-34	-37	-37	-34	-26	-13	-4
	Precipitation	in.	N/A	N/A	N/A	N/A	N/A	N/A	N/A	N/A	N/A	N/A	N/A	N/A
		cm	N/A	N/A	N/A	N/A	N/A	N/A	N/A	N/A	N/A	N/A	N/A	N/A

ACKNOWLEDGMENTS

Continued

Page 222: THE GREEN CONTINENT edited by German Arciniegas and translated by Harriet De Onis et al. Copyright 1944 and renewed by 1972 by Alfred A. Knopf Inc. Reprinted by permission of the publisher.

Page 254: Copyright © 1991 by The New York Times Company: Reprinted by permission.

Page 277: By Elvajean Hall. © 1963 J.B. Lippincott. Used by kind permission of Harper & Row Publishers.

Page 288: Copyright 1937, 1938, 1941, 1960 by The Bobbs-Merrill Co., Inc. Copyrights renewed by Macmillan Publishing Company, a Division of Macmillan Inc.

Pages 303, 306, 308: Reproduced from WE LIVE IN WEST GERMANY by Christa Stadtler with the kind permission of Wayland (Publishers) Ltd., Hove, England.

Page 307: Reprinted from HEINRICH HEINE: LYRIC POEMS AND BALLADS by Heinrich Heine, translated by Ernst Feise, by permission of the University of Pittsburgh Press. © 1961 by University of Pittsburgh Press.

Pages 324, 325: Reproduced from WE LIVE IN SPAIN by Richard Bristow with the kind permission of Wayland (Publishers) Ltd., Hove, England.

Page 328: From IBERIA by James A. Michener. Reprinted courtesy of Random House, Inc. © 1968 James A. Michener.

Page 344: Copyright © 1958, 1986 by Christine Hotchkiss. Reprinted by permission of Farrar, Straus & Giroux, Inc.

Page 363: Courtesy SOVIET LIFE MAGAZINE, 1989.

Page 366: From DR. ZHIVAGO by Boris Pasternak, translated by Max Hayward and Manya Harari, revised by Bernard Gilbert Guerney. Copyright © 1958 by William Collins & Co. Ltd. Copyright © 1958 by Pantheon Books, Inc. Reprinted by permission of Pantheon Books, Inc., a division of Random House Inc.

Page 369: Courtesy SOVIET LIFE MAGAZINE, 1991.

Page 380: Reprinted with special permission of North American Syndicate, Inc.

Page 381: By permission of Mike Luckovich and Creators Syndicate.

Page 386: Copyright © 1989 by The New York Times Company. Reprinted by permission.

Pages 397, 399: From CHERRY BLOSSOMS JAPANESE HAIKU SERIES III. Used by permission of The Peter Pauper Press.

Page 410; *Japan* by Forrest R. Pitts. © 1981 Fideler Company.

Pages 419, 422: By Peter and Babara Jenkins. Copyright © 1986 by Peter Jenkins. Used by permission of William Morrow and Company, Inc., and Sweet Springs Press.

Page 434: From THE GOOD EARTH by Pearl S. Buck. Copyright 1931 by Pearl S. Buck. Used by permission of Harper & Row Publishers, Inc.

Page 443: *Siamese Tales Old and New* by Manunet Bahhan.

Page 477: Reprinted by permission of the publishers from THE BHAGAVAD GITA, Franklin Edgerton, translator, Cambridge, Mass.: Harvard University Press, Copyright © 1944 by the President and Fellows of Harvard College, copyright © 1972 by Eleanor Hill Edgerton.

Page 491: Copyright © 1984 by The New York Times Company. Reprinted by permission.

Pages 501–502: Copyright © 1990 by Milton Viorst. Originally appeared in THE NEW YORKER.

Page 505: Reprinted by permission of the American Enterprise Institute for Public Policy Research, Washington, DC.

Page 522: Copyright © 1988 by The New York Times Company. Reprinted by permission.

Page 564: From THE AFRICANS by David Lamb. Used by permission of Random House, Inc. © 1982 David Lamb. All rights reserved.

Page 573: © 1961 by Colin Turnbull. Reprinted by permission of Simon & Schuster Inc.

CREDITS

Cover: Copyright 1993 Comstock

Country Tables: Scott Wilson **Maps:** Maryland Cartographics, Inc. **Graphs:** Richard Puder Design/JAK Graphics, Ltd. **Contributing artists:** Bryn Barnard: 48·49; Jack Brusca: 678; Susan Johnston Carlson: 44, 435; Rick Cooley: 497, 664; Len Ebert: 233, 242, 298, 473, 544, 567; Dan Fione: 112·113, 405, 589, 654; Polly K. Lewis: 216, 511; Richard Loehle: 281; Tom Powers: 104; Gary Undercuffler: 311, 368·369; Paul Wenzel: 129. **Photographs:** All photographs by Silver Burdett Ginn (SBG) unless otherwise noted. iii: Larry Lefever/Grant Heilman Photography. iv: Peter Pearson/TSW-Click, Chicago. v: Raphael Koskas/TSW-Click, Chicago. vi: Paul Chesley/Photographers Aspen. viii: Peter Timmermans/Allstock. x: M.P. Kahl/Bruce Coleman. xi: Marc Romanelli/The Image Bank. **Map Skills Handbook:** 2: Joachim Messerschmidt/Bruce Coleman. 3: t. Owen Franken/Stock, Boston; b. David Lucas for SBG. 5: Joachim Messerschmidt/Bruce Coleman; inset ©1993 David Burnett/Contact Press Images/Woodfin Camp & Associates. 11: Owen Franken/Stock, Boston. 15: David Lucas for SBG.

Unit 1 opener 22-23: Larry Lefever/Grant Heilman Photography. **Chapter 1** 24: Brian Gill/Globe Photos. 29: Kevin Schafer/TOM STACK & ASSOCIATES. 30: Michal Heron for SBG. 33: Wolinsky/Stock, Boston. **Chapter 2** 40: SuperStock. 41: NASA. 43: Campbell and Boulanger/West Light. 45: SuperStock. 47: Edward Pytlik/West Virginia University. 51: Grant Heilman Photography.

Unit 2 opener 62-63: Peter Pearson/TSW-Click, Chicago. 65: Larry Lee/ West Light. 66: Tom Algire/TOM STACK & ASSOCIATES. **Chapter 3** 72: David Barnes/The Stock Market. 74: Harrington Miller/Comstock. 75: bkgd. Stephen J. Krasemann/Peter Arnold, Inc.; t. l. Wayne Lankinen/Valan Photos; t. r. Ester Schmidt/Valan Photos; b. Johnny Johnson/Valan Photos. 76: George Hunter/ TSW-Click, Chicago. 77: Tim Graham/Sygma. 79: Bruno J. Zehnder/ Peter Arnold, Inc 80: Steve Vidler/After Image, Inc. 82: V. Wilkinson/Valan Photos. 83: Tibor Bognar/The Stock Market. 85: George Hunter/SuperStock. 86: T. Kitchin/TOM STACK & ASSOCIATES. 87: George Hunter/TSW-Click, Chicago. 88: Dan Guravich. 89: T. Kitchin/Valan Photos; inset R. Moller/Valan Photos. **Chapter 4** 96: Tony Freeman/Photo Edit. 97: Billy E. Barnes/Stock, Boston. 98: Phylane Norman/Nawrocki Stock Photos. 99: Jean-Paul Nacivet/After Image, Inc. 101: Margaret C. Berg/Berg & Associates. 102: Ronald F. Thomas/Bruce Coleman. 103: Shostal Associates/SuperStock. 108: E. R. Degginger. 109: Cary Wolinsky/Stock, Boston. 113: l. Photri; r. J. L. Atlan/Sygma. 114: © Allen Green/Photo Researchers, Inc. 117: Steve Vidler/Leo deWys. 118: Martin Rogers/Stock, Boston; inset © 1992 R. S. Uzzell III/Woodfin Camp & Associates. 119: D. Dietrich/Stock, Boston. 120-121: t. FPG International; b. Peter Menzel/Stock, Boston. **Chapter 5** 124: SuperStock. 126: Jack Kerson/DDB Stock Photo. 127: Steven D. Elmore. 128: © 1992 Robert Frerck/Woodfin Camp & Associates. 130: SuperStock. 133: Steven D. Elmore. 134: Robert Frerck/Odyssey Productions. 135: © Wesley Bocxe/Photo Researchers, Inc. 136: © 1992 Alon Reininger/Woodfin Camp & Associates. 137: © 1992 Terrence Morre/Woodfin Camp & Associates. 139: © 1992 Robert Frerck/Woodfin Camp & Associates. 140: Shostal Associates/SuperStock. 141: Bob Thomason/Leo deWys; inset George Gerster/Comstock. **Chapter 6** 144: Danny Lehman/After Image, Inc. 147: l. SuperStock; r. David Muscroft/SuperStock. 148 M. Burgess/H. Armstrong Roberts. 149: © Ed Drews/Photo Researchers, Inc. 152: Donald Dietz/Stock, Boston. 153: t. l. Ron Frehm/Wide World Photos, Inc.; t. r. Carol Francavilla/Wide World Photos, Inc.; b. Andy Hoekstra/Wide World Photos, Inc. 154: Joe Viesti/Viesti Associates, Inc. 155: © 1992 Alon Reininger/Woodfin Camp & Associates. 156: © Wesley Bocxe/Photo Researchers, Inc. 157: SuperStock. 158: AP/Wide World Photos, Inc.

Unit 3 opener 168-169: Raphael Koskas/TSW-Click, Chicago. 171: Steve Vidler/Leo deWys. **Chapter 7** 176: SuperStock. 178: Rob Crandall/Picture Group. 179: Collart Odinet/Sygma. 180: Shostal Associates/SuperStock. 181: © 1992 Robert Frerck/Woodfin Camp & Associates. 183: Capa/Magnum. 184: Patrick Rouillard/The Image Bank. 185-187: SuperStock. 189: Sebastiao Salgado/Magnum. **Chapter 8** 192: Manley Photo-Tuscon/Shostal Associates/SuperStock. 193: © Victor Englebert/Photo Researchers, Inc. 194: Don Mason/ The Stock Market. 195: r. Ernst A. Jahn/The Image Bank. 196: Robert Frerck/TSW-Click, Chicago. 196: Anna E. Zuckerman/Photo Edit. 197: l. © Victor Englebert/Photo Researchers, Inc.; r. FPG International. 198: Steele Perkins/Magnum. 200: SuperStock. 201: © H. Silvester/Photo Researchers, Inc. 202: Joe Viesti/Viesti Associates, Inc. 203: Kevin Horan/Picture Group; inset D. Donne Bryant. 205: SuperStock. 207: K. Scholz/SuperStock. **Chapter 9** 210: Pedro Luis Raota/Shostal Associates/SuperStock. 211: Claudia Parks/The Stock Market. 212: © 1992 Loren McIntyre/Woodfin Camp & Associates. 213 © Carl Frank/Photo Researchers, Inc. 215: Karl Kummels/SuperStock. 217: Hoa-Qui/Viesti Associates, Inc. 218: © Noel R. Kemp/Photo Researchers, Inc. 220: Ana MacIntyre/Viesti Associates, Inc. 221: Anna Zuckerman/Photo Edit. 222: Bill Parsons/FPG International. 223: D. Goldberg/Sygma. 224: © Suen-o Lindbland/Photo Researchers, Inc. **Chapter 10** 228: Ed Rooney/TSW-Click, Chicago. 230: Peter Frey/The Image Bank. 231: Shostal Associates/SuperStock. 232: Claus Meyer/Black Star. 234: S. Jorge/The Image Bank. 236: ©Jerry Cooke/Photo Researchers, Inc. 237: J. Messerschmidt/FPG International. 238: Shostal Associates/SuperStock. 240: deWildengen/Sygma. 241: © 1992 Stephanie Maze/Woodfin Camp & Associates. 244: Martin Rogers/Stock, Boston.

Unit 4 opener 252-253: Paul Chesley/Photographers Aspen. 255: Steve Vidler/Leo deWys. **Chapter 11** 262: Raymond Stott/The Image Works. 263: SuperStock. 264: Shostal Associates/SuperStock. 265: Randy Wells/ The Stock Market. 267: Richard Bullard/TSW-Click, Chicago. 268: Masa Uemura/ AllStock, Inc. 271: Historical Pictures Service, Chicago. 272-273: James Hargan/Leo deWys. 274: © Porterfield-Chickering/Photo Researchers, Inc. 275: Comstock. 277: Hubertus Kanus/SuperStock. 278: © Farrell Grehan/Photo Researchers, Inc. 279: Shostal Associates/SuperStock. 280: Hubertus Kanus/SuperStock. 282: l. Bruce Coleman; r. J. Messerschmidt/Bruce Coleman. **Chapter 12** 286: J. Messerschmidt/Leo deWys. 288: Floyd Holdman/The Stock Solution. 289: Rick Strange/ International Stock Photo. 292: ZEFA, U.K./H. Armstrong Roberts. 295: Kanno Shinichi/FPG International. 297: Globe Photos. 300: Neil Beer/TSW-Click, Chicago. 303: G. and M. Kohler/FPG International. 304: Messerschmidt/FPG International. 306: Terry Qing/FPG International. 307: E. Streichan/Shostal Associates/SuperStock. 308: Tony Craddock/TSW-Click, Chicago. 309: Stockman/International Stock Photo. 310-311: Globe Photos. 312: © 1992 Gernot Huber/Woodfin Camp & Associates. 314-315: Antonin Kratochvil. **Chapter 13** 318: Percy Hennell/TSW-Click, Chicago. 322: Shostal Associates/SuperStock. 323: FPG International. 324, 327: M. Thonig/H. Armstrong Roberts. 328: Robert Frerck/TSW-Click, Chicago. 329: T. Sennett/Magnum. 331: Blaine Harrington/The Stock Market. 332: SuperStock. 335: G. Clayffe/FPG International. 335: Erich Lessing/Magnum. **Chapter 14** 338: TSW-Click, Chicago. 339: Chip Hires/Gamma Liaison. 340: DPI. 341: © Photo Researchers, Inc. 342: © 1992 Momatiuk/Eastcott/Woodfin Camp & Associates. 343: Chris Niedenthal/Black Star. 344: Donald Lewis Osborn. 345: Jessie Blackburn/FPG International. 346: Luis Villota/The Stock Market. 347: Eastcott-Momatiuk/The Image Works. 348: Art Zamur/Gamma Liaison. 351: © 1992 Adam Woolfitt/Woodfin Camp & Associates. **Chapter 15** 354: Andy Hernandez/Sipa Press. 355: David Madison/Duomo. 358: © 1993 Howard Sochurek/Woodfin Camp & Associates. 359: Klaus Reisinger/Black Star. 365: Tass/Sovfoto. 366: SuperStock. 368: Focus on Sports. 369: © 1993 Heikki Saukkomaa/Woodfin Camp & Associates. 370: l. Tass/Sovfoto; t.r. Irv Beckman; b.r. Arthur Grace/Stock, Boston. 371: Peter Turnley/Black Star. 374: © 1993 Alexander Avakian/Woodfin Camp & Associates. 376: Gilles Saussier/Gamma Liaison.

Unit 5 opener 384-385: Peter Timmermans/AllStock, Inc. 387: Andrea Barrist/The Image Works. **Chapter 16** 396: Steve Vidler/Nawrocki Stock Photos. 398: TSW-Click, Chicago 399: Joe Viesti/Viesti Associates, Inc. 401: Audrey Gottlier/ Monkmeyer Press. 402: SuperStock. 403: FPG International; inset Matsumoto/Sygma. 406: Michael Hayman/Stock, Boston. 408: SuperStock. 409: Wolfgang Kaehler. 410: George Hunter/Superstock. 411: Paul Fusco/Magnum. 412: FPG International. 414: H. Kubota/Magnum. 415: © 1992 Kim Newton/Woodfin Camp & Associates. **Chapter 17** 418: Comstock. 420: Charles Marden Fitch/Shostal Associates/ SuperStock. 424: Fred Bavendam/Peter Arnold, Inc. 426: Shostal Associates/SuperStock. 429: Gamma-Liaison. 430: © 1992 Alon Reininger/ Woodfin Camp & Associates. 431: UPI/Bettmann Newsphotos. 434: Bob Thomason/TSW-Click, Chicago. 435: Michael Springer/Gamma-Liaison. 436: Robin Moyer/Gamma-Liaison. 438: © Lawrence Migdale/Photo Researchers, Inc. 439: Paul Conklin/Monkmeyer Press; inset Elisabeth Weiland. **Chapter 18** 442: © Alain Evrard/Photo Researchers, Inc. 443: D.J. Forbert/SuperStock. 444, 445: Wolfgang Kaehler. 447: Nik Wheeler/Black Star. 448: © Bruce Gordon/Photo Researchers, Inc. 449: © UPI Bettmann Newsphotos. 450: Chauvel/Sygma. 451: Wolfgang Kaehler. 452: © Emil Muench Photo Researchers, Inc. 454: J. Wishnetsky/Comstock. 456: Patrick Ward/Stock, Boston. 457: Wolfgang Kaehler. 458: © Paolo Koch/Photo Researchers, Inc. 459: Christopher Morris/Black Star. **Chapter 19** 462: Wolfgang Kaehler. 464: Shostal Associates/SuperStock. 465: Rene Born/Magnum. 467: Lorraine Rorke/The Image Works. 468: Bruno Barbey/Magnum. 470: Mimi Forsyth/Monkmeyer Press. 471: Bruno Barbey/Magnum. 472: © George Holton/Photo Researchers, Inc. 474: Magnum. 476: Mimi Forsyth/Monkmeyer Press. 478: P. Habans/Sygma. 479: Joe Viesti/Viesti Associates, Inc. 480: Sygma. 482: S. Chester/Comstock. 484: l. SuperStock; r. © 1992 Marc and Evelyne Bernheim/Woodfin Camp & Associates. 485: J. Heil/Leo deWys. 487: Bernard Pierre Wolff. **Chapter 20** 490: Stockman/International Stock Photos; l. inset FPG International; r. inset SuperStock. 491: SuperStock. 492: Michaelangelo Durazzo/Ana/Viesti Associates, Inc. 493: © 1992 Robert Azzi/Woodfin Camp & Associates. 494: © 1992 Homer Sykes/Woodfin Camp & Associates. 495: © Fred Maroon/Photo Researchers, Inc. 496: V. Lefteroff/FPG International. 497: Comstock. 498: l. Kalari/Sygma; r. C. Spengler/Sygma. 500: P. Manoukian/Sygma. 497: 501: The Image Bank. 502: Gamma-Liaison. 503: © Nancy Durrell McKenna/Photo Researchers, Inc. 504: Reuters/Bettmann. 505: Gamma Liaison. 507: Bruno Barbey/Magnum. 508: Byron Augustin/TOM STACK & ASSOCIATES. 511: FPG International. 512: Abu Hander/International Stock Photo.

Unit 6 opener 520-521: M.P. Kahl/Bruce Coleman. 523: © Arthur Gloor-Animals Animals/Earth Scenes. **Chapter 21** 532: E. Otto/FPG International. 535: Francois Dardelet/The Image Bank. 536: Robert Frerck/TSW-Click, Chicago. 538: Ted H. Funk/FPG International; r. Ian Steele/International Stock Photo. 540: M. Delledonna/FPG International. 542: Robert Winslow. 543: Erich Lessing/Magnum. 545: Michael Braid/TSW-Click, Chicago. 546: Roule Av/Sygma. 549: Hoa-Qui/Viesti Associates, Inc. **Chapter 22** 552: Dimitri Kessel/The Stock Market. 553: Magnum. 554: © 1992 Wendy V. Watriss/Woodfin Camp & Associates. 555: Dieter Blum/Peter Arnold, Inc. 556: Jacques Jangoux/Peter Arnold, Inc. 557: Shostal Associates/SuperStock. 559: Pedro Coll/The Stock Market; inset © 1992 Marc and Evelyne Bernheim/Woodfin Camp & Associates. 561: l. © 1992 Wendy Watriss/Woodfin Camp & Associates; r. Thierry Rannou/Gamma-Liaison. 562: Shostal Associates/SuperStock. 564: © Marc and Evelyne Bernheim/Woodfin Camp & Associates. 566: Yoruba/H. Armstrong Roberts. 569: Hoa-Qui/Viesti Associates, Inc. **Chapter 23** 572: James A. Sugar/Black Star. 573: Bruno Barbey/Magnum. 574: Joseph B. Brignolo/The Image Bank. 575: T. Orban/Sygma. 576: FourbyFive, Inc./SuperStock. 577: © 1992 Marc and Evelyne Bernheim/Woodfin Camp & Associates. 578: Tortoli/ZEFA/H. Armstrong Roberts. 579: Abbas/Magnum; inset © J. P. Vuillomenet/Photo Researchers, Inc. 580: Millard Thomas/Taurus Photos, Inc. 583: Hoa-Qui/Viesti Associates, Inc. **Chapter 24** 586: C. D. Flannery/Bruce Coleman. 588: Jason Laure. 590: © Dr. Nigel Smith•Animals Animals/Earth Scenes. 591: l. © 1992 Kal Muller/Woodfin Camp & Associates. 592: © Blair Seitz/Photo Researchers, Inc. 592: Robert Caputo/Stock, Boston. 593: © Bruce Brander/Photo Researchers, Inc. 595: Georg Gerster/Comstock. 596: t. © 1992 Marc and Evelyne Bernheim/Woodfin Camp & Associates; b. TSW-Click, Chicago. 598: E.R. Degginger. 599: Robert Caputo/Stock, Boston. 600: Georg Gerster/Comstock. 601: TSW-Click, Chicago. 602: b. Jason Laure; b. © 1992 Marc and Evelyne Bernheim/Woodfin Camp & Associates. 603: Wendy Bass/Viesti Associates, Inc. inset t.r. S. Franklin/Magnum; inset b. l. © 1992 Thomas Nebbia/Woodfin Camp & Associates; b.r. Peter Veit. 605: t. E.R. Degginger; b. © 1992 Stoddart/Katz/Woodfin Camp & Associates. **Chapter 25** 608: © Gregory G. Dimijian/Photo Researchers, Inc. 609: Tom and Michele Grimm/International Stock Photo. 610: Joe Viesti/Viesti Associates, Inc.; inset Jason Laure. 612: © 1992 Thomas Nebbia/Woodfin Camp & Associates. 613: Photri. 614: Dennis Cox/TSW-Click, Chicago. 615: A. Moldvay/Eriako Associates. 617: © Anthony Bannister-Animals Animals/Earth Scenes. 618: Jason Laure. 621: Shostal Associates/SuperStock. 622: William Campbell/Sygma. 624: Photri. 625: Reuters/Bettmann. 626: Jason Laure.

Unit 7 opener 634-635: Marc Romanelli/The Image Bank. 638: © 1992 David Austen/Woodfin Camp & Associates. 639: Comstock. **Chapter 26** 642: Paul Steel/The Stock Market. 644: Dallas and John Heaton/TSW-Click, Chicago. 645: Robin Smith/TSW-Click, Chicago. 646: l. Dallas and John Heaton/TSW-Click, Chicago; m. © Tom McHugh/Photo Researchers, Inc.; r. Fritz Prenzel/TSW-Click, Chicago. 647: Peter Hendrie/The Image Bank; inset Alvis Upitis/The Image Bank. 648: Historical Pictures Service, Chicago. 650: © World Copyright Pascal Rondeau/AllSport. 652: Zigy Kaluzny/TSW-Click, Chicago. 653: David Austen/TSW-Click, Chicago. 655: © 1992 Robert Frerck/Woodfin Camp & Associates. 656: © Tom McHugh/Photo Researchers, Inc. 658: Robbi Newman/The Image Bank. **Chapter 27** 662: Pete Seaward/TSW-Click, Chicago. 665: Son Smetzer/TSW-Click, Chicago. 666: FPG International. 667: Wendy Stone/Bruce Coleman. 668: © 1992 Dilip Mehta/Woodfin Camp & Associates; inset Comstock. 669: Dallas and John Heaton/TSW-Click, Chicago. 670: Jacques Jangoux/Peter Arnold, Inc. 671: © 1992 Gerd Ludwig/Woodfin Camp & Associates. 672: John Perkins/Globe Photos. 673: © Robert W. Hernandez/Photo Researchers, Inc. 674: TSW-Click, Chicago. 675: Art Wolfe/AllStock, Inc. 676: FourbyFive Inc./SuperStock. 677: © 1992 Chuck O'Rear/Woodfin Camp & Associates. 678: Grant Heilman Photography; inset George Mars Cassidy/TSW-Click, Chicago.